THE HONGKONG BANK IN LATE
IMPERIAL CHINA, 1864–1902
ON AN EVEN KEEL

VOLUME I OF
THE HISTORY OF THE HONGKONG
AND SHANGHAI BANKING
CORPORATION

THE HISTORY OF THE HONGKONG AND SHANGHAI BANKING CORPORATION

FRANK H.H. KING

For a list of contents for each volume, please see pages v–vii

Sir MICHAEL SANDBERG, CBE.
Chairman, The Hongkong and Shanghai Banking Corporation, 1977–1986.

THE HONGKONG BANK IN LATE IMPERIAL CHINA, 1864–1902

ON AN EVEN KEEL

VOLUME I OF
THE HISTORY OF THE HONGKONG
AND SHANGHAI BANKING
CORPORATION

FRANK H.H. KING

Professor of Economic History, University of Hong Kong

with

CATHERINE E. KING and DAVID J.S. KING

CAMBRIDGE UNIVERSITY PRESS

Cambridge
New York   New Rochelle   Melbourne   Sydney

Published by the Press Syndicate of the University of Cambridge
The Pitt Building, Trumpington Street, Cambridge CB2 1RP
32 East 57th Street, New York, NY 10022, USA
10 Stamford Road, Oakleigh, Melbourne 3166, Australia

First published 1987

Printed in Great Britain at the University Press, Cambridge

British Library cataloguing in publication data

King, Frank H.H.
The History of The Hongkong and Shanghai
Banking Corporation.
Vol. 1: The Hongkong Bank in Late Imperial
China, 1864–1902: On an even keel.
1. Hongkong and Shanghai Banking Corporation
– History
I. Title II. King, Catherine E. III. King,
David J.S.
332.1'2'095125   HG3354.H6

Library of Congress cataloguing in publication data

King, Frank H.H.
The Hongkong Bank in Late Imperial China, 1864–1902: On an even keel.
(The History of The Hongkong and Shanghai Banking
Corporation; v. 1)
Bibliography.
Includes index.
1. Hongkong and Shanghai Banking Corporation – History
– 19th century. 2. Banks and banking – China – History –
19th century. I. King, Catherine E. II. King,
David J.S. III. Title. IV. King, Frank H.H.
History of The Hongkong and Shanghai Banking
Corporation; v. 1.
HG1571.K56 vol. 1   332.1'5'095125 s   86–28341
[HG3338.H66]   [332.1'0951]

ISBN 0 521 32706 7

SE

CONTENTS OF VOLUMES
I, II, III, AND IV

VOLUME IV. THE HONGKONG BANK IN THE PERIOD OF DEVELOPMENT AND NATIONALISM, 1941–1984: FROM REGIONAL BANK TO MULTINATIONAL GROUP

TABLE OF CONTENTS, VOLUME I

LIST OF ILLUSTRATIONS

3C Sir Thomas Sutherland, GCMG
4C Sir Thomas Jackson, Bart, KCMG
5C David McLean

Black and white: (between p. 280 and p. 281)
  1 Various Chinese monies
  2 Albert Farley Heard
  3 View of Yokohama, circa 1870
  4 Report to shareholders for 1866
  5 James Greig 'falling between two stools'
  6 Introducing the New Year of 1875 to Mr Punch
  7 Abstract of assets and liabilities, December 1874
  8 Foreign staff, Shanghai, 1873
  9 Wang Huai-shan (Wah Sam), first Shanghai compradore
 10 The Chief Managers: Victor Kresser, James Greig, John
      Walter, George E. Noble, and François de Bovis

Black and white: (between p. 440 and p. 441)
 11 The Hong Kong Waterfront, circa 1890
 12 Hongkong Bank Office, Hong Kong, 1886 building from the
      harbour
 13 Hongkong Bank Office, Hong Kong, 1886 building, a corner
      view from Queen's Road
 14 Hongkong Bank banknotes
 15 Abstract of assets and liabilities, December 1889
 16 Abstract of assets and liabilities, December 1898
 17 Hongkong Bank Office, Shanghai, 1892
 18 China loan prospectuses, etc., 1874–1895
 19 A foreign staff group in Hong Kong, 1886
 20 Foreign staff, Hong Kong, on the eve of Sir Thomas
      Jackson's retirement, 1902
 21 Abstract of assets and liabilities, December 1901

LIST OF TABLES

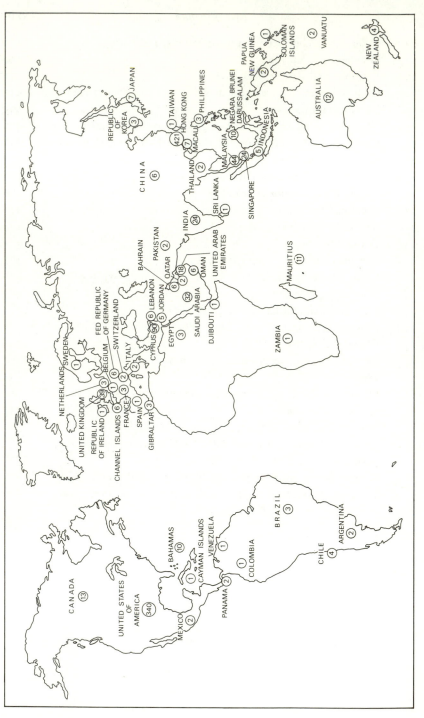

1 Hongkong Bank Group offices in 1984.

FOREWORD

SIR MICHAEL SANDBERG, CBE

Chairman, The Hongkong and Shanghai Banking Corporation

The history of The Hongkong and Shanghai Banking Corporation reflects the best pioneering tradition. The Bank first opened its doors for business in 1865 because a group of Hong Kong merchants had seen the need for a bank to service local business interests. From these relatively humble origins the Bank has grown into one of the world's great financial institutions.

I sometimes wonder if those who founded it, men of vision though they undoubtedly were, could ever have envisaged the global scale of the Bank's operations today.

It has survived more than its fair share of adversity and produced many remarkable personalities. But as well as being fascinating enough in its own right the history of the Bank commands more general interest because of the way in which it is inextricably bound up with the history of economic development of the East.

History of course is made by people, and I was concerned that the recollections of many of those who had played a prominent part in fashioning the Bank had already passed on to whatever Valhalla is reserved for bankers and had taken their memories with them. For The Hongkong and Shanghai Banking Corporation, perhaps more than any other bank, those memories were vital because so many records had vanished or been destroyed during the Second World War. One must remember that by the end of 1941 only London, New York, and San Francisco in the West and Bombay, Calcutta, and Colombo in the East remained of the Bank's 1939 establishment when the war started.

Gone were our headquarters in Hong Kong and virtually our entire China operation. We had no sooner started to reconstruct the latter in 1946 than after the 1949 Revolution we were for a time reduced to operating a single office in Shanghai.

Many who could fill the gaps left by the loss of records had themselves sadly left us. I am filled with admiration for Professor King whose scholarly research has so successfully bridged many of these gaps. I was particularly pleased that the study could be accomplished through the University of Hong Kong, with which the Bank has had such close associations over the years. I am also delighted that Frank King and Christopher Cook have obtained on tape the first-hand accounts of so many people who served the Bank both before and immediately after the war. I hope this is something the Bank can continue to do to augment the written word.

Although the Bank was fortunate to have had a very readable history written by the late Maurice Collis to coincide with our centenary in 1965, I felt we needed something in greater depth to set properly in place the role of the Bank in, and its contribution to, the commercial development of the Far East. There are political elements too. It seems to me that Professor King and his associates have accomplished this in exemplary fashion, and produced a history which is academic in the best sense of the word. Frank King has, as I had hoped, produced a work which I believe to be impartial and accurate history, a work which will be invaluable to banking and historical researchers alike.

It is in the nature of business life that those involved in it must occupy most of their time with the present and the future rather than with the past. Nevertheless, the Bank has a strong sense of tradition and takes particular pride in its history. We do not forget that the international stature which the Bank enjoys today is the result of the dedication of generations of its staff. I congratulate Professor King for capturing much of the character and initiative of the people who laid the foundations for the enterprise that is the Bank today.

This history is a fitting tribute to them.

Michael Sandberg

1, Queen's Road, Central,
Hong Kong

July 1, 1986

PREFACE

The East is that region in which 'the Bank' is understood to mean 'The Hongkong and Shanghai Banking Corporation'.

The Hongkong and Shanghai Banking Corporation was founded in 1865 by Hong Kong taipans of several nationalities; their purpose was to establish a local bank for Hong Kong and for the Treaty Ports of China and Japan. The Bank was almost immediately successful and by the 1880s had become banker and counsellor to governments, agent for Imperial China's government loans, and occasional banker to Japan's fledgling Zaibatsu. Reaching out as an Eastern exchange bank, the directors established offices in London, San Francisco, Lyons, New York, and Hamburg. In the East the Bank's financing of trade led to the establishment of offices in the Philippines, the Netherlands East Indies, the Straits Settlements, Cochin-China, Ceylon, and Burma. Its triangular exchange operations required major establishments in Calcutta and Bombay.

The absence of a full history of the Hongkong Bank has obscured analysis of key issues in the economic history of the world east of India. The present history has been commissioned as an independent academic study to fill the void which has hindered interpretation of the many crucial events in which the Bank has been a major participant.

Although founded in the East the Hongkong Bank was chartered by the Hong Kong Government in the context of British Colonial Banking Regulations. Its early ties with London, its continuing role as a British overseas bank subject to Treasury policy, and its insistence until the 1950s that its executive officers first serve in London place it within the British chartered banking tradition. London was the base of many such overseas banks; they linked the financial markets of Britain with specific parts of the Empire, South America, and Asia. Certain of these had also been founded overseas. The Hongkong Bank was unique in retaining its Head Office in the East, giving it a sense of permanence, an ability to react with understanding to the requirements of the region it was founded to serve. This was the basis of its remarkable role and its undoubted success.

The present work is a business history, the story of a corporation evolving from its status as a 'local' bank to become by the end of the last century the most important foreign financial institution in the East. Until 1959, however, the Bank remained 'regional'; then, in little more than twenty dramatic years, the regional bank become a multinational financial institution. Throughout this evolution there were questions of Board/management relations and problems relative to the control of branches, the role of Head Office, recruitment, career paths, pension plans, and the relationship with the local staff and the compradores. Sir Michael Sandberg, the Hongkong Bank's Chairman, has asked that these problems be discussed in terms of the men who made the Bank; biography, fascinating in its own right, would, as he foresaw, prove a key to a full appreciation of the issues under consideration.

The first volume describes the initial growth, despite the dramatic fall in the gold price of silver; it considers the early China loans and the efforts made to use this entrée to encourage China's development. Subsequent volumes will carry the Bank to its peak of fame as the instrument of British policy in China and Head of the international Consortium designed to finance China's requirements for railway development and administrative reorganization. In the tragedy of the Great War, the Bank under pressure abandoned its German connections and its dreams for multinational cooperative development of the East were shattered.

The post-war 'return to normalcy' described in Volume III proved a chimera; Warlord China could not be assisted. Then came the difficult times of the 1930s, tempered only by the development promises of a reunified Chinese Republic. Instead there was the war with Japan and the Bank's dramatic efforts to save China's currency, followed by its own capture at the outset of the Pacific War.

Although the Bank's Eastern branches, except for those in India and Ceylon, were occupied by the enemy and a high proportion of its Foreign staff interned, the Hongkong Bank nevertheless survived through the last minute transfer of its Head Office to London. Volume IV will describe the Bank's Babylonian Captivity, the years in London and the successful planning for the future. In 1945 the Bank returned to the East. Frustrated once again in China, the Hongkong Bank found opportunities in Hong Kong itself, financing what many consider an economic miracle. But Hong Kong was too confining; the Bank helped to meet the financial requirements of post-war development in Singapore and the Federation of Malaya; it opened for the first time in British Borneo and in Brunei, and it continued its traditional role elsewhere in the East. The Bank consolidated its position by the purchase of the Mercantile Bank Limited in 1959. Then, outgrowing its own region the Bank acquired the British Bank of the Middle East in 1960; then after steady growth, the Bank in 1980 acquired a controlling interest in New York's Marine Midland Banks – the China coast's local bank had become a multinational. The Hongkong and Shanghai Banking Corporation, now both an operating bank and a bank holding company, is one of the twenty largest financial organizations in the world.

That in summary is the story to be told in the four volumes of this history. In preparation for its centenary in 1965 the Board of Directors of The Hongkong and Shanghai Banking Corporation authorized the commissioning of two histories, a popular history for the celebrations and a 'solid' history to be written by an academic. The former was published as *Wayfoong: The Hongkong and Shanghai Banking Corporation* by Maurice Collis; the latter was not actually commissioned until 1979 when I began the research for the present study. Sir Michael Sandberg's plan was for the project to be conducted at 'arm's length' and to include 'warts and all'. The project would be housed in and administered by the University of Hong Kong, independent of, although financed by the Bank; it would be supervised subject to academic standards and principles within the University's Centre of Asian Studies.

Except during the Pacific War, the Hongkong Bank's Head Office has always been in Hong Kong. This has affected the outlook of its executives and consequently its history. Appropriately, therefore, the history project has been based on and the present study written in Hong Kong. The directional words 'here', 'there', 'go from', 'come down from (Shanghai)' or 'go down to (Singapore)', etc., must be understood in this context. Working in Hong Kong as base has made a difference to the Bank's history both as it happened and as it has been presented in these volumes.

The present work is a commissioned history of a business – the Hongkong Bank. As the project director and author, I have kept the focus on the Hongkong Bank. The events discussed in this work, therefore, were selected on the basis of their relevance to the history of the Hongkong Bank as a private-sector corporation. Whatever else this was to be, however else it might assist scholars, it must always come back to the Hongkong Bank. Accounts of world significance may appear 'interrupted' by consideration of what a Hongkong Banker had to do with it or how the local branch was affected. In fact one might well argue, with only slight exaggeration, that for a business history it is the world-shattering event that 'interrupts' the story of the Hongkong Bank.

In fulfilling this commission, the Chairman granted me 'full access' to the Bank's papers. Not all the 'secrets' of a bank, however, are their own. A bank's customers have fully protected rights of confidentiality – although, as sometimes happens, the story if of sufficient importance may be told in some independent source, possibly, and especially if there is a happy ending, by the customer himself. Furthermore the Bank is not on a 'full disclosure' basis, that is, the Bank does not report its true profits to its shareholders and it maintains 'inner reserves'. In earlier years the history can take this into account, although full recasting the accounts is not a practical task for an economic historian. In consequence, this history has in general been written on the basis of the published accounts; where possible, however, consideration has been given to the Bank's true position and its significance. With these qualifications noted, there has been no interference or censorship.

This history of The Hongkong and Shanghai Banking Corporation is itself a project within the scope of The Hongkong Bank Group History Program. In December 1981 a conference on the Bank's history was held in the Centre of Asian Studies; the papers were published as *Eastern Banking: Essays in the History of the Hongkong and Shanghai Banking Corporation* (London, 1983), the first in the Program's publications series. The papers of Sir Charles Addis, the Bank's London Manager, 1904–1922, a director of the Bank of England to 1932, and head of the China Consortium to 1944, were donated by Sir John Addis and Robina Addis to the School of Oriental and African Studies. In 1986 Margaret Harcourt Williams published a catalogue of the collection (No. 2 of the series), the preparation of which was financed by the Hongkong Bank.

Sir Michael Sandberg had in mind a history of each of the major subsidiary financial companies. Accordingly he commissioned Geoffrey Jones to research and write the history of the Imperial Bank of Persia/British Bank of the Middle East. This was published in 1986 and 1987 in two volumes: *Banking and Empire in Iran* and *Banking and Oil*.

Other works are under consideration. Furthermore the Chairman commissioned an oral history program, which, as he has stated in the Foreword, he considers of special importance. The interviews provide a source of considerable scholarly interest. The edited transcripts have accordingly been filed in the Hongkong Bank Group Archives. The Archives themselves already contained data for many specialized monographs. Indeed, the purpose of the Bank's history program has been not so much to take advantage of a privileged first look in order to press a single theme or interpretation as to take this opportunity to disseminate information which for decades has remained, through no fault of policy, inaccessible.

This particularly is the spirit in which the scope of the present work has been decided. Even when the narrative moves into the world of high finance and international policies, the corporation, the Hongkong Bank, is there. Its managers move among the Great, but they are also in Iloilo and Sungei Patani. Without the Eastern network, without the Hong Kong and Shanghai base, the world influence would have failed. In this sense the present work remains, as promised, a history focused on The Hongkong and Shanghai Banking Corporation, its policies, its projects, its failures, and, above all, the members of its Eastern staff, its Portuguese staff, and its 'native' staffs over the years 1864 to 1984.

A NOTE ON ROMANIZATION

The present official romanization system of the Chinese language as prescribed by the authorities of the People's Republic of China is *pinyin*.

In this history as a general principle all Chinese characters are either 'decoded' according to a system known as 'modified Wade–Giles' or are cited in the form customary at the time and familiar to the persons who made this history. A Glossary has been appended which relates the form in the text to *pinyin* and to Chinese characters.

I believe it is poor history to change retroactively terms and names which have become commonly understood in the English language in a particular form merely because a new system has been introduced for entirely different purposes irrelevant to the task at hand. This view is controversial. I am consistent, however, in using traditional forms with local terms and phrases of whatever origin, for example, 'godown' for 'warehouse', 'maskee' for 'never mind'.

For the period to 1949 there are exceptions to the generalization stated. The names of Chinese are romanized according to the following priorities: (i) the form they themselves used or preferred, (ii) for Hong Kong residents (or residents in the Nanyang), the Cantonese version (or the relevant romanization in the country of residence), (iii) the form generally used by foreigners, and (iv) the modified Wade–Giles romanization. The Glossary correlates the alternatives. Names of Chinese origin of residents in various countries are shown in the form used in that country.

Geographical names are given in the form normally used by English-speaking foreigners of the time. Town names are based on lists devised by G.W.F. Playfair, the Chief Manager of the National Bank of China. Geographical names not generally familiar to foreigners are in Wade–Giles. The Glossary provides the alternatives.

The names of journals published prior to 1949 are rendered in Wade–Giles unless they have another romanized form on their cover or editorial page.

By the same arguments, the names of persons, journals, and places in China today should be and are shown in *pinyin*.

FRANK H.H. KING

Centre of Asian Studies
University of Hong Kong

July 4, 1986

ACKNOWLEDGEMENTS

This history was commissioned by The Hongkong and Shanghai Banking Corporation. I am grateful to the Bank's Chairman, Sir Michael Sandberg, for his willingness not only to commission a history early in his tenure as chief executive officer, but also for his continued support as the project was extended from time to time.

The delays were partly due to the accumulation of archival material previously inaccessible, and for this credit is again due to Sir Michael and to Sir John Saunders, who authorized the establishment of an historical archive, building on the material collected by J.R. Jones in connection with the writing of the Bank's centenary history in 1964. The scope of the present collection is the consequence of the initiative of B.J.N. Ogden, the corporation's Secretary and then Controller of Group Archives. His pioneering work was consolidated by S.W. Muirhead, who took responsibility for cataloguing both Hongkong Bank and Mercantile Bank collections. The history project outlasted them both; it was left to A.I. Donaldson to undertake a final reading and see the work through the press. Margaret Lee, as Assistant Controller, possessed an intimate knowledge of the archives and provided essential support and assistance.

Both the Hongkong Bank and I are grateful to the responsible authorities of the People's Republic of China for permission to ship the Bank's major Shanghai archives for incorporation with the records in Hong Kong.

The history was an academic research project of the Centre of Asian Studies, University of Hong Kong. I am grateful to Rayson L. Huang, Vice-Chancellor, for authorizing the cooperative project, to the Committee of Management, the Director, and staff of the Centre of Asian Studies for administrative support, and particularly to the staff of the Secretary's Office and Finance Office in the University for their prompt assistance and advice.

Looking further back I acknowledge the encouragement given me in my initial studies of money and banking in China by John K. Fairbank, Sir John Hicks, Edward S. Shaw, and the late C.N. Ward-Perkins.

The present history was written in association with Catherine E. King (especially Chapters 7 and 15) and David J.S. King (especially Chapter 14); the chapters referred to reflect their respective major contributions to Volume I.

Catherine King reconstructed the early staff lists, interviewed the wives of retired staff, and generally prepared material related to the social life and personnel problems of the Hongkong Bank. In addition she acted as editorial adviser. David J.S. King was a research associate who took full responsibility for research in German archives and prepared three important studies, the first on the early China loans, the second on the various railway and other loans to China in the period 1895 to 1914 as seen through German sources and related British Government documents, and third, the Hongkong Bank's Hamburg Branch.

Elizabeth Ng Wai Yee was with the project for three years; she collected Ch'ing documents and outlined their relevance to the history of the Bank; she spent several months in London and Cambridge collecting material from several archives, especially from the Public Record Office. Her work was essential to the success of the project.

I am grateful to Leslie Pressnell who accepted the appointment of consultant to the project, read every chapter, and commented in detail on every aspect of the study. To have such an adviser virtually on call was basic to the success of the project and both the Bank and I are very much in his debt.

Sir Michael Sandberg read the drafts, and I appreciate his practical interest and comments. The main editorial burden for the Bank was carried by S.W. Muirhead, who read each chapter very carefully and made notes which varied from the substantive to sub-editorial. Earlier chapters were also read by B.J.N. Ogden, and I was also able to refer specific points to experts within the Bank who proved very patient and helpful. Certain of the later chapters were sent to retired members of the staff who had actually been involved in the events; I appreciate their reassuring statements as well as their specific corrections.

Among others who commented on parts of Volume I were Sherman Cochran, Geoffrey Jones, Ramon F. Myers, and the readers selected by the Press, whose assistance, though perforce anonymous, is none the less appreciated.

In the early stages of the project the Centre of Asian Studies held a conference, bringing together research related to the history of the Hongkong Bank. As far as Volume I of the history is concerned, that is, the period to 1902 (but excluding the indemnity and railway loans post-1895), I have first to thank Roberta A. Dayer not only for her study of the young Charles S. Addis but also for her correct assessment of the importance of the Addis Papers, now in the School of Oriental and African Studies. Although specific published contributions are found in the Bibliography, I wish to mention the studies of Peter Wesley-Smith, T.A. Lee, Carl T. Smith, Christopher L. Yip, Judith Sear, Chee Peng Lim and his colleagues, W. Evan Nelson and his Singapore assistants, J.T.M. van Laanen, H.L.D. Selvaratnam through the Marga Institute (V. Kanesalingam, Associate Director), Thiravet Pramuanratkarn, Roy C. Ybañez (through the U.P. Business Research Foundation and Dr Fanny Cortes-Garcia), N.S. Ramaswami, and Claude Fivel-Démoret.

Y.C. Jao, Reader in Economics, University of Hong Kong, has commented from time to time and chaired a series of lectures, providing a forum for further comments on early drafts of this history. Information on the Bank's Hong Kong compradores comes almost entirely from the research of Carl T. Smith. Takeshi Hamashita has provided me with considerable material in Japanese and advice on using it; his own published studies have also been consulted; Selvaratnam collected material on both the Hongkong Bank and the Mercantile Bank in Sri Lanka, submitting a useful research study; Ybañez's report covered a more extended period than his published paper.

Either David King or I have been in correspondence with scholars who have assisted my work either directly or through their own contacts. G. Kurgan-van Hentenryk was as helpful personally as was her monumental study of Belgian interests in China. Harold P. Anderson, archivist and historian for Wells Fargo, and Geoffrey Jones, the historian for the Hongkong Bank Group's British Bank of the Middle East, have been both encouraging and helpful. Leslie Hannah, the Director of the Business History Unit, London School of Economics, attended the history conference and has been available for consultation throughout.

Philip L. Cottrell provided information on Lyons and on French archives, and Stanley Chapman's advice should also be recorded. My old colleague at the University of Kansas, Grant Goodman, furnished me with references relative to the Bank's role in Philippine history, and from Liverpool Patrick Tuck sent me extracts from his notes on the Hongkong Bank and the Mission Étrangères de Paris in the East. R.G. Baird of the Royal Bank of Scotland and C.W. Munn were helpful on matters Scottish. Sir Carl Meyer was a member of the Bank's Advisory Committee; Sir Anthony Meyer kindly permitted his grandfather's letter books to be shipped to Hong Kong for examination.

In Germany Manfred Pohl of the Deutsche Bank brought our attention to several sources. We are also grateful for access to the minute books of the Ost-Asiatischer Verein in Hamburg.

In France itself I consulted with Marie-Claire Bergère and Lucien Bianco, whose works on Chinese economic history are well-known; I also met with banking historians, F. Crouzet, M. Lévy-Leboyer, and J. Bouvier. The work in France was actually done by Fivel-Démoret and D.J.S. King. On Germany we consulted Ian L.D. Forbes who provided, *inter alia*, a preliminary bibliography, and Werner Draguhn and Brunhild Staiger of the Institut für Asienkunde in Hamburg. In the course of their studies, China experts pass through Hong Kong with valuable suggestions. Among them was Robert P. Gardella, to whom I am indebted for information on the finance of the tea trade. In nearby Macau we were expertly assisted by Mariado Anjos Morais, the Directress of the Arquivo Historico.

Not all the senior assistants prepared full research papers and were able to attend the conference: Sara E. Joynes (London), Gary Watson (Toronto, J.O.P.

Bland papers), Evelyne André (Belgium), Wang Ke-wen (Hoover Institution, Stanford), R.J.H. King (Harvard and Boston area libraries), and Rakesh Kuma Verma (India).

The maps were drawn in the University of Hong Kong's Cartographic Unit, Department of Geology and Geography, by Martin Chiu, T.B. Wong, and H.K. Kwan. The figures were drawn in the University's Centre for Media Resources under the supervision of Mrs D. Lui.

Research assistants include University of Hong Kong undergraduates: Lee Chun Wah, Cheng Yim-mei (statistics and economics), Kitty Yu Wai Hing (translation), Pauline Chow Lo Sai (history), Lau Wai Keung (statistics), Anissa Ip Yau Ching, Margaret Au Yuk Han, and Maisie Cheng Mei Sze; and American students resident in Hong Kong under the American Chamber of Commerce YES program: Karen Oberheim, Wendy S. Setnicka (statistics), Kathryn T. Boland (French translation), Ralph Leonard, Paul J. Schmidt, Catherine Naumann, and Michael McCoy. In the Centre of Asian Studies I was particularly assisted by C. Kripalani-Thadani and her colleagues Carolina Chan Yuan Yee, Cathy Wong Lin Yau, Anita Lau Po Ling, and Lam Tung Chun.

The determination of G.J. Helland's nationality and biography required the assistance of the Dansk Centralbibliotek for Sydslesvig, Flensburg, Federal Republic of Germany and the Hong Kong consulates and Foreign Office archivists of Denmark, Norway, and Sweden.

The project was multi-archival in concept. In 1979 when research began, the Hongkong Bank's own historical archives, that is, the material other than in current department files, was based on material collected by J.R. Jones, the Bank's sometime Legal Adviser, who during the 1950s and early 1960s actively corresponded with retired staff in an effort to reconstruct events during the inter-war period. In this he was assisted by F.H. (Towkay) King, retired Hongkong Bank staff, who went through London Office files, and by E.C. Hutchison, then the Shanghai Manager at a time when business was not overwhelming. In addition certain correspondence files of Chief Managers had been preserved. All research began with this collection. The cooperation of the Archives staff, especially Lily Lau Fung, Margaret Woollam, and Elaine Wu was therefore particularly important. Many of the Bank's records were originally kept in London, and G. Plastow and the staff of the twelfth floor at 99 Bishopsgate in London provided additional support and assistance.

In the course of the project four important private sources appeared. First, there were the papers of Sir Charles Addis, then kept at the family home in Frant. I am grateful to Roberta Dayer for insisting on the importance of the Addis Papers and for introducing me to Robina Addis, who had for many years been concerned with maintaining her father's valuable papers; I also discussed the collection with her brother, the late Sir John Addis, a member of the Bank's London Committee, who ultimately made the decision with her to place the collection in the Archives of the Library, School of Oriental and African Studies (SOAS). Sir Michael Sandberg then commissioned a catalogue to be made for publication (in 1986), and I am indebted to the work of Margaret Harcourt Williams in this connection. Charles P. Addis, grandson of Sir Charles Addis, supplemented this collection with important items.

I am appreciative of the cooperation and hospitality received from D.C.H. McLean, grandson of David McLean, the Bank's first Shanghai Manager and subsequently London Manager, and from Mrs McLean. Their persistent searches in their home in Scotland revealed two sets of letter books as well as miscellaneous correspondence, the bulk of which was sent to SOAS; typed transcripts, made by Catherine E. King, are on file at SOAS, in the Hongkong Bank's Group archives, and with the family.

I should also record appreciation – and perhaps avoid confusion – by noting the contributions made by (Dr) David McLean, King's College, University of London, for his study of the 'political period" of the Imperial Bank of Persia and the Hongkong Bank in the years to 1914.

Rosemary Seton, the Archivist at SOAS, was helpful with the Addis and McLean papers and with other materials, including the archive of John Swire and Sons, Ltd, papers relating to the Imperial Maritime Customs, the China Association archive, and the Evans/Baker collection.

The third private collection was that of F.T. Koelle, made available through the courtesy of his son, W. Koelle of Hamburg. I am grateful for permission to have the journals xeroxed and appreciate the assistance of Peter H.A. King and the Bank's Hamburg Branch in achieving this.

The Hermann Wallich papers are in the possession of his grandson, Henry C. Wallich of the Federal Reserve Board. The letters are not directly related to the Bank; Hermann Wallich was Shanghai Manager of the Comptoir d'Escompte de Paris in the years immediately preceding the Franco-Prussian War, and he had important comments to make about banking developments in the East.

The illustrations in this volume are taken from the Hongkong Bank Group archives. These include photographs originally in the Addis Papers and the private collections of Charles P. Addis, Sir Michael Jackson, and D.C.H. McLean.

Appreciation is expressed to those who contributed various papers, photographs, and smaller collections, some of which have been deposited in Group Archives. The full autobiography of H.E. Muriel was already in the Bank's archives; permission to quote from it has been granted by his daughter, Margaret Forgan.

All of those involved in the project are indebted to librarians and archivists in various cities, companies, and universities. I should like to mention particularly R.H. Reed of the National Westminster Bank, whose bank holds the archives of the London and Westminster, the London and County, and Parr's Banks; J.M.L. Booker of Lloyds Bank for his research on the later life of the Bank's second Chief Manager, James Greig; P.H. Blagbrough, Matheson and Co., for locating and granting access to the files of the British and Chinese Corporation and the Chinese Central Railways; Alan Reid for permission to consult once again the valuable archives of Jardine, Matheson and Co. in the Cambridge University Library; J.M. Keyworth of the Bank of England; Richard G.R. Tarling, Chubb and Son's Lock and Safe Co.; Tom Ingram and M.J. Orbell of Baring Bros. C. Schultz granted D.J.S. King access to the archives of one of the Bank's founding companies, Siemssen and Co. Also in Hamburg David was assisted by Senator Jan Albers (Kunst and Albers material) and Herr Gabrielsson of the Hamburg Staatsarchiv; in Bonn Maria Keipert granted him access to the important archives of the Auswärtiges Amt. D.J.S. King was kindly granted access to the N.M. Rothschild archives by Gershom Knight, which proved invaluable for background material, especially in Volume II. We are also indebted to Peter A. Graham, the Managing Director of the Standard Chartered Bank Group, for an introduction to their archives.

Permission to use the China Trade Museum Archives in Milton, Massachusetts, was granted by H.A. Crosby Forbes with whom I was able to discuss the background of the Forbes' role in the East. These papers have been subsequently deposited with the library of the Massachusetts Historical Society, and I was grateful to John Cushing for permission to quote from the Forbes Papers. I have consulted the Augustine Heard papers in the archives of the Baker Library, Harvard Business School, over the years from 1956; R.J.H. King and D.J.S. King more recently had access for this project; our appreciation to the several archivists involved – including R.W. Lovett and Florence Bartoshesky.

The list of archives consulted as shown in the Bibliography is also a list indicating that the archivists concerned materially assisted in the success of this project.

The history is perhaps more personal than many company histories. I wish to express my appreciation to B.J.N. Ogden for initial introductions to his colleagues throughout the Hongkong Bank Group and to those officers for receiving me and Catherine King – and, on occasion, David King – and providing both assistance and hospitality. The importance of this direct contact will become more apparent in Volumes III and IV when the oral history material can be used. At that time further credits will be relevant, but for the present the appreciation is stated in general but no less sincere terms.

FRANK H.H. KING

STATEMENT ON DOLLARS AND EXCHANGE

All dollars in this history
unless specifically stated otherwise
are
HONG KONG DOLLARS.
One billion = 1,000 million
One lac = 1,00,000

The Hong Kong/London exchange rate is quoted as so many shillings and pence per dollar, e.g. $1.00 = 4s 6d. From this it follows that:

A **fall** in exchange will result in a dollar exchanging for fewer shillings and pence and is evidence of a depreciation of the Hong Kong dollar *vis à vis* sterling.

A **rise** (improvement, increase) in exchange will result in a dollar exchanging for more shillings and pence and is evidence of an appreciation of the Hong Kong dollar *vis à vis* sterling.

The Shanghai exchanges are similarly quoted in terms of a Shanghai tael.

'Silver' may refer in the popular business jargon of the day to units of account payable in silver bullion or coin. Thus a 'silver' loan is a loan denominated in e.g. Hong Kong dollars or Shanghai taels.

'Gold' may refer to sterling and/or to other currencies on a gold standard.

'The exchanges' or other similar term refers, unless modified, to the foreign exchange rates and the markets which determine the rate at which one currency can be bought in terms of another.

All dollars in this history
unless specifically stated otherwise
are
HONG KONG DOLLARS.

ABBREVIATIONS

Bank	Hongkong and Shanghai Banking Corporation
Chartered Bank	Chartered Bank of India, Australia and China
Chartered Mercantile Bank	Chartered Mercantile Bank of India, London and China (to 1892)
Commercial Bank	Commercial Bank Corporation of India and the East
d	pence
DAB	Deutsch-Asiatische Bank
DG	Disconto-Gesellschaft
D. Sassoon	David Sassoon, Sons and Co. *then* David Sassoon and Co.
HkTs	Haikwan taels
Hongkong Bank	Hongkong and Shanghai Banking Corporation
HSBC	Hongkong and Shanghai Banking Corporation
Mercantile Bank	Mercantile Bank of India, Limited (after 1892)
NA	National Association
OGSF	Officers Good Service Fund
Oriental Bank	Oriental Bank Corporation (to 1884)
P&O or P&OSNCo.	Peninsular and Oriental Steam Navigation Company
s	shillings
ShTs	Shanghai taels
(Sir)	designating a person who is subsequently knighted
TJ	Thomas Jackson
Ts	taels
TT	telegraphic transfer

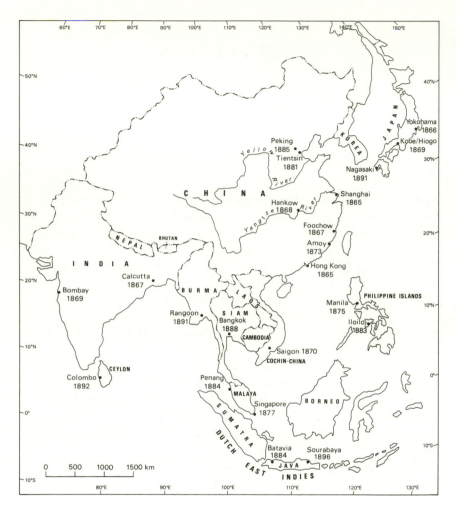

2 The Hongkong Bank's Asian offices in 1902.

1

'ON AN EVEN KEEL': THE HONGKONG BANK IN HISTORY

There are few ways in which a man can be more innocently employed than in getting money.

Samuel Johnson

THE HONGKONG BANK GROUP, 1984

At the end of 1984 The Hongkong and Shanghai Banking Corporation was reportedly the world's fourteenth largest banking group as calculated on the basis of shareholders' funds valued at $20.9 billion.[a] With 1,200 offices in 55 countries and a staff of some 45,000, the Hongkong Bank managed assets totalling $481.6 billion (= £53.0 billion or US$61.6 billion).

Ownership was widely distributed with 166,600 shareholders holding the 2.9 billion fully paid-up shares.

The Corporation was both an operating bank and a bank holding company, with subsidiary and associated companies in commercial and merchant banking, finance, insurance, related financial services, trustee and nominee services, transportation, and printing and publishing. These companies, including the Hongkong Bank itself, are referred to as the Hongkong Bank Group. Included in the Group, with name forms reflecting various modern styles, were The British Bank of the Middle East, Hang Seng Bank, Marine Midland Bank, the Hongkong Bank of Canada, the HongkongBank of Australia Limited (1986), the Wardley merchant banking group, the Wayfoong financial group, and the Carlingford insurance companies. Although Antony Gibbs & Sons, Ltd, has remained a subsidiary company, the Group's principal London-based merchant bank is the successor Hongkong Bank Limited (1986). The British and Chinese Corporation Limited, once so important in Imperial Chinese railway development, exists today only as a reminder of the Hongkong Bank's historical role.

Cathay Pacific Airways was an associated company, as were also the South China Morning Post (publishing), the Saudi British Bank, the Korea International Merchant Bank, International Commercial Bank, and the many others listed in Table 1.1. James Capel & Co., with its own group, was an associated

---

[a] Ranking banks by the value of shareholders' funds results in placing Citicorp of New York first, followed by BankAmerica Corp. National Westminster is 10th; Chemical New York Corp., 13th; and Manufacturers Hanover Corp., 15th. A listing of the top 500 banks can be found in *Euromoney* for June 1985.

Table 1.1 *The Hongkong and Shanghai Banking Corporation*
Principal operating subsidiary and associated companies, 1984[a]

	Country of Incorporation
Commercial Banking	
The British Bank of the Middle East	U.K.
Hang Seng Bank Ltd (61.48%)	Hong Kong
The Hongkong and Shanghai Banking Corporation (CI) Ltd	Jersey, C.I.
Hongkong Bank and Trust Company Ltd	Gibraltar
Hongkong Bank of Canada	Canada
Marine Midland Banks, Inc. (51.05%)	U.S.A.
Hongkong Egyptian Bank SAE (40%)	Egypt
International Commercial Bank PLC (22%)	U.K.
The Saudi British Bank (40%)	Saudi Arabia
Merchant Banking	
Equator Bank Ltd (81%)	Bahamas
Wardley Ltd	Hong Kong
Wardley Australia Ltd (80%)[b]	Australia
Wardley London Ltd	U.K.
Wardley Middle East Ltd	U.A.E.
Korea International Merchant Bank (30%)	Korea
Utama Wardley Berhad (30%)	Malaysia
Finance	
Concord International (Curaçao) NV (70.2%)	N. Antilles
Metway Ltd (51%)	Hong Kong
Middle East Finance Co. Ltd (90%)	U.A.E.
Mortgage And Finance Bhd	Brunei
Mortgage And Finance (Malaysia) Bhd	Malaysia
TKM International (Holdings) Ltd	U.K.
Wayfoong Credit Ltd	Hong Kong
Wayfoong Finance Ltd	Hong Kong
Wayfoong Mortgage And Finance (Singapore) Ltd	Singapore
FortWay Finance Ltd (50%)	Hong Kong
Insurance	
Anton Underwriting Agencies Ltd (99.8%)[c]	
Carlingford Australia Insurance Co. Ltd (82.6%)	Australia
Carlingford Insurance Co. Ltd (70%)	Hong Kong
Carlingford Swire Assurance Ltd (74.5%)	Hong Kong
Gibbs Hartley Cooper Ltd	U.K.
Gibbs Insurance Consultants Ltd	Hong Kong
Investment Holding	
Fort Hall Ltd	Hong Kong
Grenville Transportation Holdings Ltd	Hong Kong
HSBC Holdings BV	Netherlands
Wardley Holdings Ltd	Hong Kong
Wardley London Holdings Ltd	U.K.

Table 1.1 (*cont.*)

	Country of Incorporation
Investment Services	
CM&M Group, Inc. (through MMBI) (51%)	Delaware
Wardley International Management Ltd	Hong Kong
Wardley Investment Services Ltd	Bahamas
Wardley Marine International Investment Management Ltd[c] (75.5%)	U.K.
Wardley Unit Trust Managers Ltd	U.K.
James Capel & Co. (29.9%)[d]	U.K.
James Capel (Far East) Ltd (29.9%)[d]	Hong Kong
Wardley-ACLI Commodities Ltd (45%)[e]	Hong Kong
Wardley Nikko Management Ltd (50%)	Hong Kong
Financial Services	
International Treasury Management Ltd (75.5%)[f]	Hong Kong
Wardley Data Services Ltd	Hong Kong
Acceptor Enterprises Ltd (45%)	Hong Kong
Central Registration Hong Kong Ltd (50%)	Hong Kong
Dun and Bradstreet (HK) Ltd (50%)	Hong Kong
Hongkong and Shanghai Thomas Cook Ltd (50%)	Hong Kong
Trustee and Nominee Services	
Companies are located in the Channel Islands, Hong Kong, Gibraltar, India, Malaysia, Singapore, United Kingdom	
Transportation	
Cathay Pacific Airways Ltd (30%)	Hong Kong
World Finance International Ltd (37.5%)	Bermuda
World Maritime Ltd (50%)	Bermuda
World Shipping and Investment Co. Ltd (45%)	Cayman Islands
Printing and Publishing	
South China Morning Post Ltd (48.76%)[c]	Hong Kong

Notes:
Brunei   Negara Brunei Darussalam
C.I.   Channel Islands, United Kingdom
U.A.E.   United Arab Emirates
[a] Associated companies are indented. Group equity holdings are 100% except where indicated in parenthesis.
[b] Hongkong Finance Ltd (1986).
[c] sold.
[d] now a wholly owned subsidiary (1986).
[e] Wardley-Thomson Ltd (1986).
[f] Joint venture, HSBC/MMBI.

company in 1984 but had become a subsidiary by 1986.[b]

The name is evocative of the romance of the China coast, but The Hongkong and Shanghai Banking Corporation's assets were nevertheless widely diversified geographically – 39% or $188 billion were in its 'own' Asia/Pacific, but these were slightly exceeded by the $190 billion in the Americas (especially Canada, the United States, and Chile). Assets in Europe accounted for a further 11.2% and in the Middle East 4.5% of the total. This reflects the Bank and Group's evolution from a regional to a multinational operation. In 1959 the Bank had consolidated its East and Southeast Asia position with the acquisition of its erstwhile rival the Mercantile Bank (formerly the Chartered Mercantile Bank of India, London and China); then, with the acquisition of the British Bank of the Middle East (formerly the Imperial Bank of Persia) in 1960, the Bank for the first time obtained a base of operations independent of its traditional region. Throughout the 1970s the Hongkong Bank remained essentially an Eastern bank; not until its acquisition in 1980 of a majority holding in the American bank holding company, Marine Midland Banks, Inc., did it break its regional mould and become a truly multinational financial group (see Table 1.2).

The American acquisition came after a decade of steady growth. Hong Kong had recovered from the impact of Chinese Red Guards by 1970. In the years to 1984 the relevant indicators of the Hongkong Bank's growth shows a compound rate of between 21% and 26% per annum. In 1970 dividends per share (owned in 1984 and adjusted for bonus and rights issues, etc.) would have been $0.03, requiring a total distribution of $79 million; in 1984 the dividend was $0.46 costing $1,316 million. Other indicators are equally dramatic. A 24.4% compound rate of growth brought the 1970 total assets of $22.7 billion to $481.6 billion by the end of 1984; total shareholders' funds moved from $844 million at a rate of 25.75% per annum to $20.9 billion.

This is the description of a banking group which in late 1985 moved into its new headquarters building at its traditional 1, Queen's Road, Central, address. The Bank's new building is a 'hi-tech' construction designed by Foster Associates (and described in a commemorative book by Ian Lambot and Gillian Chambers). It is reputedly, at $5 billion, the most expensive office building in the world; it is a statement of the Bank's confidence in itself, in Hong Kong, and in the cost-effectiveness of the design.

[b] The names of Hongkong Bank Group companies have been listed here in their officially incorporated form. Thereafter in this volume, but with the exception of the full name of The Hongkong and Shanghai Banking Corporation (when referring to the period from 1950 on), company names will be cited in normal grammatical form, without the use of the ampersand or capitalization of the initial definite article, even when these may, were the official records thoroughly researched, prove to be part of the legally incorporated name.

Table 1.2 *The Hongkong and Shanghai Banking Corporation*
International network, 1984

	Offices		Offices
Asia and Pacific		*Europe*	
Australia	11	Belgium	1
Brunei Darussalam	10	Channel Islands	4
China	5	France	4
Hong Kong	411	Gibraltar	1
India	24	Greece	1
Indonesia	5	Republic of Ireland	1
Japan	7	Italy	2
Republic of Korea	4	Netherlands	3
Macau	7	Spain	1
Malaysia	44	Sweden	1
Mauritius	11	Switzerland	2
New Zealand	3	United Kingdom	34
Pakistan	2	West Germany	6
Papua New Guinea	2		
Philippines	4	*Middle East*	
Singapore	25	Bahrain	9
Solomon Islands	1	Cyprus	86
Sri Lanka	1	Djibouti	1
Taiwan	1	Egypt	3
Thailand	3	Jordan	5
Vanuatu	2	Lebanon	10
		Oman	6
Americas		Qatar	2
Argentina	2	United Arab Emirates	18
Bahamas	6	Yemen Arab Republic	1
Brazil	2	Saudi Arabia	24
Canada	1		
Chile	4		
Colombia	1		
Mexico	2		
Panama	2		
United States	317		
Venezuela	1		

This does not constitute a description of the Hongkong Bank as it will feature in Volume I of this history; it is an introductory review of the position at the end of 1984. This position, however, was consequent to the events to be described in the volumes which follow, beginning 120 years earlier in 1864. This introductory chapter concluded, it is to the year 1864 that the narrative will return.

THE BANK'S HISTORY, THE PRINCIPAL ISSUES

There is no simple graphical scale adequate to show the growth of the Hongkong Bank between 1864 and 1984 (see Figure 1). The statistics in Table 1.3 permit a somewhat better understanding. Between 1865 and 1957 on the eve of the Bank's first acquisition, shareholders' funds increased 72 times; between 1957 and 1984, 116 times (see Table 1.3, Figure 2, and Appendix Figures A–D). Nevertheless, as early as 1885 the Bank had become indisputably the largest bank operating on the China coast and by 1895 was reckoned as a bank of world-wide significance. This was, in the custom of the time, with reference to a geographical region; in the East the Hongkong Bank was pre-eminent.

There are two main themes in the early history of the Hongkong Bank which will help place its success in context. The first is the tradition of British overseas banking, the second the need for a sound banking institution headquartered in the East and capable of meeting directly the financial requirements of the expanding activities of Eastern based merchants and of the several colonial and sovereign governments. The Colonial Banking Regulations, in conformity to which the Hongkong Bank was eventually established by an ordinance of the Hong Kong Legislative Council, had been basic to the constitutions of colonial banks since the early 1830s. Such banks had often been first incorporated in a particular territory but, except in colonies of settlement, the bank's directors were eventually under pressure from London-based shareholders and customers to remove their head offices to London, requiring reincorporation and loss of local control. This tradition both forced the founding of a local Hong Kong bank and alerted its directors to the dangers of the London temptation.

These two themes, the colonial banking tradition and the regional focus, merged to make a unique history. Hong Kong was unusual in being a Crown Colony without representative government yet possessing an economic importance as a base for an international body of merchants who were 'decision-makers'. Similarly in other Eastern ports there was either colonial rule or extraterritorial arrangements, where, in many cases, there were firms with a resident managing partner.

The Hongkong Bank remained subject to the diminishing scope of British imperial banking policy yet, due to the continued economic independence of its Eastern constituents and its policy of retaining a significant percentage of its shares on the Eastern registers, was able to resist successfully pressures to reestablish in London. Hong Kong itself developed no significant banking laws until the 1960s, so that its major bank retained the traditions of a British overseas bank, traditions similar to those of Royally chartered banks, while maintaining the vital regional associations which were key to its continued success.

Table 1.3 *The Hongkong and Shanghai Banking Corporation*
Changes in shares, paid-up capital, and shareholders' funds, 1865–1985

End year[a]	Shares issued	Paid-up capital millions of		Shareholders' funds millions of	
		$	£	$	£
1865	20,000	2.5	0.56	2.5	0.56
1866	40,000	2.9	0.65	3.1	0.70
1867	40,000	3.0	0.68	3.4	0.77
1869	40,000	3.5	0.79	4.3	0.97
1870	40,000	4.0	0.90	4.8	1.08
1871	40,000	4.5	1.01	5.5	1.24
1872	40,000	5.0	1.13	6.0	1.35
1883	60,000	7.1	1.30	11.7	2.14
1884	60,000	7.5	1.39	12.6	2.23
1890	80,000	9.3	1.59	16.5	2.82
1891	80,000	10.0	1.60	16.6	2.56
1907	120,000	15.0	1.36	45.8	4.15
1921	160,000	20.0	2.58	81.9	10.58
1955	200,000	25.0	1.56	163.6	10.23
1957	400,000	50.0	3.13	180.1	11.25
1959	498,491	62.3	3.89	240.3	15.02
1960	632,369	79.0	4.94	321.3	20.08
1961	3,161,845	79.0	4.94	321.4	20.09
1965	6,323,690	158.1	9.88	409.2	25.57
1966	6,956,059	173.9	10.87	478.2	29.89
1969	7,651,665	191.3	13.15	591.3	40.65
1970	15,303,330	382.6	26.30	884.4	58.05
1971	16,833,633	420.8	28.93	968.9	66.61
1972	18,517,029	462.9	34.87	1,311.9	98.83
1973	224,272,510	560.7	47.74	1,508.4	128.43
1974	277,651,978	694.1	60.25	1,841.3	159.83
1975	347,064,972	867.7	85.23	1,971.4	193.66
1976	381,771,469	954.4	120.05	2,272.8	285.89
1977	419,948,616	1,049.9	119.44	2,486.4	282.86
1978	461,943,478	1,154.9	117.90	2,877.3	293.75
1979	692,915,217	1,732.3	158.06	3,709.4	338.45
1980	1,114,233,983	2,785.6	227.12	10,326.0	841.91
1981	1,559,927,575	3,899.0	360.00	14,060.0	1,296.00
1982	2,079,903,433	5,199.8	493.00	15,606.0	1,479.00
1983	2,287,893,776	5,719.7	506.00	19,586.0	1,733.00
1984	2,859,867,220	7,149.7	787.00	20,863.0	2,296.00
1985	3,145,853,942	7,864.6	700.00	21,882.0	1,948.00

Note:
[a] Years selected are those in which there are changes in paid-up capital.

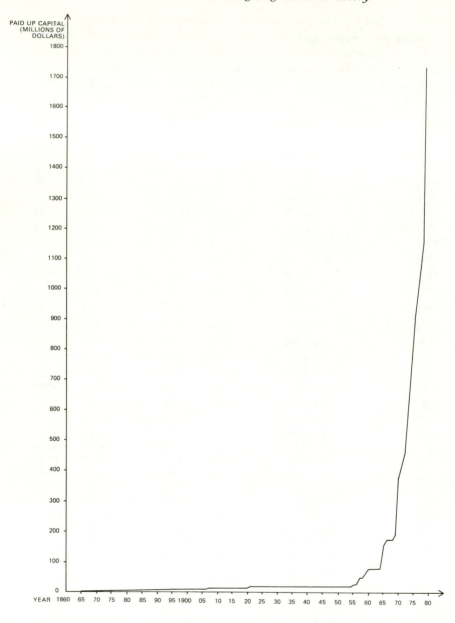

Figure 1 The Hongkong and Shanghai Banking Corporation
Paid-up capital, 1865–1979.

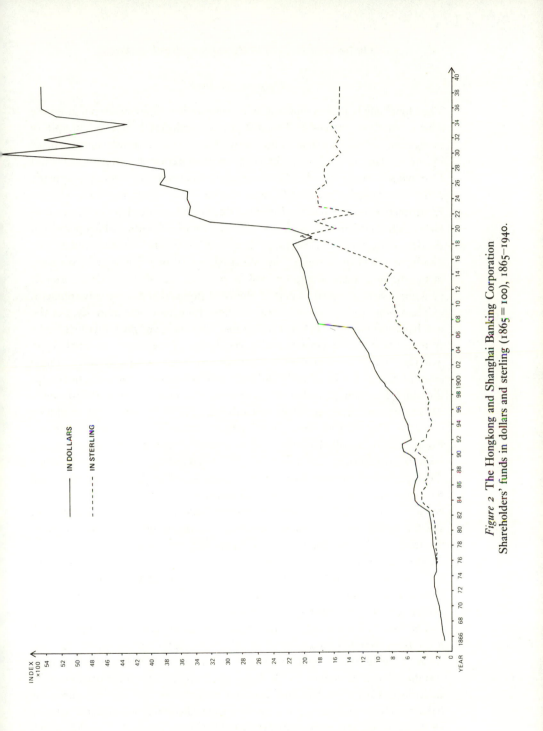

Figure 2 The Hongkong and Shanghai Banking Corporation
Shareholders' funds in dollars and sterling (1865 = 100), 1865–1940.

9

Corporate history

The Hongkong Bank was founded by representatives of the major hongs on the China coast. It was part of the Treaty Port community, of the foreign community in the East. As the merchant houses moved from simple partnerships to major business organizations, from trading to agency house to multinationals, so too did their bank. The personnel policies reflected this evolution. From a pragmatic policy of employing men available in the East, the Hongkong Bank set up a recruitment system through its London Office which involved the socialization of its 'Eastern Staff' and, through that process, a form of control which permitted the Bank to operate on the basis of geographically separated decision centres. The disadvantages of the system – the 'shutting out' of non-British from management, the long years of apprenticeship, and the lack of formal education in banking – were accepted as part of the total political and social environment.

The young banker's assistant was employed for his visible integrity, but the cost had to be minimized. There were those who perceived the limitations of the system. Some argued against specific regulations, for example, restrictions on marriage; others attempted to reconstruct the whole system of entry. These attempts failed. The banks really did need 'officers' to do clerical tasks; no receipt was valid, for example, without the signature of a member of the 'British staff'. Alternatives were, nevertheless, considered. University graduates might be recruited. This proposal was argued from time to time in the context of increased Continental, especially German, professionalism, but piecemeal reform proved impractical; there was a commonly accepted social and political structure in which the organization operated. Nor did the universities really have courses designed for undergraduates planning a business career. Business and university cooperated in the inter-war period, but the problem of university recruitment and the consequent restructuring of career patterns would not be resolved, until the total social scene changed in the 1950s and afterwards.

Attitudes to the business corporation evolved. The role of shareholders, directors, and the Bank's servants changed in response to changing attitudes. The Bank's history reflects the general course of corporate development, from personnel policy to charitable donations.

The Head Office was in Hong Kong; this limited the selection of directors and, if the Bank were to have a wide range of constituents – including the business rivals of the directors – their role had to be limited; they had to withdraw from 'hands-on' management of the Bank. By the mid-1890s the directors were able, with the presence of an able Chief Manager, to withdraw their participation in the banking activities of the corporation. In an age when this encompassed virtually all its activities, appointed managers would manage the bank. Supplementing this development was a limited broadening of management at several levels;

middle management existed. There was thus a development from the early years when the Bank was in danger of being the tool of its founding taipans and their purposes to the years from 1876 and certainly from the mid-1890s when the Bank became a true separate entity endowed with its own purposes and its own objectives as defined by self-perpetuating professional managers.

The Board existed outside management, as it were, and the paid corporate servant acted as chief executive (with profit sharing provisions), an arrangement which lasted into the 1960s. Only then did the Board and the management integrate; the Chairman was an executive chairman, the senior managers executive directors. The Bank's evolution had particular features, but they are illustrative of familiar factors in corporate development world-wide.

The Bank and Hong Kong

That the Hongkong Bank was incorporated in Hong Kong by special ordinance had special consequences. The directors, for example, had undiluted concern for success in the East; they were in the East, the Bank had been founded for a purpose and could not easily be diverted. Secondly, there were consequent limitations. Hong Kong was not the centre of Eastern entrepreneurship; that claim might be granted to Shanghai – or to Japan. The Bank enjoyed legal and communication advantages in a British colony and entrepot, but some described Hong Kong as a colonial backwater.

How the directors overcame the disadvantages and focused on the positive merits of a Head Office in the Colony is a major issue. That they were successful is evidenced by the fact that they were able to establish sound relations in the City, relations which were reinforced sufficiently over time to permit, in conjunction with the Bank's own London Office, world-significant merchant banking operations of the period 1895–1914. The directors' methods were both pragmatic and unexpected; they permitted two major centres of authority with different approaches, that of the Chief Manager reporting to the Board of Directors in Hong Kong and that of the London Manager reporting to his London Consultative Committee. This worked at least from the mid 1870s through the 1920s, with Hong Kong as the final authority. The solution was finely balanced and was eventually upset; the varying success of the solution was but a reflection of the conflict between those in the East, the men on the scene, and the central authorities, be they in the City or in the Treasury and Colonial Office.

The Bank and the regulators

Few if any banks have rivalled the Hongkong Bank in the number of jurisdictions to which it has been subject. The differences and the necessary adjustments are part of the Bank's history, particularly in the more recent days of multinational banking.

As a British overseas bank incorporated by a Colonial Government ordinance, the Hongkong Bank was subject through the provisions of the Colonial Banking Regulations to the authorized regulatory supervision administered by the Governor of Hong Kong after consultation with and/or instructions from the Treasury through the Colonial Office. As a 'foreign' corporation in other British territories, the Bank found itself subject to Indian, Ceylon, and Straits government control; in the Philippines there was first Spanish jurisdiction and then the more rigorous American regulatory provisions of the U.S. Controller of the Currency. In San Francisco and New York, State legislation prevented development; in Hamburg and Lyons, where the Bank registered according to local law, its role had been carefully restricted by the Board in Hong Kong, but local regulations were still relevant and, especially in matters of taxation, important.

In the Bank's early history the Board itself was as anxious as the authorities to limit operations in such commercially risky places as Bombay, Calcutta, and San Francisco. The American restrictions did not adversely affect operations until the early 1950s; in response the directors authorized the founding of their first banking subsidiary, the Hongkong and Shanghai Banking Corporation of California, Inc. For most of its history, however, the Hongkong Bank's principal regulator has been the British Treasury.

Royal charters or colonial ordinances of incorporation contained specific provisions which gave the Government some apparent control of the bank's operations. These provisions are discussed in Chapter 4; their administration, however, presented problems. Between the 1860s and the 1880s the concept of a uniform Imperial banking and monetary policy was virtually abandoned, the Treasury consequently lacked a consistent policy to provide the basis for administering the apparent controls which had been written into the 'charters'. The establishment of responsible legislatures in the colonies of settlement made Treasury pretensions to expertise unwelcome; regulations were disregarded or withdrawn. In the resulting confusion, practical recognition that certain colonies were still without Colonial Office control led too often to erratic implementation of hitherto forgotten rules, based, on occasion, on incorrect assumptions.

Although without an overall banking policy, the Treasury was concerned with the colonial note issue. The Treasury was consequently torn between recognition of the inadvisability of interfering with a commercial operation and the perceived need to control a corporation possessing the right to issue banknotes. The Treasury considered that it was the responsibility of the public to judge the wisdom of doing business with a private-sector bank, but, at the same time, the Treasury recognized there were sufficient provisions in the relevant legislation to give colonial residents the not unreasonable impression that the Government was taking some though unspecified responsibility.

The Treasury at times used its regulatory rights to enforce a particular but possibly unrelated policy. The Bank was required to obtain Treasury permission to open a new branch. To this the Treasury might have no objection, but as 'gatekeeper' it was able to deny the necessary permission unless the directors agreed, for example, to modify the nature of the security against the note issue. The Treasury took the opportunity to exercise its supervisory powers when the ordinance of incorporation specified the need to make routine application to Government.

The most serious of the several confusions arising from the Treasury's *ad hoc* attention to bank regulatory matters was the interpretation of colonial 'extraterritoriality', that is of the right of a colonially chartered bank to operate or even exist as a corporation outside the territory of the colonial government granting the charter. The problem of the Hongkong Bank's existence outside Hong Kong reflected a long-standing controversy which originated in the context of Treasury control of banking in the Australian and Canadian colonies; the controversy, misinterpreted and inconsistently applied, had some effect on the course of the Bank's development at least through the 1880s.

The Treasury's attitude to the issue of banknotes reflected the changes in accepted monetary theory, but for the Hongkong Bank the problem was pragmatic. The people in Hong Kong, and to a lesser extent in the Treaty Ports, preferred banknotes to an imperfect, full-bodied coinage with a high cost of usage and over which, in the absence of local mints, they had no control either of quality or of quantity. The consequent demand for banknotes soon brought the note-issuing banks to the limits of their authorized issues, and still more banknotes were required. The situation was not fully understood in London; carried to the potential extreme of a private bank finding itself providing the paper currency of all of China, it was not understood by the banks. Furthermore the Treasury was simply frustrated by the unwillingness of the Hong Kong Government to issue its own notes, an unwillingness based not on monetary principles but on the logical policy conclusion that, as the Hongkong Bank and the other two note-issuing banks were doing the job well, why gratuitously take on a very complex, time-consuming, and labour-intensive task?

By the end of the century the Treasury and Colonial Office had abandoned any thought that they were administering an Empire-wide system, but in many territories local legislation had failed to take up the task. Supervisory decisions were focused on an *ad hoc* basis on the Hongkong Bank itself, with some regard for the impact on the other main note-issuing bank, the London-based Chartered Bank of India, Australia and China. Post-1945 even Hong Kong passed banking ordinances, but the Bank's special ordinance was still seen as overriding. In the

1960s the dual approach to bank control in Hong Kong had to be abandoned in favour of subjecting the chartered banks, the foreign banks, and the locally incorporated banks to the same, increasingly detailed regulatory ordinances passed by the Legislative Council and designed for the territory.

The history of the Bank's relations with Hong Kong and British regulators may be summarized as a retreat, in confusion, from Empire-wide concepts to 'gatekeeper' type control focused on the Bank itself, to replacement of direct London interest in favour of local banking legislation applicable to all banks. In other British-controlled territories the story was illustrative of the issues already mentioned. Outside the Empire, British overseas banks were either operating under terms of treaties of extraterritoriality (extrality), as in China until 1943 and Japan until 1900, or as a 'foreign' corporation.

The regulation of the Hongkong Bank in China was based on the treaties of extrality between Britain and Imperial China. Operating under extrality did not mean operating in defiance of local laws and customs. Extrality related to the administration of justice; the foreign courts would not necessarily support policies contrary to the sovereign of the soil in matters, for example, of the currency; in commercial matters, including banking, the Courts attempted to rule consistent with local commercial practice. The Bank's China banknote issue was always relatively small; it was never legal tender and it became a nationalist complaint only in the early 1920s and then on more general political grounds.

Under these circumstances the Bank's regulator remained the Treasury, with administration implemented by the consuls and the consular courts. These were supplemented by Orders in Council and the consequent 'Queen's Regulations'. The ultimate control of the Bank's activities came from the Chinese themselves. When they refused to accept Hongkong Bank banknotes, these ceased to circulate; when the Chinese banking authorities wanted to conclude a 'Gentleman's Agreement' with foreign banks to the effect that they would accept no new Chinese customer; the Hongkong Bank would agree. Banking is a special industry; conflict with the host nation is not practical, treaties notwithstanding. The successfully restricted role of foreign banks in Japan during the shorter period of extrality is confirmation of this.

The Hongkong Bank in common with other British overseas banks was a commercial venture; in China it had Chinese customers, including high officials and the Government itself. There were many competitors; any claim to arbitrary British support would have alienated its local constituents. The Foreign Office instructed British representatives to 'keep the ring', not to actively seek new advantages or enforce previously granted general privileges in favour of a particular British bank.

The Bank and China

The Hongkong Bank has survived several Chinese regimes. Extrality was not the explanation. During the last years of the Ch'ing dynasty, from 1865 to 1911, Imperial China's resources were diverted to meet internal disturbances and to pay the cost of an unsuccessful adaptation to Western nation-state politics, especially in the field of international relations. Various provincial officials turned to foreigners for financing; the Hongkong Bank was able to assist on flexible but reasonable terms. It accepted the terms required by China and translated these into terms acceptable in the capital markets of the Treaty Ports and London; the Bank was an 'interface'. It was thus in a position to play an important role when China agreed to limited adoption of modern techniques, especially in mining and railways.

The role of the Bank in China nevertheless had special features which need full consideration in this history. It is easy to exaggerate the role of any foreign institution in this period of transition, but whatever the limitations of the Bank's impact on the history of China the latter was of essential importance in the history of the Bank. Foreign trade and financial contacts remained, at China's insistence, on the restrictive terms agreed in the so-called 'unequal treaties', but they mounted in importance during the latter part of the nineteenth century until they shook the very Throne itself.

The Bank's relations with China were dictated by the Chinese. Contacts with the merchants and officials of Imperial China tended consequently to be indirect. There was little practical access to the interior; the considerable business was done through compradores working with local banks, with the remittance or Shansi banks, with the merchants, or with officials. This last could lead to limited direct contacts on a particular issue. The Bank's Shanghai or Tientsin Manager might have dealings with a senior official; in Peking the Agent had his 'contacts' which reached into the bureaucracy, but actual official communications between the Government of China and a Western commercial bank had to pass through the British Legation; the Emperor's officials were not able to conclude major, enforceable agreements directly with a foreign merchant or banker.

The upgrading of what were, from the Hongkong Bank's point of view (and what most certainly were in the British Foreign Office instructions), private-sector business transactions to matters of sufficient apparent political importance to cross the desk of Her Majesty's Minister to China was well-received neither by the Bank nor the Minister. It is true that the Minister on occasion overstepped the restraints imposed by the Foreign Office, but officially he could do no more than 'keep (or hold) the ring'.

As long as British interests dominated and as long as, among British interests, the Hongkong Bank was the principal contender for official Chinese business, the necessity of communicating through the Legation facilitated but had little other impact on the Bank's business or on its perceived role in China. When, however, there was international competition, the British Minister found it necessary to intervene – if only to keep the ring open for British participation. But that was for British, not Hongkong Bank, participation. The British Minister obtained the opportunity for a British firm; it was then up to the British firms to secure Chinese patronage and perform according to an agreement approved by China; after a firm had been chosen by the Chinese, the Minister endorsed it as the British 'choice'. If the Hongkong Bank was usually successful, this attested to its capacity and to its relations with the Chinese; it was not a statement of a 'favoured' position relative to the British authorities.

That the Hongkong Bank's position after 1895 should be misunderstood is not surprising. The Chinese-imposed necessity of dealing through the Legation was the root cause of the confusion. Involving the Legation had eventually to involve the British Government, its relations with the other powers, and its political commitments at home. Chinese forms of foreign relations had a strange harvest.

But the confusion was compounded. The Hongkong Bank was also the British Government's banker in China, a position obtained by the commercial process of bidding for the contract to undertake 'Treasury Chest' business in a particular area. Thus it was called upon to perform banking business for the British Government, for the British armed forces, and for the consular services. As experts and government bankers, its officers were also called on to give advice. Boxer Indemnity funds were in part deposited in the Hongkong Bank; at the request of early Republican China, the Bank took custody of China's customs revenues until the establishment of the Central Bank of China. The application of guilt by association consequent to this list of its customers is not, however, a particularly fruitful approach.

That the Bank on occasion took a position described by some nationalistic writers as 'imperialist' is a further confusion. The Bank either directly or through its associated company, the British and Chinese Corporation, was trustee to bondholders and represented their interests. The Bank acted accordingly, even when the political situation suggested a softer if equally ineffective approach were preferable for long-run British political interests.

The Hongkong Bank's actual position should have been clarified in the 1930s, during the so-called 'Nanking Decade' just prior to the Japanese Incident of 1937. With the National Government established, the tasks which the Bank had been perforce performing virtually since the Revolution of 1911 were transferred primarily to the Central Bank of China. Meanwhile the Chief Manager in Hong Kong made plans for the expected end of extrality, for the imposition by the Chinese of taxation. The Bank, however, continued to be of service to the

Chinese authorities; the Shanghai Manager assisted in protecting the Chinese currency at the request of the Minister of Finance; he undertook with the agreement of the Chief Manager to co-manage loans issued for development purposes. At the same time every effort was made to continue the commercially sound basis on which business had been undertaken since 1865.

Although China had once again to depend on foreign bankers from 1937 to 1941, the end of extrality remained the goal; it was achieved in 1943 and the Hongkong Bank was the first foreign bank to receive a licence to operate under Chinese law. Post-war there would have been a role in redevelopment, but the hyperinflation caused the misallocation of resources and consequent confusion. In any case the People's Republic achieved power before foreign banks could determine the potential range of their activities under a Nationalist regime.

The first impact of the revolution on foreign enterprise was negative; the Hongkong Bank was reduced to a single office in Shanghai, although it continued to play a significant role in the finance of China's trade through its Head Office in Hong Kong. With new developments in the late 1970s following the fall of the Gang of Four, the Bank was again in a position to assist in China's development – but this time the pace would be set by China.

The Bank as a commercial operation

The Hongkong Bank was and remains a financial institution within the private sector. As a regional bank, representing the financial interests of the major business hongs in the East, its overall interests were coincident to those of the economics in which it operated. The development of those economies, the opening of new areas to trade, and thus the building of railways and their financing all led to the realization of a single objective, the increase in wealth, the consequent increase in trade, and the improved profitability of the Bank and its shareholders.

The Bank's role as Government banker indicated a commercial relationship. As a major bank it accepted responsibilities which, had there been a central bank, might well have been undertaken by such an institution. It continued its banknote issue when all other colonial issues had been taken over by the respective governments. This task was undertaken in large part because the prosperity of Hong Kong business required a note issue and the Hong Kong Government was not prepared to undertake the task. Such a role for a private-sector corporation may in general be compared with that of the early Bank of England; the latter evolved into what is understood today as a central bank. The Hongkong Bank, however, has remained in the private sector.

The Bank was also from time to time the agent of the Imperial Government of China; it regarded the Chinese authorities as a major constituent and was commercially interested in providing sound advice and in maintaining, sometimes at considerable expense, the credit-worthiness of the Chinese Government.

As a commercial bank with its Head Office in the East and its shareholders either based in the East or for the most part having Eastern interests, its presence had something permanent about it; this facilitated a long-run view. The Mercantile Bank, for example, was based in London; in 1892 it was in difficulty and withdrew from China and Japan, being represented in Shanghai for a time only by merchant agents. Other banks deserted Hong Kong in 1949/1950 as the People's Liberation Army reached the Colony's border; the Hongkong Bank remained. There was no necessary virtue or otherwise in this; it was a fact of its existence. Furthermore its Eastern base made such long-run views safe banking.

Before 1936 the Bank was, like China itself, on silver. Its handling of its currency position as between London and the East was key both to its survival and to the major role it was able to play in the finance of trade and development. This policy, described by directors and Chief Managers alike as maintaining an 'even keel', is indeed the theme of the present volume.

As an Eastern exchange bank its expertise was in silver and its operations world-wide. These developed, however, from the Bank's finance of Eastern trade and its consequent concern for a monetary system based on silver in a world turning to gold. On the basis of this experience the Bank's managers could counsel governments. Shanghai bullion operations, the assistance rendered the Indian Government, the movement of Kolchak gold following the Great War, and the defence of the Chinese currency in 1939–1941 are examples of the Bank as expert and its history is in great part the story of that expertise. Its focus on exchange was not without cost; exchange bank managers had to be their own exchange operators – even to the point where management development was hindered by this necessity.

As a corporation permanently in the East the Bank, although remaining in the private sector, could afford to provide assistance in troubled times; it could afford 'seed-money' for development finance; it gained a reputation for keeping its constituents afloat; it participated in the local money markets and on occasion acted as a clearing bank. Certainly its management was from time to time caught up in the excitement of development prospects, of the elusive modernization of China. Facilities were made available to public companies and for enterprises under terms which 'tied up' funds contrary to the theory of exchange banking; advances were made unofficially to local officials and merchants sponsoring modern enterprises often through the intermediation of the compradore or the local bankers.

The nature and extent of this primary involvement in Eastern economies provides the Bank with a broad historical importance beyond its basic significance as the major Eastern exchange bank. The particular issues varied in importance from time to time, but they can be detected throughout as connecting threads in the chronological survey which follows.

A SURVEY, 1864–1984

Colonial bank and silver

Contrary forces shaped the Hongkong Bank's first hundred years. From 1876 to 1936 the financial history of the East was dominated by the fact, not at first always recognized, of the depreciation of silver in terms of gold (= sterling), a downward trend punctuated by sudden but temporary reversals. Hong Kong itself was of the East and yet part of an Empire the political and financial centre of which was most certainly in London. When Hong Kong merchants decided in 1864 to found their own local bank, they had to conform to British imperial formalities while preparing to function in silver, on their own, from an outpost of two empires, the British and the Chinese.

The purpose of the Hongkong Bank was initially inspired by the need as perceived by its founders to finance intra-regional trade among the open ports of China, Japan, and the Philippines. This role included that of financing trading facilities, for example, local steamship lines, docks, tug boats, and small industrial enterprises. The regional focus, supported by merchants of several nationalities whose own focus was the region and who both resided there and had the authority to make decisions, kept the Board of Directors and Head Office in the East, confounding many contemporaries who misunderstood the Bank's role and underestimated its capacity to adjust.

Even from the earliest years, however, the Hongkong Bank was an exchange bank. The original promoters had Indian interests; furthermore, within months of its founding the directors had established a relationship with the London and Westminster Bank and set up an agency in the City. Exchange operations required sterling funds in London; the Bank could never afterwards afford to ignore London opinion. Those who controlled funds in Britain studied the fortunes of Eastern banks; the Hongkong Bank had then to live and flourish in two worlds, one of China and silver, the other of London and sterling. The difficulties and the opportunities were compounded as the directors also reached out to San Francisco and New York and in the 1880s pioneered in Lyons and Hamburg.

In the very early years of silver's decline, however, the Bank's extra-regional obligations remained small; this provided a breathing spell. While the great London, sterling-based exchange banks found their assets depreciating and took corrective steps too late, the Hongkong Bank suffered principally from the failure of unwise local investments.

Hong Kong and London – the China loans

Which of these two worlds, London or Hong Kong, would dominate the Bank? If the Bank needed London funds and London's good opinion, could it long retain its Head Office half the world away? Yet the Bank had been founded because, the members of the Provisional Committee claimed, mere agencies of banks headquartered elsewhere – in India or London – could not serve the financial needs of Treaty Port merchants. By the early 1880s when the question was first seen as a serious issue, that is, when additional capital was needed and raised for a silver bank but in terms of sterling, the Bank had become an integral part of Hong Kong's and Shanghai's local economies. It could not leave the East and still be 'the Hongkong Bank'. The resolution of this problem was the key to continued success.

The problem of the two worlds arose in a new form when China sought finance beyond the availability of silver funds in the East. Acting as agents of the Chinese Imperial Government, the Hongkong Bank entered the London capital market in 1875 and, through the first small loans, became established, dominating the China-loan business thereafter. By 1895 the Bank was ready to enter into agreements with foreign consortiums, beginning with the Deutsch-Asiatische Bank; by 1898 it was prepared to become bankers to a British industrial group, first through the jointly promoted (with Jardine, Matheson and Co.) British and Chinese Corporation and then through a merger of interests with the Pekin Syndicate and Yangtze Valley Company in the Chinese Central Railways. The Bank had become, as its Chinese name of 'Wayfoong' (hui-feng) suggests, a 'focus of wealth'. From here to leadership in multinational negotiations and to the inter-war headship of the prestigious but ineffective China Consortium was an apparently direct and almost inevitable progression.

All this was done in London; Head Office remained in Hong Kong, and many observers, both in London and the East, were confounded. The senior managers grew up, as it were, as the China loans became increasingly complex. A successful China office manager might receive a London assignment, where he 'grew' as the loans increased in significance and value. These men were self-taught, but they came to occupy key positions relative to Eastern finance, both as bankers and as directors of the British and Chinese Corporation and the Chinese Central Railways. Meanwhile in Peking the Bank's Agent remained, increasingly respected and effective.

Significantly these men had no successors from within the Hongkong Bank. The opportunity for self-instruction applied only to the early years; there was no system whereby new managers could gain experience. In the 1920s the Chief Manager had to bring in the first specialist.

The Hongkong Bank between 1895 and 1918 was virtually two banks. The fall in silver had forced a policy of keeping an 'even keel' but the Chief Manager, correctly assessing the long-run trend, also moved funds into sterling to build up a reserve in London equal to its silver funds in the East. From 1876 there was a London Consultative (or Advisory) Committee which kept the London Manager in touch with the City and which was, from time to time, mistaken as the Bank's Board of Directors. From at least 1890 this Committee was composed of City financiers capable of advising on loan management responsibilities.

Meanwhile in Hong Kong the Board of Directors remained in legal control, responsible to the shareholders, some 55% of whom were by now on the London register. The actual management of the Bank had devolved on the Chief Manager, Sir Thomas Jackson, and on his retirement in 1902 on a succession of able bankers competent in various degrees to bring the Bank through several Eastern-originated crises, while the London 'team' represented the Bank in the financial and political capital. Without China contacts and experience, the London business would not have existed; without London expertise and City contacts, the China loan business could not have been carried out. And underlying it all was a banking skill competent to surmount the several crises of confidence which Eastern banks experienced.

'Joss' and the Bank's nineteenth-century crises

There was, however, another element in this success which even those who admired the Bank could not refrain from observing. The Shanghai compradore called it 'joss'; many in Hong Kong were more specific – they referred to the long-term Chief Manager as 'Lucky' Jackson. With this was combined a policy which, despite occasional unwise operations, despite the support of local industry by *de facto* investment in fixed capital by 'overdraft' facilities, may be described as highly conservative.

The Hongkong Bank began with a paid-up capital of $2.5 million in 1865. The following year the Board authorized a new issue which when fully paid-up in 1872 doubled the capital. By 1875 however the Bank had lost all but $100,000 of its more than $1 million reserves, passed over the dividend, and found increasing difficulty in identifying taipans of sufficient stature willing to become directors. The cause was bad investment and uninspired exchange operations. But when the turn-around occurred under new leadership, the recovery was the faster because the losses had been fully written off and unexpectedly favourable disposal of 'dead stock' enabled the Board of Directors to reinstate the dividend and rebuild the reserves, which reached $1 million again by the end of 1877.

Riding such upswings the Board authorized rights issued at peaks of success – in 1882 and 1890, in time for new capital to offset the fall of the exchange, maintain the Bank's sterling image, and in 1892 cover exceptional losses

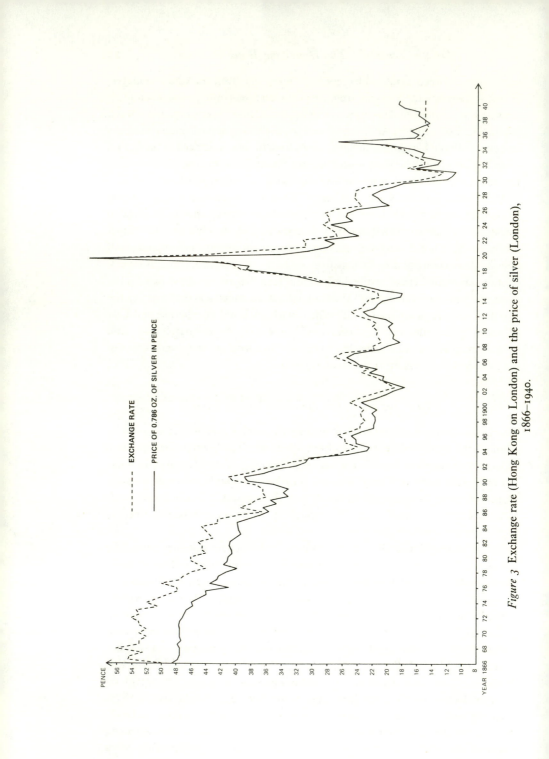

Figure 3 Exchange rate (Hong Kong on London) and the price of silver (London), 1866–1940.

consequent to the upheavals in exchange and the eventual collapse of silver. Without these issues, timed perfectly as they were, the inevitability of success is doubtful. The Bank ever had an air of inevitable success and, in banking, this in itself is a most valuable asset. The Hongkong Bank was the local bank; Chinese domestic servants depositing their dollars in the Savings Bank, taipans in Shanghai and Hong Kong negotiating credit for trade finance, and Chinese officials in Peking and Tientsin negotiating major public loans were all served by a single institution, and many of these same constituents subscribed new capital when that in turn was needed. In its first years the Bank was virtually a community 'cooperative'. It never quite lost that spirit.

Throughout these sometimes dubious years the Board of Directors and their Chief Manager were concerned with building a sound reserve. Against a background of a relatively conservative dividend policy, this involved a conservative valuation policy – writing down below market as prices moved down, writing up only reluctantly and partially when prices moved back up again. Arguing against this policy was the need to retain stable dividends in terms of sterling, the unit of account in which, for complex reasons, they were declared. The problems this created for a bank with silver accounts in a world of falling exchanges is seen in Figure 4 set against Figure 3.

On balance and with the intervention of joss Jackson not only saw the Bank through the years of doubt relative to silver, but positioned it to profit from the long years of decline until in December 1902 the semi-annual abstract of accounts was calculated at an exchange of 1s:7d, the lowest pre-Great War. The full success of Jackson's policies had, however, been revealed in 1898 when reserves in sterling were first seen as equal in value to the paid-up capital. The Hongkong Bank had 'come of age'.

The Bank as merchant bank

On a separate but not quite equal basis, the London operations took place in the years during which the Hongkong Bank was a major actor on the international financial stage. Co-managing Japanese and Siamese publicly issued sterling loans, the Bank saw its major role as furthering modernization in the East. It established itself as lead manager for Chinese Government loans to finance railways, dyke repair, mines, and, eventually and less happily, to achieve administrative reform with the funds provided by a series of reorganization loans, of which only the first, the £25 million Reorganization Loan of 1913, was issued.

Dramatic as these years were, they were not entirely satisfactory. The Hongkong Bank had developed its Chinese expertise on commercial grounds; the London and Shanghai managers had developed their position on the basis of commercial merit. They and the directors wished to keep matters that way, free

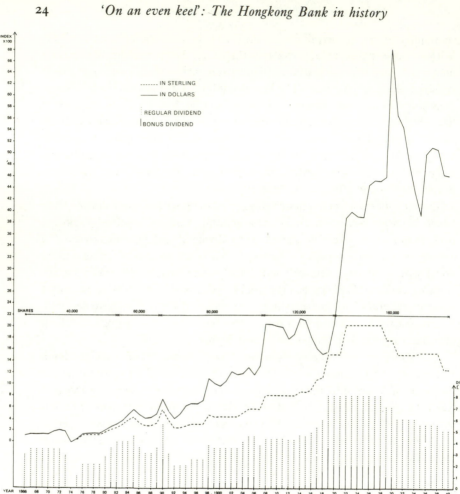

Figure 4 The Hongkong and Shanghai Banking Corporation
Sterling dividends and annual payout in sterling and dollars (1866 = 100), 1866–1940.

of political involvement. Events both political and financial made this impossible. The fear of China's financial collapse – with the examples of Egypt, Turkey, and Latin American countries well known – led the London Manager to seek to rationalize the competition for lending and to end irresponsible concession hunting with its taking of 'up-front' profits without long-run concern. The Hongkong Bank did not move into China, take its profit, and withdraw; the Bank was headquartered in the East, its financial fate appeared to be linked with China.

These attitudes were not always appreciated by a China which sought through competition to avoid being faced by a cartel of the Powers and to utilize Western disagreement to obtain what it thought would be better terms. The rationale of China's position was reinforced by the Bank's need to work in the context of understandings with the British Government, without whose diplomatic intervention the Bank could not compete at all under the system of national concessions demanded by and granted to the Powers. The British Government was traditionally opposed to granting monopoly rights to any British group; in China it had little choice. The rights the British Foreign Office had secured had to be exercised in the private sector; the Hongkong Bank, the British and Chinese Corporation, and the Chinese Central Railways, the last with French and Belgian interests, were the only commercial entities equipped to handle operations on the scale now contemplated. Nevertheless, the ultimate choice and the final terms remained within the authority of China; Britain and the Powers might obtain concessions, but in the realities of late Ch'ing negotiations, the ultimate terms became increasingly favourable to a government that never quite lost control of its relations with the foreign enterprises.

The Bank and Government

The Treasury's efforts to maintain control of British overseas banks in accordance with its changing interpretation of its own responsibilities in the context of the chartered banking system ran into the consequences of the Hongkong Bank's pragmatic interpretation of 'legitimate' banking. The major conflict was over the ability of the Hong Kong Legislative Council to grant a corporation rights outside the Colony; it was a non-issue based on unsound Treasury legal advice compounded by misunderstanding, but it clouded relationships with the British Imperial authorities.

At the same time, however, the Hongkong Bank had become bankers to the Hong Kong and Straits Settlements governments and to the British Foreign Office and military in the East. While one office of the Treasury argued against the Bank's existence outside Hong Kong, another office accepted its tender for the Treasury Chest business because, *inter alia*, of its large network and therefore superior banking facilities in the East.

The non-productive nature of the several disputes and the inability of the Treasury to give real supervision to chartered banks led to the abandonment of the chartered banking system *qua* system in the 1880s. Nevertheless it was natural that in the period from 1900 to 1914 the Bank's increasing dependence on British Foreign Office rulings in the execution of normal banking operations and its purely commercially oriented operations on behalf of the British Government as constituent would be confused with its own role as negotiator in the China loan consortiums, despite the efforts of its managers to minimize the influence of political considerations on banking decisions. To the extent the purely commercial policy was successful, the Bank would reap a strange retribution during the Great War. Among its founding committee had been Parsees, Americans, and Germans. In 1914 there were four German directors on the Board in Hong Kong; in London the senior Manager worked under agreement in cooperation with the Deutsch-Asiatische Bank; the Bank seemed to be linked everywhere to German interests. 'Scaremongers' accused it of being a German bank.

During the Great War while Hongkong Bankers served in the forces, jingoists continued their attacks. There was a natural over-reaction, but the London Manager, Sir Charles Addis, himself a reluctant convert to the necessity of the War, kept some balance. The German directors resigned in 1914, but after the War they did not return to the Board, and the Bank became, now in a narrower sense, 'British'.

When the last Ch'ing Emperor abdicated in 1912, the Bank in London reacted promptly. The dragon jerseys worn by the rugger team were changed for Republican colours; elsewhere, the changeover was more complex. From the time when Dr Sun Yat-sen called secretly on the London Manager in the immediate aftermath of the Double Tenth (October 10, 1911), managers in London, Hong Kong, Shanghai, and Canton would consider the new Republic's financial requirements. By the time the actual funds were advanced the political divisions had become apparent; by the time the Reorganization Loan was signed in 1913, financial aid had become an internal Chinese political issue. The Hongkong Bank appeared to have taken sides.

Furthermore the Hongkong Bank as banker for certain Government funds faced rival claimants; under conditions of extrality the Bank depended on the Legation in Peking or the British courts in Hong Kong and Shanghai for determination of legitimacy; its consequent disbursement of funds could affect political issues.

The inter-war years

The Hongkong Bank had every reason to support policies for a 'return to normalcy'. The Great War had interrupted the financing of China's development, the Bank's profits were based on economic recovery and trade. There were reasons to be optimistic. Silver was at an historic high and the promise of the post-war boom permitted the Board of Directors to increase the capital in 1920 with a rights issue at a premium. Once again, the issue was well-timed; there was no other year in the inter-war period during which the Bank could have obtained the new capital it required to weather the Great Depression and the other disasters through to the Pacific War. 'Joss' would once again ease the Bank through the pending crisis. There were other indicators, however, which should have provided a warning; 'normalcy' was being selectively defined. The Germans were not to be invited back into the New China Consortium and China itself was in political disarray. The Bank's role as custodian of Chinese funds continued to have a potentially significant political impact and a consequent 'imperialist' image which could not be shaken even after responsibility for the funds had been turned over to the new central bank in the period 1928–1932.

The Bank's very presence in China required it to make decisions; its financial stake biased it in favour of sound, stable government. Its Chief Manager, A.G. Stephen, became indirectly involved in what critics saw as adventurism; it was the 'return to normalcy' turned sour. Stephen died in 1924 and the Bank turned in on itself, its very prosperity endangered by the economic conditions and the political atmosphere.

Despite the Allied Victory, despite the promises of the reconstituted China Consortium, there would be no return to pre-war grandeur. The new Shanghai office, built to dominate the Bund, was an effort to reflect that grandeur, but the times had changed. The Chief Managership of A.G. Stephen was a 'last hurrah'; after 1924 there was a return from grandeur, a return to redevelopment of the Bank's continuing primary roles as exchange bank and local bank.

The China Consortium survived the reaction; the British Group had been enlarged but the Consortium's contribution proved negative; it may have prevented excessive and irresponsible lending to China, but it was never recognized by the country it was intended to benefit, and China never dealt formally with the Consortium as such.

The Hongkong Bank's inter-war role nevertheless proved to be dramatic. With the growth of authority and confidence of the National Government of China in Nanking, the Bank was able to cooperate in schemes for debt settlement and renewed development investment. When this was interrupted by the outbreak of the Sino-Japanese War, the Bank in a dramatic effort on China's behalf, attempted, virtually single-handed, to defend the currency of China.

The Bank retained its position in the East, but its position in London was eroded. With the death of Sir Newton Stabb, the Chief Manager from 1910–1921 and London Manager 1921–1932, a new London Manager was appointed; he was overshadowed by the new Chief Manager, the forceful Sir Vandeleur Grayburn, and the role of the London Consultative Committee was muted. Furthermore the

Foreign Office and Treasury, although still consulting the London managers, were no longer dependent on them for economic expertise; they sent their own representatives to China on currency and financial matters. The Bank implemented policy; its advice remained important, but it was now but one of many informational inputs.

The Bank's less significant presence in the City coincided with its expanding activity in China itself. It also coincided with the final fall of silver and the establishment of China's currency – and then of Hong Kong's – on an exchange standard. The Hong Kong dollar was linked to sterling through an Exchange Fund. Here again joss had intervened. The deterioration of China's economic position led the Board to authorize the potential write off of the Shanghai branch's capital. At the same time the stable link between the Hong Kong dollar and sterling facilitated the execution of a sterling reserve policy; the exchange risk had been minimized, thus permitting the Hong Kong dollar-based Bank to safely transfer reserves despite the consequent increase in the uncovered London position. Thus even while its energies were expended in an attempt to defend China's currency, even when War came, unprepared as Hong Kong and the Bank were for the almost immediate disasters, losses were minimized by decisions relative to sterling reserves, and its income continued even as its branches in the East were captured by the enemy.

Head Office London and the return to the East

The internment and subsequent death of Grayburn decided the succession. The new London Manager, Arthur Morse, had taken over only weeks before Hong Kong fell; he would be both the Chief Manager and serve concurrently for the first time in the Bank's history as its Chairman. With the London Committee empowered by an Order in Council to act as a wartime Board of Directors, Head Office had finally moved to London, but under the direction of a man committed to a return to Hong Kong. By mid-1942 all the offices in the East, except Calcutta, Bombay, Colombo, and a newly opened branch in Chungking, the capital of Free China, were in enemy hands.

The Head Office was reestablished in Hong Kong in mid-1946. Even with strong, able managers in London and a senior London Committee, there would not again be 'two banks'; direction from Hong Kong was facilitated by improving communications and transportation and by the changed role of London itself. The Chief Manager had returned to the East to focus on the development requirements of the East in a period of new political independence, central banking, and planning.

As in the period following the Great War, the Bank expected to play a role in China but was frustrated by deteriorating economic and political conditions.

With the establishment of the People's Government the long negotiations began whereby, and as part of 'all-for-all' settlement in 1955, the Bank virtually left China, except for a small office in Shanghai which never closed. At no time did the Bank anticipate withdrawal from China trade finance; the debate of the mid-1950s was the office from which such finance could be most effectively granted. Hong Kong seemed to be the logical choice, but in the end both China and the Chief Manager agreed that a continued presence of The Hongkong and Shanghai Banking Corporation in Shanghai was acceptable – perhaps desirable.

There were positive developments, however, which offset the loss of a major China presence. First, there was Hong Kong itself. During the Pacific War, Arthur Morse and his colleagues in London exile had participated with Government planners in considering the reconstruction of the territories in which it operated. In fact the sudden coming of peace found less destruction than anticipated, but what remained required the financial encouragement of Morse, who came to personify the enterprising spirit of the Colony. The new managers took up the challenge, and when economic overheads designed for trade were turned to support Hong Kong's industrialization, the Hongkong Bank played a major and innovative role in its finance. The Bank was once again the local bank, supporting its constituents with only marginal reference to the traditional 'real bills' doctrine of British exchange banking.

Elsewhere in Asia the Bank played a key role in reopening Sterling Area trade and through Hong Kong's open currency market provided a link with the Dollar Area. Both staff and funds were, however, limited. Although the Bank regained its pre-war position as a respected exchange bank based in the East and responsive to local requirements, a bank, that is, which would stay in the region despite temporary setbacks, competition from American and later from Japanese and other international banks became severe. The Hongkong Bank might be the doyen, respected by older political leaders, but its market share of business declined and the grand buildings in which offices and staff were housed appeared pretentious and out-of-date as urban land values rose and the Bank no longer occupied a special position.

The beginnings of the 'new' Bank

One response to American overseas banking was for the Hongkong Bank to expand its U.S. operations. Here, as noted before, regulatory authority intervened; the long-established San Francisco Agency could not accept deposits from American residents. In 1955 the Board of Directors overcame the impediments by associating the agency with a wholly-owned State bank; the Hongkong and Shanghai Banking Corporation of California, Inc.

Competition also affected other British overseas banks, and the British

Government encouraged rationalization to conform to new political realities and to provide viable corporations of sufficient size to withstand unwanted take-overs and to undertake the needed banking service. Exchange banks based in London and dealing with a particular area which had but recently obtained independence were in a particularly vulnerable position. These were facts which facilitated the Bank's acquisition of the Mercantile Bank (of India) Limited and the British Bank of the Middle East. The Hongkong Bank itself was based in British territory. If it had to withdraw from China it had ample opportunities to expand in Hong Kong and from this Far Eastern base into 'British' Borneo while intensifying its participation in the development of its traditional areas of service, especially Singapore and the new Federation of Malaya (later, Malaysia).

The acquired banks were not integrated into a single bank, and consequently the Hongkong Bank became both an operating bank and a bank holding company. As such it faced serious problems. It had first to plan, then to enforce an 'imperial view' of the new 'Group's' operations acceptable to the directors of previously independent banks with their own histories and expertise. The ultimate solution of integration took some twenty years to achieve.

The Hongkong Bank continued to serve its traditional area, albeit in new ways and in the face of new competition. The changes required to meet local requirements, including the appointment of local officers, focused management's attention on internal control and organizational structure; not until these problems were resolved could the Hongkong Bank move forward dramatically (see Table 1.3).

The year 1962 is significant in both the history and the historiography of the Bank. Sir Michael Turner, the Bank's Chief Manager and Chairman, retired. His successor, Sir John Saunders, had not been East before the Pacific War. Turner had come East in 1930, suffered internment in Singapore during the Pacific War of 1941–1945, and had presided over the Bank's fortunes in those years when the key expansion decisions were made. Nevertheless when Turner retired in 1962, the Bank and its accounts would still have been recognizable by Sir Thomas Jackson, Chief Manager for three separate terms during the years 1876 to 1902 and Sir Vandeleur Grayburn, Chief Manager 1930–1943. The Bank *per se* appeared in many respects unchanged, but the factors which would force change were already present. Afterwards the annual reports would make difficult reading even for the most recently retired; in fact, the Bank would never again be quite the same. The atmosphere of the China coast lingered perhaps – but not at the cost of business efficiency. Managers remained concerned that their offices had the correct '*feng-shui*', passers-by continued to ensure their good fortune by stroking the guardian lions, and lion dances heralded the opening of each branch and sub-branch as the network expanded in Hong Kong itself. At the same time managers were very much concerned with matters more closely related to modern banking.

The Hongkong Bank was the last of the great colonial banks to be chartered. By 1962 the peculiar features of this system as they affected the Bank – the double liability of shareholders, the special note-issuing regulations, rights to establish in British colonies, the 'gatekeeper' role of the British Treasury – had been eliminated or become irrelevant. The Bank as the China bank, as manager of the Imperial Government's public loan issues, as sponsor of railway development and currency reform, as advisers to governors and politicians had changed, although it continued to be important in the finance of the trade of the People's Republic and, significantly, the Shanghai branch remained, symbolic of the future.

As the territories in which the Bank had operated gained their independence, they no longer referred banking problems to the Colonial Office and Treasury; the Bank's operations became subject to local central bank regulations and to more severe competition, locally and internationally.

There followed the remarkable reorientation and development of the Bank as financial group after 1962. Consequently, after the reorganization between 1968 and 1977, the new executive Chairman, (Sir) Michael Sandberg, was in position to execute an 'American strategy' which would place the Group among the forefront of the world's commercial banks. In 1981 after the completion of the Marine Midland acquisition, analysts claimed that the Hongkong Bank was, for a time, the largest (as measured by the market valuation of assets) of those banks whose shares were traded. Calculated on the basis of market value of equity, the Hongkong Bank ranked for a time seventh among the world's publicly traded financial intermediaries.

ABOUT THE 'HISTORY'

The history of the Hongkong Bank not surprisingly fits with reasonable neatness into the categories which delimit 'epochs' in the financial history of the East.

The establishment of the Bank, its initial success, and its near collapse in 1874/75 is a cycle delineating Part I of the first Volume; it was also an identifiable economic period in the history of the Treaty Ports.

Sir Thomas Jackson was the Chief Manager, with interruptions, from 1876 to 1902. When he left, the Bank was in a strong position with published reserves in gold equivalent to paid-up capital, a silver reserve fund, and an inner reserve constituting a 'third line of defence'.

The Jackson era was marked by the policy of the 'even keel' countering the decline of silver; the fall ended for a time in 1903, silver prices were more erratic, and they rose during the final years of the Great War. Jackson's successors had to devise new means of implementing the Bank's even keel policy; this was the task of J.R.M. Smith and Sir Newton Stabb, described in Volume II.

Volume II is also the story of the Hongkong Bank as the 'focus of wealth' or 'Wayfoong' in the period of 'Imperialism' and War. The history in this period was affected by the dramatic role the Powers played in attempting China's development. In this the Bank participated, embarrassed by the need to deal with politics, but certain that its actions were beneficial to China. All were affected by the Great War. The Bank had ignored the anti-German 'scaremongers' and jingoists, but in August 1914 the German directors resigned and the Bank struggled to rid itself of a pro-German image. To recount the events of this dramatic era Volume II begins in 1895, overlapping in the matter of the China loans the last years of the Jackson era with Volume I; it continues through the Great War.

The 'inter-war period' is not a Eurocentric concept. China's political misfortunes developed independently of events in Europe during the Great War, but their impact on the Bank was felt most in the 1920s when the Consortium was prepared to assist China at a time when civil war prevented constructive development. This forced the 'return from grandeur' to the basic problems of exchange banking. After years of Warlordism the hopes of the Nanking Decade were dashed by the outbreak of the Sino-Japanese War. The Bank would still assist Free China, but its role ended with Pearl Harbor and the beginning of the Pacific War.

If China suffered chaos and false hopes, these were characteristics too of financial history, and the Hongkong Bank's struggle to retain its Eastern banking leadership as silver fell, depression cut its basic business, and the vagaries of sterling seemed for a time to threaten the Bank's reserve base are the topics in Volume III. The Pacific War was a time for suffering and a time for planning. The former is the subject for a final section in Volume III; the latter opens Volume IV, and there is consequently an overlap in coverage from 1941 to victory in 1945.

The Bank then returned, adjusted, developed, and made the change necessary for survival. The story concludes on the eve of the negotiations which were to promise change for the Hongkong Bank's own home territory of Hong Kong. With the implications of 1997 this history is not concerned. It is not too early, however, to at least survey more recent events or the changes which led, for example, to the acquisition of Marine Midland and transformed the colonially chartered Treaty Port bank into a major world financial group.

Each part of the history examines the performance of the corporation, its management and direction; each part covers some peculiar development which requires special consideration; and each part must pay respect to the Hongkong Bankers who made the Bank and who lived under varying conditions of hardship, with varying degrees of ambition and success, in the East. Supporting the

'Eastern Staff' were the London 'Home Staff' and the compradores and their assistants in China, the guarantee shroffs in Ceylon and their successors in the post-World War II period. The minutes of the Bank's Board of Directors are relatively brief, but there are many references to local staff and their emergency needs to which the Board gave consideration.

This work deals at one level with such technical policy problems as are implied by the promise to remain on an 'even keel'. At another level there are stories of banking under stress and emergency. One retired manager put it in the context of reactions from 'High Street' bankers at Home:

Recount of even the most elementary exchange manipulation is viewed somewhat incredulously; references to mutability of the Orient and the flexibility necessary to combat the congenital sinfulness of the Asiatic invites suspicion. Tales of domestic torts, intrigue, intimidation, religious strife, strikes, rebellion, civil war, siege, anti-foreignism, risings, revolutions, wars, massacres, internment, torture, murder are not visualized here as concommitants to Banking.

But all this is nevertheless involved in the history of The Hongkong and Shanghai Banking Corporation.

APPENDIX: NOTES FOR READERS

The tables detailing the performance of the Hongkong Bank as a corporation are based on the semi-annual (from 1915 the annual) abstracts of assets and liabilities as published for the meetings of proprietors. Accounting, at least accounting as practised on the China coast, being an inexact art, the nature of which changed considerably over the period, the published figures are difficult to interpret and as a time series they contain serious deficiencies.

That they nevertheless form the basis for the analysis in this history is due to several factors. One of the Bank's problems in presenting their case before American banking authorities in the matter of the Marine Midland Bank was the nature of their accounts – they were not compiled according to American GAAP (Generally Accepted Accounting Principles). The cost of converting the Bank's accounts could not be justified; the same principle would apply in a history project. To convert the Bank's accounts from 1865 to accord with current standards was not one of the options available.

Nor would this have solved the problem. Confidence is one major asset of a bank and this is given by proprietors and constituents in part on the basis of the published figures. Contemporary analysis was comparative. The 'corrected' figures would have been ahistorical and provided an inaccurate picture of how the Bank was seen by contemporaries. The Hongkong Bank's competitors followed roughly the same accounting procedures, and where these differ with historical consequences, they are referred to in the text.

The market reaction to the Bank's accounts suggests that contemporaries made their own estimates of inner reserves and true valuation of securities held against the Reserve Fund and that much depended on their evaluation of the Bank's ongoing policy relative to its handling of the changing exchange rates. These were subjects of newspaper and, no doubt, clubland debates; the formal speech of the Chairman at the meetings of proprietors often provided the key insights into the Bank's position which contemporaries required and, for the most part, found acceptable in the context of the expectations of the time.

The main purpose of depending on the published figures is to avoid *ad hoc* adjustments by which all contact with the reality of the Bank's accounting practices is lost or confused. Even accepting the principle of using published figures, the number of notes per table can seem overwhelming. At times supplementary tables have to be provided, but they are related to the published figures and cover a particularly complex situation.

Supplementing the tabled figures are comments in the text designed to assist in providing a more thorough evaluation of the Bank's position and policy. The minutes of the Board of Directors do contain more detailed information than is published, although to avoid conflict of interest not even the directors were necessarily always fully informed of the Bank's exchange position, constituents' accounts, or inner reserves. Using this information the basic figures can be modified for purposes of exposition but always against the consistent series of tables abstracting the published accounts.

Although the Hongkong Bank's accounts have never been made public, they have always been audited. The semi-annual accounts were not a statement of the position of the Bank on the date stated; the Bank's various offices closed their books on different days to enable the information to reach Head Office. The rates at which these accounts were 'taken over', the time lag involved in their integration with Head Office accounts, the judgement of the status of non-performing loans, the valuation of publicly quoted securities – these and other items were matters with which the auditors were concerned. There is sufficient in the archives to warrant the assertion that the managers and Board deferred to the auditors, as the signature of the latter confirms.

The figures presented in this history, taken together with the notes and explanations and supplementary information in the text, provide a fair quantitative picture of the Bank's development. Analysis, however, usually moves past this stage to judgements on performance, safety, contribution of the Bank to various sectors in each country served. This could compound the problems which are consequent to the nature of the underlying figures.

Net earnings as a percentage of shareholders' funds, for example, is a very interesting figure and the ratio has been used in this history. The ratio is, however, at best a rough estimate based on published figures and changing definitions. Shareholders' funds must exclude inner reserves; net earnings are affected by transfers to general contingencies or by an *ad hoc* decision to revalue the Bank's marketable securities.

These problems are not unique to the Hongkong Bank nor to this history. They are mentioned here by way of warning and explanation.

THE CHINESE MONETARY SYSTEM

The China orientation of this history requires the use of terms in the context of a system which is not fully understood by economic historians dealing with European problems. Although a Glossary has been provided for reference, lists of terms will not suffice when the basis on which proper interpretation depends is unknown. For this reason, and as an exception, a description of the Chinese Monetary System is included in this introductory chapter.[c]

The monetary system of China was bimetallic, copper coins were used for smaller retail transactions and silver for other monetary purposes. Although there was an ideal par rate between copper and silver, in practice the value of the coins fluctuated in terms of each other according to market forces. Because of the extreme difference in the value of the two metals, it was unlikely that one would be a competitor for the transaction usually performed by the other. For these reasons there was no question of the coins of one metal driving out or causing the melting down of the other.

The transactions in this history are denominated entirely in the silver sector of the monetary system; the copper coinage will not, therefore, be further considered.

Monetary silver in China took two forms: (i) specially shaped ingots and (ii) dollar coins. Debts expressed in a unit of account referred to in English as a 'tael' were expected to be paid in the shaped ingots, known as 'sycee', 'sycee silver', or 'monetary silver'. Debts expressed in a dollar unit of account were expected to be paid in dollar coins current in the particular market or in 'dollar silver'.

The tael system

'Tael' is the foreigners' term for the Chinese '*liang*' or ounce of weight. Thus, as with the term 'pound' or '*lira*' etc in Europe, the unit of account implies payment of a weight of precious metal. A tael unit of account in China, as the 'pound' in Early Modern Europe, expressed a debt payable (i) in a designated weight of silver, (ii) of a certain fineness as decreed by statute or custom in the market.

As the ounce or 'liang' weight was not standard from market to market, there were many tael weights in China – as there were many different ounce weights in Europe, for example, troy, avoirdupois, etc. One particular tael weight was standard for monetary purposes in any city (there were exceptions), and it was by custom associated with a specific fineness of the silver.

That the term 'tael' should refer to more than one measure was a matter of great concern to foreigners, who chose to see it as characteristic of Chinese deviousness, lack of progress, possibly even absence of true religion. In the

---

[c] For a definitive study of the Chinese monetary system in the late Ch'ing Period, see Frank H.H. King, *Money and Monetary Policy in China, 1845–1895* (Cambridge, MA, 1965); for a discussion of the various dollars and taels current in China see, for example, various editions of Edward Kann, *The Currencies of China* (Shanghai, 2nd ed. rev. 1927).

The Chinese Empire did not enjoy a unified monetary system, nor were weights and measures standardized. The statutes of the Ch'ing Dynasty provided a framework and thus the monetary system prevailing at any time or in any place could be described in terms of an ideal model to which it bore some generic resemblance.

United Kingdom today the term 'mile' designates one of five quite different lengths; 'ream' when unqualified refers to four different numbers of sheets depending on whether it is a printers ream, a writing ream, a 'news' ream, or a 'stationer' ream, although the *Economist Guide to Weights & Measures* adds a touch of realism the compradore would have appreciated: 'In practice, however, a ream usually consists of 500 sheets'. Such differences and such acceptance of variations were all the more common in the nineteenth century.

For these reasons, clarity required a statement as to the specific monetary tael in which a particular debt was expressed. Custom was sufficiently strong that in many cases contemporaries knew what tael was referred to without its being specified. This led to some confusion at the time; it leads to considerably more misunderstanding today. But the existence of different monetary taels and the method of their designation is standard to all pre-modern monetary systems based on the use of full-bodied coins as the basic means of payment.

In Foochow, for example, the weight used for monetary purposes was the *yang-p'ing liang*, and the fineness of the silver was that of the Mexican dollar coin. Debts in Foochow were expressed in Yang-p'ing taels, payable in 'dollar silver', that is silver of the same fineness as the dollar (originating from dollar coins which had been 'chopped' or stamped and defaced beyond recognition). The weight (*p'ing*) of this particular *liang* was equivalent to the weight of 1.3947 dollars. In this example a debt expressed in taels could be paid directly by a weight of dollar silver. It was theoretically possible to calculate the weight of pure silver implied in any monetary tael and make a payment in pure silver, but this was not practical. In cases where the tael weight implied payment in a silver of a fineness not current in China, the taels had in practice to be transformed, on the basis of the silver theoretically required to make payment in each tael, into a 'monetary tael' before payment could be effected.

Debts to the Customs were expressed in Haikwan taels, but payment was usually made in the monetary tael current in the Treaty Port. Or the debt might be made payable in Shanghai currency taels and thus a debt of say HkTs100 would be settled by payment of 111.4 Shanghai currency taels. Debts to the Imperial Treasury were denominated in *K'u-p'ing* (Kuping) or Treasury taels, which were slightly lower in value than the Haikwan tael and 100 would be settled by payment of 109.6 Shanghai taels.

Units of account without direct means of payment are often referred to in European history as 'imaginary units of account', or, somewhat confusingly, as 'imaginary money'.

Actual payments were made in monetary silver. In popular usage a coin is assumed to be disc-shaped and accordingly most writers claim that the Chinese in the Ch'ing period were without a silver coinage of their own. This error has caused considerable confusion. A coin is properly defined as a piece of metal of definite weight and value made into money by being stamped with an officially authorized device (*OED*).

Although there were experimental disc coins denominated in tael units of account, monetary silver in China was usually in the form of 'shoes' (because of their supposed similarity of shape to a Chinese shoe) of sycee, the weight and fineness of which was stamped in an accepted code by some designated government or market official. The essence of the definition is not the shape but the fact that silver used in payment of debts is differentiated from other silver by a process which involves expenses. Hence it has a supply and demand of its own, and the difference in its value as a coin and as bullion is the basis for covering mint charges, seigniorage, or whatever fees the process requires. It is the device whereby, indeed, the value of the coin can be totally separated from the value of the metal it contains. However, shoes of sycee passed current within a narrow range because of their silver content; China was on a silver standard.

The dollar system

Debts might also be expressed in a dollar unit of account. Certain ports used taels and shoes of sycee; others, dollars and dollar coins (by tael or weight). There were ports where both systems were used and rates of exchange existed between dollars and taels so that even if a debt were expressed as say Ts100, payment could be made in dollar coins at the market rate.

Dollar coins from Mexico were imported into China and originally payment was made by weight – in the case of the Yang-p'ing taels by a *liang* weight of dollar silver, the silver alloy of a dollar coin.

The custom developed before the mid-nineteenth century for certain debts to be expressed in a dollar unit of account. No doubt originally such a debt could be settled by tender of dollar coins on a one-to-one basis, that is, a debt of one hundred dollars could be paid by tender of one hundred dollar coins.

This remained the ideal for which foreigners strived, and discussion of currency reform usually centred on plans to provide a coin which would pass current at one coin for one unit of account.

Two developments prevented this happening in China. The deterioration of the coin through use or misuse could lead to its being accepted only by weight and not by tale. Tampering with coins could lead to their silver content being questioned, thus destroying their unique value to those engaged in the transaction.

In China, since all dollars in the Ch'ing period were imported, there was no quality control possible. Since their origins were far away and the integrity of the mints unknown, new designs or new coins might only be received at a discount. If the old designs disappeared, there might be no coin in circulation which passed current on a one-to-one basis with the dollar unit of account.

There were therefore imaginary dollar units of account.

Big and little silver

With the coming of modern mints to China in the early twentieth century, there was a tendency to over-produce subsidiary coinage. A subsidiary coin was not full-bodied; it contained less silver than its nominal value. The acceptance of a subsidiary coin at par depended on its being exchangeable at par and on demand for a full-bodied dollar coin. Over-production made this impossible, and say eleven or twelve ten-cent pieces in 'small' silver might be required in payment of one dollar 'big' silver. Hongkong Bank notes in the Straits Settlements, for example, specified they were in payment of debts expressed in 'big' silver dollar units of account.

Banknotes

Local Chinese banks issued notes in certain ports, but this survey is concerned only with the banknotes of modern-style banks, in this period almost exclusively the foreign Exchange banks of China.

The preference shown for their use depended on the user's assumption of the stability of the Bank and on their convenience. There was no weighing, testing, or 'shroffing' involved. The bearer was subject to the risk that he had been given a counterfeit, and although such cases arose, they were surprisingly infrequent. Tampering with the coinage was simpler than with security printing.

When the banknotes came to be redeemed at the bank of issue, then the bearer was exposed to the normal complexities of a metallic currency system. While he used the banknotes, he was for a time spared the problems normally associated with the Chinese monetary system.

The system as here described was time-consuming and complex, and one which, despite its logical nature, was esoteric and expensive. Transactions between markets, between taels and dollars, and between cities involved exchange operations for which the customer had to pay. Banks had to employ shroffs to handle and adjudicate cash payments, sycee coolies to move the silver from vault to vault in the clearings, and there were risks involved in the changing price of silver relative to gold.

Foreigners urged China to unify and simplify its monetary system. But until the abolition of the tael as a unit of account in 1932 and the concurrent establishment of a national dollar coin, little progress could be made. Currency unification usually follows political unification. This was true in China in the Republican Period. Under the Ch'ing, neither the political system nor the economy were organized on a national state basis and the currency reflected this delegation of executive authority under general regulations but without a single, effective control.

If nothing else the above should explain why the China loans are often quoted in apparently random amounts; expressed in the original unit of account in which the loan was negotiated, Kansu taels, Haikwan taels, etc., the sum may have been a round Ts2 million; but the loan, if in silver, might be quoted to the public for subscription in Hong Kong dollar units of account or in Shanghai currency taels (or both); hence the odd sums involved.

Part I

THE FOUNDING AND FIRST YEARS OF THE HONGKONG BANK, 1864–1876

There is nothing like this in banking history, in the same space of time . . . on a capital almost nominal, when compared with the amount of deposits, dividends and transactions.

North-China Herald, 1869

In 1864 a broadly based group of Hong Kong business leaders conceived the Hongkong Bank, formed themselves into a Provisional Committee, allotted shares to a nominal amount of $5 million, and applied to the Governor of Hong Kong for a charter of incorporation. By 1876 the Bank was already established as the principal regional bank, but during this time had experienced a cycle of growth and crisis. Having lost all but $100,000 of its $1 million reserves, a beleaguered directorate instituted a series of reforms in 1875–1876 which permitted the Bank, under the management of Thomas Jackson, to revive and, in the period to 1895, develop into the most formidable financial institution in the East.

The first part of this history deals with this early cycle; it is a story virtually complete in itself.

Significant as this particular period may be in the story of the Hongkong Bank, there are further justifications for considering the years 1864–1876 as a separate unit. The affairs of the Bank were not surprisingly a reflection of the economic and, to a lesser extent, the political events of the time. These years have their distinctive features which, though independent of the Bank, nevertheless determined the year of the Bank's foundation, influenced its success, and, in 1874, led it to the brink.

In 1864 Shanghai was recovering from the slump which followed over-speculation in real estate; Bombay was in its first months of a financial boom in speculative company promotion. In the spirit of the times Hong Kong had begun to think in terms of joint-stock enterprise and the development of regional trade. The years 1864–1866, which mark the founding of the Hongkong Bank, were a watershed in the economic history of East and South Asia.

The Hongkong Bank's early history was intimately connected with these developments, which it had indeed been in part founded to assist. Foreigners once again deceived themselves into supposing that the 'opening of China', the modernization of China's economy, was surely close at hand. Hong Kong and the Treaty Ports must be prepared; docks and other developmental overhead projects were required; modest industrial schemes in the areas under foreign control would demonstrate the effectiveness of Western methods.

Despite these underlying expectations, the Hongkong Bank was modestly perceived as designed primarily to finance regional trade, although it would be available to provide legitimate support to local industrial projects. The finance of China's modernization – reserved, promoters thought, for other and grander names – was irrelevant in this period. But even the more modest plans of the China-coast merchants were flawed, and as they foundered, the Bank was affected.

By 1876 the economy of Treaty-Port China and Japan had itself experienced a cycle; in that year a turn-around was predictable – for Hong Kong, for the companies which survived and, consequently, for the Hongkong Bank. For its first decade the Bank was to be managed by its directors in association with the Chief Manager. By 1875 the Board had dwindled and become isolated, and the dangerous dynamism and personal speculations of its first Chief Manager, Victor Kresser, had been replaced by a generally uninspired administration under James Greig. In 1876 Greig left Hong Kong; Thomas Jackson had been appointed to act in his place, and in London David McLean, the Bank's first Shanghai Manager (1865–1872), had taken over.

Silver began to depreciate in terms of gold in early 1873, but this is clear only in retrospect; in this first period the changes in the value of silver were seen by most as no greater – although potentially more serious – than the fluctuations which had occurred throughout the preceding century (see Table I.1). Attitudes changed after 1875, the Bank itself declared its dividends in sterling for the first time in June 1876, and the decline in the gold price of silver, in the sense of a possible long-term trend, became an absorbing concern. But in 1864–1876, the period covered in Part I, merchants, financiers, and the Hongkong Bank's directors and managers had other priority interests.

In this first period, the Hongkong Bank's priority was to fulfil the promises of its Prospectus. Geographically this meant a focus on Hong Kong and Shanghai, and then by stages to the other open ports of Hong Kong's trading area – China, Japan, Cochin-China, and the Philippines.

Recovering from the devastation of the Taiping Rebellion and the impact of the Second Sino-British War, China, while accepting certain of the implications of the new Treaty-Port system, was enjoying an upsurge of confidence. This was the period of the T'ung-chih Restoration. Contacts between foreigners, merchants, bankers, and diplomats would increase, but still very much on China's terms. While working through the traditional compradore system, the Hongkong Bank established initial contacts, and in 1875, as the agents of the Imperial Government, issued China's first public loan.

In Japan the Bank set up its first agencies, but its role in assisting that country's development was still modest; the close association with Japanese finance would come later.

The years 1864–1876 saw changes which would facilitate the extension of European and American influence into the Far East regional economy but at the cost of disturbance to the markets. In 1866 there was a fall in prices caused in large part by the dumping of goods which had been hypothecated to recently failed banks. Despite the consequent disruption to trade, the Hongkong Bank, as the only Eastern bank offering six-months bills, could be selective and thus relatively safe. After a good year in 1868, the tea market opened late in 1869 and the completion of the Suez Canal made as yet no impression. Again in 1870 events postponed the impact of the Suez Canal – the Franco-Prussian War and the fall in

Table I.1 *Exchange rates, 1866–1876*

(i)	Hong Kong on London: Hong Kong dollars and pounds sterling			
	1866	June 28.	6 months' sight	$1 = 4/1\frac{1}{2}$	= £0.20625
	1870	June 30.	6 months' sight	$1 = 4/5$	= £0.22083
	1874	June 30.	6 months' sight	$1 = 4/4$	= £0.21667
	1876	June 30.	6 months' sight	$1 = 3/9\frac{1}{2}$	= £0.18958
	1896	June 30.	on demand	$1 = 2/2\frac{1}{2}$	= £0.11041
	1903	June	on demand	$1 = 1/8\frac{1}{16}$	= £0.08359
(ii)	Shanghai on London: Shanghai currency taels and pounds sterling			
	1974	July 25.	6 months' sight	$Ts1 = 5/8\frac{1}{2}$	= £0.28541
	1876	July 23.	6 months' sight	$Ts1 = 5/2$	= £0.25833
(iii)	Shanghai on Hong Kong			
	par:	$Ts1 = \$1.39$			

Notes: (i) the London/Hong Kong exchange rates were quoted as so many shillings
and pence per dollar; hence a higher exchange rate indicates that more
shillings and pence will be required for the purchase of one dollar, i.e. an
appreciation of the dollar relative to sterling;
(ii) the six months rate was the standard for the period quoted.

tea and silk prices, the Tientsin riots, various rebellions in China and a general
lack of confidence disrupted trade. In 1871, however, there was a remarkable
recovery; the cable telegraph was extended to Shanghai, and the stage was set for
the heavy overtrading, that is, speculation by small traders granted new credits,
especially in teas which were sold 'to arrive'. Bought in China at high prices, tea to
an amount equal to the capacity of the London market had been sold before the
commodity ever reached the market.

These developments were paralleled by the improvement of shipping services,
including the tentative inauguration of a regular schedule from North America
across the Pacific, and the linking of financial connections around the world
through banks operating across the Atlantic and the Eastern exchange banks.
The Hongkong Bank itself would, in this first period, establish exchange links
with India, London, and San Francisco. The consequent reorganization of
mercantile practices would have an impact on the fortunes of the Hongkong
Bank, especially the 'dull' trading period following the boom in 1872, but the
main impact would be consequent to the fall in silver and affected the Bank in the
period following 1876.

In this atmosphere of improved transportation and communication, expectations relative to the growth of the China trade encouraged foreign merchants
resident in the open ports to consider the need for fixed investment, especially in

enterprises connected with shipping and with processing. The merchants turned for financial support to their new local bank – the Hongkong and Shanghai Bank.

This remains the period of British dominance in Far Eastern trade and finance. The links with British India and the strategic economic importance of British Hong Kong gave this generalization reality despite (i) the presence of the French in Cochin-China and Shanghai and the role of their bank, the Comptoir d'Escompte de Paris, (ii) the presence of several German Hanseatic trading firms, and (iii) the potential challenge from long-established American firms anxious for a major role in the lands across the Pacific.

In the minutes of the Bank's Court of Directors, the Franco-Prussian War is hardly referred to. Nevertheless, as a consequence the French directorate of the Comptoir d'Escompte discharged their German staff, and the former Shanghai manager, Hermann Wallich, played an important role directing the Asian aspirations of the new Deutsche Bank. But in this period the threat of German competition did not materialize; the Deutsche Bank's role in the East lasted from 1873 to 1875, little more than two years.

The role of American merchants in the East was, at least until 1875, relatively stable. In that year Augustine Heard and Co. failed, and with the departure of A.F. Heard the last member of the Bank's founding Committee had gone. Later in 1875 Russell, Sturgis and Co., the Bank's Manila agents, also failed. Meanwhile, schemes for increased American involvement in Eastern finance had proved lacking in substance, although the leading American houses continued their interest in development projects.

After the shake-out of British and Indian exchange banks in 1866, the banking scene in the East changed little. The reconstructed Agra Bank returned with diminished capital; otherwise business not handled by the Hongkong Bank was left to the veteran and still prestigious Oriental Bank Corporation, to the smaller Chartered Mercantile Bank of India, London and China with its primarily South Asian orientation, and to the Chartered Bank of India, Australia and China (see Table II.2).

This then is the setting for Part I.

2

THE PROVISIONAL COMMITTEE AND THE FOUNDING OF THE HONGKONG BANK, 1864–1865

Notwithstanding the very extensive foreign trade with China and Japan [the Hongkong and Shanghae Banking Company (Limited)] is the first Bank locally started or in which the majority of our Merchants are directly interested ... the chief inducement which the promoters had in view was to supply an absolute want arising out of inability of the Branch Banks established here to meet the varied requirements of local trade. This trade implying the business between Hong Kong and the open ports in China and Japan is now of the most extensive character and requires a more special mode of dealing than any Bank Agency can possibly supply.

In this respect the promoters of the Hongkong and Shanghai Bank believe that from the experience of its Directors and the sources of information at their disposal arising from the fact of the proprietors being connected with every branch of trade in this country, they will be enabled most materially to aid the legitimate working of business.

Francis Chomley, Chairman, Provisional Committee[1]

With this clear statement of intent, the Chairman of the Hongkong Bank's Provisional Committee applied to the Governor of Hong Kong in December 1864 for a charter of incorporation. This was to be the fulfilment of plans many times considered and many times abandoned. The cause of the new resolve was on board a P&O mail steamer which, on July 22, 1864, had sailed into Hong Kong and changed banking history.

News from Bombay

The Hong Kong Superintendent of the Peninsular and Oriental Steam Navigation Company, Thomas Sutherland, had boarded the mail steamer *Singapore* in from Bombay. The formalities concluded, Sutherland, no doubt with a hospitable word, was about to disembark when the Captain motioned him to the cabin. There was news from Bombay.[2]

The news concerned a 'local' bank even then in the process of promotion in Bombay. What made the news exceptional was that this bank, the Bank of China, was to have a head office in Hong Kong and finance regional trade between Hong Kong and the treaty ports of China and Japan.

The merchants of Hong Kong would understand the need – indeed, none better. This was 'an idea which had frequently been talked up here for discussion and as often dropped for want of someone to push it'.[3] And now, in the privacy of the Captain's cabin, Sutherland was to be told the news first – a Bank of China floated in Bombay to do just those things which the Hong Kong merchants had so often talked of. Here was the opportunity for a speculation, to be among the first subscribing to the shares of the proposed bank which would, even before allotment, fetch more than 70% premium. Sutherland knew enough of Bombay to recognize this possibility; he knew that to be allotted shares was to be assured immediate gain – the stags would benefit; they could sell almost immediately to considerable advantage.

There was an alternative, although not one which the ordinary shipping agent might consider. But then, as his subsequent career proved, Sutherland was not an ordinary agent. He would become, at the age of fifty, the Chairman of the P&O, but first he would found the Hongkong and Shanghai Banking Corporation.

Sutherland's immediate reaction to the news from Bombay was critical of his Hong Kong friends – 'I thought they would deserve whatever fate might befall them.' Fortunately, he reconsidered.

In addition to its regular cargo, a coastal steamer, like a floating doctor's waiting room, apparently carried collections of ageing magazines. In 1864 while on a voyage by the SS *Manila* between Hong Kong, Swatow, Amoy, and Foochow, Sutherland had come across an article in a twenty-year-old edition of *Blackwood's Magazine* on the advantages of Scottish banking. On the basis of this he concluded that founding a bank on Scottish principles would not be difficult.[4] Recalling this article and recognizing that the founding of a local bank had now become a matter of urgency, he decided to fill the want complained of; he would be the one to 'push' the establishment of a local bank.

Given the competitive nature of the Hong Kong mercantile community, perhaps only a man standing outside it, but serving it, could have overcome the rivalries and suspicions of the independently minded merchants and pushed such a project through. Against the background of the traditional rivalry between Jardine, Matheson and Co. and Dent and Co., between Russell and Co. and Augustine Heard and Co., there were the new rivalries stemming from the promotion of rival docks, rival insurance companies, rival shipping firms. Now more than ever they needed banking facilities, but under whose control, and for what purposes? Sutherland was not a wholly innocent bystander; he was sufficiently involved to lend credibility, independent enough to command respect.

To be successful, a local bank would have to meet the diverse needs of the community and gain constituents from rival firms because it promised to serve them all. It would need to become the main depository of local funds; firms would have to open their own treasuries and deposit their silver bars and sycee with the new bank. The local bank would then extend credit . . . but to whom, for what purposes, and under whose control?

But if the merchants watched each other closely, they were also proud of Hong Kong. When they heard of Bombay's Bank of China the 'news caused considerable talk and excitement . . . as it was thought to be cheeky'.[5]

If this were a merchant's view, the local press, commenting on the recent past, was more outspoken.

Thus it came to pass that a few enterprising Parsees and Scotchmen in Bombay invented and achieved so many banks in China. They had little money but they had eyes in their heads and sense too. They saw a clear field before them with a lot of small donkeys browsing on it, and they turned it to pretty good account.[6]

The writer was perhaps thinking of the Agra and United Service Bank, the Bank of Hindustan, China and Japan, the Commercial Bank Corporation of India and the East, the Asiatic Banking Corporation, and the more firmly established Oriental Bank Corporation and Chartered Mercantile Bank of India, London and China. These, however, were exchange banks extending their Indian based business to China and thus, it could be argued, offering credit on competitive terms with little risk to the independence of the local merchant.

Now, however, came the Bank of China to be a 'local' bank, to hold the government accounts, finance local industry, to be to Hong Kong and Shanghai what the Presidency banks – the Bank of Bengal, for example – were to their respective Indian regions. The Hong Kong community was once again, it seemed, unable to take the initiative. Soon, it was promised, a Neale Porter, emissary of the Bank of China, would visit Hong Kong to recruit directors, line up business, and accept subscriptions for the few shares which the Bombay promoters had graciously reserved for the China-coast.[7]

The formation of the Provisional Committee

The editorial cited had been inspired by the prospectus of the Bank of China published in the same paper on July 28, 1864. But Sutherland had 'pushed' and the Prospectus of the Hongkong and Shanghae Banking Company Limited together with a list of the promoters was published in the *China Mail* that same day. The shipping lists indicate that the last Bombay mail steamer must have arrived on July 22, giving a maximum of five days for the rallying of the leading merchant houses and undertaking the preliminary work necessary for the founding of a $5 million bank.

But that is not, in fact, quite what happened. Sutherland worked fast, but he was also realistic.

On July 27 Albert Farley Heard, managing partner in China for the American trading firm of Augustine Heard and Co., was writing a letter to Charles A. Fearon, his former partner in London and a director of the Asiatic Bank, about the firm's connection with this newly established exchange bank. In passing he mentioned that:

A bank is being started here to compete with outsiders, Hong Kong and Shanghae Banking Corporation or some such name. I am urged to be one of the provisional committee with Chomley, Maclean, Lapraik, Sutherland and others . . . nothing yet is settled and I don't intend to take a very prominent part in promoting it.[8]

The following day, after the publication of the Prospectus, Heard wrote in a different tone to his formidable uncle and founding partner, Augustine Heard, Sr: 'Today I see my name down on a Bank committee started here rather suddenly after having been taken up and dropped several times.'[9] After a further day's reflection he wrote to his brother John:

The appearance of the Bombay [Bank of China] prospectus stirred up those interested in the Hong Kong scheme and in consequence the Hong Kong scheme has been put forward hastily in a prospectus concocted by Pollard and Sutherland in the last 48 hours. I have never favoured the scheme save in a very general way and when applied to for my name on the Provisional Committee I did not refuse it nor did I agree to it. In fact I was, I confess, rather taken by surprise this morning to see it all in print, my name on the list . . .[10]

With his colleague George B. Dixwell in Shanghai, Heard, writing on the eve of the first meeting of the Provisional Committee, was even more explicit:

The first time I saw the prospectus it was in the paper. I had not given consent for the use of my name but hesitated and did not decline, supposing it would be open for discussion after the mail. [E.H.] Pollard however rushed the matter thus in order to have it go to India and check mate a plan originated in Bombay for a Bank of China to come on here for just that purpose and object which the Hong Kong bank intends to fill.[11]

The tone of these letters may be partly explained by the fact that the Heards already were involved in several joint-stock companies and consequently reflected A.F. Heard's concern that his distant partners might not approve of his involvement with yet another promotion, with the 'locking up' of funds, or with prejudicing the firm's relations with their already established banking connections, for example, the Comptoir d'Escompte de Paris and the Asiatic.

But the confession that 'I did not refuse . . . nor did I agree', correctly reflects the mercantile attitude which Sutherland had to overcome. He achieved his goal by presenting publicly an apparent *fait accompli* – 'apparent' because the published members of the Provisional Committee did not, in fact, meet and declare themselves so until August 6. Heard would seem to be indignant as to the way the matter was rushed and cautious as to his future role. His real attitude is pride that the 'house' had been approached as the representative American firm in China and resignation to the inevitable – with just the hint that he might yet make something good of it all.

That none withdrew is a comment on Sutherland's correct reading of the situation. Public sentiment was at last behind the scheme and those who for so long had discussed it and set it aside had now been committed to a responsibility they found difficult to evade, and once committed they did not, be it said in fairness, attempt to do so.

There is a tradition that the Hongkong Bank was founded at a dinner party. There may well have been a dinner at which the participants were unaware they were founding a bank. Sutherland took the sense of the conversation and published the Prospectus without further consultation. Or, if this is being too charitable to the story, something of the kind must have occurred – the known facts are not in substance much different from the legend.

In his own account Sutherland states that he wrote up a draft prospectus overnight, took it to his legal adviser, E.H. Pollard, and together they solicited support. They moved so rapidly, indeed, that the Hongkong Bank Prospectus, which had to be drawn up *ab initio*, was published on the same day as the Bank of China prospectus, which had arrived in Hong Kong fully prepared. Heard writes of a 48-hour period, and certainly the maximum, given the arrival of the P&O steamer *Singapore* on the 22nd and Heard's knowledge of the project on the 27th, would seem to be but four days.

There is, however, a limit to credibility. How could the P&O agent, however brilliant, design a successful banking project in so short a time? What in fact did he achieve; what was the 'Prospectus'?

The Prospectus was neither a charter nor a deed of settlement, but was rather a general statement of intent. As such it reviewed the history of the scheme, stated the overseas direction of the existing bank branches, and gave a positive description of the proposed Hongkong Bank as a local bank concerned with the finance of local, that is, Hong Kong, Shanghai, and inter-port, business, adding, '[Experience] clearly shows that the largest profits are obtained by those Public Companies which possess an interested local body of Proprietors and Shareholders whose support naturally forms a chief element of remunerative success.'

'The Bank', A.F. Heard was to write shortly afterwards, 'would succeed because of its local support.'[12]

Whatever other argument the promoters might put forward – the ending of the compradoric system, the reform of the currency, the encouragement of local business as opposed to exchange operations – the key to the Bank's success lay in its local support. While this was to be true in the long history of the Bank, its immediate relevance was as a counter to any claim the Bombay-promoted Bank of China might have to a legitimate role on the China coast.

The language of the Prospectus suggests that either Sutherland or Pollard had access to comparable documents and, not surprisingly, to that of the Bank of China itself. Both prospectuses make comparison between the Presidency banks and the proposed China-coast bank; the Hongkong Bank adds a legitimate comparison with the local Australian banks. The Hongkong Bank Prospectus does contain specific reference to conditions in Hong Kong, confirming that this was not merely a flash reaction but was the promotion of an enterprise 'in contemplation for a very long time'.

At some point in the early negotiations a necessary but potentially dangerous decision was made.

Sutherland's advantage was his standing outside the mercantile community, but the prospective bank needed a base, a sponsor, to move it beyond the realm of a vague promotion to the immediate semblance of organization. Thus it was that the Prospectus was signed, not by Thomas Sutherland or indeed by any individual, but by the leading British merchant house of Messrs Dent and Co. In a community where the managing agent system had already developed, there was a danger that the bank might become the creature of – or at least be dominated by – a powerful company and, by this association, find itself opposed by the major hongs while at the same time losing the support of smaller companies and individual entrepreneurs.

The opposition from the rival hong of Jardine, Matheson and Co. materialized immediately, primarily in the form of legislative opposition to the proposed companies ordinance.

As it happened, the Provisional Committee by chance or instinct kept their new bank relatively independent, while the failure of Dent and Co. in 1867 removed the danger at a critical point.

If the bank's base were to be British in a British colony, the choice was Dent or Jardine Matheson, and, by approaching Dent's first, the promoters put Jardine's in opposition. But there may have been little choice. Jardine's banking aspirations were well-known, and it may have been that Dent's, already detecting their own weakness, felt they had more to gain than lose from sponsoring a banking institution.[13]

In accepting this traditional assumption, based as it is on the well-known rivalry of the two British hongs, there is a danger in overlooking the competition between Jardine Matheson and other firms interested in the Indian trade, especially Messrs D. Sassoon, Sons and Co., but including also P. and A. Camajee and Co. and P.F. Cama and Co., all of whom signed the original Prospectus. The role of the Sassoons will be considered further below.

With the Prospectus and the organizational sponsorship determined, Sutherland and Pollard solicited support. Since they were willing to accept an equivocal response as sufficient authority to include the name in the published list of the Provisional Committee, this should not have been difficult. Thus the timing is sufficiently explained, and the focus must now be on the organizational activities of a committee formed under such exceptional circumstances.

The members of the Provisional Committee and their priorities

The Provisional Committee gave first priority to getting started. This, as it turned out, was to be another key to success, a principle which might be described as taking responsible action and formalizing it afterwards. The Bank opened for business on March 3, 1865, but the formalities of its incorporation were not concluded until July 1867. The Bank established agencies and branches, on the basis of cautious business assessment, as required and in good faith; certain of these actions did not receive full legal recognition, however, until the revision of the Bank's ordinance in 1889. The problem was Treasury misinterpretation of the doctrine of extraterritoriality as it applied to the acts of a colonial legislature. This the promoters and directors of the Bank could not be expected to foresee. And, in fairness to Colonial Office and Treasury officials, virtually from the time the Bank's initial request for a charter reached the Treasury in London, these civil servants accepted that they were dealing not with a speculative promotion but with an operating bank. This official attitude – the Bank has done what it ought not to have done, but how can the problem be corrected without damaging either the Bank or its constituents – would prove decisive throughout.

The Hongkong Bank was to be a local bank. To ensure this three policies were pursued: (i) there had to be broad local representation on the Board of Directors, and, before that, on the Provisional Committee, (ii) there had to be local support through a proper allocation of shares, and (iii) the Board of Directors had to be located where the Bank operated.

By 'local' the Bank's supporters did not mean Hong Kong only, but Treaty-Port China and Japan. The stress was on China, and the Shanghai branch was to open virtually simultaneously with that in Hong Kong; there was to be no 'chief' manager, and the Shanghai Manager would operate under a local committee. As the Bank evolved, it is true, direction devolved to Hong Kong whose Manager became 'Chief Manager' in 1868 and the committee at Shanghai disappeared; nevertheless, the Shanghai Manager retained access to the Board of Directors and he and the Hong Kong Manager were in a sense partners, the former would as the years passed be in control of the Bank's resources in China, the latter would control the world-wide distribution of the Bank's staff and funds. The Hong Kong Manager would become the ultimate arbiter under the directors; he would be the 'chief', yet the Bank would remain both a Hong Kong and a Shanghai institution. Development in Japan would be significant, but the Bank was primarily China-oriented.

To be successful the Bank's promoters had to be representative of or acceptable to potential constituents. Who then were the members of the Provisional Committee?

There was the founder, (Sir) Thomas Sutherland (1834–1922), who was to become MP for Greenock (1884–1890), GCMG, chairman of the P&O in 1884, then chairman, London Board of the Suez Canal Company and a director of the London, City and Midland Bank. In 1864 he was Superintendent of the P&O – and one of his major customers would be D. Sassoon and Sons – and in 1865–

Table 2.1 *The Hongkong and Shanghae Banking Company (Limited)*
Provisional Committee, 6 August 1864–2 March 1865

Francis Chomley, Chairman	Messrs Dent and Co.
Thomas Sutherland[a]	Superintendent, P&O SN Co.
William Adamson[a]	Manager, Borneo Co., Ltd
Robert Brand	Messrs Smith Kennedy and Co.
Rustomjee Dhunjeeshaw	Messrs P.F. Cama and Co.
Pallanjee Framjee	Messrs P. and A. Camajee and Co.
Albert Farley Heard	Messrs Augustine Heard and Co.
George Johann Helland[b]	Messrs John Burd and Co.
Douglas Lapraik	
Henry Beverley Lemann	Messrs Gilman and Co.
George Francis Maclean	Messrs Lyall, Still and Co.
Woldemar Nissen	Messrs Siemssen and Co.
Arthur Sassoon	Messrs D. Sassoon, Sons and Co.
Waldemar Schmidt	Messrs Fletcher and Co.

Note:
[a] These members did not necessarily represent a particular firm.
[b] Known as 'John' on the China Coast.

1866 he was a member of the Hong Kong Legislative Council. Without him there is no reason to suppose the Bank would have been started. Already active in the economic life of Hong Kong, in 1863 Sutherland had become the first chairman of the Hongkong and Whampoa Dock Company and in this venture was closely associated with Jardine's and Douglas Lapraik.[14] Yet he would, in establishing the Provisional Committee, prove equally able to win the confidence of Francis Chomley of Dent's and A.F. Heard of Augustine Heard and Co.

The credit for leading the Committee through the initial complexities must go to the man unanimously elected Chairman, the Hon. Francis Chomley, senior partner in China of Dent and Co. Dent's were at the time agents in China for the Scinde, Punjaub and Delhi Bank, but this would appear to have had no impact on their role in the founding of the Hongkong Bank.

Dent's prominent role did not lead to the eclipse of Sutherland; there was no crude takeover from an inexperienced initiator, for indeed Sutherland, who remained influential in matters affecting the Bank, was to be elected Deputy Chairman of the Bank until his departure for Shanghai in April 1866, *de facto* acting Chairman of the Bank during Chomley's absence from May to December 1865, and member of the Board until his own departure from China in November 1867.

The success of the Hongkong Bank, however, undoubtedly rested from the first on the broad international base of its directorate. This was a British bank in a British colony on whose founding committee eight of the fourteen members were not from Britain, and which, for some four months in 1875, was without a single British director. In 1864 the goal was to develop the China trade and the Treaty Ports; there was room for all, not the least for German traders from the Hanseatic City of Hamburg or for American merchants from Ipswich, Massachusetts, with long-standing China connections. Thus on this first Provisional Committee (see Table 2.1) Siemssen and Co. and Augustine Heard and Co. were represented, and they would soon be joined by Wm Pustau and Co. and other German companies and by Russell and Co., the senior American firm in China. In addition, Helland was Norwegian, and Schmidt was apparently German.

This tradition lasted until 1914. The American companies which had participated in the Bank's early fortunes had by then left the China coast. The Germans, however, remained until the Great War not only forced their removal but challenged the basis for the Bank's early success – its open accommodation to merchants of all nations. For a time the Bank yielded, but the logic of commerce on the China coast forced the Bank back to its historical role even during the constraining times of the inter-war period. The German connection would in time of war be misunderstood – a problem inconceivable as Sutherland and Pollard made their rounds in 1864. But all that must wait for full consideration in Volume II.

There were five British trading partnerships represented on the Provisional Committee. The manager of the Borneo Company, Wm Adamson, who had a long career in Singapore and Siam (he introduced Anna to the King of Siam), and Douglas Lapraik, a vigorous and independent entrepreneur, completed the British contingent. Lapraik, who was an early settler in the Colony, had begun his career as a watchmaker and the metamorphosis by which he became a shipbuilder, the owner of a shipping service on the China coast, the promoter of dock companies and the owner of the baronial Douglas Castle at Pokfulam on Hong Kong Island is told in Austin Coates' study of the Hongkong and Whampoa Dock Company.[15] Here was a man who, like A.F. Heard, represented the new spirit of development in Hong Kong. They would provide stimulus to the Bank, but their requirements would need to be controlled.

Three of the initial fourteen members represented Bombay interests, of whom two were Parsees and one, Arthur Sassoon, was from the Jewish house of David Sassoon, Sons and Co. The son of the more orthodox David Sassoon (1792–1864) of Bombay, he was known to his father as Abraham, but in Hong Kong he wore Western-style clothes and was something of a man-about-town, preferring the name 'Arthur'.[16] His firm's initial heavy investment in the shares of the Bank gave the Sassoons a long-term financial interest in the success of the new institution; his own and later his brothers' close involvement in the Court of Directors' Standing Committee may well have provided a much needed stabilizing influence, balancing to some extent the enthusiasms of the entrepreneurs, but it confirmed the Hongkong Bank's role in the finance of trade between India and China, which, so long as it remained legal, involved the finance of opium exports to China.

The complete list is in Table 2.1; and it can be seen that not all firms were or could be represented. Indeed at fourteen members the Committee was apparently considered unwieldy for, when two stated their intention not to become directors, the Committee agreed on a maximum of twelve and a minimum of seven as appropriate.

The only absences which provoked general comment were those of Jardine Matheson and Russell and Co. The reasons for the first have been touched on; Jardine's was rightly concerned at the formation of any company in a speculative atmosphere and they probably resented the leadership in the project assigned to Dent's. But there must surely have been a more specific reason involved.

The underlying factor causing Jardine's to withhold support from the Hongkong Bank at its founding was probably their concern at the presence on the Provisional Committee of India trading firms, especially their main competitors in the opium trade, D. Sassoon and Sons. In the first years of the Bank's operations, the members of the Court of Directors would have access to the accounts – an apparently obvious comment, but descriptive of a situation which could not last. Jardine's, as Swire's at a later period, did not wish to be involved too closely in a bank of which their business competitors were directors holding the right of access to their banking accounts.

To avoid this kind of situation in a small community, one of two developments would eventually prove necessary – either the removal of the Board of Directors to a distance, to London, or the withdrawal of the directors from direct banking involvement. The latter course could be dangerous, since the directors could not absolve themselves of responsibility to their shareholders; nevertheless to the surprise of some observers they indeed took that course. Why they did so and why they were able to do so are told in this history.

The withdrawal of the directors from direct involvement would alone have been sufficient to enable Jardine's to reconsider their attitude to the Hongkong Bank. Moreover the changed composition of the Board, the obvious inability of any firm to handle its own banking affairs, and Jardine's own change of direction, all combined to encourage the then taipan, William Keswick, to reconsider. The 'change of direction' is a reference to Jardine's withdrawal from major financing of the opium trade, following the successful activities of Sassoon interests, at least by 1871.[17]

Russell and Co.'s indecision has never been satisfactorily explained. It is tempting to make a parallel with the Dent/Jardine rivalry: Russell's objected to the prominent role played by Augustine Heard and Co., whose founder, Augustine Heard, Sr, had left Russell and Co. in 1836 to found his own firm. There is, however, no evidence to support this. More likely it was a question of general caution, or, possibly, the need to consult distant partners. If the Heards had taken the same precaution, they too might not have dared join the Provisional Committee. In any case Russell and Co.'s hesitation was temporary since they pledged general support for the Bank from the beginning and their senior partner in fact accepted election to the Bank's Court of Directors in September 1866.

The Provisional Committee held 23 meetings between August 6 and the following March 2, and in a workmanlike manner, often, as A.F. Heard wrote to his partners, taking up most of the afternoon, they moved step-by-step through the routine of founding a company.[18] Attendance rates were high, although Heard was out of the Colony during key periods and Lapraik's record was somewhat erratic.

By March 1865 the Committee had established a bank and their work endures, but the fate of their own firms proved mixed. That this should be so is perhaps a further commendation of their work, for which, incidentally, and contrary to the custom in those speculative times, they neither reserved shares to themselves personally – beyond the regular allocation – nor accepted any promoter's fee.[19]

David Sassoon and Co., Ltd as a successor firm remained in Hong Kong until 1956 and their Hong Kong taipan served continuously, except during World War II, on the Hongkong Bank's Board of Directors. Gilman and Co., a major Hong Kong agency house, were also serving post-war. Sutherland was on the Committee in his personal capacity, as indeed were Douglas Lapraik and William Adamson of the Borneo Company. One of Adamson's successors, H. Nicaise, was not permitted by his directors to remain on the Bank's directorate in 1875 – a problem the Bank had to face in recruiting managers of overseas corporations to the Board.

For the others, the record is one of failure.

Dent and Co. failed in early 1867; the speculations in Bombay brought down many Indian houses, and by July 1866 both Parsee members had left Hong Kong. Fletcher and Co. failed in 1865, Lyall, Still and Co. and Smith, Kennedy and Co. in 1866, while Augustine Heard and Co. collapsed in 1875.

Although the development is slow and subtle, such a falling away of the companies represented on the original committee cannot but have affected the power structure which determined the effective direction of the Bank, giving a greater independence to senior staff, particularly to the Chief Manager and the Manager Shanghai. Continuity, given a changing directorate and the uncertain future of the constituents they represented, would eventually be provided by the bankers.

Ensuring local support

The Provisional Committee was, then, as representative of Hong Kong's mercantile interests as was possible under the circumstances. The next step in ensuring local support was the allotment of shares on the principle that the Bank's shareholders would be its constituents and, conversely, shares should be allocated to those most likely to be constituents. The Bank of China's chance of success on the China coast may always have been minimal, but it was not enhanced by the failure of the Bombay promoters to reserve sufficient shares for allotment to China-coast merchants and so involve them in the fortunes of the enterprise.

The presence of 'decision-makers'

'Local support' suggests that there is someone local who can make financial decisions. If the traders of Hong Kong had been but junior agents of firms headquartered in London, Hamburg, or New England with banking connections established at Home, a Hong Kong-based bank would have had little chance of obtaining business beyond token allocations – on a friendship basis 'at equal rates' – to the extent such allocations remained within the discretion of the local manager. When the Hongkong Bank opened in Colombo in 1892, for example, the Agent was to find that he had little room for manoeuvre; the major banking decisions of the British trading firms were long-established and made in London. London Office had to solicit business on behalf of the Bank's Colombo agency.

Hong Kong not only had firms whose senior partners made independent decisions, it was also a base for those companies looking north to China and Japan and thus seeking a bank with the same orientation. Even if these firms had connections with the India-oriented exchange banks, they would still value a bank with headquarters in Hong Kong. Surprisingly, Hong Kong was the base for Catholic missionary finance. In 1847 the Mission Étrangères de Paris established their Procure Générale in the newly founded British Colony – it came to handle the funds of all the mission for all Asia east of India. The Procureur banked with the Hongkong Bank.[20]

As for the commercial hongs, Augustine Heard and Co. began in China and partners returned to Massachusetts, and, while they offered advice, they left the responsibility for most decisions to the partners remaining on the China coast. Siemssen and Co. had been founded on the China coast in 1846 and was first established in Hong Kong in 1858. When the founder, Georg T. Siemssen, returned to Hamburg, one of his successors Woldemar Nissen, who had himself been on the China coast since the early 1860s, became the senior partner in China; only with the return of Nissen in 1868 was a separate co-partnership formally opened in Hamburg. The decision-making for the Hong Kong partnership remained, however, in Hong Kong. Thus Heinrich Hoppius, who was eventually to succeed Nissen on the Hongkong Bank's Court of Directors, and like Nissen serve for a time as Chairman, remained the senior partner in the Eastern firm with full authority.

This was a Hong Kong/London pattern, as for example with Jardine, Matheson and Co./Matheson and Co.; Gilman and Co./Ashton and Co.; Gibb, Livingston and Co./T. and A. Gibb and Co.; Wm Pustau and Co./Pustau and Co.; Melchers and Co./C. Melchers and Co. Decisions were made in Hong Kong by senior partners of the Hong Kong partnerships; they needed a bank which could similarly make decisions in Hong Kong.

The allocation of shares

If then the Bank were to depend on local support, the Provisional Committee had to make a wise allocation of shares. While the Committee did ensure that their 'friends' were given all consideration, this was not inconsistent with reserving shares for potential 'constituents'; there was still opportunity to ensure that shares were reserved for leading firms, that the major proportion went to those interested in the China trade, and that sufficient were reserved for India and, later, London.

At its first meeting on August 6, 6,000 shares had been applied for by 158 persons, and the Committee confirmed that the authorized and issued capital should be $5 million in 20,000 shares of $250.[21] Initially only half the capital was to be paid up, in two calls – $25 on allotment and $100 three months after allotment. The balance was to be called at intervals over a period of two years, and it was noted that this would be governed by Colonial Regulations of which the Committee were apparently vaguely aware even from the first. These figures were confirmed on August 15 and the acting Secretary, E.H. Pollard, who was also the Committee's counsel, was instructed to place advertisements for applications in the newspapers of Manila, Java, Singapore, India, Japan, and elsewhere, with a deadline set for October 31.

Some 8,000 shares were reserved for Shanghai for allotment by a local committee organized through Dent and Co., however these shares were undersubscribed probably because firms consolidated their requests through Hong Kong. Two thousand shares were to be specifically reserved for India and allotted entirely at the discretion of the Bank's agents in Bombay, B. and A. Hormusjee, whose senior partner became chairman of the Indian Peninsular, London and China Bank, and who had themselves only been selected on December 26 – by a majority of one.[22] Meanwhile the Provisional Committee itself was to handle the bulk of the allocations, including 2,000 for Japan, the Philippines, and other ports. Approximately 1,000 were reserved for as yet unidentified but potential constituents and for errors or oversights in allocation, a precaution which was responsible for rumours that the directors had allocated shares to themselves.

All China or Japan applicants for ten shares or less were allotted the number requested, and in subsequent meetings minor allocations were made on an *ad hoc* basis; a special reservation of 100 shares at par for Russell and Co. was not taken up. The task was rendered more difficult by the considerable over-subscription; Heard reported to his brothers that applications had totalled 34,000 by the end of November.[23]

A limit on ownership was established at 500 shares or 2.5% of the subscribed capital, a measure possibly reflecting not only the number of applications but probably also confirmation that Committee members were concerned over the question of control. This 'poison pill' – and it would remain in the Bank's regulations in modified form throughout – would prevent any pretension of control by a large shareholder; it would also, in more dangerous times, deter those who might consider an unfriendly take-over. Less absolutely, the broad distribution of shares which the many applications made possible – and which subsequent regulations enforced – confirmed the broad base of the Bank's ownership and of its constituency. This in turn would affect the relationships of the directors and the senior management of the Bank, in the latter's favour.

Not everyone was satisfied with the Committee's decisions, and a special meeting was called in March 1865. The public wished to assure itself that the directors had reserved nothing to themselves as 'promoters' and that the system had been fair; on both counts the Chairman, Francis Chomley, and his deputy, Thomas Sutherland, defended their colleagues successfully.

Profit sharing

In these matters the Provisional Committee had acted on the basis of conventional wisdom in their efforts to ensure the acceptance of the Bank in the China-Japan trading area.

They now made an unusual decision. At the meeting on January 7, 1865, it was resolved that:

> The principle of appropriating a certain percentage of the profits shall be admitted and included in the terms of the Deed of Settlement; that such a percentage shall not exceed one-fifth of the nett profits but that the mode of dividing this reserved portion shall be decided hereafter.

Although this allocation of profits to customers would happen but once, that is, only during the existence of the initial Deed of Settlement and the 'Company, Limited', this decision is dramatic evidence that the Bank was conceived of almost as a community enterprise – 'cooperative' is perhaps too precise a term – which would not only respond to the needs of local enterprise but would return the profits to both shareholders and ordinary customers. The latter would receive a payment related to the Bank's records of their fixed deposit or current account interest, which reflected their contribution to the Bank's disposable funds. Since the proposal was made by the German member of the Provisional Committee, it is possible that he was influenced by the success of cooperative banking in

Germany, but the provision was out of place in the constitution of a chartered bank. Its main significance was as a gesture of intent, a declaration of purpose.

This was the local bank.

'Company Limited' or 'Corporation' – registration or charter

The Prospectus does not state the method by which the promoters intended to obtain corporate status with limited liability. There was at the time no general companies or banking ordinance in the Colony, and the immediate supposition was that the proposed Bank would seek a 'colonial charter'.

The Indian Presidency banks had been incorporated by special ordinances of the Indian Government, but the model which appears to have been considered appropriate by the promoters of the Hongkong Bank was a Royal charter, similar to that issued to the Asiatic Bank and to that applied for by the Bank of China, although these (i) defined an exchange bank and (ii) assumed a head office in the United Kingdom.

The account of the Hongkong Bank's incorporation under the Colonial Banking Regulations is found in Chapter 4, but a summary here of the role of the Provisional Committee is necessary to complete its history and provide a preliminary understanding of the position when the Bank commenced business in March 1865.

There is nothing in the minutes of the Provisional Committee which is relevant except the single instruction to Pollard to proceed with the application for a charter. At the same time the name given the bank in the Prospectus, 'The Hongkong and Shanghae Banking Company (Limited)', suggested registration under a local companies ordinance, but this is probably coincidence.

As the matter evolved, two contradictory courses were pursued simultaneously, the one – although eventually disallowed – permitted the Bank to begin immediate operation, the other, which took longer, was then available as a fallback.

The Provisional Committee realized from the first that their bank would require (i) limited liability and (ii) the right to issue notes payable on demand (banknotes), acceptable at the Colonial Treasury. By December 1864 they had been informed that to achieve these ends, if combined with a Hong Kong Head Office and directorate, a special ordinance, containing provisions similar to those in a Royal charter and conforming to the relevant colonial regulations, would have to be passed by the Hong Kong Legislative Council. This the Committee appeared to accept, but, due to the requirement that all capital be subscribed before application for a charter, their initial request for such an ordinance was not sent to the Government before December, and thus, had they but known it, with the procedures requiring at least eighteen months, the Hongkong Bank could not have begun operation with limited liability much earlier than mid-1866.

Before the full implications of this were realized either by the members of the Committee or by those who had subscribed for shares, an apparently immediate solution presented itself independently of the Committee or the Bank. Company promotion was promising large rewards not only in the United Kingdom but also in India, a slump in the Shanghai real estate market was dissipating, and in the Treaty Ports and Hong Kong there were legitimate enterprises whose promoters sought the broader capital base of a joint-stock company and the protection of limited liability. Both Chomley and Sutherland were members of the Legislative Council and there they supported passage of a general companies ordinance sponsored by the Chamber of Commerce, the provisions of which included, contrary to the stipulations of the Colonial Banking Regulations, the registration of banking companies with limited liability.

When the charter or special ordinance was seen to be delayed, the Provisional Committee, without necessarily changing its position relative to the desirability of ultimate incorporation by charter – or special ordinance – sought registration under the new general ordinance. This enabled the Bank to begin operations with its status as a limited liability company if not secured then certainly assured; the Bank would then await the outcome of negotiations with the Colonial Office.

Indeed, the Committee itself had little to do in respect to these latter negotiations, which were carried out between the Hong Kong Government, the Colonial Office, and the Treasury.

But also on the Legislative Council was Jardine's James Whittall, and he, together with William T. Mercer, the Colonial Secretary, opposed the companies ordinance on general and specific grounds. They feared, not without reason, the speculative forces such legislation might unleash, and Whittall argued that there were related dangers inherent in the new bank. Jardine's position was both reasonable, given the common knowledge of the situation in Bombay, and consistent – the firm turned down proposals from its correspondents in Bombay to look favourably on the projected Bank of China.[24]

After the initial rejection of the ordinance in February, a delay which adversely affected prices of Hongkong Bank shares, the passage was completed two days after the Bank became operational, and it was left to the Court of Directors to take the steps necessary for registration.

Preparing to commence business

The routine of establishing a joint-stock business includes the formulation of a Deed of Settlement, obtaining suitable premises, employing at least the senior management, and securing appropriate corporate registration. This last, as noted above, proved to be a continuing project concluded long after the commencement of business. No copy of the Deed of Settlement for the Company Limited has survived, but as it had to be drawn up on the basis of models available in Hong Kong, Pollard may be assumed to have followed the examples of one of the existing exchange banks. Thus the unamended or initial Deed of Settlement for the eventual (1866) Corporation should prove a reasonable guide to the contents of the original, with the possible exception of any clause dealing with the distribution of profits to customers.

The Provisional Committee set up a sub-committee – Sutherland, Lemann, and Nissen – to identify potential managers and an Accountant; from time to time the sub-committee was assigned other tasks, but, as in the main they had to report their findings to the full committee for decision, their recommendations were fortunately recorded. There is, however, no record of the Shanghai Committee set up through Dent and Co. to deal with preliminary problems, including the Shanghai Manager's contract, in that port.

The Provisional Committee appointed E.H. Pollard, their counsel, as acting Secretary, an appointment which, given the absence of any Bank staff, was essential for the handling of correspondence between the Committee and the public and for negotiations with the Government. Once the Bank was established the Court of Directors dealt through the Hong Kong or Chief Manager. There was no full-time Secretary until 1969.

The first employee of the Hongkong and Shanghai Bank was John Grigor, whom the sub-committee were empowered to take on nominally as Accountant in Hong Kong but with the understanding that his services might be available for any purpose required by the Committee. Some eleven days later, on September 24, 1864, the Committee balloted for the post of 'Manager, Hong Kong', and Victor Kresser, a Swiss national then local manager of the Comptoir d'Escompte de Paris, received eight votes to three for J.W. Maclellan, the manager for China of the Commercial Bank Corporation of India and the East and subsequently financial editor and then editor of Shanghai's best-known newspaper, the *North-China Herald*.[25] Nissen, who noted that Kresser's appointment had been opposed on grounds of nationality by certain of the British members of the Committee, considered him the most able banker available.[26]

The fact that he was an exchange banker did not escape the notice of Hong Kong observers, and the future of the projected Hongkong Bank as a 'local bank', one willing to lend on the securities of local shares and otherwise assist local enterprise, was queried.[27] As it happened the critics were wrong; Kresser's downfall would come on just that issue – he was himself involved and he committed the Bank too far in its support of local enterprise.

David McLean, the acting manager of the Oriental Bank Corporation's Shanghai branch, had not been a candidate. Word had apparently reached him that his application would be welcome, but he was at first unwilling to leave the Oriental, where he considered his prospects good. On learning of the prospective salary, however, he commented, 'I wonder who will get the appointment – $1,000 a month is not to be picked up every day but I don't like the idea of applying.' But when McLean learned that he would probably be replaced in Shanghai and transferred to Yokohama, his views changed and he applied for a manager's post on November 16; on the 18th the Committee unanimously voted him Manager Shanghai.[28]

Although the Provisional Committee appointed merchant agents in Bombay, Calcutta, and Singapore, they planned no further branches or Bank-staffed agencies. Arrangements had been made with Ashton and Co., Gilman's London friends, to establish appropriate London connections. These were finalized later in the year. Thus, with the appointment of the two key managers, the Provisional Committee's main task in this area had been concluded. Hereafter staff recommendations, however initiated, were a function of management; appointment was to remain a responsibility of the Court of Directors.

Another early task was the acquisition of an appropriate building for the new bank. The sub-committee considered several possible sites, but the preference from the first, actually approved on October 28, 1864, was for a property of D. Sassoon, Sons and Co., Wardley House, named after W.H. Wardley, an early Shanghai merchant, and available for rent at $500 per annum for two years certain – the Bank purchased outright in 1866.[a] Situated in Victoria at No. 1, Queen's Road, the main thoroughfare of the Colony, the building backed onto a small path, later developed as Des Voeux Road, across which was the sea.

From this base the Bank was to expand along Queen's Road by the purchase of the neighbouring Chartered Mercantile Bank building and laterally to include part of the old City Hall site. After the Praya reclamation the Bank's headquarters would hold a commanding position at the southern end of Central District's main open space. The Provisional Committee had chosen well and, quite incidentally, had acquired a name, Wardley, which became not only the Bank's telegraphic address but also – some 120 years later – the title of its merchant bank subsidiary.

The Shanghai premises are a subject for the following chapter.

Final acts

When Thomas Sutherland first received news of the projected Bombay bank, the P&O captain advised him to await the arrival of Neale Porter, the Bank of China's envoy. Porter in fact arrived in Hong Kong, armed with a formal introduction to Jardine, Matheson and Co., on the P&O's *Emeu*, on October 26, but, as

---

[a] W.H. Wardley had been a clerk with Gibb, Livingston, and Co. in Canton in 1847, but in 1850 founded his own W.H. Wardley and Co.; he died in Shanghai in 1853. According to information supplied by Carl Smith to the Bank's Archives, a branch of his firm, which survived him, was established in Hong Kong in 1855; it did not prosper and Sassoon's closed on the mortgage to the property at 1, Queen's Road.

Sutherland recalled the events fifty years later, '[Porter] could not get anybody to take a single share in his capital; he could not discover a possible director anywhere . . .' He eventually returned empty-handed to Bombay.

The Bank of China's promoters, with the full agreement of their shareholders, who had bought at a high premium, determined nevertheless to proceed, first by seeking to merge with the Hongkong Bank. Their proposition was considered seriously. Indeed, the Provisional Committee's meeting of December 21 was adjourned 'to consider the proposal of Neale Porter that they amalgamate with the Bank of China'. Two days later the Committee resolved that they 'declined to entertain' the proposition.

The *London and China Express* commented, 'Why shouldn't local merchants profit through dividends from the business they give the local bank? The Bombay people are petulant.'[29]

This dismissal of Porter's proposal would seem a natural consequence of developments since July 1864. But there were relationships which might have complicated the Provisional Committee's deliberations. Neale Porter had originally gone to India as managing director for the Scinde, Punjaub and Delhi Bank Corporation, of which William Dent, Jr, 'late Messrs Dent and Co., China', was a director. In 1864 this bank intended to open branches in China with Dent and Co. as agents. Porter had left the Delhi Bank under circumstances which were questioned at a General Meeting and came to Hong Kong on behalf of the Bank of China armed with a letter of introduction to James Whittall of Dent's great rival, Jardine, Matheson and Co., although Jardine's never gave either Porter or the Bank of China encouragement. In 1866 steps would seem to have been taken to join the business of the Delhi Bank with that of the successful National Bank of India, Ltd.[30]

Here again is evidence of a sort of miscellaneous bank promotion proclivity, so apparent with the Heards, but with no obvious follow-through. The Sassoons avoided involvement in the Bombay banking speculations which were the consequence of the Back Bay (Bombay) share mania, but they would appear to have had long-run investment interest in exchange banking and were certainly involved as shareholders in the Bank of Hindustan, China and Japan; many houses however – always excepting Jardine's – appear to have been caught in the fever.[31]

To appreciate the full meaning of the Hongkong Bank's success, an understanding of this speculative atmosphere, this promotion of banks that merged, failed, or changed direction, is essential; when, as in this case, it involves members of the Hongkong Bank's Provisional Committee and early merchant agents, the facts are all the more relevant. But the Provisional Committee did their work well; such overtures and connections had no impact on the 'local' Bank's history.

Indeed, in the case of the Bank of China it is difficult to imagine what, other than unneeded subscribed capital and the offer of Indian agencies – which in any case the Committee had already selected – the Bombay promoters had to offer. They certainly could provide neither customers nor direction, and the status of its shareholders, given the speculative situation in Bombay, could not be relied upon.

But the Bank of China's promoters had much to lose, and Neale Porter attempted once again to seek an agreement with the Provisional Committee; on February 27, 1865, less than a week before the commencement of business, he was again rebuffed. The Bank of China after two years of ineffective efforts to obtain a charter began the process of 'winding up' in October 1866, a decision precipitated by the failure of the Asiatic Bank in which their capital funds had been deposited. Their chief expense had been Rs27,312 for Mr Porter's visit to Hong Kong.[32]

The Provisional Committee resolved on January 9, 1865, that they would provide the first direction of the new banking company, that each director should hold 50 shares of the 20,000 subscribed, and that the first Chairman of the 'Court of Directors' should now be elected. Accordingly there was a ballot in which Francis Chomley of Dent and Co. received twelve votes to one vote for A.F. Heard. In the election for Deputy Chairman, Thomas Sutherland received seven votes to Heard's five and H.B. Lemann's one. The sponsoring company had the key position of Chairman of the new local bank; the honour – a working honour as it turned out – of Deputy Chairman went to the Bank's respected 'founder'. Heard's support is difficult to understand given his long absence in Shanghai, but there is evidence that the Heard brothers were personally respected and popular on the China coast and this, rather than any British versus non-British sentiment, is the more likely explanation.

The Committee spent considerable time on the question of their remuneration and while voting not to receive fees as promoters agreed to set aside $25,000 maximum at the end of each year, a figure modified at a subsequent meeting by a complicated formula which never, in fact, came into effect. The arrangements made under the original Deed of Settlement in any case lapsed in December 1866 when the Bank's business came under the terms of its special ordinance. The Committee also left over the preliminary expense account as a charge against future profits and voted Pollard $15,000, which he felt insufficient and in response claimed $30,000. This dispute went eventually to arbitration. The result is, however, not recorded. In view of Pollard's large holding of Bank shares it is possible that the final settlement included an additional allotment at par. In any case, as Pollard remained Counsel at an unusually high fee, there must have been an agreement which later comments suggest the Court considered very much to have been in Pollard's favour.

Concurrent with consideration of the Deed of Settlement were discussions on the rules under which the managers would conduct business, including the problem of credits to directors, the inspection of individual accounts by directors, and the maximum credit to any single customer, but the conclusions, being embodied in the Deed, are unfortunately not recorded in the minutes.

With the original Deed of Settlement finally agreed and signed by the Committee members present on March 2, 1865, and with a resolution earlier passed that business was at such a time to commence without delay, the Provisional Committee declared its proceedings closed and minuted that the Court of Directors of the Hongkong and Shanghae Banking Company Limited were to meet forthwith.

Four basic questions – the names and the dates

1 How did the Bank receive its English name?

On the eve of the publication of the Bank's Prospectus, A.F. Heard wrote about the new bank as the 'Hongkong and Shanghai Banking Corporation or some such'; and the Prospectus refers to 'The Hongkong and Shanghae Banking Company (Limited)'.[33] No other name appears in any article, manuscript, or document. The use of a geographical name to denote the area of operation was usual at the time. Contemporary sources indicate that from the earliest period the bank which became 'The Hongkong and Shanghai Banking Corporation' was referred to on the China coast and particularly in Hong Kong as simply 'the local Bank', or in conversation as 'the Bank'.

Despite this apparently eventless history of the Bank's name, there were three potential sources of trouble: (i) 'and' or '&', (ii) 'The' or 'the', and (iii) 'Hongkong' or 'Hong Kong'. The choice in (i) was seen as a matter of design or convenience; the Bank itself authorized the ampersand on its banknotes. The capitalization of the 'T' depends, among other factors, on whether the definite article is recognized and accepted as part of the incorporated name; in the case of the Bank and with the exception of the equivocal wording of the initial ordinance and Deed of Settlement, this was generally not the case. The Court of Directors specifically omitted the article in their December 29, 1866, motion. The third problem arose from the early custom of writing the names of familiar Chinese cities as one word, for example, Shanghai (or, earlier, Shanghae), Peking, as opposed to Shang-hai, Pei-ching. The British authorities, however, usually referred to their colony as 'Hong Kong' and, therefore, to the Bank as the 'Hong Kong Bank'. When writing the full title of the Bank both Government officers and Bank officers were wholly inconsistent.

In the late 1930s the Hong Kong Government attempted to preempt any further discussion by referring to the 'Hong Kong and Shanghai Banking

Corporation' in the ordinance. The Bank's post-war Chief Manager and Chairman, Sir Arthur Morse, simply refused to accept this as a *fait accompli*, and, as a result of his forceful representations, an amendment was included in a 1950 miscellaneous provisions ordinance (No. 37), which for the first time officially acknowledged the Bank's (or possibly Morse's) preferences: 'The Hongkong and Shanghai Banking Corporation'.

This 1950 ordinance, however, did not automatically standardize the names of the Bank's trustees and nominee subsidiaries, which had been incorporated in forms using one or more of the disapproved variables. These matters exercised the minds of several chief executives, who felt strongly on one point or the other and who were frustrated by the considerable disinterest of all but those within hearing. In 1980, on the eve of success, the corporate image experts took charge, and the problem developed new and costly dimensions which must surely be the only justification for the full consideration given the matter here.

2 How and when did the Bank receive its Chinese names?

Foreign firms usually adopted 'officially recognized' Chinese names, which might not be the same in each port. For example, the Asiatic Bank was known as 'Ho yin-hang' 曷銀行 , 'Heard's Bank', in Hong Kong; it was known as 'Li-hua yin-hang 麗華銀行' in Shanghai. As *ho* 曷 is literally an interrogatory, it is inexplicable as the name of a bank unless one knows that their agents are Augustine Heard and Company and that this is the standard Chinese name of the trading company – it is also helpful to know that 'ho' in revised Wade-Giles romanization is pronounced 'hê'. Parenthetically, this may answer A.F. Heard's plaintive query as to why people assumed some close association between the Asiatic and his company!

At some stage a firm might decide on a single Chinese name. The name might be literal translation or a phonetic approximation of the name of the company, its agent or manager. Alternatively the company might attempt to create a more traditional Chinese image, acting in consultation, perhaps, with a Chinese scholar.

According to contemporary business directories, the Hongkong Bank was first known by a literal translation – 'Hsiang-kang Shang-hai yin-hang' 香港上海銀行 but by the mid-1870s directories for Shanghai included the characters *hui-feng* 匯豐 meaning, possibly, 'focus of wealth', conjuring up a vision of streams of wealth flowing towards . . . the Hongkong Bank. Meanwhile in Hong Kong the Bank's Chinese name had come to include the characters *hui-li* 匯理 or 'regulated' as opposed to the Chartered Mercantile's Shanghai name *you-li* 有利 or 'profitable'.

As nothing on the subject appears in the early records of the Bank, the banknotes, which are at least bi-lingual, provide the only guide to change. The

Chinese names printed on the notes must have had some management sanction; they cannot but have influenced popular usage.

The Chinese name on the Bank's early notes includes the term *hui-li* (Waylee) 匯理, giving the sense of 'high principled' or, more prosaically, 'regulated'. This may have been inspired by the earlier Agra and United Service Bank, whose Chinese name was 'Ho-chiu-la *hui-li* yin-hang' 呵加剌匯理銀行, which compares with the Hongkong Bank's 'Hsiang-kang Shang-hai hui-li yin-hang' 香港上海匯理銀行. The practice of combining *hui* 匯 with another character to provide a bank with a significant name is also seen in the Commercial Bank Corporation of India and the East's *hui-lung* 匯隆 and the Central Bank of Western India's *hui-yüan* 匯源. The Hongkong Bank's Shanghai notes had, in addition to the standard name, which included *hui-li* 匯理 written across the top, an alternative name, 'Ying-shang hui-feng yin-hang' 英商匯豐銀行, printed vertically. This also is in the *hui-* 匯 pattern and could be translated, very literally, 'British merchants' focus of (abounding in) wealth bank'

From 1888 all Hongkong Bank notes, whether issued in Hong Kong, Shanghai or, later Penang, Singapore, Tientsin, Hankow, etc., adopted the Shanghai variant term *hui-feng* 匯豐. In popular Cantonese romanization this becomes 'Wayfoong', which has recently been given the more literal but a-historical translation, 'abundance of remittances'. It is unlikely that such a colourless name would have been advised in the nineteenth century; Jardine's for example used Ewo (I-ho) 怡和 'upright and harmonious'.

Today 'Wayfoong' and 'Waylee' are used as the English-language name of the Bank's launches and of certain Hongkong Bank subsidiaries, as, for example, Wayfoong Finance, Ltd or Waylee Investments, Ltd.

When the 1888 change occurred, the Shanghai banknotes dropped their additional, vertically printed name, and the text at the top of the note was amended to include *Ying-shang* 英商 thus: 'Ying-shang Hsiang-kang Shang-hai hui-feng yin-hang' 英商香港上海匯豐銀行. The phrase *Ying-shang* was also used in the official name of the Bank in the Straits Settlements.

The only available explanation for the change comes from a manuscript comment on a specimen old-style Shanghai note held in the Bank's archives, and actually used to illustrate an article on the Bank's notes. There is an inked arrow pointing to the character *li* 理 in the phrase *hui-li* 匯理 with the smudged comment, 'not so good, means regul[ated?] Corporation'; similarly, by the character *feng* 豐 in the phrase *hui-feng* 匯豐, the comment reads, 'better, means abounds'. The date, which is obscure, is pre-1888.[34]

There is a tradition that the characters *hui-feng* on the banknotes were written in 1881 by the Chinese Minister to London, Tseng Chi-tse 曾紀澤, a skilled calligrapher and friend of the Hongkong Bank.

These are 'officially recognized' names, but a foreign company might be referred to in a Chinese text in quite unpredictable, and sometimes uncomplimentary, ways. The Hongkong Bank was sufficiently well-known, however, that some uniformity was ensured. Thus by the end of the century, the Bank was known either by a literal translation, for example, 'Hsiang-Shang yin-hang' 香上銀行 or by some variant which included the characters *hui-feng*, as, for example, 'Hui-feng yang-hang' 匯豐洋行 , literally 'Wayfoong foreign company'.

3 When was the Hongkong Bank founded?

The first step is to request that the name be completed: the Hongkong and Shanghae Banking Company, Limited, or the Hongkong and Shanghai Banking Corporation? Or the question might be rephrased before answering. The Corporation assumed the assets and liabilities of the Company without cessation of business or management, so that, for ordinary purposes the question is really, when did the continuity of business of the present Hongkong Bank begin?

But rather than speculate on what is meant by the question, this is an opportunity to provide the dates for several beginnings as a prelude to the history proper of the Hongkong Bank, both company and corporation, though not, at this stage, of the 'Group'.

The first Deed of Settlement of a Hongkong Bank was signed on March 2, 1865, and the first meeting of the Court of Directors of the Hongkong and Shanghae Banking Company, Limited was held on the same day. But the Bank did not open for business until March 3 and was not registered under the Limited Liabilities or Companies Ordinance (which alone gave it the right to the term 'limited') until August 5, 1865.

The earliest possible date for the 'founding' would be the first meeting of the Provisional Committee on August 6, 1864, but few would find this an acceptable date. On the other hand, a case could be made for saying the Bank was founded on January 1, 1865, for it was from that date Victor Kresser took office as Manager and the directors calculated the remuneration due them under the Deed of Settlement, notwithstanding the fact between January and March they referred to themselves as 'promoters' and members of the Provisional Committee.

The Hong Kong Government was instructed by the Treasury in London not to accept the Bank's notes until it had been in operation six months and it could be decided whether it had gained the confidence of the populace.[35] The Government's decision to accept the notes from July 31 is based on a letter from Victor Kresser stating that 'the establishment of the Bank dates from 31st January last upon which day the Deed of Settlement was signed and operations commenced by the Company'.[36] This statement is surprising as the Deed of Settlement was signed on March 2 and business was not commenced until the following day. The established facts require that it be ignored.

Of the choices available therefore, March 2, 1865, would appear the most appropriate.

The beginnings of the Hongkong and Shanghai Banking Corporation are found in the approval by the Legislative Council of the Hongkong and Shanghai Bank Ordinance (No. 5 of 1866) on August 14, 1866. Although this ordinance incorporated a bank known as the Hongkong and Shanghai Banking Corporation, the latter was a mere shell; it could not commence business until certain specified requirements were met and proclaimed by the Governor, nor did it have any shareholders – all those interested in the Bank had shares in the Hongkong and Shanghae Banking Company. The relevant Proclamation was duly published in the *Hongkong Government Gazette*, dated December 15, 1866. The Court of Directors, however, did not meet until December 29, and it was on that date the Court, noting publication of the Proclamation, resolved:

that the present denomination of the Bank be changed forthwith into that of the 'Hongkong and Shanghai Banking Corporation' [and] that the Corporation assume and take over all the liabilities, contracts, and obligations of the 'Hongkong and Shanghai [sic] Banking Company Limited', the latter from this time ceasing to exist.

At this point the Company's shareholders became shareholders of the Corporation which was, at the same time, to commence business.

The Corporation existed, therefore, as from August 14, 1866. The December 15 date merely granted permission for the Corporation to undertake business. The December 29 date is the operative one; the empty shell of the Corporation was filled and became an operating bank on December 29, 1866.

Colonial ordinances dealing with money and banking are 'reserved', that is, they are subject to disallowance by the Sovereign on the advice of Her constitutional advisers. Disallowance might indeed have been the fate of the Hongkong Bank Ordinance had not all concerned been willing to allow the necessary amendments to be incorporated into a new Deed of Settlement, the terms of which could not be amended without the consent of the Governor in Council and which was not agreed in substance until early July and was declared signed by a sufficient number of shareholders only on July 30, 1867. At this meeting the directors minuted that the ordinance was now in full effect; the Deed was however forwarded to London, where it was finally approved by the Treasury in January 1868.

But the ordinance remained in full effect throughout, the only difference being that after the Treasury's decision that the Deed could be revised rather than the ordinance amended, a decision which in fact confirmed the latter's official but conditional 'confirmation' of November 24, 1866. The ordinance would no longer be disallowed. At no time had there been an annulment of the Bank's incorporation or suspension of its business.

Thus August 14 and December 29, 1866, as the dates of the Corporation's birth and commencement of business respectively, must stand. However, for the banking historian neither of these dates are relevant. Clause XXX of the Hongkong Bank's Ordinance is so worded that, as far as the courts are concerned, all activities carried on by the Company before the ordinance are treated as if they had been carried on by the Corporation. In a sense this clause has the effect of making incorporation retroactive to the commencement of operations by the Company.

From this it follows that with reference to the question 'When was the "Hongkong Bank" founded?', the most meaningful response, the date the enquirer was probably seeking in the first place, is March 2, 1865.

4 What is the date of the establishment of the oldest company in the Hongkong Bank Group?

If the previous question were intended to refer to the Hongkong Bank as the holding company of some 400 subsidiary and associated companies, that is, to the origins of the Hongkong Bank Group as it stood in 1984, then within the Asian region the trail leads back through the Mercantile Bank of India Limited, incorporated in 1892, to the Chartered Mercantile Bank of India, London and China, chartered in 1857, and beyond that to the Chartered Bank of Asia, 1853, and the Mercantile Bank of India, London and China founded in Bombay in 1853. Before its registration it had been originally entitled the 'Bank of India'.[37]

The business of the Mercantile Bank had however been completely transferred to the Hongkong Bank by 1984 and the corporate shell sold to Citicorp so that the latter might use its banking licence in Bangkok. The historical tradition – and the Mercantile Bank's archives – remained with the Hongkong Bank. The discussion above remains relevant.

One can take another course, back through Marine Midland Banks, Inc., to the history of the many separate banks which came under the holding company since its founding in 1929. The Marine Midland Trust Company of the Mohawk Valley, for example, could trace its origins to the President, Directors and Company of the Bank of Utica (New York State), founded in 1812.[38]

The Group's third banking candidate, the British Bank of the Middle East, goes back only to the Imperial Bank of Persia, chartered in London in 1889.

The oldest member of the Group, now operating under the Wardley name, is found through the merchant bank channel, to Antony Gibbs and Sons, which was founded as a London firm in 1808, with even earlier origins in Exeter and Spain. In 1986 James Capel and Co. became a wholly-owned subsidiary; its history can be traced back to the mid-1770s. Using stricter criteria, however, the date of the partnership of James Capel in the firm of Antrobus and Wood would argue for 1813, leaving the claim of Antony Gibbs and Sons still standing.[39]

APPENDIX: THE PROSPECTUS OF THE HONGKONG AND SHANGHAE BANKING COMPANY, LIMITED

The Scheme of a Local Bank for this Colony, with Branches at the most important places in China, has been in contemplation for a very long period.

The local and foreign trade in Hongkong and at the open ports in China and Japan has increased so rapidly within the last few years that additional Banking facilities are felt to be required.

The Banks now in China being only branches of Corporations, whose headquarters are in England or India, and which were formed chiefly with the view of carrying on exchange operations between those countries and China, are scarcely in a position to deal satisfactorily with the local trade which has become so much more extensive and varied than in former years.

This deficiency the Hongkong and Shanghae Banking Company will supply, and will in fact assume the same position with relation to this Colony as the Presidency Banks in India, or the Banks of Australia in their respective localities.

The Establishment of a Mint in Hongkong, providing an adequate supply of proper currency, will render a local Banking medium essential to carry out its operations, and the almost certain disappearance of the existing Compradoric system (so far as money is concerned) will also ensure Banks becoming in course of time the exclusive medium for the transactions of the monetary operations connected with trade.

For the anticipated success of this enterprise there are therefore ample grounds; and the great prosperity which has attended the working of other local associations in China clearly shows that the largest profits are obtained by those Public Companies which possess an interested local body of Proprietors or Shareholders, whose support naturally forms a chief element of remunerative success.

The Bank will commence operations simultaneously in Hongkong and Shanghae, and as the importance of its business at the latter place must be very great, it is intended to establish a local Board of Directors there for more effectually meeting the work. As circumstances render it advisable the Bank will establish Branches at other places.

In the distribution of Shares Hongkong and Shanghae will equally participate. Shares will also be reserved for the other ports in China and Japan and for persons residing elsewhere, who are directly interested in the China Trade.

Applications for Shares must be addressed, until further notice, to the Provisional Committee, care of

Hongkong, July 29, 1864   Messrs DENT & CO.

3

THE HISTORY OF THE HONGKONG AND SHANGHAE BANKING COMPANY, LTD

> Resolved unanimously that the Company commence business forthwith.
> Court of Directors, March 2, 1865

The history of the 'Company Limited' begins with the first meeting of its Court of Directors on March 2, 1865, two days before passage of the Companies Ordinance (No. 1 of 1865) and continues until December 29, 1866, when the formalities required for incorporation under the Hongkong Bank Ordinance (No. 5 of 1866) had been completed and the directors passed the appropriate resolution dissolving the company and transferring its business to the corporation.

The transition from company to corporation was immediate and the business of the Bank continued uninterrupted. This chapter is, therefore, not so much a history of an interim operation or preface to the main story but an integral part of the Hongkong Bank's history, an account of the very beginnings of the Bank, differentiated only slightly by the nevertheless significantly different legal context. It is in this spirit that the history of the Hongkong and Shanghae Banking Company, Ltd, is told.

General principles

The first recorded banking decision had in fact been made by the Provisional Committee on January 7, 1865. With the first call on shares payable by January 31, the Committee resolved, subject to legal objections, to have the Manager, Victor Kresser, invest the paid-up capital in bank or mercantile acceptances or other first class securities – subject to the approbation of the sub-committee.

Now there were more fundamental questions to decide. Was the Bank a 'local bank' and like the Presidency banks able to issue notes but barred from operating in exchange? Was the Bank to be run on Scottish principles? What in fact were its duties to its local constituents and in particular to the Chinese traders and native banking institutions? What, in view of the promises in the Prospectus, would the Bank do about the currency system . . . about the compradoric system? A formidable list of questions indeed, but perhaps two contrasting statements of A.F. Heard, written only six weeks apart, will put the situation in better perspective:

(i) '[The Hongkong Bank will] limit its business to loans, discounts and deposits, etc, and local exchange operations without competing in English and Indian exchanges with the other banks.'[1]

(ii) '[The Hongkong Bank will] feel its way along and get into every form of banking business.'[2]

Significantly, the first statement, reflecting the sense of the Prospectus, was written before the second statement after the first meetings of the Provisional Committee. Apparently the discussion had not followed faithfully the terms of the Prospectus.

If such development occurred in the early meetings, concepts could be expected to become even more flexible by March 1865 and, with the failure of many exchange banks in the following two years, fear of the wrath of the survivors was even less a moderating force. The Hong Kong merchants wanted a bank to serve their needs; they were not concerned with nice distinctions nor were they impressed with theoretical arguments as to the difference between an exchange and a 'local' bank. Furthermore, and perhaps very much to the point, the majority were not concerned with loyalty to existing branches of overseas exchange banks. The directors, being publicly associated with the new Bank had more to fear. Distant partners of Augustine Heard, for example, would caution against antagonizing present banking connections.

What has been called 'department store' banking appealed early to Hong Kong, and neither the Companies Ordinance nor the Colonial Regulations were sufficiently restrictive to prevent a natural pragmatic development. Exchange banks dealt in acceptances and were, therefore, 'merchant banks' – although in this history the term is used mainly in connection with the Bank's public loan and consortium operations.

There were precedents for all required operations. What Hong Kong needed was a bank alert to local financial requirements, locally directed and responsive. The parallel with the Indian Presidency banks was illustrative but not exclusive.

The Hongkong Bank, then, operated in the exchanges from the first, nor, given the appointment of Victor Kresser as Hong Kong Manager, were the public surprised; they were only concerned that support of local companies might be neglected. As already noted small local banks had been founded in England for the purpose of supporting local enterprise, including companies in which the bank promoters had a financial investment. There was nothing unusual, certainly nothing questionable about such a purpose for the Hongkong Bank. Whether such support were wise is another matter.

The public's fears that due to Kresser's background with the Comptoir d'Escompte, the Hongkong Bank would become interested exclusively in exchange operations proved groundless. Members of the Court of Directors and their Hong Kong and Shanghai managers were directly connected with public companies and other ventures for which risk capital was more appropriate than bank credit, and the Bank's involvement would result in serious, almost fatal, losses during the financial crisis of 1874. That is a later story; in the period of the 'Company, Limited', losses on all accounts were minimal; the Bank began soberly and profitably.

Exchange banking works for a rapid turnover of funds; a lock-up of funds is to be deprecated. What a local bank needed to develop was a balance suitable to the banking environment and to be given the liquidity needed for sound operations. By the 1880s (Sir) Thomas Jackson would find this balance, but even he was to find it a delicate one.

The Bank would then be a 'local bank', but did it operate, as Sutherland had intended, on Scottish principles?

James Gilbart described a Scottish bank as (i) joint stock, (ii) a bank of issue, (iii) characterized by a branch system, (iv) granting interest on current accounts, (v) lending on the basis of cash credits.[3] The *Blackwood* article which had been Sutherland's introduction to banking stressed the importance of a cash-credit system based on notes of less than £5 in value, a right English private banks had lost in 1829; the Hongkong Bank would be able to go down to the rough equivalent of £1 but not to $1.00 without the special authority of the Governor, and, when the permission was granted, its usefulness was restricted by the Treasury, a problem to be considered at a later stage of this history.[4]

Although these comparisons are useful in placing the Hongkong Bank in context, and although the Bank's operations were not incompatible with Scottish principles, there is little point in pursuing the argument. Scottish banks, moreover, operate under Scottish law; the Hongkong Bank's legal environment was English. Scottish banks had developed systems of control through inspection and internal audit; in the Hongkong Bank such measures, except temporarily in Shanghai, were far in the future. The question is more subtle than Sutherland imagined and in the Treaty Ports of China a bank had to determine its own 'tradition'. Perhaps more important than Scottish principles in the colonial context, was the fact that the Bank was to operate within the framework of the colonial Banking Regulations. Heard's general appreciation of the Bank's pragmatic philosophy is perhaps the operative characteristic of its policies.

Finally, the Prospectus noted the early establishment of a mint in Hong Kong.[5] This, it was expected, would require the assistance of a local bank and in consequence there would be a 'certain disappearance of the existing compradoric system (so far as money is concerned)'. The Prospectus concluded by declaring that banks would become in course of time the exclusive medium for the transaction of the monetary operations connected with trade.

The Hongkong Bank began operations little more than a year after the Hong Kong dollar had been declared the official unit of account for the Colony.[6] This abandonment of an Empire-wide attempt to force acceptance of pounds-shillings-pence as the universal unit of account and the positive policy implied in the decision to establish a mint in Hong Kong suggested that a reform of the Colony's complex currency system might soon be accomplished. Plans for the mint were well advanced when the Hongkong Bank was first announced and the establishment of a local bank was confidently expected to facilitate the achievement of any such reform, a view to which the Prospectus gave voice. Hong Kong merchants saw the confused state of the currency as a deterrent to trade, and the Promoters of the 'local bank' considered it their duty – and one of the attractions of the proposed Hongkong Bank – to play a role in supplementing the improvements which were assumed to be underway. The more optimistic also expected the operations of the Bank would naturally cause a related reform, the end to the so-called 'compradoric system'.[7]

As for the currency, the Provisional Committee and, afterwards, the Court of Directors stressed the importance of the note issue, and the success of the Hongkong Bank's notes, which quickly exceeded the total of the issue of all other banks, was surely part of what was hoped might prove to be a new currency system. The metallic coinage, however, resisted reform and by 1868 the Hong Kong Mint had been proved a financial burden and its closure scheduled. These developments together with consideration of the surprisingly controversial one-dollar note issue are subjects for a separate consideration.

In predicting the certain disappearance of the 'compradoric system', the Prospectus was careful to confine itself, albeit parenthetically, to the system in relation to the currency. Foreign establishments, including the Hongkong Bank, had Chinese managers responsible for hiring and guaranteeing the Chinese staff and for attracting Chinese business. The Promoters certainly did not have in mind the dismissal of all compradores, but rather a lessening of the foreign merchant's dependence on them. The utter dependence of the merchant on the compradore for the handling of cash was particularly aggravating; the power of the shroffs in determining the value of the coins was resented, especially as it seemed at times to be arbitrary. Foreigners recognized that this was partly at least because they did not understand the system, nor could they evaluate the various coins – Carolus or Republican (Mexican) dollars, shoes of sycee, bits of monetary silver, chopped dollars. Knowledge of this basic but esoteric system seemed restricted to the Chinese who invented it, perhaps, many thought, especially to confuse foreigners. (See Chapter 1 for a brief explanation.)

Thus a reform or simplification of the currency was seen as essential to ending the hold of the compradore over the merchants' transactions in cash or bullion.[a] Then, too, given the need for the merchant house to rationalize the holding of reserves – a need the Bank could immediately fulfil – the power of the compradore could, at the same time, be diminished, and his role, though still vital, be redefined.

[a] When the monetary system was rationalized, the Chinese shroff, working under and guaranteed by the compradore, continued to handle the Bank's cash. The shroff could, however, be monitored.

The Hongkong Bank had compradores from the first, and the title remained until 1960 when Peter Lee Shun Wah, the last of the Bank's Hong Kong compradores (retired in 1965), became, more appropriately for both his contribution and the age, the Chinese Manager. This subject, too, requires separate development, but suffice to say at this point that the Hongkong Bank's role did much to rationalize both the monetary and the compradoric systems.[8]

The Bank's immediate recognition

By the end of 1868 the Hongkong Bank was described in glowing, almost awed terms normally reserved for companies which had proven their stability over a period of years. The virtually immediate recognition of the Bank as a leading financial institution can be partially explained by the very fact of its survival – it seemed indeed to have risen phoenix-like from the ashes of older banks and bubble companies which crashed in the wake of the Bombay financial collapse and the Overend-Gurney crisis in England. Writing of the Hongkong Bank as if it had been a financial monument of many years standing, the *North-China Herald*'s economic editor – probably the same J.W. Maclellan who had unsuccessfully offered himself as the Bank's Hong Kong Manager in 1864 and who obviously bore no grudge – gave evidence of the recognition which the 'local institution' achieved in a surprisingly short period of time. His comments also provide the basis for discussion of the Bank's development in its earliest years.

Projected at a critical period in the financial history of Shanghai, its career has been one of steady progress. It is true that its projectors and managers had before them, as both warning and a guide, the utter collapse of a large number of houses of the highest reputation, as well as of several banks; and they have escaped the entanglements of disastrous failures. This Bank was established in the very midst of the financial storm which swept away a large proportion of the Shanghai mercantile houses, but it was not taken unawares. It passed through the crisis under cautious and judicious management, and it has wrought up to magnificent success. As a London contemporary observes in reference to it,

'There is nothing like this in banking history, in the same space of time, except the large business done, the great profits realized, and the important position achieved by the London and Westminster Bank, on a capital almost nominal, when compared with the amount of its deposits, dividends and transactions . . .'

The object of the Bank is to make money for the public by making money out of the public; this is one of the principal secrets of its success. Banking is a business undertaken as a favour to the mercantile community; and one of the results of recognizing this policy, is that the Hongkong Bank has attained to a position of remarkable and almost impregnable strength. There is no scheme in the East that promises better, as a safe and lucrative investment . . . There are few institutions in the East which, take them all in all, will bear equal comparison with the Hongkong and Shanghai Bank, in point of rapidity and genuineness of success, of influence and stability, and of a prosperous future.[9]

The course of business

The reports of the Court of Directors reflect the troubled times; indeed, they seem almost to ascribe the Bank's success to the foresight in doing as little business as possible. Opening in March and April 1865 in Hong Kong and Shanghai respectively, the Bank's two offices were 'not in fair working order' until the middle of May. By the end of the year two directors had resigned due to business failures and the Court considered the most encouraging news was that 'up to the present time the Bank has suffered no losses whatever'. Reflecting on the first half of 1866 the directors congratulated the shareholders on satisfactory results in what had been a period of continued and increased depression. Again the emphasis was on escaping from loss, and, although noting for the first time the temporary lock-up of funds, they predicted, correctly, that the Reserve Fund of $100,000 would remain intact. The Bank held bills of the failed Agra and Masterman's Bank, which explains the relatively large sum of $45,700 carried over in the Profit and Loss account (see Table 3.1). But by the end of our period, that is, at just that time when the Company had received its charter and become the Corporation, the directors expressed some long-run optimism and noted the Bank's growing credit, the steadily increasing confidence and support of its numerous constituents – and the disappearance from China of no less than six banks. Table 3.1 contains the abstract of the Bank's accounts; Table 3.2 provides key information through 1875, consistent with the format provided throughout this history.

Of the ten banks actually operating in Hong Kong when the Hongkong Bank was promoted, only five remained when the Corporation succeeded the Company in 1866, and certain of these had sustained losses which made their directors more cautious, their resources less dominating (Table 3.3). The survivors – the Comptoir d'Escompte, the Chartered Mercantile, the Chartered Bank of India, Australia and China, and the Oriental Bank Corporation – were formidable exchange banks, but their direction was in Europe and, with the exception of the Comptoir, their primary focus was on South Asia and the Straits. The Asiatic, Agra and Masterman's, and the Commercial Bank Corporation of India and the East had had their origins as joint-stock banks in India; they had in fact been weakened by their move to London, and they suffered fatally from the financial climate in both areas. The Agra and Masterman's Bank was reconstituted under general banking legislation as the Agra Bank, Ltd, and survived until 1900. The Commercial Bank was the only one whose failure was primarily the consequence of events in the East – the over-speculation of Shanghai real estate – and the unauthorized investment of the bank's funds by their San Francisco manager in California mining enterprises. Even this understates the magnitude of the failures. Table 3.3 lists in addition some eleven banks which were planning a China business, some of which never commenced operations, some failed, others postponed their plans. There were also three institutions which had agencies in Hong Kong and either failed or withdrew. There must, then, be some appreciation of Jardine Matheson's scepticism of yet another banking institution founded in that speculative year.

Table 3.1 *The Hongkong and Shanghae Banking Company, Limited[a]*
The semi-annual abstract of accounts, 1865–1866

end of:	December 1865	June 1866	December 1866
Assets and liabilities			
(in millions of dollars)			
Assets			
Cash on hand and with banks	1.25	1.54	1.94
Discounts, loans, credits	3.14	4.75	4.07
Exchange remittances	5.55	4.72	9.20
Branches and agencies	3.39	–	–
Preliminary expenses	0.03	0.02	0.02
Dead stock	0.01[c]	0.03	0.03
Premises	–	–	0.06[d]
Total: assets = liabilities	13.40	11.07	15.32
Liabilities			
Paid-up capital	2.50	2.50	2.50
+ Paid-up (new shares)	–	0.04[e]	0.39
+ Reserve Fund	–	0.03	0.10
= Shareholders' funds	2.50	2.57	2.99
Deposits and notes	3.38	3.81	4.13
of which: banknotes[b]	0.80	0.73	0.93
Exchange acceptances	5.73	4.43	7.86
Branches and agencies	1.55	–	–
Profit and loss			
(in thousands of dollars)			
By balance of undivided profits	–	12.3	45.7
By amount of profits	193.4[f]	210.4[f]	278.3[f]
= Total funds to be allocated[f]	193.4[g]	222.6	324.0
To preliminary expenses, etc	6.4	5.8	5.0
To bonus to customers	8.2	–	–
To dividend	132.2	100.0	180.0
To directors' remuneration	–	4.4[h]	28.0[i]
To reserves	33.3	66.7	75.0
To balance carried forward	12.3	45.7	35.9

Notes:
[a] the accounts for 31 December 1866 are for the 'Corporation', but actually refer to business done under the 'Company'.
[b] these figures are from the *Hongkong Government Gazette* and may not be compatible with the figures derived from the Bank's semi-annual published accounts.
[c] sundries.
[d] Wardley House at cost.
[e] $38,775 paid in anticipation.
[f] net of rebate on bills not due: (i) $31,697, (ii) $35,573, (iii) $23,133.
[g] for 8 months (rather than 6).
[h] for Thomas Sutherland as Deputy Chairman on leaving Colony.
[i] of which $20,550 due from 1 January 1865 to 30 June 1866; $7,500 from 1 July to 31 December 1866; plus $4,444 = total remuneration of directors.

Table 3.2 *The Hongkong and Shanghae Banking Company, Limited*
The Hongkong and Shanghai Banking Corporation
Key indicators, 1865–1875

(in thousands of dollars)

Half-Year	Assets	Reserves	Net earnings	To			
				(i) Reserve Fund	(ii) Dividends		
					Payout	Rate % p.a.	Payout ratio
1865 Dec.	13,400	33	225	33	132	8	58.7
1866 June	11,070	100	246	67	100	8	40.7
1866 Dec.	15,330	175	301	75	180	12	60.0
1867 June	15,560	250	260	75	180	12	69.2
1867 Dec.	20,960	375	378	125	180	12	47.6
1868 June	18,930	500	340	125	180	12	52.9
1868 Dec.	21,450	700	390	200	180	12	46.1
1869 June	22,840	700	252	0	180	12	71.4
1869 Dec.	28,070	800	257	100	210	12	81.8
1870 June	27,530	800	278	0	210	12	75.5
1870 Dec.	38,050	800	367	0	160	8	43.6
1871 June	38,060	900	366	100	240	12	65.5
1871 Dec.	40,500	1,000	368	100	270	12	73.4
1872 June	46,240	1,000	397	0	270	12	68.0
1872 Dec.	53,670	1,000	220	0	300	12	136.0[a]
1873 June	54,070	1,000	339	0	300	12	88.5
1873 Dec.	51,140	1,000	204	0	200	8	98.0
1874 June	44,960	775	104	−225	0	0	−
1874 Dec.	42,910	100	113	−675	0	0	−
1875 June	36,320	100	260	0	0	0	−
1875 Dec.	34,630	100	231	0	150	6	64.9

Shareholders' funds (1865 Dec.) = $2.5 million
Shareholders' funds (1875 Dec.) = $5.2 million

Note:
[a] Paid out from net earnings and retained earnings.
Source: Semi-annual abstract of accounts

Table 3.3 *Commercial banking in Hong Kong, 1864–1865*

A. *Banks in Hong Kong, 1864–1865*
CHARTERED:
Chartered Mercantile Bank of India, London and China (7)
Chartered Bank of India, Australia and China (2)
Oriental Bank Corporation (6)
Commercial Bank Corporation of India and the East (3)
Asiatic Banking Corporation (1)
ACTS OF 1844–1862:
Agra and United Service Bank, Ltd, which in 1864 became Agra and
    Masterman's (4)
ACT OF 1862:
Bank of Hindustan, China, and Japan Ltd (4)
INDIAN LEGISLATION (Act VII of 1860):
Bank of India (3)
Central Bank of Western India (2)
FRENCH LEGISLATION:
Comptoir de'Escompte de Paris (2)
HONG KONG ORDINANCE NO. 1 OF 1865:
Hongkong and Shanghae Banking Company, Ltd (2)

B. *Agencies of banks doing Eastern exchange business in Hong Kong*
Bombay Trading and Bankers Association Ltd (Agents: Central Bank of Western
    India)
Scinde, Punjaub and Delhi Bank Corporation (Dent & Co.)
Eastern Exchange Bank (Chartered Bank)
Asiatic Banking Corporation (Augustine Heard & Co.)
Bombay General Credit and Financial Corporation (Commercial Bank)

C. *Banks planning to establish in Hong Kong and/or China and Japan*

FROM INDIA	FROM LONDON
Bank of China, Ltd	Imperial Bank of China, Ltd
Imperial Bank of India and China	Imperial Bank of Japan, Ltd
then Indian Peninsular, London and China Bank	Imperial Bank of China, India, and Japan
National Bank of India, Ltd	British and Netherlands India Bank, Ltd
Royal Bank of India	
Alliance Bank of Bombay	Eastern Exchange Bank
Bank of Baroda, Ltd	(Liverpool)

Note:
(Figures in parenthesis are the number of staff on the jury list, and therefore give
some indication of the size of the operation.)
Source: The table is compiled from information in the local Hong Kong newspapers,
the jury lists in the HKPRO, A.S.J. Baster, *Imperial Banks* (London, 1929) and his
'The Origins of British Exchange Banks in China', *Economic History* 3: 140–51
(1954), as well as the *Bankers' Magazine* and *Journal of the Money Market and
Commercial Digest*, etc.

But the Hongkong Bank began business just a little too late to get into trouble. By mid-1865 the need for caution seemed obvious even to directors who themselves were not all successful in avoiding commercial failure. The Bank was moreover able to profit from the crises, not only in facing less competition but by recruiting trained bank staff, for example future Chief Managers James Greig from the Asiatic, Thomas Jackson from Agra and Masterman's, and G.E. Noble from the Commercial Bank Corporation of India and the East.

On the other hand, it can be reasonably argued that since the Bank, while building up its reserves, was able to pay dividends at the rate of 8% per annum for the first year (on an eight month basis this is 5.33% or $6.66 per share) and at 8% per annum for the first six months of 1866, 12% for the second, some business must in fact have been done, however cautiously.[b] While the published accounts, which are compatible with those reported to the directors, are not informative in detail, the almost immediate build-up of deposits suggests that the Bank's local support was of a practical nature.

The business of an exchange bank included (i) the buying and selling of bills of exchange, (ii) granting of credits extended against goods purchased abroad, (iii) acceptance of current and deposit accounts, (iv) purchase and sale and movement of bullion, (v) circulation of banknotes.[10] The Hongkong Bank's source of funds for trading was deposits and banknotes in circulation, indicating how dependent the Bank was on the good will of the community and how susceptible, particularly in the early years, to public evaluation of its stability.

The Hongkong Bank began business with its capital fully subscribed, giving it 20,000 shares of $250 for a nominal capital of $5 million. On the shares $125 was called and paid up in two tranches for a total of $2,500,000. This was the Bank's initial capital.

The relevant ratios hardly suggest the need for additional capital, but there was a question of the Bank's credit. Anticipating the need for greater accommodation in London and, hopefully, better trading conditions, the Court in December 1865 voted to increase the capital by the issue of 10,000 new shares of $250 at a premium of 5%, payable on allotment; the premium was to be credited to the Reserve Fund. The first call on the new shares was $37.00, which with the premium of $12.50 per share, required payment by allottees totalling $49.50 per share.

As it happened, after the first call (see Table 4.1) and due to the need to accept the conditions of a special ordinance, the Court decided to reorganize the Bank's capital for issue in a somewhat different form. For that reason further consideration is postponed until the next chapter. Sufficient to note here that, due to poor trading conditions, not all the 10,000 new shares were subscribed, and the directors agreed to accept, as part of their approved remuneration, all

[b] Dividends were quoted as a percentage of paid-up capital at an annual rate, and the payment in August was considered interim.

unsubscribed shares at par in order to meet the standard requirement that all shares be subscribed before the new ordinance could take effect.

To turn now to the other sources of the Bank's funds, even during the recession in the first half of 1866, deposits – as opposed to banknotes – increased slightly, and there was another slight gain in the latter half of the year, with confidence in the Bank, as reflected in the increased holding of banknotes, being particularly marked. This is all the more interesting when one recalls that the essential element of limited liability was missing during the major part of the Company's history, and rumours concerning and actual problems in obtaining the charter would normally create an uncertainty which would, in turn, be reflected in the accounts. That the public was nevertheless willing to hold the Bank's banknotes, however, may be explained by the Hong Kong Government's treating the Bank as a chartered institution in anticipation of Treasury approval. If, as contemporary observers often stated, foreigners rarely carried cash anyway – they relied on 'compradore's orders' and, to a lesser extent, on cheques drawn on current accounts – the banknotes were held by Chinese, reflecting perhaps the chaos and consequently the cost of the metallic currency. This was the origin of the custom which led to Hongkong banknotes becoming, by the beginning of the twentieth century, the preferred currency of Hong Kong and of large areas in the Liang Kwang provinces (Kwangtung and Kwangsi) and along the railway line from Canton to the north.

The Bank's funds had to be paid for. The Bank advertised interest on both fixed deposits (3% for 3 months, 5% for 6 months, and 6% for 12 months) and, in a tradition not inconsistent with Scottish banking, on current accounts – 2%. As noted in Chapter 2, the Company also paid a bonus at the end of 1865; the bonus was equivalent, it is true, to only 3.4% of profits but it was nevertheless calculated to improve the Bank's relations with constituents, ensuring a sound deposit base for its initial operations. The bonus was granted on the basis of 1% per annum increase in the interest paid on all fixed deposits then on the books and 1% additional to current account holders calculated on the basis of interest already entered into the passbooks.

The Hongkong Bank was proving itself the 'local bank'.

The same statement may be made of the Bank's uses of funds, illustrated dramatically by the sudden growth of earning assets during the second half of 1866. Exchange remittances increased nearly 100% from $4.72 million to $9.2 million, significant despite the decline in activity of the preceding six months which, in any case, reflected the general trade conditions rather than anything particular about the Hongkong Bank. One explanation for the Hongkong Bank's success in exchange business stresses the local factor in the finance of international trade by short-circuiting delays in referring bills to houses in Bombay and faraway London.[11] But the more obvious way in which the

Hongkong Bank proved itself designed to meet the requirements of its local constituents was in its early defiance of an agreement by the other exchange banks to shorten the usance period on bills from six to four months, a defiance which had both short- and long-term significance.[12]

The ostensible reason for the decision by the London and Paris based banks was the not unreasonable belief that long usance periods encouraged speculation and over-trading and that, with the consequences of this very visible on all sides, any support of such activity ought to cease. This caused no argument as far as finance bills were concerned, if they could be distinguished; the usance for trade bills, however, ought to be geared to the specific requirements of the business, and, while the finance of India/London trade, with which the Hongkong Bank was not then involved, might possibly operate on a four-month credit basis, the new agreement was inappropriate for the China trade.[c] This could objectively be shown to require closer to six months. Consequently the Hongkong Bank declined to join the agreement.

The major Eastern trading hongs still commanded considerable funds and could finance their own trade on a six-month basis, but it is fair to conclude that this was not the main influence in the Bank's decision. The Hongkong Bank was responding to the legitimate requirements of its constituents for appropriate accommodation.[14] That it was able to meet their requirements was due to a Hong Kong headquarters whereby (i) the Bank could escape from the pressures of the then more influential banks and (ii) have first-hand knowledge of the local trading scene.

But London was powerful; it could not be ignored without some precaution. Consequently the Court's resolution of August 21, 1866, was firm – 'unless [compliance was] insisted upon by the Company's London Bankers'.

At the various semi-annual meetings the Bank's Chairman made much of the issue, as for example in 1867. The Bank, he said, had 'established further claims on the sympathies of the mercantile community . . . adhering to a liberal policy . . .' and indeed he went further by claiming that the 'diminished competition on the market for six-months' bills afford[ed] the Bank a wider and more profitable selection'.

The immediate results are reflected in the end-1866 balance sheet. Furthermore the Hongkong Bank received new customers who stayed with the Bank subsequently. As a contemporary later observed:

The bank rapidly improved its position in China and Japan – it had then no branches in India – and gained the favour of the mercantile communities. While the agreement among the other banks lasted, a lucrative part of the business of the Hongkong [Bank] was to purchase six months' paper, and sell its own drafts on London at four months' sight to its

---

c Finance bills are drawn e.g. to finance the carrying or processing of stocks of raw materials; trade bills cover the movement of goods.[13]

competitors at a good profit, which was sometimes the only way in which they could obtain remittances. This action on the part of the Hongkong Bank immensely strengthened the Hongkong [Bank].[15]

The Hong Kong managers of the other banks recognized the likely impact of the new policy and attempted to delay implementation of their instructions, but eventually they had to obey not the dictates of their experience and the needs of their customers but the rules of a London or Paris directorate making a policy which, while not without basis, was unwisely applied in this situation. The Hongkong Bank's orientation and loyalties were proving significant.[16]

The first government loan

Reverting again to the original declaration that the Bank would be modelled after the Presidency banks, it is certain that the promoters and directors hoped to do business with the Hong Kong and other governments. In the initial period the local government's business and the United Kingdom Treasury Chest accounts were with the Oriental Bank; if the Hongkong Bank wanted the business, it would need to bid for it. There is no purpose in paying to obtain deposits beyond the needs of legitimate banking requirements. In the period of the Company Limited, the Bank made overtures, but full success came later. For the present the Bank would begin with a credit to the Hong Kong Government.

Embarrassed by the financial burden of the Mint and facing the annual military contribution of £5,000 in the absence of previously anticipated revenue from land sales, the Government required accommodation and accordingly approached the banks. The Oriental, the Commissariat's bank, showed a 'very great disinclination' to assist and, the Governor added, 'a disinclination manifested lately in several instances without, as far as I am aware, any reason whatever to justify it'.[17] Robert Hart, Inspector-General of the Imperial Maritime Customs in Peking, would write in the same vein over the Oriental Bank's attitude towards loans to the Chinese authorities.[18]

In any case, only the Hongkong Bank responded favourably (at 4% below the current merchant rate), and, in consequence, Victor Kresser signed an agreement to open a credit for Her Majesty's Government of the Island of Hong Kong in the sum of $100,000 for six months at 8% per annum on the outstanding balance, interest to be paid monthly. This was consistent with Scottish banking. But, and this too was to be characteristic, the Bank took advantage of the situation to obtain, however temporarily, a monopoly:

All remittances made through a Bank to England on behalf of the Government of Hong Kong shall be made through the Hongkong and Shanghai Banking Company except in such cases where Her Majesty's Government in England shall specially direct that the said remittances shall be otherwise made through any of the Banks of Hong Kong.[19]

This expresses the principle on which exchange banks are supposed to operate. Whatever else is done and at whatever bargain rate, it is done to obtain the exchange business. The turnover of funds and the margins implied in exchange are the basis of the Bank's profits; large funds on loan do not turn over. With Kresser as manager this was known and implemented from the first.

The Court of Directors – membership and role

Initial role and policy

Although praise for the management of the Hongkong and Shanghae Banking Company by its Court of Directors must be tempered by the knowledge that at some point, certainly before 1870, they became unwisely involved in local company development, certainly in the present period they remained cautious and on course.

The Court's conservatism took several forms: (i) as promoters they had accepted no remuneration, and now as directors they postponed taking directors' fees until advised by the August 1866 Semi-Annual General Meeting of Shareholders to accept the amount of remuneration to which they 'are entitled under the Deed of Settlement', (ii) recognizing the dangers of too rapid expansion they limited themselves to Bank branches in Hong Kong and Shanghai, while they appointed merchant agents in selected Treaty Ports, specifically delaying any development in India which could lead to premature involvement, (iii) as the Bank's international credit standing would initially be significantly affected by their choice of London agent, the directors' London friends were sufficiently astute to secure a relationship with the prestigious but cautious London and Westminster Bank – and when this proved mutually unsatisfactory, the Court of Directors were sufficiently reactive to obtain the equally respectable London and County Bank's cooperation.

At the same time the directors initiated a positive policy of loans to governments, first to Manila and secondly, as described above, to Hong Kong itself. While the Philippine administration withdrew its request before completion of the negotiations, a principle had been established, and the Court responded readily to the Hong Kong Government's application some months later. During the period of the Company Limited, the Bank's relations with the Hong Kong Government were focused mainly on the task of obtaining the charter, and the uncertainties involved were not conducive to a closer relationship, which developed later. Nevertheless, the Government already dealt with the Bank as the 'local bank' in terms consistent with the *North-China Herald*'s panegyric of 1869 and accepted the Bank's banknotes at the earliest opportunity consistent with their interpretation, which was biased in the Bank's favour, of Treasury instructions.

The Bank had two highly qualified managers in Kresser and McLean, but supporting staff was limited and the directors, through their sub-committee, remained closely involved in the details of the business, much in the style of a London joint-stock bank.

An examination of the Court, its membership and policy, is therefore essential at this time.

By the end of 1866 only five of the original fourteen members of the Provisional Committee remained on the Court; both the chairman and his deputy had left the Colony. It would be well, then, to trace these and related changes in some detail. While it is too early to note the establishment of long-term patterns of selection, who was on the Court and why are particularly important questions in these early days when the Bank's business was closely overseen by the directors (see Table 3.4).

Resignations

The initial Court was composed of the members of the Provisional Committee, excepting Brand and Adamson, who had previously announced their intention not to participate further. The failure of founding firms meant the departure from the Court of Waldemar Schmidt, G.F. Maclean, Rustomjee Dhunjeeshaw, and Pallanjee Framjee. Despite the excellent record and obvious interest of the latter two members, no Parsee was again elected to the Court.

The independent Douglas Lapraik resigned on leaving the Colony, as did the first Chairman, Francis Chomley. H.W. Wood of the Borneo Company, first appointed in January 1866, resigned in July on reassignment.

The Bank's founder Thomas Sutherland was no longer at board meetings after his transfer to Shanghai, but he did not in fact resign until his return to the United Kingdom in 1867. The Court nevertheless voted him a special remuneration of £1,000 (= $4,444) in April 1866; the sum was in anticipation of the vote for directors' fees and was subtracted from the total available for allocation.

Elections

If the resignations were the result of outside factors, failures and transfers, over which the Court had no control, the choice of replacement was theirs.

The minutes suggest that the Court began their policy of electing a director to 'replace' one who had resigned from the same company; thus H.W. Wood replaced, after an interval, Wm Adamson of the Borneo Company. While F. Chomley of Dent and Co. was absent from Hong Kong temporarily he was not replaced, but John Dent was elected on the former's final departure and resignation. The Court also took the opportunity of a resignation to expand representation by electing Caleb T. Smith of Smith, Archer and Co. and W.H. Forbes of the previously hesitant Russell and Co. The latter, however, does not

Table 3.4 *The Hongkong and Shanghae Banking Company, Limited*
List of directors

(Provisional Committee members not joining the Court

Robert Brand	Smith, Kennedy and Co.
Wm Adamson	Manager, Borneo Co.)

Courts of Directors of the Hongkong and Shanghai Banking Company, Ltd

first court		(resignations)
F. Chomley (Chairman)	Dent and Co.	23 April 1866
Thomas Sutherland[a]	P&O SN Co.	23 April 1866
(Deputy Chairman)		(on leave)
A.F. Heard	Augustine Heard and Co.	
G.F. Maclean	Lyall, Still and Co.	21 August 1866
Douglas Lapraik		13 August 1866
W. Nissen[a]	Siemssen and Co.	
H.B. Lemann	Gilman and Co.	
W. Schmidt	Fletcher and Co.	12 April 1865
Arthur Sassoon[a]	D. Sassoon, Sons and Co.	
Pallanjee Framjee	P. and A. Camajee and Co.	17 July 1866
G.J. Helland	John Burd and Co.	
Rustomjee Dhunjeeshaw	P.F. Cama and Co.	4 November 1865

members elected subsequently with dates		
H.W. Wood (23 Jan 66)	Borneo Company	17 July 1866
C.T. Smith (18 Apr 66)	Smith, Archer and Co.	
John Dent (23 Apr 66)	Dent and Co.	
W.H. Forbes (25 Sept 66)	Russell and Co.	

last court		
John Dent	Dent and Co.	Chairman
W. Nissen[a]	Siemssen and Co.	Deputy Chairman
A.F. Heard	Augustine Heard and Co.	
H.B. Lemann[a]	Gilman and Co.	
Arthur Sassoon[a]	D. Sassoon, Sons and Co.	
G.J. Helland	John Burd and Co.	
Caleb T. Smith	Smith, Archer and Co.	
W.H. Forbes	Russell and Co.	
Thomas Sutherland	(on leave)	

Note:
[a] indicates members of the Court's sub- or Standing Committee.

appear to have taken his seat until the December 1866 meeting, by which time the Company had been transformed into the Corporation.

The changes may be seen in tabular form in Table 3.4; the last Court of the Company is the same as the first of the Corporation.

Chairman, Deputy Chairman, and the sub-committee
At their first meeting, a practical minded Provisional Committee unanimously voted Francis Chomley of Dent and Co. to the chair. When the Provisional

Committee turned its attention to the Bank's future management, it again voted Chomley as Chairman. When Chomley resigned, the Court elected John Dent both a director and the Bank's Chairman at the same time – there was no question of seniority or rotation. Dent's provided the Bank its initial continuity. They were apparently able chairmen, the state of affairs in their own hong notwithstanding.

The first Deputy Chairman, Thomas Sutherland, was the Bank's founder. When he resigned his post on leaving the Colony, there were several members of equal seniority. Some may have been disqualified by reason of imminent departure – Lapraik and Framjee are examples – but there remained choices. The Hamburg merchant Woldemar Nissen was elected. No reason is given in the minutes and there was no ballot; but Nissen, Lemann, and Sassoon had been members of the Court's sub-committee, Lemann was still on leave, and Sassoon joined with Lapraik to propose Nissen. He had, after all, been active in the Bank's affairs throughout, and he was a major shareholder.

The first sub-committee 'to advise the managing officers of the Bank and inspect the accounts' was composed of Sutherland with nine votes, Sassoon eight, and Nissen five, and there is a temptation to speculate why.

The members, while apparently acknowledging the special role of Dent and Co., were obviously unwilling to elect Chomley to a committee with the duties including inspection of accounts – but he was 'in the running' and received three votes. The American A.F. Heard was absent, as he had been on several previous occasions, and was not nominated – nor were Lapraik or the Indian members. The preference for Sutherland reflects partly the respect in which he must have been held and partly his independent position. A few years later the Court would observe on the 'interest' D. Sassoon, Sons and Co. had in the Bank as the basis for election; Arthur Sassoon was said to be popular in Hong Kong and he was, as Nissen had been, a major shareholder. He too had played an important role in the Bank from its beginnings.

The Provisional Committee had considered the question of individual directors inspecting particular accounts. It was by no means the last time the issue would be before the Court, and these initial decisions would support the view that the first directors were very conscious of the problem of confidentiality and were determined to maintain the confidence of constituents.

Two directors revealed in correspondence

There were indications that directors, no matter how public spirited or far-seeing, would have problems being intimately involved in the management and fortunes of the Hongkong Bank. An examination of the directors' role in the Bank's first years should be more meaningful after consideration of the directors individually and their attitudes to the Bank and related matters. The correspondence of two directors survives. It provides a touch of reality, an insight into the limits of their altruistic promotion of the Bank for the general commercial welfare. This is particularly useful if the directors' subsequent – and lesser – role is to be understood.

Both A.F. Heard of Augustine Heard and Co. and Woldemar Nissen of Siemssen and Co., members of the Provisional Committee and the first Courts of Directors, have in their surviving papers provided an insight into their attitudes and expectations, or at least so much as they wished to report to their partners in Massachusetts and Hamburg. The content of their correspondence often contrasts with their actions – both need exposition and explanation if the initial success of the Hongkong Bank is to be understood in the context of the role of the directors.

Albert Farley Heard

In setting out his company's strategy, A.F. Heard made it clear that, while he saw the wisdom of setting up a local bank and of pooling resources, he expected a direct return, primarily in the granting to Augustine Heard and Co. of several of the Bank's projected outport agencies and of the patronage of Manila and possibly New York. Specifically Heard hoped to be appointed agent for the Hongkong Bank at Yokohama, Hankow, and Foochow (in order of priority).[20] Heard reminded Dixwell, his Shanghai partner, that the firm would also have the agency for the Commercial Bank at Bangkok and Kiukiang, the agency for the Asiatic at Foochow and Hankow, and possibly the agencies for the Asiatic and Hongkong banks in Japan. Heard was not only keeping his connections with the Asiatic Bank and the Commercial Bank Corporation but also hoping to act as their agents in several ports. From Shanghai A.F. Heard urged his younger brother, G.F. Heard, then in Hong Kong, to continue this policy of maintaining relations with several banks, mentioning in particular the Comptoir d'Escompte.[21]

In a sense, it is true, this attitude and program were consistent with the idea that the Hongkong Bank would not be an exchange bank, which the Asiatic certainly was, but would be a local bank – in the sense previously defined – the need for which arose from the development of Shanghai and Hong Kong, the Yangtze ports, and the coastal trade. This is the context in which Heard wrote to his former associate, Charles A. Fearon of the Asiatic Banking Corporation in London, asking if the new bank, the Hongkong Bank, could be of any use to him, implying a complementary relationship between an exchange bank (the Asiatic) and a 'local bank' (the Hongkong).[22]

With his firm's merchant activities running into increasing difficulties, A.F. Heard's overall policy involved promoting a multiplicity of projects, both practical and visionary. In 1865, for example, A.F. Heard and his brother Augustine, Jr, were corresponding about a projected American 'China and Japan Banking Association', backed by American capital and designed to handle U.S. State Department, Naval, and indemnity funds as well as 'incidental local business'. The bank would be incorporated under the U.S. National Banking Act and would not actually, Heard suggested, open a branch in the East (for which in any case no provision existed in the Act); Augustine Heard and Co. would handle that part of the enterprise.[23]

The Heards had earlier been holding futile discussions in Peking with Robert Hart, the Inspector-General of the Chinese Imperial Maritime Customs, in connection with a telegraph scheme and China loan. A.F. Heard and his brother George in Hong Kong were involved with insurance companies, docks and steamship lines, both local and trans-Pacific; R.I. Fearon, their partner in Shanghai, was a director of the North-China Steam Carriage Company. In the late 1860s A.F. Heard became enthused with a grand comprehensive scheme to develop China, a company to have its headquarters in Brussels and be called the China International Banking Company, or, more grandly, the China and Japan International Banking Company.[24] No wonder one brother, probably John, wrote in despair to Augustine, Jr:

I have no objection to joint-stock companies so far as the insurance company and such steam companies as may tend to reduce our interest in steam are concerned. But I do object to Manila loans, China loans, Borneo Companies, Coolie Companies, Formosa Companies, petroleum schemes, camphor contracts in Formosa, lead mines and everything of this kindred.[25]

Brother John in Ipswich, Massachusetts, could not refrain from advising A.F. Heard in terms of Washington's Farewell Address – no entangling alliances![26]

From all this two points may be made. First, the Hongkong Bank was not the only venture in which the Heards were interested. Second, the success of the Hongkong Bank may be explained by contrast – the Bank did not try to develop China, build its railroads, finance its mines (at least not yet) or even undermine or support its government; the Bank instead developed its own 'regular banking business'. Its few adventures into direct involvement with Hong Kong industrial finance would prove sufficient to endanger its future.

For Augustine Heard and Co. reality was disappointing. Despite voluminous correspondence with his brother George in Hong Kong, A.F. Heard's expectations were dashed in part at least because his wanderings in the north caused him to be absent from the key Court meetings at which the majority of agencies were decided. They were designated agents only at Kiukiang on the Yangtze – Heard was present at that Court meeting! When the Asiatic and the Commercial banks failed in 1866, the Heards, even with their friendly relations with the Comptoir d'Escompte intact, were left heavily dependent on the Hongkong Bank; they could no longer hope to play off the banks or have them be 'made cows of and sucked at'. Heard was 'disgusted'. At one point he wrote in frustration, 'Hang the Bank!'[27]

But, and this is the actual long-run business decision, the Heard brothers, or some other senior partner, continued to serve on the Hongkong Bank's Court until the firm's failure in 1875; and they remained 'constituents'. Merchants like the Heards made the Bank, but it was not to remain their tool. It served them, but only consistent with what the Manager – and, in fairness, the Court's Standing Committee – considered sound banking. The failure of so many Eastern banks had taught the need for sound banking at the same time as the consequent relative lack of competition made such banking practices enforceable to some small degree. Even then the Bank survived only by a hair's breadth.

Woldemar Nissen

As for Woldemar Nissen of Siemssen and Co., he would appear from his correspondence to have been primarily concerned with selling a piece of Shanghai property to the Bank for its branch there, and like A.F. Heard, he downplays the importance of his role in the establishment of and his subsequent directorship in the Hongkong Bank. 'It doesn't mean much more than if you see my name mentioned in connection with the Sailors' Home or any such institution.'[28]

Nissen, who in mid-1867 had over 1,000 Bank shares, was very much interested in their changing value and in the allocation to 'friends' in Germany, although in this he, like Heard, foresaw the success of the Bank; the shares might be used for speculation, but he also expected long-run growth.[29]

Each director had public and private motives for his role in the Court, and thus the importance of the part played by the independent Thomas Sutherland can be easily appreciated – he was part of a larger 'scene', the world of the P&O, yet he played a leading and respected role in Hong Kong, acting as an individual without either sanction or apparently hindrance from his managers in London. The Chairman, F. Chomley, was probably voicing the views of even the most cynical when, on Sutherland's retirement, he spoke of his 'distinguished service in the creation and organization of the Bank' and again of 'the valuable and efficient service rendered by him to the Bank from the time of its commencement up to his resignation of the post of deputy chairman'.

Nevertheless, whatever private grief they may have expressed, perhaps intemperately, in letters to their associates, there is nothing as yet suggesting they should not sit around a directors' table, guiding the initial fortunes of a Bank which, after all, was being ably managed by Kresser and McLean. The effective conflict of interest would come later, when the Bank was established and the public companies of Hong Kong needed financial support.

Shanghai and developments in the East

It would be nearly sixty years before the Bank's Shanghai Manager, A.G. Stephen, would order the architects to design a building which would 'dominate the Bund'. In 1865 the Bank's first premises on the river front at the corner of Nanking Road 'were flanked on the one side by old fashioned Hongs, and on the other by the picturesque but dilapidated Chinese Yamen which then did duty for a Custom House'. A.M. Townsend looking back sixty-seven years to his first Eastern assignment with the Bank in 1870 recalled that the Shanghai office was 'surrounded in summer with a bamboo and mat verandah; it was called the "Mat Shed"'.

Here on April 3, 1865, the Hongkong and Shanghae Banking Company, Ltd opened for business under David McLean. Kresser in Hong Kong was also 'manager'; there was as yet no 'chief'. The 'and' in the Bank's name brought together two equals, of which Shanghai, in that first year of operation, brought in the larger profit – $193,000 to Hong Kong's $168,000.

Indeed, the Court relied on McLean not just for the Shanghai operations, but also for direction of the Bank's activities in central China and in Japan. A local committee had been set up through Dent and Co. in 1864, and now that business had started it was reestablished and stood virtually in the same position to the Court on the one hand and the local manager on the other as the Court's own Standing Committee of Advice and Inspection in Hong Kong. The Court also appointed a Shanghai auditor. All this was consistent with Scottish banking practice.

In the spirit of currency reform the Court authorized a Shanghai issue of banknotes, denominated in Shanghai currency taels. The one-tael note would become a matter of controversy under the provisions of the charter. A reserve in specie equal in value to one-third of the value of notes issued was ordered, but this too would be subject to renegotiation under British Treasury regulations.

In May 1865 the Court of Directors, on McLean's recommendation, appointed Messrs Macpherson and Marshall the Bank's agents in Yokohama, but only a year later the Bank's own branch was set up under the management of W. Robert Brett. Later Singapore and Manila would become the focus of regional operations, but for the early years the Bank with but three branches remained a China-coast and Japan institution, its agents elsewhere – Bangkok, Manila, Singapore, Saigon – were justified as part of Hong Kong's trading orbit; those farther afield in London, Paris, San Francisco, and Sydney as the key terminals to long-distance trade and finance (see Table 3.5). India was much thought of, but prudence, as the Bank's Chairman told an 1866 meeting of shareholders, suggested postponement of business for the present. As for Chile, the Bank's agents in Valparaiso are mentioned once, but Chile apparently does not feature again until the opening of the Bank's own branch in 1983!

Table 3.5 *The Hongkong and Shanghae Banking Company, Limited*
Initial branches, agencies, and agents, 1865–1866

Branches and Bank agencies

Hong Kong	3 Mar. 1865	Victor Kresser, Manager
Shanghai	3 Apr. 1865	David McLean, Manager
London	26 July 1865	W.H. Vacher, Special Agent
Yokohama	23 May 1866	W. Robert Brett, agency Manager

Agents

Bombay	26 Dec. 1864	B. and A. Hormusjee
Calcutta	9 Jan. 1865	McKillop, Stewart and Co.
Singapore	9 Jan. 1865	Borneo Co., Ltd.
Foochow	25 Mar. 1865	Gilman and Co.
Manila	25 Mar. 1865	Russell, Sturgis and Co.
Amoy	12 Apr. 1865	Tait and Co.
Swatow	12 Apr. 1865	Bradley and Co.
Paris	12 Apr. 1865	La Société Général de Crédit Industrial et Commercial
Ningpo	17 May 1865	D. Sassoon, Sons and Co.
	25 Sep. 1865	Davidson and Co.
Kiukiang	17 May 1865	Augustine Heard and Co.
Yokohama	17 May 1865	Macpherson and Marshall
Hankow	9 June 1865	Gibb, Livingston and Co.
San Francisco	25 Sep. 1865	Bank of California[a]
Sydney/Melbourne[b]	25 Sep. 1865	Union Bank of Australia
Valparaiso, Chile	25 Sep. 1865	Messrs Th. Lachambre and Co.
Bangkok	9 Nov. 1865	Messrs Pickenpack, Thies and Co.
Saigon	2 Jan. 1866	Messrs Behre and Co.

Notes:
[a] failed in 1875, not related to the present Bank of California.
[b] also for other Australian towns where the Union Bank was located.

The original Provisional Committee had three members with Indian connections, and it is not surprising that agents in Bombay and Calcutta were selected even before the Bank was opened; so too, with a Borneo Company manager on the Committee, the early choice of an agency in Singapore is explicable. But the order of selection did not denote priorities, for each area had its own requirements and logic. Manning ports, as it were, along the China coast and Yangtze was first priority, for just as the trading firms which composed the Court had headquarters in Hong Kong and secondary bases in Shanghai, undertaking business with, for example, the Chinese tea merchants in Amoy and Foochow, so the Bank had to parallel that structure to effect their finance.

San Francisco, where the Commercial Bank Corporation's agent had succumbed to speculative temptation, was necessary for bullion operations and to complete the world-wide financial links through, perhaps, the London and San Francisco Bank. This latter bank had, in fact, made overtures to the Hongkong

Bank, which the directors had considered promising. The Bank, founded in 1865, had sound backing through Bischoffsheim, Goldschmidt and Co., and J.S. Morgan and Co. in London and the California financier John Parrott in San Francisco, but the depression of 1866 forced a decision to close while its capital was virtually intact.[30]

France was already represented in the East by the Comptoir d'Escompte, and Kresser, as their former Hong Kong manager, would recognize that, for those financing silk, representation in France was essential. Lyons was preferable, but the Hongkong Bank first tried Paris. Sugar took the Bank to Saigon and Bangkok, but further on that later; sugar would also affect the Bank's fortunes in Manila, which was part, and yet a distinct and separate part, of the East Asian trading network – the Bank's agency with Russell, Sturgis and Co. was a link with Canton trading days but, for the present, little more.

And there was London, where W.H. Vacher was confirmed as Special Agent in July of 1865.

Although the Hongkong Bank was by the end of 1865 virtually 'in place', this was true only of the first stage; the Bank had after all only two branches and one special agency; a third branch in Yokohama was to come in 1866. The business of the Bank in other ports was handled by merchant or banking agents, which was not a long-run solution. If the problem of confidentiality arose when directors examined the accounts of constituents, it was compounded when a merchant house actually handled the banking business of a rival firm. When the withdrawal of facilities by the Asiatic Bank forced Augustine Heard and Co. to find other sources to finance their tea trade from Foochow, they turned to the Hongkong Bank, but only if the account could be handled in Hong Kong.[31] Their rival, Gilman and Co., was the Hongkong Bank's agent in Foochow.

But the decision of the Bank to develop in this way had several favourable consequences: first, and most obvious, it was able to do business within its designated area almost immediately; secondly, as the agents were usually constituents the policy of the Bank making money by helping others make money was reinforced; and thirdly, the Bank was able to delay opening agencies staffed by its own personnel until, indeed, it was able to find, employ, and train them. There were to be, as a result of the events of 1866, bank clerks and managers available, and some proved suitable for the Bank, but there were also juniors to be taken on and a whole staff policy to be determined, slowly, sometimes painfully, through experience.

The merchant and banking agents were, over time, replaced either as business grew and Bank staff became available or when the failure of the agents forced the decision. But Yokohama and London could not wait.

In May 1866 the Court of Directors appointed W. Robert Brett, the former Yokohama agent of the Chartered Mercantile Bank, to be the Hongkong Bank's first Agent in that same city. Brett had actually left the Chartered Mercantile for speculating in Japanese coins; he left the Hongkong Bank for the same reason.

At the time the foreign trade of Japan totalled under Yen26 million – it was to reach Yen59 million within twelve years. The Bank settled at 62 Yamashita-cho in premises which it subsequently bought, probably in 1870, for just over $20,000. The Bank was established then in the year of the Satsuma-Choshu coalition which presaged the Meiji Restoration two years later. The foreigners, still under Shogunate rule, were more concerned with the immediate problem of the currency; the villain, as usual, was the 'compradoric system', which there, as in Hong Kong, was in the hands of the Chinese. While not unique to Yokohama, the difficulties are vividly described by the pioneering Far East journalist, J. R. Black:

The plan the wily Celestials adopted was this: They were in the habit of buying up, and even importing, inferior dollars, paying as a rule $94 first class for $100 inferior. The latter they paid away, as opportunity offered, to the public. Thus the inferior dollars were always kept in circulation. But the crafty fellows would receive none but the best themselves and consequently were always supplied with the means of purchasing the inferior ones. This was a ready way of coining money, for six per cent stuck to their fingers whenever they touched a dollar . . . Until at last a public meeting was held . . . it was one of the most numerously attended meetings ever assembled in Yokohama. All the bank managers, most of the merchants and shopkeepers, and many of the foreign citizens were present . . .

A solution, proposed by Mr Septimus Short, manager of the Chartered Mercantile Bank, and seconded by Mr W.R. Brett, manager of the Hongkong and Shanghai Bank, was unanimously adopted.[32]

This apparently is the first time in the history of the Hongkong Bank that one of its managers advised on and assisted in the formulation of policy with reference to the currency. Brett, who was otherwise to prove an unsuccessful manager, was in this instance setting a precedent for Thomas Jackson and A.M. Townsend in Japan itself, for David McLean in London, W. Adams Oram in Manila, Robert Wilson in Colombo, and many others to the present time. But to return to Yokohama in 1866: the solution, to which both the Foreign Ministers and the Japanese authorities agreed, was that the Custom House would accept in payment of duties all *bona fide*, full weight, unchopped, uncracked Mexican dollars at par – if the banks would do the same.

The report that the crisis was over within the year would seem too simple, since arguments as to the coins ought surely to have continued. What had been established was a generally accepted unit of account, thus narrowing the range of controversy and permitting the Hongkong Bank to facilitate reform by the issue of banknotes, denominated in Mexican dollars and acceptable at par. Brett indeed acted so quickly on the matter that the first notes, in the name of the Company Limited, had been designed for Hong Kong and were overstamped 'Yokohama'. Useful as these banknotes proved – they were reissued in the name of the Corporation under Thomas Jackson when Yokohama Manager in 1873 – they were not accepted as legal tender by the Government and circulation ceased with the termination of extraterritoriality in 1899.

The London question

A 'local bank' might not need an establishment in London; the Indian Presidency banks did not. However, with strong Indian representation on the Provisional Committee it was likely that the Hongkong Bank would finance the India/China trade, and once involved in providing Indian exporters with rupees, there was logic in some representation in London where tri-lateral exchange operations – London, Hong Kong/Shanghai, and Calcutta/Bombay – would be possible.

Whatever pretences the Hongkong Bank had on the eve of its promotion, by the third meeting of the Provisional Committee the decision was made for the new bank to become, *inter alia*, an exchange bank seeking an imperial charter. An exchange bank must have facilities at the 'other end', and some arrangement was necessary not only with London but also with Calcutta, Bombay, and San Francisco.

Despite the Hongkong Bank's Hanseatic connections, no agency was, however, established in Germany until the Hamburg Branch in 1889, and there is no discussion on this question recorded in the minutes. The assumption was that German trade could continue to be financed through London.

London presented a special problem, being both an essential development and a potential threat. The promoters and first directors of the Hongkong Bank were well aware of the precedents. Banks started in India and flourishing were 'lured' to London and reorganized under imperial charters or general companies acts with, no doubt, greater capital and a broader constituency but beyond the control of the founding merchants and others the bank had originally served in say Bombay or Colombo.

In 1866 and after the Hongkong Bank's promoters and then directors, if not aware before, would see the dramatic consequences of this loss of control. Eastern exchange banks failed, although not in all instances could it be proved that the distant London head office was the proximate cause. Directors in Hong Kong could, however, choose to believe so. Whatever the cause of failure, the directors would note the powerlessness of the original constituents and shareholders to become involved in the liquidation. The available funds were distributed in Britain on orders of a British court.

Hong Kong merchants wanted a local bank, and whatever else they understood by the term they meant one in which decisions were made in the East, in Hong Kong, in Shanghai, and in Yokohama. That is one positive reason for a Hong Kong headquarters. Over the Bank's history others were revealed.

Then what was the danger? What could move the Bank?

Merchants in the East retired relatively young; if they survived, they might remain interested in the Bank they had founded and encourage its move to England; shareholders, originally on the China coast, would eventually move to the United Kingdom taking, in many cases, their shares with them. The very success of the Bank might force an increase of capital beyond the capabilities of the local capital markets and so shift the balance of power to Europe. All these threats to a Hong Kong Head Office were to occur during the history of the Hongkong Bank, but their impact was delayed sufficiently for the advantages of a Hong Kong base to be clearly seen, especially after the decline in the price of silver. The Hongkong Bank at appropriate times foresaw the pitfalls and avoided them; one they could not conceive of did in fact force the Head Office to London temporarily, but that was not until 1941.

The lure was real even though avoided; it will be seen in connection with shareholder 'requisitions', with the financial importance of London in the negotiations relative to the China loans, and with the prestige of the Hongkong Bank's London Consultative Committee. The importance of London would require a skilled and forceful manager, but he might himself challenge the management in Hong Kong.

When the Provisional Committee and the first Court of Directors sat to consider the London connection, they could not have had all the factors clearly in mind, but the decisions they reached then and their successors reached subsequently were fundamental to the constitution of the Bank. What the promoters/directors wanted was a suitable presence in London – and San Francisco – without the dangers of becoming involved. This proved impractical in London from the first; their London correspondent insisted on the Hongkong Bank opening an operating agency in the City. In San Francisco the failure of the Bank's agents and the increased volume of business forced the decision to open an agency, but by that time the directors felt more self-assured.

As the directors moved from the selection of a correspondent London bank to the appointment of an agent, a London share register, the establishment of a branch, the appointment of a London Committee, the question of the denomination of the Bank's capital, in silver or in sterling, the increasingly important relationship with the Foreign Office after 1895, the question of control was never far away; the pressures mounted but were held in check.

Whatever the concern of the directors, in 1865 they had to forge a London connection and they inherited from the Provisional Committee preliminary arrangements with the London and Westminster Bank. They had also planned to recruit Walter Ormiston, formerly of the Chartered Mercantile Bank, as their London Agent, but this had fallen through. The directors instead obtained the assistance of their colleague H.B. Lemann, then on leave. He in turn secured the cooperation of R.J. Ashton of Messrs Ashton and Co., Gilman's London friends, of Thomas Dent, and, possibly, of John Dent, the future Bank Chairman. They successfully approached William Herbert Vacher, the retiring Shanghai partner of Gilman and Co. and a merchant highly regarded on the China coast.

Vacher, who took up his appointment as Special Agent of the Bank on May 29, 1865, opened an office in two small rooms on the third floor of Gresham House, 25 Old Broad Street, hired two clerks – neither of whom remained through 1866, and immediately faced a problem with the London and Westminster Bank.[33]

That this particular bank should have been approached is fully understandable, that it should have agreed to act is less so. The reputation of the Westminster was of the highest and many overseas banks attempted, unsuccessfully, to establish agency relations. In 1868, for example, the Comptoir's Shanghai manager, Hermann Wallich, sought similar accommodation and was informed by Théodore M. Dromel, the French bank's London agent, 'that a favourable response was highly unlikely as the Westminster was reluctant to be drawn on by a foreign domiciled bank'.[34] The underlying problem was the Westminster's reluctance to handle foreign acceptances, but in 1865 this would have been reinforced by the increasingly critical banking situation. Nevertheless they did agree, perhaps because one of the partners of Messrs Ashton and Co., Charles Freeman, was also a director of the Westminster.

As early as February 1865 the London and Westminster replied to the approaches made on behalf of the Provisional Committee in a letter co-signed by Freeman:

The Directors of this Bank have considered the offer you have been good enough to make to them of the London Agency of the Hong Kong and Shanghai Banking Company Limited and though they have of late declined similar proposals from Establishments in the East, yet in the present instance from the very high standing of those connected with the China Bank the subject has been favourably entertained.[35]

The description of the Hongkong Bank as being connected with those of 'very high standing' – including, of course, Gilman and Co. – must, in this context, be taken as more than a formal politeness.

The terms were, *inter alia*, that the London and Westminster would accept bills drawn by the Hongkong Bank up to a maximum of £500,000 covered by approved bank or mercantile paper at or under six months' sight (with roll-over permitted) and an uncovered position of a further £100,000 for *exceptional* purposes or circumstances, while the Hongkong Bank would keep on deposit a minimum balance of £10,000 without interest.[36]

By the end of May, 1865, however, the Hongkong Bank was seen to be operating outside the terms of the agreement, the exceptional uncovered position being used immediately and the facilities requested being in excess of those agreed. The problem in Hong Kong was apparently that a change in the exchange rate had made it unprofitable to remit funds to London. The directors, however, informed the London and Westminster that the sums called up from shareholders would provide the source of funds necessary to meet the terms of the agreement.[37]

The London and Westminster protested and, after an exchange of letters, served notice that it would terminate the agreement with the Hongkong Bank in six months.[38] This was extended for a further three months at the end of which the Hongkong Bank's account had moved from a £90,000 uncovered overdraft to a credit balance of £3,000.

The London arrangements had been made before the Bank's requirements could have been fully understood, and the directors, now that they examined the situation, were dissatisfied with the limitations of the agreement with the Westminster. Accordingly, on receiving the Westminster's decision, they authorized Vacher to seek other banking relationships, and he in turn began negotiations with the equally prestigious London and County Bank – which were successful.[39]

The London and County initially approved a £1.5 million covered accommodation with an additional £100,000 uncovered (or less than the Hongkong Bank requested) but agreed to modify a requirement for a £20,000 minimum deposit to £10,000.[40] Thus the facilities granted were on balance enlarged, as the Hongkong directors had wished, and they would be, over the years, modified as the need arose. The Hongkong Bank at this time would still have preferred that their main London activities be handled by a clearing bank as 'agents', but this the London and County refused to undertake, advising that it was in any case not in the interests of the Hongkong Bank, which should rather enter into a correspondent relationship while establishing their own operating office in London.[41]

The directors would also have preferred to remain with the London and Westminster, and while the Hongkong Bank did retain an account relationship with them, the final outcome of the negotiations was a break with that bank and the establishment of long-term relations with the London and County as confirmed in December 1865.[42] But since the London and County and the London and Westminster banks subsequently merged, it is correct for today's National Westminster Bank PLC and the Hongkong and Shanghai Banking Corporation to talk of more than 100 years of banking cooperation.

The history of the Hongkong and Shanghae Banking Company Limited ends on December 29, 1866. For all the while the Company was operating, sometimes with and sometimes without limited liability, the process of obtaining a charter was continuing, even, at times, without the knowledge of the Court of Directors. The important fact is that, whatever the corporate status of the Bank, it continued operating. There is no suggestion in the correspondence that the matter ever concerned either the London and Westminster or the London and County; the Hong Kong Government treated the Bank as if it were already chartered. The approximately 550 shareholders however showed their concern more visibly in the market, but then the market was very thin and times were difficult.

Nevertheless the Company did become the Corporation; the Bank was incorporated by a special ordinance. The processes by which this occurred and the significance of the change are subjects for the following chapter. As an introduction to the subject it will be necessary in Chapter 4 to return to a consideration of the Prospectus of July 28, 1864 (see Appendix to Chapter 2).

4

THE HONGKONG BANK'S SPECIAL ORDINANCES – TO 1873

> . . . nothing herein contained shall restrict the said Company . . .
>
> from Ordinance No. 5 of 1866*

By 1858 British banking legislation relative to the formation of joint-stock banks had relaxed the stringent provisions of 1844. That this attitude was not immediately transferred to the system of colonial chartered banks is due at least in part to the two privileges the latter were seeking through the charter: (i) the right to issue notes *which would be accepted by the Colonial treasuries* and (ii) the right, subject to successful tender, to hold government funds. The Treasury, however, was not yet prepared to permit a non-representative colonial legislature to pass general banking legislation which granted limited liability to locally incorporated banking institutions whether or not they sought the privileges referred to. Colonial bank promoters requiring limited liability had therefore the choice of incorporating under a Royal charter, conforming to Colonial Banking Regulations and thereby obtaining the related privileges, or of registering under British banking legislation with limited liability but without the privileges of note issue.

For a Hong Kong promoted bank, either of these courses would require the board of directors and the 'effective' head office to be situated in Britain.[a] The promoters of the Hongkong Bank had decided on a Hong Kong domicile; they had seen banks originated in India move back to London on being chartered; they had witnessed the loss of control of the founders and, in too many cases, the failure of the bank. The Treasury were sufficiently flexible to meet this requirement by authorizing a special Hong Kong ordinance incorporating the provisions of the Colonial Banking Regulations; they would not, however, alter their position on general colonial limited liability legislation. This latter point was not at first clear to all those involved with the incorporation of the Hongkong Bank.

* Reprinted in the Appendix, pp. 625–33.

[a] There was no legal impediment to the geographical separation of the Board and the Head Office; it was simply unlikely that real authority would remain in the area of operation. For example, the Imperial Bank of Persia's Board were situated in London and its head office in Tehran; similarly the Deutsch-Asiatische Bank's Board sat in Berlin and its head office was in Shanghai. Policy, however, was made in and orders sent out from London and Berlin and the associated London and Berlin office respectively, by whatever name, was the effective *de facto* 'head office'.

Having accepted the alternative of a local ordinance as 'charter', the parties concerned − Treasury, Colonial Office, Hong Kong Government, and the Court of Directors of the Hongkong Bank − were uncertain as to exactly what had been created, how, that is, the powers of the new corporation could be exercised consistent with the principles of the several relevant legal concepts. This uncertainty was further complicated by the tendency of official minute-writers to be unfamiliar with the background, or to neglect consideration of some key provision, or simply to ignore files which were unindexed and thus difficult to locate.

The Hongkong Bank was affected by these uncertainties, but not to any significant extent. The directors might be worried, even annoyed; the legal discussions would not seem, however, to have had long-run operational impact. It was almost as if the clause, 'nothing herein contained shall restrict the said Company', actually related not to a specific provision quoted out of context but to the entire ordinance. This is, however, an exaggeration. At least by 1880 the Treasury sought to be relieved of the responsibilities inherent in the provisions of a Royal charter or, by extension, a special ordinance; this was not to prove a simple matter. While the Bank's banknote issue continued, the Government could not ignore the Hongkong Bank. While several of the discussions initiated in the early days of the Hongkong Bank's corporate existence were settled by 1890, others continued at least to the Great War.

This chapter considers the initial provisions and first settlement of problems as they arose from the Provisional Committee's original decisions and from the consequence of the disallowance of the banking provision of Hong Kong's first general companies ordinance of 1865.

Following the pattern set by the Bank's early directors, who first commenced business and then settled the matter of incorporation, this chapter outlines therefore the complex question of the Bank's charter, the issues involved and their resolution. The story is continued through the abortive attempts to solve the problem of the extraterritorial status of a bank incorporated by a colonial legislature, thus placing the issue in perspective and taking the story up to the eve of the final solution, the Bank's revised Ordinance (No. 29 of 1889), when the Bank's operations may be said to have been put on an agreed and sound legal footing.

In detailing these events, the question of the issue of banknotes will be touched on, but full consideration of this subject is reserved for Chapter 11.

The last colonial charter

The original Prospectus of the Hongkong and Shanghae Banking Company (Limited) published on July 28, 1864, makes no specific reference to the method of incorporation, that is, how the Bank intended to obtain limited liability.[1] However, A.F. Heard writing the previous day to Charles Fearon in London stated that the Provisional Committee, which had neither been formed officially nor had it met, intended to apply for a colonial charter.[2] The question would appear to have been resolved at the August 14 meeting (the second) of the Provisional Committee. But the context in both cases is not clear. Heard would seem to have been referring to a charter for a 'Presidency' type bank, as might be inferred from the Prospectus itself. The Committee's minute merely instructed their Counsel, E.H. Pollard, who would himself be one of the Bank's major shareholders, to take the necessary preliminary steps to apply for an ordinance.

In the Provisional Committee minutes the matter is never alluded to again.

At this time in Hong Kong there were branches of British and Indian banks operating under the terms of Royal charters, various United Kingdom joint-stock company acts between 1844 and 1858, the Companies Act of 1862, and the Indian Act VII of 1860. (See Table 3.3.) The proposed Bank of China intended to (i) obtain a Royal charter and (ii) register under the Companies Act of 1862 while waiting for the former to be granted. The Hongkong Bank would in effect parallel the plan of the Bank of China, first incorporating under the Hong Kong Companies Ordinance (No. 1 of 1865) and then by a special ordinance (No. 5 of 1866), with complications discussed in earlier chapters.[3]

The existence of banks with varying legal origins does not imply that the promoters of the Hongkong Bank were or could be aware of the subtleties of these differences. Nor indeed would it necessarily be possible to discover how best to proceed. Fortunately for the Bank, the chairman of the Provisional Committee, presumably on the advice of the well-qualified Pollard, did make a formal application for a colonial charter to the Colonial Secretary on December 23, 1864, and from then on the Committee and Court were virtually passive; developments were subject to administrative and legislative processes.[4]

The Hongkong and Shanghai Banking Corporation was the last colonial chartered bank (excluding provincially chartered banks in Australia and Canada). As such it represents the climax of a system developed primarily from 1833 to control the development of banking in the colonies, a system rendered to a great extent superfluous by general banking legislation in the United Kingdom and India and considered with increasing disfavour by the Treasury as the implications of government's responsibilities for a chartered bank became clearer.[5] As for so-called 'foreign chartered banks', that is, banks designed to operate in foreign countries but which, for some reason, had a claim to United Kingdom incorporation, these continued to be chartered on an *ad hoc* basis. The last was the Imperial Bank of Persia in 1889; it is now (1986) the British Bank of the Middle East and a member of the Hongkong Bank Group.

The schedule

Hong Kong was a small community. With the then current interest in joint-stock company promotion, it is inconceivable that the several issues were not matters of discussion following the dramatic publication of the Prospectus in July. The newly appointed Hong Kong Manager, Victor Kresser, had personal access to the Governor, Sir Hercules Robinson. And David McLean, who certainly planned to come down to Hong Kong from Shanghai to visit the promoters of the new bank and other bank managers, with Sutherland, Chomley, Pollard, A.F. Heard, and (Sir) Julian Pauncefote as business and legal experts, and W.T. Mercer, the experienced Colonial Secretary and former Treasurer, would all contribute to pooled information.

In consequence when the Hon. Francis Chomley, the chairman of the Provisional Committee, all the Bank's nominal capital having been subscribed for, finally applied for a charter on December 23, 1864, he was able to show some knowledge of the requirements. Nor would the Government appear to have been taken by surprise, for the application together with the Governor's comments was forwarded to the Colonial Office on December 29.[6] Major despatches were not undertaken so rapidly without there having been considerable prior discussion.

No banking charter could be recommended without the approval of the Treasury. Accordingly, on March 1, 1865, the Colonial Office forwarded the correspondence to the Treasury noting that the 'profits of issue' were involved.[b] The British Government was now aware that the promoters of the Hongkong Bank sought a charter; they were soon to learn that the Bank was actually operating, information which, far from being considered *ultra vires* or unsound, was regarded as evidence of the bona fide nature of the proposals. At this point two levels of correspondence were maintained, the one dealing with the progress towards incorporation, the other with the interim problems, the acceptance of the Bank's banknotes for example, in the full expectation that, eventually, a charter or special ordinance would be granted.

Given the Provisional Committee's decision for the Hong Kong headquarters, a Royal charter was inappropriate. The provisions of a Royal charter could, however, be incorporated either in a general Hong Kong *banking* ordinance, under which the Hongkong Bank could then register, or in a special ordinance for the Hongkong Bank alone. The former was never in fact considered. The Hong Kong public were strongly in favour of a local bank, but there was no demand for a general ordinance which might lead to the speculation which James Whittall of

---

[b] The profits of issue are those which arise from the right to issue demand liabilities in the form of banknotes while holding only a required one-third reserve in specie. Banknotes represent a free source of funds to the Bank; two-thirds of these funds could be used to purchase earning assets.[7]

Jardine's so feared. Indeed, Bombay's rival Bank of China would have been able to register under such a general banking ordinance!

The actual provisions found in the Royal banking charters varied to meet the evolving requirements established by the Colonial Banking Regulations, a version of which was available in the Hong Kong Government.[8] The Hongkong Bank's proposed special ordinance had, then, to incorporate the current regulations as adjusted for the particular situation in Hong Kong. After informal correspondence between the Colonial Office and the experienced George Arbuthnot in the Treasury, the latter decided to send the relatively new charter of the Asiatic Banking Corporation as a model, stating that its provisions 'would of course be unobjectionable'.[9] It had already served as a model for the proposed Bank of China charter.

With this response the Hong Kong Government had the necessary basis for proceeding. The Colonial Office requested that Hong Kong send a draft of the proposed ordinance Home for comment; this instruction the Government overlooked and in consequence the Bank had to face the need for amendment later.[10] The special ordinance was drafted under instructions of the Court of Directors of the Hongkong Bank by Pollard who coordinated the Committee's progress with the requirements of the Government, working with the gifted Attorney General, Julian Pauncefote – later to be Britain's highly respected minister and then first ambassador to the United States.[11] The draft was submitted to the Governor in March. The ordinance as first introduced in April was objected to by Whittall of Jardine's and was amended to meet various objections of the Government; final passage was on August 14, 1866.[12]

Thus the actual process from the application to incorporation required nearly twenty months. Completing the procedures would take a further twelve months.

The events up to the actual drafting of the special ordinance apparently affected the formal meetings of the Committee and Court but little. There was discussion of relevant problems: facilities to directors, the issue of banknotes, the transfer of shares, etc., but these were matters which had in any case to be covered and, as they were for the most part found satisfactory by the Treasury, they had presumably been made after consideration of the Colonial Banking Regulations.

In August 1865 the Court learned that, in response to their December application, the requirement of double liability would not be waived. They would be required to draft a 'model charter' and revise their current Deed of Settlement. In November 1865 Pollard presented his drafts to the Court for discussion but decision was postponed, and on December 8 the Court made the potentially dangerous decision to 'perfect Registration under the Colonial ordinances' while leaving the charter application in abeyance.

The Court's decision was fortunately couched in such terms that Pollard did not actually withdraw the application. The Hong Kong Government meanwhile kept the Court informed of developments as if a charter were still being sought. Thus when on February 6, 1866, the Court was informed that the Bank could not in fact register under a general companies ordinance, no time had been lost. The news obviously did cause some concern and the Court resolved to send a deputation consisting of Sutherland, Maclean, and Nissen to wait on the Governor to (i) ascertain the conditions of a special ordinance and (ii) urge that nothing less favourable than the provisions incorporated in the charters of the Asiatic and other chartered banks be insisted upon.[13]

Thenceforth, the Court would take an active interest in the proceedings which would affect, *inter alia*, decisions on the capital structure of the Corporation.

The lack of concern which the minutes would appear to reflect, at least from mid-1865 to February 1866, requires a review of the Bank's apparent alternative line of action. This in turn provides an introduction to the substantive issues involved.

Even as the Provisional Committee were holding their first meetings in September 1864, proposals were being put forward for a Hong Kong general companies ordinance which would permit registration of joint-stock companies and grant them the privilege of limited liability. These proposals were formulated into a draft ordinance which, much to the consternation of its supporters, including the Hong Kong General Chamber of Commerce, was defeated in February 1865.

The Provisional Committee were apparently not influenced by these proceedings. The main delay in their application for a charter was the need to allot the 20,000 shares to intending subscribers, a task which had to be completed before a charter could be applied for, and which was prolonged by failure of some applicants to subscribe when shares were allotted to them. This was, in part, the origin of the rumours that the members of the Provisional Committee had allotted themselves shares; they subscribed as promoters (not as directors) to shares not subscribed to by the deadline or which they had held back for allocation under special circumstances.[14]

Throughout the days of the Provisional Committee and certainly as late as March 1865 Francis Chomley and Thomas Sutherland declared publicly in favour of a 'charter' in the form of a special ordinance of incorporation.

With Francis Chomley and now Thomas Sutherland on the Legislative Council, the Governor introduced an amended general companies ordinance, No. 1 of 1865, which was actually passed on March 4, 1865, the day after the Hongkong Bank opened for business.[15] The ordinance covered all joint-stock companies, including banks, and the Hongkong Bank, as already described, took steps to register, steps which were not completed until August and seemed in question as late as December 1865.

The Bank's decision relative to the Companies Ordinance was not necessarily a comment on its plans relative to the charter; the former could be a temporary measure to give limited liability while waiting for the special ordinance. Sutherland stated his view that the latter conferred superior benefits.

The general Companies Ordinance, although not inconsistent in purpose with the general Companies Act in the United Kingdom, which also covered banks, including those with London head offices operating in the colonies, was at variance in this respect with the provisions of the Colonial Banking Regulations.

The ordinance as a whole was formally protested by Whittall on the grounds that it encouraged speculation. The Governor refused to withdraw a measure so fully supported both by United Kingdom and colonial precedent and by the mercantile community. The ordinance was accordingly passed and sent to London with Whittall's objections. These were considered worth examining by David Jardine, MP, who sought the support of John Abel-Smith, MP, the banker, and John Pender, MP, who had interests in the Oriental Bank. In fairness Jardine did inform Smith that he was unable himself to form an opinion; he simply did not want the matter to go by default.[16] In consequence of this intervention, the objections were taken seriously in London and reviewed by the Colonial Office, the Treasury, and the Board of Trade.

The Treasury immediately noted a difficulty, and the Governor was advised that, while the ordinance was approved in principle, the clause permitting the registration of banking companies had to be excluded.[17] The ordinance was repassed in March 1866 as No. 2 of 1866 but in a form excluding banks, thus forcing the 'de-registration' of the Hongkong Bank and providing it with the necessity of incorporation by special ordinance. That the Court may have entertained last minute hopes that banks might yet be permitted to continue their registration under the general Companies Act is evidenced by Sutherland's lone opposition to the amended ordinance. But the Court was preparing for the inevitable and its considerably enhanced interest in a charter dates from February 1866.

The principal issues

The concern of the Treasury was a vestige of London's 'tutelege' on matters related to the monetary and banking system of the Empire and of the attempt to regulate and control on a central basis. With the coming of responsible local legislatures in the colonies, this approach had to be modified at the practical level to one of advice. But London was left with two responsibilities, the banks previously chartered and the colonies which, like Hong Kong, still had appointed legislative councils.

In 1880 the whole chartered banking system was reviewed. The Treasury had come to realize that, on the one hand, it was virtually impossible to maintain the kind of control of the chartered banks which might reasonably be expected by the public on the basis of certain specific charter clauses (see below), or that, on the other, it was difficult to refuse to renew or amend charters once granted for fear of damaging the prestige and therefore the business of the particular bank – or so the chartered banks chose to argue. Chartered banks might fall by the wayside, might amalgamate with larger banks organized under general legislation, or might be forced to reorganize in consequence of developments within the corporation, as in the case of the Chartered Mercantile in 1892. In this way the system, as a system, eventually disappeared, leaving individual survivors, each no doubt of considerable importance, but safely handled on a case by case basis within the new regulatory systems.

In 1864–1867 the Treasury, however, was still very much involved with its responsibility to respond on the basis of the Colonial Banking Regulations. The Treasury had in 1864 recommended disallowance of a general companies ordinance in British Guiana for including banks, and their reaction to the Hong Kong ordinance had been automatic.[18]

The Regulations required the inclusion of specified provisions in the Deed of Settlement, including details which the British Act of 1862 left entirely to the consideration of promoters and prospective shareholders. The trend of legislation was to remove government from the discussion and therefore from the responsibility. That this was not seen as appropriate for the non-self-governing colonies would seem to be due in large part to the special relationship which might develop between the managers and directors of chartered banks and the local governments. The need for caution, and hence for double liability, was seen as consequent on the colonial government's placing funds in and accepting the banknotes of the chartered bank. This latter privilege was important: the Bank had the assurance that its banknotes would be received at government treasuries; without this, the note issue, it was generally agreed, would not be accepted by the public.

When, for example, the Hong Kong Government sought Colonial Office advice on the acceptance of the Hongkong Bank's banknotes at the Colonial Treasury, the affirmative reply assumed that the Bank was to be incorporated eventually by special ordinance under the Colonial Banking Regulations and not under the provisions of a general companies act.[19]

These points alone justify Thomas Sutherland, then the Deputy Chairman of the Bank, in declaring to the shareholders at the Extraordinary Meeting of March 27, 1865, that a charter, 'which was hoped would be obtained in a short time would in many respects secure more advantages to the company than mere registration under the Limited Liability Ordinance'.[20]

There had been other advantages to incorporation by Royal charter, and it would be useful to consider these in the context of the Hongkong Bank's requirements.

First, the charter had been the only method by which a bank designed to operate in the colonies might incorporate with limited liability. Second, the charter was issued by Imperial authority and it could be, and usually was, made valid for operation in several colonies, although always within a specific region.[c] In this latter restriction the regulators were probably well-advised, since both directors and managers were insufficiently experienced and communications relatively undeveloped.

When, however, local legislatures took over control of banking or colonial governments began issuing their own currency notes, the charters, hedged in with rights reserved to the Crown, offered no more than any general companies act. A bank's right to operate in a particular territory had become subject to compliance with the applicable local laws as a 'foreign corporation', whether it had been incorporated by Royal charter or under a general act.

For the Hongkong Bank, however, even these additional if emasculated benefits were not applicable. The Hong Kong legislature as it turned out was not competent to authorize the Hongkong Bank to operate outside the Colony, although it could not, by the same reasoning, effectively forbid such operations.[21]

The Court of Directors, true to Scottish banking principles, sought the right to have the Bank's banknotes accepted. They also required a Hong Kong base. Hence, they had no alternative but to seek a special ordinance of incorporation containing the relevant features of a Royal charter, specifically those of the Asiatic Banking Corporation (which failed in November 1866), consistent with the Colonial Banking Regulations.

Limited liability and the capital structure

The members of the Provisional Committee were sufficiently aware of the provisions of bank charters to request, in their initial letter to the Governor, exemption from two provisions, (i) the requirement of double liability and (ii) the time limit within which subscribed capital had to be fully paid up. The former was denied. The Treasury 'saw no ground for relieving the shareholders from the liability imposed on the shareholders of all the banks in the Colonies incorporated by Royal charter . . .'; the latter, being a matter for a more pragmatic approach, was subject to successful negotiation.[22]

The apparent change in emphasis of the Court of Directors between mid-1865 and February 1866, although no doubt partly a response to the fact that the Bank had apparently secured limited liability under the Companies Ordinance, was undoubtedly due to the requirement that shareholders agree to a double liability.

Briefly, the regulations required that the applicant bank's capital be fully

---

[c] Shareholders and, more to the point, banknote holders could not be expected to judge a bank whose activities were too widespread, a consideration presumably off-setting any advantage to be obtained from diversity of risk.

subscribed and one-half paid up before commencement of business – that this had been done in the case of the Hongkong Bank was the subject of the Governor's Proclamation of December 15, 1866. The balance of the capital had to be paid up within two years from the commencement of business, but, as just noted, could under reasonable circumstances be postponed.[23]

Double liability and the note issue

Shareholders were, however, liable on the winding up of the company to the extent of their subscribed capital and an equal additional amount. That is, assuming the nominal value of a share were, as in the case of the Hongkong and Shanghae Banking Company (Limited), $250 of which $125 were paid up, the shareholder would be liable for an additional $125, being the unpaid balance of his subscribed capital, plus $250, or $500 total.

This requirement was standard, although it had been waived by the Treasury in the case of the Colonial Bank, chartered in 1836, on the grounds of its size – its subscribed capital was £2 million compared to the Hongkong Bank's approximately £1.1 million equivalent.[24] The basic reasoning behind this requirement was stated in a minute by the Treasury's James Wilson in 1857. He observed the 'leverage' involved in banks' acquiring assets in excess of their capital, thus differing from other joint-stock companies and creating additional risks.

Banks differ from other joint-stock companies in as much as they are not only Trustees for money deposited with them, but are also dealers in money deposited, and the money with which they deal is to a great extent the property of others. In the case of ordinary trade the risk incurred is generally proportioned to the capital invested, but in the case of Banks unless the amount of debts to be contracted by them is restricted, the amount of their liabilities arising from the use of deposits may greatly exceed the amount of the subscribed capital and in the event of fraudulent and improvident management that capital alone would afford inadequate security to depositors and other creditors.[25]

Colonial banking charters consequently had contained provisions limiting 'debts' to 'deposits plus three times the paid-up capital', which means in effect that earning assets must not exceed cash and bullion (and other liquid assets) plus three times the paid-up capital.[26] But this limitation was dropped at least by 1864. Security was to depend on double liability.

Another common reason stated for double liability, however, was protection of the bank's banknote holders, although they were not given priority as creditors on the winding up of the bank.

Experience suggested they were still inadequately protected. Indeed on the failure of the Oriental in 1884, the Government of Ceylon had to guarantee that bank's note issue to prevent public unrest, and in Singapore the other note-issuing banks took responsibility for the local issue. As another reason for double liability, the Treasury had noted in the 1851 charter of the Oriental Bank Corporation a clause requiring the winding up of the bank when one-third of its capital was lost. The Treasury observed that without double liability this would in effect be a guarantee that creditors would receive only £0.67 for £1 as a maximum.[27]

It can be argued that double liability could be achieved by leaving half the subscribed capital unpaid as a 'reserved liability' (to use the 1879 term), but it was within the power of the shareholders to authorize or the directors to determine to call up all or part of the unpaid balance. This problem could be countered by a stipulation, frequently employed after the failure of the City of Glasgow Bank, which would prohibit the use of the additional shareholder liability provision except on the wind-up of the company. This was the effect of the provision for double liability in the Hongkong Bank ordinance.

The Treasury in any case preferred banks to operate on a fully paid-up basis. By requiring chartered banks to prove their capital was fully subscribed before commencing business and to trade on the basis of their subscribed capital, which was to be fully paid-up within a brief specified period, the Treasury hoped to relate the level of activity to the capital resources actually available and so prevent over-trading by a bank's directors based on the assumption that the balance of the capital could be paid up in an emergency – an assumption often proved dangerously unrealistic. The policy of operating with fully paid subscribed capital would prevent the necessity of making calls on the shareholders for further capital at just that time when financial difficulties made it all too likely the calls would go unpaid. The double liability provision was seen as being a measure available only to meet the ultimate emergency; in the absence of a central bank the shareholders were to be their own 'last resort'.

In either case the presence of an additional or reserve liability was, in the early days of limited liability, considered necessary by creditors of such incorporated companies. There was the problem of whether subscribers would meet the additional calls, and for this reason the public was normally provided access to the list of shareholders. The Hongkong Bank's ordinance, in common with the Royal charters, made no provision for this, probably, since the Colonial Banking Regulations predate general liability legislation, through oversight.

The failure of the Regulations to provide adequate protection to the holders of a bank's banknotes did not escape the observation of either James Whittall or the Governor, and the Hongkong Bank was faced either with giving a priority to banknote holders, a measure which the Court of Directors considered would have affected their general credit, or accepting unlimited liability for the note issue, as in the British Act of 1862.[28] The Court of Directors accepted the latter. The shareholders of the Hongkong Bank were thus subject both to double liability overall and unlimited liability on a rateable basis on the Bank's note issue.

In January 1865 the Provisional Committee had resolved that the liability of shareholders would not be more than double the amount of subscribed capital, except on the resolution of an extraordinary meeting, and this presumably became part of the original Deed of Settlement. The decision was overriden, in effect, by Ordinance No. 5 (see Appendix), to which the shareholders acquiesced by signing a new Deed of Settlement. They had little choice; with the redesign of the Companies (or 'Limited Liability') Ordinance in 1866, the Hongkong Bank could be reincorporated only under the terms of its special ordinance.

Capital structure and limited liability

The immediate success of the Bank suggested the need to obtain access to additional accommodation in London. This would be facilitated by increasing the Bank's paid-up capital, and in December 1865 both Vacher, the Bank's Special Agent in London, and McLean, the Bank's Manager in Shanghai, urged the Court to take action.

In January 1866 the Court of Directors of the Company Limited, apparently secure under the terms of the 1865 Companies Ordinance, resolved to call an extraordinary meeting of shareholders to approve an increase in the capital of the Company by the issue of 10,000 new shares of $250, $37.00 paid up plus a premium of 5% on the par value of the share, that is $12.50 per share making a total of $49.50 per share. Had this been carried through the subscribed capital of the Company would have been $7.5 million, of which paid-up capital after the first payment referred to would have been $2.875 million with the premium of $125,000 allocated to the Reserve Fund. Uncalled but subscribed capital would have been $2.5 million of the original share issue and $2.125 million of the new share issue, that is, $4.625 million.

The hypothetical figures in Table 4.1 imply that the Board's ultimate intention was for further calls to be made until all subscribed capital was 50% paid up.

Before the extraordinary meeting could be held, however, the Court had recognized that the ordinance under which they were incorporated would be disallowed and the Hongkong Bank would have to be reincorporated under the Colonial Banking Regulations which would require a double liability. The Court accordingly revised its capital plans in time for consideration by the shareholders on March 3. At the same meeting the shareholders were also able to approve a revised Deed of Settlement – although this would need to be further amended the following year.[29] The changed capital plan reflected the Court's recognition of the impact of the double liability requirement.

The existing capital of $5 million was at that time comprised of 20,000 shares of $250, of which one-half or $125 was paid up. The liability of the shareholder was $250 per share.

The Court resolved that the capital should instead be 40,000 shares of a nominal value of $125, and that the present shares would be redesignated accordingly; as a consequence they would automatically become fully paid up.

This would leave the liability of the then shareholders unchanged at $250, twice the nominal value of the share. To this would subsequently be added the additional rateable liability for the note issue.

Under conditions of normal single liability the shareholder's liability of $250 per share was explained by the nominal value of the shareholder's subscribed capital; now that the shares were to be declared fully paid up at $125, the $250 shareholder liability per share would be explained by the provision of double liability required by the Colonial Regulations to be incorporated into the Bank's special ordinance.

The Bank's *new* capital was now to be obtained by the issue at par of 20,000 newly created shares, also of $125 nominal value, on which an initial $25 would be called up July 1. Holders of these shares would be liable in the event of winding up for the balance of their subscription plus $125, that is for a total $250 per share. When the new shares were eventually fully paid up, there would be no difference between them and the original shares. The Court agreed that this new issue should be a rights issue.

The subscribed capital would remain at $5 million.

The Court noted that, under the circumstances, this was better than the original plan of increasing subscribed capital.

The two schemes can be summarized – the former, which was never implemented, is in parenthesis (see also Table 4.1):

Subscribed capital $5 million ($7.5 million) in 40,000 shares (30,000) of $125 nominal value ($250), of which 20,000 shares are declared fully paid up and 20,000 with $25 paid up (of which 20,000 shares are unchanged and $37 + $12.50 are paid up on the 10,000 new shares), **resulting in a total paid-up capital initially of $3 million, eventually of $5 million ($2.875 million plus reserve fund of $125,000 = $3.0 million).**

Both methods achieve the same total increase in shareholders' funds, but the method agreed in March and subsequently implemented assumed that all payments for new shares were for capital account; there was no provision for a premium, and consequently the subscribers to the new shares participated in rather than contributed to the Reserve Fund, a matter of some slight importance when, as will be explained below, the allocation plans were changed – the new issue would no longer be a rights issue.

Allocation of the increased capital
Although the records are not quite clear, that there should be a change in allocation plans is explicable. Poor business conditions did not make a rights issue an unqualified advantage. The Court could take advantage of this situation by allocating new shares directly to new constituents, including some resident in

Table 4.1 The Hongkong and Shanghae Banking Company, Limited
The Hongkong and Shanghai Banking Corporation Initial capital, 1865–1872

I. The Hongkong and Shanghae Banking Co., Ltd

| | Shares | | par value | Capital (millions of dollars) | | | Shareholders' reserve liability, etc.[a] | |
	issued	new	$	subscribed	paid-up	surplus	per share $	total millions of $
A INITIAL POSITION								
1865 March	20,000		250.00	5.000	2.5	—	125	2.5
B THE ABORTIVE PLAN								
1866 January decision		+10,000	250.00	+2.500	0.375	+0.125		
intended eventual result	30,000		250.00	7.500	3.75	0.125	125	3.75
C ACTUAL PLAN								
1866 March decision (i)			125.00					
result	20,000		125.00	2.500	2.5			unlimited[b]
decision (ii)		+20,000	125.00					
					Paid-up capital old + new = total			
results 1866 July 1	33,000		125.00	4.125	2.5 + 0.039 = 2.539			unlimited[b]

II. The Hongkong and Shanghai Banking Corporation

| | Shares | | par value | Capital (millions of dollars) | | Shareholders' reserve liability, etc.[a] per share | | |
	issued	new	$	subscribed	paid-up	old	new	total millions of $
1866 Dec.	40,000		125.00	5.000	2.5 + 0.385 = 2.835	125	230.75	7.115
1867 June	40,000		125.00	5.000	2.5 + 0.500 = 3.000	125	225.00	7.0
1869 Dec.	40,000		125.00	5.000	2.5 + 1.000 = 3.500	125	200.00	6.5
1870 Dec.	40,000		125.00	5.000	2.5 + 1.500 = 4.000	125	175.00	6.0
1871 Dec.	40,000		125.00	5.000	2.5 + 2.000 = 4.500	125	150.00	5.5
1872 Dec.	40,000		125.00	5.000	2.5 + 2.500 = 5.000	125	125.00	5.0

Notes:

[a] Uncalled capital plus shareholders' reserve liability to which must be added the value of the note issue.

[b] Double liability provision of the ordinance was not yet effective; the company was operating without the protection of either the

London and, for the first time as a separate group, to its own directors and officers. Thus the final allocation of which there are details and on the basis of which the actual allotments were made was probably – to present shareholders 10,000, to directors and Company Officers 1,000, to applicants in London 1,000, in Bombay 2,000, in Calcutta 2,000, in Shanghai 2,000. There remained 2,000 for later allocating as required.[30]

The authorized capital of the Hongkong Bank was put at $7.5 million, that is, the subscribed or 'original' capital of $5 million could be increased by $2.5 million on the decision of the directors – with the consent of the Governor but without the need for shareholder approval or a revised ordinance. A further provision in the ordinance permitted an increase of capital to $10 million subject to the consent first of the Governor and then by a general meeting of shareholders. Any increase of capital beyond this would require an amendment to the ordinance.

By August 1866 the Court was faced, on one hand, with the need under the terms of the ordinance to once again declare all shares fully subscribed and, on the other, with the knowledge that 7,000 shares were in fact not subscribed for and, given the economic conditions, were unlikely to be. The directors themselves were not all in a position to subscribe, which suggests that this may have been the point when the allocation plan was changed. The broader-based appeal and the improved economic conditions caused the number of unsubscribed shares to decline to 822 by December. The Court of Directors was able to handle this much diminished number by assigning a sufficient sum from the remuneration due them as directors from January 1, 1865, including the amount to become due for the six months to the end of 1866, to cover the cost of the first call of $25. As the apportionment of directors' remuneration was to be undertaken by a formula which included payment for each meeting attended, the actual allocation was not undertaken until early 1867. Consequently, the 822 shares were subscribed for by John Dent, the Bank's Chairman, as trustee for the directors.

The decision relative to the unsubscribed shares was minuted on December 29, and it is therefore not clear how the Court could have certified to the Governor that the capital had in fact been subscribed in time for the Proclamation on December 15. Preliminary decisions were made earlier, and it is possible that these were considered binding. As there is no record of a meeting of the Court between September 25 and December 29, a most unlikely situation, the only conclusion is that some part of the story is missing. In any case, the Company became the Corporation under these circumstances at the December 29 meeting.

The special ordinance – other provisions

The Hongkong and Shanghai Bank Ordinance (No. 5 of 1866) was modelled after the charter of the Asiatic Banking Corporation, but with exceptions appropriate for Hong Kong. Neither the Treasury nor the Colonial Office spelt out these exceptions and indeed refrained from sending a draft ordinance. A copy of the Asiatic's charter was, however, sent in response to the Governor's plea for guidance. The matter was left to the Hong Kong Government and the Bank, with the expectation, not in fact fulfilled, that their draft would be sent back to London for comment before enactment.[31]

There are several references in the Court minutes to discussions on drafts of the ordinance at various stages, but, unfortunately, with no details. The final result, however, was a fair copy of the Asiatic's charter with the necessary adjustments, including the controversial provisions for the Bank's overseas operations and particular detail to cover the winding up of the Corporation, a necessary addition due to deficiencies in the existing Hong Kong legislation. The provision for unlimited liability for the note issue, not found in the Asiatic's charter, was also added.

The business of the Bank

The Bank was incorporated to undertake the business of banking for 21 years (Clause IV). Restricting the effectiveness of the charter to 21 years was usual, but, as noted, the charter would normally be extended, probably incorporating requirements consistent with the latest colonial regulations. An extension provision, similar to one first found in the Oriental Bank charter and also included in the Asiatic's, is in Clause XXIX of the ordinance.

Neither the charter of the Asiatic nor the ordinance, however, state positively what banking consists of, although earlier charters do make the attempt. The more recent charters played a prudential role; they outlined what banks must *not* do in the interests of sound banking, for example, advance on the security of their own shares (Clauses XIV–XXII).

The Deed of Settlement in fact permits the Hongkong Bank not only to undertake banking but also 'all other business usually transacted by Bankers . . .' (Article 12).

Although most of the clauses relate to specific categories of transactions, Clause XIV is more general in its impact:

[The total amount of debts and liabilities] shall not at any time exceed the aggregate amount of the then existing *bona fide* assets and property of the Company and the sums for which its shareholders are liable under the provisions herein contained [double liability plus unlimited liability for the note issue].

This may be contrasted with a provision in previous charters (and actually in the draft of the Asiatic, but replaced as above), which states that:

[The total amount of debts and liabilities] over and above the amount of deposits for remittance and monies due on Banking Accounts with the Company's Establishments shall not at any time exceed three times the amount of the Capital of the said Company which for the time being shall have been actually paid up.[32]

The latter would seem an attempt to control activity, specifically the acquisition of earning assets, by relating total liabilities to paid-up capital. This is consistent with strictures to trade at a level related to paid-up capital. But it does not take account of the consequences of a decline in the value of assets. The former provision, the clause actually in the charters of the Asiatic and Hongkong banks, would protect shareholders by requiring assets to be written down to actual worth and for this to be reflected either by a corresponding contraction of liabilities or else by changes in shareholders' funds.

Area of operation

The Treasury had informed the Governor that there would be no objection to the incorporation of a bank to operate in China and Japan. The special ordinance (Clause IV) words this in the negative. The legislature had no extraterritorial jurisdiction and could not therefore give positive permission for the Bank to operate outside Hong Kong, but by (i) stating that nothing in the ordinance should be construed as preventing the Bank from operating outside the Colony and (ii) listing the places the Bank might operate with permission, the ordinance suggests the area of operation. 'If we could tell you where you could operate it would be these places . . .' In consequence of this approach the Bank was apparently left free to operate anywhere without restriction except, paradoxically, in the area actually intended by the Government, that is, where Treasury permission was required. The key phrase is 'nothing herein contained shall restrict the said Company . . .'

The Asiatic's charter refers to 'Eastward of the Cape of Good Hope' and specifically mentions Australia and New Zealand; the Hong Kong ordinance is more specific relative to China and Japan and omits reference to Australasia, presumably with no disagreement from the Court of Directors of the Bank. Both charter and ordinance refer to agencies for exchange, deposit, and remittance in India; for the Hongkong Bank, this was to be amended in the Deed of Settlement.

The note issue (Clauses XII–XIII)

Although this subject is better handled separately (see Chapter 11), no discussion of the Hongkong and Shanghai Bank Ordinance would be complete without noticing the initial provisions. The note issue privileges and the ability to bid for government accounts were, after all, the main surviving advantages of a Royal charter/special ordinance.

The Hongkong and Shanghai Bank Ordinance ran parallel to Royal charters in limiting the total issue to the amount of the Bank's paid-up capital, forbidding the issue of notes of less than \$5 in value without special authorization, and requiring a reserve in specie equivalent in value to one-third of the note issue.

At this point the extraterritoriality problem again intervened. The Royal charters assume that notes might be issued in more than one territory and make arrangements for the specie reserve to be held proportionately in each principal place of issue. Provision is also found for encashment of notes at the head office at the rate of the day. The Hongkong Bank's ordinance could not, it was thought, be specific about places outside the Colony. The problem was again avoided by stating that nothing in the ordinance should prevent the Bank from issuing in other places where, by some authority or other, it in fact found itself. The Hongkong Bank was instructed to keep its reserves against note issue at the head office, presumably because the legislature did not consider itself competent to instruct otherwise. The Court of Directors had, sensibly and pragmatically, already instructed David McLean to hold a one-third reserve against his Shanghai note issue in Shanghai; it would be uneconomical to hold a one-third reserve in each of two locations.[33] McLean had in fact issued one-tael notes, which was a banknote of less than $5 in value. The consequences of all this were to be complex.

The Royal charters required a bank wishing to issue notes of less than £1 in value, or the equivalent in other currencies, to obtain permission of the Treasury; the Hongkong Bank's ordinance names the Governor as the authority. He was expected, apparently, to consult with the Treasury before granting permission; when he did not but instead acted immediately on the advice of his Executive Council, another complex situation arose.

The Reserve Fund

An early version of the Colonial Banking Regulations states that no dividends shall be paid out of 'any other Funds than the surplus profits accruing periodically from the transactions of the Bank', and the charter of the Agra and United Service Bank would take this a step further by declaring that the Reserve Fund is to be considered part of the capital of the Bank. On the other hand, a Reserve Fund could also be authorized for the purpose of 'equalizing dividends', a totally opposite concept; an example would be Art. 122 of the Deed of Settlement of the Bank of Hindustan, China and Japan, incorporated under the Acts of 1857 and 1858.[34]

This subject is not one of those surveyed in the 1880 Report of the Select Committee on Chartered Banks, and this difference of approach was to continue.

In the case of the Hongkong Bank the purposes of the Reserve Fund are specifically stated to include equalization of dividends (Arts 151–58 of the Deed of Settlement). Nor is there any limitation on the amount of current profits which may be set aside into such a separate fund, as for example is found in the Oriental Bank's charter, which stated that up to 25% of the net profits could be paid into a Reserve Surplus Fund, provided a dividend of £5 per cent had been declared. The handling of the Hongkong Bank's Reserve Fund would seem to be entirely at the discretion of the Court, and when, for example, the directors considered the

A View of Hong Kong, Victoria West, by George Chinnery (d. 1852) – from the Hongkong Bank's Collection.

Sir THOMAS SUTHERLAND, GCMG (1834–1922).

Founder of the Hongkong Bank
– a portrait by J. S. Sargent (1898); copy by Robert Swan (1964).

Sir THOMAS JACKSON, Bart, KCMG (1841–1915).
Chief Manager, Hongkong Bank, 1876–1888, 1889–1890, 1893–1902;
Chairman, London Consultative Committee, 1902–1915
– a portrait by Howard Barron.

DAVID McLEAN (1833–1908).

Manager Shanghai, 1865–1873; Manager London, 1875–1889.
'Presented to David McLean, Esq. on his retirement from the management of the
Hong Kong & Shanghai Banking Corporation as a token of sincere regard & esteem
from many friends. November 1889'
– a portrait by Sir George Reid, P.R.S.A. from the private collection of D. C. H. McLean.

Fund sufficiently large to meet possible losses etc., they were permitted to propose paying out their estimated 'surplus' in dividends.

The Reserve Fund of the Hongkong Bank was not considered, then, part of the Bank's capital for purposes of legal analysis or compliance with the provisions of the ordinance, for example, the limiting of the note issue to paid-up capital. Nevertheless, in reality, losses met by withdrawals from the Reserve Fund constitute a diminution of shareholders' funds and would affect both the credit of the Bank and the price of the shares. Nor was it practical to consider paying dividends from funds appropriated from Reserves. When at the August 1869 General Meeting it was noted that large undistributed profits had been carried forward rather than any sum being appropriated to reserves, George F. Heard, the Chairman, explained that the directors were uncertain of being able to declare a year-end dividend from projected earnings and that 'it would look bad to withdraw any money from the Reserve Fund after it had been paid in'.[35] The short-fall in current net earnings was a reality in 1872 and the directors recommended a payout of an amount equivalent to 136% of the year's net earnings (see Chapter 3 and Table 3.2), a recommendation made possible by the existence of undistributed funds in Profit and Loss Account.

Later in the 1880s another fund would be established specifically for the equalization of dividends – and so named. But this was to answer the special problems caused by what was then considered an unusually severe decline in the gold price of silver.

Government accounts

The Treasury must of necessity have been more flexible on this question, the more so since in some areas in which the diplomatic service operated, for example, there might not be a chartered bank. On the other hand, a chartered bank did not, solely because of its charter, receive deposits of government funds. Commissariat and other government business was awarded on the basis of bids, which by 1872 the Hongkong Bank would be successful in winning.

The required revisions

When the Treasury received the Hongkong and Shanghai Bank Ordinance for comment, it referred to it as a 'draft', in accordance with its previous instructions. As already explained, however, in the event and possibly using a precedent established in the case of the charter of the Commercial Bank Corporation and at the request of the Bank supported by the Governor, the ordinance was allowed to stand on condition that the Deed of Settlement was amended as directed.[36] The Deed could not then be changed without the sanction of the Governor of Hong Kong. The relevant correspondence stresses the potential impact of disallowance on the successful business operations of the Bank.

The note issue – the location of reserves
Colonial Banking Regulations required that a chartered bank make provisions to ensure the ability of the public to encash the bank's banknotes, which were not legal tender. The Hongkong Bank's specific problem arose from the fact that it issued notes not only in Hong Kong but also, at that time, in Yokohama and Shanghai. Where was the legal tender cash to be kept – and in what proportions?

That the Treasury dealt with the question at all provides further proof that the Lord Commissioners were well aware that the Hongkong Bank was already operating and would continue to operate outside the Colony of Hong Kong.

The Treasury's contribution to the solution, while logical, proved to be costly and was later further amended. The Bank was to be required to redeem its notes not only at the place of issue but also at the Head Office, where the ordinance instructed the cash reserve should be kept. In the original ordinance, redemption of notes issued elsewhere was to be at the rate of the day (Art. 12).

This revision is consistent with the provisions of the Asiatic and most other charters. A London-headquartered chartered bank with a banknote issue in Ceylon, for example, would have the principal office for that colony in Colombo. Notes issued at a branch in, say, Jaffna, would be payable both in Jaffna and Colombo – but not, in the normal course of business, at the head office in London. If one considers the Treaty Ports of China and Japan as an area comparable for purposes of this discussion to Ceylon, the parallel is obvious: a note issued in Yokohama must be payable in Yokohama and Hong Kong.

This analogy, while explaining the Treasury's decision, does not alter the fact that the Bank could not sensibly issue notes in Shanghai and Yokohama, and later in Singapore and Bangkok, without adequate cash reserves in those places; the transfer of funds from Hong Kong to these ports was more time-consuming and expensive than moving funds from Colombo to Jaffna.

In consequence the Bank was obligated by prudence if not by statute to keep cash reserves both at the branch of issue and at Head Office. At first it neglected the latter obligation (except for its Hong Kong issue); when the omission was discovered, the problem was admitted and the ordinance revised. The statutory cash reserves would be held only at the principal branch of issue; the Ceylon example cited was the model.

Prudential requirements
Certain prudential requirements relative to the borrowing powers of directors, advances on shares, and the payment of dividends from earnings were required to be tightened to accord with the Regulations. The limitation on borrowing by directors seemed to the Governor so enormous that he protested eloquently and at great length to the Treasury. He was advised, in rather abrupt language, that the limitation applied to total borrowing by all directors, not by one individual.[37]

Agencies in India

Since the granting of the Asiatic Bank's charter, the Indian Government had again protested and the Treasury had agreed that overseas banking institutions should be required to comply with Indian regulations before being permitted to establish either branches or *agencies* in India. This, as the Governor pointed out, Hong Kong could not have been expected to know, and the appropriate amendment was put in the Deed of Settlement.

When the Hongkong Bank did apply to the Treasury for permission to open in India, it was referred to the Indian Government and registered under the Indian Companies Act of 1866 on April 7, 1869. This obvious solution to the extraterritorial problem was not recognized as such, and that argument continued.

Branch and agency – a terminological digression

The charters refer to branch banks, branches, and agencies, and the distinctions are designed in part to distinguish various legal obligations relative to current accounts, bills of exchange etc. as between one office of the overall banking institution and another. But a general distinction between a branch and an agency was considered useful, especially since, in many cases, charters stated that agencies could be opened without specific permission while plans for a new branch had to be referred to the Treasury.

Conceptually a branch was seen as an operation complete in itself, competent to perform all varieties of banking operations permitted by the bank's charter and by the authorities of the territory in which the branch was located. The branch lacked total independence only in the fact that it was subject to the general direction of a corporation head office and/or the board of directors.

An agency was defined as something less than this. 'An agency does not issue notes, cash drafts or pay money over the counter' was one 1854 definition.[38] In the charters and the Bank's ordinance, as if to confirm that ambiguity existed, an agency is defined as being for 'Exchange, Deposit and Remittance'. Or, more generally, an agency existed to service a branch.

The problem of determining an exact delineation between the functions of a branch and those of an agency forced the India Office to insist that the Indian Government be given the final right to extend its powers to include not only determination of whether a bank might open a branch in India but also whether it might open an agency. This change had to be incorporated into the Hongkong Bank's revised Deed of Settlement.

A bank requiring facilities in a city or territory where no branch of the same institution existed might take one of the following steps, any one of which can be referred to, confusingly, as an agent or agency: (i) establish an office staffed by employees of the bank, that is, an agency as defined in the charter or ordinance of incorporation, (ii) appoint an individual member of the bank's staff to be the bank's agent under his own name, (iii) appoint another bank or company to undertake agreed tasks for a fee and commission, designating it the bank's 'agents' – a bank staff member might be sent to assist, but he would work as part of the agent's firm, who would remain listed as the 'agents of the bank', or (iv) simply set up a 'correspondent' relationship. This last is a standard relationship which is not considered further in this section.

Category (ii) is a legal variant of (i) used by the Hongkong Bank in San Francisco and initially in Manila and Hamburg for reasons to be considered later. The main distinction is then between (i) the Bank-staffed office or 'agency' and (iii) the Bank's 'agents', implying another business entity acting for the Hongkong Bank.

The head of a branch was referred to as 'Manager'; of a Bank-staffed agency, usually but not always, as 'Agent'.

In attempting any generalization, especially in dealing with the history of the Hongkong Bank, the existence of exceptions requires caution; for example, although the Yokohama office was established in May 1866 as an agency, the Bank officer in charge was designated 'manager' and he did issue banknotes.[d] In 1867 the Board agreed to Vacher's recommendation that he be styled London 'manager' rather than agent.

The banking functions of an agency might increase to the point that the activities were indistinguishable from those of a branch. Nevertheless, it is usually true that an agency (i) had neither the autonomy of a branch nor (ii) did it maintain its own exchange position. An agency was usually under the control of a 'parent' branch; the accounts of an agency would be incorporated with those of its branch before being forwarded to Head Office. Thus the Manila accounts would incorporate Iloilo's; if the 'parent branch' were Head Office, Head Office's Hong Kong accounts would parallel the case cited by incorporating those of its direct agencies.

Exceptions might arise due to the delay in changing status. Change on the other hand might be made for reasons of prestige, and the world of sub-agencies and mini-banks presents further problems of differentiation. As with the Foreign Service where 'ministers' virtually all became 'ambassadors', so in the 1950s the fashion for all agencies to be designated branches and 'agents' to become 'managers' or, in the United States, 'vice-presidents', was not always related to changes in their functions.

A merchant agent of the Hongkong Bank might develop services which made the operation indistinguishable from a Bank agency but for the fact that the

---

[d] Small issues of Hongkong Bank banknotes were issued from other agencies, for example, Amoy, Foochow, Hankow, Tientsin, Penang, and Bangkok (see Table 11.1).

persons dealing with the Bank's business were employees of the merchant and not of the Bank. The merchant might even maintain current account facilities; he might, if business warranted it, designate a separate entrance or counter. If business reached this stage, there would have to be some particular reason to explain the Bank's unwillingness to take over the operation with its own staff. But it did happen; Chemulpo (Inchon), Korea, in the late 1890s would be an example.

Extraterritorial problems may have affected the Court of Directors' decision as to whether to term a new office 'branch' or 'agency'. In the case of San Francisco, the directors stated that their ordinance gave them no rights, presumably on the erroneous grounds that it was not mentioned in the ordinance, and resolved therefore that their Agent would operate initially under his own name. Banking regulations in California and New York contained provisions relative to agencies and branches, to which the Hongkong Bank had to conform.

The responsibilities of Government[39]

The first word in the charter of the Asiatic Bank is 'Victoria'. The ordinary investor not versed in the working of the constitution might be excused for supposing that the imposing preamble to bank charters had a real significance. In the days when many still understood the Crown in a personal context, the fact that Britain's beloved Queen had by Her Grace granted a charter – even though the listed promoters were no longer, as in earlier bank charters, referred to as 'trusty and well-beloved' – gave rise to the suggestion that somehow the Royal prestige was involved.

Those who examined the text further could find confirmation that several of Her high advisers were apparently involved in ensuring that the company was properly managed – the Lords of the Treasury, the Colonial Secretary, the Board of Trade, the several Governors. As the Treasury well knew and so informed the Parliamentary Committee in 1880, neither they nor the other branches of government could fulfil the obligations reasonably implied from the terms of the charter, nor would Parliament expect the Government to accept responsibility if management proved inefficient or corrupt, resulting in loss to customers and shareholders. An exception has been noted in the case of the collapse of the Oriental Bank Corporation and the payment and underwriting of their banknote liabilities by the Government in Ceylon, but this is a good example of just the sort of situation the Treasury felt unable to control and wished to avoid.

The Hongkong and Shanghai Bank Ordinance does not refer to the Queen; it merely states that it is enacted by the Governor of Hong Kong with the advice of the Legislative Council thereof, but the ordinance and the Deed of Settlement contain clauses that would appear to make Government responsible for its operations – otherwise, any reasonable observer might argue, why are they there?

In a sense the whole ordinance reflects the Treasury's concept of how a bank should be organized, what prudential measures are necessary, what restrictions on its business, the roles of directors, employees and shareholders, the nature of the required information, etc. To the extent that these define relations within the corporation and between the corporation and the public, they are of a different order from the present discussion. The issue here is the visible and apparently continuing relationship of the bank with Government and the responsibility of the latter implied by particular clauses.

The sanction of the Governor of Hong Kong was required by the Hongkong Bank Ordinance for the following: (i) an increase in subscribed capital, (ii) the issue of notes of less than $5 denomination, (iii) changes in the Deed of Settlement, and (iv) the acquisition of property, where allowed at all, over a yearly value of $30,000. The Governor must be sent semi-annual statements of accounts drawn up according to his requirements, and he may require access to the accounts on which the statements are based, etc. The Governor may, with the advice of the Legislative Council, extend the term of the charter at the end of the initial 21 years. The Governor must be informed when capital is paid up and he must proclaim this through the *Government Gazette*; he is also involved in the winding up of the Bank in various ways.

These powers were properly exercised either by the Governor with the advice of his Executive Council or, perhaps in particularly controversial matters, after advice from the Colonial Office and the Treasury, thus involving the Home Authorities.

The Bank had to inform the Colonial Secretary within fourteen days of the price of any property sold over $30,000 yearly value. This it omitted by oversight to do until involved in the purchase of 9, Gracechurch Street, London, in 1912.

The sanction of the Lord Commissioners of the Treasury was to be obtained before opening branches in specified places and before opening agencies in India.[40]

Whatever the merits might be of the supervision implied, neither the local colonial Government nor the Treasury were equipped to handle it. The difficulty involved in inferring the state of a bank from its half-yearly statements was already well-known. The judgements involved in interfering with the development of a private undertaking by, for example, giving or withholding permission to open a branch, were neither consistent with the philosophy of the time nor with the level of supervisory capability – two factors not wholly unrelated.

By 1880 the Treasury had another and, in a sense, opposite reason for advocating an end to the charter system.

A Royal charter had been a particularly effective document since it was originally granted for the incorporation of banks intending to operate in one or more British colonial territories, particularly where there was as yet no banking legislation. The existence of banks whose charters incorporated the control measures then thought desirable thus obviated the need for local legislation; or, alternatively, if the local colonial legislature attempted to impose its own regulations limiting the privileges of the chartered bank, the Treasury could advise, as it did in the case of Hong Kong Companies Ordinance (No. 1 of 1865), that the relevant ordinance be disallowed.

The development of self-governing colonies changed the relationship between colonial executive and legislature, the latter resenting interference in their decisions by the imperial Treasury in London. To an extent this attitude could be noted in colonies where the legislature still had an official majority, especially on the question of the note issue.

Thus in addition to the objection that the Treasury lacked the capacity for true bank supervision, recent political realities had relegated the Treasury in many areas to one of merely advising. The Hongkong Bank would find that the role it was permitted to play in the various economies of the region depended on local legislation rather than on its Hong Kong ordinance, however the extraterritorial problem might be interpreted.

It would, however, be going too far to state that the requirements were altogether useless. The objection was that they could be misleading, but properly understood they required the directors of a bank to acknowledge their public responsibilities while the authorities would use the relevant provisions in their role as 'gatekeepers'. Thus when the Hongkong Bank requested an increase of capital or permission to open branches, it had to approach Government; at such a time the progress of the Bank could be, and usually was, reviewed, and the opportunity taken of negotiating changes in other regulations or in business methods.

Later and consequent developments

Capital

Under the terms of the ordinance the full amount of the 'original capital', $5 million, was to be paid-up within two years from December 15, 1866. At the time of the Corporation's establishment by special ordinance in 1866 the old shares of $125 were fully paid, but only $25 had been paid on each of the 20,000 new shares, leaving a balance of $2 million. With the authority of the Court, Victor Kresser, then Hong Kong Manager of the Bank and *de facto* secretary to the Court, wrote to the Governor in December 1867, stating that although the shareholders had been granted an exceptional three years to pay, he nevertheless requested a further extension.

In the present unfavourable circumstances of the China trade the Directors do not see the probability of the Bank requiring, or being able to employ profitably, more Capital than has already been paid up: viz. three millions of dollars, the depression prevailing would cause serious inconvenience and loss to the Shareholders of the Corporation in the event of fresh calls being made upon them at any early period . . .[41]

The letter received the favourable recommendation of the Governor and, not unexpectedly, was approved by the Treasury, who were concerned that were the Bank required to call up superfluous capital the directors might be tempted to make unsound investments to maintain the dividend. Accordingly a further five years was granted from December 15, 1869.[42]

The Court drew up the actual schedule at its January 26, 1869, meeting. Payments totalling $500,000 every six months were required, and the total subscribed capital of the Bank was to be fully paid up on January 1, 1873, some two years before the new deadline. Prepayments were to receive 6% interest and the Court reserved the right to amend the schedule in an emergency.

In 1882, $2.5 million, the balance of the capital of $7.5 million permitted by the special ordinance subject to the Governor's permission but without the need of extraordinary sanction of the shareholders, would be authorized by the Governor on the advice of his Executive Council. The proposed terms were announced in a circular signed by Thomas Jackson as Chief Manager on September 13.[43]

This will receive consideration in a chronological context, but it may be noted further at this point that, following sanction by the required extraordinary meeting of shareholders, a further $2.5 million, bringing subscribed capital up to $10 million, the total permitted within the terms of the original ordinance, was authorized, subscribed, and fully paid up by the end of 1891 (see Table 1.3).

The problem of extraterritoriality
Before the Bank became subject to the provisions of the Hongkong and Shanghai Bank Ordinance, it had opened a branch in Shanghai, an agency in Yokohama, and a special agency in London. Throughout the negotiations between the Hong Kong and United Kingdom authorities, no question arose as to whether the Bank would in fact operate outside Hong Kong, that is, in China and Japan. This was the basic purpose of the Bank, and the Treasury accepted the fact in positive terms. The Treasury's insistence that the Bank's banknotes be encashable at the head office as well as at the place of issue was required specifically because the Bank would be operating outside the Colony.[44] The actual ordinance had been carefully worded to permit these developments without ascribing an authority to the Colonial legislature which was considered *ultra vires*. For, as Wesley-Smith has put it, a lack of competence to permit (branches outside Hong Kong) entailed also a lack of competence to prohibit.[45]

The Court of Directors were responsible for developing the Hongkong Bank to serve the requirements of Hong Kong, China, and Japan's local trading area. This would include, in the early years, the Treaty Ports, London, San Francisco, and ports in the Netherlands East Indies, India, the Philippines, the Straits Settlements, and Cochin-China. In August 1867 the directors wrote to the Governor in terms of the ordinance for permission to open branches at Shanghai, Foochow, Yokohama, and Nagasaki and agencies in Bombay and Calcutta. The only response discovered is a letter, forwarding the ruling of the India Office, instructing the Bank to seek approval direct from India with reference to the agencies, with which instruction the Bank, as previously noted, complied.[46]

The Bank was already operating outside Hong Kong with the full knowledge and agreement of the Colonial Office and Treasury when the original charter or special ordinance was confirmed, and the Bank continued to open agencies and even branches, as required by its business.

If this is so, why did the Bank feel it necessary to 'rectify' its position?

Uncertainty must no doubt have arisen when the Bank wrote to the Governor for authority to open branches and received no satisfactory reply. Word must have reached the Court of Directors that their status was being challenged; this cannot but have created a sense of unease, for the charter, after all, was only for 21 years. The Court made three attempts to adjust the *ad hoc* situation: (i) a request for a supplemental charter in 1870, (ii) a supplemental ordinance (No. 1 of 1872) which was disallowed, and (iii) a draft ordinance in 1873 which was emasculated by the Treasury before enactment and withdrawn. The Treasury, which had approved the original ordinance as effectively amended by the Deed of Settlement, came to believe that those provisions which called for the Treasury to 'authorize' overseas branches were virtually 'waste paper'.

Extension of the Bank to Saigon and Manila under the terms of the draft ordinance of 1872 was objected to on the grounds that a colonial legislature was attempting to sanction the foundation of establishments in foreign countries. There is some justification for the objection since the claim was made by counsel that the draft ordinance was designed to 'grant facilities' to the Bank for opening in Saigon and Manila. Technically this was an unfortunate way of expressing the Bank's position.[47]

The Treasury's position, as stated in minutes relative to consideration of the 1872 and 1873 draft ordinances, was based on a confusion. The provision in the Hongkong and Shanghai Bank Ordinance that the Bank seek Treasury approval for the establishment of branches was designed to reinstate the Imperial Government's control, which Royal charters provide but which the Colonial legislation was thought unable to include or enforce itself. The Treasury approval was intended for proposed actions of the Bank; it was not supposed that such approval would or could preempt the legislative prerogatives of other jurisdictions – colonial, Indian, or foreign – within which the Bank planned to operate. To actually establish a branch after receiving Treasury approval the Bank would have to comply with local requirements, as it did in India and as it also did in Singapore. The Treasury might in fact determine the views of the appropriate local authorities before granting its own approval to the Bank, but this was purely a procedural matter which could and did vary with the circumstances.

But the Treasury at times seemed to go one step further and claim that, because the Bank was incorporated by Colonial legislation, it did not or could not *exist* outside Hong Kong, a proposition wrong in law and inconsistent with the Treasury's own advice, but sufficiently obscure as to have had no influence on the Bank's eventual development.

Indeed a Colonial Office minute of 1874 following Treasury disapproval of the draft ordinance of 1873 suggested that all this didn't really matter. The Bank had been, for example, operating in Saigon for two years and the Government in Hong Kong, even with the requisite power, would never interfere with the Bank wherever it went. On the other hand 'The Bank will never get anything out of the Treasury', the minute commented.[48] The inescapable implication is that the Colonial Office, the Hong Kong Government, and the Hongkong Bank became perforce unconcerned with the issue and its implications. Having attempted to meet the new Treasury position and failed, those involved continued practices already authorized, waiting, perhaps, for the Treasury to employ a new legal adviser.

The Bank received the cooperation of the Hong Kong Government whose legal advisers were formidable and had correctly interpreted international law. The Hongkong Bank's rights were confirmed when the Bank established a branch in Singapore without special Singapore legislation on the Treasury-stated grounds that a bank incorporated and possessing the appropriate powers under the law of one colony could establish a branch in another colony – if the laws of the latter did not forbid it.[49] When all was set aright, it was this doctrine, extended to foreign countries, which was to prevail.

The matter was finally settled by passage of Ordinance No. 29 of 1889, which was necessitated by a crisis in Manila and involved a total review of the case. This will be considered in its appropriate chronological place. Sufficient to conclude here that, although the Bank did not always present its case consistently and although the Treasury interpreted the law incorrectly, the Bank in any case established itself wherever its directors decided, and they were not rashly over-expansive. They were challenged in Manila by the local courts, but not by British Home or Colonial authorities.

The confusion in London is, however, explicable. The question of a bank incorporated in one colony operating outside that colony had been a matter of policy concern relative to both Canadian and Australian provincial banks. The general sense of the Treasury files (T.7) from the early 1830s to the mid-1860s is that the Treasury, having abandoned its control to the local legislatures, had not abandoned its own principles. If it could not control provincial banking legislation, it could prevent a provincially chartered bank from operating in another province. The test was whether the bank had been incorporated under regulations similar to the Colonial Banking Regulations; if it had, then it might operate outside the province of incorporation as a 'foreign corporation', subject to the laws of the host jurisdiction.

The issue had been one of policy as Empire-wide Treasury control became increasingly limited. On the basis of these principles the Hongkong Bank, chartered by a colonial legislature but in conformity with Colonial Banking Regulations, should not have been impeded by the Imperial authorities. Once it had complied with local registration requirements in the Philippine Islands, the Spanish Government accepted the bona fides of the Bank. The British authorities had apparently been confused by wording which was subsequently seen to present no particular problem; either that or the Treasury had misplaced their files.

The Hongkong and Shanghai Banking Corporation was, in this lengthy, leisurely, and in part contentious way, properly incorporated by special ordinance within the terms of the Colonial Banking Regulations. But all this was an aside. The Bank had been and continued functioning. As the 1866 ordinance had been, in effect, retroactive, so also was the final solution of 1889.

5

THE COURT AND ITS POLICIES, 1867–1875

> The growth of business has been remarkable, and shows conclusively that the Bank has met a want of the time.
>
> quoted in the *North-China Herald*, December 19, 1872

During the first twelve years of its existence, the Hongkong Bank played out the roles described in its Prospectus. The unqualified praise bestowed on the Bank as early as 1868 continued. The following extract from the London *Bullionist*, which deals with the Bank in mid-1872, is perhaps typical:

> The fourteenth [semi-annual] balance sheet of [the Hongkong Bank] discloses a preposterous condition of business . . . The net profits are returned as $397,474 after paying working charges and interest and after making provision against ascertained and doubtful deposits. The result compares favourably with the best returns, as it does not appear that so large an amount of net profits has before been realized . . . The growth of business has been remarkable, and shows conclusively that the Bank has met a want of the time. It has been carefully managed by competent men well versed in the trade of the locality, and has attracted the confidence of the community for whose service it was founded.[1]

And so indeed it seemed.

At the end of 1871 net profits were sufficient to permit an allocation of $100,000 to reserves, bringing the total up to the directors' declared goal of $1 million. By mid-1872 the Bank's earning assets totalled $37 million, of which exchange remittances were $26 million; there was $7 million in cash and bullion, and total balance sheet footings were $46 million. The calls on the new shares were being met on schedule, and paid-up capital had reached $4.5 million or approximately £1 million; confidence in the Bank was reflected in the circulation of its notes ($1.5 million) and in the volume of its deposits ($13.7 million). But profits were inadequate to pay more than the previous 12% rate of dividend and, in the following half-years, with net profits down and capital finally fully paid-up at $5 million, there was no question of increasing the rate (see Tables 3.2, 6.2, and 6.3).

Between mid-1872 and 1875, moreover, the Bank was destined to lose all but $100,000 of its reserves and see its deposits decline, while the poor level of earnings became insufficient to justify a dividend. The causes of this real crisis in the history of the Bank and the course of events leading to the non-payment of dividends for three successive half-yearly periods in 1874/75 is considered in

Chapter 6, although frequent reference is made to the 'crisis' in the present chapter. The Court of Directors and individual members were severely criticized, and their morale must have been further tried as the ordinary turnover of directors and company failures forced the Court's membership down below the minimum required by the Deed of Settlement.

This then is the history of the Bank's attempt to follow the promises of its Prospectus under the direction of the founders and their immediate successors. The crisis of 1874–1875 forced a reassessment of methods and personnel at a time when the Court itself needed replenishing. Thus the return to prosperity began under a virtually new Court operating under new rules, with a strong management team of Thomas Jackson in Hong Kong, David McLean in London, and Ewen Cameron in Shanghai, unencumbered by the pronouncement of its founding, but still the local bank, still fully supported by its constituents. By 1878 the Reserve Fund was again to reach $1 million and the Hongkong Bank would achieve new successes in new contexts with corrective, if potentially dangerous, setbacks.

The early directors made serious errors in the fulfilment of their conception of the Bank's role. They appear, however, to have recognized the risks and maintained a policy of dividend limitation which proved adequate, if barely, to save the Bank. No doubt if they had not acted in support of local industry, they would have been accused of betraying their constituents, whose continued support can alone account for the ultimate survival of the Hongkong Bank.

Under the terms of its ordinance the Hongkong Bank was established for the purpose of carrying on under the management of a Court of Directors, and although David McLean in Shanghai operated with considerable authority and autonomy, especially after the disappearance of the Shanghai Committee in 1868, the fortunes of the Bank in Hong Kong itself in the decade 1867 to 1876 remained very much the direct responsibility of the Court operating through its Standing Committee. The experience was a sobering one. The Committee could neither control Victor Kresser's speculations nor improve on James Greig's unprofitable operations. They were nevertheless in charge.

The story of the first ten years of the Corporation is the subject of the following three chapters. In the present chapter the focus is on the directors as managers, the composition of the Board, their conception of the Bank's role, and their policies in the context of the Prospectus. In the following chapter the story is told in narrative form, leading up to and detailing the crisis of 1874–1875 and the very beginnings of the revival. Finally, the history must return to the beginning and examine the stories of the first men who devoted their careers to the fortunes of the Hongkong Bank and to the early personnel policies which set the stage for the Bank's subsequent expansion.

THE SHAREHOLDERS

The Provisional Committee declared themselves the first directors of the company; the ordinance proclaimed the then directors of the company to be the first directors of the Corporation – until the February 1867 General Meeting. Here for the first (and until 1946 the last) time the shareholders would be voting on the election of each of the directors at the same meeting, that is, they would be determining the entire direction of their company. But who were the shareholders?

Much has already been written in this history concerning the care with which shares were allotted. The Provisional Committee determined that in Hong Kong and the Treaty Ports, shareholders ought also to be constituents; the success of the Bank was as a mutual enterprise. The obvious question follows: who were in fact the early shareholders?

Unfortunately, there are only two extant sources, both of which have defects. First, there is the list of signatories to the Deed of Settlement in July 1867. While the list is explicit, including the number of original and new shares held, it stops when holders of 50% of the $5 million subscribed capital have signed, this being the legal requirement for the Deed's validity. Any *a priori* reasoning as to who might be more likely to sign first is not particularly helpful, and any comment must be based on what is in the record, without speculation as to what is not.

Secondly, there is the Shanghai share register, but it deals mainly with the period 1871–1873 and is not the most important register since many shares held in China and Japan were on other registers, mainly Hong Kong.

Before examining the sources, three points need to be made: (i) shares priced at $125 with a reserve liability of $125 were expensive – a fully qualified clerk's salary might be as low as $100 per month; (ii) five shares were necessary to entitle the shareholder to one vote; thereafter the entitlement was one vote for every twenty shares; and (iii) the maximum permitted holding of any one shareholder was 4,000 or 10% of the then total outstanding.[a]

In the context of the high value/low value share controversy, where did the Hongkong Bank stand, how did the promoters see the role of the shareholder? If by high value shares of £1,000 are indicated, or by low value £1 equivalent, then the Hongkong Bank had taken a middle road, not out of line with other banks formed in the period immediately before 1865.[b]

---

[a] Deed of Settlement, Art. 72. This would subsequently be lowered and by 1929 was 2,000 shares, or 1.2% of the then paid-up capital.

[b] Contemporary sources give the following nominal values and paid-up amounts for bank shares in 1865: Asiatic £20, paid up £5; Agra £50, £25; Chartered £20, £20; Chartered Mercantile £25, £25; Commercial Bank Corp. £25, £25; Delhi and London £50, £25; Bank of Hindustan £100, £25; Oriental £25, £25; Scinde, Punjaub and Delhi £20, £10.[2]

Attendance at the Bank's semi-annual general meetings was at least until 1874 reportedly light, say about 30 excluding directors and staff.

These comments coupled with the data available suggest that the promoters did not intend that any one person or group should reach a position where, by their shareholdings, they could dominate the Bank. In this they were successful. Furthermore, there were two main social categories of shareholders, the business leaders and small-holders. The latter invested for steady income, holding perhaps one to five shares; they would be heaviest hit when in 1874–1875 the dividend was passed over three times. The small-holders were mainly Portuguese but included ship's officers, members of the Imperial Maritime Customs Service, HM Consular officers, and Chinese compradores.

The directors were running what was virtually a community bank. They were responsible for both the financial support of their major constituents and the protection of the investment of the clerks and minor officers, whose retirement, whose families, in the absence of savings banks and other 'safe' opportunities for small savers, were from thenceforward dependent on the performance of the Hongkong Bank. Sir Thomas Jackson, the Bank's long-time Chief Manager, was to proclaim, 'Nothing is too big and nothing is too small for the Hongkong Bank.' This dictum extended to the shareholders; it was a great responsibility and one which the directors, though barely, were in the end to meet.

Despite the limitations of the sources, some look at the details should be of interest. The following were among the first to invest in the Hongkong Bank.

The major shareholders on the Hong Kong register in mid-1867 (*among those signing*) were E.H. Pollard, the Corporation's counsel, 1,258; 'Provisional Committee and Court members: Arthur Abraham D. Sassoon, 2,456; Woldemar Nissen, 1,086; Albert F. Heard, 530; George J. Helland, 470; Julius Menke, 470; George F. Maclean, 410; W.H. Foster, Jr, 302. Also with large holdings were Siqua – presumably Siemssen's compradore and signed for by Nissen – 500; Rustomjee Dunruttenjee, 324; Herman Melchers, 326; and Gustav Overbeck, 303. Directors had to hold 50 shares to qualify, and several subscribed for a further 50 under the terms of the rights issue. There were many holders in the 100–400 range, including such well-known Treaty Port figures as James B. Deacon in Canton, 300; Jonathan Russell of Russell, Sturgis in Manila, 300; Dr J. Murray, the contentious Colonial doctor in Hong Kong, 260; and Henry Kingsmill, barrister, 195.

The above is not, however, an accurate measure of voting power, since many held the proxies of those in their company or of 'friends' who lived in the outports. A.F. Heard's holdings, for example, should be reckoned together with G.F. Heard's 72, A.M. Daly's (Foochow) 20, and Jonathan Russell's 300.

In making generalizations from this source, it must be remembered that Woldemar Nissen was then Chairman of the Bank. Nevertheless, the strength of the German holdings is significant – William Pustau in Hamburg had 120, G.T. Siemssen 50 – totalling at a rough estimate some 3,420 shares plus, perhaps, influence over the 500 shares of Siqua. This is not a matter of control since all the German shares listed could be outvoted by Pollard and Sassoon in combination, but the German interest is nevertheless important.

One conclusion is possible: the directors were unlikely to meet any concerted opposition, subject to reasonable management.

The list deals only with shares on the Hong Kong register, but the others were probably of little significance as yet, especially since some firms encouraged their associates to apply through Hong Kong. In any case the number of shares belonging to those giving London, New York, San Francisco, and even German addresses is negligible. Manila subscribers seem to have been friends of Augustine Heard, there are but three or four residents of Japan subscribing.

There were few Bank employees at this time, and even fewer signed the Deed of Settlement. Kresser himself had 320 shares with another 60 for members of his family, including minor children.

Two further observations should be made. First, there are only six Chinese whose names appear on the list, and only Siqua had a significant holding. D. Lapraik's compradore Acheong and Dent's Alai in Hong Kong and Ah Lee in Foochow are listed; there are also a Shanghai merchant, a ship's compradore, and a Macau trader. From this observation nothing further should be or can be deduced. Secondly, there are several holders with less than ten shares, especially Portuguese, tending to confirm the observations made above and the generally held opinion in the China-coast newspapers that Hongkong Bank's shares were looked upon as sound investments by clerical wage-earners, promising a steady income. Certainly David McLean in his correspondence with James Greig in Hong Kong stressed the importance of a steady 12% dividend.

Moving ahead five years and to Shanghai, the register contains some 300 names, resembling a Who's Who of foreigners in China: for example, John Fryer of the Kiangnan Arsenal, Prosper Giquel of the Foochow Arsenal, William Kaye of the Chartered Bank, Lethbridge of the Oriental, Edward Maccall of the Agra, and five Portuguese.

There were few Chinese holders, and these, as in Hong Kong, were mainly compradores, with the Hongkong Bank's Shanghai compradore, Wah Sam (Wang Huai-shan) holding 350, the only substantial Chinese holding, although the head shroff, Wu Jim Pah or 'Jim Crow' (Wu Mao-ting), held 38. In 1875 Wah Sam also held shares in joint account with McLean and Ewen Cameron, the then Shanghai Manager. Not surprisingly the Shanghai register shows evidence of a large turnover of shares by brokers and by two or three members of the staff, especially the Manager, David McLean, and John Walter and William Murray. The Bank's staff were holders of shares; they were also possessed, in the tradition of the times, with insider information.

The holdings of ten brokers, including James R. Anton, C.A.L. Dunn, William Mitchell, Henry Morriss, and James Septimus Daly, are listed. There are foreign officers training Chinese forces, Indian merchants, and a few residents of other open ports – Ningpo, Hiogo, Yokohama, Hankow, Kiukiang, Foochow, even Manila.

These then were some of the proprietors of the Hongkong and Shanghai Banking Corporation in 1867 – and in the early 1870s. In February 1867 the shareholders elected their directors, and it is to the directors that this history must now turn.

THE COURT OF DIRECTORS – MEMBERSHIP

The failure of Dent's and initial adjustments

With the failure of Dent and Co. in early 1867 the Hongkong Bank was freed of further obligation to its organizing base. Until this time the senior partner of the company had been Chairman first of the Provisional Committee and then of the Court. What was to be the policy of the Court, whose powers included the election from among their number of the Chairman and the Deputy Chairman? (see Table 5.1).

At the first Ordinary General Meeting of Shareholders under the new Bank ordinance, held February 11, 1867, and with the prior announcement of the resignation of W.H. Forbes of Russell and Co., Edward Cunningham, senior partner in Hong Kong of the same company, was elected a director, and at the next meeting of the Court he was elected Chairman. Granted that Cunningham was both well-known and highly regarded on the China coast, he was new to Hong Kong. In any case, this was no decision by rotation; Russell and Co. were the most influential house then represented on the Court.

Cunningham, however, never attended a meeting and left the Colony soon after his election. Woldemar Nissen of Siemssen and Co. had been elected Deputy Chairman, possibly on seniority (although other founder members could make an equal claim) or possibly on the grounds of his shareholding or his impending departure. In any case he now became Acting Chairman, and a key question for contemporary observers might have been whether this was merely an interim appointment until the next Russell and Co. representative was appointed director and elected Chairman. It may be that this was considered, but in the event, although W.H. Foster joined the Board in June, the following month Nissen was confirmed Chairman. And when Nissen returned to Hamburg in November, G.J. Helland (John Burd and Co.) was elected Chairman on the declared principle of seniority. He was also elected for a fixed term, until the end of 1868. Both decisions are evidence of a radically new approach – there was no longer the undisputed leadership of a single hong whose taipan was automatically elected to the chair; the chairmanship of the Court and therefore of the Hongkong Bank was to be, in general, on a rotation by seniority principle. This would affect the relationship of the Court and its senior manager, especially in the period after 1875 when Thomas Jackson proved able and successful.

The seniority principle continued with the election of Arthur Sassoon as Deputy Chairman under Nissen; he did not succeed to the chairmanship, however, because he planned to leave Hong Kong. Instead George F. Heard, who had earlier replaced his brother A.F. Heard and was already the next senior, became Deputy Chairman under Helland and, in January 1869, Chairman. George wrote that this was strictly on a rotation basis and indeed, well-liked as he was, George made no pretence of being a brilliant businessman. His brother had once written to him, 'Don't get in a funk about it – you know just as much as I do and you have only to look wise and tell people that you "will take it into consideration" and "will see" and they think you are all right.'[3]

With this principle of selecting the chairman and his deputy generally agreed if not rigidly established, one may turn to the question of membership in general (see Table 5.2).

The last member of the original Provisional Committee to serve continuously on the Court was G.J. Helland of John Burd and Co.; he was Chairman of the Bank in 1868. Although his firm was always represented, A.F. Heard himself did not serve throughout, but, when Augustine Heard and Co. failed in 1875, his final departure might be said to mark the end of the Bank's early years.

The successors

The Court held to the principle that its members should be representative of trading interests in Hong Kong. This meant in practice that (i) the replacement of a director leaving the Colony would usually, but not always, be found from the same firm, (ii) the principle of a national quota, specifically a 'German quota', was implemented, (iii) representation from new firms was actively sought, and (iv) there was room still for a particular individual. As for the last policy, in 1868 E.R. Belilios, commonly reputed to be a large holder of Bank shares, asked to be elected, and the Court recommended him favourably to the General Meeting; he was to play a long and active role as director.

As for the various firms represented, the succession was often forced by the transfer of partners, by Home leave, and other factors solely matters of concern to the firm itself. For example, Augustine Heard and Co.'s representative was first A.F. Heard, then his younger brother George, followed by G.F. Weller, and back to A.F. Heard. The succession was about to return to George when the firm crashed in 1875. Russell and Co. began with W.H. Forbes and, after the interval

Table 5.1 *The Hongkong and Shanghai Banking Corporation Chairmen and Deputy Chairmen, 1867–1876*

Chairman	Deputy Chairman
1867	
John Dent (Jan.-Feb.)	Woldemar Nissen[b] (Jan.-June)
E. Cunningham[a] (March-May)	
W. Nissen[b] (June-Nov.)	Arthur Sassoon (July-Dec.)
G.J. Helland[c]	
1868	
G.J. Helland[c]	G.F. Heard[a]
1869	
G.F. Heard[a]	Julius Menke[b]
1870	
H.B. Lemann	J.B. Taylor (Jan.- July)
	R. Rowett (July-Dec.)
1871/2	
R. Rowett	Thomas Pyke
1872/3	
Thomas Pyke	S.D. Sassoon
1873/4	
S.D. Sassoon	W.H. Forbes[a]
1874/5	
W.H. Forbes[a]	R. Rowett
	A. von André[b] (Jan. 75)
1875/6	
A. von André[b]	A.F. Heard[a] (Feb.)
	W.H. Forbes[a] (Feb.-Jan.)
	E.R. Belilios (Feb. 76)
1876/7	
E.R. Belilios	A. von André[b]

Notes:
[a] An American director.
[b] A German director.
[c] A Norwegian director.

with Cunningham and W.H. Foster, brought him back again in 1872 in time to be Chairman during the crisis year of 1874. Gilman's and Sassoon's had a succession of brothers, with H.B. and William Lemann alternating five times in the period until, again in the crisis year of 1874, William Lemann insisted on resigning. Meanwhile Arthur Sassoon was replaced by his brother Solomon D., who in turn gave place to F.D. Sassoon in 1875. C.T. Smith of Smith, Archer and Co. was replaced by J.B. Taylor, and Nissen of Siemssen's first by A. Joost and then, after

Table 5.2 *The Hongkong and Shanghai Banking Corporation*
Selected Courts of Directors, 1867–1876

26 January 1869: 11 members

*G.F. Heard	Augustine Heard and Co.	Chairman
*Julius Menke	Wm Pustau and Co.	Deputy Chairman
Wm Lemann	Gilman and Co.	
J.B. Taylor	Smith, Archer and Co.	
*S.D. Sassoon	D. Sassoon, Sons and Co.	
A. Joost	Siemssen and Co.	
*Jas. P. Duncanson	Gibb, Livingston and Co.	
W.H. Forbes	Russell and Co.	
R. Rowett	Holliday, Wise and Co.	
E.R. Belilios		
G.J. Helland	John Burd and Co.	

27 March 1873: 9 members

*S.D. Sassoon	D. Sassoon, Sons and Co.	Chairman
*W.H. Forbes	Russell and Co.	Deputy Chairman
*A. Joost	Siemssen and Co.	
E.R. Belilios		
H.B. Lemann	Gilman and Co.	
*Thomas Pyke	Birley and Co.	
R. Rowett	Holliday, Wise and Co.	
A.F. Heard	Augustine Heard and Co.	
A. von André	Melchers and Co.	

Note: * indicates a member of the Standing Committee

an interval, by Heinrich Hoppius, another long-serving director. Similarly Adolf von André eventually succeeded to the place of H. Melchers, J.F. Cordes to the place of J. Menke.

Reference to Hoppius, André, and the other German Court members is a reminder of the German quota, a matter first raised in reference to J.F. Cordes's application to become a director in July 1873. He was told that he would be given 'favourable consideration the next time there is a German vacancy'. At that time there were two Germans on the Court, although for six months from August 1871 of the nine members there had been three Germans – Joost, Menke of Wm Pustau and Co., and Melchers – and but three from Britain. As Cordes was actually applying for the Pustau and Co. representation vacated the previous year by Menke, the quota would seem to represent an effort to actually reduce the German membership. The existence of the self-imposed limit of two Germans would appear confirmed when Joost resigned; Cordes was elected into what had been the 'Siemssen vacancy', and when Hoppius of that firm applied in February 1874 he was told, as Cordes had been told before him, that he must wait for a 'German vacancy'. Hoppius's election would come sooner and for other reasons – but that is another story.

The new firms represented were Holliday, Wise and Co., Melchers and Co., Wm Pustau and Co., and Birley and Co. Jas P. Duncanson of Gibb, Livingston and Co. had been a member of the Shanghai Committee until his move to Hong Kong in late 1868; he was elected to the Court in January 1869 but died within the year. Jardine, Matheson and Co. were not as yet ready.

The Court was to consist of a maximum of twelve members and a minimum of seven, although, fortunately for the Bank, the Court could operate temporarily on the basis of a quorum, set by the Deed of Settlement at four. In fact the Court never exceeded eleven, arguing at one point that it did not need further strengthening. This attitude led to a slow rate of replacement, and the Bank entered the year of 1874 with a Court of but nine members.

The resignation of William Lemann

On July 25, 1874, with the storm clouds gathering, William Lemann submitted his resignation. The Court refused under Art. 128 to accept it on the grounds that, coming just before the General Meeting of Shareholders, this would further shake confidence in the Bank. On August 4, Lemann insisted on resigning and having the resignation fully publicized; the Board agreed.

To understand Lemann's behaviour, first consider the riddle posed in a *China Punch* poem entitled 'Yarn of the "Broker Swell"', sub-titled 'A dismal lay of the future'.

Oh, I am the Hongkong and Shanghai Bank,
The Docks, and the Indo-Chinese,
The Steam-boats, the Piers – I own it with tears –
And also the Dis-tilleree.[c]

These are references to various joint-stock companies then in difficulties, several of which will feature later in Chapter 6.

The 'Broker Swell' obligingly continues his story: with all the problems the companies faced, the brokers were in difficulties.

For months we'd scarcely made a cent,
But we hit on a bright idee,
To sue the Directors who didn't protect us
From losing our coin, d'ye see?

So first we fell on the Rum Mill Board,
(And the Jury was werry kind,)
Then the Bank so Strong, – they didn't take long,
The few as was left behind.[4]

---

[c] That is to say, the Hongkong and Shanghai Banking Corporation, the Hongkong and Whampoa Dock Company, the Indo-Chinese Sugar Company, the Hongkong, Canton and Macao Steamboat Company, the Hongkong Pier and Godown Company, and the Hong Kong Distillery.

The last two lines are in the future; the Rum Mill Board, better known as the Hong Kong Distillery, and the suit referred to, *Whittall v Bell and others*, in which the jury were 'werry kind' and awarded damages against the directors of the company – these were very much matters of the present.

The fault of the Distillery Company's directors was not that they had made positive and purposeful mis-statements, it was rather their failure in their annual accounts to present a true overall picture of the state of the company. Thus James Whittall of Jardine Matheson was induced to take action he would not otherwise have taken; he provided the company molasses on credit.[5]

In finding for Whittall, the special jury was split five to two; William Lemann was a member of the jury and, it may reasonably be supposed, one of the minority. Whether his resignation from the Court of Directors of the Bank was an act of frustration in the light of the jury's majority decision, a principled response to the views expressed by Chief Justice Sir John Smale (the most likely), or whether he had, perhaps, particular concern with the Hongkong Bank's accounts is not recorded.

William Lemann was determined not to be one of 'the few as was left behind'. He was permitted to resign.

The search for an 'English' director

At the same meeting of the Court of Directors, August 4, 1874, Thomas Pyke announced his intention of resigning after the General Meeting. He was simply leaving Hong Kong. This would put the Court at seven members, the minimum permitted (see Tables 5.3A–C).

But H. Hoppius had previously asked to be elected. Ironically he had been on the special jury with Lemann but had presumably voted with the majority. Now he too could express his principles – by joining the Court. Despite any limitations imposed by a so-called 'German quota', Hoppius was elected in time to face the shareholders on August 12.

After this meeting the resignation of Thomas Pyke was effective, and R. Rowett also resigned on leaving the Colony, thus leaving the Court without a single British director. At a meeting on January 30, 1875, the Court resolved to find some, but it was not to prove easy. There were rumours that James Whittall of Jardine Matheson would join the Court, but Heard commented simply, 'There is no question of [his] joining the direction of the Bank.'[6] Of the two the Court invited, one was a civil servant and unable to accept and P. Ryrie had to consult his partners – nothing further is recorded.

In the meantime Adolf von André, a German, was elected Chairman and A.F. Heard, an American, Deputy Chairman for 1875/76, the terms now running from the February general meeting. In February Heard announced his intention to

Table 5.3A *The Hongkong and Shanghai Banking Corporation*
The Court of Directors during the crisis, 1874/75
(*12 August 1874*)

9 members		
*W.H. Forbes	Russell and Co.	Chairman
*R. Rowett	Holliday, Wise and Co.	Deputy Chairman
E.R. Belilios		
Thomas Pyke	Birley and Co.	
*Adolf von André	Melchers and Co.	
A.F. Heard	Augustine Heard and Co.	
J.F. Cordes	Wm Pustau and Co.	
*S.D. Sassoon	D. Sassoon, Sons and Co.	
H. Hoppius	Siemssen and Co.	

Note: * indicates a member of the Standing Committee.

leave Hong Kong but, using their authority under Article 118, the Court refused to accept his resignation. The Court was again down to the minimum number.

The failure of Augustine Heard and Co. in April 1875 meant the automatic disqualification of A.F. Heard under Art. 119 (Art. 118 notwithstanding), and the Board was consequently composed of but six members – below the minimum but still enough for a quorum. There were three Germans, one of whom was Chairman, an American as Deputy Chairman, and two members who had come originally from South Asia.

The Court again turned its attention to securing an 'English' director and the meeting agreed to invite H. Nicaise, manager of the Borneo Company in Hong Kong. He accepted but had to offer his resignation at the following meeting since his superiors would not permit him thus to spend his time – a problem the Bank would face again. Once more the Court invoked Art. 118; Nicaise was not permitted to resign as this would again put the Court's membership below the minimum authorized.

The crisis was resolved when, on August 14, Alexander McIver, the superintendent of the P&O, came to the rescue. This released Nicaise and the Court of the Hongkong and Shanghai Banking Corporation had at last found a British subject of British descent both willing and, equally important, able to serve.

For some observers the crisis raised the question as to whether the Hongkong Bank was, in fact, a British bank. The available records indicate that the majority of the shares were held by British subjects and the Bank was incorporated by ordinance in the British Crown Colony of Hong Kong. The staff was British. The

Table 5.3B *The Hongkong and Shanghai Banking Corporation*
The Court of Directors during the crisis, 1874/75
(*20 April 1875*)

6 members		
*Adolf von André	Melchers and Co.	Chairman
*W.H. Forbes	Russell and Co.	Deputy Chairman
E.R. Belilios		
J.F. Cordes	Wm Pustau and Co.	
*H. Hoppius	Siemssen and Co.	
*F.D. Sassoon	D. Sassoon, Sons and Co.	

Note: * indicates a member of the Standing Committee

Table 5.3C *The Hongkong and Shanghai Banking Corporation*
The Court of Directors after the crisis, 1874/75
(*3 February 1876*)

7 members		
*Adolf von André	Melchers and Co.	Chairman
*E.R. Belilios		Deputy Chairman
J.F. Cordes	Wm Pustau and Co.	
H. Hoppius	Siemssen and Co.	
F.D. Sassoon	D. Sassoon, Sons and Co.	
A. McIver	P&O SN Co.	
S.W. Pomeroy	Russell and Co.	

Note: * indicates a member of the Standing Committee.

Hongkong Bank was a British overseas bank seeking an 'Englishman' from 'Home' willing to sit on its Court of Directors.

Even then the Court was slow to restore its membership, although the search for British directors from the United Kingdom continued. With the election of E. R. Belilios as Chairman and A. von André as Deputy – on the seniority principle – the Court was ready for redevelopment of the Bank in the 'Jackson Era' (see Part II). The above merely sets the stage for a discussion of the period 1867–1875, which must be considered in detail.

THE COURT IN ACTION

Continuity on the Court had been provided, not by the great British hongs, but by D. Sassoon, Sons and Co., Siemssen and Co., Russell and Co., and, until April 1875, by Augustine Heard and Co. But there was continuity, and the promises of the first years were well in mind. In the following section, then, the focus is on the policies pursued by the Court, relating them, where appropriate, to the initial intentions or purposes of the Hongkong Bank, particularly as declared in its Prospectus.

The Shanghai Committee

The Prospectus stated that the Hongkong Bank would open simultaneously in Hong Kong and Shanghai, 'and it is intended to establish a local Board of Directors there for more effectively meeting the work'. Initial developments in Shanghai were undertaken by a committee of unrecorded membership, appointed through Dent and Co., whose duties included, *inter alia*, arranging terms with David McLean.

The existence of this preliminary Shanghai Committee presumably ceased with the establishment of the Hongkong and Shanghae Banking Company, Ltd, for in September 1866 the Court minutes that a Committee of Advice and Inspection is to be constituted there and accordingly appointed George Tyson, Shanghai partner of Russell and Co., Alexander Turing, partner of Dent and Co., and James P. Duncanson of Gibb, Livingston and Co. That the Court considered them a local board of 'directors' may be supposed from the fact that they each received a flat fee of $400 per annum – equivalent to that of a director, paid from the $20,000 allocated for directors under the terms of the Deed of Settlement. They were not, however, directors in the sense intended by the ordinance, nor were they subject to election by the shareholders.

At first the Court apparently intended to continue the Committee, for, when Turing left as a consequence of Dent's failure, the Court appointed H.B. Lemann, who had resigned from the Court on leaving Hong Kong for Shanghai. The Shanghai Committee was given the responsibility of auditing the accounts of the branch and was asked to undertake preliminary negotiations for improved premises in Shanghai. The first Court discussion of an agency in Hankow, May 1867, notes that it was urged by 'our Shanghai colleagues'.

Less than a year later, in March 1868, the Court recorded that all members of this Committee had left Shanghai, presumably within weeks of each other, and that the Court's own Standing Committee was to look into the question of new appointments. J.P. Duncanson had in fact become a director in Hong Kong in February.

The new appointments to the Shanghai Committee were never made. The Committee simply ceased to exist.

With the exception of London the Court of Directors never again appointed a local committee. The directors were ultimately responsible to the laws of Hong Kong; perhaps they were unwilling to share that responsibility. Shanghai may have been too close and too similar to Hong Kong; there are references in McLean's early letters to suggest differences of opinion. Whereas a London Committee could advise on British firms, a Shanghai Committee would compound the problems of confidentiality the Bank already faced. Even in the case of London, where contact was essential, the Court was hesitant; the subject is mentioned as early as 1867, but the decision to go ahead was not taken until 1875, when it was forced as another consequence of the events of 1874–1875.

Perhaps it is not a coincidence that the year of the Shanghai Committee's disappearance, 1868, was also the year the Hong Kong Manager was designated as 'Chief Manager'.

Control and inspection

Branch banking had not been without its critics. Gilbart's opinion was that branches were feasible – the Scottish banks offered proof – provided there were a capable administrator and sufficient discipline. He added that joint-stock banks had grown faster than efficient potential managers could be found and that, with the Scottish banks raising the salaries of their staff, they could not be bid away.[7]

Scottish managers were however attracted to the East. There demand outgrew supply, or growth outran discretion. In the failures of the new Eastern banks during the period 1865–1867, embattled directors accused managers and managers, directors. Investigation revealed strange happenings. These were not times for careful reflection on the problems. But the Hongkong Bank had no need to reflect. The dangers were revealed and obvious. Control was a key problem.

The Court, it must be admitted, was not always able to control itself. Thus when it resolved to meet regularly twice a month on specified dates, it did not, for many months afterwards, actually meet on those dates. When it resolved to meet at least monthly the records show unaccountable gaps. Setting down a seniority principle or a German quota, the Court would seem to have revised its procedures whenever the need arose. In many ways it was, not unreasonably, feeling its way.

The problems of 1874/75 naturally provoked questions as to the care the directors had taken in exercising their responsibilities. Certainly the directors were concerned and increased the number of meetings; furthermore the minutes prove reasonable attendance records for members of the Court and exemplary ones for the Standing Committee. And it was through the Standing Committee that the directors controlled the details of the Corporation's activities.

The figures in Table 5.4 indicate that the number of meetings increased as the problems of the Bank developed. But the remuneration of the directors was fixed at $20,000 by the Deed of Settlement and apportioned on a flat fee basis plus an allowance for each meeting attended. This meant, ironically, that the proposal by

Table 5.4 *The Hongkong and Shanghai Banking Corporation*
Number of meetings: Court and Standing Committee

	1867	1868	1869	1870	1871	1872	1873	1874	1875
Court	12	11	9	18	12	12	15	18	19
Committee[a]	9	22	22	34	35	39	42	55	43

Note:
[a] There is no record of the total number of Committee meetings; these figures are consequently understated.

Charles May at the General Meeting of February 1875 that the directors take a smaller remuneration was, as far as each individual's work was concerned, automatically achieved – especially for the over-worked members of the Standing Committee. The records also reveal that the Sassoon brothers attended almost all meetings, the Bank Chairman was almost always present, and members of the Standing Committee were most likely also to attend the full Court.

In the early months of the Bank's history the Chairman, a partner of Dent and Co., had not been elected to the important Standing Committee which met more frequently than the full Court. He had nevertheless access to customers' accounts and to the branch and agency records, and in general supervised the work of the Bank.

Then in 1867 the pattern changed. Nissen as Chairman and Sassoon as Deputy were both members; the third was G.J. Helland. This arrangement – Chairman and Deputy Chairman *ex officio* plus one elected member – was confirmed by the Court in early 1868, and held, with one interesting amendment, throughout the period. In 1869 the Court ruled and subsequent meetings confirmed that Sassoon, 'because of his large interest in the Bank', should be an additional member.

Exceptionally in 1871 Sassoon was not a member of the Standing Committee. Belilios had refused appointment as Deputy Chairman on the grounds that, as this would make him a member of the Standing Committee *ex officio* and if Sassoon were also a member, there would be two members from the same profession. The minutes do not record a decision, but attendance records show Belilios as a member of the Committee and no Sassoon.

As the Court was active in management, it follows, as noted above, that the Standing Committee actually oversaw the decisions of the Manager and, therefore, had access to the accounts and credit requests of customers. There are instances of individual directors enquiring about specific accounts – always those, incidentally, that proved to warrant attention – and the director was invited to the next meeting of the Standing Committee.

The fact of access to customer information by directors, especially in a 'local bank', is a matter of serious concern. Nissen enjoyed being on the Court, he wrote, because of the information it provided him; later, G.F. Heard learnt for the first time how much of his company's paper had been bought by the Hongkong Bank.[8] On the other hand the Heards had not been so pleased at the thought of Gilman and Co. learning of their activities in Foochow. The problem would be a continuing one; John Swire's refusal in 1892 to seek financial support from the Hongkong Bank for his Taikoo Sugar Refinery Company, for example, was explained by the fact that the Board included Jardine's representative and 'to seek assistance from this bank would therefore be to play directly into Jardine's hands'.[9] In contrast, the Hongkong Bank's success in attracting small, local firms in Lyons has been ascribed to its being a foreign bank without intimate local contacts and thus more likely to be able to maintain secrecy.[10]

Here was a dilemma which had not been satisfactorily resolved in the United Kingdom; directors, if actively involved, would know too much of the secrets of their competitors and would have to make a decision on loans intended for their own or rival companies; but if they delegated responsibility for key banking functions they nevertheless remained responsible. There seemed to be two possible lines of solution: (i) appoint directors who were not in business – hardly possible in Hong Kong, or (ii) let managers handle the problems, referring only a limited and clearly defined range of problems to the Board and then in such a way as to minimize identification. The first solution had been tried in England and, as Gilbart noted in his famous study of banking, had led to failure since a director not involved in business might not know anything about business; the second depended for its success on the wisdom of management and on the Board's proper selection of a chief manager.[11]

The larger Hong Kong trading firms had a tradition of banking, but, with the exception of Heard and, perhaps, Nissen, the directors were new-generation merchants brought up in the era of the India and London based exchange banks. The Hongkong Bank's directors were nevertheless experienced, hard-working, and knowledgeable. From the point of view of control it is fair to conclude that the Court identified the problem accounts; the crisis in the Bank – the passing of the dividend – arose from the decisions the directors then made. The decisions were often based, it is fair to add, on the advice the Court received from their Hong Kong Manager and from his colleagues in other offices.

Thus the only alternative the directors had – abdication to the paid managers – was not as yet viable nor were the directors yet ready for it.

The minutes confirm that the directors dealt directly with the shortcomings of senior staff. For example, two Yokohama managers, W. Robert Brett in 1867 and John Grigor, the Bank's first employee, in 1871 were removed for violating instructions; Thomas Jackson was taken to task for directly circulating the

London shareholders with a reassuring memo during the 1875 crisis; David McLean was criticized for issuing the Imperial Loan on the London market in 1875 without first consulting the Court; and Henry Smith, agent at Hiogo, was discharged while on leave for poor performance – he returned to Hong Kong at his own expense and was reemployed 'on trial', which he amply justified as Chief Accountant, the task he performed until his death in 1882. At the time of his death he had been for some time the senior (longest-serving) member of the Eastern staff.

Senior managers were conscious of the Court's role and that they operated under their direction. When Ewen Cameron succeeded David McLean as Manager Shanghai he inherited the practice of making clean or 'chop' loans (*ch'e-p'iao*) to native banks in Shanghai. Cameron reported this in 1873; it was contrary to the standing instructions. The Court on the recommendation of the Standing Committee approved the chop loans as 'tried and appropriate business', a decision which, incidentally, confirmed the Hongkong Bank's major role in the Shanghai money market.

In the absence of the Standing Committee's records, details of the directors' role must be based on matters brought before the full Court. The following would seem typical – and not particularly surprising: (i) staff appointments, transfers, and terms of service, (ii) sovereign risk loans, (iii) new agencies and branches, buildings, and accommodation, (iv) special rules in developing problem areas, for example, loans to joint-stock companies in Hong Kong, (v) shareholder relations, including share registers and presentations, notices, or correspondence to shareholders, (vi) policy towards the Hong Kong and British Governments, especially in relation to the charter, and (vii) relations through the London Office with the City and the Stock Exchange.

As early as September 1867 the Court confirmed that the Bank was in general banking business and that anything outside this, including such business undertaken on an unusual scale, long-term loans which would lock up funds, and large dealings in bullion and exchange, must be brought to the Court. The retiring Thomas Pyke, who had served three years on the Standing Committee, brought up supervisory problems at his last meeting in February 1874. But by this time the Court were already in trouble.

The Court inspected the accounts and considered the recommendations of the auditors, they dealt with charitable requests and special situations, such as compensating the family of the Chinese who had died assisting in protecting Bank property during a fire in Foochow. And obviously they dealt with their own internal affairs – remuneration of directors, replacement of directors, and the election of the Chairman and Deputy Chairman and members of the Standing Committee.

Those familiar with business methods on the China coast will have certainly noted an omission, the relationship of the Court with the Bank's compradores. There is no reference to a compradore in the extant records of the Bank during the period under discussion. This is surprising; the Bank most certainly had compradores, in Shanghai, Wang Huai-shan (Wah Sam), in Hong Kong, Lo Pak Sheung, who held the post from 1865 to his death in 1877 and was succeeded by his son.[12] The subject requires further consideration in Chapter 14.

Under the terms of the ordinance the Bank's accounts were to be audited, and the Bank in addition appointed auditors in Shanghai. Otherwise there was not, until the event of 1874 forced a reassessment, an internal inspection system beyond the scrutiny of managers and the Standing Committee in the normal course of business, or the survey made by a trusted officer on a circuitous route Home.

But, it may be argued, the Bank's problems were in Hong Kong. Actions contrary to standing instructions in Yokohama and Hiogo were promptly settled; even Vacher's misuse of funds in London to make unauthorized investments on the Bank's and his own account could have been absorbed. The difficulties in Hong Kong, however, arose not by oversight or lack of control but as the consequence of unsound decisions by the Court themselves.

Branches and agencies

The Bank pursued a conservative policy relative to the establishment of Bank-staffed agencies, while the question of branches was clouded by the interpretation of the Bank's ordinance relative to its existence outside the Colony of Hong Kong, the 'extraterritorial' question, and the failure to secure a clarifying amendment either in 1872 or 1873. The significance of this uncertainty was mitigated (i) by the fact that there was no clear distinction between an agency and branch in respect to the Hongkong Bank's activities, and (ii) the Hong Kong Government was not expected to interfere, nor did it wish to do so. For a list of the Bank's offices in 1876, see Table 5.5.

The Bank's 'trading area'
The growth of business prompted the Court to replace the merchant-agents with Bank-staffed agencies in the Treaty Ports of Foochow (1867), Hankow (1868), and Amoy (1873); to expand in Japan with the establishment of agencies in Hiogo (1869) and Osaka (1872), where the machinery from the defunct Hong Kong Mint had been sent and a business in bullion developed. Hong Kong's precarious sugar industry and Kresser's personal involvement led the Bank to establish its own agency in Saigon (1870) and, at a date not specified, to appoint the Bank of Rotterdam its agent in Singapore and Batavia. In 1869 the Court resisted pressure to replace its merchant-agents in Manila, partly because of the confused

Table 5.5 *The Hongkong and Shanghai Banking Corporation Branches and Bank-staffed agencies, 1876*

	opened		opened
Hong Kong	1865	Hiogo (Kobe)	1869
Shanghai	1865	Saigon	1870
London	1865	Osaka	1872
Yokohama	1866	Amoy	1873
Calcutta	1867	Edinburgh (?)	1874
Foochow	1867	Manila	1875
Hankow	1868	San Francisco	1875
Bombay	1869		

interpretation of the Bank's ordinance, and partly because the Court was basically not expansion-minded. However, the failure of Russell, Sturgis and Co. in 1875 forced the Court's hand, and, without reference in the minutes to the legal problems, appointed the relatively junior C.I. Barnes as Agent, presumably to operate under his own name as special agent of the Bank, a fine point soon forgotten in the routine of business.

Indeed, the announcement of a new agency was often accompanied with the assurance that its functions would, in some way, be well-controlled and strictly limited, or that it would be 'small'. The Bank saw itself as a regional bank based on China and Japan. However, as Hong Kong's entrepot trade and the requirements of its industry developed, there was justification for expansion in Indo-China, the Philippines, and Netherlands East Indies.

Agencies for exchange operations

The Hongkong Bank was also an exchange bank, justifying a special agency in London and a banking agent in San Francisco. As previously noted, the Bank had arranged for agents in New York and consciously avoided competing with, for example, Baring's in the North Atlantic exchanges.[13]

The Bank did not have its own staffed agency either in France or in Germany. The latter omission is particularly interesting as there were German directors on the Court and potential competition in the early 1870s from the newly established Deutsche Bank's Far Eastern branches and from the Deutsche National Bank at Bremen, for whom Melchers were agents in Hong Kong and Siemssen's in Shanghai – both these firms being represented on the Hongkong Bank's Court.[14] When the Deutsch-Asiatische Bank was preparing to open in Hamburg in the late 1880s the Hongkong Bank did respect the challenge and established its own agency there in 1889; but for the present the German banks proved no threat and London Office with its correspondents apparently served the Bank's European requirements.

As for San Francisco, when the Bank of California failed in 1875, the Court had to reconsider its position, and, after consultations with David McLean, by then Vacher's replacement as Manager London, and the newly appointed London Committee, they agreed to establish a Bank-staffed agency, taking special precautions that the Agent would not speculate with Bank funds – the failure of the Commercial Bank Corporation had been due in large part to their San Francisco agent's mining speculations, and this remained an unhappy memory on the China coast.

Even then the Bank hesitated, attempting to work out an exclusive relationship with the Bank of Nevada.

When this was declined, the Court made the unusual decision, 'due to our good standing with the Chinese and [consequent] large business done between San Francisco and China and facilities for bullion', of pressing ahead with the San Francisco special agency, even if it should, for a time, operate at a loss.

The Court recorded its admission that the charter 'doesn't permit us to open a Branch' – and by this they meant 'branch or agency'; W.H. Harries, then the Manager in Yokohama, who was appointed Special Agent, was therefore instructed to advertise under his own name, thus: 'W.H. Harries, Agent, Hongkong and Shanghai Banking Corporation', as opposed to 'Hongkong Bank, W.H. Harries, Agent'. Legally there was or was thought to be a distinction; in fact, Harries operated as any agent would and the distinction was not maintained in the Bank's internal documents. Not until 1912 did the Bank acknowledge and the State of California accept a San Francisco agency in the usual way.

In February 1876 the Bank's Chairman, Adolf von André, announced the decision to the shareholders with the usual declaration of intent: 'It may be satisfactory to you to know that we have prohibited all local advances being made in San Francisco, and that the agency has been established for the sole purpose of exchange business.'

Expansion to India

The most significant development was the Bank's early replacement of its merchant agents in Calcutta (1867) and Bombay (1869). The Bank had early declared its interest in India, making a special allotment of shares to potential constituents there, but then holding back during the financial crisis and following uncertainties of 1865/66. With Indian interests represented on the Court – and one of the public arguments for later electing E.R. Belilios to the Court would be his Indian connections – the Bank confirmed its intention and then set up its own agencies cautiously, for exchange purposes only. Nevertheless, the operations would be sizeable and Kresser urged the Court to make a further call on the unpaid capital of the 'new shares' as a precaution; as noted in Chapter 4, the schedule of calls was indeed agreed in January 1869 with the next call being set for July 1.

Typically, the Bank appointed its first agent in India virtually at the same time it wrote the Indian Government for permission to operate; he was fully established by the time the permission was in fact granted in October 1868. Robert Stevenson, formerly manager of the Asiatic Bank in Shanghai, had been sent to Calcutta in December 1867. When in 1869 the development of the business of the Corporation through India required the establishment of an agency in Bombay, Stevenson was placed in charge; Calcutta became subsidiary to Bombay and was managed by Ewen Cameron, who had previously been the agency's Accountant.

The importance of India to the Bank was based on the requirements of (i) its constituents, for example D. Sassoon and Sons, who required rupees to finance imports, mainly opium and cotton from India to China and (ii) its own exchange operations in cases where a tri-lateral operation would, with favourable combinations of rates, prove profitable. The Hongkong Bank in Hong Kong or Shanghai could provide rupees to importers by drawing on Calcutta or Bombay and covering by buying sterling which could then be sold against rupees, putting the Bank back in funds.

The banker turned financial journalist, J.W. Maclellan, has explained:

The operations were, as a rule, simultaneous; that is, the bank invested the produce of its drafts on India in sterling exchange, which it remitted to London by the same mail. The profit was made by the Indian branches providing funds with which to pay the draft from China at cheaper rates than the equivalent given by the remittance from China in sterling bills.[15]

Such an operation could result, however, in the Bank running an overdraft in India and holding additional cash in China, in Hong Kong and Shanghai. Whether the dollars or taels could be profitably invested was another factor in the equation. To provide an available margin on deposit and means of credit to facilitate these Indian operations, the Court announced at the General Meeting in February 1868 that it had invested £100,000 in Indian Government paper; a year later the Chairman announced that the entire Reserve Fund was so invested. To handle transactions of any magnitude the Bank obviously had to have offices in Calcutta and Bombay, but their function, as the Bank's Chairman put it in the end-1868 report, was 'strictly confined to Exchange, the Bank not in any way entering into transactions of a local character', the Court have previously authorized only those operations 'specifically initiated or sanctioned by the Head Office' – and Kresser had confirmed that Stevenson's instructions included this stricture. In 1866 there had been 24 banks in Bombay and 22 in Calcutta undertaking exchange business; in 1867, of these 46 banks, only 7 remained. The Court's cautious approach was understandable, but eventually the rules were relaxed and the Hongkong Bank played a role, though relatively modest, in the finance of Indian trade and industry.

The Bank of Rotterdam withdrew from Singapore and Batavia in 1873, but the Court, as if to stress the Bank's self-definition of its region, did not in this period press to open in Singapore. Although the question of a Bank-staffed agency in Singapore was agreed in principle as early as 1869, the Court did not pursue the matter, apparently considering that the Straits Settlements belonged to another region. Certainly it was not required for exchange operations, and as yet the Straits had not developed economically significant connections with China through the overseas Chinese. Nor did the Bank yet venture north of the Yangtze or into the international political uncertainties of Korea. In the tradition of British overseas banking the Hongkong Bank's region was restricted and well-defined but, even within this region, expansion would be both cautious and consciously based on changing trade patterns and requirements. In these early years new agencies had to show their role in the context of a financial and trading complex of which either Hong Kong or Shanghai was the hub.

Developments in Britain

One of the many questions the British Treasury considered in the granting of Royal charters was the role of the exchange banks in London. In general the charters limited the scope of their operations in England to those necessary in connection with banking operations in their main geographical area. Thus the chartered banks could not undertake general banking in the United Kingdom. Courts had been liberal in interpreting this restriction, but it is clear that there were limits, and the Agra and United Service Bank had combined, fatally as it turned out, with Masterman, Peters, Mildred and Co. in order to gain access to the London clearing house.

The Hongkong Bank's ordinance, for reasons already discussed, did not touch on the matter and apparently the Bank's expanding operations in London were never challenged. As a small beginning, in May 1867 the Court of Directors accepted their London Agent's recommendation that he be styled 'manager'.

The Edinburgh agency

Even before the depreciation of silver in terms of gold, the Bank sought to obtain funds in Britain to finance its bill operations; accordingly at an early date agents were appointed in Edinburgh to attract Scottish deposits. With the breakup of the partnership that had handled the Bank's affairs and with the retirement from the East of Robert Stevenson, the Court in 1874 took the opportunity to state their intention of opening a Bank-staffed agency in Scotland's capital, with the former Bombay Agent in charge. There is no record that this was ever accomplished and, by 1881/82 at the latest, Stevenson would appear to have dropped from the story. James Hill, the surviving partner of the original agents, was proving troublesome. As the then London Manager, David McLean, felt the business could be handled from the London Office, the Edinburgh operation was closed until the Bank's establishment of a branch in the Scottish capital in 1977.[16]

Meanwhile relations with the London and County Bank, the Hongkong Bank's London correspondents, continued to develop. As the Bank expanded its activities to include the finance of the China trade with India and Australia and development of the triangular pattern described above, the Bank requested additional accommodation from the London and County Bank. Indeed in February 1869 the London and County Bank suggested that the Hongkong Bank seek additional facilities from another London bank.[17] The loss of control over the Hongkong Bank's operations which would have resulted from this advice was sufficiently obvious that within a month the London and County Bank reversed itself and agreed to an extension of facilities on the condition that the Hongkong Bank not deal with any other London correspondent.[18] From this point on the London and County Bank's records show a continued series of letters negotiating various extensions of facilities, and special and temporary arrangements, in fact a sound and developing business relationship which has continued with the eventual successor National Westminster, which, as previously noted, remains the Hongkong Bank's London clearing bank.

One could argue that the Hongkong Bank's sound relations with the London and County Bank for a time obscured the need for a London Committee. In 1871, for example, when the Court was considering renting 24 Lombard Street for three years at £2,300 per annum with the option to renew at £2,500 and authority to sub-let excess office space, the Court recorded the approval of the London and County Bank. They were also consulted with reference to the Bank's involvement in the Bank's first public China loan of 1874, a matter to be considered in the next chapter.

The London share register

The Provisional Committee of the Hongkong Bank had secured a constituency by careful allotment of shares to potential customers (constituents) and by providing for share registers first at Hong Kong and then at Shanghai and Calcutta. The decision to raise additional capital in 1866 provided another opportunity for controlled allotment. There is no record, however, as to when this thorough vetting of ownership ceased, but there was specific provision in the Deed of Settlement for such control, including the limitation of the number of shares which may be beneficially owned by any one shareholder.

Trading in Bank shares was presumably freed from formal scrutiny, transaction by transaction, in 1867. A strongly worded minute dated September 1874 shows that the concept of control had not lapsed; an angry Court of

Directors claimed that a George McBain had been circulating rumours to depress the share and instructed the Chief Manager to close his account. McBain was not, the Court added, a desirable person to be allowed to hold any of the Bank's shares in his name.

In July 1867 the Court instructed its London Agent, W.H. Vacher, and the Bank's counsel, E.H. Pollard, to nominate a London Committee and to make arrangements to have the Bank's shares quoted on the Stock Exchange. There is the assumption that these two instructions are linked, that is, a Stock Exchange listing required the existence of a London Committee. However as late as 1874 the Court resisted the appointment of such a committee, although the shares had been listed since 1867. The only condition set by the Stock Exchange Committee would seem to have been that shares once transferred to the London register should not be transferred back to the East, the purpose presumably being to ensure a minimum number available on the London market, although the Stock Exchange Minute Book merely records the 'marking' of 5,000 old and 5,000 new shares of the Hongkong Bank's 40,000.[19] This at least was the interpretation of the Court of Directors. As an alternative the Court resolved at their December 1867 meeting that a required minimum of shares, without 'marking', would be kept on the London register. This policy was adopted without, apparently, any Stock Exchange objection.

The shares were required to be assigned a nominal value in sterling, and the Hong Kong dollar value of $125 was converted, at the rate of 4s:6d, to £28.125 (£28:2s:6d). As dividends were declared as a percentage of the paid-up capital calculated at the par rate of 4s:6d, shareholders consequently received non-comparable amounts depending on whether their shares were on the London or Hong Kong register and whether the exchange was above or below 4s:6d. By 1875 these differences had become intolerable and the directors decided to state the dividend as a fixed sum. The directors were advised, rightly or wrongly, that if dividends were declared in dollars they would be payable in London to shareholders with shares on the London register at the same rate of exchange, 4s:6d; their purposes would thus be frustrated, especially when the trend of falling exchanges became apparent and silver entered its long decline.

For the time, the unequal dividends proved acceptable. The solution to the Board's problem was not found until 1876, as described in Chapter 8. Meanwhile a decision to authorize the London Office by cable to pay dividends simultaneously with Hong Kong was a minor but welcomed improvement, and provision was made for a second Corporate seal to be used by the London Manager.

THE HONGKONG BANK'S EARLY RELATIONS WITH GOVERNMENTS

To pick up another thread from the Prospectus, the Bank was to be similar to an Indian Presidency bank, which implied close connections with, but not in this case shareholding by, the Hong Kong Government; by extension it implied such connections with the government of any territory in which the Bank operated. Even before incorporation the Bank had extended to the Hong Kong Government a credit line of $100,000; in the period under discussion two developments require particular attention, (i) the Bank's offer to save the Hong Kong Mint and (ii) the question of the deposit of government funds.

Informal contacts with the Hong Kong Government were doubtless facilitated by the presence, at different times, of Bank directors and officers on the Legislative Council – the directors Thomas Sutherland, Francis Chomley, John Dent, Jas. P. Duncanson, R. Rowett, and the Chief Manager, James Greig. On the other hand, relations do not seem to have been hampered by the very visible foreign leadership existing in the Bank from time to time, and this subject would never appear to have been mentioned in despatches from the Governor to the authorities in London.

As for China, the Court was from time to time called upon to make policy decisions on tentative proposals or feelers from the local authorities at Foochow, culminating eventually in China's first publicly issued loan, the Chinese Imperial Government 8% Foochow Loan of 1874 for £627,615, equal at the agreed but arbitrary exchange rate of 2 million taels.

In Shanghai a reorganization of the Shanghai Recreation Fund, a product of the land speculation of the early 1860s, was ordered by the Supreme Court in 1874, and the Manager of the Hongkong Bank was *ex officio* one of the four trustees. It was financial support from this fund which made possible the reclamation of the land in front of the British Consulate-General as a park for the use of foreigners; the park today remains a Shanghai landmark.

In 1875 the Bank also concluded an agreement to lend $176,000 to the Government of Macau. The loan was for five years, secured on the revenues of Macau and, secondarily, on the revenues of Portugal.

In Japan, however, the Oriental Bank remained the agents and advisers to the various authorities, and although the advice of Robert Brett, John Grigor, Thomas Jackson, and John Walter was added on specific issues and the Hongkong Bank was closely involved with the financing of bullion shipments to the Osaka Mint, its real role in that fast developing country began in the period after 1876.[20] Indeed, the Hongkong Bank's involvement with financing China's Taiwan defences precluded financing arms shipments to Japan, and the Court in September 1874 sent John Walter to Yokohama to cancel the arrangements already made with Messrs E. Fischer and Co. Meanwhile the Bank contented itself with establishing its agencies and with surviving – a goal not achieved by the other British exchange banks. Consequently with the closing of the Mercantile Bank in 1984, the Hongkong Bank, which was already the oldest continuously operating (the Pacific War excepted) foreign bank, is today the doyen of the foreign banks in Japan.

The Bank and the Hong Kong Government – the Mint

One of the promises of the Prospectus was currency reform and, indeed, the Hongkong Bank and the Mint were spoken of together when this subject was discussed. The Mint would turn out a standard dollar coin and reliable subsidiary coins accepted throughout the East, the Hongkong Bank would issue banknotes in denominations of $5 or more, and the foreign merchants would thereby be released from the tyranny of the compradoric system – the control of cash transactions by the compradore and his staff.

Unfortunately, the assumptions on which an economical operation of the Mint were based depended on rates of exchange which would bring silver to the Mint for coinage at a 2% seigniorage. By early 1868 the heavy overheads of the Mint had, in the absence of such exchange rates and with the consequent under-utilization of the Mint, placed a heavy financial burden on a Colony whose revenues had fallen due to a decline in land prices and whose expenditures had increased due to payment of the defence subsidy. Indeed, these were the problems which had driven the Government to obtain the 1866 credit from the Hongkong Bank.

In February 1868 the Governor, Sir Richard MacDonnell, obtained authority from London to close the Mint unless public sentiment were opposed and, at the same time, willing to meet the costs from local sources. Accordingly the Governor called a meeting of members of his Executive Council and the bankers to ask if the latter, who in a sense would have the benefit, were willing to subsidize operations. The Chartered Mercantile and the Hongkong Bank meanwhile placed sufficient orders with the Mint to pay its way for two months – time to (i) receive replies from the bankers and (ii) give notice to the Mint staff. The Governor was realistic.

The sense of the meeting was summed up, pithily in the Governor's opinion, by W. Jackson, manager of the Chartered Mercantile Bank, who is reported as stating that, 'as a banker, he would be glad that the Mint should continue open, but as a colonist, he would say decidedly that the Mint ought to be closed.'[21]

There was no support for continued subsidy of the Mint from public funds, and the only real question was whether the exchanges were likely to turn thus making it profitable for silver to be imported and leave a margin to pay the seigniorage, and, if so, whether even then sufficient silver would be brought to the Mint for coinage.

The bankers left the meeting and replied separately. William Kaye, manager of the Chartered Bank and later Sub-Manager of the London Office of the Hongkong Bank, felt that there was insufficient reason even to refer the matter to his directors in London. The Chartered Mercantile Bank confirmed that it was unable to assist; the Oriental Bank did not reply, and only the Comptoir d'Escompte made a gesture by offering an annual subscription of $3,000 towards meeting the deficit.[22]

At this point Victor Kresser, who had earlier expressed the view that the exchanges would not change for some time to come, put forward a comprehensive proposal from the Hongkong Bank. The Bank would agree to contribute $60,000 per annum, for a maximum $300,000 over five years provided that the Mint coin 25,000 dollars daily (or their equivalent in subsidiary coins) on the following conditions:

[The Bank] to have exclusive control of the coinage and profits accruing therefrom, with the power to raise the seigniorage on dollars to 2.1 per cent (pre-melting charges included); to regulate the issue of subsidiary coins and to undertake any lawful work on account of foreign Governments upon such terms as they may think proper.[23]

The Lords of the Treasury reacted sharply: 'They would consider to be objectionable any arrangement which would place the coinage, in any of Her Majesty's possessions, under the control of private individuals or commercial firms.'[24]

The Bank insisted that they should study with the Government means of reducing costs. This was non-controversial. But the Bank also called for (i) the exclusive right to issue banknotes in Hong Kong for a period of five years, and (ii) the right to hold all government funds for the same period. The former was inadmissible from the start and was so characterized both by the Governor and the Colonial Office. A colonial government might be empowered to take over the task of issuing notes, in which case it could by ordinance prevent all the chartered banks from exercising their note-issuing privileges, but it could not authorize a monopoly in favour of any one bank.

The Bank was playing for high stakes merely to keep the Mint open for another five years – in case something turned up. The Government refused the terms and Kresser replied that the proposal consequently 'must fall to the ground'.[25] Nevertheless, the Bank had made a daring response. At least Government could never complain, as it did of the Oriental, that the Bank did not react. The Hongkong Bank could be depended upon to react, to advise, to play a role in the community. It was, after all, the local bank.

The Mint was closed, the machinery sold to Japan and the building to Wahee Smith and Co. to be used as a sugar refinery. With both the new Japanese Mint and the sugar refinery the Bank established financial relations, the first brought it good will and remunerative business, the second near disaster. Meanwhile the coinage remained in chaos, and the Hongkong Bank tried another solution, the issue of one-dollar banknotes. Approved by the Governor in Council in 1872, the issue of banknotes of a denomination less than $5 brought down on both Governor and Bank the full wrath of the Treasury, but, backed (somewhat unwillingly) by its rivals in Hong Kong and supported by public sentiment, the Hongkong Bank fought a rearguard action, limiting the damage the Treasury's attitude would cause.

The Bank and Hong Kong Government funds

In May 1872 the Government of Hong Kong transferred its current account from the Oriental Bank to the Hongkong and Shanghai Banking Corporation. Government fixed deposits were distributed with the Hongkong Bank holding $342,285 at 5%, the Chartered Mercantile $30,000 also at 5%, and the Oriental $40,000 at only 4%. But handling the current monies made the Hongkong Bank, only seven years after its founding, the Government's banker.

As recently as 1869 the Oriental had agreed with the Government on terms to continue its hold on the Colony's funds; the Oriental was to pay 2% but the balance was to be maintained above $35,000. This proved inconvenient. When the Government decided to open a second current account, they were informed that, virtually as a concession, the Oriental would treat the two accounts as one for purposes of the minimum balance but reduce the interest to 1%. This enabled the Governor to reopen the question, and, as he wrote to the Secretary of State in London:

I have not been slow to enter into an agreement with the Hongkong and Shanghai Banking Corporation by which the current account will be kept with them and two per cent will be allowed on the minimum daily balances. There is no condition as to the amount at which that balance must be kept. . . . The Executive Council were firmly of opinion that the opportunity of obtaining the more favourable terms of the Hongkong and Shanghai Bank should be seized without delay, and as that Bank stands on such a sound basis, and is accounted so highly in commercial circles, I had no hesitation in agreeing to what I have reported.[26]

The Hongkong Bank was earning a reputation for cooperation. But then it could use the funds, and a bank cannot sensibly pay interest for funds it does not require in its business. As far as the Oriental was concerned, this was virtually saying that it could no longer compete locally.

The close connections of the Bank with the Hong Kong Government would lead to informal discussions which are not necessarily in the public records. As the acting Auditor General put it in 1889, '. . . the amount of gratuitous assistance we received from the Hongkong and Shanghai Bank is very considerable'.[27] As an example, there is correspondence in 1868 explaining that the Hongkong Bank made practical proposals to assist the Post Office's money order remittances in a way both beneficial to the Post Office and the public and remunerative to the Bank.[28] This was a formula for success.

Treasury Chest business in China and Japan

The agreement with the Hong Kong Government covered only the current funds of the Colony. In June 1874 the Court noted, however, that the Bank had been successful in obtaining H.M. Government's Treasury Chest business in China; the Bank had become bankers to the Diplomatic and Consular Services and to the armed services, to the extent included within the term 'Treasury Chest'.

In 1869 the Treasury had called for tenders and, since the other terms offered were virtually identical, the contract had been awarded to the Chartered Mercantile Bank on the basis of the higher interest rate that bank was willing to pay on minimum balances. The contract was thereby transferred from the Oriental for a differential of $\frac{1}{2}\%$. Before considering the tenders the Treasury minuted the present value of the various banks' shares: at that time, in common with the others, the Hongkong Bank's were at a premium, its London registered shares, £28.125 (£28:2s:6d) par, being quoted at £37, a 32% premium over par.[29]

But the Hongkong Bank confused the issue by presenting different tenders in Hong Kong and London, the former from Kresser through the Hong Kong Government secretariat. The Hong Kong authorities explained to the Treasury that this procedure was necessary because the Bank had its Head Office in Hong Kong rather than London. Meanwhile Vacher, the London Manager, had also sent in a tender, presumably on his own responsibility – and on less favourable terms. If the Hongkong Bank were to be taken seriously in City or Imperial affairs, its London Office would have to assume certain head office responsibilities on a coordinated basis. That the Hongkong Bank could accomplish this without either abdicating to the City or moving its head office to the Imperial capital constitutes an achievement which will require closer examination in the days of Thomas Jackson and David McLean.

Although the terms of the Bank's 1874 Agreement with the Treasury are not available, one may assume them to be identical to those of the Bank's successful 1878 tender, which in turn closely resembles, except in the rate of interest offered, their unsuccessful 1869 bid.

In its 1869 tender the Hongkong Bank stipulated that it have the monopoly of the business during the period of the contract, a typical but wholly unnecessary demand. The Treasury Agreement was exclusive, but the Hongkong Bank never neglected an opportunity. The 1878 correspondence is not to hand, and the exclusive arrangement is inferred by the Agreement itself.[30] This stated, *inter alia*, the account was to be held at Hong Kong, interest payable on the minimum monthly balance at $4\frac{1}{2}\%$ per annum, no commission to be charged and brokerage only when actually incurred, charges for shipment of specie only when the Bank makes an actual outlay, receipt and payment to be made by weight without charge, dollars when required at the consular ports in China or Japan to be supplied (if procurable) at the rate of the day, negotiation for all bills relative to movement of funds to be conducted by Treasury Chest officers, and strict confidentiality to be maintained. Furthermore, 'Upon like terms as all the foregoing, the Bank shall, while this Agreement continues in force, wherever it may have its Branches in China or Japan, conduct any Business within the limits of its charter, which may be required on account of the Imperial Treasury.'[31]

These negotiations had taken place in London and the Agreement was signed by McLean, the London Manager.

The Treasury, having twice refused a revision of the Bank's charter or ordinance, was now acting on the basis that the Bank had the capacity to accept responsibilities which assumed branches and agencies outside the Colony of Hong Kong, although admittedly in China or Japan, foreign countries with which Britain had treaties granting extraterritorial jurisdiction. This geographical qualification, however, had more to do with the Bank's actual capacity, which was, as a matter of fact, negligible outside this area, rather than with the theory of the Hong Kong legislature's extraterritorial jurisdiction and the related implications relative to the provisions of the Bank's ordinance.

Loans to China[32]

The Court of Directors had confirmed as early as 1867 that the Hongkong Bank was in 'regular banking' and ruled that loans for long periods should be referred for its consideration. This would also apply to clean loans proposed on the signature of government officials.

In 1867 and 1868 there were two loans arranged, by his merchant-agent in Shanghai, Hu Kwang-yung, on behalf of Tso Tsung-t'ang, then Governor-General (or Viceroy) of Shensi and Kansu, for his Northwest campaigns. There is no indication that the Hongkong Bank participated.

Then in 1869–1870 there were rumours that a third and larger loan would be raised, this time for Ts4 million, also to be arranged in Shanghai. The Hongkong Bank's Court of Directors authorized the Chief Manager to participate to the extent of $1 million – although some directors argued for a limit of $750,000 – at an interest of 14%, subject to approval of the loan signified by an Imperial edict and a security based on the customs revenue, both conditions being an early recognition of the importance of Imperial sanction and of the security provided by the Imperial Maritime Customs. The negotiations would be the Bank's first contacts with Hu Kwang-yung, a merchant and banker, who would later be characterized by (Sir) Robert Hart, the Inspector-General of the IMC, as the 'great friend of the Hongkong Bank'.[33]

The loan was never made and there is nothing further in the Court's minutes relative to Chinese Government loans until 1874, when negotiations in Foochow for China's first publicly issued loan reached their final stages. But it is true that small, short-term loans to provincial authorities would not necessarily come before the full Court if they conformed to the regulations of the Bank or were sufficiently routine to be handled by the Court's Standing Committee.

The Foochow Loan was finalized in two agreements, signed on November 28, 1874, and June 5, 1875, for a total of £627,615, and is discussed in more detail in Chapter 14. As far as policy is concerned, the Court had to consider the position of its London correspondent, the London and County Bank, and their willingness to include the bonds resulting from such a loan as cover against credit they had extended to the Hongkong Bank. Advised by the London and County Bank to act only as agents for the Chinese Government, the Hongkong Bank had then to determine the terms and conditions which would be acceptable in the London market. This led to the conclusion that the Bank had to ensure the loan was secured on the customs revenues on a basis approved by an Imperial edict.

But typically the Hongkong Bank also attempted to secure a monopoly position and in the preliminary agreement such a clause was in fact included. Protested by the manager of the Oriental Bank to Thomas F. Wade, the British Minister in Peking, the clause was also found objectionable by Robert Hart.[34] The clause did not appear in the final agreements.

While the negotiations for the Hongkong Bank's Imperial Chinese Government 8% 'Foochow' Loan of 1874 were continuing, the Bank's Agent in Foochow, Alexander Leith, received a request from the Foochow Arsenal in September 1874 for an advance of $285,000 for two months at 12% per annum against the seals of various local officials and the guarantee of the local Man Kin Bank. The Court of Directors in approving the loan began to set precedents which would be guidelines, not binding requirements, for future negotiations. A.F. Heard reported that the loan was actually concluded.[35]

In 1875 two further loans were sought by the Arsenal on guarantees similar to those of September 1874, and in April the Court agreed to lend 100,000 taels for three months at 12%. In May the Court agreed to what was apparently a credit line of $500,000 a year and refused to consider a one million tael, two-year loan to the Foochow authorities at 11–11½%. In 1876 three further loans were in fact negotiated, for 100,000 taels for three months at 12% in March, for 200,000 taels in April, and for 500,000 in May.

With the exception of the publicly issued loan, these operations can hardly be described as satisfactory in themselves. Assisting China's modernization through financing the Foochow Arsenal was no doubt attractive in a general sense, but James Greig, then Chief Manager, pointed out 'the great undesirability of locking up the Bank's funds for so long a time in unconvertible security'.[36] The Bank in 1874–1875 was not in a position to be expansive, but Leith was urged to maintain friendly relations with the local officials despite the Bank's unwillingness to meet all their requirements.

These are not particularly dramatic beginnings for a bank which, at least until the outbreak of World War II, was to feature internationally as the leader in China finance. While reserving these developments to later chapters, a few introductory comments belong here.

The Prospectus of the Hongkong Bank had been relatively modest, when compared, for example, with that of the 'Imperial Bank of China' – the one promoted unsuccessfully by Robert Montgomery Martin in 1864.[37] Despite Western expectations of Chinese railway development, despite the formation of the China Railways Company in 1865, there was nothing tangible that a court of bank directors could consider. Nor, had the Chinese been otherwise receptive, would this particular company have inspired their confidence; John Dent and George Lyall on the eve of their bankruptcies were the leading promoters; A.F. Heard considered the most noted of the company's directors, Sir Macdonald Stephenson of Indian Railway fame, a 'humbug'.[38]

China development finance was not, then, part of the immediate rationale of the Bank's founding. Nevertheless, the Hongkong Bank once *in situ* was available, and, as merchant houses fell, the gold price of silver declined, and many London-based exchange banks retreated, it became pre-eminent in the field.

In the period to 1874 the merchant houses, including Augustine Heard and Co., whose senior partner in China sat on the Hongkong Bank's Court, remained very much involved. The legitimate hopes of the merchant were that assistance in small financial requirements might lead to a larger contract involving the actual supply of development goods, rails, telegraph equipment, ships, etc. But this, which must surely be, they thought, around the corner, was ever in the future. To meet purely financial demands the merchant had, contrary to all principles, to tie up funds. The small loans could not be issued to the public, although they might be shared with 'friends'; larger loans required formal agreements with financial 'syndicates', which, when the merchant actually approached with the proposal, might prove illusory. In brief, the merchants did not have ready access to funds for China loans; the banks, potentially at least, did.

The London-based banks had other problems; their directors were not on the scene, the local manager had to compete with other voices who might have the ear of the Board, and their capital and their major sources of funds were denominated in gold units of account.

The Hongkong Bank won the contracts and then the confidence of the Hong Kong and, to an extent, the Home Governments. Similarly, in China the Bank cooperated where possible and was seen by the authorities as flexible and available. The Hongkong Bank, it was said, understood how to negotiate with the Chinese. Since no senior member of the Bank's staff – until the Peking management of E. Guy Hillier and, to a lesser extent, Charles S. Addis from the mid-1880s – spoke adequate Chinese or had any grounding in the country's history or culture, and since the regular business with Chinese customers was handled through compradores, it is difficult to give precision to or a specific defence of this claim.

Let the defence be built up in the history.

For the present it is sufficient to note that 'understanding' did not imply violating sound banking practices, but it did require some knowledge of the structure of the Chinese Government, of the practical limits to foreign influence, and of the need to accommodate to meet Chinese financial preconceptions. At the same time the Bank was willing to recommend alternatives which, while respecting the wishes of their constituent – Imperial China – would make the proposal more acceptable in Western capital markets.

As important as 'understanding' was the fact that the Hongkong Bank had funds to advance in anticipation of the concluding of an agreement. The Bank's few but strategically located offices made it possible to meet sudden official demands for specie or bullion.

When the China loans became of higher value and required coordination with London, both the Chinese Government and the Hongkong Bank had established themselves there with sufficient authority to permit the Bank to compete successfully with London-based rivals and merchant banks. The Bank's reluctant but steady development in London was to pay off.

APPENDIX: CHANGES IN THE PROVISIONAL COMMITTEE AND BOARD OF DIRECTORS

A The Provisional Committee

6 August 1864

F. Chomley	Dent and Co.	Chairman
*Thomas Sutherland	Super. P&O SN Co.	
A.F. Heard	Augustine Heard and Co.	
G.F. Maclean	Lyall, Still and Co.	
Douglas Lapraik		
*W. Nissen	Siemssen and Co.	
*H.B. Lemann	Gilman and Co.	
W. Schmidt	Fletcher and Co.	
Arthur Sassoon	D. Sassoon, Sons and Co.	
Robert Brand	Smith, Kennedy and Co.	
Pallanjee Framjee	P. and A. Camajee and Co.	
Wm Adamson	Manager, Borneo Co.	
G.J. Helland	John Burd and Co.	
Rustomjee Dhunjeeshaw	P.F. Cama and Co.	

14 members

* = members of sub-committee for *ad hoc* assignments.

28 November 1864: a Shanghai 'Provisional' Committee is in existence.

9 January 1865: first direction of company to be same as Provisional Committee until 1 July 1866; Chomley elected Chairman 12 to 1 (Heard); Sutherland, Deputy Chairman, 7 to 5 (Heard) and 1 (Lemann)

21 January 1865: term of first directors extended to 31 Dec. 1866

26 January 1865: Brand and Adamson resign as directors, i.e. not from Provisional Committee. Adamson states he is leaving colony.
Directors to be 12 maximum and Deed of Settlement will require 7 minimum.

B Court of Directors, Hongkong and Shanghae Banking Company, Ltd.

2 March 1865

F. Chomley	Dent and Co.	Chairman
*Thomas Sutherland	Super. P&O SN Co.	Deputy Chairman
A.F. Heard	Augustine Heard and Co.	
G.F. Maclean	Lyall, Still and Co.	
Douglas Lapraik		
*W. Nissen	Siemssen and Co.	
H.B. Lemann	Gilman and Co.	
W. Schmidt	Fletcher and Co.	

APPENDIX TO CHAPTER 5 (*cont.*)

*Arthur Sassoon	D. Sassoon, Sons and Co.
Pallanjee Framjee	P. and A. Camajee and Co.
G.J. Helland	John Burd and Co.
Rustomjee Dhunjeeshaw	P.F. Cama and Co.
12 members	

A committee of three directors established to advise the managing officers of the Bank and to inspect the accounts. In subsequent years the actual membership varies. Voting for the first committee was as follows: Sutherland 9, Sassoon 8, Nissen 5, Maclean 4, Lemann 3, Chomley 3, Helland 1. Members are indicated by an asterisk.

12 April 1865

Waldemar Schmidt resigns – due to failure of Fletcher and Co.?

F. Chomley	Dent and Co.	Chairman
*Thomas Sutherland	Super. P&O SN Co.	Deputy Chairman
A.F. Heard	Augustine Heard and Co.	
G.F. Maclean	Lyall, Still and Co.	
Douglas Lapraik		
*W. Nissen	Siemssen and Co.	
H.B. Lemann	Gilman and Co.	
*Arthur Sassoon	D. Sassoon, Sons and Co.	
Pallanjee Framjee	P. and A. Camajee and Co.	
G.J. Helland	John Burd and Co.	
Rustomjee Dhunjeeshaw	P.F. Cama and Co.	
11 members		

From 17 May 1865 to 19 December 1865 inclusive Thomas Sutherland is Acting Chairman of the company.

4 November 1865

Rustomjee Dhunjeeshaw resigns due to position of Cama and Co.

F. Chomley	Dent and Co. (on leave)	Chairman
*Thomas Sutherland	Super. P&O SN Co.	Acting Chairman
A.F. Heard	Augustine Heard and Co.	
G.F. Maclean	Lyall, Still and Co.	
Douglas Lapraik		
*W. Nissen	Siemssen and Co.	
H.B. Lemann	Gilman and Co. (leave granted for one year)	
*Arthur Sassoon	D. Sassoon, Sons and Co.	
Pallanjee Framjee	P. and A. Camajee and Co.	
G.J. Helland	John Burd and Co.	
10 members (8 effective)		

23 January 1866

H.W. Wood of Borneo Company elected vice Dhunjeeshaw

Hon. F. Chomley	Dent and Co. (on leave)	Chairman
*Thomas Sutherland	Super. P&O SN Co.	Deputy Chairman
A.F. Heard	Augustine Heard and Co.	

APPENDIX TO CHAPTER 5 (*cont.*)

G.F. Maclean	Lyall, Still and Co.
Douglas Lapraik	
*W. Nissen	Siemssen and Co.
(H.B. Lemann	Gilman and Co.)
*Arthur Sassoon	D. Sassoon, Sons and Co.
Pallanjee Framjee	P. and A. Camajee and Co.
G.J. Helland	John Burd and Co.
H.W. Wood	Manager, Borneo Company

    11 members (10 effective)

18 April 1866

Caleb T. Smith of Smith, Archer and Co. elected

Hon. F. Chomley	Dent and Co. (on leave)	Chairman
*Thomas Sutherland	Super. P&O SN Co.	Deputy Chairman
A.F. Heard	Augustine Heard and Co.	
G.F. Maclean	Lyall, Still and Co.	
Douglas Lapraik		
*W. Nissen	Siemssen and Co.	
(H.B. Lemann	Gilman and Co.)	
*Arthur Sassoon	D. Sassoon, Sons and Co.	
Pallanjee Framjee	P. and A. Camajee and Co.	
G.J. Helland	John Burd and Co.	
H.W. Wood	Borneo Company	
Caleb T. Smith	Smith, Archer and Co.	

    12 members (11 effective)

23 April 1866

Chomley retires, John Dent elected director and Chairman, and Sutherland leaving Colony, so Nissen elected Deputy Chairman, all as of 1 May 1866. However, exceptionally, Sutherland does not resign until 18 November 1867 when he leaves China. His name is therefore in parenthesis as on leave.

8 May 1866

John Dent	John Dent and Co.	Chairman
*W. Nissen	Siemssen and Co.	Deputy Chairman
A.F. Heard	Augustine Heard and Co.	
G.F. Maclean	Lyall, Still and Co.	
Douglas Lapraik		
(H.B. Lemann	Gilman and Co.)	
*Arthur Sassoon	D. Sassoon, Sons and Co.	
Pallanjee Framjee	P. and A. Camajee and Co.	
G.J. Helland	John Burd and Co.	
H.W. Wood	Borneo Company	
Caleb T. Smith	Smith, Archer and Co.	
(Thomas Sutherland)		

    12 members (10 effective)

APPENDIX TO CHAPTER 5 (*cont.*)

17 July 1866
Wood transfers to Shanghai, Framjee leaving Colony. Lemann has returned from leave and is elected to sub-committee.

John Dent	John Dent and Co.	Chairman
*W. Nissen	Siemssen and Co.	Deputy Chairman
A.F. Heard	Augustine Heard and Co.	
G.F. Maclean	Lyall, Still and Co.	
Douglas Lapraik		
*H.B. Lemann	Gilman and Co.	
*Arthur Sassoon	D. Sassoon, Sons and Co.	
G.J. Helland	John Burd and Co.	
Caleb T. Smith	Smith, Archer and Co.	
(Thomas Sutherland)		

   10 members (9 effective)

13 August 1866
Douglas Lapraik resigns on leaving Colony.

John Dent	John Dent and Co.	Chairman
*W. Nissen	Siemssen and Co.	Deputy Chairman
A.F. Heard	Augustine Heard and Co.	
G.F. Maclean	Lyall, Still and Co.	
*H.B. Lemann	Gilman and Co.	
*Arthur Sassoon	D. Sassoon, Sons and Co.	
G.J. Helland	John Burd and Co.	
Caleb T. Smith	Smith, Archer and Co.	
(Thomas Sutherland)		

   9 members (8 effective)

25 September 1866
Shanghai Committee of Advice and Inspection: Turing, Tyson, and Duncanson. Maclean's last meeting was 21 August 1866, presumably due to failure of Lyall, Still and Co.
Election of W.H. Forbes of Russell and Co. but does not attend (and presumably does not accept) until 29 December 1866 meeting.

C   *Court of Directors, The Hongkong and Shanghai Banking Corporation*

---

29 December 1866

John Dent	John Dent and Co.	Chairman
*W. Nissen	Siemssen and Co.	Deputy Chairman
A.F. Heard	Augustine Heard and Co.	
*H.B. Lemann	Gilman and Co.	
*Arthur Sassoon	D. Sassoon, Sons and Co.	
G.J. Helland	John Burd and Co.	
Caleb T. Smith	Smith, Archer and Co.	
W.H. Forbes	Russell and Co.	
(Thomas Sutherland)		

   9 members (8 effective)

APPENDIX TO CHAPTER 5 (*cont.*)

21 January 1867
Forbes to resign on leaving Colony; Edward Cunningham elected to replace him, effective next meeting.

11 February 1867 Ordinary General Meeting of Shareholders
Under Art. 60 of the original Deed of Settlement all directors' terms expire and the following are reelected (note, this does not include John Dent).

E. Cunningham	Russell and Co.
A.F. Heard	Augustine Heard and Co.
George J. Helland	John Burd and Co.
H.B. Lemann	Gilman and Co.
Woldemar Nissen	Siemssen and Co.
Arthur Sassoon	D. Sassoon, Sons and Co.
Caleb Tangier Smith	Smith, Archer and Co.
(Thomas Sutherland)	
8 members	

7 March 1867
A.F. Heard resigns; G.F. Heard elected; Cunningham elected Chairman, Nissen Deputy Chairman. Sub-committee confirmed with membership unchanged.

E. Cunningham	Russell and Co.	Chairman
	(not present)	
*W. Nissen	Siemssen and Co.	Deputy Chairman
*H.B. Lemann	Gilman and Co.	
*Arthur Sassoon	D. Sassoon, Sons and Co.	
G.J. Helland	John Burd and Co.	
Caleb T. Smith	Smith, Archer and Co.	
G.F. Heard	Augustine Heard and Co.	
(Thomas Sutherland)		
8 members (7 effective)		

10 May 1867
Cunningham resigns on leaving Colony and thus apparently never presided over a Court meeting. Election of Chairman postponed.
Julius Menke of Wm Pustau and Co. attends first meeting, election authority not found.

*W. Nissen	Siemssen and Co.	Acting Chairman
*H.B. Lemann	Gilman and Co.	
*Arthur Sassoon	D. Sassoon, Sons and Co.	
G.J. Helland	John Burd and Co.	
Caleb T. Smith	Smith, Archer and Co.	
G.F. Heard	Augustine Heard and Co.	
J. Menke	Wm Pustau and Co.	
(Thomas Sutherland)		
8 members (7 effective)		

21 June 1867
Elect William H. Foster, Jr. of Russell and Co.
H.B. Lemann resigning and elected to Shanghai Committee vice Turing (resigned).

APPENDIX TO CHAPTER 5 (*cont.*)

Notice is taken of the failure of Dent and Co., so John Dent is certainly no longer a director.

*W. Nissen	Siemssen and Co.	Acting Chairman
*H.B. Lemann	Gilman and Co.	
*Arthur Sassoon	D. Sassoon, Sons and Co.	
G.J. Helland	John Burd and Co.	
Caleb T. Smith	Smith, Archer and Co.	
G.F. Heard	Augustine Heard and Co.	
J. Menke	Wm Pustau and Co.	
W.H. Foster	Russell and Co.	
(Thomas Sutherland)		
9 members (8 effective)		

Shanghai Committee of three elected: H.B. Lemann, Tyson, and Duncanson.

30 July 1867

Elect Wm Lemann in room of his brother. Nissen elected Chairman and Arthur Sassoon Deputy Chairman.
On the Standing Committee, Helland vice Lemann.

*W. Nissen	Siemssen and Co.	Chairman
*Arthur Sassoon	D. Sassoon, Sons and Co.	Deputy Chairman
G.J. Helland	John Burd and Co.	
Caleb T. Smith	Smith, Archer and Co.	
G.F. Heard	Augustine Heard and Co.	
J. Menke	Wm Pustau and Co.	
W.H. Foster	Russell and Co.	
Wm Lemann	Gilman and Co.	
(Thomas Sutherland)		
9 members (8 effective)		

13 August 1867 Ordinary General Meeting of Shareholders
All directors' terms expire and the directors are reelected as in 30 July list above, according to Art. 122 of the new Deed of Settlement.

18 October 1867

James Banks Taylor of Smith Archer replacing C.T. Smith of same company.

*W. Nissen	Siemssen and Co.	Chairman
*Arthur Sassoon	D. Sassoon, Sons and Co.	Deputy Chairman
*G.J. Helland	John Burd and Co.	
G.F. Heard	Augustine Heard and Co.	
J. Menke	Wm Pustau and Co.	
W.H. Foster	Russell and Co.	
Wm Lemann	Gilman and Co.	
J.B. Taylor	Smith, Archer and Co.	
(Thomas Sutherland)		
9 members (8 effective)		

18 November 1867
Nissen resigns on leaving Colony. Helland elected the Bank's only Norwegian Chairman as the senior member and for a term of office, i.e. until the end of 1868. These are firsts.

APPENDIX TO CHAPTER 5 (*cont.*)

Thomas Sutherland resigns, having been on leave since April 1866, and he is now leaving China.

Wm Lemann elected member of the Standing Committee.

*G.J. Helland	John Burd and Co.	Chairman
*Arthur Sassoon	D. Sassoon, Sons and Co.	Deputy Chairman
G.F. Heard	Augustine Heard and Co.	
J. Menke	Wm Pustau and Co.	
W.H. Foster	Russell and Co.	
*Wm Lemann	Gilman and Co.	
J.B. Taylor	Smith, Archer and Co.	
7 members		

18 January 1868

Arthur Sassoon resigns and his brother Solomon D. Sassoon is elected.

George F. Heard is elected Deputy Chairman.

The Standing Committee is to be composed of the Chairman, the Deputy Chairman ex officio and one other elected.

*G.J. Helland	John Burd and Co.	Chairman
*G.F. Heard	Augustine Heard and Co.	Deputy Chairman
J. Menke	Wm Pustau and Co.	
W.H. Foster	Russell and Co.	
*Wm Lemann	Gilman and Co.	
J.B. Taylor	Smith, Archer and Co.	
S.D. Sassoon	D. Sassoon, Sons and Co.	
7 members		

10 February 1868

A. Joost of Siemssen is elected vice Nissen.

*G.J. Helland	John Burd and Co.	Chairman
*G.F. Heard	Augustine Heard and Co.	Deputy Chairman
J. Menke	Wm Pustau and Co.	
W.H. Foster	Russell and Co.	
*Wm Lemann	Gilman and Co.	
J.B. Taylor	Smith, Archer and Co.	
S.D. Sassoon	D. Sassoon, Sons and Co.	
A. Joost	Siemssen and Co.	
8 members		

14 February 1868

Jas P. Duncanson (formerly of the Shanghai Committee) is elected.

*G.J. Helland	John Burd and Co.	Chairman
*G.F. Heard	Augustine Heard and Co.	Deputy Chairman
J. Menke	Wm Pustau and Co.	
W.H. Foster	Russell and Co.	
*Wm Lemann	Gilman and Co.	
J.B. Taylor	Smith, Archer and Co.	
S.D. Sassoon	D. Sassoon, Sons and Co.	
A. Joost	Siemssen and Co.	
Jas P. Duncanson	Gibb, Livingston and Co.	
9 members		

APPENDIX TO CHAPTER 5 (*cont.*)

2 March 1868
Shanghai Committee: all have resigned on leaving Shanghai. This is in fact the end
of the Committee as they are not replaced.

2 June 1868
W.H. Foster of Russell and Co. resigns and is replaced by W.H. Forbes.
R. Rowett of Holliday, Wise and Co. offered a seat.

*G.J. Helland	John Burd and Co.	Chairman
*G.F. Heard	Augustine Heard and Co.	Deputy Chairman
J. Menke	Wm Pustau and Co.	
*Wm Lemann	Gilman and Co.	
J.B. Taylor	Smith, Archer and Co.	
S.D. Sassoon	D. Sassoon, Sons and Co.	
A. Joost	Siemssen and Co.	
Jas P. Duncanson	Gibb, Livingston and Co.	
W.H. Forbes	Russell and Co.	
9 members		

17 July 1868
The decisions of 2 June are given effect.

*G.J. Helland	John Burd and Co.	Chairman
*G.F. Heard	Augustine Heard and Co.	Deputy Chairman
J. Menke	Wm Pustau and Co.	
*Wm Lemann	Gilman and Co.	
J.B. Taylor	Smith, Archer and Co.	
S.D. Sassoon	D. Sassoon, Sons and Co.	
A. Joost	Siemssen and Co.	
Jas P. Duncanson	Gibb, Livingston and Co.	
W.H. Forbes	Russell and Co.	
R. Rowett	Holliday, Wise and Co.	
10 members		

8 August 1868
E.R. Belilios asks for a seat. Has to be at Annual General Meeting as the Court
cannot add a member; it can only replace.

18 October 1868
Belilios was elected at the Annual Meeting.

*G.J. Helland	John Burd and Co.	Chairman
*G.F. Heard	Augustine Heard and Co.	Deputy Chairman
J. Menke	Wm Pustau and Co.	
*Wm Lemann	Gilman and Co.	
J.B. Taylor	Smith, Archer and Co.	
S.D. Sassoon	D. Sassoon, Sons and Co.	
A. Joost	Siemssen and Co.	
Jas P. Duncanson	Gibb, Livingston and Co.	
W.H. Forbes	Russell and Co.	
R. Rowett	Holliday, Wise and Co.	
E.R. Belilios		
11 members		

APPENDIX TO CHAPTER 5 (*cont.*)

23 December 1868
Election of Chairman for 1869, G.F. Heard; Deputy J. Menke, on seniority basis.
Standing Committee for 1869: Sassoon because of his large interest in the Bank and
Duncanson by ballot. Thomas Pyke interested in joining Court. As there was no
need to strengthen the Court now, the directors minuted they would bear his interest
in mind.

26 January 1869
As a result of the decisions of 23 December:

*G.F. Heard	Augustine Heard and Co.	Chairman
*Julius Menke	Wm Pustau and Co.	Deputy Chairman
*Wm Lemann	Gilman and Co.	
J.B. Taylor	Smith, Archer and Co.	
*S.D. Sassoon	D. Sassoon, Sons and Co.	
A. Joost	Siemssen and Co.	
*Jas P. Duncanson	Gibb, Livingston and Co.	
W.H. Forbes	Russell and Co.	
R. Rowett	Holliday, Wise and Co.	
E.R. Belilios		
G.J. Helland	John Burd and Co.	
11 members		

17 January 1870
W. Lemann resigns, elect his brother H.B. Lemann. Election of new Chairman etc.
postponed.

*G.F. Heard	Augustine Heard and Co.	Chairman
*Julius Menke	Wm Pustau and Co.	Deputy Chairman
J.B. Taylor	Smith, Archer and Co.	
*S.D. Sassoon	D. Sassoon, Sons and Co.	
A. Joost	Siemssen and Co.	
*Jas P. Duncanson	Gibb, Livingston and Co.	
W.H. Forbes	Russell and Co.	
R. Rowett	Holliday, Wise and Co.	
E.R. Belilios		
G.J. Helland	John Burd and Co.	
H.B. Lemann	Gilman and Co.	
11 members		

25 January 1870
Election: Chairman H.B. Lemann, Deputy J.B. Taylor on the expiration of the terms
of office of previous Chairman and Deputy.
Standing Committee: Chairman, Deputy, Joost and Sassoon. These are the seniors.
Jas. Duncanson has died. Replaced by Thomas Pyke.

*H.B. Lemann	Gilman and Co.	Chairman
*J.B. Taylor	Smith, Archer and Co.	Deputy Chairman
*S.D. Sassoon	D. Sassoon, Sons and Co.	
*A. Joost	Siemssen and Co.	
W.H. Forbes	Russell and Co.	
R. Rowett	Holliday, Wise and Co.	
E.R. Belilios		

APPENDIX TO CHAPTER 5 (*cont.*)

G.J. Helland	John Burd and Co.
G.F. Heard	Augustine Heard and Co.
Julius Menke	Wm Pustau and Co.
Thomas Pyke	Birley and Co.
11 members	

23 July 1870
J.B. Taylor and W.H. Forbes leaving Colony, resign.
Rowett elected Deputy Chairman vice Taylor.

*H.B. Lemann	Gilman and Co.	Chairman
*R. Rowett	Holliday, Wise and Co.	Deputy Chairman
*S.D. Sassoon	D. Sassoon, Sons and Co.	
*A. Joost	Siemssen and Co.	
E.R. Belilios		
G.J. Helland	John Burd and Co.	
G.F. Heard	Augustine Heard and Co.	
Julius Menke	Wm Pustau and Co.	
Thomas Pyke	Birley and Co.	
11 members		

30 December 1870
Election for 1871: Chairman, R. Rowett. Belilios elected Deputy but refuses on the ground that Sassoon ought to be on the Standing Committee and you do not need two on the Standing Committee in the same line of business. T. Pyke elected. No mention of Standing Committee changes, but Joost is not a member, and it is apparent from remuneration of directors for first-half 1871 that Belilios has been elected.

27 January 1871
In consequence of previous decisions:

*R. Rowett	Holliday, Wise and Co.	Chairman
*Thomas Pyke	Birley and Co.	Deputy Chairman
S.D. Sassoon	D. Sassoon, Sons and Co.	
A. Joost	Siemssen and Co.	
*E.R. Belilios		
G.J. Helland	John Burd and Co.	
G.F. Heard	Augustine Heard and Co.	
Julius Menke	Wm Pustau and Co.	
*H.B. Lemann	Gilman and Co.	
9 members		

5 April 1871
G.F. Heard resigns and is replaced by George F. Weller; H.B. Lemann resigns and his brother Wm Lemann elected, effective next meeting.

*R. Rowett	Holliday, Wise and Co.	Chairman
*Thomas Pyke	Birley and Co.	Deputy Chairman
S.D. Sassoon	D. Sassoon, Sons and Co.	
A. Joost	Siemssen and Co.	
*E.R. Belilios		
G.J. Helland	John Burd and Co.	

APPENDIX TO CHAPTER 5 (*cont.*)

G.F. Heard	Augustine Heard and Co.
Julius Menke	Wm Pustau and Co.
H.B. Lemann	Gilman and Co.
9 members	

23 May 1871
Sub-committee: Wm Lemann elected vice H.B. Lemann.

*R. Rowett	Holliday, Wise and Co.	Chairman
*Thomas Pyke	Birley and Co.	Deputy Chairman
S.D. Sassoon	D. Sassoon, Sons and Co.	
A. Joost	Siemssen and Co.	
*E.R. Belilios		
G.J. Helland	John Burd and Co.	
Julius Menke	Wm Pustau and Co.	
*Wm Lemann	Gilman and Co.	
George F. Weller	Augustine Heard and Co.	
9 members		

29 August 1871
Helland resigns on leaving Colony to settle in Denmark and Hermann Melchers is elected 'in his stead'. This suggests that Helland was considered part of the German quota – perhaps, therefore, 'Continental' quota is a more accurate term.

*R. Rowett	Holliday, Wise and Co.	Chairman
*Thomas Pyke	Birley and Co.	Deputy Chairman
S.D. Sassoon	D. Sassoon, Sons and Co.	
A. Joost	Siemssen and Co.	
*E.R. Belilios		
Julius Menke	Wm Pustau and Co.	
*Wm Lemann	Gilman and Co.	
G.F. Weller	Augustine Heard and Co.	
H. Melchers	Melchers and Co.	
9 members		

9 February 1872
W.H. Forbes again elected director effective after the annual meeting.
Election: Pyke as Chairman vice Rowett, Sassoon as Deputy. Seniority.
Standing Committee: Wm Lemann and Forbes elected.

29 February 1872
Menke resigns on leaving Colony. R. Rowett does not attend a meeting for approximately one year and is reported as having resigned before the August meeting of shareholders.

*Thomas Pyke	Birley and Co.	Chairman
*S.D. Sassoon	D. Sassoon, Sons and Co.	Deputy Chairman
A. Joost	Siemssen and Co.	
E.R. Belilios		
*Wm Lemann	Gilman and Co.	
G.F. Weller	Augustine Heard and Co.	
H. Melchers	Melchers and Co.	
*W.H. Forbes	Russell and Co.	
8 members		

APPENDIX TO CHAPTER 5 *(cont.)*

27 April 1872
Wm Lemann resigns and his brother is invited effective following meeting.

2 July 1872
H.B. Lemann accepts. A. Joost is elected, senior, to the sub-committee.

*Thomas Pyke	Birley and Co.	Chairman
*S.D. Sassoon	D. Sassoon, Sons and Co.	Deputy Chairman
*A. Joost	Siemssen and Co.	
E.R. Belilios		
G.F. Weller	Augustine Heard and Co.	
H. Melchers	Melchers and Co.	
*W.H. Forbes	Russell and Co.	
H.B. Lemann	Gilman and Co.	
8 members		

31 January 1873
Officers elected for 1873: S.D. Sassoon, Chairman; W.H. Forbes, Deputy.
To take effect after the annual meeting.

8 February 1873
Rowett reelected to the Court; taking his seat at the next meeting.

27 March 1873
Adolf von André elected vice Melchers, leaving Colony.
Weller resigned at the Annual Meeting; A.F. Heard elected.

*S.D. Sassoon	D. Sassoon, Sons and Co.	Chairman
*W.H. Forbes	Russell and Co.	Deputy Chairman
*A. Joost	Siemssen and Co.	
E.R. Belilios		
H.B. Lemann	Gilman and Co.	
*Thomas Pyke	Birley and Co.	
R. Rowett	Holliday, Wise and Co.	
A.F. Heard	Augustine Heard and Co.	
A. von André	Melchers and Co.	
9 members		

29 July 1873
Cordes applies to be director and told that he would be favourably considered the next time there is a German vacancy.

21 October 1873
Wm Lemann vice H.B. Lemann.

*S.D. Sassoon	D. Sassoon, Sons and Co.	Chairman
*W.H. Forbes	Russell and Co.	Deputy Chairman
*A. Joost	Siemssen and Co.	
E.R. Belilios		
R. Rowett	Holliday, Wise and Co.	
*Thomas Pyke	Birley and Co.	
A. von André	Melchers and Co.	

APPENDIX TO CHAPTER 5 (*cont.*)

A.F. Heard   Augustine Heard and Co.
Wm Lemann   Gilman and Co.
    9 members

2 February 1874
Joost resigns as he is leaving Colony.
Elections: W.H. Forbes, Chairman; R. Rowett, Deputy. This is not seniority. André
and Sassoon to sub-committee – effective after the annual meeting.
Hoppius applies, but told to wait for German vacancy as J.F. Cordes is filling the
present one.
*S.D. Sassoon   D. Sassoon, Sons and Co.   Chairman
 W.H. Forbes   Russell and Co.   Deputy Chairman
 E.R. Belilios
 R. Rowett   Holliday, Wise and Co.
 Thomas Pyke   Birley and Co.
 A. von André   Melchers and Co.
 A.F. Heard   Augustine Heard and Co.
 Wm Lemann   Gilman and Co.
 J.F. Cordes   Wm Pustau and Co.
    9 members

12 March 1874
The Court after the meeting is as follows:
*W.H. Forbes   Russell and Co.   Chairman
*R. Rowett   Holliday, Wise and Co.   Deputy Chairman
 E.R. Belilios
 Thomas Pyke   Birley and Co.
*Adolf von André   Melchers and Co.
 A.F. Heard   Augustine Heard and Co.
 Wm Lemann   Gilman and Co.
 J.F. Cordes   Wm Pustau and Co.
*S.D. Sassoon   D. Sassoon, Sons and Co.
    9 members

25 July 1874
Wm Lemann wants to resign owing to a Supreme Court decision relative to the
responsibilities of directors. He is asked to remain until after the Annual Meeting
and his request is refused on the basis of Art. 128 of the Deed of Settlement.

4 August 1874
Lemann 'insists' on resigning. Board agrees and elects Hoppius although this is not a
German vacancy.
Pyke announces he is leaving Colony and will resign after the Annual Meeting.
*W.H. Forbes   Russell and Co.   Chairman
*R. Rowett   Holliday, Wise and Co.   Deputy Chairman
 E.R. Belilios
 Thomas Pyke   Birley and Co.
*Adolf von André   Melchers and Co.
 A.F. Heard   Augustine Heard and Co.

APPENDIX TO CHAPTER 5 (*cont.*)

J.F. Cordes	Wm Pustau and Co.
*S.D. Sassoon	D. Sassoon, Sons and Co.
8 members	

12 August 1874
Hoppius takes his seat.

*W.H. Forbes	Russell and Co.	Chairman
*R. Rowett	Holliday, Wise and Co.	Deputy Chairman
E.R. Belilios		
*Adolf von André	Melchers and Co.	
A.F. Heard	Augustine Heard and Co.	
J.F. Cordes	Wm Pustau and Co.	
*S.D. Sassoon	D. Sassoon, Sons and Co.	
H. Hoppius	Siemssen and Co.	
8 members		

7 January 1875
S.D. Sassoon resigns and his brother F.D. Sassoon is elected effective the following meeting.

15 January 1875
R. Rowett resigns prior to leaving Hong Kong.
Election for Deputy Chairman: André vice Rowett.
Sub-committee: Heard and Hoppius vice Sassoon and Rowett.

*W.H. Forbes	Russell and Co.	Chairman
*Adolf von André	Melchers and Co.	Deputy Chairman
E.R. Belilios		
*A.F. Heard	Augustine Heard and Co.	
J.F. Cordes	Wm Pustau and Co.	
H. Hoppius	Siemssen and Co.	
F.D. Sassoon	D. Sassoon, Sons and Co.	
7 members		

30 January 1875
Board resolves on need to secure English directors.

4 February 1875
Elections effective after annual meeting: Chairman A. von André; Deputy Chairman A.F. Heard; sub-committee is elected by ballot after discussion and Belilios, Cordes, and Sassoon decline to vote – Hoppius and Sassoon elected.

12 February 1875
Resolve to appoint a London Committee to supervise the transactions of the Branch.

22 February 1875
A.F. Heard resigns both as Deputy Chairman (and thus never functions as such on the main board) and director as he is leaving the Colony but suggests one of his brothers would be a director if elected. Board accepts his resignation as Deputy

APPENDIX TO CHAPTER 5 (*cont.*)

Chairman but not as director as they would be below the minimum number.
W.H. Forbes elected Deputy Chairman vice Heard.

*Adolf von André	Melchers and Co.	Chairman
*W.H. Forbes	Russell and Co.	Deputy Chairman
A.F. Heard	Augustine Heard and Co.	
E.R. Belilios		
J.F. Cordes	Wm Pustau and Co.	
*H. Hoppius	Siemssen and Co.	
*F.D. Sassoon	D. Sassoon, Sons and Co.	
7 members		

20 April 1875

Augustine Heard and Co. have failed, so A.F. Heard no longer a director by Art. 119 of Deed of Settlement.
H. Nicaise, Manager, Borneo Co. invited to become a director.

*Adolf von André	Melchers and Co.	Chairman
*W.H. Forbes	Russell and Co.	Deputy Chairman
E.R. Belilios		
J.F. Cordes	Wm Pustau and Co.	
*H. Hoppius	Siemssen and Co.	
*F.D. Sassoon	D. Sassoon, Sons and Co.	
6 members		

11 May 1875

H. Nicaise accepts.

*Adolf von André	Melchers and Co.	Chairman
*W.H. Forbes	Russell and Co.	Deputy Chairman
E.R. Belilios		
J.F. Cordes	Wm Pustau and Co.	
*H. Hoppius	Siemssen and Co.	
*F.D. Sassoon	D. Sassoon, Sons and Co.	
H. Nicaise	Manager, Borneo Company	
7 members		

29 June 1875

Changes in the sub-committee: Belilios and André vice Sassoon and Hoppius.
Nicaise offers resignation as Borneo Company will not permit him to remain as a director – all his time is to be devoted to the company. Board refuses to accept until a substitute is found, but he does not attend meetings after this.

*Adolf von André	Melchers and Co.	Chairman
*W.H. Forbes	Russell and Co.	Deputy Chairman
*E.R. Belilios		
J.F. Cordes	Wm Pustau and Co.	
H. Hoppius	Siemssen and Co.	
F.D. Sassoon	D. Sassoon, Sons and Co.	
H. Nicaise	Borneo Company	
7 members		

APPENDIX TO CHAPTER 5 (*cont.*)

14 August 1875
Alexander McIver, who was nominated in previous meeting, has accepted and this releases Nicaise.

*Adol von André	Melchers and Co.	Chairman
*W.H. Forbes	Russell and Co.	Deputy Chairman
*E.R. Belilios		
J.F. Cordes	Wm Pustau and Co.	
H. Hoppius	Siemssen and Co.	
F.D. Sassoon	D. Sassoon, Sons and Co.	
A. McIver	P&O SN Co.	
7 members		

14 September 1875
London Committee appointed: A.H. Phillpotts, Director, London and County Bank; E.F. Duncanson, Messrs T. and A. Gibb; Albert Deacon, partner, E. and A. Deacon.

25 January 1876
Forbes resigns and S.W. Pomeroy of Russell and Co. elected effective next meeting. Election: Deputy-Chairman is E.R. Belilios, longest serving member of the Court.

3 February 1876
As a consequence of these decisions:

*Adolf von André	Melchers and Co.	Chairman
*E.R. Belilios		Deputy Chairman
J.F. Cordes	Wm Pustau and Co.	
H. Hoppius	Siemssen and Co.	
F.D. Sassoon	D. Sassoon, Sons and Co.	
A. McIver	P&O SN Co.	
S.W. Pomeroy	Russell and Co.	
7 members		

Election: E.R. Belilios as Chairman, postpone election for Deputy.
Effective after the annual meeting.

10 February 1876
Election of Deputy Chairman: after discussion agreed it should be based on seniority except in exceptional circumstances, so elect A. André.

22 February 1876
Sub-committee is cancelled.

E.R. Belilios		Chairman
Adolf von André	Melchers and Co.	Deputy Chairman
J.F. Cordes	Wm Pustau and Co.	
H. Hoppius	Siemssen and Co.	
F.D. Sassoon	D. Sassoon, Sons and Co.	
A. McIver	P&O SN Co.	
S.W. Pomeroy	Russell and Co.	
7 members		

* members of the Board's Standing Committee

6

SUCCESS, CRISIS, AND
REORGANIZATION, 1867–1876

What shareholders were crying for was to know the worst . . . We have full confidence the worst has been at last declared.

North-China Herald, 28 August 1875

The Corporation ended the half-year in June 1867 with its first intimation of any considerable trading loss. The fall of the Bank's 'founding company', Dent's, had created difficulties throughout the community and the Hongkong Bank's Chairman, Woldemar Nissen, was heard at the General Meeting of Shareholders without criticism. Indeed there was room for an expression of regret at the passing of Jardine's rival. The shareholders could afford such an attitude, for, despite the losses, the Bank was able to pay a dividend at the annual rate of 12% with sufficient remaining to add to the Reserve Fund.

If this proved the Bank were not immune to problems, it was a fact which hardly seemed relevant in the next two years as the dividend continued at 12% and the reserves grew to $800,000 by the end of 1869. Indeed at the mid-1868 meeting the Chairman, G.J. Helland, felt it necessary, in his very brief report, to defend the dividend policy:

The growing success of the Bank . . . would have justified the Court in recommending the distribution of a larger dividend . . . but, faithful to the policy to which they have always adhered, the Directors consider it more conducive to the true interests of the Corporation to continue strengthening the Reserve Fund by a liberal appropriation out of realized profits; a course of action likely to be thoroughly appreciated by the general public; and a steady perseverance in which must further raise the credit and standing of the Bank.

Six months later, George F. Heard, then Chairman, had again to stress the necessity of paying into the Reserve Fund: 'The Directors are of opinion that when the Reserve Fund shall have reached a Million of Dollars, the time will have arrived when they can with safety recommend the division of a larger proportion of the profits in the shape of Dividend . . .'

When that time came – at the February 1872 meeting – there were other things to think about.

The first real problems manifested themselves in 1870. During the first half-year's trading profits were low, but although these improved the Court had to report potential losses on securities held and set aside $268,600 in a contingent account, reducing the interim dividend to 8% on an annual basis.

The Bank picked up again, and at the end of 1871 the reserves had reached the goal of $1 million. They were to stay at this level through a difficult period through December 1873. The Bank was, however, on the margin straining its resources to pay dividends at the annual rate of 12%; in 1872, for example, the dividend was maintained only by drawing from retained earnings (or Profit and Loss Account balance), with the consequence that the payout ratio was 136% (see Table 6.2). By early 1874 the directors recognized the Bank was in difficulties and accordingly cut the year-end dividend to 8% at an annual rate. Their concern was justified but the problems were underestimated. Before mid-1874 a series of losses converged; the Reserve Fund itself was drawn on and the balance fell to $100,000 by the end of the year. No dividend was recommended at the next three half-yearly meetings.

Recovery was apparent in the latter half of 1875 when a full dividend was again declared, but not until 1876 was the Bank able to augment the reserves. Yet so strong was the revival that the Bank's reserves again reached $1 million by the end of 1877.

Had the Bank been in danger? Possibly. Succeeding chairmen announcing bad news were usually quick to point to the continued public confidence in the Bank as witnessed, for example, by the growth of deposits and the holding of banknotes. A.F. Heard had predicted, 'The Bank will succeed from its local support,' but in January 1875 he was advising an associate, 'Pay as much as possible to sell your coast and local drafts to some other bank than the Hongkong. The Bank's accounts are very bad. The dividend will not exceed 2% and the Reserve Fund will be reduced to $200,000. Don't mention it.'[1]

Yet Heard was also complaining, despite his insider knowledge of the Bank's admittedly weak condition, about the expected failure to pay a dividend – 'their illiberal policy arises from Greig's and Cameron's funk'.[2] (Cameron was McLean's successor as Shanghai Manager.)

If these were the views of a founding director, a member of the Bank's Standing Committee and Deputy Chairman elect, there must have been some validity to the view expressed in the newspapers that, had the Bank passed the dividend for the fourth half-year, there would have been a general loss of confidence. But just as the Bank's varied misfortunes converged in 1874 so its success in negotiations with the Chinese Government succeeded, and the profits from that loan, together with the writing off of the Bank's past, permitted an unburdened recovery which might legitimately be described as spectacular.

The business was always there; it was potentially profitable if well-managed. The Hongkong Bank inherited certain obligations from its Prospectus; the Bank had also to test both management systems and managers. This chapter must then, in addition to chronicling the history through the accounts, examine (i) the involvement of the Bank, its directors and its managers in specific joint-stock companies and (ii) the effectiveness of the management of the routine – if such a word is appropriate – of exchange banking. The companies have already been referred to – the Sugar Refinery or Wahee Smith and Co., the Indo-Chinese Sugar Company, and the Pier and Godown Company. And before these there had been the venture of Heard's and Dent's in the Union Dock Company. Victor Kresser, able exchange banker that he was by all contemporary accounts, was personally involved in joint-stock enterprises; James Greig, experienced as he was on the China Coast, lost the confidence of management through his handling of the Hong Kong office. Stevenson in Bombay retired in the normal course of events; the directors' faith in W.H. Vacher, the London Manager, had been misplaced; of the top management only David McLean came through.

The period from 1874 to 1876 was one of reorganization – the dismissal of Vacher in London triggered the appointment of a London Committee, strengthened the resolve for an inspector, and forced a reconsideration of the role of the Court of Directors itself. Then on February 23, 1876, the Court appointed Thomas Jackson Acting Chief Manager at the age of 35. When he left Hong Kong finally in 1902, the Hongkong Bank had become a powerful financial force in the region. But that is a story to be told in the following chapters; the date of Jackson's appointment is an appropriate point at which to end this account of the Bank's first years.

A CHRONICLE FROM THE BANK'S REPORTS AND ACCOUNTS, 1867–1873

Growth and first problems, 1867–1871

Not all growth is progress. The increase in cash in the second-half of 1867 is indicative of the dullness of trade and should be set against the fall in 'discounts, loans and credits' from $4.07 million at the end of 1866 to $3.37 million a year later. Or, more generally, the Bank's success in attracting and keeping deposits, even when interest rates were lowered, was unrelated to the demand for funds with a consequent negative impact on the Bank's profitability. Or, more obviously, the growth in loans made in order to save past investments may be, and in some cases certainly was, unsound.

By the end of 1872 the staged payment of calls on the subscribers to the new shares had been completed and the authorized $5 million of subscribed capital fully paid up. From 1867 through mid-1869 a semi-annual dividend at the annual rate of 12% cost the Bank $180,000; this rose in stages to $300,000 as the paid-up capital reached $5 million, whereas net profits did not increase consistently and certainly not to the extent necessary to sustain the Court's policy of both a 12% dividend and augmentation of reserves.

The problem lay not in the capital policy itself. The growth of the Bank after 1876 is sufficient evidence that the Bank's level of trading required a strong capital base, and, once subscribed, capital had to be paid up within the time-limit agreed by the Treasury. The initial progress of the Bank justified the payment schedule; the time-limit for payment had already been extended. Unfortunately, the increase in capital coincided with the Court's need to offset losses which were, with dull trading, responsible for the low level of allocatable profits. This combination of events suggested a modification of the dividend policy in the early 1870s. However, it was just at this time that the Reserve Fund reached the magic figure of $1 million, the point at which the Court had promised to consider recommending a higher dividend; thus remaining at the same level was seen, psychologically, as an admission of difficulties. Any lowering of the rate might have forced the exposure of problems which the directors hoped, not unreasonably but – as it turned out – wrongly, would be cured by time.

In late 1867 the Hongkong Bank's competitors were forced to return to granting bills at six-months' sight and the Bank's Chairman welcomed them back, noting that:

The position which the Corporation has acquired in the meantime with its constituents, and the considerable extension which it has occasioned to its Exchange business, an ample compensation for the cessation of the temporary advantages which the Bank derived throughout [1867], from being the only large operator on the market for six months' sight paper.

Exchange remittances as shown in the semi-annual accounts had increased from $9.2 million to $13.3 million.

In a sense the Hongkong Bank's fortunes were those of the community it served; when trading was slack the turnover of funds, which were the source of profits to an exchange bank, naturally declined; when firms failed some loss was borne by the Bank. The key indicators – exchange remittances and deposits – showed the Bank increasing proportionately its financial role in Hong Kong and Treaty-Port China and Japan; the Bank's danger lay elsewhere.

The information in Table 6.1 is, unfortunately, available only for the period stated; its interpretation is difficult because nothing is available on assignment of profits from intra-Bank operations, including for example Hankow, which may be assumed to be under Shanghai, and London. Nor can costs be broken down and the difference between gross and net explained in detail. The statement rests as a comment on the performance of both Company and Corporation to mid-1868.

The relatively poor performance in 1869 was ascribed to the late opening of the tea market, the general depression and inactivity of trade, and then the unremunerative turn taken by the exchanges. At the February 1870 semi-annual meeting, however, the Chairman assured shareholders that a revival was then

Table 6.1 *The Hongkong and Shanghae Banking Company, Ltd*
The Hongkong and Shanghai Banking Corporation
Performance, 1865 to 30 June 1868[a]

(in thousands of dollars)

Profits			
By Hong Kong Office	1,953.9	To: dividends	953.2
Shanghai	894.2	reserves	500.0
Yokohama	34.4	prelim. expenses[c]	32.3
Foochow	15.9	directors	60.0
Total gross	2,898.4	constituents[d]	8.1
Total net[b]	1,624.2	undivided	70.7

Notes:
[a] The period covers seven half-years.
[b] The items reducing gross to net are not stated in the source.
[c] Expenses incurred by the Provisional Committee to 2 March 1865.
[d] 'Profit sharing' by the 'Company Ltd', see Chapter 3.
Source: Hongkong Bank Court Minutes, 28 August 1868.

apparent both in China and Japan. The failure of the Bank to improve its performance in 1870, therefore, needs examination.

The fact is that in 1870 the Bank not only failed to add to the Reserve Fund but was forced in the second half to reduce dividends by $50,000, from an annual rate of 12% to 8%. The assignment of $268,600 to contingency account despite the considerably improved performance of net earnings is the key. The Bank had from time to time written off losses or made allowances for bad or doubtful debts before stating net profits; apparently something more serious had occurred.

The Union Dock Company, formed in 1864, was a combination of Augustine Heard, Dent, and other interests.[3] By 1867 the company had become known as the 'Dis-union Docks' with its shares at 17% discount. In November George Heard, already a director of the Bank, was chairman at a fateful Docks meeting referred to as the 'suicide' of the directors, following which Victor Kresser was granted permission by the Court of the Hongkong Bank to become a director of the Union Dock Company to 'look after the Bank's and his own interests'.

In June 1868 James Duncanson questioned Kresser about the Dock Company's account with the Bank and, although officially reassured, was able to obtain his fellow directors' consent to set a limit to any further advances beyond the then outstanding $61,675, except with the sanction of the Standing Committee. A year later Helland went so far as to ask if the Chief Manager had in fact obeyed the limitations; the latter's explanations were 'formally' accepted, but the Standing Committee was asked to draw up rules for the 'better guidance of the Chief Manager'. Obviously something was very wrong; in 1870 the Augustine Heard-sponsored Union Dock Company, succumbing to a price war from the

Jardine-dominated Hongkong and Whampoa Dock Company, went into voluntary liquidation.

Also at the June 1868 meeting of the Court, the Hon. R. Rowett requested to see the accounts of Messrs Landstein and Co.; Landstein was, at least in mid-1867, a large shareholder. Rowett reported himself 'satisfied with the measures agreed upon with the [Standing] Committee for the further conduct of the account'. In May 1870 Landstein's was in debt $506,000 to the Bank against securities, presumably of Hong Kong and/or Shanghai companies, then valued at $100,000, but which, the Court hoped, could over time be sold without loss.

In May 1869 the Court began consideration of Victor Kresser's complex involvement 'in a private capacity' with a telegraph scheme through Saigon, but this apparently affected Kresser's career rather than the Hongkong Bank and need not be considered further in this chapter.[4] But a general sense of unease resulted in the Court resolving that: 'no loans to public companies may be made without first referring to the Standing Committee for sanction and if they disagree among themselves then referral to the full Board.' (September 3, 1869).

In January 1870 Kresser stated his terms for renewing his contract: Kresser defended his request – a $5,000 indemnity for entertainment, $10,000 bonus for reengagement, and $10,000 in lieu of an annual bonus, plus his then salary of $15,000. The Court rejected these as extravagant. Kresser defended his demands on the basis of the growth of the Hong Kong office which in 1869 had handled transactions totalling $275 million and had shown a gross profit of $3 million. The terms sound more as if Kresser were in need of capital to finance 'schemes'. The Court extended felicitations relative to the statistics; they confirmed their refusal of the terms and in April minuted that:

Future chief managers were to devote all their time to the Bank, were not to take part in trade, or become partners in any public company or private firm or to invest in shares (other than Government) or property other than 'Land Houses' except with the express permission of the Court. (April 15, 1870)

Available evidence is conclusive that this rule was not for long enforced.

Although the rule was also made applicable to the Bank's agents in general, it would seem to reflect the Court's sense of dissatisfaction not only with Kresser's contract demands but also with certain of his activities. At the August 1870 meeting announcing Kresser's 'intention to retire', the Chairman added that the directors 'felt it their pleasant duty to record their high appreciation of Kresser's very able and successful conduct of the Bank's business'.

In April 1871 Kresser requested the Court to confirm this statement; the Court declined.

This adverse conclusion had long been foreseen by the Bank's Shanghai Manager, David McLean. McLean had frequently disagreed with Kresser's purely banking operations, but he had also been critical of his involvement in company speculations. More specifically McLean had evidence that Kresser granted favourable rates of interest to companies represented on the Standing Committee and that this had made the members less critical of Kresser's overall activities.[5]

The Standing Committee acted as a filter; when therefore the 1870 minutes of the full Court deal with problem loans, it is a fair assumption that there were others handled at the lower level. Wahee Smith and Co.'s (China Sugar Refinery) indebtedness totalled $620,000, two loans to Chinese constituents were to be discussed with Kresser on his return from Saigon, and the Indo-Chinese Sugar Company was applying for up to $150,000. Meanwhile there was bad news from Shanghai due to the shipment of spurious Japanese 'niboo' coins and an eventual loss of some $30,000. .

The Court adhered to a policy of writing off losses as they occurred and, by setting aside nearly $270,000 in a contingency account, the Court, for the time at least, solved its problems. The accounts for 1871 appear unencumbered, with a somewhat increased profitability; this made possible a restoration of the 12% dividend rate – even with the increased paid-up capital – and the assignment of $200,000 to reserves, bringing the Reserve Fund to the $1 million goal. But the question of an enlarged dividend did not immediately arise.

The Bank and the public companies[6]

As James Whittall of Jardine, Matheson and Co. and Attorney General J. Smale had warned on the Executive Council when the general companies ordinance was being considered in 1865–1866, limited liability was to prove a mixed blessing, but in 1865 Hong Kong had been swept not simply with a speculative fever but by a feeling that its time had come. China was opening up and, if the Colony were not ideally suited for exploitation of the Yangtze Valley, it could nevertheless perform the role of depot, way station, business centre. And docks were one obvious need; another, equally appealing, was the sugar industry. The Union Docks have been noted; the rival company was well administered through Jardine's. The focus here is on the Bank's involvement with sugar and with the not wholly unrelated Pier and Godown Company.

The figures already considered suggest that a merchant community could ill afford to tie up funds in joint-stock companies. Although no specific case studies are available, the Bank's concern with the revaluation of securities held and its calls for increased margins on loans outstanding confirm this generalization. Those who did invest in shares found it necessary to borrow against them; these funds the banks provided; they were – willing or not – suppliers of liquidity to the market. If the purposes for which the companies had been established were endangered, the share prices could fall spectacularly in a thin market at a time when the merchant borrower would be unable to put up further collateral.

There were two consequences to this situation. First, the Bank by advancing against potentially unmarketable shares rather than self-liquidating trade bills or gilt-edged securities, was depending on its 'permanent deposits' and was thus in danger of a loss of confidence, an impossible demand for funds and therefore the 'passing' of the dividend – at the least. Secondly, since the same companies whose shares were being given liquidity by the Bank were themselves unable to meet their liabilities to the Bank, the Bank, not for the last time in its history, was running, or getting involved in the running of, an industrial enterprise, the sugar refinery of Wahee Smith and Co., the docks and the sugar estates of the Indo-Chinese Sugar Company in Cochin-China and Siam.

Indeed the Bank's problem loans were interrelated. The Western merchant was aware of the market deficiencies of Chinese sugar; he was informed of the inefficient Chinese production and processing methods. Here then was an opportunity to prove the worth of progress, for in the end, it was argued, the benefit would be as much to the Chinese producer as to the foreigner. These thoughts gave rise to three companies: the Indo-Chinese Sugar Company would obtain a supply of the crop, Wahee Smith and Co. would obtain refining equipment and place it in the old Mint buildings, and the Hongkong Distillery would make rum. To link all together, one could add that perhaps the Pier and Godown Company expected to be useful in the handling of both the refined sugar and the rum.

A number of the Bank's directors were involved as company directors; no doubt others were investors.

The supply of sugar was not, however, so easily obtained. Chinese merchants, including those investing in the company, held out for higher prices. Attempts by the Indo-Chinese Sugar Company to harvest their own crops in estates at Bien Hoa in Cochin-China or 'Laconchaisu' in Siam ran into mounting difficulties and costs; the former was sold at a loss of $80,000, the latter suffered natural disasters until the company's working capital of $400,000 was lost, and it borrowed $382,000 from the Bank against further calls from shareholders in 1872.[7]

The Bank's total involvement with the Indo-Chinese Sugar Company, Ltd was confirmed at a Court meeting on October 23, 1871. The Bank's Chairman was Richard Rowett, who was personally involved, and the decision to continue support was made only with his casting vote. The involved settlement included a guarantee for the deferred payments to the sugar company by Wahee Smith and Victor Kresser, a further advance of $119,000 to the sugar company to see it through the season, and an advance to Kresser against enumerated shares which eventually declined drastically in value. Belilios was one of those who opposed.

Two years later the Bank went in a further few steps, assigning $80,000 to market previous crops, undertaking supervision of sales in London, controlling the finances of the company, and agreeing to further advances of $20,000, if necessary. The Bank accepted the assignment of all capital calls due and to become due.

The Bank eventually sent its own 'special agent', C.I. Barnes, a junior clerk just out from London Office, to report on the Siam estate; this led to Barnes's becoming a 'sugar expert' and his subsequent assignment to Manila, where he was Manager during the Bank's sugar losses in the late 1880s.

The Sugar Refinery was also in trouble. Europeans too often had to relearn the unpleasant truth that just being a European was insufficient qualification for supervision of an industrial enterprise and that, even if a qualified man were brought out, methods used in England could not necessarily be duplicated with success on the China coast. In August 1870 the Bank was involved in supervising an experimental refining of 5,000 piculs of sugar, by which it may be inferred that it had considerable financial interest in the company. In April 1871 the Court minuted to keep the company's account as it then was with the exception of financing the purchase of the new sugar crop. During 1872 the Bank was involved in negotiations with Jardine Matheson for running the refinery, but in both semi-annual reports the Chairman of the Hongkong Bank was forced to make specific references to the Bank's commitments. Sums set aside at the end of June proved insufficient, and further allocations to meet obligations were announced at the February 1873 meeting of shareholders.[8]

The Bank in fact was caught. After two specific references to the shareholders – a most unusual procedure – the directors had the choice of losing all or financing further operations; not to work the machinery would be, in the view of many directors, ruinous. So, with E.R. Belilios objecting, a further advance of $60,000 was approved in March 1873 to operate at half-capacity. Victor Kresser with his Saigon connections and partnership in Wahee Smith and Co. was still very much involved, but negotiations to resolve his indebtedness, provide him with funds to invest in the Bien Hoa plantations of the Indo-Chinese Sugar Company, and clear off his responsibilities to the Bank, do not appear to have been resolved satisfactorily, although the records are incomplete.

At the mid-1873 meeting it was the Pier and Godown Company which attracted public interest and the Bank's involvement was acknowledged.

With regard to the Pier and Godown Company, the affairs of which, as the shareholders no doubt knew, were in a very precarious position, the Company had secured to the Bank by a mortgage and bill of sale, the sum of about $100,000, and when he stated that the property cost $290,000, the shareholders would see that it was not likely that any loss would accrue.[9]

Not likely, perhaps, but at auction the property was bought in at $80,000 and the Bank only rid itself of this dead stock sometime after 1875.

Shortly after the mid-1873 meeting, the *China Punch* published a cartoon depicting James Greig, the Bank's Chief Manager, literally falling between two stools, the one labelled 'Pier and Godown $11 . . .[?]', the other 'Indo Chinese $300,000'.[10] The charge was just. The Bank was becoming more and more involved in the affairs of both these companies, with those of Wahee Smith and Co.'s East Point refinery and to a lesser extent of the Hong Kong Distillery.

The Distillery was completed in 1872 but, with its capital expended, required credit to operate. By June 1873 it was insolvent with debts of $18,000 and the Hongkong Bank a major creditor. The Bank also held the company's then worthless shares in connection with credit advanced to Wahee Smith. Jardine's had become involved with supplier's credits, and Whittall sued the Distillery directors in their personal capacity with favourable results – as described in connection with the *China Punch* poem quoted in the previous chapter.

Once capital had been run down and debts written off, various schemes were attempted to revitalize the activities of these companies on a more modest basis – not without success. But this would little benefit the Hongkong Bank in its 1874/75 crisis. The inter-involvement of these companies, often offering the shares of one as security for a loan to another, caused almost total collapse when their legitimately conceived activities proved flawed in execution. Other equally meritorious enterprises from brick making to rice milling, all attempting to introduce modern methods, suffered similar fates, but with less impact, apparently, on the fortunes of the Hongkong Bank.

Events to 1874, a summary (see Tables 6.2–4)

The Shanghai succession

When the Court in January 1870 confirmed their unwillingness to accept Victor Kresser's terms, they resolved in May to appoint David McLean as the Bank's Chief Manager. McLean, however, was content in Shanghai and argued that it was in the Bank's interest that he remain. He was already planning to leave the East no later than 1873, and he saw no reason to move to Hong Kong for the additional title of 'chief', although he offered to be 'chief' if he could remain in Shanghai – a most unlikely situation.[11] McLean would not be the last to refuse the offer of the chief-managership of the Bank, and his decision was respected. He retired from the East as planned in 1873 and accepted appointment as Sub-Manager (salary £1,000 per annum) in the London Office under W.H. Vacher. The Shanghai vacancy, which had at first been offered to William Kaye of the Chartered Bank and then, on McLean's urging, to Thomas Jackson, was filled by the Bank's Calcutta Agent, Ewen Cameron, whose management was to prove distinguished.

The appointment of Cameron to Shanghai was something of a last minute decision, as Jackson, the Yokohama Manager, successfully argued against his

(in millions of dollars)

Table 6.2 *The Hongkong and Shanghai Banking Corporation*
Assets and liabilities, 1867–1870

end of:	1867		1868		1869		1870	
	June	December	June	December	June	December	June	December
Assets								
Cash on hand and with banks	2.64	3.95	2.83	4.23	6.59	4.25	5.29	10.18
Discounts, loans, credits	3.64	3.37	4.83	4.38	4.37	4.76	6.73	8.11
Exchange remittances	9.14	13.29	10.91	12.00	10.82	17.98	14.56	16.67
Government securities	—	0.24	0.24	0.72	0.94	0.94	0.82	2.95
Other[a]	0.14	0.11	0.11	0.12	0.12	0.13	0.13	0.14
Total: Assets = liabilities	15.56	20.96	18.92	21.45	22.84	28.07	27.53	38.05
Liabilities								
Paid-up capital	2.50	2.50	2.50	2.50	2.50	2.50	2.50	2.50
+Paid-up (new shares)	0.50	0.50	0.50	0.50	0.50	1.00	1.00	1.50
+Reserve Fund	0.175	0.25	0.375	0.50	0.70	0.70	0.80	0.80
=Shareholders' funds	3.175	3.25	3.375	3.50	3.70	4.20	4.30	4.80
Deposits and notes	4.72	6.28	6.76	7.06	7.86	7.81	8.66	11.11
of which: banknotes[b]	1.09	1.22	1.02	1.11	1.41	1.76	1.51	1.71
Exchange acceptances	7.37	11.04	8.39	10.42	10.96	15.68	14.25	21.67
Profit and loss	0.30	0.39	0.40	0.46	0.32	0.37	0.32	0.46

Profit and loss

(in thousands of dollars)

By balance of undivided profits	35.9	14.2	57.3	70.7	63.2	116.8	46.3	99.4
By amount of profits	245.8[c]	368.1[c]	328.4[c]	382.6[c]	243.5[c]	249.5[c]	273.1[c]	361.7[c]
=Total funds to be allocated[c]	281.7	382.3	385.7	453.2	306.8	366.3	319.4	461.1
To preliminary expenses	5.0	10.0	—	—				
To Contingent account								268.6
To dividend	180.0	180.0	180.0	180.0	180.0	210.0	210.0	160.0
To directors' remuneration	7.5	10.0	10.0	10.0	10.0	10.0	10.0	10.0
To reserves	75.0	125.0	125.0	200.0	0.0	100.0	0.0	0.0
To balance carried forward	14.2	57.3	70.7	63.2	116.8	46.3	99.4	22.6
Reserve Fund: new balance	250.0	375.0	500.0	700.0	700.0	800.0	800.0	800.0

Notes:
[a] includes: preliminary expenses (run down by June 1868) dead stock ($32–54,000) and bank premises ($60–77,000).
[b] in this table banknote figures are based on the semi-annual accounts and are compatible.
[c] net of rebate on bills not due.

193

(in millions of dollars)

Table 6.3 *The Hongkong and Shanghai Banking Corporation*
Assets and liabilities, 1871–1874

end of:	1871 June	1871 December	1872 June	1872 December	1873 June	1873 December	1874 June	1874 December
Assets								
Cash on hand and with banks	9.95	9.35	7.10	8.10	13.00	11.26	11.04	8.55
Discounts, loans, credits	8.53	7.65	10.72	11.03	13.64	9.84	13.02	9.76
Exchange remittances	17.20	21.31	25.70	32.22	24.71	26.95	18.73	21.87
Government securities	2.23	2.04	2.58	2.16	2.55	2.82	1.87	2.48
Other[a]	0.14	0.15	0.15	0.16	0.17	0.26[b]	0.29	0.32
Total: Assets = liabilities	38.06	40.50	46.24	53.67	54.07	51.14	44.96	42.91
Liabilities								
Paid-up capital	2.50	2.50	2.50	5.00	5.00	5.00	5.00	5.00
+ Paid-up (new shares)	1.50	2.00	2.00	+ Marine Insurance account		0.03	0.03	0.03
+ Reserve Fund	0.80	0.90	1.00	1.00	1.00	1.00	1.00	0.10
= Shareholders' funds	4.80	5.40	5.50	6.00	6.00	6.00	6.03	5.13
Deposits and notes	12.77	12.58	15.24	16.07	18.26	18.77	16.21	19.80
of which: banknotes[c]	1.67	1.52	1.51	2.37	1.26	1.96	1.45	2.24
Exchange acceptances	20.10	22.12	25.08	31.26	29.49	26.13	22.59	17.86
Profit and loss	0.39	0.40	0.42	0.34	0.36	0.24	0.13	0.12

Profit and loss

(in thousands of dollars)

					By Amount from Reserve Fund			
By balance of undivided profits	22.6	31.3	18.3	122.8	19.2	36.8	225.0	675.0
By amount of profits	358.8[d]	367.0[d]	384.5[d]	206.4[d]	327.4[d]	199.7[d]	99.8[d]	112.7[d]
=Total funds to be allocated[d]	381.3	398.3	402.8	329.2	346.6	236.3	351.0	794.8
To Contingency Fund							334.0	781.0
To dividend	240.0	270.0	270.0	300.0	300.0	200.0	0.0	0.0
To directors' remuneration	10.0	10.0	10.0	10.0	10.0	10.0	10.0	10.7[e]
To reserves	100.0	100.0	0.0	0.0	0.0	0.0	0.0	0.0
To balance carried forward	31.3	18.3	122.8	19.2	36.6	26.3	7.0	3.1
Reserve Fund: new balance	900.0	1000.0	1000.0	1000.0	1000.0	1000.0	775.0	100.0

Notes:

[a] includes: dead stock ($59–91,000) and bank premises ($82–230,000).

[b] there is a significant growth in both dead stock and bank premises from this year.

[c] in this table banknote figures are based on the semi-annual accounts and are compatible.

[d] net of rebate on bills not due.

[e] includes rebate on bills not due, $0.7.

195

(in millions of dollars)

Table 6.4 *The Hongkong and Shanghai Banking Corporation*
Assets and liabilities, 1874–1877

end of:	1874		1875		1876		1877	
	June	December	June	December	June	December	June	December
Assets								
Cash on hand and with banks	11.04	8.55	8.07	4.36	5.12	4.45	5.22	5.72
Discounts, loans, credits	13.02	9.76	9.53	9.25	12.52	8.67	10.06	10.34
Exchange remittances	18.73	21.87	15.50	18.15	19.63	28.92	25.41	34.01
Government securities	1.87	2.48	2.90	2.55	1.47	0.93	1.03	2.31
Buildings	0.20	0.23	0.23	0.23	0.22	0.22	0.21	0.21
Dead stock	0.09	0.09	0.09	0.09	0.09	0.10	0.10	0.10
Total: Assets = liabilities	44.96	42.91	36.32	34.63	39.06	43.29	42.05	52.71
Liabilities								
Paid-up capital	5.00	5.00	5.00	5.00	5.00	5.00	5.00	5.00
+ Marine Insurance Account	0.03	0.03	0.04	0.05	0.06	0.07	0.06	0.07
+ Reserve Fund	1.00	0.10	0.10	0.10	0.10	0.20	0.50	0.65
= Shareholders' funds	6.03	5.13	5.14	5.15	5.16	5.27	5.56	5.72
Deposits and notes	16.21	19.80	13.52	13.41	14.78	13.07	15.97	22.36
of which: banknotes[a]	1.45	2.24	1.35	1.88	1.62	1.31	1.23	2.04
Exchange acceptances	22.59	17.86	17.38	15.74	18.78	24.44	20.16	24.08
Profit and loss	0.13	0.12	0.26	0.34	0.33	0.50	0.36	0.55

Profit and loss

(in thousands of dollars)

By amount from Reserve Fund	225.0	675.0	0.0	—	—	—	—	—
By balance of undivided profits	26.3	7.0	3.1	106.0	19.1	38.1	11.0	14.0
By amount of profits	99.8	112.0	257.0	228.1	306.8	460.7	340.8	535.0
=Total funds to be allocated[b]	351.0	794.0	260.0	334.1	325.9	498.8	351.8	549.0
To Contingency Fund	334.0	781.0	154.0	145.0	—	—	—	—
To dividend	0.0	0.0	0.0	150.0	177.78[c]	177.78[c]	177.78[c]	177.78[c]
To directors' remuneration	10.0	10.0	0.0	20.0	10.0	10.0	10.0	10.0
To reserves	0.0	0.0	0.0	0.0	100.0	300.0	150.0	350.0
To balance carried forward	7.0	3.1	106.0	19.1	38.1	11.0	14.0	11.2
Reserve Fund: new balance	775.0	100.0	100.0	100.0	200.0	500.0	650.0	1000.0

Notes:

[a] in this table banknote figures are based on the semi-annual accounts and are compatible.

[b] net of rebate on bills not due.

[c] dividend declared at £1 per share, exchange rate set at 4/6 per $; offset not shown in published accounts.

own transfer on the grounds that the development of Japanese business required his continued presence. In any case Jackson went Home on leave in March 1874 and was available in London. Kaye also had plans to leave the East and was eventually given the post of the Hongkong Bank's London Sub-Manager after McLean had succeeded Vacher in 1875.

The appointment of James Greig as Chief Manager

With McLean remaining in Shanghai the Court then turned to its Hong Kong Sub-Manager, James Greig, formerly a manager of the Asiatic Bank, who had joined the Hongkong Bank as late as 1869. No other name is mentioned in the minutes. Writing after the events of 1874–1876, David McLean commented, 'I rather pitied [Greig] being left with such a load of old things by Kresser, but ...' his exchange operations were not always on a sound basis.[12] Greig was designated as the prospective Chief Manager in June 1870 at $10,000 per annum, but with Kresser still in Hong Kong to advise; when Kresser's wife died in September, he was permitted to return Home with his several shareholding children and the following month the 34-year-old Greig was in sole charge. In July 1871 Greig was confirmed as Chief Manager and reappointed in October 1873 at $15,000.

A 'Bank of China', 1872

In January 1872 there came the first threat of a rival Eastern-based bank. McLean wrote to Thomas Jackson in Yokohama, 'A new Bank is likely to be established here.'[a] He even toyed with the idea of being its London manager, news of which gave Greig the idea of offering him the sub-managership Vacher claimed was needed. McLean, however, did not really expect that the promoters had the necessary funds for the new bank. Furthermore he foresaw real obstacles: (i) there was no way a local company might register with limited liability in Shanghai, and (ii) the Hong Kong Government would probably not receive favourably a request for a second special bank ordinance. The promoters would, therefore, have to incorporate in the United Kingdom with a board of directors in London. They would risk loss of control.

There was a temporary revival of interest in April with news that the promoters of the new bank should apply for a charter in London and with indications that they would be successful. Hongkong Bank shares dropped for a

---

[a] The first list of promoters included: A.A. Hayes of Olyphant and Co., Behn of Pustau, David Reid and Co., Chas J. King of Chapman, King and Co., R.W. Little and Co., and F. Hormusjee. Capital was first announced as ShTs3 million, but only Hormusjee really had funds, and he kept McLean informed of developments. The major hongs apparently notified the promoters in advance that the new facilities were not needed.[13] The Eastern exchange banks might be in difficulties, but they, including the reconstituted Agra Bank, still provided facilities which the well-established companies considered adequate and sufficiently competitive to meet their needs.

day or so, but recovered. McLean once again dismissed the matter. But the project reappeared on July 6, 1872, with an announcement in the *North-China Herald* that the 'Hua-li yin-hang' (Bank of China, Ltd) was to be formed under the British Companies Act of 1862 with a board of directors in London, a management committee in Shanghai, and an initial paid-up capital of Ts2.5 million. Both foreign and Chinese shareholders were to be represented on the local Shanghai Committee.[14]

By August 27 the idea had been given up. The Hongkong Bank remained without a locally based rival.

The promotion was the first of a series of 'Bank of China's; there would be another in 1882 and yet another in 1890; this last, as the National Bank of China, was actually established. It would survive without marked success to 1911.

Shanghai business

David McLean informed the Court of Directors in 1872 that the branch had paid 12% on its capital since 1866 and had in addition remitted $186,000 in 1871 'towards the Reserve fund'. His correspondence provides evidence of the thinness of the Shanghai share and bullion markets. A careful analysis of the position of each bank would enable McLean to manipulate the exchanges to his advantage and his extraordinary successes not only affected profits but also gave the Bank a strong competitive base from which to develop. Up-country information would come from, *inter alios*, the Shansi (or remittance) bankers, with whom McLean did 'a large business occasionally'.[15] McLean was fortunate in being the first banker to note that Shanghai sycee silver contained small quantities of gold. He was thus able to ship sycee to London at rates which were apparently unprofitable, but the gold made the difference.

One task of an exchange bank was to move the 'full-bodied' currency to points where it was needed; anticipation of the market requirements for monetary metal and the probable movements of world bullion prices were keys to success. McLean's letters from Shanghai are replete with examples, usually involving triangular exchange operations via India. A simpler Shanghai example may be helpful in understanding McLean's approach.

In the 1870 tea season McLean decided on the basis of personal investigation in Shanghai and correspondence with Hongkong Bank agents that there would be a shortage of sycee relative to the requirements of the tea exporters. The tea exporters in Shanghai sold pounds sterling against sycee, using the latter to pay the teamen. McLean let the other banks buy the teamen's pounds (or remittances) at relatively low rates, providing them with sycee at say 6s:1d, but, when banks had sold their sycee and had no immediate prospects of obtaining further bullion (and McLean watched for signs that silver bars would be imported) and since the tea exporters were still trying to obtain increasingly scarce sycee, the tea exporters' search for sycee had the consequence of bidding up its price in terms of sterling; that is to say, it raised the exchange rate; or, put another way, a greater number of shillings had to be given for the same amount of sycee. McLean did considerable business at 6s:8d; he sold sycee and obtained six shillings and eight pence per tael as opposed to the other banks' earlier rates of approximately six shillings and one penny.[16]

That McLean was the master is reflected in the figures he submitted. This the Court of Directors acknowledged with an additional bonus of $1,300.[17]

Hong Kong and the public companies

This period was dominated, as far as the directors were concerned, by their investments in public companies. The Hongkong Bank was weakened. The published accounts show an allocation of profits to contingency account recommended at the February 1872 meeting. This was apparently necessary because the Court's decision was made in January, after the accounts for 1871 had been closed. There were however subsequent transfers which took place before disclosure of profits, and by the end of 1873 a total of $730,000 had been so utilized. In 1874 the position of the Bank was too well known and its profitability questioned; therefore once more the Court had to assign funds to meet contingencies from published profits.

This suggests, however, that the Bank's profits had been understated during 1872 and 1873, accounting in part at least for the otherwise inexplicable drop in declared profits at the end of the latter year.

Normal losses could be met from net profits before publication. In years of extraordinary losses, especially if these arose from transactions in previous accounting periods, the Court had a choice: it could either write off the losses and present a low figure in the profit and loss account or it could recommend allocation of net profits to a contingency fund at the General Meeting. The former resulted, as noted above, in charges of poor performance in general, the latter exposed the unwise decisions of the directors. If the losses were sufficiently heavy, the directors had little choice – they had to declare the situation to the shareholders.

Whether a loss has occurred or is contingent depends on one's expectations, and with respect to the public companies, the directors were generally over-sanguine. Although they had followed the wise policy of meeting losses as they arose, their support of Hong Kong's floundering industry – and, to some extent, their own investments therein – would cause further losses until a policy change was effected or the utter hopelessness of the situation became obvious. This occurred in 1874.

THE CRISIS OF 1874/75

The problems which the Hongkong Bank faced were the consequence of events on the China coast. The Bank had been involved in financing fixed investments which had proved unprofitable. The timing of the 'crisis' in the Bank's history suggests the influence of economic problems in the United States and Europe in 1873, and there may have been an impact on the profitability of James Greig's operations (see below) or on the ability of China-coast merchants to find alternative sources of funds from London friends. This would affect the Bank's ability to handle its main problems. What should have been simply a period of questionable profitability from trade finance became a test of the Bank's ability to survive. As stressed throughout, the causes for this were to be found in the Bank's activities in the East.

Developments through the August 1874 meeting

First the good news.

The Hongkong Bank was successful in its bid to obtain the Treasury Chest business in China and Japan.

The bad news may be divided into three categories: (i) trading account, (ii) public companies, and (iii) Vacher's share transactions in London. Although all relevant information was not made public until the August General Meeting by the Hongkong Bank's American Chairman, W.H. Forbes, Hong Kong was a small community and the price of Bank shares began to decline in early 1873; the shares, which had once been at a premium of 75%, had dropped to 20% by May 1874. At the June meeting of the directors, Forbes stated there was no reason for the decline and that no big losses were expected. A month later the Court faced a surprising loss due to transactions in London which should have been, but unfortunately were not, noticed by the auditors in their previous examination of the accounts. Even without this unexpected development Forbes had been overly optimistic.

Net profits for the first six months of 1874 were 50% of the previous half-year's published figures – from which latter figure $25,000 had already been deducted for contingencies. This poor performance was ascribed by the Chairman to the sudden advance in exchange on India, for which the Bank was unprepared and which disrupted the triangular exchange business previously described, and was explained by the famine in that country. Shanghai exchange operations were unremunerative due to the early collapse of the produce markets. The Hongkong Bank made funds available in Shanghai and Hankow to meet the requirement of the tea exporters; with the early decline in prices the Bank had to remit surplus funds to London at a 'considerable loss'. Finally the usually profitable operations with Japanese currency, buying the metallic currency cheaply at the beginning of the year and then selling when the price rose, had been upset by the unexpected issue of paper currency by the Japanese Government.

There were also losses anticipated through the failure of trading firms. E.H. Pollard, the Bank's first counsel, was in financial difficulties, and the Bank anticipated losses on his account. There was some hope that a claim against the King of Annam might be successful, although the relevant documents had been mislaid between two offices in the Hong Kong Government, an incident which the Court deplored.

From this weak base the directors were required to handle the continuing problems of its investments in the Pier and Godown Company, the Sugar Refinery, and the Indo-Chinese Sugar Company.

The attempt to float a new public company to take over and work the property of the Pier and Godown Company in early 1874 had not surprisingly failed, and the Bank's attempt to auction the property had resulted in a bid of under $80,000 which the Bank, unwisely in the view of some commentators, rejected. But the whole had in any case been written off. The Sugar Refinery, which the Court thought had been fully provided for at the February 1874 meeting, incurred further losses due to market conditions. Current operations were reported as being profitable, and the books of the company were made available for inspection by shareholders of the Hongkong Bank. The problems of the Indo-Chinese Sugar Company were still unsolved, and the Court resolved to warn the shareholders that a possible maximum loss of $275,000 might yet be suffered by the Bank in the latter part of 1874.

Most shareholders must have been aware of the Bank's problems with the limited liability companies. But the unauthorized activities of W.H. Vacher came as a surprise. That they came also as a surprise to the directors of the Bank was a legitimate subject for discussion.

At the General Meeting in early 1875, the Hong Kong barrister, Henry Kingsmill, put the problem this way:

He had known Mr Vacher in China and knew that he had a character for uprightness and ability, and he would not have been surprised at individuals trusting in him, but he *was* surprised at the Board having put such trust in him, and they had fully verified the truth of overtrust not being good policy.

The directors' only defence was that when you placed a man in such a position of responsibility he had to have the authority to act and he had therefore to be trusted. They had stated a classic management dilemma, one which they would face again in almost identical circumstances in 1889 with E. Morel, their Lyons Agent.

The Court had from time to time commented favourably on Vacher's undoubted contribution to the Bank's development in London, and his engagement with the Bank had been twice extended. The Bank's growth depended to a considerable extent on the continuing confidence of its London correspondent, the London and County Bank, and in fostering this confidence Vacher's role must have been considerable.

The Court were then ill-prepared for the news that their London Manager had been engaged in 'considerable transactions' in bonds and securities outside of English and Indian Government paper. The loss was then estimated to be £20,000, which was fully provided for in the allocation to the Contingency Fund the Court recommended in August 1874. But the directors did not have the full story and would have to come back to the shareholders at the following meeting with further losses to report on this account.

All this was reported fully to the General Meeting. In recommending the allocation from published profits of $334,000 to a Contingency Fund with only $116,000 available, the directors were forced to face the withdrawal of $225,000 from the Reserve Fund. The possible losses from the Indo-Chinese Sugar Company might, the directors warned, have to be covered by a further withdrawal of $275,000 – this was to prove an underestimate.

The shareholders present – and attendance was unusually high – received the reading of the Chairman's report and additional comments with 'much applause'. Contemporary editorial comment ascribed this not so much to a sort of naive innocence as a recognition that other Hong Kong companies had been unable to declare a dividend, that the misfortunes of the Bank reflected those of the community it served, and that the directors had done all within their competence to contain matters. When this came to be questioned, the directors would have to be certain of their answers.[18]

Developments through the February 1875 meeting

The confidence of the Bank's constituents as reflected in their use of the Bank was apparently unshaken. In the six months following the events described, not only did deposits increase but by the end of 1874 the circulation of the Bank's banknotes had recovered, while exchange business moved upwards with the improvement of trading conditions, although the Bank's profits were to remain stagnant. Share prices on the other hand continued to decline and, in reaction to the end-1874 report, renewed a downward trend; they were quoted at a discount throughout 1875 – more than 20% discount between March and October.

Perhaps the public needed a simple issue they could come to grips with. Exchange rates, problems of public companies – these are complex and the problems developed understandably over a period of time. The directors always seemed to have an answer. Then in January 1875, with problems continuing on all fronts, the Court of Directors of the Hongkong and Shanghai Banking Corporation made a decision of heroic proportions: they would furnish the Bank's new Shanghai premises at a cost of £4,000 ('shame'). The cost of furniture, it turned out, was something the average shareholder felt competent to take a position on, and furniture accordingly featured prominently in the stormy February General Meeting. But there were other matters to which it would be useful to turn.

This time the good news cannot be so quickly stated.

In October 1874 James Greig went to Foochow; there, while the directors dithered, he committed the Bank to a loan of £627,615 – equivalent at the agreed but arbitrary exchange rate to 2 million taels, and immediately advanced 60,000 taels 'on account'.[19] That the loan was made to 'His Majesty Tung Chih, Emperor of China' was a matter of some mirth to at least one of the Bank's critics, but it affected neither the validity of the agreement nor its terms.[b]

The Court in Hong Kong, fearing their inability to float a Chinese Government loan in London if hostilities should break out between China and Japan over Formosa and unaware that a peace treaty had already been signed, wired Greig on November 6 to advance no further funds. Once the war threat was known to have disappeared, the directors authorized the concluding negotiations, and final agreements for the Chinese Imperial Government 'Foochow' Loan of 1874 were signed in two stages – November 28, 1874, for the 'first issue' of £539,748:18s:0d and June 5, 1875, for the 'second issue' of £87,866:2s:0d. In January 1875 the first portion (or tranche) was issued to the public in Hong Kong and Shanghai at 95 in ten-year, 8% sterling-denominated bonds. The Bank had pre-paid the full amount of the loan to the Chinese authorities on December 19, 1874.

The Bank's net profit on the loan, based primarily on the difference between the rate the funds were made available to China and that at which the bonds were sold to the public, amounted to approximately $125,000 'up-front', which may be compared to the Bank's total profits in the second half of 1874 of $112,800, or, for the following six months, $257,000.[21]

Comments in the minutes of the Court, confirmed by the Chairman at the General Meeting, suggest that the Bank credited a high proportion of the profits

---

b Charles Rivington, a share broker, claimed he had been harshly dealt with by John Walter, in 1878 acting Manager, Shanghai, and for some ten years wrote to the directors in complaint. His more immediate comment dealt with the wording in the loan agreement and he was sarcastic. Indeed it was a little pretentious – 'the Hongkong Bank and the Emperor of China'! Furthermore 'T'ung-chih' was not the *name* of the *Emperor*; the Bank, scoffed Rivington, had made a loan agreement with a reign title, not with the Emperor – who anyway had died. On this latter point, the critic himself can be faulted; the Emperor Mu-tsung died on January 12, 1875, six weeks after the loan agreement was signed.[20]

of the loan to the end-1874 Profit and Loss Account. This is the only explanation of the confession that: 'the half-year's results have been so unsatisfactory . . . had it not been for the China Loan there would, I regret to say, have been no profit available'.

China Punch caught the mood. For its New Year's cartoon, Father Time is shown emerging from the gloom of 1874 bringing in the New Year, a bag of silver dollars with legs and clearly marked '1875 Loan . . . £675,615'.[c] A significant episode in the history of the Hongkong Bank, the early China loans are considered as a single topic in Chapter 14; suffice it to mention here that the conclusion of the loan was clearly seen as a factor of importance in the Bank's immediate future.

But this leads directly to the bad news.

As the Bank agreed to advance the 2 million taels – equivalent to $2.8 million – to the Foochow authorities regardless of the success of any public issue, the amount is shown in the December 1874 accounts under 'discounts, loans and credits'. This implies that the Bank's 'regular' business was but $7 million, down $5 million compared with the end-June figures. At the same time the value of interest-bearing deposits actually increased by approximately 17% – a 'double disadvantage', as the Bank's Chairman put it.

With current operations running virtually at a loss, the directors had to inform shareholders that the $275,000 mentioned at the previous meeting had indeed been taken from the Reserve Fund, together with a further $400,000 – the shareholders were being told, not asked. This, when added to the published profits, presumably from the China loan, permitted an allocation of a necessary $781,000 to the Contingency Account – and, as shareholders were not slow to notice, $10,000 for the remuneration of the directors.

The directors were now open to the emotionally appealing but not wholly accurate charge of withholding information, of bringing up their follies one by one. 'Let us know once and for all where we stand!' But this the directors could not state with certainty. Questions put to the directors elicited the response that many problems were of such long standing that not one of the diminished directorate had been present when the original decisions were made, but this did not satisfy. Indeed, in anticipation of a difficult meeting, Henry Kingsmill, a prominent Hong Kong attorney and shareholder, who played a tough but constructive role throughout, had sent the Court a list of questions he intended to put. The Chairman's speech covered many of the points raised. The Chairman spoke frankly, his information being consistent with that recorded in the minutes

---

[c] The 'official' is none other than Mr Punch, dressed in the robes of a 'Taiping' (or rebel) Mandarin. This Mr Punch is the China-coast manifestation of the Italian puppet Punchinello, through Punch of Punch and Judy shows, as transformed in *Punch or the London Charivari* (there was a Paris *Charivari*), and brought to the East in the short-lived *China Punch*.[22]

of the Court of Directors. The task was not an easy one, and the directors would have to come before the shareholders twice more and set aside a further $300,000 before the backlog of problems was overcome.

The problems were again (i) the dullness of trade, (ii) the affairs of the public companies, and (iii) the new dimensions of the Vacher affair.

The books of the three 'bug-bears', as they were referred to, were made available for inspection by shareholders, and the Chairman noted the amounts written off while he received criticism for not disposing of the Pier and Godown Company for the $70,000 plus offered at the auction. The worst news had come from London where the losses sustained by Vacher's unauthorized advances against American railway and Spanish bonds now totalled £71,000 of which only £38,000 had been written off; there was thus approximately $160,000 needed for this account alone.

On the new Shanghai premises the Chairman, W.H. Forbes, was on stronger ground. He could convincingly show that the previous offices were inadequate and that the amortized cost of the new structure would be less than paying rent for the necessary space. Unwisely Forbes added that 'at the time the building was sanctioned, the Bank was in what he supposed even Mr Kingsmill would have called a very flourishing condition'. To which the good barrister, for the only laugh of the meeting, replied, 'Ah, but you've got into the hands of architects and builders.'

The shareholders were then left with two issues to play with: (i) the cost of furniture – and in the end the Shanghai Manager, Ewen Cameron, simply moved in with a neighbour – and (ii) the directors' remuneration, which Police Commissioner Charles May thought the directors ought under the circumstances to forgo. This developed into a procedural struggle and, despite some caustic comments, the meeting in the end left the matter in the hands of the directors. They confirmed the allocation of $10,000 but subsequently postponed their January–June 1875 fees until the end of the year when the Bank appeared about to turn the corner. The maverick E.R. Belilios, who throughout had taken a more conservative position on the Bank's policy towards the public companies, refused to accept his fees for the second half of 1874. With considerable reluctance shown by his colleagues and public praise at the next shareholders' meeting, his repayment was accepted and acknowledged.

REORGANIZATION AND RECOVERY, 1874–1876

Realization that their Bank was in trouble did not immediately suggest to the directors what course ought to be taken. In 1874, for example, they twice resolved not to appoint a London Committee and they were slow to recognize that their Chief Manager might be open to criticism. However, both the full Court and the Standing Committee were active and their program of reorganization, partly self-initiated, partly forced by events and outside pressures, proved in the end successful. The directors first moved to tighten controls and restate the basic nature of the Bank's business; they then turned to an examination of the state of the Bank and began to focus on James Greig's operations – had 'dullness of trade' become a phrase hiding 'dullness of management'? In 1875 the directors faced the by then urgent need for a London Committee, and finally in 1876 they made changes in the procedures of the Court itself.

David McLean was to play the key role with Thomas Jackson waiting.

Postmortem

If the directors were not sure of their course, editors and their correspondents were quick to offer comment and advice. Some writers thought the directors deserved criticism but not abuse; others were unwilling to make so nice a distinction. The content of these articles and letters followed a predictable pattern.[23]

There was a general expression of surprise and annoyance that the shareholders themselves had never raised points of significance at the semi-annual meetings, that is, not until February 1875. This, many felt, put them in a weak position, since they had acquiesced by default in what had happened or, alternatively, failed to ask questions likely to provide information necessary for informed comment. The August 1874 meeting was undeniably passive, but then very few attended, and the Court at one time was concerned over the problem of a quorum.

Most were agreed that the Bank had proved there was legitimate business for it to undertake and that, if it confined itself to banking properly defined, it would prosper. There was a question, however, as to whether the present directors and/or managers were qualified to redirect the Bank into sound practices.

There was no problem identifying the source of the Bank's major difficulties – support of the three bug-bears, especially the Indo-Chinese Sugar Company, which one correspondent estimated the Bank had financed to an extent in excess of one-fourth of the company's paid-up capital. There was recognition of the path down which the directors had wandered by supporting an enterprise and then continuing the support rather than face the financial consequences of its collapse, but some modified their criticism by considering whether this had not on balance been a reasonable course for the Bank to take. Withdrawal of support might have had a dramatic effect on the entire economy.

Perhaps the most unrealistic criticism was the suggestion the directors 'knew' of the problems and withheld information. Here correspondents were frustrated by the failure of shareholders to ask for the information at the time. The directors' defence would be that (i) the problems of the joint-stock companies and the Bank's involvement were well-known, (ii) the Chairman had informed the shareholders in a general way, and (iii) the directors themselves could not predict the losses, given their optimistic hopes for the companies and, in the case of Vacher, the failure of the auditors to note the unauthorized investments.

Observers were aware and noted specifically that the Bank was without British directors in a British colony, but it was not accurate to state that the British directors had all resigned when trouble loomed; only William Lemann reacted to the combination of Bank losses and the case of *Whittall v Bell and others*, and his motivation has already been discussed in Chapter 5. The others left as a result of normal turnover. Fault might instead be found with those, unknown, who declined to become directors when approached.

Several writers were critical of the Bank's role in lending against shares, especially against its own, and so fuelling speculation. The critics correctly pointed to David McLean for initiating this business, but the focus of complaint was Hong Kong. McLean might be a director of the North-China Steam Carriage Company and heavily involved in Shanghai company promotion, but the losses which had endangered the Bank were correctly attributed to Hong Kong. The inflated prices of shares proved them to be inadequate as security when prices fell. By lending against shares the Bank gave a false sense of liquidity to the economy, and yet the projected enterprises required fixed capital financing and the merchants required funds for carrying on their normal business. The merchants invested their trading funds in fixed capital, turning to the Bank for liquidity and presenting their shares as security. If, in so thin a market, key enterprises were unsuccessful or trade unusually unremunerative, this practice became a recipe for disaster; if the Bank did not accommodate its constituents, it was not fulfilling its promised role; if lending against shares in this way were improper, then the whole basis of industrial development (restricted as it was) in Hong Kong and Shanghai was put in question and the wisdom of those who had passed the General Companies Ordinance challenged.

There was a solution: (i) redefine the Bank's legitimate role more conservatively, (ii) write off previous mistakes, and (iii) institute internal reforms within the Bank to guard against repetition of past errors.

Interestingly, in stressing the need for the Bank to return to 'legitimate' banking, observers failed to comment on the poor performance reflected in the Bank's semi-annual statements. But this too would be noted and acted on before the shake-out had been completed.

Inspection and control, the first stage

Although the extent of the London losses was not yet fully realized, the Court in September 1874 resolved on a series of control measures. Their purpose was to ensure an improved and independent flow of information to the directors. Important as they were, they would not have avoided the 1874 crisis which was in the end traceable to the directors, their involvement, and their decisions. The Court needed the controls, but they also needed a strong and able Chief Manager.

The directors confirmed that the business of the Bank be strictly confined to general banking; advances to individuals or firms in excess of $100,000 to require the directors' consent, and all accounts exceeding $100,000 to be submitted to the Court monthly for review. Then, arising directly from the still-developing Vacher affair the Court resolved (i) to appoint an inspector at a rank higher than that of a branch manager, (ii) to require surety bonds from the staff, and (iii) to cause the second officer in any branch or agency to be equally responsible for all transactions. McLean, who was already Sub-Manager in London, had been at first unaware of Vacher's unauthorized transactions.

These resolutions were, however, flawed in execution. After a hiatus of some six weeks, presumably because of the absence of Greig in Foochow, the Court appointed a retiring director, Richard Rowett, as Inspector. The directors, noting the 'strong feeling existing at home [London] against the Directors and General Management', then decided that Rowett should not take up the appointment until July 1875. But feeling was also high in the Colony, and their decision suggests that the directors had been misled by the apparently favourable reception of the Chairman's August report and were out of touch with the strength of local resentment at the Bank's performance. Rowett, who had been Chairman at the 1871 decision relative to the Indo-Chinese Sugar Company, was also involved with other public companies, the Distillery in particular, and he was a particularly unfortunate choice. At the January 1875 meeting the Court had to withdraw the offer and compensate Rowett.

In the end the Court, as described below, turned to McLean to make a special, 'one-time' inspection. The decision was undoubtedly correct, but once McLean had reported, the Court neglected to appoint a permanent inspector until the former Chief Accountant, G.R. Johnston, became 'Acting Inspector of Branches', in 1885.

Reorganization and inspection

The appointment of Rowett had been part of an overall scheme, best described by Heard in a letter of December 1874.

The Bank have decided to make some changes to content angry shareholders and appease especially those in London. They have telegraphed for McLean to come out and on his arrival he will be made temporarily Chief Manager and as such have an opportunity of seeing and knowing everything, and Greig goes to London to replace him there and he may there satisfy any inquiring minds and himself study up again London banking.[24]

This first reorganization plan was aborted when McLean twice refused to accept appointment as Acting Chief Manager, despite the Chairman's cabled appeal that it was in the 'interests of the Bank'. His stated reason was health, an unwillingness to spend another summer in China. To this must be added the family tradition that his real concern was for his family. The Court recorded they 'feel much dissatisfaction at Mr McLean's second refusal to accept for a year the chief managership of the Bank in Hong Kong'.

However the directors chose to see a bright side to the refusal. Their plan had been offered, as Heard correctly stated, in part response to pressures from shareholders in London and had involved the voluntary but temporary resignation of James Greig, who was, in any case, due for leave. The Court recorded that they were 'pleased at not having to act on the praiseworthy offer of Mr Greig which was only entertained with a view to satisfy some of the London shareholders'. The Standing Committee had reaffirmed their 'entire confidence' in Greig and the prospect of the London managership was held out to him on his retirement from the East.

As in the case of Victor Kresser, the Court were shortly to withdraw these endorsements.

A 'Circular to Directors' from London shareholders was in fact widely published on the China coast – for example in the *North-China Herald* on December 31, 1874 – 'suggesting' that David McLean should be appointed Inspector, but confirming their conviction that 'the fundamental resources of our Bank are still solid and merely require patient and judicious development to realize all, and more than all our former prosperity'. The problems of the Hongkong Bank were a very public affair.

The Court were well aware of this 'suggestion' and of the London shareholders' strong opposition to any further advances to the Indo-Chinese Sugar Company. They made McLean the offer and he accepted. Newspaper comment naturally questioned the wisdom of appointing a servant of the company as inspector, but the results fully justified the Court's decision. McLean's ability to offer a critical and totally unbiased opinion is a characteristic manifest in all he wrote.[25]

With Greig remaining in Hong Kong, McLean on inspection, and Vacher's resignation from the Bank effective in January, London was left to the temporary management of Thomas Jackson, who had fortuitously been in Ireland on leave. In February 1875 Jackson took the unusual and unwise step of circularizing the London shareholders on the soundness of the Bank, using information he had just received by cable from Hong Kong on the semi-annual meeting at a time when the shares remained at a significant discount on the London market. Jackson's statement, as reported in the press, ended with the following optimistic summation: 'I am assured that the most ample provision has been made for all possible losses, which statement the shareholders may fully rely upon.'[26]

This was more than a normal press release. Jackson was by-passing the Court and offering a personal endorsement of the Board's integrity. On April 25, 1875,

Greig was accordingly instructed by the Court to inform Jackson that 'his circular to shareholders was greatly objected to, while duly appreciating his good intentions in reassuring the shareholders, the Court must inform him his action was ill-judged'.

The receipt in January 1875 of a 'circular' or requisition from 26 London shareholders holding 1082 shares (and referred to above) must have given proof that London could exert pressure with or without a London Committee.[27] Indeed, it might have been argued that such a committee would have diverted the attack which could thereby have been contained, although this was not always to prove the case. Nevertheless, in February the Court resolved, again unanimously, this time in favour of a London Committee and in May confirmed their decision, adding that its three members were to be nominated by McLean.

McLean's detailed report was before the Court in May with the conclusion that losses of $117,000 would have to be provided for on June 30 and a further $340,000 at the end of the year. Although the details are unavailable, this erred on the side of caution, but it was essential that the report allow for every possible problem. The Bank could not afford new discoveries. As it happened only $300,000 was set aside from published profits; not all McLean's non-performing loans resulted in losses. The essence of McLean's report was available to the shareholders at the August 1875 meeting and McLean himself was confirmed as London Manager at a salary of £2,000 per annum plus an additional £500 for his inspection trip – 'both,' wrote McLean to Greig, 'highly satisfactory to me & for which please convey my best thanks to the Directors.'[28]

By comparison with the February meeting, tempers had cooled by August. The Bank's 1875 Chairman, Adolf von André, was able to begin, 'I am somewhat more fortunate than my predecessor in this Chair . . .' As the *North-China Herald* commented:

The [mid-1875] report of the Hongkong and Shanghai Bank seems to have very generally re-assured shareholders as to the soundness of its position. Irritated and alarmed beyond measure by the successive disclosures of losses which had swept away the Reserve Fund, the shareholders insisted, last year, on an authoritative inspection and exposition of the real state of the Bank accounts.

. . . What shareholders were crying for was to know the worst . . . We repeat, therefore, that we have full confidence the worst has been at last declared . . . The inconvenience which has been caused in many cases by the cessation of dividends has been cruel; but we trust those who have been able to weather the storm may now look forward to an early relief from their difficulties.[29]

Further reorganization

London Committee

The decision relative to a London Committee had been announced to the shareholders in August 1875; a month later the Court agreed to appoint A.H.

Phillpotts, a director of the London and County Bank, E.F. Duncanson, formerly of Shanghai and then with T. and A. Gibb and Co., and Albert Deacon, partner in E. and A. Deacon and Co.

McLean first described the duties of the Committee informally in reply to a query from Phillpotts. Reporting to Greig he wrote: 'I told [Phillpotts] that the duties would be to examine the bill Schedules sent home & those sent out and to give me the best information about the names etc. and also the general working of the London office.'[30] However, McLean continued, Phillpotts suggested that the Committee should get all the returns from Head Office and branches for inspection. The problem with this proposal was that the Hongkong Bank in fact made many of its advances upon shares. McLean was concerned that if the London Committee objected, were overruled, and resigned, 'it would play the devil with us'.

McLean himself became concerned with the problem of lending on the ultimate security of Bank shares. The question would be resolved in the Bank's favour in a razor's edge decision in the case of the Trustees of the *Estate of Augustine Heard and Company v The Hongkong Bank*, February 23, 1876. The Court agreed with the Bank that it could make a cash advance to a shareholder while retaining under Article 28 of the Deed of Settlement a lien on the shares owned by the borrower without violating the clear prohibition against lending on the security of its own shares contained in Article 29.[31] This nice distinction confirmed the basis on which much Hong Kong business was done, but its reception in London was uncertain.

The duties of the London Committee evolved over time with its role expanding as the China loans became of increasing importance, as the Hongkong Bank's role in the City developed, and as the decline in the gold price of silver undermined the position of the London-based Eastern exchange banks.

Whatever the subsequent hesitations, the decision had been made and the Bank was to have the advice and the pressures of a local committee based in the world's financial centre, the City of London.

The dismissal of James Greig

When McLean summarized his report for the shareholders he included his opinion that the Bank was sound, operating on a safe basis generally, and that the staff were efficient and expenses being kept down. Omitted was the comment that the general business was not earning as before.[32]

In October 1875 McLean, by then London Manager, was writing critically to Cameron in Shanghai and Jackson back in Yokohama on Greig's exchange operations, especially as they related to India. McLean's expectations relative to profits for the half-year were not fulfilled, and with Greig's departure from Hong Kong on leave in February 1876, he began writing advice to Jackson, by then

Acting Chief Manager in Hong Kong. These were private letters, and it must be remembered that McLean at 43 was senior to both Jackson and Cameron; he had been Jackson's Manager in Shanghai in the early days of the Bank and had pushed Jackson's career by advocating his promotion and appointment to key positions to two Chief Managers. Furthermore, McLean was now the senior serving officer and his role in 'saving' the Bank made him the '*éminence grise*', a role which he continued to play until Jackson was very firmly established.

By May of 1876 McLean was warning Jackson that the London shareholders were considering sending a requisition dealing with Greig's management and that E.F. Duncanson had been approached.

One thing is pretty certain that if you do well the second six months 1 July to 31 December his chance of returning as Chief is gone. I strongly recommend that you should have a fair trial before Greig is allowed to return to the East. I know what the result will be.[33]

The semi-annual accounts show published profits as follows: end 1875, $228,000; mid-1876, $307,000; end-1876, $461,000.

Greig arrived in London in mid-May of 1876. After Arthur Sassoon, a former member of the Bank's founding Provisional Committee then resident in London, had complained to McLean, the latter determined to put the matter to Greig.

I told Greig what the London shareholders opinion is of his management and that they were going to protest against his return to headquarters. Also the report is that he lost a lac [1,00,000] of dollars in rupee transactions . . . the best thing he can do is to resign as I am sure he will never get back to H[ead] O[ffice] as Chief.[34]

Greig appeared to be aware of his precarious position and manoeuvred to get a senior position in the London Office. He first proposed – and he was, after all, still titular Chief Manager – that McLean go to Shanghai for a year to relieve Cameron; McLean refused. He then suggested that William Kaye, who had accepted the post of London Sub-Manager in March 1875, go to San Francisco and that Harries, who was relatively junior, should return to London. This too McLean vetoed, recognizing that once a London vacancy existed, however temporary, Greig would attempt to get himself entrenched.[35] But Greig certainly showed no signs of resigning.

Under mounting pressure both in China and London, the directors did not wait for the end-1876 results. Jackson's mid-year report apparently satisfied them, and in July they conducted a survey of Greig's record. The Court noted that in the six years 1871–1876 profits at Head Office had been $889,176 and that losses had been $1,685,000. Given the history of the Bank's involvement with unwise Hong Kong investments, which were at least partially the responsibility of Kresser and/or the directors, these figures might well, in fairness, need adjustment; nevertheless, Greig's performance had not been satisfactory. The Court, which had less than two years previously confirmed confidence in and appreciation of their Chief Manager, now requested his resignation.

The Board . . . being also well aware of the strong feeling against his retention in the Bank's service shown by the public interested in the establishment, are unanimously of opinion that Mr Greig should be requested to resign entirely from the service of the Bank, and that an intimation to that effect be conveyed to him by the Chairman through Mr McLean. (11 July 1876.)

Instead McLean first wrote privately to Greig urging him to resign; only when this failed did he forward the Chairman's letter. The Hongkong Bank's second Chief Manager resigned on October 9, 1876, clearing the way for the confirmation of the then Acting Chief Manager, Thomas Jackson.

A reassessment of Greig

Was Greig sacrificed? Was he responsible for the unprofitable Head Office operations? The only specific description of Greig's transactions is contained in McLean's letter to Ewen Cameron in Shanghai.

It is impossible to make money by his operations – the moment he remits £10 to London he draws on India for the equivalent. This would no doubt suit if Exchange in India happened to be high when he entered upon the operations, but it cannot always pay. India has been at death's door for funds ever since my arrival [1874] and the cry has been send funds at any price while H[ead] O[ffice] has been chokeful of dollars.[36]

In other words he was, in effect, (i) buying £10 in Hong Kong by paying out Hong Kong dollars, (ii) recovering the dollars by selling rupees to an equivalent amount, thereby creating an overdraft in India on Head Office account. He must then sell the £10 for rupees at a rate which will more than cover the overdraft if the set of transactions is to be profitable. For this to happen, the rate for rupees in London must be high, that is, rupees must be cheap. McLean states that the contrary was in fact the case: India was 'crying' for funds at any price, that is, they were demanding rupee remittances at any price, thus driving up the price of rupees in terms of sterling and making Greig's operations unprofitable. McLean commented, '[He] seems to have got off the rails if one may judge by the last half-year's operations – no money having been made by H.O. for sometime past.'[37]

McLean continues the charge that Greig had been mishandling the exchange operations in letters covering the period through June 1876 and concludes, 'Greig's management the last 12 months has been lamentably bad . . .'[38] The shareholders were holding him responsible for the loss of a lac of dollars solely in ill-judged rupee operations.[39]

The Court of Directors' first investments for the Reserve Fund had been in Indian rupee securities to serve as security against exchange operations involving overdrafts in India, as in the operation described. McLean did not state that this type of operation could never pay, but that it had not paid at least in 1874/75, implying that Greig had not reacted properly when the London/India exchange rate changed.[d]

McLean treated Greig's operations as if they were simultaneous, but there is implied a longer run approach which, in more modern terms, can be reexpressed as follows:

instead of utilizing Hong Kong dollars, of which he had plenty, to purchase sterling, Greig preferred to sell rupees, funding this by way of an overdraft. His view was that rupees would depreciate sufficiently to make this short position profitable, notwithstanding the high rate of interest on rupee overdrafts. McLean thought this view speculative, as it would only be profitable if the rupee were overvalued at the time of the transactions. McLean also held the view, with which most modern bankers would probably concur, that it made more sense to employ surplus funds in Hong Kong rather than pay heavy interest charges in India against the hope of an exchange rate movement in his favour.[40]

Assuming that the Bank, in order to meet the legitimate trade requirements of its constituents had to (i) buy sterling bills on London and (ii) provide rupee exchange, and given also that McLean considered Head Office to be 'chokeful of dollars', his solution would apparently have been to ship silver to India.

As far as present information permits a judgement, the conclusion must be that there was substance to the criticism of Greig as Chief Manager. The question of the Court's timing in relation to the reassessment however remains, and on that it may be supposed that the directors needed the perspective of time – and distance – to properly perceive this.

The Court of Directors

The directors had been subjected to considerable pressure and the record of meetings confirms high rates of attendance. But, as recorded previously, there had been problems both with particular incidents, for example Belilios's refusal to accept his fees and his opposition to allocating the full year's fees for 1875. On policy, there had been discussion on the criteria for electing members to the Standing Committee. The Court were in danger of isolation and efforts to secure an 'English' (a term used in contemporary documents to include Scots) director were successful only after at least three failures.

In February 1876 after considerable discussion the directors confirmed that election to the position of Chairman and Deputy Chairman would normally be on a seniority basis except in 'exceptional circumstances'. The following month they took the significant steps of abolishing the Standing Committee and resolving to

---

[d] To test McLean's criticism with random figures for 1875, take the following rates for June: $ = 4/1¼, $100 = Rs227, Rs = 1/10 3/16, then with the hypothetical £10 (= $48.70) transaction London can buy Rs108.2, but Greig would have sold Rs110.5 for $48.70, a loss of approximately 2%. Rates for December give the same results. To lose a lac of rupees in this way would involve a turnover of some $2.1 million, a not impossible figure.

hold weekly meetings of the full Court, with each director told off to inspect the accounts of assigned agencies and branches.

This latter step was surprising, but it may have been that the directors considered their position had been endangered by decisions of the Standing Committee and that problems had been referred to them too late. McLean's private accusations, cited earlier, relative to Kresser's 'intimacy' as Chief Manager with members of the Standing Committee, specifically the reference to more favourable rates of interest granted their firms, may by this time have been more generally known. There is no supporting evidence, however, and it is equally likely that the burden of a director's personal responsibility was a factor in the decision. For otherwise involved merchants to meet weekly to solve all matters referred to them was however over-ambitious. This solution might well lead to the screening process taking place not in a sub-committee of the Court but in the offices of the Bank's Chief Manager and branch managers.

As for the other problems of the Hongkong Bank, exchange business fluctuated in reaction to the state of trade, the decline in deposits was thought not to reflect a lack of confidence in the Bank, and McLean's judgement that the business was basically sound proved correct.

The Bank took steps to rid itself of responsibilities relative to the Indo-Chinese Sugar Company, the Hong Kong Distillery was under new management, the property of the Pier and Godown Company was again auctioned and again bought in, while legal cases continued in the complex affairs of the Sugar Refinery. Although the Hongkong Bank had still to extricate itself from management responsibilities, the financial losses had been written off. New problems would arise: in 1875 Augustine Heard and Co. failed, followed in Manila by Russell, Sturgis and Co. – leading to the establishment of an agency there under the Bank's 'sugar expert' C.I. Barnes; in San Francisco the Bank of California failed; the Bank had £8,500 in clean bills outstanding when several Lyons firms failed; the steamship *Calibar*, with which the Bank had become involved, was a financial burden; and documents dealing with the Bank's claim on the King of Annam remained lost somewhere between the chambers of the Chief Justice and the chambers of Mr Justice Snowdon.

With its Reserve Fund still at $100,000, its Court trying desperately to keep at least at the minimum level, recruit 'Englishmen', and work out a new method of handling the increasingly complex affairs of the Bank under a new Chief Manager, the Bank was in a sense beginning again. As in 1864 it could be predicted with equal certainty that the Bank would succeed from its local support. And now it was independent of sponsors, its ties with the past and early role concepts forgotten, and its options entirely open. The Bank began its new era.

Perhaps the critical Charles May summed it up at the February 1877 meeting:

We may, gentlemen, perhaps, in after years, be rather proud of our having sacrificed a million for the furtherance of local enterprises (laughter); and I think, gentlemen, there has been enough done for those enterprises so far as this Bank is concerned (renewed laughter).

7

THE EARLY HONGKONG BANKERS

> It was a common fault with Banks to put their managers in too prominent a position and lodge them palatially as if they were partners in the business. Now this was not the position the manager of a joint-stock company should occupy.
>
> H. Kingsmill at the February 1875 Meeting.

This chapter is about the Bank's servants and the directors' policies towards them.

The Hongkong Bank's newly appointed Hankow agent, A.M. Townsend, found the American captain of the Yangtze River steamer surprised that he was English. The captain had thought all bank men were 'Scotch'. They were so in the Oriental Bank . . .

'Well,' he concluded, 'I suppose the Hongkong Bank being a local bank is not so particular.'[1]

Finding qualified bank staff had been one of the major problems confronting the directors of the newly established exchange banks in the early 1860s, as indeed it apparently was for the Deutsche Bank in 1872 despite the Comptoir's discharge of all its German executives.[2] This was true even though these banks had been established in Europe – or at least in Bombay – where there was access to potential staff of varying qualities, but the Hongkong Bank was, as the Captain rightly stated, a local bank. At the beginning it had to recruit locally.

Fortunately the task was facilitated by the failure over a period of years of several Eastern exchange banks, so that the Hongkong Bank could recruit staff as its business grew and more assistance was required. And, in the course of this, Englishmen, Irishmen, a German, a Swiss, even an Australian – a mistake as it turned out – were acquired along with the Scots.[3] The Bank was to acquire high quality ledgers and a safe or two from the same source.

This process is illustrated in Table 7.1. In the period through 1875 the Bank's long-term staff policies were initiated, but before they could be implemented, there was immediate need for recruitment. Senior positions required experience, preferably Eastern experience, and coupled with the dictum that good merchants don't make good bankers, in the period 1864–1876, 20 of the 27 men accepting appointments which assumed some experience came from other Eastern banks. The record suggests, however, that not all the bankers were successful: of these twenty, four died and ten either retired, resigned, or left for reasons of health; five were discharged, asked to resign, or failed to have their contracts renewed; one left after two years for reasons unknown. Only nine of the twenty lasted with the Bank more than ten years, a reflection at least in part of their seniority and of the serious health problem.

By 1875, as a survey of that year's Staff List in the Appendix will indicate, the Bank had been able to modify its policy and, although continuing to take on a few juniors in the East, no longer needed to accept the more senior staff of the then faltering Eastern banks, despite the many requests received. There was one (successful) exception – M.C. Kirkpatrick.

However small the staff may have been in those early years, policies had nevertheless to be developed. Even seniors needed, for example, Home leave; they needed assistants and, eventually, replacement. These and other related matters required consideration by the directors. For junior staff the Bank took advantage of the presence of young men on the China coast, but it also began to develop a system of recruiting in Britain, training in London Office, and then calling the juniors out East as need for them arose.

This chapter is an account of the early development of staff policy, an opportunity to provide vignettes of life and biographical details which do not easily fit into the banking chapters. This is not, however, a digression; the story of the Hongkong Bank's bankers is key to understanding its history – and its success.

THE DEVELOPMENT OF PERSONNEL POLICY

Salaries and other payments

Salary scales were based on those of other exchange banks and in this period the directors did not formally establish or minute a scale of payments related to length of service and post. Various *ad hoc* decisions were made, but with a small staff, the directors were able to set salaries in part on the basis of personal knowledge.

Managers and agents were paid an annual bonus which approximated one to two months' salary. There were no pension or Provident Fund provisions in this period, but staff leaving the service, including those requested to resign, were granted 'gratuities' of varying amounts on a basis which must have changed from case to case. That this was unsatisfactory is evidenced by the reconsideration the Court was willing to give to requests for a further 'gratuity'.

The personal factors involved in each staff decision and the variation from port to port suggest that the details are best considered in connection with each specific case. A more systematized discussion must be reserved for Chapter 15.

Table 7.1 *The Hongkong and Shanghai Banking Corporation*
Former positions and careers of early Hongkong Bank officers

		Position from which employed	Senior position in HSBC		
(i) from other Eastern banks					
1864	Grigor, John	Acct, Bank of Hindustan, China and Japan	Manager Yokohama	f	1871
1865	Kresser, Victor	Manager, Hong Kong, Comptoir d'Escompte	Chief Manager	cnr	1870
1865	McLean, David	Act. Manager Shanghai, Oriental Bank	Manager Shanghai, London	r	1889
1865	Louden, John S.	Agra and Masterman's Bank, Shanghai	Agent Foochow	h	1873
1866	Noble, George E.	Shanghai, Commercial Bank Corp of India[a]	Chief Manager, Manager London	r	1897
1866	Brett, W.R.	Manager Yokohama, Chartered Mercantile	Manager Yokohama	f	1867
1867	Jackson, Thomas	Banker's asst HK, Agra and Masterman's Bank	Chief Manager	r	1902
1867	Cameron, Ewen	Acct. liquidator, HK, Bank of Hindustan	Manager Shanghai, London	r	1905
1867	Riddell, W.S.	Manager Hong Kong, Asiatic Bank	Act. Chief Acct, Hong Kong	d	1877
1867	Stevenson, Robert	Manager Shanghai, Asiatic Bank	Manager Bombay, Edinburgh	r	1874
1869	Greig, James	Manager Hong Kong, Asiatic Bank	Chief Manager	f	1876
1870	Turner, Alfred L.	Acct, Hong Kong, Commercial Bank Corp[a]	Manager Yokohama	d	1878
1871	Hodgson, John G.	Asst Cashier, Comptoir d'Escompte de Paris	Agent Calcutta	f	1886
1871	Leith, Alexander	Chartered Mercantile Bank, Calcutta[b]	Agent Tientsin	h	1891
1871	Willaume, N.	Comptoir d'Escompte, Hong Kong	Act. Agent Saigon	?	1873
1872	Morriss, Edward	(liquidator) Shanghai, Agra and . . . Bank	Manager Yokohama	d	1890
1873	Winton, J.J.	Manager Singapore, Asiatic Bank	Manager Singapore	d	1883
1875	Jordan, Paul	Chartered Mercantile Bank	Banker's asst, Hong Kong	re	1882
1875	Kaye, William	Manager Shanghai, Chartered Bank	Sub-Manager London	r	1889
1875	Tompkins, M.M.	Exchange clerk San Francisco, Bank of California	Accountant San Francisco	r	1913

1884	Kirkpatrick, M.C.	Oriental Bank Corporation, Singapore	Agent Batavia	r	1909
(ii) from merchant houses					
1865	Moody, Gifford D.	Torrey and Co. Hong Kong	Act. Agent Hiogo	h	1871
1867	Cope, Herbert	Barnet and Co. Shanghai	Agent Singapore	f	1879
1868	Walter, John	Dent and Co. Shanghai	Act. Chief Manager; Mgr Yokohama, Shanghai; Inspector; Sub-Manager London	r	1902
1869	Stewart, Henry Kirk	Siemssen and Co. Hong Kong	Agent Saigon	d	1871
1870	Abendroth, Hermann E.C.	Landstein and Co. Hong Kong	Agent Amoy, Act. Agent Manila	f	1880
(iii) former Eastern employment unknown					
1865	Smith, Henry C.		Chief Accountant	d	1882
1866	Murray, William		Act. Agent Calcutta	re	1872

Notes:

[a] Commercial Bank Corporation of India and the East.

[b] Recruited by Cameron; Leith had left the Chartered Mercantile and was a school teacher.

cnr = contract not renewed; f = discharged or requested to resign for poor service; d = death; r = retired due to age even if health also a factor; re = resigns voluntarily; h = health.

Sources: China directories, Hong Kong jury lists, minutes of the Court of Directors of the Hongkong Bank, various advertisements in China-coast newspapers, Private Letter Books of David McLean, official Staff Lists after 1891, lists for 1864–1891 reconstructed by Catherine E. King, and biographical materials in the HSBC Group Archives.

Leave and marriage

On the question of leave and marriage the directors took the easy way out. In 1870 after making several *ad hoc* decisions and noting that similar requests were likely to occur from time to time, the Court decided to consult other banks.

The directors agreed to fall in with current practice. Home leave was to be granted for one year after five years' service in the East; it was to be at half-pay, all travelling and personal expenses paid by the officer. These were by later standards tough conditions which eventually evolved into eleven months leave, the first half of which was on full pay, the balance on half-pay, and passage paid. Acting officers received half their own plus half the salary of the person they were relieving. The expense of leave was modified by the fact that passage was paid, by the Bank, first class and included room and board on the ship – possibly one-fifth of the total leave time.

Also from the first there were exceptions – David McLean, for example, was granted leave on full pay.

On the other hand the marriage policy although apparently clear-cut was in fact confused. European officers under the rank of 'Accountant' had to obtain the Court's permission to marry.[a]

Whatever the directors' qualifications might be, they were not competent marriage counsellors, and Chief Managers often less so. The nature of bank employment made a minimum salary rule for marriage practically universal – certainly there were rules for London Office staff. In the East, however, the rules were more formal and were formulated not only from concern over the Bank's image in a closed foreign society but also over matters of expense – housing and passages. A mess was cheaper than providing married quarters; one passage was cheaper than two. Certain of the smaller ports had no suitable married quarters, and transfers might be made without warning.

In the early days of the Bank promotion came relatively early. Under all circumstances, however, a young man's desire to marry could become a matter of priority to him. The consequence of the Court's decision was, therefore, that the minutes became cluttered with contradictory judgements on the age of (Hongkong Bank) consent and the statement of 'final' policy decisions which

---

[a] 'Accountant' came to be the standard term for the assistant manager; in large branches he would be junior to any Deputy or Sub-Manager. Usually it was the first 'appointment', that is, the first assignment made in the name of and with the ultimate approval of the Court of Directors. Bankers below this level were undifferentiated; they were known as 'juniors' or 'banker's assistants' – despite the considerable responsibility that the 'junior' in charge of a large department in a major branch might undertake. The capital 'A' is used to differentiate the title from an 'accountant' by profession. The duties of the Hongkong Bank 'Accountant' included management of the office routine and personnel as well as banking decisions not requiring reference to the manager.

would not, in fact, be final. But these problems developed later as promotion became slower.

Three tiers

The reference to 'European' staff suggests correctly that there were other varieties. The term 'European' included North Americans, of which there were probably three on the Bank's pre-World War II Eastern staff.

There were 'non-Europeans' in the Bank, however.

From 1865 the Hongkong Bank both in Hong Kong and Shanghai recruited locally. The new staff included Chinese, employed through the compradore, but the policies determining their terms of service were not a matter for the Court of Directors. The Bank also employed Portuguese, and there is information on their early role but mainly from the Shanghai records. A three-tiered system developed immediately: (i) the foreign staff or 'Eastern Staff' composed of those whose origins were not in the East and who could be transferred at the discretion of the Court, (ii) the Portuguese staff, primarily clerical, long-serving, loyal, and usually recruited to remain in the local office, and (iii) the Chinese or compradore's staff. This was already a pattern in other banks, indeed in other firms on the China coast; the Hongkong Bank merely complied with the custom. The pattern prevailed until the 1950s.

The categories require three modifications.

First, there were Europeans recruited in the East. In the early days of the Bank these were probably intended for category (i); later they would be known as 'local British staff' (although not all would be British) and may be included in the functional sense with (ii). They would not be eligible for an 'appointment' by the Court of Directors, that is, appointment as 'Accountant' or higher, although they might be promoted by a branch manager to be the head of a department within the branch.

Second, there were Chinese who were not on the compradore's staff and may have been recruited independent of him. This development came later in the Bank's history when Shanghai, for example, required virtually a second shift of bookkeepers.

Third, the categories are 'China-coast' oriented. The equivalents of (ii) and (iii) were found elsewhere; there might even be a local office manager – in Japan, a *banto* – as well as a Chinese compradore. In Ceylon the 'burghers' took the place of the 'Portuguese'; in India, native staff were employed consistent with caste rules; they were supervised by a native employee with responsibilities similar to that of the compradore. The guarantee shroff in Ceylon, as the name suggests, took responsibility for the business introduced.

In the early days of the Bank the demarcations were not always clearly seen.

They formed nevertheless a series of unspoken but almost assumed realities which were later formalized. The success of the Hongkong Bank is a reflection of the work of all staff. Nevertheless, it was the Eastern staff, the Foreign staff, (i) in the above categories, who were the decision-makers and who eventually became the Accountants, Sub-Managers, Agents, and Managers – and eventually Chief Manager. Naturally, a history of the Bank must focus on their contribution and therefore on Court policies relative to their recruitment, training, and development.

The fundamental policies

At this point two basic policy decisions should be introduced:

(i) 'the Board supported the view that, as far as possible, the berth [Hankow agent] should be occupied by an officer taken from the present staff of the Bank – it being the wish of the directors to afford to the Corporation's servants every chance of encouragement and promotion [1867]'; and

(ii) 'the strong opinion was expressed that in future all clerks joining the service of the Bank should go through the London Office, save under very exceptional circumstances and then the consent of the Board must be obtained [1876]'.

The first policy was initially stated in connection with Thomas Jackson's appointment to Hankow, the wisdom of which had been questioned purely on the grounds of his youth.

The two statements together have *de facto* the consequence that, once London was able to generate enough juniors to meet the Bank's requirements for executive staff in the East, local recruitment of 'Eastern Staff' would virtually cease. Then, almost without exception, only those normally resident in the United Kingdom would be taken on as potential members of the Eastern staff of the Hongkong Bank. The policy of promotion from within was also strictly adhered to and had a supporting effect.

These policies would permit recruitment of the French François de Bovis (East in 1872) and the apparently stateless German F.T. Koelle (East in 1894), both of whom resided in England and had English mothers. De Bovis even became, for a short time, Chief Manager. It would be fair to conclude, however, that, although the composition of the Court of Directors would draw from many nationalities, the executive staff would, with very few exceptions, be British.

The London requirement would effectively argue against promotion of local non-British staff to the executive officer rank, that is, to the Eastern staff, and indeed the policy came to be so used. While the rule was not totally without exception, it became increasingly inflexible; even after World War II those leaving the armed forces in China were told to apply in London and in consequence at least two preferred to join the Mercantile Bank of India in the East (see Volume IV). In the 1950s the first local staff scheduled for appointment as officers were sent to London for orientation. London would play a varied role in the history of this Hong Kong-based Eastern bank.

There were relatively few exceptions to the 'London rule' after the initial years and until the 1950s. These exceptional appointments were made to relatively senior men with special qualifications, for example, E. Morel (1881) in Lyons, Archibald Maccoll (1884) in Batavia, Julius Brüssel (1889) in Hamburg, and the Bank's inter-war political advisers, G.E. Hubbard and W.C. Cassells. Morel and Brüssel were citizens of France and Germany respectively employed specifically to be branch managers; they and M.M. Tompkins (1875) (see Table 7.1), who was the San Francisco Accountant, were the equivalents of today's 'regional officers'. Maccoll had been the senior partner in Batavia of Martin and Dyce, the Bank's Netherlands East Indies agents; Maccoll's appointment was, in David McLean's view, a mistake – as indeed it proved to be.[4]

These are names which will appear again in this history. But as the only American on the Eastern staff to be recruited in the period 1865–1876, Tompkins requires additional comment.

Born in New York State in 1836 Tompkins attempted at the age of twenty to reach California overland, was turned back by Indians, and sailed to Panama, crossing the Isthmus by mule and eventually reaching San Francisco in 1858 where he worked for a time as a messenger with Wells Fargo. In 1863 he joined one of the two partnerships which in 1865 amalgamated as the Bank of California, a State bank with paid-up capital of $2 million, advertising 'banking and exchange business within this and neighboring states and Mexico; also . . . China'.[5] When the bank failed in 1875 Tompkins, who had been working as an exchange and bullion clerk, was taken on in the new Hongkong Bank agency in San Francisco as Accountant and as a member of the Eastern staff.

In his attempt to secure his own London appointment, James Greig made the proposal, opposed by McLean, that W.H. Harries (East in 1870), the Bank's San Francisco Agent, return to London and Tompkins take over in San Francisco.[6] As stated before, the Court did not agree, but whether as Agent or Accountant Tompkins was unknown to his colleagues, and McLean proposed to Jackson:

[that] it would be very desirable that the Directors & yourself should see Mr Tompkins . . . if you want to see Tompkins wire and I'll advise Harries [on leave in England] to send him on to China. (September 8, 1876)

I would advise you to send him home this way [via London]. I would like to see him about the business & perhaps a little talk will do more than a year's correspondence . . . (3 November 1876)[7]

A letter suggesting a new officer in a responsible position be sent around the world would not, in 1976 perhaps, be worthy of special notice; written a hundred years earlier it is of interest. Tompkins, who retired in 1913 – a year after Harries, was for his last year second in seniority (to Wade Gard'ner) on the Eastern staff of the Hongkong Bank.

The Hongkong Bank might seek the advice of consultants, but it did not employ experts as full members of its staff. One exception would be E.G. Hillier, trained in the Chinese language, employed at a junior level in the East in 1883, and, until his death in 1923, Agent in Peking. He was followed, as noted above, by two political advisers in succession, secured from the Foreign Service. These advisers, if remembered at all by retired staff, are dimly seen; they were 'not one of us'. Indeed they dealt only with the Shanghai, Hong Kong, and London Managers.

The pattern then to which the Bank was heading may be simplified as follows: a young man with two recommendations and say two years' apprenticeship in a British bank would be interviewed, examined, and taken on in London, usually before he reached 21. There he would remain as a London junior but destined for the East when the call came. This could be perhaps in two to three years, depending on demand and on the junior's previous experience. Once in the East he would serve some 30 years, health permitting; he would take eleven months' leave every five years, wars and related crises permitting. He would not marry before his mid-thirties.

Stated thus, the pattern is premature, but it is told here to set against the realities of the Hongkong Bank's first years.

THE FIRST HONGKONG BANKERS – THE SENIORS

No history can afford the luxury of a year-by-year analysis, especially since by 1875 the Eastern staff already numbered 44 (see Appendix to this chapter) and by 1914 some 214. But there is a legitimate interest in 'the first' who worked for a successful corporation (see Tables 7.2A and B). The more successful will receive appropriate coverage, but the others, whether successful or not, deserve in this history the courtesy of a brief reference.

The first

The first servant of the Hongkong and Shanghae Banking Company, Ltd, was John Grigor, taken on by the Provisional Committee in 1864 before the selection of either Kresser or McLean. He became Accountant in Shanghai in 1867, but in 1871 as Manager he was responsible for losses on an advance made contrary to the Bank's standing regulations. The Court ordered him recalled to Hong Kong, but, unwilling to serve under James Greig, he resigned to become a broker in Japan.

Kresser, McLean, Jackson, Noble, Vacher, and Townsend are mentioned separately. What then was the fate of the other early 'European' recruits?

John Louden, after serving in Shanghai and Hong Kong, opened the agency in Foochow in 1871. The last reference to this early officer of the Bank is in 1873; he

Table 7.2A *The Hongkong and Shanghae Banking Company, Limited*
First 'European' staff, 1864–1865

(i)	(ii)	(iii)	(iv)
Eastern staff recruited in the East			
1864 Grigor, John	13 September, Accountant, Hong Kong	f	1871
1865 Kresser, Victor	1 January, Manager, Hong Kong	cnr	1870
1865 Louden, John S.	25 March, Accountant, Shanghai	h	1873
1865 McLean, David	March, Manager, Shanghai	r	1889
1865 Moody, Gifford D.	9 March, Asst. Accountant, Hong Kong	h	1871
1865 Smith, Henry C.	28 December, clerk, Hong Kong	d	1882
Staff recruited in London			
Vacher, W.H.[a]	26 July 1865, Agent, London	f	1875
de St Croix, George[b]	1865, clerk; 'terminated'	–	1865

(i) seniority in the service; for staff recruited in the East, this is the date of
recruitment; for staff recruited in London, the date of arrival in the East; (ii) place
and date of recruitment and position; (iii) f = discharged, cnr = contract not renewed
(see text), r = resigned, h = left Bank's service on health grounds, d = death; (iv) year
of leaving the Bank for reason stated in (iii).

Notes:
[a] Vacher did not work for the Bank in the East.
[b] A George de St Croix is taken on as a junior in 1869, went East in 1872 but the
evidence indicates this is another person.

returned Home to Britain in very ill health. Gifford Moody was an Assistant
Accountant in Hong Kong until 1868, he then went to Yokohama as Accountant.
In January 1871 he replaced Henry C. Smith as Agent Hiogo, but in September
had to leave the East on grounds of health. Smith had remained in the Hong Kong
office until 1869, when he was sent to open the agency in Hiogo. While he was on
leave in 1871, his performance was evaluated and his contract was not renewed.
Smith, however, returned to Hong Kong at his own risk, was taken back on
probation, was confirmed with strong recommendations, and served as Chief
Accountant until his death in 1882; he became the senior member of the Eastern
staff from 1873, the year McLean left Shanghai to be Sub-Manager, London,
and thus a member of the Home staff.

And in 1866

In 1866 the Bank employed five new 'Eastern' staff in the East, while in London
the first two 'London juniors', David Moncur and Alfred M. Townsend, both
marked for Eastern service, were taken on.

W.R. Brett had been manager of the Chartered Mercantile Bank in Yokohama

Table 7.2B *The Hongkong and Shanghai Banking Corporation*
First Eastern staff, 1866

(i)	(ii)	(iii)	(iv)
Eastern staff recruited in the East			
1866 Mackintosh, Lacland	23 January, Hong Kong, clerk	t	1867
1866 Noble, G.E.	February, Shanghai, clerk	r	1897
1866 Brett, W.R.	23 April, Manager, Yokohama	f	1867
1866 Jackson, Thomas	2 August, Hong Kong, clerk	r	1902
1866 Murray, William	April, Shanghai, clerk	r	1872
1866 Flowerdew, William	Shanghai, clerk	f	1867
Staff recruited in London			
1877 Burnett, G.H.[a]	8 June, Accountant	r	1899
1871 Moncur, David[b]	July, clerk	d	1873
1870 Townsend, A.M.[b]	October, clerk	r	1911

(i) seniority in the service; for staff recruited in the East, this is the date of recruitment; for staff recruited in London, the date of arrival in the East; (ii) place and date of recruitment and position; (iii) f = discharged, r = retired, t = temporary, d = death; (iv) year of leaving the Bank for reason stated in (iii).

Notes:

[a] Burnett was an experienced banker and was not originally recruited for Eastern service.

[b] The first London Office juniors, recruited to go East. Moncur was recruited before Townsend but went East after him.

and returned there for the Hongkong Bank, but he was dismissed for misconduct in 1867. William Flowerdew transferred to Yokohama and shortly afterwards was discharged.

William Murray is remembered by Townsend as primarily interested in his own investments on the embryo Shanghai stock market – 'Maun,' he would say when asked a question about the 'books', 'just go away and think a little – think a little and don't bother me'; Murray had been appointed Accountant in Shanghai in 1868, transferred to Calcutta as Agent in 1871, and resigned the following year. He is probably the Agent notorious in the folklore of that latter city for chalking the buying and selling rates on the soles of his shoes, propping up his feet on the desk and taking a long after-tiffin sleep without fear of being wakened by enquiring exchange brokers. Once out of the Bank's service and back in London Murray kept closely in contact with David McLean and, as a leading broker in Hongkong Bank and other Eastern shares, is often referred to in the correspondence.

Few among the first flourished. Victor Kresser had gone by 1870, W.H. Vacher by 1875, and, of the others who joined in 1864 and 1865, in the East only

Smith served out his years, in London there was David McLean. But the staff list already included names of those who starred in the Bank's development – David McLean, Thomas Jackson, G.E. Noble, A.M. Townsend – and, if one adds but one more year, in 1867 there came Ewen Cameron and Robert Stevenson, and then in 1868 John Walter.

Some of the early departures shown in Table 7.1 are quite explicable; Stevenson, for example, was already senior and, given his earlier connections first with the Commercial Bank Corporation of India and the East and then with the Bombay-originated Asiatic Banking Corporation, had most probably been trained in India; if so, he was the obvious choice for opening the Hongkong Bank's agencies first in Calcutta and then Bombay. In 1874 he returned Home on retirement, but is referred to in the Court minutes in connection with the 'Edinburgh agency'; then he too is mentioned no further.

A similar assumption of earlier Indian training might be made concerning Edward Morriss, whom the Bank sent to India and then to Yokohama, where he died from exhaustion in 1890.

Herbert Cope went to Singapore to open the Bank's agency in 1877 but was not successful; discharged, he decided to become a farmer and, according to McLean, emigrated to Iowa. J.J. Winton took over the Singapore management in 1879 and went far to setting the new branch on sound lines, but, already ailing, he left on leave in 1883, only to die at sea a few days out. John G. Hodgson rose in the normal way from Accountant in Yokohama, Agent Foochow, Agent Amoy, Agent Bombay in the emergency absence of the Agent James M. Grigor, a former London junior, and finally Agent Calcutta. Unfortunately, he was not successful in his exchange operations there and was asked to resign in 1886.

Hermann Abendroth was appointed Agent Amoy in 1874, but his role there was criticized as early as 1876, mainly on the charge that he was unpopular and failed to further the business interests of the Bank. Abendroth was German and a Jew; there is certainly a question of prejudice. Recruited in 1870 on the China coast, probably in Hong Kong, he was 40 years of age when he was sent to Shanghai at McLean's urgent request for assistance. McLean in particular wanted British juniors out from Home; he found Abendroth merely satisfactory. Behind this was McLean's objection to Kresser's alleged policy of picking up miscellaneous recruits on the China coast. 'I have asked HO to get out Assistants from your [London Office],' McLean wrote to Vacher, 'and the other day I applied for one and they send me [instead] a German [Abendroth]. He may be a good hand, but I don't want foreigners. I want English, or Scotch, nothing like sticking to one's colors.'[8]

Despite this uncertain reception and subsequent mediocre reports, Abendroth was granted leave that year and, on his way back to Head Office in 1877, he inspected Saigon. After discussions in Hong Kong with Jackson he returned to

Amoy and in April 1880 was sent to Manila to relieve C.I. Barnes when the latter went on leave. However, Abendroth himself became ill and proved unable to handle the Manila assignment. He was granted emergency sick leave to Europe in October and was asked to resign with a gratuity 'not to exceed' $10,000, equivalent to approximately two years' salary.

There is a clear indication that neither the directors nor the Chief Manager were as yet alerted to the fact that banking was a complex profession, that a man might do well in certain tasks, poorly in others.[b] Thus Smith, who had performed well as Accountant in Hong Kong, was sent as Agent in Hiogo where he was unsuccessful; but he was to be highly praised for his subsequent work as Chief Accountant. Hodgson rose to authority in ports where exchange was not a key operation but did poorly in Calcutta. Morriss on the other hand did better in Calcutta than in the totally different atmosphere of Yokohama.

But it might also be said in the defence of management that they had little room for manoeuvre, for trial and error. John Grigor, for example, when offered a 'second chance' in Hong Kong after failing to follow general instructions in Yokohama, refused it. The pressure was to appoint senior men to the next senior post, even if it were totally different in its requirements or in an area with which the officer had little or no experience. It would be a long time before the Bank both realized the problem and had a sufficiently large staff to permit flexibility and specialization. As a practical matter it was rarely possible to consider a man's qualifications and assign him to a back-room position, to China or to India according to his abilities and experience. In a 'service' it was not always desirable to do so.

There were exceptions: W.K. Dods (East in 1889), for example, was left in Calcutta for the major part of his career – assigned briefly to Hong Kong he told Jackson, 'The snipe shooting is terrible here – send me back to Calcutta.' Jackson agreed. In North China E.G. Hillier remained in Peking. In general, however, personnel policy of this kind – with career development concepts – was a product of the post-World War II period.

THE FIRST HONGKONG BANKERS – THE JUNIORS

The younger staff must be considered (i) as recruited in the East and, as this policy is phased out and (ii) as recruited in London. Indeed their story if told entirely here would carry the history to 1932, for in that year A.M. Townsend, who in 1870 was the Bank's first 'London junior' to go East, retired from the London Committee; he died in 1939 at the age of 93.

[b] At this time the complexity of various professions was being gradually acknowledged; the Institute of Bankers, however, was not founded until 1879.

Juniors recruited in the East, 1868–1880

The Hongkong Bank developed a system which was based on early recruitment in London and continuous service through to retirement in the early fifties, a retirement age standard in the East but young for Europe. A United Kingdom-based youngster made a major decision in joining London Office – he could anticipate a career in the East and was no doubt told early to expect good and bad assignments, advances and setbacks as he progressed up the seniority list. (The terminology used is listed in Table 7.3.)

The China-coast Britisher made no such major decision. He was there and selected the Bank as one of several local possibilities. There were a number of 'transients' or short-serving staff among the Eastern recruits – the majority of these would later have been recruited as 'Local British Staff', for example J.D. Woodford (see Table 7.4).

Table 7.1 lists those of the Hongkong Bank's early officers who came into the Hongkong Bank with some significant experience. In Table 7.4 there is a list of those who came with little or no experience, (i) from merchant houses, (ii) on their own from Britain, and (iii) 'Eastern juniors', apprentices on less than full pay. These last, when placed on full pay, were the equivalent of a first-tour clerk (banker's assistant), the category which would soon be exclusively recruited in London and come out after experience as a London junior. When this policy was formalized, then the recruits in the East, especially in a large branch, would be 'Local British Staff', not transferable into the 'career' service. In London the parallel would be recruitment into the 'Home Staff'.

The major advocate of the London junior policy was McLean; Kresser, a Swiss recruited in Hong Kong, was not supportive. McLean's experience with China-coast juniors had not been satisfactory, and he opposed British juniors from India on the grounds that they expected even the more important ledger work to be done by 'the natives'; McLean wanted it done by a member of the Eastern staff. He also opposed non-British – he just preferred British, or, to read behind his letters, Scottish-trained lads. His experience led him to see positive benefits from homogeneous recruitment; this indeed was his strongest argument – that and the fact he was very persistent.

Of the 21 listed as on the Eastern staff (excluding Cope and Walter who are in Table 7.1) only five served more than ten years. Many served no more than a year or two (see Table 7.4). Five Eastern juniors – in the sense referred to in Table 7.3 – can be identified: Beveridge, Barton, Dare, Maitland, and probably Mitchell.

What is the history of these juniors recruited in the East?

Their stories

C. H. Beveridge was the son of McLean's National Bank of Scotland manager in Dunfermline. Had he applied a few years later, he most certainly would have been taken on trial as a London Office junior. Although he was paid the full minimum salary of Ts150 a month from the beginning, he came out with the promise of an appointment under McLean's sponsorship, and he cannot have been much more than 21 years of age, with minimum experience. He was eventually assigned to Foochow, but unhappily he did not succeed, and, despite McLean's surveillance from London and Jackson's attempt to assist in Hong Kong, the young man had to return to Scotland in 1878 from where his father attempted in vain to have him reinstated.[9]

Another junior, **C. Barton**, is first listed in the Shanghai Charges Account below the Portuguese and with a smaller salary – Ts50. This appointment reflected McLean's urgent need for additional 'junior' staff. Barton was *de facto* an Eastern junior who required the sort of apprenticeship others, similar to him, would obtain in London Office. He lasted only three years, having been granted a terminal payment of Ts450, equivalent to six months' salary.

The firm of Maitland and Co. was operating in Shanghai in the 1870s, and in 1874 **Andrew Wright Maitland** is listed in the Shanghai branch charges book on a salary of Ts50. His seniority in the Bank dates from 1876, so in those two years he too was the equivalent of a 'London junior', training for the Eastern staff. In 1886 Maitland was the Bank's Chief Accountant and in 1891 became Agent of the important Tientsin office, but he is best known for his involvement in Sheng Hsuan-huai's 1897 Imperial Bank of China, modelled after the Hongkong Bank 'in everything', with Maitland as the manager of the Shanghai head office working with a Chinese compradore under Chinese managing directors.[10]

Another successful Eastern recruit was **G.R. Johnston**, who began in Shanghai in 1873 at the minimum salary and rose to be Chief Accountant in Hong Kong, went out to Bombay as Agent when James M. Grigor was taken ill in 1884, and then was appointed the first Inspector of Branches in 1885. Unfortunately his health broke down and he retired on leave in England in 1886. In 1919 at the age of 68 he was destitute, and the Court voted him an annual gratuity of £150.

F.W. Mitchell, Jr was the son of Hong Kong's Postmaster General and joined the Bank in Hong Kong in 1869, presumably as an Eastern junior. The records show he served in Foochow and Hankow before becoming Agent in Saigon in 1876 where he died in 1881.[11]

C.B. Rickett, who is mentioned by Townsend for his supporting role in the Hiogo office in 1876–1877, retired only in 1904 after many years as Agent Foochow; he is thus the longest serving of the Eastern junior recruits.

The last junior to be recruited in the East was **A.H. Dare**, a relative of Thomas

Table 7.3 *The Hongkong and Shanghai Banking Corporation Staff designations used, 1864–1914*

Eastern staff (sometimes 'Foreign staff')	The career service from clerks to Chief Manager serving in the East, not in theory confined to a single branch. As policy evolved, Eastern staff assigned to London Office or a European office – Hamburg or Lyons – might be taken off the Eastern staff list if the assignment were permanent, e.g. McLean, Koelle, de Bovis.
Home staff	Those taken on in London, not intended to be sent East.
Local staff	Clerical staff employed locally, usually referring to local citizens.
Local British staff	Those 'Europeans' taken on in the East for service in one office.
Junior	The broadest definition is a member of the Eastern staff who has not yet received an appointment by the Board of Directors as Accountant, Agent, or Manager.
London Office junior	A young man appointed in London with the intention that he be sent East when 'trained' and called for.
'Eastern junior'	A term used in this history to designate a young man appointed in the East on a basis similar to a London junior – applicable only in the early years of the Bank, (i) narrowly defined as one earning less than the usual minimum salary; but, as the system at first was not so sharply defined, also (ii) broadly defined as one employed at the minimum salary, relatively inexperienced but a member of the Eastern staff.
Portuguese staff	A clerk from the local Portuguese community employed for work in the local office.
Compradore's staff	The Bank employees engaged and guaranteed by the Bank's compradore at that particular branch or agency.
Chinese staff	Used interchangeably with 'compradore's staff' but actually and especially in larger branches a broader category to include Chinese in bookkeeping and certain technical jobs; they were not necessarily guaranteed by the compradore.

Jackson's wife, and his entire career (with the exception of a year in Amoy in 1883) was spent in Japan, although he received leave to England and was on the Eastern, not the 'Local British Staff'. He resigned in 1893; the Court subsequently learned that the reason had been health and consequently voted him a gratuity of £1,000.

Others are unfortunately but names on a list, staying a year or two and then departing. But even one or two of these will feature in the narrative which follows.

Meanwhile the London juniors were preparing for their assignment to the East.

Table 7.4A *The Hongkong and Shanghai Banking Corporation*
Junior staff recruited in the East

(i)	(ii)	(iii)	(iv)	(v)
1866 Mackintosh, L.		Hong Kong	t	1867
1866 Flowerdew, W.	Ts150	Shanghai, Yokohama	f	1867
1867 Cope, Herbert[a]	Ts150	from Barnet and Co., Shanghai; Agent Singapore	f	1879
1867 Smith, Elliot R.		Hong Kong	?	1868
1868 Beveridge, C.H.	Ts150	from Scotland; Shanghai, Foochow, Hong Kong	f	1878
1868 Walter, John		from Dent and Co., Shanghai; Act. Chief Manager	r	1902
1869 Ellis, G.J.		passage paid from Yokohama; Shanghai	f	1872
1869 Laurence, H.A.	Ts150	from Rothwell, Love & Co., Shanghai; May–Aug.	re	1869
1869 Mitchell, F.W. Jr[b]		Hong Kong, Foochow, Hankow, Agent Saigon	d	1881
1870 Gibson, F.F.		Act. Accountant, Hong Kong	f	1871
1872 Barton, C.[c]	Ts60	Shanghai junior, Hankow	f	1875
1874 McMahon, J.P.		Yokohama, Foochow	?	1874
1874 Rickett, C.B.[c]		Yokohama junior from 1872; Agent Foochow	r	1904
1872 Symonds, J.W.		Hong Kong, Shanghai	f	1878
1873 Johnston, G.R.	Ts150	Shanghai; Chief Accountant, Inspector	h	1887
1873 Morrison, John		Hong Kong, Agent Amoy, Agent Hiogo	f	1881
1873 Skelly, T.D.		Hong Kong	?	1873
1873 Thevenin, C.		Saigon . . . later wine merchant, Hong Kong	?	1873
1874 Gunn, D.A.M.		Hong Kong, Shanghai, Hangkow	f	1881

1874	Smith, A.J.		Yokohama, Asst. Accountant	re 1878
1876	Maitland, A.W.^c	Ts50	Shanghai junior, 1874; Agent Tientsin	r 1895
1876	Nelson, R.A.		Hong Kong; Manila	h 1878
1880	Dare, A.H.^c	$125	Yokohama junior, 1878; Sub-Manager Yokohama	re 1892
1867	Woodford, J.D.^d		from R.S. Walker and Co., Hong Kong; books	f 1884

(i) Seniority in the service, based on date of recruitment in the East (except for Eastern juniors), or date of first arrival in the East, or date of going on 'full pay' in the East; (ii) First monthly salary (only Shanghai known); (iii) Previous employment, highest positions; (iv) Reasons for leaving the Bank: t = temporary, f = discharged, r = retired, re = resigned on own volition, d = death, h = left for health reasons; ? = unknown; (v) The year last mentioned on the Eastern staff.

Notes:

a Also listed in Table 7.1. Ages are unavailable and some cross-listing cannot be avoided.
b Mitchell was a junior and probably at less than full pay, but the records are insufficient.
c Juniors on less than full pay, seniority from date of full pay.
d Possibly what would later be called 'Local British Staff' (see text).

Sources: Shanghai Charges Account Book, Minutes of the Court of Directors, various biographical materials, HSBC Group Archives; various contemporary directories, Hong Kong jury lists, letters of David McLean. Salaries are only available for Shanghai; China Directory information is not always reliable.

Table 7.4B *The Hongkong and Shanghai Banking Corporation*
Staff recruited in London before 1876 who went East

(i)	(ii)	(iii)	(iv)	(v)
1866 Moncur, David	1871	Act. Accountant Calcutta, Yokohama	d	1873
1866 Townsend, A.M.	1870	Shanghai; Manager New York, London	r	1911
1866 Burnett, G.H.	1877	Accountant London	r	1899
1868 Cook, R.H.	1872	Yokohama, Agent Hiogo	d	1904
1869 Harries, W.H.	1870	Hong Kong, Agent San Francisco	r	1912
1869 de St Croix, G.[a]	1872	Hong Kong, Agent Tientsin	r	1886
1870 Greig, W.G.	1870	Hong Kong, Manager Singapore	f	1888
1870 Grigor, J.M.	1871	Hong Kong, Agent Bombay	d	1885
1870 Veitch, A.	1871	Shanghai, Agent Calcutta	d	1893
1870 de Bovis, F.	1872	Hong Kong, Chief Manager, Manager Lyons	r	1922
1870 Haselwood, A.H.C.	1873	Shanghai, Agent Foochow	d	1888
1871 Hardie, D.	1871	Hong Kong, Agent Saigon	d	1874
1871 MacNab, J.	1872	Hong Kong, Agent Iloilo	r	1897
1872 Edger, J.S.	1876	Hong Kong, Manila	d	1882
1872 Moore, H.	1873	Shanghai, Accountant New York	d	1883
1872 Simpson, J.B.	1874	Bombay	?	1875
1872 Barnes, C.I.	1873	Shanghai, Agent Manila	r	1887
1872 Gard'ner, J.P.W.	1873	Hong Kong, Manager Singapore, Shanghai, New York	r	1919
1872 Cope, A.E.	1873	Hong Kong, Agent Saigon, Manila	f	1891

1872	Broadbent, J.F.	1878	Hong Kong, Agent Amoy	r 1900
1873	St John, R.N.	1877	Hong Kong, Yokohama	re 1883
1873	Creyk, J.G.G.	1874	Hong Kong, Cashier Hiogo	re 1880
1873	Permewan, R.T.	1874	Hong Kong, Accountant Singapore	f 1883
1874	Townsend, G.H.	1878	Hong Kong, Agent Bombay	d 1900
1874	Oxley, E.H.	1874	Hong Kong, Agent Hankow	r 1903
1874	Robinson, G.G.	1878	Hong Kong, Yokohama	r 1890
1874	Bevis, H.M.	1875	Hong Kong, Manager Yokohama, Shanghai, Acting Chief Manager	d 1906
1874	Anton, P.W.	1877	Hong Kong, Accountant New York	h 1884
			rehired for London Office 1888	? 1895

(i) Date of entry into London Office; (ii) Seniority in the service, based on date of first arrival in the East; (iii) First assignment, highest position; (iv) Reasons for leaving the Bank: f = discharged, r = retired, re = resigned on own volition, d = death, h = health reasons, ? = unknown; (v) The year last mentioned on the Eastern staff.

Note:
a See also Table 7.2A.
Sources: London Office staff ledger; Private Letters, David McLean Papers.

BIOGRAPHICAL SKETCHES AND NARRATIVES

Victor Kresser, David McLean, and James Greig

Victor Kresser's position as Hong Kong manager of the Comptoir d'Escompte de Paris and his close connections with French officials, especially those in Cochin-China, supports the common but erroneous assumption that he was French.

There are two independent sources which force the conclusion that he was, in fact, Swiss. In his autobiography Hermann Wallich, the French bank's Shanghai manager, makes the sweeping but possibly accurate generalization that the French did not make good exchange bankers; French banks had to employ either German Jews or Swiss Calvinists. A survey of the Comptoir's managers suggests that the Swiss Calvinist must be Kresser in Hong Kong. Woldemar Nissen, commenting on Kresser's selection as Hong Kong Manager for the Hongkong Bank, states definitely that he is Swiss.[12]

Kresser's life has not been fully researched, although he is known to have come East as early as 1861 with recommendations to authorities in Saigon. He was involved in two Cochin-China based projects, a telegraph scheme and sugar growing and processing. The former, which was active in 1869–1870 when Kresser was with the Hongkong Bank, was unsuccessful; a rival project succeeded, and the Governor in Saigon, aware that Kresser's company had been caught up in political intrigues, undertook to repurchase certain equipment.[13]

The sugar venture also originated while Kresser was still with the Bank, and his subsequent but inconclusive negotiations have already been referred to; he received additional support from the Comptoir d'Escompte, but in 1873 there was a reassessment of the company's prospects leading to the withdrawal of support from Hong Kong and increased pressure from the French bank for repayment. In the end the Saigon Government repaid the Comptoir and declared Kresser, who had become a partner in the associated Wahee Smith and Co., forfeit of all his rights. Later developments were more successful, but by then Kresser had returned to Europe.

Before leaving the East Kresser was to make a significant contribution to French banking by submitting a memorandum to the French authorities which would form the basis for the constitution first of the Banque de la Nouvelle-Calédonie and then of the Banque de l'Indo-Chine. His recommendations were based on the Hongkong Bank's ordinance and regulations, especially with reference to the banknote issue, a particular concern of the French authorities in Saigon.[14]

There is a sad reference to Kresser passing by the Bank's London Office in 1876 and borrowing £100 – which McLean did not expect to see again. '*Maskee* poor devil am sorry for him.'[c] In 1883 McLean wrote to Jackson that Kresser had died of brain fever.[15]

This does not read like the biography of a banker, and yet those on the Provisional Committee preferred him to Maclellan, despite his non-British nationality, by a vote of seven to three, and Nissen has been quoted as considering him the best exchange banker available. The only letter of his extant is to McLean, dated virtually on the eve of his departure from Hong Kong, that is July 25, 1870. It is a point-by-point technical answer to complaints made by McLean in the latter's usual forthright style; Kresser's letter suggests competence.[16]

Thomas Jackson long afterward remembered him as: 'a marvellously clever man, of immense energy, and it would have been impossible to find anyone better able to start a venture of the kind. He was full of zeal and threw himself heart and soul into the work . . .'[17]

Perhaps, indeed, that is the point. Kresser was an organizer and understood exchange, but he was, compared to the Scots with whom he was associated, undisciplined. His outside projects – whatever their intrinsic merit or whether successful or not – were more worthy of finance by risk capital than by a banker. Given the interests of the directors under whom he served, it would be unfair to suggest he led the Bank single-handed into difficulties, but he did not stay them, and there are Court minutes which suggest even the directors felt the need to watch their Chief Manager carefully. In the end they refused, when specifically requested by Kresser, to endorse his management of the Bank.

David McLean was a banker; he was furthermore a successful banker. Born on February 4, 1833, at Scotswall Farm, Dunfermline, Fifeshire, he was apprenticed at the age of sixteen to the National Bank of Scotland; on his retirement from the Hongkong Bank in 1889, the newspapers noted that the Dunfermline agent had been – and still was – William Beveridge.[18] McLean was, like his contemporary Andrew Carnegie, apparently right in supposing that opportunities for advancement were more likely overseas. In 1858 he set out for Australia, and, finding his intended ship had been wrecked, embarked for Hong Kong where, it was correctly rumoured, there was a need for bankers.

He joined the Oriental Bank Corporation, the doyen of Eastern exchange banks, then with its overwhelming reputation intact. McLean served in both Hong Kong and Shanghai, becoming acting manager, Hong Kong, in 1862 and acting manager in Shanghai from July 18, 1864, just before publication of the Prospectus of the Hongkong and Shanghae Banking Company was announced and a rumour circulated that his name was mentioned as a likely candidate for its

---

[c] 'Maskee' (Pidgin English) was used in Shanghai in the sense of 'never mind, it's all right', thus the impact of McLean's comment is that he is sorry for Kresser and doesn't mind (or forgives him) the probable loss of £100. The loan was a personal one.

senior managership. 'They'll need to tempt me with a stiff amount to leave the old ship. I have very good prospects in the OBC and am not going to throw them overboard merely for the sake of changing.'[19] McLean did not apply.[20] Apparently, however, the Provisional Committee neither approached McLean formally nor tempted him – possibly his position was known.

McLean, however, was mistaken in his estimation of his prospects with the Oriental; they did not confirm him as manager Shanghai, nor was he told of his next posting; it would in fact have been manager Yokohama. Two factors may have been involved. First, the directors had never met McLean; he had joined in the East and had not yet been Home on leave. Secondly, even in his early management days, he was taken to writing letters which, while of great value to the historian, may not have been so highly esteemed by those who considered themselves his superiors. In any case McLean was suspicious of the Oriental Bank's intentions towards him and disgusted at the treatment he was receiving. Consequently, he no longer felt tied to the Oriental; he applied for and was unanimously appointed to the position of Manager Shanghai branch of the new Hongkong Bank.

His subsequent activities have been covered to the extent the sources permit. His contract was renewed, he was given Home leave with full pay, and he was offered the chief managership in Hong Kong in 1870. But he had already resolved to leave the East within a few years, he expected that he would have saved £50,000, he had marriage in mind, and he was often to refer to the heat of the China-coast summer. The Court was not interested in his proposal to spend two summers in England and then return; instead, they offered him the sub-managership of the London Office. There he uncovered, where the auditors had failed, Vacher's improper transactions. In 1874 he was again offered the position of Chief Manager, but agreed instead to inspect the Bank, virtually at the demand of the London shareholders, most of whom would have known him in Shanghai; meanwhile, Jackson held down the London Office before returning to Yokohama.

Of **James Greig**'s early life unfortunately little is known. He was born in 1837 and certainly served in the East with the Asiatic Banking Corporation, whose Hong Kong manager he was in 1865. As the Asiatic had only then been founded, he must have had previous experience; he is undoubtedly the James Greig listed by Buckley as being the Singapore accountant for the Chartered Bank of India, Australia and China in 1864.[21]

He became the youngest Chief Manager of the Hongkong Bank at the age of 34 and was at first on very good terms with David McLean who had taken an almost older brother attitude to his activities, communicating with him relative to Kresser's more speculative activities. Greig had seemed to carry the Court with him. Thus when in 1876 he was subjected to criticism in London by leading shareholders, Greig, not unreasonably, found it difficult to accept that the directors had turned against him, virtually in the time it took him to travel between Hong Kong and London, and he resisted all McLean's recommendations to resign voluntarily.

There follow a few later references to him in the McLean correspondence. In 1877 he subscribed £50 for Riddell's widow, left with six children to care for; later in the year McLean notes that he is a partner in Blockley, Greig and Co. and comments that, on the basis of the bills he is handling, 'I don't think he had a good start . . .'[22]

A tradition in the Greig family maintained that he retired as the manager of a branch of Lloyds Bank. In fact the story is more complex.

Blockley, Greig and Co. apparently did sufficiently well for Greig to reside in Chislehurst – the sometime home of Thomas Jackson; on the train from Beckley to London he became acquainted with John W. Cooper, partner in the London private bank of Brown, Janson and Co., which had Leeds connections as William, Williams, Brown and Co., founded in 1813; he was invited into the partnership. The office was on Abchurch Lane and the bank itself was taken over by Lloyds in 1901; the following year Greig retired – and in this brief interim was one of the two joint managers of the Cheapside Branch.

Greig was remembered by T.S. Allen, a former employee, as:

a shortish, round-faced man with closely clipped white beard and always clad in black vicuna . . . he introduced methods of moneylending new to the ancient institution of 1813, however, as far as the clerks were concerned, they benefitted, for almost from his first Christmas they received in addition to the Christmas Fund distribution a Bonus . . .[23]

Greig's grandson, Hugh Alistair Greig (1904–1983), who served with the Hongkong Bank from 1925 to 1954, recalled that he smoked black Burma cheroots and died of throat cancer in 1911.

It was McLean who advised the Court of Directors that **Thomas Jackson** would be a suitable Acting Chief Manager, realizing that James Greig was not likely to return. McLean's opinion of Jackson was not unique. Jackson had worked in Hong Kong under Greig and his record alone would have entitled him to consideration. With Stevenson retired from the East and Cameron taking over in Shanghai only one other name could be considered – William Kaye of the Chartered Bank, but he was leaving the East and wanted an assignment in London where McLean would be pleased to see him as Sub-Manager. Thus Jackson became Acting Chief Manager in 1876 and, with (i) his own brilliant performance and (ii) Greig's forced resignation, he became the substantive Chief Manager of the Hongkong Bank in 1877.

Thomas Jackson and Ewen Cameron

Sir Thomas Jackson, Bart – 'Lucky' Jackson – these titles belong to a later section. Here there is the beginning – a young man from County Armagh and Belfast. His father, four generations from a landholder who around 1750 had lost all, was a teacher in the local school; his mother was an educated woman of Huguenot ancestry. Among their children they had two sons, Thomas and David, who were to serve the Hongkong Bank, but the younger was to die in 1903 while Manager Yokohama.

Thomas Jackson was born in 1841, the second son of David Jackson of Urker, Crossmaglen, County Armagh. Educated privately he became a clerk in the Bank of Ireland, Belfast, in 1860. In 1864 he signed an agreement with the Agra and Masterman's Bank under which he was to go to Hong Kong as clerk for a period of three years with a salary of $200 per month. The passage money of £137:10s was repayable if he broke the engagement, a strong inducement to remain as the one-way fare was itself equivalent to 28% of the annual salary.

This bank was a 'merger' of the Agra and United Service Bank and the private bank of Messrs Masterman, Peters, Mildred and Co., as agreed in May 1864. The new trading name became effective on July 1, 1864, although the new corporation was only in existence legally some months later. Jackson's contract was signed on July 28 and must have been one of the first under the new regime. Unfortunately, many in the City were unreconciled to the Agra Bank's thus becoming both a member of the Clearing House and an Eastern bank, and adverse rumours were circulated. The merger had itself led to a loss of accounts, and a bear raid on the shares caused a withdrawal of funds leading to a suspension of business on June 7, 1866.[24] The bank was subsequently reconstituted as the Agra Bank, Ltd.

Jackson was accordingly released from his contract. On July 28 he wrote to A. Hay Anderson, the Agra's Hong Kong manager:

> You are aware that I have an appointment from the Hongkong and Shanghai Bank and as there is very little for me to do consequent upon the suspension of this bank, I should take it as a great favour if you allow me to leave as soon as you conveniently can.[25]

The Hongkong Bank's records indicate his service began on August 2, 1866.

The promotion nearly a year later to Accountant Shanghai cannot be explained by shortage of available staff. The Hongkong Bank began 1867 with twelve Eastern staff and, in the course of the year, took on a further five in the East. Brett was dismissed from Yokohama in May and this caused some disruption, but William Murray was in Shanghai and at least two others were senior to Jackson. When in 1868 and with full support of McLean he was first appointed Agent in Hankow and then Manager in Yokohama, there had obviously been concern at Board level that he was too young or possibly too inexperienced for the responsibilities being assigned him.

Certain directors had friends among the 'available' bankers, and it was at this point and under these pressures that the Court of Directors formally declared the policy of promotion from the staff – where possible. Jackson's early recognition and promotion could only have been based on observed ability; no other explanation is possible.

In Yokohama Jackson married Amelia Lydia Dare in 1871. She was one of nine children of Captain George Julius Dare, a well-known Singapore resident who died in England in 1856; one of her sisters married Dr William Hartigan of Hong Kong who was (at least in 1890) doctor for the Hongkong Bank - his recommendation that European staff be provided summer accommodation on the Peak is on record.[26]

After the event a successful appointment often appears as if it had been inevitable. Jackson was able and he proved to be a great Chief Manager; in summary, after a successful first administration Jackson attempted to retire from the East in 1886 but took the helm temporarily from 1888 to 1889 and again in 1890 to 1891; he then returned in 1893 to lead the Bank to an assured prosperity, retiring from the East in 1902 to become Chairman of the London Consultative Committee until his death in 1915. There seemed to be no need therefore to question the process by which in 1876 he had been chosen. The mantle of inevitability fell easily on a man of his ability once proven and his later career as the Bank's third Chief Manager was such that the question seemed irrelevant. This is poor history. In the mid-1870s, after all, Jackson's public success had yet to be achieved; there were other men of ability in the Bank and Jackson's appointment must be placed in context.

John Grigor was clearly senior to Jackson, but there is no overall statement in the records of Grigor's ability; certainly he was criticized by McLean for some aspects of his Shanghai work; he was later faulted for his Yokohama operations, but officers were reprimanded, as were Thomas Jackson and Ewen Cameron, and yet rose to the most senior positions. Had Grigor returned as ordered to Hong Kong in 1870, he might have provided the only internal threat to Jackson's eventual appointment as Acting Chief Manager in 1876. But he had gone. G.E. Noble, who eventually succeeded Jackson in 1889, was in fact seven months his senior and had experience similar to Jackson's – Shanghai, Hong Kong, and then Accountant in Bombay. Cameron was actually an Acting Manager before Jackson's appointment in Yokohama in 1870, but he was in India. Thus Jackson was 'available' first for the Yokohama appointment and then for the offer of Shanghai.

In 1872 with McLean's retirement imminent, the Court instructed Greig and McLean to approach William Kaye of the Chartered Bank and offer him the Hongkong Bank's Shanghai management, despite McLean's arguments that Jackson was qualified. Kaye, however, wanted to return to England. The Court then actually appointed Jackson Manager Shanghai. However, Jackson requested permission from the Court to remain in Yokohama to handle the Bank's growing business there; Cameron was appointed to Shanghai instead. Had he taken the Shanghai position, would he have retained it in preference to Hong Kong as did other Shanghai Managers before and after McLean's time? Jackson was the right man, but he was also in the right place.

Although Jackson was promoted on the basis of ability – he made practical the Court of Directors' policy to promote from within the ranks – the Bank was young; say ten years later, no amount of ability would have resulted in so fast a rise, or in appointment to Chief Manager after only ten years in the East. Nor was Jackson at 36 the Bank's youngest Chief Manager; James Greig had been only 34 on appointment. (A.G. Stephen, the Bank's oldest Chief Manager on appointment, was 58 in 1921, but that too was exceptional; see Volume III.)

The Bank in the 1880s was not expanding at the same rate relative to the number of staff, as men of the C. S. Addis seniority, say 1883, would complain. Each of Jackson's successors, G.E. Noble (in 1888), F. de Bovis (in 1891) and J.R.M. Smith (in 1902), had been in the East with the Hongkong Bank approximately twenty years when they became Chief Manager. Each generation thought themselves less fortunate.

Ewen Cameron was also born in 1841. The son of William Cameron of Muckopie, Inverness-shire, he was apprenticed in the Caledonian Bank in 1859, joined the Bank of Hindustan, China and Japan and first went East in 1866. He apparently succeeded John Grigor as the accountant of their Hong Kong branch and, when in 1866 the bank suspended payment, Cameron stayed on as liquidator.[27] His ability, therefore, had already been recognized, and in early 1867 when he accepted an appointment in the Hongkong Bank, he was in charge of Hong Kong current accounts for only a brief time before being posted as Accountant to assist the experienced Robert Stevenson in opening the new Calcutta agency, an example of the convenient phasing by which qualified bankers became available to the Hongkong Bank at the moment the need arose. Two years later, when Stevenson moved to Bombay, Cameron became Agent in Calcutta.

While in Calcutta, Cameron recruited J.J. Winton (later Manager Singapore) and Alexander Leith to the Bank's service. Leith had come East with the Chartered Mercantile Bank but had left it to teach in Doveton College. He was Agent Foochow during negotiations in 1874 for China's first public loan; as Agent Tientsin he suffered a mental breakdown, forcing his retirement from the Bank in 1891. He would later recover.

Although Cameron had had a sound and quite traditional introduction to Eastern banking, he did not serve long in Head Office nor did he work under either McLean or Jackson. That he was nevertheless appointed to succeed McLean in Shanghai is evidence that he received good recommendations from Stevenson and that Stevenson himself was respected. His record as Agent in Calcutta must have received the endorsement of McLean, and his relative independence of Jackson would make him particularly valuable as Jackson came to dominate the affairs of the Bank. They would work as a team, and the strong position of the Shanghai Manager and of the Shanghai branch in the management of the Bank's developing China network would remain unimpaired.

Thus in 1876 the team which would turn the Bank around was in place.

THE SHANGHAI BRANCH, 1866–1875

Only by examining the sole surviving charges account, that of the Shanghai branch, is it possible to fit in the Portuguese and Chinese staff in those first years. This section provides both a summary and new insights.

In 1866 the Manager, David McLean, received a monthly salary of Ts750 (@1.39 = $1,042), his only European assistant, John Louden, Ts300. The Manager's bonus, which in 1869 was Ts1,800 and was awarded by the Court before published profits, is not listed as a 'Shanghai charge'.

The Portuguese clerk, M.A. de Carvalho, in what was certainly an exceptional situation, had his passage paid from Hong Kong. Carvalho initially received Ts85 a month, by which it may be assumed he was experienced. In December 1879, his last month of employment, his salary had risen to Ts140, but this was still less than the Ts150 received by the lowest-paid European junior on full-pay status. On January 8, the Court of Directors took notice of de Carvalho; describing him as a 'very old and valuable clerk', they approved an expenditure of $300 to pay for an operation on his eyes and a pension of $100 a month. The charges account for January 1880 shows an item: Extra medical attention for M. Carvalho, Ts25; there is nothing more until his death is noted in 1913.

To put this somewhat in perspective, Louden at Ts300 per month was earning in salary (excluding housing allowances, *pro rata* leave pay etc.) approximately six times that of his rough counterpart, G.H. Burnett, at £175 per annum in the London Office. A Portuguese clerk at say Ts100 per month was paid more than his counterpart at £100 per annum in London.

The Hongkong Bank's Shanghai compradore, Wang Huai-shan, known familiarly as Wah Sam or Wah Sung, was paid a 'salary' of Ts150, but with more precise bookkeeping practices he and the Chinese staff were soon placed in a separate column headed 'wages'. The monthly payment, and there would be thirteen of them a year, was the least important part of the compradore's remuneration, which came in the main from commissions.

Wah Sam was from the Shao-hsing district of Chekiang Province and in the course of his travelling as a merchant had been in contact with foreigners. One story, which has never been substantiated, is that a British merchant invited Wah Sam to subscribe in a bank he intended to form; the foreigner left China promising to return in nine months, but only after three years did he return to inform Wah Sam he was now head of a new bank, the Hongkong Bank, and to invite Wah Sam to be its first Shanghai compradore at the age of 28.[28] The story is not impossible, although the planned bank and the Hongkong Bank need not be the same; indeed, the story points to a Dent partner, since Dent's were both interested in other banks and provided the Chairman for the Hongkong Bank's Shanghai 'Provisional Committee'.

In any case Wah Sam's background, with its broad mercantile contacts, was ideal for the assignment, and his record with the Bank is brilliant as his Chinese nickname, 'K'uai-fa-ts'ai' ('get rich fast') attests.[29]

In addition to the compradore, there were five shroffs, nine coolies, and one boy, for total wages of Ts92 per month. Two additional staff were presumably for the manager's quarters. At first the head shroff is merely listed by title; then the name 'Jim Pah' is given – he was known familiarly, and inevitably, as 'Jim Crow'; finally the full name 'Wu Jim Pah' is stated, and he can be identified as Wu Mao-ting, from Anhui Province (as was the great Viceroy Li Hung-chang). Wu became the Bank's Tientsin compradore in 1883 and as railway director and factory owner played a practical role in China's modernization.[30]

In 1867 Thomas Jackson came up to Shanghai as Accountant with a salary of Ts250, or $148 more than the basic $200 promised him by the Agra and Masterman's Bank; working with him were William Murray, George Noble, and Herbert Cope. There were now seven shroffs, and a second Portuguese had been employed.

By 1872 there is differentiation among the Chinese. In addition to the eleven shroffs, the head shroff was listed, as already noted, separately by name with a wage of Ts25, and one of the coolies was designated 'lamp coolie', his task being to both keep the lamp filled and the wick trimmed. Further differentiation had taken place by 1875 when there were seven 'sycee' coolies, men specifically employed to move the heavy silver bullion (sycee) not only within the Bank's vaults, but also for shipment and inter-bank, there being no clearing house in Shanghai. These were usually Shantung men, traditionally strong and relatively large of stature. There were also three 'chit' coolies who would today hold the more dignified title of 'messenger', their task being to carry correspondence between desks and offices with a 'chit book' in which receipt was noted.

The Shanghai branch in 1875 already employed five Portuguese and the most senior had begun to be paid a salary higher than that of a European junior. Ewen Cameron was then the Manager, with salary unchanged at Ts750; he now had a Sub-Manager, John Walter, at Ts450, and his staff included Andrew Veitch whose contributions on the silver content of the Shanghai monetary tael are quoted in Edward Kann's classic study.[31] There were five 'first-tour' juniors who had come through the London system, and three who had been employed as juniors in the East.

The branch was responsible for Hankow, and there were staff movements back and forth during the busy season. Hankow might also be a testing ground for a particularly bright young man, Thomas Jackson or A.M. Townsend, for example, whose promotion thereafter could be immediate.

Although the 'Eastern Staff' lists have been reconstructed by Catherine King and a close estimate made of the location of each member of the 'Foreign Staff', Shanghai remains unique in that the records indicate not only in-grade promotions but also the size and composition of the Portuguese and Chinese staffs. The affairs of other branches must have had the same proportions, subject to consideration of the need for sycee coolies.

The Shanghai charges account also details the rise of the Junior Mess, the price of its furniture, beverages, rent, and servants.[d] Items are listed separately, as, for example, the cost of winding the clocks. But at this point the story must turn again to the Bankers, to those who were part of the new pattern, to the coming of the London juniors.

TOWNSEND AND THE FIRST LONDON JUNIORS

At the age of 90, A.M. Townsend wrote his memoirs, 'Early Days of the Hongkong and Shanghai Bank'; they are remarkably accurate. Only a few weeks before Townsend's death in 1939, Sir Charles Addis (1861–1945), who had succeeded him as senior London Manager in 1912 and had himself retired from the London Consultative Committee in 1933, noted in his diary, 'Mr Townsend (93) deaf and blind, unable to walk but memory good and full of interest and chat. What memories!'[32] These are captured in the quotations below.

He recalls that on joining the London Office of the Hongkong Bank in October 1866 there were, in addition to W.H. Vacher, the Accountant G.H. Burnett and a clerk (David Moncur).

Moncur, the first 'London junior', was less experienced than Townsend and went East only in 1871. Sadly he died in Yokohama in 1873.

As for Burnett, he was already a qualified bank accountant; under the later more formal system he would have been clearly designated 'Home Staff' and would not have been considered for the East. Burnett was, however, asked to go as a leave replacement for H. Cope in 1877; and he agreed on condition that it be for one year only. Jackson then offered him an appointment as Sub-Manager,

---

d The Shanghai junior mess was later discontinued. Shanghai juniors lived in 'chummeries' or small messes they organized themselves, often with non-Bank juniors.

Hong Kong office, which he accepted, but after examination by the Bank's doctor in Hong Kong, Burnett was required to return to London in late 1878, where he was reinstated in the London Office.[33]

Townsend in London Office

Townsend himself was born in 1847 in Searby, Lincolnshire, the son of the vicar. Educated at Caistor Grammar School and the Merchant Taylor's School, at seventeen he joined the Bradford branch of the Yorkshire Banking Company, in which his father owned shares. Penmanship, or simply 'writing', was a prime qualification and this skill the young would-be banker lacked. He took twelve lessons for a guinea, but samples of his handwriting suggest the money was misspent.

Ellis Gilman, senior partner in Ashton and Co., the London 'friends' of Gilman and Co., a founding firm of the Hongkong Bank, was related by marriage to Townsend's father. Gilman's partner, Charles Freeman, was a director of the London and Westminster Bank. Thus it was that Townsend received a nomination to the great London joint-stock bank and joined their head office in July 1866. These details underlie the realities of personnel policy. Family and school, these were the links which provided the introduction, the bona fides; without it employment in a status leading to preferment was extremely difficult. Ironically, at the same time there were Westerners in China commenting adversely on the effects of the Oriental family system.

Of course there was an examination. Townsend had to (i) read an article of *The Times* aloud, (ii) write a letter of application, and (iii) add a column of figures. Like many others so examined Townsend was shrewd enough to guess his examiners did not themselves know the correct answer. One is tempted to conclude that this examination – literally reading, 'riting and 'rithmetic – was a pure formality and that the introduction must be 'everything'. Unhappily for the state of British education there were those who failed the simple exam.

Ashton and Co. had early represented the Hongkong Bank in London and it was their former Shanghai partner, W.H. Vacher, who was the Bank's London Manager. Shortly after Townsend had joined the prestigious London and Westminster Bank, he found himself 'released' and both invited and encouraged to join the Hongkong Bank as a clerk. Although there is nothing specific in his memoirs to confirm this, the context is clear – he was one of the first two juniors recruited to go East and this latter point was quite understood by him. Nevertheless, he wrote:

I rather squirmed at leaving so important an Office as the Westminster Bank and joining such a small one, where there was, besides the Agent, only the Accountant, [G.H.] Burnett, who was none too civil, and one clerk [David Moncur], a nice fellow but very shy and silent; and, as there was very little to do, my position was not at first much more than Messenger Boy.[34]

In 1870 Townsend was head of the London Office Inward Bills Department; juniors, even those destined for the East, might play a substantive role in London until the development of the Home staff. Indeed, the London Manager might delay their departure for the East because of their Home responsibilities. In addition to Rodham H. Cook, W.H. Harries, David Moncur, and George de St Croix, all of whom went East, there were two others in the office, a clerk and messenger, and further recruitment brought London Office to a total of fifteen that year, in addition to Vacher and Burnett. Townsend notes that they had moved out of the initial cramped quarters into the old Agra Bank Offices in Nicholas Lane. London Office would later move first to 23 and then to 31 Lombard Street, where it remained until 1913 and the move to 9, Gracechurch Street.

A brief note on others

Before Townsend left for the East in July 1870 with the but recently joined William G. Greig, whose older brother James Greig was within days of being appointed Acting Chief Manager, London Office had recruited François de Bovis, James M. Grigor, A.H.C. Haselwood, and Andrew Veitch.

Townsend states that these four juniors were in London Office with him, but the London records suggest they came in a month or so after he had left for the East with young Greig. It may be that Townsend met them during the recruitment process, or, knowing these bankers so well in after years, he may simply have confused the timing.

In 1869 the Bank had taken in the 28-year-old W.H. Harries from J.S. Morgan and Co. as a 'general clerk' at £175 per annum, compared to Townsend's initial £100 and £140 in 1870. The London junior system had not as yet been formalized; young men were taken in with varying levels of experience; Harries was, in fact, one of the more experienced young bankers to be appointed in London *and* intended for the Eastern staff during this period. After serving eleven months in London Office he left for the East in June 1870, a few weeks before Townsend.

His initial assignment was Hong Kong, where he remained approximately one year before being assigned to Hiogo as Agent; in 1875 he was Acting Manager Yokohama, relieving John Walter, and then opened the San Francisco 'agency' in 1875.

In San Francisco he married an actress by declaring the fact before her sister and the stage manager, a proceeding which, McLean noted, was being supplemented by some further rite in the United Kingdom. Harries returned to

San Francisco, acknowledging in 1902 that he had become the No. 1 on the 'Eastern Staff' list but expressing the understandable wish to remain in California the rest of his days.[35] He retired in 1912 and died in 1915 at the age of 72.

David Hardie became a London junior in January 1871 with a salary of £130. This implies he had had some experience, and, indeed, he went East in August and became Agent Saigon in 1874. Shortly afterwards he committed suicide.

There were many brief careers; those Bankers who survived moved slowly up the list, and their story will be told in Chapter 15.

First trip East – via North America

Townsend and Willie Greig went East via New York and San Francisco, recording a visit to Salt Lake City en route and noting that the train had no dining car but stopped for meals, then across the Pacific to Japan, with a fine view of Fujiyama as they approached the coast. And so to Yokohama and the Bank office.

[Thomas Jackson] welcomed us in his pyjamas, gave us breakfast, provided us with a guide to show us all the sights of the town, and, in the evening, got ponies and took us for a ride round Mississippi Bank, finishing up at the Barracks on the Bluff, where an English Regiment was then stationed. We were hospitably received in the Mess Room. And then to dinner with Jackson, who dressed me up in one of his white cotton suits . . .

The next morning when we returned to our steamer, we found to our surprise in our cabin a case containing champagne and other wine, with Jackson's good wishes. This was the beginning of a life-long friendship with him, and I began to get a glimpse of the new life opening before me.

'. . . of the new life opening' – how many times is this phrase repeated in reminiscences by Bank retirees! That first trip East, be it the unusual route across North America or the traditional P&O via Suez, was a lasting memory for a Hongkong Banker. Other voyages tended to fade the one into the other; always the first is clear, and Townsend, the first junior to go East, was to remember it well in his old age.

The arrival in Hong Kong was somewhat unusual. The two juniors were met by both the Chairman of the Bank and the Acting Chief Manager; the former was H.B. Lemann of Gilman and Co. who had been advised of Townsend's arrival; James Greig was there to greet his brother.

An intimate glimpse at Hong Kong office

The diary of C.J. Gonsalves
The first junior had arrived in Hong Kong in time to be formally introduced to Victor Kresser, the first Chief Manager, and to attend the funeral of Mrs Kresser; Townsend also experienced a severe typhoon in which, he recalled, many lives

were lost and much damage done. He remained in Hong Kong for six weeks and was then assigned to Shanghai, and was probably unaware of the undercurrents in the Hong Kong office.

Until the founding of Hong Kong in 1841 the British merchants were dependent on the sometimes reluctant hospitality of the Portuguese in Macau; the two communities were separated, partly by political factors, but largely by religion. In Hong Kong the British then had their own Colony, and the Portuguese followed across the Pearl River Estuary first as interpreters and later to found a new Portuguese community, which developed to a degree independent of Macau. Although individual members of this community achieved status – in the professions, by success in business, especially printing and publishing – those who chose to work for 'foreign' firms found themselves in a category from which promotion to executive rank was impossible. Yet the implications of this were not so clear at the beginning; politically they received equality under British law and, eventually for the majority, as British subjects. Nor would their initial assignments betray any bias; the routine of clerical duties was common to all 'juniors'.

But the realization of the subordinate status and the resignation to the inevitable are reflected in the brief diary of Constancio Joaquim Gonsalves, covering only two months of 1871, but enough to bring a hidden world to temporary life.[36]

Gonsalves joined the Bank as a clerk at the outset, almost certainly in early 1865; his salary was increased from $80 to $100 in January 1866, compared to a locally employed 'European', Gifford Moody, who began at $100 with quarters provided in the Bank building. Moody's cash remuneration was subsequently increased to $200.

The first entry in Gonsalves' diary provides a confirmation of Scottish banking. January 1 was a holiday. The following extracts reflect the routine, the social awareness, and comments on colleagues.

On the first working day of the new year, Gonsalves was 'writing to Shanghai' and 'registering a lot of shares. Office closes at 6 o'clock p.m.' The next day 'Mr Woodford applied for assistance. I was too busy with my own work. Very light mail for Europe by French steamer.' There are then several references to the problems of bookkeeping:

I was trying to balance my Register, but could not succeed – share brokers and other shareholders did not give me time to attend to my work. They were bothering me for information relating to shares etc.

I am balancing my Registers . . . The Manager appears not to like the system of keeping the General Sterling Progressive Ledger. The fault is not mine. [It] cannot be kept in the other way.

I wrote out 71 drafts and made out 5 slips besides my own work. Woodford assisted us by 4 o'clock.

The brokers and buyers of shares wait for the last moment to hand in their deeds. I am still unable to balance my books. I commenced but yesterday to take out a trial balance and lost all my time today to catch 110 shares short. Until now 6 o'clock I cannot succeed to balance my books and am short of 10 shares. [F.F.] Gibson this morning solicited my assistance and was rather rude in his expressions. What have I to do with the Accountant's Department? . . . I could not give any assistance to the *acting accountant*. I myself am too busy and nobody assists me. They always want my assistance but they never assist me. Very *nice* fellows they are and very *slow coaches* too.

Sunday. Hard working day. I and [F.B. do] Rozario in the office since one o'clock. I succeed to balance my books.

On January 12, 1871, the Hongkong Bank tackled the problem of smoking in the office.

By 12 o'clock the Manager said no business to smoke in the office excepting when people come back from tiffin with cigar. I could have replied that I have seen several times that everyone was smoking in office time, but I kept quiet.

The remark by the Manager was, as I consider, not of a reprehensive character. The tone was moderate and polite. It only means that smoking does not look well in a public establishment like this Corporation.

There are in the records of the Hongkong Bank several comments on the policy towards staff borrowing and indebtedness, but the Gonsalves diary presents the case from the clerk's viewpoint. 'My current account debt balance shows $131.62 including 6 mos. interest $7.83. I and [A.] Jorge bought one dozen porto wine off J.J. Remedios and Co.'

When Gonsalves wrote a cheque for $32 to pay his rent, the Manager refused to initial it; 'he says that I cannot overdraw out of my pay.' But a few days later Gonsalves wrote that the Manager 'seems inclined to grant me a loan of $350 to meet any debts. I was told to make out a B/Sale of my furniture.' The Manager apparently relented on the $32 cheque, stating that 'it was not his doing. The Directors compelled him to act in the way he did for the interest of the Bank.' The problem was one of security, and Gonsalves responded, 'I will be prepared to give him security against my overdrawing if he would consent me to overdraw some hundreds dollars to meet my debts payable before the arrival of the Chinese New Year.'

The matter of the bill of sale of furniture was again raised, but eventually it would appear that Gonsalves received the loan, a reflection of the narrow margin the salary afforded. There is no reference to any further indebtedness; but other clerks were not so fortunate. At just this time Carvalho wrote from Shanghai under the impression that Hong Kong clerks were being paid at higher rates. Gonsalves commented, 'How wrong the Shanghai people are!!!'

But the most dramatic entry involved the staff presentation of a 'memorial' to Victor Kresser. Woodford told Gonsalves that their names had been excluded from the List.

We cannot understand such exclusion. It is very unfair and irrational. Pride and injustice are the order of the day in this Establishment. [A.A.?] Pereira being a Portuguese and Macao Portuguese, like I, Jorge and Rozario, has not been excluded from the List. Why? Because his father is a rich man? And because he was recommended by Dent? Why Mr Kresser said once that we are all equal in this Bank? Why such difference then?

There is no response.

Names are mentioned, tantalizing, and they are gone.

Woodford seedy and left office about 12 o'clock.

This fellow Gibson is always seedy and does not appear to be a quick hand. He takes Cod liver oil every day with half glass sherry on account of his disease.

F.F. Gibson joined the Bank in Hong Kong in 1870; he signed the semi-annual accounts of June and December 1870; in April 1871 he was discharged.

There is a single reference to Harries, and the directors loom a distant threat with their meetings and requirements. And then the diary ends, but not without having noted J.J. Remedios' birthday and the soirée *dansante* that night.

The career of J.D. Woodford

The references to Woodford require some further consideration. James Daniel Woodford joined the Bank in 1867 and a superficial glance suggests he was a member of the Eastern staff. Instead he is more associated with the Portuguese staff and indeed had married Rozaura F. Ferreira in Macau in 1857. As head bookkeeper he was noted by the Court of Directors as a valued employee and in 1877 he was authorized, as a special concession, to borrow $3,000 to buy property and build a home at 223, Spring Gardens, Wanchai. His salary was raised the following year to $300 per month, a maximum the Court decreed, but generous for a 'local' employee.[37]

Woodford was not, apparently, a 'back-room' bookkeeper. At the February 15, 1881, meeting of shareholders, A.P. McEwen, in summarizing the role of the staff of the Bank in its recent successes, stated: 'that from the shareholders was due to the staff at head office a special recognition of the invariable courtesy received by those who had business to transact at the Bank. He especially mentioned the name of Mr [H.] Smith and Mr Woodford.'

Unfortunately in 1883, seriously in debt, Woodford was granted permission to borrow a further $3,500, but in February the following year, having reportedly speculated in shares, he was convicted in bankruptcy court and sentenced to six months in prison. The Court of Directors were apparently willing to recognize his long service and his contribution to the Bank, and their concern for his welfare is shown by their continuing to pay the equivalent of his salary to his wife while he remained in jail, and, afterwards, by their awarding him twelve months salary as a gratuity following the eventual and virtually mandatory discharge from the Bank's service. Woodford was replaced by a member of the Eastern staff.

Woodford died in 1892 in Kobe, Japan. A sad story, a very personal one perhaps, but nevertheless part of the history of the Hongkong Bank.

Early assignments

Meanwhile the sometime London junior, A.M. Townsend, had long since set off for Shanghai.

I was landed on the rather muddy frontage of the Bund in a sampan. . . . I joined the Mess, then in rather poor quarters in Hongkew, having given up their better house outside the Settlement owing to Native troubles. David McLean was manager, Scotch, shy, silent, but very kind hearted and very able; one of the best and strongest of the early bank Managers. He lived, a bachelor, very simply, over the Bank offices . . .

In the office many of the Staff had been recruited locally; among them, fortunately, was John Walter – who was clever and served the Bank well in many important branches, finally reaching the position of [Acting] Chief Manager at Hong Kong [1886–1887 and 1892]. There was also [Gerald J.] Ellis – a young man from Australia – of uncertain capacity and habits. One day calling the head Shroff (Jim Crow) [Wu Mao-ting] to check some figures, he lost his temper and hit him a blow in the face.

This provided David McLean a long-sought opportunity. McLean objected to random recruitment in general – 'don't send me duffers' – and to Ellis in particular. Ellis's general incompetence had been a subject of frequent complaint in McLean's letters, but a general shortage of staff had delayed action.[38] Then, as Townsend remembered it, 'In an instant the whole native staff was in an uproar and rushed into the Manager's room, headed by the compradore, with the result that Ellis was dismissed.'

When Townsend arrived in Shanghai both the Bank and the local share market were prospering, and there was already a scheme for a modern-style Chinese bank with Chinese shareholders – the Hua-li yin-hang (Bank of China, Ltd), as described in Chapter 6.[39]

Townsend's reports were favourable, so much so that, much against the wishes of both McLean and Townsend, the latter was sent to Bombay a year later as Accountant and as leave replacement for G.E. Noble.

[He was billeted with two] charming Scotsmen, Robert Stevenson, Agent, and his friend Anthony Morrison, who had been manager of the Asiatic Bank. . . . We had quarters on the first floor, above Treachers, the chemists, consisting of dining and drawing rooms, billiard room and three bedrooms, and two other rooms for the Bank Offices, with one other small room in which Stevenson had a lathe, with which he spent some time, as there was not much to do in the Office.

Townsend, after describing the snipe shooting and other diversions, was nevertheless glad to receive orders to return to Shanghai after only nine months in Bombay; he took Murray's place as Accountant. His new salary of Ts225 was clear indication that he had been promoted over Willie Greig and several others of greater seniority, including C.H. Beveridge, who had been in Shanghai since 1868.

In March 1873 Townsend was given a further sign of recognition – he became Agent Hankow, replacing John Walter, who after leave would be Sub-Manager Shanghai. In his memoirs he tells another story that rings true: at a rowdy farewell party the table collapses and the chinaware is broken, 'which was unfortunate, as my Boy had borrowed it from the Hong next door'.

Townsend remained in Hankow for two years and then Home on leave by P&O. En route he spent a night with Jackson, possibly in Shanghai, and recalls that 'after dinner he [Jackson] undertook to run 100 yards against Andrew Veitch running 50, with the portly A. Leith on his back – Jackson won'.

Shanghai had changed since Townsend had left for Hankow, at least in one important aspect. The *Celestial Empire* had predicted – upon good authority, the editor insisted – that the new Bank building would be an ornament on the Bund. For a time the editor was in doubt; then in January 1875 he wrote, 'The latest addition, however – the finishing touch of the master's hand, has put an end to our suspense. It is impossible to gaze unmoved upon those quaint Egyptian pillars, with their appropriate Grecian chapters, which now grace the entrance to the Bank . . .'[40]

In Hong Kong, however, the shareholders were looking at the bottom line, and as already stated, objected to the cost of the furniture. As a result Cameron moved in with a friend, a partner of Russell and Co., who lived next door. And Townsend continued on to England.

On leave Townsend married Ewen Cameron's wife's sister and:

As my leave was nearly up we had a brief and busy honeymoon, preparing for the East and visiting and saying goodbye to friends and relatives. We sailed by P&O steamer, March 1876, for Kobe where I was appointed Agent, being kindly entertained en route at Colombo, Penang, and Singapore, and we were heartily welcomed at Hong Kong by [Acting Chief Manager] Thos. Jackson . . .

This was the beginning of a career which would lead him to Agent New York and to Senior Manager London Office.

Townsend's story has formed the basis for an introduction to the East and to the Bank; his reminiscences foreshadow so many that are similar – the friendships, the Bank hospitality en route to the East, life in the mess, the weekend shooting, the rides through the country . . . And there is the after-dinner story of Jackson's physical prowess maintaining the legend of an invincible chief.

But even if Jackson were not to reach quite the perfection suggested in the legend, nevertheless the next part of this history is the Age of Jackson.

Appendix to Chapter 7. The Hongkong and Shanghai Banking Corporation

List of Eastern staff in 1875 with career information

Seniority		Position in 1875	Origins	Final Positions	Data
1865	Smith, Henry C.	Accountant Hong Kong	?	Chief Accountant Hong Kong	d 1882
1866	Noble, G.E.	Agent Bombay	banking	Chief Manager, Manager London	r 1897[a]
1866	Jackson, Thomas	Manager Yokohama	banking	Chief Manager, Manager London	r 1902[a]
1867	Cameron, Ewen	Manager Shanghai	banking	Manager Shanghai, London	r 1905[a]
1867	Cope, Herbert	Sub-Manager Hong Kong	merchant house	Agent Singapore	f 1879
1868	Walter, John	Act. Manager Yokohama; Sub-Manager Shanghai	merchant house	Inspector, Act. Chief Manager	r 1902[a]
1868	Beveridge, C.H.	Shanghai	Eastern	clerk Hong Kong	f 1878
1869	Greig, James	leave from April, titular Chief Manager	banking	Chief Manager	f 1876
1869	Mitchell, F.W. Jr	leave	Eastern junior	Agent Saigon	d 1881
1870	Abendroth, H.E.C.	Agent Amoy	merchant house	Act. Agent Manila	f 1880
1870	Harries, W.H.	Act. Mgr Yokohama; Special Agent, SF	London banking	Agent San Francisco	r 1912
1870	Townsend, A.M.	Agent Hankow; leave	LO jr 1866	Manager New York, London	r 1911[a]
1870	Greig, W.G.	Accountant Shanghai; leave	LO jr 1870	Manager Singapore	f 1888
1870	Turner, A.L.	Agent Foochow; leave	banking	Manager Yokohama	d 1878
1871	Grigor, J.M.	Act. Accountant Bombay	LO jr 1870	Agent Bombay	d 1885
1871	Veitch, Andrew	Shanghai, trips to Chefoo, Tientsin	LO jr 1870[b]	Agent Calcutta[c]	d 1893
1871	Hodgson, John G.	Accountant Yokohama	banking	Agent Calcutta	f 1886
1871	Leith, Alexander	Agent Foochow	banking/teaching	Agent Tientsin	h 1891
1872	de Bovis, François	Shanghai (in Tientsin to July)	LO jr 1870	Chief Manager, Manager Lyons	r 1922
1872	Cook Rodham Home	Yokohama	LO jr 1868	Sub-Mgr Yokohama, Agent Hiogo	d 1904
1872	MacNab, John	Yokohama	LO jr 1871	Agent Iloilo	r 1897
1872	Morriss, Edward	Agent Calcutta	banking	Manager Yokohama	d 1890
1872	de St Croix, George	Shanghai	LO jr 1869[d]	Agent Tientsin	re 1886
1872	Symonds, J.W.	Yokohama	?	clerk Shanghai	f 1878
1873	Barnes, C.I.	Agent Manila	LO jr 1872	Agent Manila	re 1887
1873	Haselwood, A.H.C.	Shanghai	LO jr 1870	Agent Foochow	d 1888
1873	Johnston, G.R.	Shanghai; Hankow	?	Chief Accountant, Inspector	h 1887
1873	Gard'ner, J.P.W.	Foochow	LO jr 1872	Manager Singapore, Shanghai, New York	r 1919

Year	Name	Location	Origins	Post	Status
1873	Moore, Horace	Shanghai	LO jr 1872	Accountant New York	d 1883
1873	Cope, A. Edward	Hong Kong	LO jr 1873	Sub-Manager Hong Kong[e]	f 1891
1873	Morrison, John	Act. Agent Saigon	?	Agent Hiogo	f 1881
1873	Winton, J.J.	Accountant Calcutta; Act. Agent Hiogo	banking	Agent Singapore	d 1883
1874	Permewan, R.T.	Hong Kong	LO jr 1873	Act. Accountant Singapore	f 1883
1874	Simpson, J. Bell	Bombay	LO jr 1872	clerk Bombay	? 1875
1874	Rickett, Charles B.	Yokohama	Eastern junior 1872	Agent Penang, Foochow	r 1904
1874	Creyk, J.G.G.	Hong Kong	LO jr 1873	cashier Hiogo	re 1880
1874	Oxley, E.H.	Hong Kong	LO jr 1874	Agent Hankow	r 1903
1874	Gunn, D.A.M.	Hong Kong	?	clerk Hong Kong	f 1881
1874	Smith, A.J.	Yokohama	?	Yokohama	re 1878
1875	Bevis, H.M.	from London, November	LO jr 1874	Manager Shanghai, Yokohama, Act. Chief Manager	d 1906
1875	Tompkins, M.M.	Accountant San Francisco	USA, banking	Accountant San Francisco	r 1913
1875	Jordan, Paul	Hong Kong	banking	Hong Kong	re 1882
1876	Maitland, A.W.	Shanghai	Eastern junior 1874	Agent Tientsin	r 1895
	Woodford, J.D.[f]	Hong Kong	merchant house	chief book-keeper, HO	f 1884
	Barton, C.[g]	Shanghai	Eastern junior	clerk Shanghai	f 1875

Notes:

r = retired, possibly due to ill health, but usually through age.
re = voluntary retirement.
h = resigned due to health where this is the main factor.
f = discharged or requested to resign.
d = death while on the Eastern staff or before resignation is effective.

[a] made a member of the London Committee on retirement.
[b] Veitch joined the Chartered Mercantile Bank as a junior in 1864.
[c] Veitch was appointed Manager Yokohama, but died three days after arrival before assuming the post.
[d] a George St Croix was employed by London Office March 1866, resigned September 1866, but he was probably more senior.
[e] had been Agent Saigon, Agent Manila, then demoted on grounds of poor health, then discharged in 1891.
[f] Woodford is probably associated with the Portuguese staff, see text.
[g] Barton was never a member of the Eastern staff.

'banking' indicates a move from another Eastern bank unless otherwise stated.
LO jr = London Office junior.
Eastern = employed in the East probably without significant experience.
Eastern junior = employed in the East at less than full salary.
? = unknown. Where this refers to 'origins', assume that the actual engagement is made in the East.

257

Part II

THE AGE OF JACKSON, 1876–1902, AND THE FALL OF SILVER

Now, **here**, you see, it takes all the running **you** can do, to keep in the same place. If you want to get somewhere else, you must run at least twice as fast as that!

Lewis Carroll, *Through the Looking Glass*

Sir Thomas Jackson was to direct the fate of the Hongkong and Shanghai Banking Corporation from 1876 to 1901, with an interregnum from 1889–1892. His triumphant final departure from Hong Kong was in early 1902.

In Hong Kong's Statue Square, only his statue remains – on Bank-leased land set aside for public use while Jackson was Chief Manager. And, if the Bank is associated with any one person, with any one Chief Manager, it is with Jackson. No one man ever dominated the Bank. The Bank's success in this period was due not only to Jackson but also to Ewen Cameron in Shanghai and London, David McLean and William Kaye in London, and to many others whose names will appear in this history. Accepting this and a Board of Directors (as the Court was by now generally known) who, especially in the earlier years, were still very active in Hong Kong, this was nevertheless the Age of Jackson.

Banking history in the East was dominated in this period by the fall in the gold price of silver from a December 1875 high of 56⅝d an ounce to a pre-Great War low of 21⅞d in February 1903, a 61% drop. The rate of exchange, Hong Kong on London, was set on the basis of the London silver price, taking into account various market forces and cost components, a causal relationship which, when tested statistically, provides a coefficient of determination of over 0.98 (see Table II.1 and Figure 3).[a]

Long-established Eastern exchange banks closed their doors – the Oriental Bank Corporation in 1884, the Comptoir d'Escompte in 1889, and the Agra Bank in 1900. The Oriental was reorganized as the New Oriental Bank Corporation, Ltd, but this failed in 1892; the French bank was reorganized as the Comptoir National d'Escompte but was virtually replaced in the East by a 'colonial bank', the Banque de l'Indo-Chine. The Chartered Mercantile Bank never closed its doors, but it was reorganized as the Mercantile Bank of India, Ltd in 1892, and from 1959 to 1984 was part of the Hongkong Bank Group. The Chartered Bank of India, Australia and China, however, came through the period in a strong competitive position and from 1969 has been merged with the Standard Bank (of South Africa) to form the Standard Chartered Bank. The fortunes of the British exchange banks are summarized in Table II.2.

But as the Hongkong Bank's traditional competitors disappeared or were weakened, there were threats from new directions. The Chinese were anxious to develop their own modern banks and attempted to do so either with the support of government in the *kuan-tu shang-pan* (official supervising, merchant undertaking) system as in the 1898 Imperial Bank of China or with 'compradore

---

[a] The graph suggests a positive relationship between the exchange rate for the dollar on London and the price of silver against time. A statistical test using regression analysis confirms that when the appropriate equation is written to determine the exchange rate on the basis of changes in the price of silver, 98.25% of the variations can be explained, and further tests indicate the hypothesis is significant.

Table II.1 *Exchange rates amd silver*

	(i)	(ii)		(iii)
1872 (June)	4/6	100	(June)	100
1876 (December)	4/2	115	(December)	109
1880	3/8	122		116
1885	3/4	135		128
1890	3/5	132		121
1895	2/1⅝	211		195
1900	2/1	215		201
1901	1/10¼	242		233
1903 (June)	1/8	269	(February)	269
1914	1/10⅝	237	(June)	228

Notes:
(i) Rate per $, Hong Kong on London
(ii) Index based on (i) but indicating number of dollars per pound, with 100 = 4/6, i.e. £1 = $4.44; at 269, £1 = $11.96
(iii) Index of ounces of silver purchasable with £1; 100 = 60d/oz, 269 = 22 $\frac{5}{16}$d/oz.
Source: rates as given in the Semi-Annual Hongkong Bank abstract of accounts

Table II.2 *British exchange banks in China, 1870–1914*
(in millions of pounds sterling unless otherwise stated)

	1870	1880	1890	1900	1910
Hongkong and Shanghai Banking Corporation					
Capital ($ millions)	4.0	5.0	9.3	10.0	15.0
Shareholders' funds ($ millions)	4.8	7.0	16.5	24.7	48.5
Capital	0.9	1.1	1.6	1.6	1.4
Shareholders' funds	1.1	1.3	2.8	2.6	4.4
Agra Bank					
Capital	1.0	1.0	1.0	–	–
Capital + Reserves	1.0	1.2	1.2	–	–
Chartered Bank of India, Australia and China					
Capital	0.8	0.8	0.8	0.8	1.2
Capital + Reserves	0.8	1.0	1.0	1.3	2.8
Chartered Mercantile Bank of India, London and China then *Mercantile Bank of India, Ltd*					
Capital	0.75	0.75	0.75	0.56	0.56
Capital + Reserves	0.79	0.81	1.00	0.60	0.84
Oriental Bank Corporation then *New Oriental Bank Corporation, Ltd*					
Capital	1.5	1.5	0.6	–	–
Capital + Reserves	1.9	1.5	0.6	–	–

capital' in association with foreign interests, as in the National Bank of China, Ltd of 1891. With the tendency to associate the Hongkong Bank with British interests came the desire for foreign banks to represent other national interests. The Deutsche Bank had found its Eastern branches unprofitable, but with a base in Indo-China the French Banque de l'Indo-Chine, founded in 1875, flourished; the Japanese entered the international banking field with the Yokohama Specie Bank in 1880, then came the Deutsch-Asiatische Bank in 1889, and the Russo-Chinese Bank in 1895. Not all the new banks remained. The Crédit Lyonnais left India in 1899 after three unsuccessful years, consequent to the same exchange uncertainties which caused the Agra Bank to be wound up in 1900 on grounds of unprofitability. The Hongkong Bank remained the dominant European financial institution in the East.

Following the crisis of 1874–1875, the Hongkong Bank, with a capital of $5 million and reserves of $100,000, resumed the payment of dividends at the rate of £2 (= $9.80) per annum through December 1879, when the rate was increased. This represented a payout (dividend distribution) ranging from $392,000 to $427,000, or a payout of 48% to 65% of net earnings depending on the exchange rate.

By 1901, Jackson's last full year in Hong Kong, the dividend for the year was £3:10s (= $36.90) – representing a payout of approximately $3.0 million, for with the fall in the value of the Hong Kong dollar the dividends in sterling had in this period increased by only 75%, yet they cost the Bank in dollars 7.6 times the amount paid out in say 1877.

The Bank was indeed in the land of the Red Queen.

The impact of the falling exchanges was manifold and dominated economic events in the East throughout the period covered in this Part of the history. Not only did the depreciation of the London-based exchange banks' silver assets force bank boards to write down these assets but it also dictated the withdrawal of funds remaining in the East. If these banks were to continue in business they would have to seek Eastern silver deposits, just as the Hongkong Bank sought sterling (gold) funds. In this search for silver funds, however, the Hongkong Bank had the locational advantage and its local contacts proved overwhelming. Nevertheless, in the 1890s when a general distrust of Eastern banks affected the Hongkong Bank's ability to obtain sterling deposits, it too had to move funds to London, that is, into the 'other' currency area, restricting for a brief period its ability to service the 'legitimate requirements' of its constituents and leaving it 'uncovered'.

The fluctuations in exchange led to merchants fixing exchange as an integral part of an import deal involving sterling. The task of the exchange bank was to provide this exchange, sterling, and then cover by a reverse transaction, selling dollars against sterling bills on London. Timing was essential and cover was not always available. In 1886, for example, the Hongkong Bank, having laid down funds in Hankow in anticipation of receiving cover from the finance of tea exports, was caught uncovered when a heavy and unexpected decline in the exchanges occurred on the eve of 'the season'.

The uncertainty hindered the export of capital to the East. Those seeking investment funds on the China coast had either to borrow in sterling – and take the exchange risk – or borrow from the limited funds on the China coast and pay the higher interest rates. The higher interest could offset the fall of the exchanges, if only the extent of the latter could be estimated. The offset, which was in the nature of a speculation, possessed a particular attraction whenever silver appeared to have stabilized or when international conferences, U.S. legislation etc. appeared about to reverse the long-run trend. Those that yielded to this speculative temptation were unwise – unless they could, as many did, unload before others recognized that depreciation of silver had once again resumed.[1]

Those who expected China and Japan to modernize and trade to expand never lost their long-run enthusiasm. Thus when the Hongkong Bank sought to increase its capital in 1882 and 1890, despite the need to raise the funds at least in part in the London equity market, the new shares were subscribed for at a premium. The Bank's capital was thus increased to $10 million, and the Bank, surmounting and indeed benefiting from the problems created by the falling exchange, continued to prosper. Year-end 1901 shareholders' funds totalled $25.9 million, compared to $5.3 million in 1876. There was a doubling of paid-up capital; shareholders' funds in 1901 were virtually five times their 1876 value. At the same time the Bank's assets had increased from $39 million to $248.8 million, or slightly more than six times; its deposit liabilities, from $13 million to $190 million (or 14.6 times); its note issue, from $1.6 million to $13 million (or 8 times) – all significant growth indicators.

Until the mid-1890s the Hongkong Bank itself was very much the same, operating within the self-imposed boundaries set by the first directors (see Chapter 10). The Bank did position itself in North China (Tientsin and Peking), but it did not establish its own staff in Korea, being content to operate through a merchant agent reporting to Nagasaki. Its expansion into the Straits Settlements was an important development – Singapore became another decision base and in 1884 the Bank opened in Penang. The Hongkong Bank was cautious in moving beyond Penang, and the Chartered Bank took the lead. Certainly the Bank established its own staffed agencies in, for example, Batavia and Iloilo – but the Bank never opened in Madras, although it extended its operations to Rangoon in 1891; it resisted suggestions to open in Colombo until 1892.

As in the early years, expansion was the result of growth of trade within the Bank's self-defined region, on occasion forced by the failure of a merchant agent.

The move into North China, however, was primarily a decision to be near the seat of the Imperial Government, waiting for the opportunities modernization would create. And, foreshadowing an era of national rivalry, the opening in Bangkok in 1888, while it could be justified on a business basis, was timed by information from the British Legation that a French rival might preempt the Bank's opportunities in the Kingdom.

The Bank also opened agencies in New York (1880), Lyons (1881), and Hamburg (1889), and although these strengthened the Bank's regular banking business, and were thus part of the Bank's well-established practice, the European branches were both an admission of foreign competition in the East and an example of the bold, pioneering steps which the Hongkong Bank could take when necessary. With the exception of a Canadian bank in New York, the Hongkong Bank was the first foreign bank in each of these cities.

Jackson's management and the impact of the fall of silver provide the continuity to this second period of the Bank's history. In 1902 the very year Jackson left Hong Kong the price of silver hesitated and then, within a year, had begun a slow recovery. The coincidence is convenient. To this extent Volume I is made a unit describing the Bank's establishment and 'coming of age', the focus on the silver/gold problem justifies the title, 'On an even keel', describing the Bank's policy in these years.

The Hongkong Bank was a China bank. Between 1865 and 1895 the Chinese authorities had several opportunities to call on the Bank's financial advice and facilities. The Bank stood prepared to assist China. The Bank planned for possible Imperial decisions favouring railroads and other development projects; it stood by with advice to provincial officials; yet events in this period were very much under the control of the Chinese authorities.

The history of the Bank in China up to 1895 is told in Chapter 14.

The Sino-Japanese War of 1894–1895 affected relations with China. The dramatic economic developments from 1895 to 1914 are complex and important, requiring separate and continuous narration, despite the overlap of years (1895–1901). When the Great War had been concluded the Bank attempted a return to pre-war days; it had, however, inherited a past in China which has to be understood. For these reasons the history of the Hongkong Bank in China, the Bank in the era of concessions, railway loans, indemnity funding, and revolution and reorganization is assigned to a second volume, 'The Bank in the Period of Imperialism and War, 1895–1918'. This is a prelude to the events – or non-events – of the inter-war period.

After 1895 and until the European Powers became absorbed in the Great War, the political condition of China and the economic pressures to which that country was subjected placed the Hongkong Bank in a special position, while colonial developments elsewhere in the region and the requirements brought about by the self-development of Siam would affect the history of the Bank. At virtually the same time extraterritoriality in Japan was ended. These are developments which, together with the continued history of the Bank as corporation, must be considered, beginning roughly from 1895, in Volume II.

As for Part II of Volume I, the next two chapters will describe the fortunes of the Hongkong Bank during Thomas Jackson's first administration. Jackson took his first 'leave' as Chief Manager in 1886. Had all gone well, he would not have returned. He was, however, officially on leave and his successor was 'acting'. Jackson did return to handle problems, many of which had arisen from his own earlier decisions. The period 1876 to 1888, the year of Jackson's second departure, is then one of management continuity. For purposes of the history, the most useful break occurs in 1882 when the Board agreed on a rights issue which would increase the Bank's paid-up capital to $7.5 million.

Chapter 8 is described by its title. The Bank's paid-up capital remained at $5 million throughout, but the setting in which the Bank operated had changed.

Chapter 9 deals with the decision to increase the Bank's capital and the course of events in the increasingly complex times through 1888. The difficulties of the gold-based Eastern banks and the continued fall in silver led to concern for the welfare of the Hongkong Bank. This in turn led to public analysis of exchange banking. The Bank's Board and Chief Manager described their policy of matching sources and uses of funds, a policy felicitously described as keeping the Bank on an 'even keel'.

The Hongkong Bank often acted first and had to work out the legal implications later. Thus in Chapters 10 and 11 there is the account of the Board of Directors coping with the forces which were propelling the 'local China bank' to world prominence. Not the least of the Board's problems, which it apparently little understood, would be those created by the Imperial Treasury in London, always jealous of its supposed expertise and concerned at the independent development of a bank growing beyond Treasury control and attempting to serve its constituents in ways the Treasury could not or would not understand.

Although there were special factors, including the successful conclusion of three relatively important China loans, which partially explained the Hongkong Bank's rapid recovery in the early years of Thomas Jackson's administration, his own record and contribution were already fully recognized.

In 1888 Jackson turned over management to a contemporary, G.E. Noble, in anticipation of the eventual succession of the next generation – specifically, François de Bovis. Again there were problems and again Jackson returned. Then in 1891 the chief-managership of the Hongkong Bank was once again passed on; Jackson left the task to de Bovis and returned to head the London Office. All this, as Chapter 12 relates, was to prove an interregnum, and Jackson was brought back in 1893 to find the Bank once more in crisis.

The recovery and final establishment of the Bank, the triumph of Jackson's management, is told in Chapter 13, thus carrying the history of the Bank as corporation to 1901. Always Jackson returned to success. This was a measure of his ability as a banker, but contemporaries sensed that with this ability there was an additional factor – they called him 'Lucky Jackson'.

At this point two special subjects are introduced. In Chapter 14, as noted above, there is an account of the Bank in China – but only until 1895. In the final chapter, the story of Chapter 7 is up-dated; an account of Hongkong Bankers in the Age of Jackson is provided.

The complexities of these developments and the significant qualitative differences in each of several time periods force the conclusion that analysis over grand sweeps of time is not helpful in understanding the history of the Hongkong Bank. The story will therefore be taken one stage at a time and the characteristics of each set down in context.

JACKSON'S FIRST TERM, I: RECOVERY AND GROWTH, 1876–1882

The business of the Corporation is sound and prosperous . . .
W. Keswick, Chairman, the Hongkong Bank, August 1880

This and the following chapter cover Thomas Jackson's first administration as Chief Manager.

The justification for ending this initial period in 1882 is, as previously noted, the Board of Directors' September decision to increase the Bank's capital from $5 to $7.5 million, itself a statement of the Bank's condition and expectations.

As shown in Table 8.1A the average annual net earnings of the Hongkong Bank in the period 1876 to 1882 were $946,000, but the wide annual variations render this figure of relatively little significance and each year has to be separately considered. The Bank began 1876 with a capital of $5 million and reserves of $100,000. The Board declared its first post-crisis dividend in February 1876, and in August was able to put the dividend on a £2 per annum basis. Additions to the Reserve Fund were renewed in June 1876, and by December 31, 1877, the Fund had again reached $1 million. In the years immediately following they continued to grow.

In Chapter 9 the Bank's growth will be seen as continuing: new capital was paid-up to a total of $7.5 million by early 1884, with reserves reaching a maximum of $5 million in June 1886. (See tables in Chapter 9.) Despite the increased capital, dividends were maintained at a level of £2 through June 1886, with a bonus of 10 shillings in December 1885. Then from Manila came bad news and the Bank's fortunes were temporarily reversed; the book value of shares which had reached $214.4, a premium of 72% over par, fell to $194.5 by December before rising again slowly to $224.4 in June 1891 – beyond the period covered in this and the following chapter.

The Bank's growth can be explained in part by the development of trade based on the open ports of China and Japan, by more intensive coverage of this area, and by increased activity in what the Bank's Chairman would refer to as the 'South', the Straits Settlements. The failure or weakness of its once fearsome rivals, the Oriental Bank and the Chartered Mercantile Bank, and the development of new business were also important factors. The Bank benefited from, first, the

Table 8.1A *The Hongkong and Shanghai Banking Corporation*
Key indicators, 1876–1882
(in millions of dollars)   (in thousands of dollars)

Year	Assets	Deposits + banknotes	Reserve Fund	Net earnings	To reserves	To dividends
1876 June	39.06	14.78	0.20	315 + 22	100	@ £1 = 200
1876 Dec.	43.29	13.07	0.50	465 + 14	300	192
1877 June	42.05	15.97	0.65	347 + 24	150	202
1877 Dec.	52.71	22.36	1.00	539 + 26	350	204
1878 June	55.92	21.05	1.20	401 + 31	200	209
1878 Dec.	53.42	24.49	1.30	300 + 40	100	218
1879 June	53.45	18.75	1.40	277 + 36	100	213
1879 Dec.	52.13	24.95	1.50	304 + 31	100	209
1880 June	44.89	22.92	1.60	336 + 39	100	£1:5 = 261
1880 Dec.	48.01	26.14	1.80	462 + 61	200	£1:10 = 327
1881 June	48.02	31.92	1.90	386 + 57	100	324
1881 Dec.	58.23	35.17	2.10	639 + 76	200	£2 = 431[b]
1882 June	59.16	37.74	2.35	527 + 53	250	£1:10 = 320
1882 Dec.	68.59	43.29	2.50	703[a] + 114	250	£2:10 = 558[b]

Notes:
+ Reserve for Equalization of
dividends   0.10

[a] the December 1882 data are
calculated on the basis of the rate
of the day.

[b] £1:10 plus bonus.

Net Earnings: as in published accounts plus amount subtracted to offset the cost of dividends as calculated at 4/6 but paid at the rate of the day. After 1882 this practice was discontinued and the adjustment would prove unnecessary. The figures are found in a circular from the Chief Manager written in support of an increase in capital, stating the true cost of dividends.

Dividends: Actual cost of dividends, i.e. published cost of dividends at 4/6 plus difference due to lower exchange rate. The difference is shown as the second figure under 'net earnings'.

successful sale of property connected with the three 'bug-bears' and related problems, and then the continuing returns from the Bank's loans to China.

But there were serious offsets. The Bank's exchange operations were at first still subject to criticism and, in common with other banks in the region, the Hongkong Bank suffered considerable losses in the ordinary course of business.

Most serious of all was the need to react to the falling gold value of silver, to the fall in the exchanges on London. Indeed, to understand the Bank in this period, the new setting, the impact of the silver exchanges, must be described.

SILVER, THE EXCHANGES, AND THE FALL OF THE ORIENTAL

This complex subject is introduced by explaining that the Hongkong Bank, with Head Office in Hong Kong and its accounts in a silver unit of account, the Hong Kong dollar, nevertheless quoted its dividends in a gold unit of account, the pound sterling. When the Board decided to increase the capital, the new shares, with a declared par value of $125, were nevertheless offered to shareholders in terms of sterling at £40.

The following case study will support the proposition that although the Hongkong Bank was a 'silver bank', its relations with sterling could never be ignored.

Dividends and the sterling unit of account

The Hongkong Bank's capital and balance sheet were expressed in terms of Hong Kong dollars, and a fall in the gold value of silver *per se* was irrelevant *arithmetically* to the solvency of the Bank. The need to consider the sterling equivalents in this period is due (i) to the fact that, when the Bank issued London registered scrip, it gave a nominal value of £28:2s:6d to the shares, thus assuming a rate of 4s:6d to the dollar, and this rate, the Bank was advised (rightly or wrongly), had to be maintained in the payment of dividends, (ii) the inability of the Bank to raise all the required new capital funds in silver-using areas, and (iii) the need to hold funds in London.

The existence of London shareholders, who tended to judge the Bank on the basis of its sterling growth and dividends and the knowledge that the City would base its evaluation of the Bank in terms of sterling, were factors reinforcing the need for the Bank to consider the sterling implications of its balance sheet.

The Hongkong and Shanghai Banking Corporation was not operating isolated in a distant colony; it was a bank which financed the Eastern trade world-wide, acted as merchant bankers for the Imperial Government of China, and held British Treasury and Colonial funds in the East. Whatever the denomination of its balance sheet unit of account, the Bank needed London and its good opinion.

The quotation of the dividend – an example of the problem

The importance of these factors grew as the exchange rate fell from 4s:6d to 1s:10¼d for the December 1901 accounts. However, the problem first manifested itself in 1876 over the quotation of the dividend. The Bank's legal advisers concluded that, because the scrip, that is, the London issue of the Bank's shares, contained the statement that the exchange rate was taken at 4s:6d, the dividend payable to shareholders on the London register had to be paid at 4s:6d. If the dividend were declared to be, say, $5 as for the six months ending June 30, 1876, the shareholders in Hong Kong would receive $5 (= £1 at the rate of the day $1 = 4s:0d), but the London shareholders would receive £1:2s:5d, since the Bank, as advised, was legally obligated to pay out at the rate of 4s:6d.

Or, to show the unfair situation that had developed, assume two residents of Hong Kong: one has a share on the Hong Kong register, the other on the London register. The former would be paid $5, which he could remit his dividend to London and receive £1. The latter would receive £1:2s:5d, which he could then remit back to Hong Kong and obtain $6 (less commissions etc.). Whether the shareholders want dollars or pounds sterling, the shareholder with shares on the Hong Kong register is the loser.

The solution, first recommended by David McLean, was for the Bank to declare the dividend in the number of pounds sterling equivalent, at the rate of the day, to the number of dollars the Bank intended to pay out per share. The sterling-denominated dividend would be payable to Hong Kong and other Eastern shareholders at the rate of the day. To revert to the previous example, if the Board were to declare a dividend of £1.00, the London shareholder would receive £1 and the Eastern shareholder $5.00.[a]

This solution is reflected in the accounts.

From 1876 to 1882 dividends are shown at the rate of 4s:6d, the adjustment necessary to cover the additional cost due to the depreciation of silver (in the example above the rate was 4s:0d) being deducted from gross profits; thus published profits are net of this amount. This is clearly misleading as it understates both profits and the cost of the dividends, and from 1883 both the nominal amount and the exchange adjustment amount are shown separately in the allocation of profits. The circular of 1882 announcing the proposal to issue new capital shows the actual cost of dividends for the period 1876–1882, so the accounts can be easily adjusted for purposes of comparison. This requires an adjustment to the figures as described in the notes to Table 8.1A; the impact of the exchanges on the cost of dividends is fully developed in Table 8.1B.

McLean's solution was an answer to the particular legal situation, but it created a new problem which, while not perhaps as inflexible, was nevertheless at times of critical importance. To the extent it proved desirable for the Board to maintain a stable dividend policy, it was the sterling value which became the basis of public judgement. Thus for policy reasons a degree of inflexibility reappeared. Indications of stability are most important in times of crisis; maintaining the dividend would be one such indication. However, it is at just such times that maintaining a dollar-determined dividend, in itself a difficult feat, would be

---

[a] From May 1876 until mid-1914, in view of the small amounts involved, the London shareholders received dividends free of tax, a fact ignored in the above illustrations. There was no tax on dividends in Hong Kong.

Table 8.1B The Hongkong and Shanghai Banking Corporation
Dividends, 1876–1882

Year	Interim £ = $ @		Final £ = $ @		Bonus[a] £ = $		Total £ = $		Total payout £ = $ (millions)		Payout ratio (per cent)	Total Dividends as % of book value £ (per cent)	$
1876	1:00 4/0	5.00	1:00 4/2	4.80			2:00	9.80	0.08	0.39	48	6.9	7.0
1877	1:00 3/11½	5.05	1:00 3/11	5.11			2:00	10.16	0.08	0.41	44	6.7	6.7
1878	1:00 3/10	5.22	1:00 3/8	5.45			2:00	10.67	0.08	0.43	56	6.8	6.6
1879	1:00 3/9	5.33	1:00 3/10	5.22			2:00	10.55	0.08	0.42	65	6.3	6.3
1880	1:05 3/10	6.52	1:10 3/8	8.18			2:15	14.70	0.11	0.59	66	8.6	8.4
1881	1:10 3/8½	8.09	1:10 3/8¼	8.09	0:10	2.70	3:10	18.88	0.11	0.76	66	10.3	10.3
1882	1:10 3/9	8.00	2:00 3/7	11.16	0:10	2.79	4:00	21.95	0.16	0.88	34	11.4	11.2
1883b	2:00 3/7½	11.03	2:00 3/8	10.91			4:00	21.94	0.19	1.04	79	10.8	10.9

Notes:

Bold face = $ equivalent

[a] Bonus is at same rate of exchange as final dividend.
[b] Figures include pro rata dividends etc. on 20,000 new shares.

Source: Table 8.1A.

inadequate. The dividend was quoted and would be measured by the public in terms of sterling, and sterling was appreciating. Stability in the public mind meant increasing dollar dividends sufficient to offset the fall in exchange. A graphical representation of this problem, that is, the increasing dollar cost of a sterling-declared dividend, has been shown in Figure 4, p. 24 (see also Introduction to Part II).

Even in the context of McLean's solution a minor irritant remained. In periods of significant exchange rate changes, there would be a possibility of loss (or gain) to the Eastern shareholder resulting from a change in the rate, one way or the other, between the day the accounts were published and the day the dividend was paid. In response to a question at the February 1891 meeting, the Chairman stated that shareholders on the Eastern registers could opt for payment in sterling in London but that the option had to be exercised some months in advance.

The Hongkong Bank remained in one sense a silver bank, although many contemporaries noted that it operated on a gold basis, a distinction which the following chapter will make clear. Then too from 1877 one-half its shares were by decision of the Board of Directors on the London register; from 1892 the balance was upset – 55% of the shares were eligible for registration in London.

The Bank's need for credit in the City gave prominence to the views of its London Committee. The Bank needed funds in London for use in London. There were those who did not always differentiate between Eastern banks which were sterling based and those on silver; there were those who did not fully understand the use to which the Hongkong Bank put its sterling deposits, fearing that they were sent out to the East, where a fall in silver would thus endanger their value.

The Bank needed to be understood in London.

Silver and the exchanges

By later standards the decline in the gold price of silver from $56\frac{1}{8}$d an ounce at the end of 1875 to 50d at the end of 1882 was not spectacular – some 12% over seven years (see Table 8.2). To contemporaries the situation was one which bore watching, but the outcome was not foreseen. Nor is there any reason why it should have been. The average price of silver during this period was 52d, with a standard deviation of $1\frac{1}{2}$d; but if the period 1880–1882 is taken separately, the average price was $51\frac{11}{16}$d with a standard deviation of only $\frac{1}{2}$d.

Thus the contemporary could view the changes in price as a movement to a new level; indeed, there were two plateaus, from mid-1876 to mid-1878 and from 1880 to 1882 (and beyond to end-1884), the latter being the more convincing. The view that silver would remain at a level of approximately 52d would find

Table 8.2 *The price of silver and the Hong Kong exchange, 1876–1882*

Year	d/ounce of silver	Hong Kong on London	
		$\$ = x$ s/d[a]	% change in 6 months
1866 Dec.	60.8	4/6½	–
1868 June	60.4	4/8	–
1872 June	60.0	4/6	–
1873 Dec.	58.1	4/2½	–
1875 Dec.	56.1	3/11¾	–
1876 June	56.0	4/0	0.5
1876 Dec.	55.2	4/2	4.1
1877 June	54.0	3/11½	– 5.0
1877 Dec.	53.8	3/11	– 1.1
1878 June	52.5	3/10	– 2.1
1878 Dec.	50.7	3/8	– 4.3
1879 June	53.0	3/9	2.3
1879 Dec.	52.3	3/10	2.2
1880 June	52.2	3/10	0.0
1880 Dec.	51.6	3/8	– 4.3
1881 June	51.7	3/8½	1.1
1881 Dec.	52.0	3/8½	0.0
1882 June	51.9	3/9	1.1
1882 Dec.	50.9	3/7	– 4.4
1883 Dec.[b]	50.5	3/8	–

Notes:
[a] from June 1876 the rate is as quoted in the Hongkong Bank semi-annual abstract of accounts.
[b] for post 1882 figures, see Tables 9.3, 12.1, and 13.1.

support from the restraint Germany had begun to show in the sale of her silver, from the passage over a Presidential veto of the 1878 Bland-Allison Act in the United States, and from the apparent ability of the silver-using countries, especially India, to absorb newly mined silver, production of which was, while admittedly increasing, as yet having only a minor impact on the world's total stock.[1]

While European nations were still concerned over the price of silver, there was no practical indication of a return to bimetallism. The market had already taken this factor into account, and thus the inconclusive ending to the 1881 Paris Monetary Conference in April would not appear to have had any noticeable impact.

The next significant decline in silver began at the end of 1884 and continued, with at least one significant interruption, to 1903. The increase in silver production, the failure of subsequent international conferences, the move to a gold monometallic standard by other nations (including Japan), the continued ineffectiveness of the Bland-Allison Act were among the factors responsible for the trend; on the other hand, such events as the Sherman Silver Purchase Act of 1890 (repealed in 1893) and new gold discoveries were offsets which accounted for the interruptions in the trend.

The Hongkong Bank's interest in silver was based on silver's role in providing the basis for the exchanges, for the need to anticipate bullion requirements either as cover for operations or for delivery in accordance with the terms of loan or related agreements in China. Senior Hongkong Bank managers had to become silver experts. The correspondence of David McLean with Jackson and other managers, although only McLean's out-letters survive, reveals the development of an expertise. McLean attended Parliamentary debates on Indian monetary affairs, stayed away from the Kirk one Sunday to be on hand when a special messenger brought news reports on major silver legislation, and urged A.M. Townsend, then Agent in New York, to attend relevant Congressional debates.[2] McLean's evaluations, changing from time to time, were not always correct, but it is obvious that a great deal of his time was devoted to collecting, assessing, and exchanging with his Eastern colleagues information and advice on silver.

Between countries on the same metallic standard, exchanges in normal times fluctuate around a par value and are limited by the prices at which it would pay to ship bullion. While the principle is basically the same between a country on gold and one on silver, the par value varies as the gold price of silver changes, and the exchange rates lie within a band around this changing par rate.[b] Determining the exchange rate of a currency on silver with one on gold involved further risks and uncertainties. At least two months might pass between the initiation of a silver shipment and the realization of any consequent sale. Dealers recognized that the price of silver might change and that consequently there was a potential for exchange fluctuations beyond the theoretical import/export points as determined at one moment in time. The custom developed of calculating in terms of the (two months) forward price of silver, as providing a more accurate estimate of the point at which shipment of silver would be profitable. Thus for Hongkong Bank managers, the gold price of silver was just the beginning of their problems; they were concerned with how this translated into an exchange rate.

The average rate for Hong Kong on London during the period 1876–1882 was 3s:9½d, with a standard deviation of 1½d; for the shorter period 1880–1882, the

---

[b] For the silver exchanges the par rate may be defined as the product of the London price of silver and the silver exchange constant; consequently the par rate is determined by multiplying the London price of silver bullion per ounce troy .925 fine by the ratio between the number of grains of pure silver in an ounce troy as sold in London, 444 grains, and the number of grains of pure silver which will satisfy a debt expressed in the foreign unit of account – this ratio is termed the 'silver exchange constant'.

average was 3s:8½d and the standard deviation only 1d. This is not surprising as it conforms to the previous description of silver prices.

For a London-based bank keeping its books at 4s:6d this would represent a serious enough depreciation of silver to cause concern, especially if this rate, which had not been realistic since 1872, had been used to take over silver assets for the annual accounts; indeed, as will be described below, when the Oriental and Chartered Mercantile banks eventually decided, partially at least, to make the adjustment, their entire position was threatened.

The Hongkong Bank's accounts were in silver, but this did not in practice solve the problem. The decline in silver even if recognized as a dominant trend did not negate the probability of a sudden if temporary change in direction, as in the first half of 1879; indeed, McLean at one time thought an increase in silver to a price as high as 60d was quite possible. Expectations depended on which factors affecting the gold–silver relationship were prominent at the time.

What was new then in the monetary scene of the late 1870s and early 1880s was not so much the depreciation of silver *per se* but recognition that the gold–silver relationship could not be assumed to be 'in normal times' stable – the long-run direction, if any, of change was for the consideration of speculators, the fact of change for bankers.

Bankers needed to develop a more careful approach to the handling of funds. It has become obvious to those looking back that a bank based on London, keeping its accounts in sterling and with a sterling source of funds was highly exposed to an exchange risk if it 'sent out' these funds for employment in the East in silver.

It was equally speculative for a Hong Kong bank, with accounts in Hong Kong dollars, to encourage the growth of its fixed sterling deposit liabilities in London for employment in the East. Also a bank in a silver area requiring sterling funds for use in London would, at least in principle, be exposed to an exchange risk unless cover were available. The Hongkong Bank required funds in London to finance exports from Europe; its London Register shareholders required to be paid dividends at a fixed sterling rate.

As a silver-based bank, it is true, the Hongkong Bank had the **bookkeeping** advantage that its accounts were in the depreciating currency, but its real advantage was that its main source of funds and a high proportion of its financing were in silver. This also constituted a 'real' advantage provided its shareholders were similarly based on silver; but by the end of the century, as already noted, over 50% of the shares were registered in London – the advantage had become partial; as noted before, for this and other reasons the Bank had cause to consider its accounts in terms of both silver and sterling.

The China sterling loans called for repayment in silver, the currency of the Bank's area of operations, but at the rate of the day *vis-à-vis* sterling, thus providing the Bank, which serviced the loans, a hedge against depreciation in the sterling value of its 'permanent' silver deposits, while ensuring a supply of funds in the East. Indeed, Ewen Cameron saw that one source of demand for China bonds issued in Shanghai and Hong Kong would be as 'exchange operations', that is, a way for European residents on the China coast to remit funds to England by buying the interest-bearing bonds with local currency and selling them (or having them eventually redeemed) at a time convenient to themselves in sterling.

Furthermore the Hongkong Bank did not have to 'fear' silver deposits; it could afford to employ them in the East, even if the higher rate of interest – which, if allowance were made for the higher cost of funds and greater risk, were to an extent illusory – failed to offset the rate of silver depreciation. Thus the Hongkong Bank could bid successfully for government accounts and could tolerate a lock-up of funds in the East which would have been potentially dangerous for sterling-based banks. Indeed, the Hongkong Bank's problem was to be a shortage of available funds in the East; it needed additional resources, and these had to be found in part in London.

To the extent that the Bank required sterling funds for employment in London, for payment, say, of telegraphic transfers (TTs) on London in the financing of 'outward' business, no problem was caused by seeking fixed deposits in sterling. Indeed, the safest policy was to match sources of funds in a particular currency (silver or gold) with uses in that particular currency. In June 1882, for example, the Bank's London deposits were approximately £2.26 million, which with the dollar at 3s:9⅝d, was equivalent to $11.6 million or 30% of the Bank's total deposit liabilities.[3]

This matching of sources with sterling uses of funds by sterling sources of funds – and similarly in silver – was to be known as 'keeping on an even keel' – and became the declared policy of the Bank.

The problem arose when the Bank's demand for silver resources to finance the Bank's legitimate general business in the East exceeded the available supply. At this point, which, in the opinion of the directors and the Chief Manager, was reached certainly by 1881, the sound policy of matching sources and uses of funds by currency necessarily limited the Bank's options; the short-fall in silver funds could not be corrected by moving gold funds to the East without involving an exchange risk.

The only alternative available to the directors was to recommend an increase in the capital of the Bank. This was true even though some proportion of the capital would come from the London market. As this was equity capital and not a deposit liability in sterling, the risk of silver depreciation was being borne by the individual shareholder; that is, if the Bank's earnings failed to increase sufficiently to both offset the falling value of silver and pay an acceptable dividend in sterling, the value of the shares would be likely to fall. While this could be dangerous – encouraging under adverse circumstances a withdrawal of sterling deposits – it also put pressure on management to perform, but it did not in itself endanger the Bank's solvency.

In practice, however, the increasing percentage of shares being held in London and the actual quoting of dividends in a sterling unit of account combined to limit the Bank's flexibility. The directors had to give priority consideration to maintaining the dividend in terms of sterling, despite the exchange; although it was the spectacular growth of dollar earnings which the Board rightly stressed, growth in terms of sterling was equally as important if the Bank were to remain in a position to raise additional capital in London or maintain an adequate level of sterling deposits at a reasonable rate of interest. Both were essential to its growth and operations; while the Bank had undoubted advantages as a silver-based bank, it could never neglect its sterling position.

Thus silver and the exchanges were the underlying problems which, if unsolved, would prevent the Bank from performing its basic purposes – the finance of trade and, as merchant bank, the finance of industry and governments. The most successful of the Bank's managers were in consequence exchange operators in the narrow sense; they actually operated. Whether in all cases this provided a balanced management was one of the problems confronting the Bank throughout its history.

The fall of the Oriental

The £25 shares of the Oriental Bank Corporation stood at approximately £45 in the London market of the mid-1870s. With book value at about £32.5, the market/book ratio or multiple ranged between 1.29 and 1.45 in the period 1871–1877. In 1877 and 1878 the bank's reserves fell from £444,000 to £13,672 mainly as a result of writing down by 17% its holdings of short-term assets denominated in Eastern currencies.[4] This move forced the directors to reveal old losses, including a Chilean loan; current losses in Ceylon and Cape Colony, where the Oriental had made an unfortunate investment in 1874, completed the picture.[c] So weak did this leave the bank that its directors determined not to write down the value of its capital 'fixed in the East', which was therefore kept on the books at the unrealistic par rates of 2s per rupee, 4s:6d per dollar, and 5s per tael, a decision of desperation unconvincingly defended by stating that the Bank had no intention of winding up.[5]

As a result, the Oriental's shares began falling, and by the end of 1879 the market/book ratio was less than 1 – and it so remained to the end. As early as 1879 David McLean, the Hongkong Bank's London Manager, was predicting the Oriental would be forced to wind up; he advised the Chief Manager, Thomas

---

[c] The Hongkong Bank Board wrote off all losses in the half-year they occurred; this policy appears to have been maintained throughout.

Jackson, against buying their paper. While the Oriental Bank remained open, it was naturally treated as the 'doyen'; in January 1881 a meeting of Indian exchange banks was to be held at the Oriental to decide whether to stop paying brokerage on outward bills (they so agreed).[6]

In 1881 the Oriental Bank lost £20,000 in Ceylon and Singapore; the following year the bank, attempting to pick up local business in Hong Kong, lost some £40,000 through their compradore, at least in part by taking over clean advances to local banks, apparently at the same time the Hongkong Bank was withdrawing on the eve of a commercial crisis. Year-end efforts to window-dress the accounts to show a highly liquid position were detected by the observant.[7]

The demise of the bank was foreshadowed by a serious decline in deposits, a series of bad coffee crops in Ceylon dealt a final blow, and the once great Oriental closed its doors in May 1884.

While many customers had switched to the Hongkong Bank, two at least remained loyal up to the very eve of the collapse – and after. Just before the end McLean had written to Jackson:

I think [the Oriental] must go. No sane man will leave deposits with shares at £5 and a lock up of £2 million Sterling [in Mauritius and Ceylon estates] and perhaps a good deal more. I recommend you to try and secure the whole of the Customs accounts in the event of their changing bankers . . .[8]

But Robert Hart, the Inspector-General of the Imperial Maritime Customs in Peking, and his London Office chief, James Duncan Campbell, made no move. Fortunately Robert Hart was warned by a consular cable only hours before the Oriental's China agents were instructed to cease business; he was just in time to withdraw the Customs funds in China – but not in London, where both he and Campbell lost officially and personally.[9]

Despite the clear indications over the previous four years, Hart was taken by surprise and at first could not believe the news. His positive opposition to the Hongkong Bank and blatant favouritism of the Oriental Bank are referred to in the McLean correspondence. Dr S.H. Macartney of the Chinese Legation in London, for example, alerted McLean to Hart's plan to move funds exclusively through the Oriental Bank to pay the Russian indemnity in 1883.[10] Nevertheless, on sighting the cable Hart was sufficiently alert to act immediately, transferring the China accounts of the Imperial Maritime Customs to the Hongkong and Shanghai Banking Corporation, 'which lucky establishment,' he wrote, 'will probably long flourish as the leading bank out here. . . . Le Roi est mort; vive le Roi!'[11]

The Chartered Mercantile followed much the same course, but it had not the same backlog of unrevealed losses nor was it as heavily involved in Ceylon coffee; consequently it survived. Nevertheless both the Chartered Mercantile and the Oriental had by 1879 decided to cut back their Far Eastern business, withdrawing from Yokohama and Foochow in the first quarter of the year. The Hongkong Bank seized the opportunity to gain new constituents, and the Board noted the immediate increase of 71 new accounts with deposits of $306,864 in its Yokohama office. The Bank also bought property, for example, the quarters of the Oriental in Foochow and, for $80,000 in 1881, the next door Chartered Mercantile office in Hong Kong, the latter purchase preparing the way for a new Head Office building to be completed in 1886.

The Chartered Bank of India, Australia and China had been able to write down its Eastern silver assets without endangering its operations. The continued weakness of silver, however, led to subsequent (1885) instructions to branches that, to the extent possible, managers were to remit Home any funds in excess of trade finance requirements, as a consequence of which their capital in the East fell from £550,000 to £225,000 before the silver crisis of 1886 (see Chapter 9).[12] Nevertheless lack of funds in the East put the Chartered Bank at a competitive disadvantage, and managers were active in seeking silver deposits.

While it is difficult in every case to quantify the impact this withdrawal of the old banks had on the Hongkong Bank's business, it was, however, considerable and was one of the arguments advanced for the augmentation of capital voted in 1882. The weakening of so many Eastern banks put the Hongkong Bank in an enviable position. At the same time the fate of the Oriental could be used as a cautionary tale for shareholders anxious for high dividends; the events were a warning for management in general.

The fall of silver had exposed the Oriental and the Chartered Mercantile. Once past miscalculations and the resulting exposure had been remedied, however, the fall in silver need not of itself have caused these banks further problems had not their managers taken a surprising position as to the expected outcome of the 1881 Paris Monetary Conference – they assumed it would be successful in establishing bimetallism.

The years 1881 and 1882 were in fact relatively profitable for the Hongkong Bank.

The accumulated problems already noted plus the bullish position taken by the managers during these two years ensured the Oriental Bank's failure upon the renewed fall of silver in 1884. The Chartered Mercantile survived although weakened, and found it necessary to reorganize in 1892 under the Companies Act with the consequent relinquishment of its charter in 1894. McLean cast much of the blame for the Oriental's failure on its management, and this view found support in the press.[d] More objectively, the changing methods of business,

---

[d] McLean may have been biased. These were the managers who had failed to confirm him as their manager in Shanghai in 1864. But when in 1879 McLean had been arguing for an increase in his salary, his disapproval of Oriental management practices did not prevent him from listing the Oriental as one of the London banks paying their manager a salary higher than that paid by the Hongkong Bank.[13]

1 Various Chinese Monies. Sycee, shoes of silver, Ts5 and Ts10; a British trade dollar; a Spanish dollar; a string of cash.

2 Albert Farley Heard, Augustine Heard and Co. Member of the Hongkong Bank's Provisional Committee, Director 1865–1867 and 1873–1875.

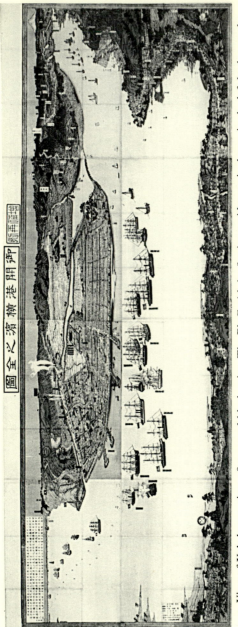

御開港横濱之全圖

3 View of Yokohama, circa 1870, wood block print. The Bluff with its foreign residences is shown in the left background.

HONGKONG & SHANGHAI BANKING COMPANY, LIMITED.

Report of the Court of Directors

TO THE

General Meeting of Shareholders,

TO BE HELD AT THE BANKING HOUSE OF THE COMPANY,

WARDLEY HOUSE,

HONGKONG,

On Monday, the 12th of February, 1866.

To the Proprietors of the

Hongkong & Shanghai Banking Co., Limited.

GENTLEMEN,—In accordance with the terms of the Deed of Settlement the Directors have now to submit to you their First annual Report on the position of the Company's affairs.

The first call of $25 per Share was made on the first of January 1865, and the Second call of $100 was due on the 31st of March; these payments were made with great promptness.

The Company's Offices at Hongkong and Shanghai were opened for the transaction of business in the month of April last, but were not in fair working order until the middle of May. The operations of the Bank to the 31st December have therefore extended over a period of less than eight months.

The following is the statement of accounts, which have been duly audited by the Honorable W. H. Rennie and Caleb T. Smith, Esq.

Abstract Statement of Liabilities and Assets of the Hongkong and Shanghai Banking Company Limited, on the 31st December, 1865.

LIABILITIES.		ASSETS.	
Paid up Capital ($125 on 20,000 shares),	$2,500,000.00	Cash Balance on hand and at Bankers,	$1,250,338.78
Deposits and Notes in circulation,	3,384,876.62	Discounts, Loans, credits, &c.,	3,144,446.75
Exchange acceptances, &c.,	5,731,434.62	Exchange Remittances, &c.,	5,554,279.13
Branches and Agencies,	1,548,219.18	Branches and Agencies,	3,393,430.75
Profit and Loss account,	225,055.93	Preliminary Expenses,	32,827.62
Sundries,	7,069.07	Sundries,	21,332.39
Total,	$13,396,655.42		$13,396,655.42

PROFIT AND LOSS ACCOUNT.

To Dividend at the rate of 8 per cent. per annum, or $6.66 per share,	133,200.00	By amount of Profit for the Eight months ended 31st December 1865, after deducting all expenses and interest paid and due,	$ 225,055.93
Amount carried to Reserve Fund,	33,300.00		
Amount written off Preliminary Expenses, Bonus to constituents and Depositors, &c.,	14,577.97		
Rebate on Bills not due,	31,696.96		
Balance being undivided profit carried forward to next half year,	12,281.00		
	$ 225,055.93		

We have examined and audited the above accounts and find them correct.

(Signed) W. H. RENNIE,
C. T. SMITH,
Auditors.

4 Report to Shareholders for 1865 with Abstract of Assets and Liabilities.

'OH!'

5 James Greig 'falling between two stools' – *China Punch* (August 30, 1873)
reprinted with the permission of The British Library.

6 Introducing the New Year, 1875, to Mr Punch in the dress of a Taiping
Official – *China Punch*, 1875.

ABSTRACT OF ASSETS AND LIABILITIES, HONGKONG AND SHANGHAI BANKING CORPORATION.

31st December, 1874.

ASSETS.		LIABILITIES.	
Cash and Bullion,	$ 8,550,804.92	Paid-up Capital,	$5,000,000.00
Government Securities,	2,478,885.74	Reserve Fund,	100,000.00
Bills Discounted, Loans and Credits,	9,759,524.26	Marine Insurance Account,	33,981.06
Exchange Remittances,	21,797,957.84	Notes in Circulation, ...$ 2,242,170.92	
Bank Premises,	229,967.09	Deposits, ... 17,554,726.80	
Dead Stock,	91,922.55		19,796,897.72
		Exchange Acceptances,	17,858,398.20
		Profit and Loss Account,	119,785.42
	$42,909,062.40		$42,909,062.40

PROFIT AND LOSS ACCOUNT, HONGKONG AND SHANGHAI BANKING CORPORATION.

31st December, 1874.

Dr.		Cr.	
To AMOUNTS WRITTEN OFF:		By Balance of Undivided Profits, 30th June, 1874,	$ 7,042.19
Remuneration to Directors, ...$10,000.00		By Amount of Net Profits, for the Six Months ending 31st December, 1874, after deducting all Expenses and Interest paid and due,	112,743.23
Rebate on Bills not due, ... 725.98	$10,725.98		
To CONTINGENT ACCOUNT:		By Amount from Reserve Fund,	675,000.00
Amount set aside to meet Losses, (referred to in half-yearly Report of 12th August, 1874), ...$275,000.00			
Amount set aside to meet Losses, ... 506,000.00	781,000.00		
To BALANCE:			
Carried forward to next half-year,	3,059.44		
	$794,785.42		$794,785.42

RESERVE FUND.

To Amount transferred to		By Balance on 30th June, 1874,	$775,000.00
Profit and Loss Account to meet Losses,...$675,000.00			
To Balance on 31st December, 1874, ... 100,000.00	$775,000.00		$775,000.00

JAMES GREIG, *Chief Manager.*
H. SMITH, *Accountant.*

Wm. H. FORBES,
ADOLF ANDRÉ, } *Directors.*
H. HOPPIUS,

We have compared the above Statements with the Books, Vouchers and Securities at the Head Office, and with the Returns received from the various Branches and Agencies, and have found the same to be correct.

P. RYRIE,
F. W. MITCHELL, } *Auditors.*

Hongkong, 12th February, 1875.

7 Abstract of Assets and Liabilities, December 1874.
Note the transfer of $650,000 from the Reserve Fund and the absence of a dividend.

8 Foreign Staff, Shanghai, 1873.
(Left to right, back row) C. I. Barnes, A. Veitch, A. H. C. Haselwood, J. M. Grigor, F. W. Mitchell, Jr.
(front row) W. G. Greig, Ewen Cameron (Manager designate), David McLean (Manager),
A. M. Townsend, C. H. Beveridge.

9 Wang Huai-shan (Wah Sam), first Shanghai Compradore.
A picture taken in November 1874 for Mrs David McLean when Wah Sam was
37 years of age – from the private collection of D. C. H. McLean.

10 The Chief Managers.
Victor Kresser (1864–1870), James Greig (1870–1876),
John Walter (1886–1887), George E. Noble (1889–1890), François de Bovis
(1891–1893). (See separate illustration of Sir Thomas Jackson.)

especially the practice of remitting by telegraphic transfer (TT) as opposed to bills of exchange, required the Eastern banks to hold large deposits at either end, and the high level of competition forced the banks to offer 'options', which permitted customers to take up exchange contracts at their convenience, often at times unprofitable to the banks.

And yet it is true that the increase in regional trade, the handling of government monies, and the involvement in local business within the silver using area all implied the holding of silver assets liable to depreciation in terms of sterling. The banks which could surmount this problem would gain the ascendancy, and the Hongkong Bank's accounts were in any case denominated in a silver unit.

In the last desperate years of the Oriental, proposals had been put forward for an amalgamation of the Indian banks – the Oriental, the Chartered Mercantile, and the Chartered – but these had been resisted by the respective boards of directors. The 'local China bank', the Hongkong Bank, was usually singled out in the Press by way of contrast, and the point made then, as it had been from the first, that the Hongkong Bank's prosperity could be explained by the business loyalty of its local constituents.[14]

FACTORS IN THE RECOVERY

The role of the China loans[e]

The story of the Oriental has not been told as a diversion but rather to provide a control against which to discuss the more fortunate activities of the Hongkong Bank. But before continuing the chronological narrative which illustrates the contrast in management policies, the difference in capital structure, and the relative experience with customers, this history must admit and quantify the role of the Hongkong Bank's China loans.

Between 1876 and 1882 the Hongkong Bank undertook three major loans to the Chinese Imperial Government, the 1877 Kansu Loan for £1,604,276:0s:10d (= 5 million Haikwan taels); one-half of the 1878 Kansu Loan, HkTs1,750,000 (= £490,000 approx.) – see Table 14.2; and the 1881 Silver Kansu Loan for Kansu Taels 4 million (= £1,115,000 approx.). The immediate profits from these loans and the 1874 8% Foochow Loan accounted for some 60% of the total net earnings of the Bank allocated to the Reserve Fund during this period. This is but part of the earnings from the loans, which would include commissions on

---

[e] The material in this section is taken from D.J.S. King's report on 'China's Early Loans, 1874–1895, and the Role of The Hongkong and Shanghai Banking Corporation', and will be more fully considered in a subsequent chapter. Only the profit figures are of concern at this point. The Haikwan Tael was an imaginary unit of account; payments were made in Shanghai taels at the rate ShTs111.4 = HkTs100.

related exchange operations and capital gains from bonds held and subsequently sold. These benefits, direct and indirect, are difficult to quantify and even more difficult to time; indeed in the absence of sufficient information, only the calculations of the direct earnings can be attempted.

Profits on the 1877 Loan consisted of (i) the difference in exchange at which the funds were paid over to the Chinese authorities and the rate of the day and (ii) the difference between the rate of interest paid by the Chinese to the Bank and the rate paid by the Bank to the public. The former was up-front; the latter spread over the seven-year life of the loan. The 1878 Loan was denominated in a silver unit of account and the profit was obtained solely from the differential in interest rates (12% and 8%) over approximately six lunar years. The 1881 silver loan, however, was issued at an average of $103\frac{3}{4}$ and paid over to the Chinese at 100, the difference, $3\frac{3}{4}\%$ of the nominal amount of the loan, ShTs208,240, being up-front profit; there was also a profit over the life of the loan from the interest differential, 1.75% of the outstanding nominal amount.

Any evaluation of the Hongkong Bank's performance should seek to differentiate between earnings from regular or general banking business and from unusual circumstances. McLean, for example, in discussing the question of increasing the Bank's capital in 1882, noted the high and increasing rate of earnings but asked if these could be maintained in the event that lending to the Chinese Government were suddenly to cease.[15] Or, put another way, what would the earnings have been without the loans? For reasons stated above, this cannot be stated accurately, but in Table 8.3 an attempt is made to list the direct loan earnings by half-year periods. The result is indicative rather than definitive.

The finance of trade

Basic to the regular operations of the Bank was the finance of the China trade. The adjusted total value of China's imports and exports grew from 140 million Haikwan Taels in 1875 to HkTs166 million in 1881, declined significantly through 1884 and rose again to exceed HkTs300 million by 1895. These dates are selective, but for the period under consideration, 1876 to 1882, growth, based on adjusted figures, was but 5% overall, only a percentage point greater than the rate of decline in the average sterling value of the Haikwan tael between the relevant years.[f]

The tael value of tea exported declined over the period from HkTs36.6 million in 1876 to 31.3 million in 1882, reaching a pre–World War I low of 18.5 million in 1902. Exports of raw silk fluctuated considerably but the average for the period

---

[f] The unit of account used by the Imperial Maritime Customs was the Haikwan (Customs) Tael (100 = Shanghai currency taels 111.4), and the average annual exchange rates used were $5/11\frac{3}{8}$ and $5/8\frac{1}{2}$ for 1876 and 1882 respectively.[16]

Table 8.3 *The Hongkong and Shanghai Banking Corporation*
Net earnings and China loan profits, 1876–1882

(in thousands of dollars)

	(i) Net earnings	(ii) Direct loan earnings	(i)–(ii) Balance	(ii) as % of (i) Per cent
1876 June	337	0	337	0.0
1876 Dec.	479	40	439	8.4
1877 June	371	0	371	0.0
1877 Dec.	565	284	281	50.3
1878 June	432	57	375	13.2
1878 Dec.	340	72	268	21.2
1879 June	313	100	213	31.9
1879 Dec.	335	50	285	14.9
1880 June	375	100	275	26.7
1880 Dec.	523	140	383	26.8
1881 June	443	78	365	17.6
1881 Dec.	715	300	415	42.0
1882 June	580	104	476	17.9
1882 Dec.	817	129	688	15.8

Source: D.J.S. King's report, cited. Net earnings figures for December 1882 may not be comparable as they are taken at the rate of the day.

was HkTs22.7 million, the take-off in the trade occurring in the late 1890s, presumably with developments in the Canton Delta region. The fortunes of the silk and tea trade suggest difficulties for the firms involved and little growth potential for the banks financing them. The import trade reflected no dramatic trend, the values ranging from HkTs62 million in 1876 to an unusual high of 80 million in 1881, but the figures had topped 100 million by 1888.[17] China was fortunate in that she imported no tobacco goods; she did, however, import opium, and whereas the accuracy of the statistics can be questioned, the Customs figures indicate values ranging from HkTs28 million in 1876 to a high of 37.6 million in 1881, a figure not again reached until another exceptional year, 1903. The only other import category of statistical significance – cotton and cotton goods – was HkTs25 million in 1876 and 29 million in 1882; these two categories, opium and cotton and cotton goods, account for 82% of China's 1882 imports.

The fluctuations in the export staples were the despair of old China hands, the dependence of the import trade on opium was feared to be hampering 'legitimate' imports which would be directed, it was thought by the most hopeful, for the modernization of China. There was general dissatisfaction, matched in some cases by optimism which can only have been based on the *a priori* expectations of Victorian political philosophy. In the meantime opium was a vital element in the prosperity of Treaty Port China, and the financing of the opium firms linking India with the East, even in the absence of supporting figures, must be accepted as crucial. The opium traders were represented on the Board of the Hongkong Bank.

Although the trade of Japan increased significantly in this period, 36% for exports and 26% for imports, total trade at Yen 71 million in 1882 was but 30% of China's HkTs148 million (= $229 million).

The explanation and analysis of growth

The explanation of the growth of the Hongkong Bank's regular business in this period is to be found in (i) the transfer of business, including government accounts, from other banks, especially from the Oriental and the Chartered Mercantile as they withdrew from the Far East, (ii) the increase in local and regional business and the development of business with the Chinese through the compradores and local Chinese banking institutions – developments which are impossible to quantify, (iii) the ability of the Bank to keep abreast and adjust professionally to new methods of trading and new financial requirements, and (iv) an improvement in the Bank's geographical coverage and facilities offered.

The Hongkong Bank's early development in Singapore, beginning as an agency in 1878, was slow, but a full branch was finally authorized by the authorities in 1881; there were the beginnings of expansion in China, with Tientsin opening in 1881 and the first move to Peking in 1885; outside the region the New York agency was established in 1880 and Lyons in 1881.

The Hongkong Bank was an exchange bank and Thomas Jackson considered the greatest of exchange bankers. There is some question, however, as to whether Jackson was able to free himself soon enough from the pattern established by Greig which, catering to those who required rupees for the import of both cotton and opium into China, subjected the Bank to exchange problems if not losses. This at any rate was the often and forcefully expressed view of David McLean; unfortunately, Jackson's and Ewen Cameron's responses (the latter was Shanghai Manager) are not available. Certainly there were years in which the Bank's performance was not brilliant and the image of 'inevitable' growth maintained only by its extraordinary operations in silver, China loans, and government securities. If there is some justification to McLean's criticisms in the early years of Jackson's administration, the Bank's performance in 1881 and 1882 certainly suggests that he had matured and the Bank was at last standing firm on its banking record.

The years under discussion were marked by considerable speculation in Hongkong Bank shares, by brokers, by large holders in the East, and by officers of the Bank using insider information. There were frequent transfers from Eastern registers to the London register, but, as the figures in Table 8.4 indicate,

Table 8.4 *The Hongkong and Shanghai Banking Corporation
Earnings and share prices, 1876–1882*

Year	(i) $ ooo Net earnings[a]	(ii) £ Divi- dend/ Share	(iii) $ Book value	(iv) £ Book value	(v) Share price Shanghai	(vi) London	(vii) $ M/B ratio	(viii) £ M/B ratio
1876 June	337	1	132	26.5	$128	£24	0.97	0.91
1876 Dec.	479	1	140	29.1	154	32	1.10	1.10
1877 June	371	1	143	28.3	171	33	1.20	1.17
1877 Dec.	565	1	152	29.8	196	37	1.29	1.24
1878 June	432	1	158	30.2	219	40	1.39	1.32
1878 Dec.	340	1	161	29.5	194	32	1.20	1.08
1879 June	313	1	163	30.6	200	38	1.23	1.24
1879 Dec.	335	1	166	31.9	204	37	1.23	1.16
1880 June	375	1¼	169	32.5	200	36	1.18	1.11
1880 Dec.	523	1½	174	31.9	219	40	1.26	1.25
1881 June	443	1½	176	32.7	254	45	1.44	1.38
1881 Dec.	715	2	182	33.9	274	50	1.51	1.47
1882 June	580	1½	189	35.9	278	50	1.47	1.39
1882 Dec.	817	2½	195	35.0	344	59	1.76	1.69
Increase	142%		48%	32%	169%	146%		

Notes:
[a] The sum of the two figures in Table 8.1A, which contains an explanation
(i) Net earnings in thousands of dollars from Table 8.1A.
(ii) Dividends declared in pounds sterling, see Table 8.1A.
(iii) Book value = shareholders' funds, i.e. paid-up capital + reserves (including amounts paid in from net earnings) + retained profits, divided by 40,000 (the number of shares).
(iv) Column (iii) converted into pounds sterling at rate of day.
(v) Shanghai shares were quoted at so much percent premium, which is added to $125 (the par value of shares); the date is mid-July and mid-January.
(vi) London prices for shares on the London register.
(vii) Equivalent to (v) divided by (iii).
(viii) Equivalent to (vi) divided by (iv).

arbitrage did not equalize prices. The generally higher Shanghai market/book value multiple could well reflect the lesser importance Eastern shareholders in general placed on a potential decline in silver, not necessarily a more favourable expectation relative to the price of silver. The relatively great differential in 1878–1879 probably reflects the growing awareness of the Oriental's problems, of the public's awareness of the falling price of silver and of their growing distrust of Eastern banks. There is evidence that share speculations received some financial encouragement from the Eastern banks, including in the early years, the Hongkong Bank itself, but the resulting activities would not be confined to shares on the Eastern register.

The important observation relative to Table 8.4, despite the shortcomings of its statistical base, is that although the market/book multiple was linked to performance, the impact of the Oriental and Chartered Mercantile's position resulted in a general distrust which was reflected in the share market.[g]

Poor performance would naturally result in a fall in share prices; this could trigger a withdrawal of funds, crippling management, and leading step-by-step to failure. The Hongkong Bank was fortunate in that its mid-1870 crisis, although reflected in the market, did not affect the confidence of local constituents; a turn-around was therefore easier. The Hongkong Bank had, moreover, written off its past and begun its own recovery when the temporary revival in economic activity in 1879, and beyond, brought about a more optimistic atmosphere generally; the Oriental and the Chartered Mercantile, on the contrary, chose that moment to reveal their weaknesses. Not only did this affect confidence, but depositors had the Hongkong Bank to turn to.

Dividend policy

The directors had to resolve the policy conflict between increased dividends and a large reserve fund.

Major shareholders and those holding for speculative purposes were probably inclined to support the directors in their desire to build up the reserves, since the former were concerned for the growth of the Bank in the sense of its ability to meet their financial requirements, and both groups recognized that increased reserves themselves affected the price of the shares.

Against this was the attitude of the small investor, who was valued by the Bank as a constituent (i) likely to keep a 'savings' balance with the Bank and thereby permit some lock-up of funds giving the Bank more flexibility in its investment loan policy, for example, certain China loans, (ii) willing to hold on to shares in difficult periods, thereby stabilizing the Bank's credit rating in London. This class of shareholder often expected an income commensurate with the Bank's earnings.

The Chairman of the Hongkong Bank had little difficulty persuading shareholders that a Reserve Fund of $1 million was wise policy; this had long been accepted. That goal was reached, however, as the result of decisions made in February 1878. The recommendations the following August, despite the fact that $200,000 was to be added to the reserves, did not include a dividend increase.

g The problem is that, as the market for Hongkong Bank shares was thin, it is difficult to select a meaningful market price. The market price is related in this analysis to the book value at the end of the half-year, but, as this value was not immediately known, the share prices would reflect performance only with a lag of perhaps as much as six weeks, depending on leaks. This too is a matter of judgement, and, if mid-January figures are too early, the ratio as calculated in Table 8.4 may be understated.

F.D. Sassoon, the then Chairman, while admitting that profits would permit a dividend in excess of £1, stated:

The Directors however attach great importance to still further augmenting the Reserve Fund, and have no doubt that Shareholders generally will approve of their policy. (Applause) It should be borne in mind that a feeling of stability and confidence will be given which will fully compensate Shareholders for present comparatively small Dividends.

The reduced earnings of the Bank in the following half-years, the problems of the Oriental and Chartered Mercantile banks, and the consequent careful watch on 'Eastern banks' by London correspondent banks dampened any enthusiasm for immediate increased dividends. With the passing of the $1.5 million mark in February 1880, however, the matter could not be further delayed, and the directors increased the dividend to £1:5s on the basis of the June accounts, William Keswick, the Bank's Chairman, stating that he felt the 'increased rate would be maintained if not still further increased'.

Keswick's caution in August gave way to enthusiasm at the February 1881 meeting when he raised the dividend to £1:10s and announced that the directors had voted the staff a 10% bonus. A dividend bonus of 10s was voted after the extraordinary results of 1881, which included the up-front profit of the 1881 Loan, an amount in the range of $220,000. Meanwhile the Reserve Fund continued to be augmented and at the end of December 1882 had reached $2.35 million. The extraordinary earnings of June–December 1882 permitted a bonus payment of £1 and allocation to reserves of $250,000.

The allocations made in February 1883 were undoubtedly connected with the Bank's decision to increase its capital from $5 to $7.5 million. The premium at which the new shares could be sold depended on both the Bank's Reserve Fund, which now had reached the latest goal of $2.5 million, and the rate of dividends (see Table 8.1B).

The directors, however, were also concerned with their ability to maintain the semi-annual dividend of £1:10s in view of the decline in silver and the agreed increase in capital. The Reserve Fund was legally available for the equalization of dividends, but there was a psychological problem; it was thought, probably correctly, that the Reserve Fund proper could not in fact be touched without undermining confidence in the Bank. Therefore a fund specifically labelled for the purpose of equalization was established with an initial funding of $100,000.

The Board's conservative policy must be understood in the context of a complex of factors, not the least being the extent of non-recurring income. As previously noted, of the $2.5 million set aside to reserves, some $1.5 million or 60% was derived from the immediate and direct profit on loans to China. This was the reasonable cause of McLean's unnecessary concern as to whether the dividend, requiring a larger payout in consequence of a larger capital, could be maintained. Extraordinary income could not be depended on, but in the history of the Hongkong Bank it was to reoccur regularly.

THE HONGKONG BANK'S RECORD, 1876–1882

Clearing up the past and related developments

To return to a more general consideration of the Bank in the years 1876–1882, it has been noted that after allowances for the unpredictable China loan business, the adjusted record of net earnings is still not one of steady growth. There is a good first year, then a decline followed by improvement culminating in an exceptional 1882.

These movements can be explained in the following general terms. During the second-half of 1876 the profits of the Indo-Chinese Sugar Company were noted by the Board of Directors to be 'paying off the position'. The Bank sold to the China Merchants' Steam Navigation Company the steamship *Calabar*, which, having lost $120,000 in 1875, was a fortunate transaction at $32,000. A sum of $60,000 was accepted for the Annamite claim in early 1877, and the Bank's interest in the China Sugar Refinery was bought out for $300,000 by a new company in January 1878. The Bank had successfully left its past behind it, but the data also require a more critical assessment of the profitability of the Bank's ordinary business under Jackson's early administration.

The middle years were years of commercial uncertainty, highlighted by the failure of the City of Glasgow Bank in 1878, which temporarily tied up £48,000 of the Bank's funds, and sustained by uncertainty over the course of silver. The Bremer firm of Wm Pustau and Co., represented on the Board of Directors from 1867 to 1872 by Julius Menke, failed in 1878, taking several companies with it.

The withdrawal of the Oriental and Mercantile in 1879 left the Hongkong Bank as the only Eastern exchange bank in Japan. That same year the Japanese needed assistance in encouraging the use of their silver yen; they turned to the Hongkong Bank Manager, A.M. Townsend. In return for its assistance the Bank was to receive Japanese Government deposits of $300,000 interest free for three years. The Bank, since in any case it favoured a role for the silver yen, agreed to cooperate.

The weakness of the Oriental no doubt was also one of the factors which enabled the Hongkong Bank to compete successfully in 1879 for a share of the Imperial Treasury business in Singapore.

The magnitude of the improvement in 1882 cannot be fully explained, but it would appear that Jackson, with the encouragement of McLean, revalued Head Office sterling assets. Certainly Jackson was under pressure to show a favourable result with dividends to match as he sought to raise £2.5 million in additional capital, and the semi-annual figures depend to a great extent on the rates at which balances in the various currencies are 'taken over'. Indeed one difficulty in evaluating the Bank year-by-year arises from the possibly arbitrary timing in which unrealized exchange gains might be taken over, and McLean often commented critically on the rate at which a branch 'took over' its balances – that is, expressed them in terms of Hong Kong dollars. Each manager determined the rate at which he would take over his accounts, while the Chief Manager determined the method by which he would evaluate government securities. An example of this latter problem is evident in the second half of 1880, during which the Bank sold India stock and realized a significant capital gain.

A consideration of the accounts

The total assets of the Hongkong Bank increased 76% in the years between 1876 and 1882, and with annual increases in the reserves, the dollar book value of the Bank's shares rose from $132 to $195 or 48%. The sterling book value rose only 32%. Deposits and notes outstanding increased 193%, loans 93%, and bills receivable 81% (loans plus bills receivable increased 86%), and the general picture given in Tables 8.4 and 8.5 is obviously one of growth, reflected in the extraordinary increase in the price of the Bank's shares.

Unfortunately, the balance sheets and the information behind them are not so straightforward.

One example of this, for which see Table 8.5, will be found in the Bank's holdings of cash. Over the period the modal cash/assets ratio would appear to be 0.11 and no trend is observable, McLean's injunctions to be economical in the holding of cash, given improved communications, not as yet having any visible impact on the accounts.[18]

What is striking, however, is the apparently random movement in the ratio, including a high of 0.23 in June 1881. In general the unusually high holdings of cash and bullion can be ascribed to the timing, or mistiming, of the China loans. The delays which followed implementation of the final agreement for the 1878 Kansu Loan, for example, would account for the Bank having additional bullion on hand on June 30, 1878, and for its being drawn down before the end of the year. Less explicable is the large holding of cash and bullion at the end of June 1879; this may reflect in part holding of payments made when the bonds were allotted to the public in April, and there is mention in the McLean letters of shipments of silver by the Bank to India in July. The extraordinary holdings in June 1881 are clearly the consequence of the Kansu Silver Loan in 1881, the proceeds of which were to be paid out early in the second half of that year.

The China loans may also be reflected in the columns headed 'Loans, etc.', since the Bank advanced funds to the Chinese before receiving them from the

(in millions of dollars)

Table 8.5 *The Hongkong and Shanghai Banking Corporation*
Cash, selected balance sheet items, and ratios, 1876–1882

Year	Assets	Index[b]	Cash and bullion	C/A ratio	Net E	E as % of A	Deposits + notes	Loans etc.	Loan/D ratio	Bills rec	BR index	Bills pay	BP index
1876 June	39.06	100	51.16	13	0.337	0.86	14.78	12.5	0.85	19.6	100	18.8	100
1876 Dec.	43.29	111	44.47	10	0.479	1.11	13.07	8.7	0.67	28.9	147	24.4	130
1877 June	42.05	108	52.20	12	0.371	0.88	15.97	10.1	0.63	25.4	129	20.2	107
1877 Dec.	52.71	135	57.26	11	0.565	1.07[a]	22.36	10.3	0.46	34.0	173	24.7	131
1878 June	55.92	143	89.60	16[a]	0.432	0.77	21.05	14.2	0.67	30.9	158	28.4	151
1878 Dec.	53.42	137	68.01	13	0.340	0.64	24.49	15.0	0.61	28.2	144	22.3	119
1879 June	53.45	137	102.05	19[a]	0.313	0.59	18.75	13.7	0.73	25.8	131	28.0	149
1879 Dec.	52.13	133	78.89	15	0.335	0.64	24.95	13.2	0.53	27.2	139	20.3	108
1880 June	44.89	115	75.65	17	0.375	0.84[a]	22.92	16.5	0.72	17.8	91	15.0	80
1880 Dec.	48.01	123	64.36	13	0.523	1.09[a]	26.14	12.8	0.49	28.3	144	14.6	78
1881 June	48.02	123	109.96	23[a]	0.443	0.92	31.92	18.6	0.58	18.0	92	8.8	47
1881 Dec.	58.23	149	59.09	10	0.715	1.23[a]	35.17	20.9	0.59	30.1	153	15.4	82
1882 June	59.16	151	66.29	11	0.580	0.98[a]	37.74	24.4	0.65	26.6	135	13.6	72
1882 Dec.	68.59	176	68.21	10	0.817	1.19[a]	43.29	24.1	0.56	35.6	181	17.0	91

Notes:
[a] Ratios affected by China loan operations.
[b] Index of total assets, June 1876 = 100.

Bills Rec = BR = bills receivable.

E = earnings   D = deposits + notes
A = assets.
Loans etc = bills discounted, loans and credits.
Bills pay = BP = bills payable, incl. 'drafts on London Bankers and short sight drawings on our London Office against bills receivable and bullion shipments'.

public and held an undisclosed number of the bonds on its own account.

Despite these uncertainties, one may conclude that, after making allowances for the years indicated in Table 8.5, earnings were a relatively high percentage of assets. The changes in the ratio of loans to deposits suggest that the Bank's liquidity was sound, but the McLean correspondence, especially in 1879, warned Jackson that the Bank was locked-up because it was lending heavily against shares and especially against its own shares, contrary to the spirit of the charter. With Jackson apparently responding that this problem had his attention, and with the general revival of trade and economic conditions on the China coast in 1880–1882, the growth of the Bank may be assumed to have been on a sounder basis.

The final columns in Table 8.5 deal with bills receivable and payable, and these show contrary trends. Certainly the 81% growth in bills receivable is a key indicator on the 'legitimate' role of the Bank in the finance of Far Eastern trade. The decline of bills payable (as fully defined in the Table) should be seen against the growth of TT drawings to finance imports into China and accordingly of the need for London sterling deposits to meet them; this would be reflected in the growth of overall deposits – almost 90% in the last $2\frac{1}{2}$ years.

The figures for government securities also appear erratic, but can be explained in part by the expression of opinion by the Board in 1876 that as many of the Bank's securities as possible should be in sterling both in India and London, subject to the decision of the managers. As Indian rupee paper was held against overdrafts in Bombay and Calcutta, and as prices and expectations changed, the Bank engaged in transactions which are not possible to follow. However the 1880 decision by the Board, on the recommendation of the London Committee, to realize its gains on Indian rupee securities and invest, over a period of time, £250,000 in British government paper, is clearly seen in the semi-annual accounts. This operation was only completed in the second half of 1882.

From the semi-annual meetings

The story of these years as reflected in the Chairman's speeches at the semi-annual general meetings does not alter the picture gained from an examination of the accounts. The meetings themselves were not particularly well-attended – typical of years of success – and one speaker noted that he would not have to raise his voice to be heard. The Chairman noted for 1876 the sale of dead stock, and the tone for the next two years is optimistic with Thomas Jackson acknowledging the vote of thanks to the Chief Manager and staff for the first time in February 1878.

And it was in 1878 that very quietly the Hongkong Bank agreed to conform to the London banks' decision to reduce usance from six to four months for China, Japan, and the Straits and three months for India. By this time the move was more in accord with legitimate mercantile requirements.

The next two years were acknowledged as being less profitable – unfavourable changes in the exchange and losses in the tea trade – but with the Reserve Fund passing $1.5 million shareholder pressure, from both London and Shanghai and, no doubt, less formally in Hong Kong, took the form of circulars to the directors. In July 1880 the London Committee wrote that as the reserves had reached $1.5 million the time had arrived 'when a moderate increase in dividends may be made to advantage of all interests'.

The directors promised to give all this their 'earnest attention'. Indeed, despite the Chairman's reference to the example of the Oriental Bank and an appeal for caution, he had in February 1880 virtually promised the increase. Performance for the first half of 1880 being sufficient to permit a move from £1 to £1:5s, the Chairman, W. Keswick of Jardine, Matheson and Co., both optimistic and cautious, declared at the August 1880 meeting:

The business of the Corporation is sound and prosperous, and without taking too sanguine a view of the future, we have reason to anticipate that the increased rate of dividend will be maintained if not still further increased. [Applause] I may mention, too, that in view of paying the larger dividend now recommended a specially careful examination of all outstandings of the Bank has taken place, and that all known or anticipated losses have been fully provided for. [Applause]

The February 1881 meeting was the first since the crisis of the mid-1870s which can be called 'exuberant'. Net 'earnings' were high at 1.1% of assets – due in part to profits from the China loans and, it should be added, from the sale of Indian securities involving the realization of a considerable capital gain. Again in response to shareholder pressure, the interim dividend was raised from £1:5s to £1:10s indicating the Board's intention to pay out £3:0s per annum (see Table 8.1B). This, moreover, did not prevent an allocation of $200,000 to reserves; the payout ratio itself was virtually unchanged at 66%. The Board had already declared their goal to be a Reserve Fund of $2.5 million, and with the Reserve Fund now at $1.8 million that target was within reach with even higher dividends, it was hoped, not far away. The meeting accepted with applause the decision of the directors to grant a bonus of 10% of salary to the staff, and Thomas Jackson once again rose to acknowledge the praise:

I am remarkably gratified by this vote of thanks. It has been my very great good fortune to be surrounded by earnest, capable men, and to our united efforts the success we have attained is due; and many of them – I may say this publicly – deserve as much credit if not more than I do for the result. The present position of the Bank is a source of pride and pleasure to everyone of us, and I hope to be able to meet you here for many years, and to submit, year after year, as satisfactory a report as that which the Chairman has now read to you. [Applause]

It was natural that the focus of praise in Hong Kong should be the Hong Kong Manager, and it was just that Jackson commented on the team. There were McLean in London writing letters of advice and ably assisted by William Kaye, Cameron in Shanghai dealing with the Chinese on whom so much depended, de

Bovis soon to open Tientsin, Edward Morriss and G.E. Noble in India, J.J. Winton in Singapore, Harries in San Francisco, and Townsend developing the New York agency. There were also Henry C. Smith, soon to die, and J.D. Woodford – both of whom received special mention for the courteous performance of the business of the Hong Kong office.

At the end of 1881 the Board recommended a dividend bonus of ten shillings. The mid-1882 speech took note of the growth of the Bank's regular business as reflected, for example, in the rise in deposits, but it also noted a financial crisis among the 'native banks' in Hong Kong, the withdrawal of credit, and the careful role the Hongkong Bank had played, so that:

Owing to the discreet tact of your Chief Manager, the Bank has passed through the ordeal, avoiding in the first place any loss whatever from its local loans, and in the second place putting itself in this position without in any way incurring ill-feeling among the large and valuable native constituency of the Bank.

This is a reminder that the Chairman's speech is inadequate as a full explanation of the progress of the Bank. Behind the favourable growth figures was the development of business with the Chinese and Japanese through the compradores and local financial institutions, but – and not for the last time – the Hongkong Bank was unable to act as a central bank, finding it necessary to withdraw facilities to preserve its own resources. If, as in this case, credit had been extended unwisely by local banks, there would be failures and resulting commercial distress.[19]

The figures and the speeches nevertheless confirm that the Bank had taken over the business of the retreating Eastern banks – the state of the China trade permits of no other explanation. As yet, the Bank's operations in Singapore, the Philippines, and Batavia could hardly account for the favourable changes of the past few years.

Optimistic as the successive chairmen had been, it was the speech dealing with the end-1882 accounts which seemed designed to introduce the new era.

First, there was acknowledgement of the extraordinary growth of business; secondly, an announcement of a 10% bonus to the staff with shareholder tributes to Jackson –

the service Mr Jackson has given to the Bank has been of a kind which no money could buy and that his energy and ability [applause], backed – as we have every reason to believe it has been – by like energy and ability on the part of the other managers, has brought about our present prosperity . . .

– which he once more suitably acknowledged. The need for new capital had already been considered and approved at a special meeting in December 1882, and thus the announcement of plans for a grand new Head Office building in Hong Kong, the cost of which was underestimated at 3 lacs of dollars, seemed wholly appropriate.

Even in this heady atmosphere the Board of Directors remained conservative.

Their goal of \$2.5 million was easily reached and the dividend raised from £2 per annum plus bonus to £4 per annum. Indeed, with the payment ratio at only 34% an additional bonus could have been paid. The directors, having set and reached a target for reserves, might be supposed to have had their hand forced, but instead, as explained earlier in this chapter, taking note of the instability of silver and the burden of paying dividends on increased capital, they successfully proposed and funded a new reserve 'for the equalization of dividends'.

A new stage in the Bank's history was to begin.

9

JACKSON'S FIRST TERM, II: NEW CAPITAL AND GROWTH, 1882–1888

The principle of banking is to turn over money, and not bury it in the East.

North-China Herald, 10 September 1886

This chapter is a continuation of the story of the Hongkong Bank during Thomas Jackson's first years as Chief Manager. The success of the period 1876–1882 led to the need for additional capital, but this created both opportunities and problems. Jackson solved the latter for the time, but during his leave in 1886–1887, old problems came to the front and new ones developed. In the final sixteen months of his administration, Jackson set the Bank back on course; he then returned to London, apparently for the remainder of his service and with the intention of becoming David McLean's successor as London Office Manager.

THE INCREASE IN CAPITAL

In a circular dated September 13, 1882, the Hongkong Bank's Chief Manager, Thomas Jackson, informed shareholders that the directors had, after careful consideration, decided to recommend an increase of 50% in the capital of the Bank, from $5 million to the maximum $7.5 million authorized in Article V of the ordinance of incorporation (No. 5 of 1866).

The argument for the increase was based on the growth of the Bank's business as reflected in the declining ratio between shareholders' funds and the Bank's liabilities (including the note issue). The decision was complicated by realization that the funds required were probably not available on the China coast and that capital for a silver bank would have to be raised at least in part in the London capital market. The directors had to be assured that the operation was feasible and that the increased London interests would not endanger the directors' determination that the Head Office should remain in Hong Kong. Furthermore the operation would have to be timed and carried out so that present shareholders' equity was not disturbed. Relative share prices and premiums therefore became important.

The increase in capital was to be accomplished by a rights issue of 20,000 new shares with a par value of $125 per share to present shareholders on a one for two basis at £40, representing a premium of 77% over par at the rate of exchange used in the Bank's end-1882 accounts.[a]

The Governor's authority, granted on an urgent basis without reference to the Colonial Office in London, was received on September 19, and the shareholders approved the arrangements at a special meeting on December 30.[1] The additional capital was paid up in four equal payments of £10 at the end of each 1883 quarter – hence it is referred to in this history as the capital increase of 1883. Payments had not been quite completed by the end of 1883, but by June 1884 the accounts indicated a paid-up capital of $7.5 million and an addition to the Reserve Fund from the premium on new shares of $1.86 million.

Despite the strongly expressed misgivings of the London Committee, the operation proved successful. Shareholders' funds totalled $12.6 million and the 60,000 shares had a book value of $209, 166% of par; the market price in a financially shaken Shanghai was $271 equivalent or 217% of par, and the consequent market/book ratio had fallen to a more realistic 1.31. Seen in terms of sterling equivalents, shares on the London market at £51 were 220% of par (of $125 at current exchange rates) and the M/B ratio was also 1.31 (see Table 9.1).

The proposal to increase the Bank's capital had been put forward in a period of local China-coast optimism and share speculation; by the time all the new capital had been paid up, prices in Shanghai had fallen to a more realistic level. Shanghai was, in fact, recovering from a financial crisis marked by the failure of the great banker/official and friend of the Hongkong Bank, Hu Kwang-yung.

The shareholder who exercised his right to buy for £40 a share at the ratio of one new share for every two old shares owned did not realize any capital gain, but his equity per old share had increased by £19.5, for which increase he had in effect paid £20. This apparent 'watering' was more than accounted for by a fall in the exchange from 3s:7½d to 3s:6½d or 4.7%. Aside from this aspect of the operation, there is little doubt but that the move on the part of the directors was generally well-received.

The Hongkong Bank's new capital position made it one of the world's largest financial institutions; on the China coast its nearest rival was the Chartered Bank with shareholders' funds of approximately $5.4 million equivalent (£1 million). The Agra Bank, with $6.5 million equivalent, was basically an Indian bank, the Chartered Mercantile's capital was less than £1 million, and the Oriental Bank Corporation had fallen.

---

[a] The 77% figure is the premium on the dollar par value of $125 using an exchange rate of 3/7⅛. The par value of the shares in London was £28.125 at the stated rate of 4/6; thus the sterling premium would be only 42%. This latter calculation has no operative significance; it is an example of the confusion which the Bank had got itself into as a result of (i) stating the rate of exchange on its scrip and (ii) accepting what may have been poor legal advice.

Table 9.1 The Hongkong and Shanghai Banking Corporation: The capital increase of 1883

	Authorized = Paid-up capital	Reserve funds	Shareholders' funds	Capital/ assets ratio	Book value	Share price	M/B ratio	Exchange rate $1 = x s/d = £x
				%	$	$		
A. Actual		in millions of dollars						
40,000 shares								
Dec. 1882	5.00	2.60	7.82	11.4	195.5	344.0	1.76	
60,000 shares								
June 1884	7.50	4.80	12.56	16.6	209.4	271.0	1.29	
		in millions of pounds			£	£		
40,000 shares								
Dec. 1882	0.90	0.47	1.40	11.4	35.0	59.0[a]	1.68	3/7$\frac{1}{8}$ 0.17969
60,000 shares								
June 1884	1.39	0.89	2.33	16.6	38.8	51.0[a]	1.31	3/8$\frac{1}{2}$ 0.18541
B. Hypothetical – using the December 1892 exchange rate		in millions of pounds			£			
40,000 shares								
Dec. 1882	0.68	0.35	1.06		26.6	–	–	2/8$\frac{3}{4}$ 0.13646
60,000 shares								
June 1884	1.02	0.66	1.71		28.2	–	–	2/8$\frac{3}{4}$ 0.13646

Notes:
[a] This is the London price in pounds sterling.
M/B = ratio of market price to book value of shares.

The official explanation

The growth of the Hongkong Bank's regular business is reflected in the increase in deposits and notes in circulation from $13.4 million at the end of 1875 to $35.2 million at the end of 1881. The consequence of this as seen from various ratios over time was erratic. There was no certain trend. The capital/assets ratio at the end of 1881 was 12%. The problem was liquidity. Alternatively the Bank could approach the matter as one of 'over-trading' on the basis of its capital, a matter of particular importance if the directors foresaw a period of further growth.

The percentage which the Bank's capital and reserves bore to liabilities and notes in circulation, the ratio which guided the Board's decision, had fallen from 38% to 20% – by mid-1882 the percentage had fallen further to 19%. It was these figures that provided the published basis for the directors' decision to seek a larger capital, and, by the standards of the time, this argument alone would be convincing.

The Bank was fortunate that such a justification existed. The increase in capital came not only on the eve of a stock market crisis in Shanghai – this was a matter of lucky short-run timing – but also before the downward trend in silver prices was generally accepted as such. If a hypothetical calculation be made, converting, for example, December 1882 shareholders' funds into sterling at the rate prevailing ten years later (December 1892, $1.00 = £0.13646), the sterling book value, *pari passu*, would have been £26.6 or less than the actual £35.00 value (see Table 9.1). Furthermore this hypothetical book value of £26.6 would have been even less than the theoretical par of £28.125, calculated at the 4/6 rate.

A further indication of the problem faced by the Bank can be shown by taking June 1884 shareholders' funds, after the new capital and the premium had been paid up and additional sums added to the reserves, and then using the same 1892 rate. Other things being equal, the £39 book value shown in Table 9.1 would have been reduced to £28.2, or only marginally more than the par of £28.125.

A glance ahead at Table 13.1, which shows the June 1883 rate of 2s:6d to be the highest in the decade, will reinforce the point made in the previous paragraph.

The Bank had to grow in dollar terms to remain credit-worthy in terms of sterling. Growth could only proceed from a larger capital base. But increased capital, a significant portion of which was subscribed for either from the United Kingdom itself or by those whose long-run thinking was in terms of sterling, could only be obtained at a reasonable price under certain conditions – a high level of reserves, a sound dividend policy and, most important of all, reasonably optimistic views on the future of silver. Timing was therefore all important.

The decision to increase the capital had not been unanimous. In July 1882, less than two months before the favourable decision, the London Committee had recommended that the Board postpone action for twelve months unless the

Hongkong Bank were being challenged by the prospects of a new bank on the China coast. Conveniently the Board could provide evidence of such a threat, and the plan for an increased capital proceeded – successfully.

The London dimension

The very fact of the new shares being quoted in a sterling unit of account, payable by shareholders in the East in dollars at the rate of the day, is itself a witness to the changed times and the role of London. The method of quotation did not, however, mean that the Bank was about to state its accounts in sterling; that was not at this time discussed. As with certain of the China loans, the directors were aware of the trend in the exchanges and were unwilling to float new capital over a period of time when conditions might unduly favour shareholders on the London register. But the Board's decision also meant that on the conclusion of the operation the Bank would have received a given amount of sterling, and it was the sterling value of the capital which remained one of the principal concerns of the Bank. To examine how this came about is an essential preliminary to an understanding of the Bank's position.

The growth of London deposits shown in Table 9.2A was not a matter of chance. David McLean required sterling; he actively sought sterling deposits, even encouraging constituents either presently in or recently returned from the East to open current accounts, despite the additional work and its associated costs. There had been discussion in the early days as to what banking activities such a bank, chartered to operate in the colonies, might legitimately undertake in London, but that had ceased to be an issue for all practical purposes.[b] The finance of the Bank's outward business was straining the sources of funds available; the growth of this business was occurring at just that time when Eastern banks were under suspicion and, despite the presence of a London and County Bank director on the Hongkong Bank's London Committee, the Hongkong Bank could not obtain what McLean considered 'sufficient' accommodation. McLean's correspondence, especially in 1878 and 1879, frequently refers to a critical shortage of funds with instructions that branches were not to draw on him by telegraphic transfer (TT) until funds were actually in London to cover – 'surplus on the water', wrote McLean, 'is no use to us'.[2]

The London and County Bank had confirmed its agreements with the Hongkong Bank in April 1879, including the limit of credit to £2.5 million, and the uncovered credit of £100,000. This could be increased by a further £100,000 for exceptional purposes, but the London bank now requested the Hongkong

---

[b] This was the issue which had brought about the union which became the ill-fated Agra and Masterman's Bank in 1864. But the former Agra and United Service Bank had wanted to become a clearing bank; the Hongkong Bank was not seeking this privilege.

Table 9.2A *The Hongkong and Shanghai Banking Corporation London deposits, 1878–1882 and 1888*

	£	$ equivalent	% D[a]	£1 = $x
30 April 1878	485,898	2,527,000	13	5.2
31 October 1878	509,616	2,905,000	13	5.7
30 April 1879	475,145	2,471,000	14	5.2
24 December 1879	512,000	2,662,000	12	5.2
30 June 1881	1,372,000	7,409,000	25	5.4
31 December 1881	1,823,000	9,844,000	30	5.4
23 June 1882	2,143,000	11,272,000	32	5.3
17 May 1888	4,015,591	26,770,607	36	6.7

Note:
[a] London deposits as a percentage of total deposits.
Source: Occasional references in David McLean Papers, MS 380401, Library, School of Oriental and African Studies and the minutes of the Board of Directors; hence the random dates. Total deposits and the exchange rate are taken from the closest semi-annual report.

Bank to seek permission to use this on each occasion – and not to exceed it. Other cautions were added to the communication.[3] Then in July 1883, with the Hongkong Bank's increase of capital in process, there was one breakthrough; the Hongkong Bank was permitted to obtain advances against documentary mercantile acceptances to the extent of £750,000, an increase of £50,000.[4] McLean had been obtaining advances from other banks in addition to the London and County, but, preferring to do all business with the latter bank alone, he had, on that basis, requested and obtained the additional credit. 'The bulk of these bills run off within three months. They get the bills with two names, full documents and the endorsement of the H&SBC and in addition a margin of 5%. Why the security is as good as a Bank of England note.'[5]

The London and County Bank's committee minutes contain, however, many instances of special requests, covered usually by the offer of appropriate security, all of which appear to have been granted – there is the probability that requests which the manager considered unsuitable were not pressed by McLean.[6] With a director on the Bank's London Committee there was intercommunication, but the London and County had its own obligations and the Hongkong Bank could not expect unlimited facilities.

Despite this need and consequent search for funds, McLean was watching their cost and in the process cancelled the agreement with the Bank's agents in

Scotland.[c] By 1882 McLean had decided that the Bank could attract funds directly and save the commission; after a dispute over the right of James Hill to receive a commission on renewals, a dispute resolved in the Bank's favour, direct representation in Scotland appears to have ceased.

The main issue, however, was the dependence on the amount of the Bank's shareholders' funds as a factor in attracting deposits. In the first instance an increase in the reserves would appear to have met McLean's sound belief that the ability to attract further deposits depended on the level of the reserves. In the absence of deposit insurance, depositors rightly considered shareholders' funds, that is, paid-up capital, reserve funds, Marine Insurance Fund, and the balance of P&L Account, as a measure of their security. The proprietors of the Hongkong Bank had a reserve liability equal to paid-up capital, but with the failure of City of Glasgow Bank fresh in people's minds and the consequences of the new Banking Act of 1879 untested, little weight would be given to the practical value of such a provision.[d] In January 1882 McLean was writing to Jackson that, given the Bank's increased reserves, any amount of deposits needed by London operations could be obtained at 5% on which he made a net income ranging from $\frac{1}{4}$% to 1%, sufficient to attract the attention of the income tax commissioners and force submission of a tax return for the first time in the Bank's history (see Table 9.2B).[8]

The objection to new capital was (i) the inflexibility of the dividend payout and (ii) the inability of the Bank to sell new shares at Jackson's proposed price of £47 in instalments covering only a twelve month period.

The first objection appears to contradict the nature of equity capital and dividends, but McLean as an investor in Hongkong Bank shares was well aware that inability to maintain the rate of dividends would be likely to result in a fall in the market value of the shares; as London Manager McLean feared this would spill over into the Bank's ability to raise funds through fixed deposits. On the other hand, when business was poor and funds no longer required, interest rates could be lowered and deposits discouraged.

---

[c] The agency 'opened' by Robert Stevenson in Edinburgh is nowhere mentioned, and it must be assumed that it was short lived – indeed, despite Bank records, it may in fact never have existed. In any case it was to be operated in conjunction with Hill, the former agent, and with Stevenson dropping out the arrangements reverted to the *status quo ante*.

[d] This Act, 42 and 43 Vict. c. of 76 of 1879, designed to encourage the movement from unlimited to limited liability banking, made possible the effective creation of a reserve liability by authorizing incorporation with paid-up capital limited by agreement to less than subscribed, except on the winding up of the company. The average British bank shareholder in 1885–1886 is estimated to have had a reserve liability of four times the amount paid-up, thus virtually recreating the problems of unlimited liability – the whole premise of the Act was questionable. As Clapham has observed, 'Security lay not in the law but in the management' – but management was reflected in the very policies McLean referred to.[7]

Table 9.2B *The Hongkong and Shanghai Banking Corporation*
Increase in London Office business, 1875–1881

Fixed deposits		*Total deposits in £*	
31 Dec. 1875, No. of depositors	247	266,000	
31 Dec. 1881, do	1,547	1,821,000	
Increase	1,300		1,555,000
Bills receivable			
31 Dec. 1875, No. of bills	5,897	6,861,000	
31 Dec. 1881, do	20,862	20,472,000	
Increase	14,965		13,611,000
Outward bills remitted			
31 Dec. 1875, No. of bills	3,936	1,721,000	
31 Dec. 1881, do	15,400	4,381,000	
Increase	11,464		2,660,000
Current accounts		*Debit balances*	*Credit balances*
31 Dec. 1875, No. of accounts	150	24,900	30,300
31 Dec. 1881, do	400	93,200	111,200
	250	68,300	80,900

Source: D. McLean to the Hongkong and Shanghai Banking Corporation Board of Directors, 17 February 1882, in his papers MS 380401, SOAS, IV, 24.

Nor was it sufficient for Jackson to show an improved rate of dividends; both he and McLean knew that this was in great measure the consequence of profits from the China loans, and, as McLean pointed out, there was no guarantee that China would continue borrowing through the Bank. In fact China did contract new loans. The later interruptions to the normal rates of dividend payments were due to unforeseen business hazards and to fluctuations in exchange – events which would have proved even more dangerous to an undercapitalized bank.

The second objection was really a matter of timing; McLean advised waiting until the reserves were $2.5 million and the dividends at £4 per annum. Unlikely as it seemed in early 1882, these goals were in fact reached at the end of the year, that is, after the decision to increase the capital but before the new shares were available in the market.

Source of funds – gold or silver?

There was a limit to the availability of funds in China, either as deposits or as equity capital. Primary deposits might grow with trade and with the development of the Treaty Ports and the Straits Settlements, but these were not at the time a sufficient basis for the expansion of banking operations without increasing the capital. There is evidence, certainly accepted by McLean, that bank shares were maintaining their value due to the questionable practice of accepting them as security for loans. McLean, Jackson, and Cameron, often acting with or in the name of the London Office Accountant, Burnett, and sometimes with John Walter, speculated in Bank shares – if dealing with insider information can be so termed. Their operations tended to stabilize the market, but there were other forces operating, some of them close to Jackson and the members of the Board, and the situation was fraught with potential abuse and danger.

The obvious remedy was a broader capital base, but this could only be achieved by raising capital in London and risking loss of control in Hong Kong. As McLean was to put it later:

Our great success depends upon the Eastern people being interested in the Bank, besides if more than one-half were on this register the London shareholders might some day, for some reason or other, attempt to get H[ead] O[ffice] transferred to London, which in my opinion would not be for the good of the concern.[9]

The latter danger has already been discussed; it was to become an arithmetical possibility before the turn of the century, but it was never to be realized.

McLean's solution was to encourage further sterling deposits at 5%, but to this there were several objections. First, this could only meet London's needs and depended on building up the Bank's uncapitalized reserves to a level unacceptable to shareholders. They would press for increased dividends. Secondly, as McLean acknowledged, London funds could not be 'used in the East' because of the exchange risk. Finally, the cost at 5% was excessive – the Board urged McLean to reduce the London rate of interest even below $4\frac{1}{2}$%; but at 4% the Bank was to lose deposits and at the end of the decade London was offering $4\frac{1}{2}$%.

These arguments might be countered by noting that the rate of dividends was higher and, legally at least, discretionary, but cost of funds in London affected the rate of interest charged to branches on their overdrafts and apparently distorted the decision-making process despite various accounting devices to minimize 'costs' as defined in London Office books.[e] The Board felt that branches and agencies were letting exchange operations 'pass them' because of the cost of their London overdrafts.

This impasse could only be surmounted by offering new shares at a price sufficiently low to attract London investors despite the exchange risk, but sufficiently high to obtain the support of present shareholders.

Funds were in fact needed both in London and in the East, and any increase in the Bank's capital, which was in silver, would facilitate McLean's borrowing in London in gold, while the Bank itself could remain on an even keel. But the real success of the plan depended on the China loans. If these were to continue and if

e   An example would be crediting of interest from securities in the special London Reserve to London Profit and Loss account instead of to Head Office.

there could be a mix between sterling and silver loans, the Bank would have both long-term sterling cover and a continuing stream of repayments in silver. This, in fact, is what happened.

The making of the decision

Jackson's discussions by letter with McLean continued throughout the first half of 1882, but the latter, while acknowledging that London funds could not be used in the East, remained unconvinced. The London Committee supported McLean. Nevertheless, the Board continued its preparations.

On July 4, 1882, the Board of Directors noted for the first time news of a rumoured new bank in Shanghai and it is this which may have affected the balance. Jackson's September circular to shareholders had in fact been approved as early as July 25, but still the Board hesitated. On August 29 they noted receipt of the negative advice cabled from the London Committee and resolved to wait for their letter, but a week later the Board had become aware of dissatisfaction among Shanghai shareholders at the rumoured delay and the question of whether indeed plans for a new bank were moving ahead became the key to the Board's decision.

The Board cabled Ewen Cameron, the Bank's Shanghai Manager, asking whether the report that plans for a new bank had been cancelled were in fact true. Cameron wired back that the report was false. The prospectus for the new bank was at that moment with the printers. With the receipt of this information the Board resolved on September 6 to increase the capital of the Bank to $7.5 million, but the £10 instalment represented another disagreement with London who had insisted that the market would accept nothing more than £5 over a longer period. As it developed the Hong Kong Board had a better feel for the situation.

McLean was to grumble afterwards, not without some basis, that the threat of the new Shanghai bank never really existed. The 1882 bank, to which no reference has been found in the newspapers, was presumably a product of the speculative atmosphere developing in what Shanghai residents enjoyed calling the 'model Settlement'. It was presumably planned to depend heavily on Chinese, probably 'compradore', capital and would have been formed with unlimited liability since facilities for incorporation in Shanghai with limited liability did not then exist.[10] Thus the size of the bank would have been restricted, and its chances of success, given the reputation of banks with unlimited shareholder liability, following the City of Glasgow Bank disaster, were hardly worth considering.

In all this McLean was correct. He had witnessed a previous Shanghai effort to create a local 'Bank of China' in 1872, but the attempt to bring in compradore participation was new, and a National Bank of China was indeed founded in 1890.

Cameron was right to show concern. Furthermore, even the temporary promotion of such a bank could have diverted sufficient capital to add to the problems of floating the Hongkong Bank's new $2.5 million issue – and the directors were anxious that as high a proportion of the capital as possible should be raised in the East. Furthermore delay under such circumstances could have caused doubts as to the Hongkong Bank's directors' long-run view of their Bank. If it were to remain the local bank it needed to expand its capital base. Inaction might have been interpreted as either inability to recognize this fact or, much worse, an abdication of the Bank's role in the East.

But the Board did act and proved successful.

CONTINUED GROWTH, 1883–1885

During the next three years, 1883–1885, the Hongkong Bank's total assets increased by 55% and its net earnings by 65%. The Bank's reserves totalled the Board of Directors' newly declared goal of $5 million, and dividends at the rate of £4 per annum had not only been successfully maintained but a premium had been approved – in 1885 total payout at £4:10s per share had been $1,360,000, equivalent to 18% of paid-up capital or 10.6% of shareholders' funds.

The management of Thomas Jackson, up to this point, must be judged an unqualified success.

In early 1886 the Chief Manager went on leave. The Acting Chief Manager, John Walter, had to withdraw $300,000 from the fund for the equalization of dividends in order to maintain the £2 semi-annual rate, and for the next two years shareholders' funds declined, and the semi-annual dividend was reduced to £1:10s. These and subsequent misfortunes cannot be ascribed to John Walter; they had their origins in the good years, and for them Jackson must take some responsibility.

The fortunes of the Bank did not increase evenly through the period, but that was a fact influenced by exogenous factors, including the distrust caused by the fall of the Oriental, the Sino-French War, the accelerated fall in the exchanges by nearly 5% in the second half of 1884, and serious losses in Japan and Batavia. On the other hand certain positive developments depended on Ewen Cameron's inspired management of the Bank's China affairs, including the negotiation of new China loans, the development of contacts in Tientsin, and the tentative establishment of an agency in the imperial capital of Peking. Certain of the loans were contracted with the Canton authorities, and with these the Hong Kong Head Office and Jackson were directly involved.

Having said this much, the fact is that the years 1883 to 1885 justified Jackson's support of an increased capital, and his handling of a complex series of problems, not as rule of his own making, gained him the name 'Lucky' Jackson. His taking of leave a moment before the Bank's affairs changed direction would confirm the title.

Dividend vs reserves

The growth of business justified the increase in capital. Nevertheless the consequences of attempting to maintain a rate of £4 per annum strained the resources of the Bank under conditions of a depreciating dollar, and to this extent the Hongkong Bank had to face the same problems as a sterling-based bank. The clearest evidence is in the payout ratios, which began at 79% and rose to 102% in 1886 (see Table 9.5C). It might be argued that this is hindsight, that the Bank on the basis of its gross income could easily have met the dividend payments. This would have been true (i) if the stability of the dividend rate could have been measured in dollars and (ii) if there had been no serious losses. The fear that China would not continue borrowing proved unfounded, but the Bank could not withstand the impact of the fall in silver and heavy business losses – write-offs in the second-half of 1883, for example, were $282,786 or 26% of net profits before losses.

The relatively high rate of interest in the East was not a sure road to grand profits; rather it reflected, *inter alia*, the degree of risk.

McLean as London Manager received information of projected branch profits and on the basis of these would project dividend levels not only for the immediate half-year but for the years to come. As a conservative banker he anticipated first £2 per half-year, with a bonus of 10 shillings at the end of the year; after this he expected £6 per annum on a regular basis. But his hopes were dashed by losses; furthermore the 1886–1887 events in Manila (see below) forced priority consideration to rebuilding the reserves. When that task had been completed, new capital was required, silver continued to fall, and the hoped-for £6 dividend materialized only after the Great War – and inflation. Given these exaggerated expectations and calculations relative to an immediate improvement in the dividend rate, the pressures on the Board of Directors can be better understood.

Although the Board continued to give prominence at semi-annual general meetings to the need for a large reserve, the policy was sacrificed at least in December 1884 and December 1885 to maintain the dividends. Indeed, it would be fair to say that dividends were being paid from the extraordinary, sometimes up-front income from China loans.

Of the $5 million reserves in December 1885, $500,000 were in a fund for the equalization of dividends, and, with the Bank's unpublished contingency fund virtually committed, the payment of a bonus seemed almost as if the Board – or Jackson – wished a dramatic exit line for the Bank's first successful Chief

Manager. McLean had urged building up the reserves while good business lasted – he might have called it 'good luck'; the tide turned in the Spring of 1886 with the Reserve Fund at $4.5 million. News of a £20,000 loss in Manila, which the Agent, Charles I. Barnes, had failed to report the previous half-year when profits had been extraordinary, reached the Board on February 25, 1886, two days before the semi-annual meeting. Perhaps a last minute withdrawal of the dividend bonus would have been overly dramatic and misinterpreted. The fact remains that the high dividend was paid out on the eve of new disasters in Manila and a dramatic fall in the exchange, which the Reserve for Equalization of Dividends proved totally inadequate to handle.

But the Bank had grown. Jackson had been the Chief Manager during its years of growth. Had he been on hand in the less fortunate months which followed, he might well have modified the impact of events. In any case, the Board could do no less than make a gesture fully supported by the shareholders and, one suspects, by the Hongkong Bank's constituents and the community at large. Before Jackson left Hong Kong on leave in March 1886 the Board granted what he referred to as a 'munificent gift' of £8,000.

Silver and the exchanges

Silver was relatively steady at about 50d per ounce until the last two months of 1884. It then declined some 15% to 42⅝d by August 1886, with a brief recovery to 47d in early 1887 (see Table 9.3, which cannot reflect the fluctuations within the six-monthly intervals chosen). During 1885 silver was affected by the fear the United States would cease minting the Bland dollar; this was also the year the productive Broken Hill mine in New South Wales was opened. The movements in the Hong Kong/London exchange rate, despite its naturally high correlation with the London price of silver, were affected by additional factors; the impact of the Sino-French conflict (1884–1885), for example, would be more direct.

The first reference to the exchanges at the semi-annual meetings was in February 1886 – Jackson's last before leave, when the Chairman referred to the rate of 3s:4d as 'unprecedentedly low', but, as already noted, this did not prevent the Board from declaring a £2 dividend plus bonus of 10 shillings. Perhaps he was right in feeling confident; the increase in the Bank's deposits during the previous half-year were, he stated, mainly in London – the loss of confidence in the Hongkong Bank as an Eastern bank had been overcome; sterling deposits could increase in the face of a decline in silver. Given the policy of the Bank to employ sterling funds in London, depositors were correct in their view, but it was reassuring nevertheless to see it expressed practically.

Table 9.3 *The price of silver and the Hong Kong exchange,*
1883–1888

Year	d/ounce of silver	$\$ = x$ s/d[a]	% change in 6 months
1882 Dec.[b]	50.9	3/7	–
1883 June	50.1	$3/7\frac{1}{2}$	1.2
1883 Dec.	50.5	3/8	1.1
1884 June	50.6	$3/8\frac{1}{2}$	1.1
1884 Dec.	49.5	$3/6\frac{1}{2}$	– 4.5
1885 June	49.0	$3/6\frac{1}{2}$	0.0
1885 Dec.	46.9	3/4	– 5.9
1886 June	45.4	$3/0\frac{1}{2}$	– 8.8
1886 Dec.	46.4	$3/3\frac{1}{2}$	8.2
1887 June	44.2	3/2	– 3.8
1887 Dec.	45.1	$3/1\frac{1}{2}$	– 1.3
1888 June	42.2	3/0	– 4.0
1888 Dec.	42.9	$3/0\frac{1}{2}$	1.4
1889 Dec.[b]	44.2	$3/1\frac{1}{2}$	–

Notes:
[a] rate quoted in the Hongkong Bank's semi-annual reports.
[b] for pre-1883 figures see Table 8.2; for post-1888 figures see Tables
12.1 and 13.1.

The China loans, 1883–1888

As may be assumed from Table 9.4 the previously contracted China loans were
being repaid and interest from this source declined through 1884. The problem
of continued income from new China loans, which had so concerned McLean,
seemed confirmed. The Hongkong Bank however was asked to meet China's new
loan requirements, particularly to finance the Northwestern campaigns of
Viceroy Tso Tsung-t'ang and then the requirements caused by the Sino-French
conflict. The loan for the China Merchants' Steam Navigation Company was
reflected in the 1886 accounts.

Table 9.4 understates total profits in this period for the special reason that the
Hongkong Bank was unsuccessful in its initial issue of its silver loans and in
consequence held them as an investment, selling them off 'as opportunity arose'
at profitable prices. On the other hand, with the exception of the CMSNCo loan,
the greater part of the profits were received over the life of the loans, thereby
minimizing the erratic impact on total earnings.

In 1884 the Hongkong and Shanghai Banking Corporation made two loans of
one million Canton taels each to the Viceroy of the Liang-Kwang provinces,

Table 9.4 *The Hongkong and Shanghai Banking Corporation*
Net earnings and China loan profits, 1883–1888

(in thousands of dollars)

Year	(i) Net earnings	(ii) Direct loan earnings	(iii) (i)-(ii) Balance	(iv) (ii) as a % of (i)
1883 June	575	91	484	15.8
1883 Dec.	739	80	659	10.8
1884 June	797	75	722	9.4
1884 Dec.	701	186	515	26.5
1885 June	878	96	782	10.9
1885 Dec.	948	61	887	6.4
1886 June	547	102	445	18.6
1886 Dec.	770	384	386	50.0
1887 June	561	159	402	28.3
1887 Dec.	599	134	465	22.4
1888 June	700	103	597	14.7
1888 Dec.	864	256	608	29.6

Source: derived from D.J.S. King's report, cited.

Chang Chih-tung; they were designated 'A' and 'B' and issued in Hong Kong in dollars at the standard par rate of 717 Canton taels = 1,000 dollars. The loans, which totalled $2,789,400, were redeemable within three and six years respectively and bore interest at 0.75% per tael per lunar month or approximately 9.3% per Western year. The Bank intended issuing the loans to the public at 8% and par, profits depending on the difference in interest rates. In fact only 5% of the bonds were tendered for at par and the Bank for a time held the balance.

In December of 1884 the Hongkong Bank made a further silver loan, referred to as the 'C' Loan, for 1,143,400 Canton taels of which 143,400 taels was to enable China to repay the indemnity for the destruction caused during the Shameen Incident of 1883. The total, equivalent to $1,594,700.14, bore interest at approximately 9.3% and was repayable commencing October 1888 in five annual instalments. The Bank never formally issued the loan in a public offering but rather sold it at par or above on an 8% basis as opportunity arose.

These silver loans, issued as they were in politically disturbed times, had to be held at least initially by the Hongkong Bank. The Chairman reported the Bank held a total of $2.6 million of the A and B Loans; after several transactions including paying the Chinese for the C Loan in the form of A and B Loan bonds, some of which were then resold to the Bank, the Hongkong Bank held a maximum of $3.8 million worth of bonds from these three loans. This amounted to a sum equivalent to 30% of shareholders' funds and had to be explained at the semi-annual meeting.

In February 1886 the Chairman, F. D. Sassoon, announced that the bonds were being 'disposed of gradually at a handsome premium', which may be partly reflected in the following figures from Table 9.4, at the same time illustrating the inadequacy of calculating 'profits' from the China loans on the sole basis of direct profits as stated in the agreements:

	(i) Net earnings	(ii) Direct loan earnings	(iii) (i)–(ii) Balance	(iv) (ii) as a % of (i)
1885 Dec.	948	61	887	6.4
1886 June	547	102	445	18.6
1886 Dec.	770	384	386	50.0

Six months later, the new Chairman, M. Grote of Melchers and Co., was able to assure shareholders that all bonds in the A, B, and C series had been sold, although the Bank now held bonds from a small issue to the Canton Hoppo (the [Chinese] Controller of the Kwangtung Maritime Customs). Grote was referring to the so-called 'D' Loan for 300,000 Canton taels agreed on July 9, 1886, and issued successfully at a 5% premium in December.

An 'E' Loan for 700,000 Peking Kuping taels for China's Kaiping mines was signed by the Bank in October 1886.

Of more consequence were the Canton Loan of 1885 for £505,000, repayable in ten years in Hong Kong at the rate of the day at 0.75% per lunar month or 9% per Western year plus approximately 0.75% every three years for the intercalary month, the 1885 Foochow Loan of £1 million – although the amount actually agreed with the Chinese was 4 million Shanghai taels, equivalent at the agreed arbitrary rate of 5s:1d to £1,016,666:13s:4d – and the Imperial Government 6% Loan of 1885 for £750,000, issued at 98. The calculations for the Foochow Loan were complex, involving interest, exchange rate, and timing differentials, but net profit was probably in the order of £67,600 over the ten year period of the loan.

An 'F' Loan for Kuping Ts 1 million was signed between the Bank's Tientsin Agent, Alexander Leith, and Viceroy Li Hung-chang in June 1888. The purpose was to pay for works on the Yellow River at Cheng Chou Fu in Honan. The impact of this loan on the Bank's accounts was subsequent to the period now under consideration.

The bulk of these loans had been made, as previously noted, in connection with the Sino-French War. Of more interest to China's development was the Bank's loan of £300,000 to the *kuan-tu shang-pan* enterprise, the China Merchants'

Steam Navigation Company.[f] The agreement was signed in July 1885 and called for delivery of 1,180,327.8 Shanghai taels, which at the agreed rate of 5s:1d was equal to £300,000. The loan was issued in Shanghai in silver at the rate of 4s:8d to 1 Shanghai tael.

The Bank's profits on this loan were all up-front and included the exchange rate differential, and the difference between par (at which the funds were delivered to the company) and 105, at which the bonds were issued to the public. McLean wrote that London Office had made a profit of £39,000 less expenses or Tls175,000, probably in the second half of 1885.

The course of business (Tables 9.5A–7)

The various indicators from the Hongkong Bank's accounts during the period from the increase in capital to Jackson's first leave as Chief Manager confirm the accelerated growth of the Bank which began with the crisis in confidence in Eastern banks and the trade crisis of 1884. The impact on the Hongkong Bank of share speculation, merchant-banker Hu Kwang-yung's unsuccessful attempt to corner the supply of silk, the withdrawal of chop loan facilities by the Hongkong Bank, and the resulting crisis in the Shanghai and Chekiang Province banking industry in 1883 was minimized due to the assistance of Wah Sam (Wang Huai-shan), the Bank's Shanghai compradore, a role acknowledged by the Board with a 'gift' of $10,000 in 1885.[11]

The continuation of China loan business underpinned the Bank's earnings and the various ratios suggest liquidity, growth, and confidence. The large cash and bullion holdings may be assumed to relate in part to China loan operations; but they also suggest a less than optimum use of funds and the interest inelasticity of the supply of funds, that is, the inability to control deposits by varying interest rates.

The Bank's reserves were invested in British and Indian Government securities, usually carried on the books at less than market value. While the bulk were domiciled in London and a special reserve kept, on the insistence of the London and County Bank, with and by the advice of the Bank of England's Chief Cashier, certain rupee securities were in Bombay and Calcutta as cover for Indian, the Straits, and Java operations.

The growth of the Bank's earnings was also ascribed by the Board to 'Southern' operations, that is the Straits Settlements – Singapore and, from 1884, Penang – from which base there was business both with the Malay States and with Siam. In the second half of 1887, for example, Singapore, Penang and Batavia accounted for 13% of net profits (see Table 9.9).

[f] For an explanation of the Chinese term and its relation to the CMSNCo, see A. Feuerwerker's biography of Sheng Hsuan-huai, *China's Early Industrialization* (Cambridge, MA., 1958).

There were other developments. In 1884 the Hongkong Bank opened the 'Hong Kong Savings Bank' after successful experience running such 'banks' in Shanghai and Japan. They were actually savings 'departments' (see Chapter 10). The opening of the Iloilo agency in 1883 was forced by the threat of competition, and the Batavia agency was established in 1884 after the costly failure of the Bank's merchant-agent, Martin Dyce and Co. But these last mentioned ventures were also to create problems before the end of the decade and their contributions in this period were mixed. The tentative opening of a Peking agency in 1885 had as yet little impact.

Branches and agencies both contribute to the corporation as a whole and are little 'banks' in their own right. The first part of this story only is told here; their specific contribution in this period is found in Tables 9.8–10 below, and their development in their own territory is described subsequently.

In October 1885 the Hongkong Bank entered into a transaction of interest if only because of its magnitude and impact. The Bank bought bar silver above the market at $49\frac{1}{4}$d per ounce in order to facilitate delivery of silver in Peking under the terms of a £1.5 million loan managed by Baring's in association with Jardine, Matheson and Co. Silver worth £700,000 in excess of the amount required had to be diverted for sale in Calcutta, where it was sufficient to depress the Eastern exchanges to $47\frac{5}{16}$d. The Bank's losses were offset by a gain in interest account, but the associated transactions caught John Hodgson, the bank's Calcutta Agent, unprepared, and further losses were recorded, leading eventually to Hodgson's early retirement.

The Chairman's reports for the first few meetings after 1882 noted the poor prospects in the China trade and the continued growth, despite the problems, of the Hongkong Bank. The Sino-French conflict affected trade, but apparently had little other impact on the Bank's fortunes – except perhaps that the Agent in Saigon was ordered to be especially careful. Thereafter the main topics noted were (i) the Bank's holdings of various China loans and (ii) the position of the Bank's holdings of British and Indian government securities.

However, at the Ordinary Half-yearly General Meeting of Shareholders, February 27, 1886, on the eve of Thomas Jackson's leave, the Chairman, F.D. Sassoon, made these comments:

Mr Jackson, the Chief Manager, has applied for twelve months' leave of absence, which has been granted. I take this opportunity of recording the immense services Mr Jackson has rendered to the Bank by his unremitting energy and ability during the ten years he has been the chief management. [Loud and prolonged applause]

When Mr Jackson first took charge of the Bank at the beginning of 1876 we had a Reserve Fund of only $100,000; today we have $4,500,000 reserve and $500,000 for equalization of dividends [renewed applause], our assets were $34,634,364.75 against $104,798,836.51; our Marine Insurance Account was $50,006 against $233,917.43; notes in circulation $1,881,906 against $4,662,736; deposits $11,526,203 against $65,615,078.

Table 9.5A *The Hongkong and Shanghai Banking Corporation*
Key indicators, 1882–1888
(in millions of dollars)   (in thousands of dollars)

Year	Assets	Deposits and notes	Reserve funds[a]	Net earning	To reserve[c]	To dividend	Rate $1 = xs/d$
1882 June	59.16	37.74	2.350	580	250	£1:10 = 320	3/9
1882 Dec.	68.59	43.29	2.600	817	250	£2:10 = 558	3/7
1883 June	67.69	48.82	3.398[b]	575	100	£2 = 469	3/7½
1883 Dec.	77.60	49.23	4.363[b]	739	100	573[f]	3/8
1884 June	75.59	49.62	4.800	797	145[d]	647[f]	3/8½
1884 Dec.	85.65	56.73	4.800	701	0	678	3/6½
1885 June	85.43	57.83	**5.000**	878	200	678	3/6½
1885 Dec.	104.80	70.28	5.000	948	0	£2:10 = 900[g]	3/4

Shareholders' funds (1885 Dec.) = $12.798 million (@ 3/4 = £2.13 million)

(Thomas Jackson on leave)

Year	Assets	Deposits and notes	Reserve funds[a]	Net earning	To reserve[c]	To dividend	Rate $1 = xs/d$
1886 June	101.67	71.10	4.700	547	−300	£2 = 789	3/0½
1886 Dec.	104.84	74.32	4.500	770	−200	£1:10 = 547[h]	3/3½
1887 June	104.58	75.56	3.900	561	−600	568	3/2
1887 Dec.	105.95	76.87	3.900	599	0	576	3/1½

(Thomas Jackson returns from leave)

Year	Assets	Deposits and notes	Reserve funds[a]	Net earning	To reserve[c]	To dividend	Rate $1 = xs/d$
1888 June	103.53	79.73	4.000	700	100	600	3/0
1888 Dec.	114.64	82.36	4.300	864	300[e]	592	3/0½

Shareholders' funds (1888 Dec.) = $12.11 million (@ 3/0½ = £1.8 million)

Notes:
[a] Includes the Reserve Fund and the Fund for Equalization of Dividends.
[b] Includes the premium received from new shares £40 less $125 par, as paid up, and from June 1884 on.
[c] Includes sums allocated to (i) the Reserve Fund, so called, and for the years 1882–1885 (ii) the Reserve for Equalization of Dividends Account (ED A/c). The division is found in Table 9.5B.
[d] $45,000 to Reserve Fund to round it up to $4.8 million with premium from new shares.
[e] Includes write-up of Indian government securities ($88,000), see Table 9.5B.
[f] Includes dividends for new shares pro-rated on basis of paid-up capital.
[g] £2 plus a bonus of 10 shillings.
[h] Rate changed to £1:10s.
Rate: for 1882 the rate of the day from market reports; for 1883–1888 and for shareholders' funds the rate as shown in the semi-annual reports.
Dividend: paid at the rate of £2 per fully paid-up share, pro-rated for the new shares; bonus of 10 shillings on basis of December 1885 accounts. From December 1886, the rate was £1:10s per share.
See also: Table 9.5B.

Table 9.5B *The Hongkong and Shanghai Banking Corporation*
Reserve appropriations, 1882–1888

(in thousands of dollars)

	(i) To reserves	(ii) For ED A/c.	(iii) ED A/c. balance	(iv) For Reserve Fund	(v) Reserve Fund balance	(vi) Total reserves	(vii) To pub. contingencies[a]
Balance at:							
1881 Dec.			–		2,100	2,100	
Subsequently:							
1882 June	250	–	–	250	2,350	2,350	
1882 Dec.	250	100	100	150	2,500	2,600	
1883 June	100	100	200	$0 + 698^e$	3,198	3,398	–
1883 Dec.	100	100	300	$0 + 865^e$	4,063	4,363	–
1884 June	145	100	400	$45 + 292^e$	4,400	4,800	–
1884 Dec.	0	0	400	0	4,400	4,800	–
1885 June	200	100	500	100	4,500	5,000	–
1885 Dec.	0	0	500	0	4,500	5,000	–
1886 June	− 300	− 300	200	0	4,500	4,700	–
1886 Dec.	300^b	$− 200^b$	0	0	4,500	4,500	$− 500^b$
1887 June	0	0	0^d	$− 600^f$	3,900	3,900	$− 600^f$
1887 Dec.	0	–	–	0	3,900	3,900	–
1888 June	100	–	–	100	4,000	4,000	–
1888 Dec.	$212 + 88^c$	–	–	300	4,300	4,300	–

Notes:
 (i) Amounts assigned from (+) or to (−) P&L account to or from either (ii) or (iv) or both, but see notes 'b' and 'c'.
 (ii) Amounts from (i) transferred to (+) or from (−) the Reserve for Equalization of Dividends Account (ED), but see note 'b' below.
 (iii) Balance in the Reserve for Equalization of Dividends Account.
 (iv) Amounts from (i) transferred to (+) or from (−) the Reserve Fund, but see note 'f' below.
 (v) Balance of the Reserve Fund.
 (vi) Balance of the sum of the Reserve for Equalization of Dividends Account and the Reserve Fund.
 (vii) Funds transferred to published contingencies as noted in 'b' and 'f'.
 [a] Credit is (−).
 [b] Of the $500,000 set aside in published contingencies, $300,000 came from P&L Account and $200,000 from the Reserve for Equalization of Dividends Account.
 [c] $212,432 from P&L Account and $87,568 from writing up Indian Government sterling loan from £86 to £95.
 [d] This account is not mentioned again.
 [e] The allocation from P&L Account + the share bonus.
 [f] The $600,000 from the Reserve Fund was transferred to published contingencies.
Source: Table 9.5A and semi-annual statements of account.

Table 9.5C The Hongkong and Shanghai Banking Corporation Dividends, 1883–1888

Year	Interim £ = $ @	Interim $	+	Final £ = $ @	Final $	+	Bonus £ = $	Bonus $	=	Total £ = $	Total $	Total payout £ = $	Total payout $ (millions)	Payout ratio %	Total dividend as % of book value £	Total dividend as % of book value $ (per cent)
1883[a]	2:00 3/7½	**11.03**		2:00 3/8	**10.91**					4:00	**21.94**	0.19	**1.04**	79	10.8	**10.9**
1884	2:00 3/8½	**10.79**		2:00 3/6½	**11.29**					4:00	**22.08**	0.24	**1.33**	89	10.8	**10.5**
1885	2:00 3/6½	**11.29**		2:00 3/4	**12.00**		0.10	**3.00**[b]		4:10	**26.29**	0.27	**1.58**	86	12.7	**12.3**
1886	2:00 3/0½	**13.15**		1:10 3/3½	**9.11**					3:10	**22.26**	0.21	**1.34**	102	10.4	**10.9**
1887	1:10 3/2	**9.47**		1:10 3/1½	**9.60**					3:00	**19.07**	0.18	**1.14**	98	9.9	**9.8**
1888	1:10 3/0	**10.00**		1:10 3/0½	**9.86**					3:00	**19.86**	0.18	**1.19**	76	9.8	**9.8**
1889	1:10 3/0½	**9.86**		1:10 3/1½	**9.60**		0:10	**3.20**[b]		3:10	**22.66**	0.21	**1.36**	72	10.8	**10.9**

Notes:
Bold face = $ equivalent
[a] Figures include pro rata dividends etc. on 20,000 new shares.
[b] Bonus is at same rate of exchange as final dividend.
Source: Tables 9.3 and 9.5A.

Table 9.6 *The Hongkong and Shanghai Banking Corporation*
Earnings and share prices, 1882–1888

Year	(i) $ 000 Net earnings	(ii) £ Dividend/ share	(iii) $ Book value	(iv) £ Book value	(v) Share price Shanghai	(vi) Share price London	(vii) $ M/B ratio	(viii) £ M/B ratio	(ix) Rate $1 = xs/d
1882 June	580	£1:10	189	35.9	278	50	1.47	1.39	3/9
1882 Dec.	817	£2:10	196	35.0	344	59	1.76	1.69	3/7
1883 June	575	£2	198^a	35.9	330	59	1.67	1.64	3/7½
1883 Dec.	739	£2	201^a	36.9	306	58	1.52	1.57	3/8
1884 June	797	£2	209	38.8	271	51	1.30	1.31	3/8½
1884 Dec.	701	£2	210	37.2	281	48	1.34	1.29	3/6½
1885 June	878	£2	213	37.8	325	59	1.53	1.56	3/6½
1885 Dec.	948	£2:10	213	35.6	336	63	1.58	1.77	3/4
(Thomas Jackson on leave)									
1886 June	547	£2	209	31.8	345	62	1.65	1.95	3/0½
1886 Dec.	770	£1:10	205	33.7	322	58	1.57	1.72	3/3½
1887 June	561	£1:10	194	30.8	299	50	1.54	1.62	3/2
(Thomas Jackson returns from leave)									
1887 Dec.	599	£1:10	195	30.4	313	50	1.61	1.64	3/1½
1888 June	700	£1:10	196	29.4	325	52	1.66	1.77	3/0
1888 Dec.	864	£1:10	202	30.7	320	52	1.58	1.69	3/0½

Notes:

(i) Net earnings in thousands of dollars from Table 9.5A.
(ii) Dividends declared in pounds sterling, see Table 9.5A.
(iii) Book value = shareholders' funds, i.e. paid-up capital + reserves (including amounts paid in from net earnings) + retained
profits, + Marine Insurance Account divided by the number of shares, i.e. 40,000.
(iv) Column (iii) converted into pounds sterling at rate of day.
(v) Shanghai shares were quoted at so much percent premium, which is added to the par value of shares, i.e. $125; the date is mid-July
and mid-January.
(vi) London prices for shares on the London register.
(vii) Equivalent to (v) divided by (iii).
(viii) Equivalent to (vi) divided by (iv).
(ix) For 1882, the rate of the day; for other years, the rate used is the semi-annual Hongkong Bank accounts.
^{a} Book value is based on shareholders' funds pertaining to the old shares, i.e. less partial amounts (and bonus) paid on new shares.

Table 9.7 *The Hongkong and Shanghai Banking Corporation*
Cash, selected balance sheet items, and ratios, 1882–1888

(in millions of dollars)

Year	Assets	Index[a]	Cash and bullion	C/A ratio	Net earnings	E as % of A	Deposits + notes	Loans etc.	Loan/D ratio	Bills rec.	BR index[b]	Bills pay	BP index[b]	Rate $1 = xs/d
1882 June	59.16	87	6.63	0.11	0.58	0.98[c]	37.74	24.40	0.65	26.60	88	13.58	154	3/9
1882 Dec.	68.59	101	6.82	0.10	0.82	1.19[c]	43.29	24.10	0.56	35.59	118	17.02	193	3/7
1883 June	67.69	100	8.13	0.12	0.58	0.85	48.82	27.48	0.56	30.16	100	8.84	100	3/7½
1883 Dec.	77.60	115	7.70	0.10	0.74	0.95	49.23	29.96	0.61	36.90	122	16.04	181	3/8
1884 June	75.59	112	8.68	0.11	0.80	1.05[c]	49.62	35.25	0.71	27.89	92	12.75	144	3/8¼
1884 Dec.	85.65	127	12.42	0.14	0.70	0.82[c]	56.73	36.01	0.63	34.31	114	15.61	177	3/6½
1885 June	85.43	126	12.71	0.15	0.88	1.03	57.83	35.70	0.62	33.84	112	14.15	160	3/6¼
1885 Dec.	104.80	155	12.51	0.12	0.95	0.90	70.28	40.79	0.58	46.58	154	20.79	235	3/4
(Thomas Jackson on leave)														
1886 June	101.67	150	13.83	0.14	0.55	0.54	71.10	37.72	0.53	44.94	149	11.21	127	3/0½
1886 Dec.	104.84	155	8.98	0.09	0.77	0.73[a]	74.32	36.81	0.50	54.77	182	17.20	195	3/3½
1887 June	104.58	154	14.07	0.13	0.56	0.54	75.56	33.88	0.45	52.24	173	16.17	183	3/2
1887 Dec.	105.95	157	13.37	0.13	0.60	0.57	76.87	33.18	0.43	54.89	182	16.82	190	3/1½
(Thomas Jackson returns from leave)														
1888 June	103.53	153	8.74	0.08	0.70	0.68	79.73	46.19	0.58	43.95	146	11.43	129	3/0
1888 Dec.	114.64	169	9.15	0.08	0.86	0.75	82.36	52.16	0.63	48.54	161	19.57	221	3/0½

Notes:
[a] Index of total assets, June 1883 = 100.
[b] June 1883 = 100.
[c] Ratios affected by China loan operations

Bills rec. = BR = bills receivable

E = net earnings D = deposits + notes.
A = assets.
Loans etc. = bills discounted, loans and credits.
Bills pay = BP = bills payable, incl. 'drafts on London Bankers and short sight drawings on our London Office against bills receivable and bullion shipments'.

317

Considering the strides the Bank has made and the important position it has attained, your Board of Directors intend to present the Chief Manager on his departure with an honorarium of £8,000 [loud applause], and we trust that, after enjoying his well-earned holiday, he will return to his post to devote many more years to the service of the Bank.

I am confident that this mark of recognition of Mr Jackson's eminent services will meet with the hearty approval of all shareholders. [Cheers and applause]

One of the Bank's juniors, Charles Addis, was present at the meeting. He made these observations in a letter to his father:

Poor Jackson looked most uncomfortable, fidgeting in his chair, and looking ready to cry. But he was soon on his legs and replied with feeling and modesty . . . What a fellow he is. Sound to the core. Straight in all his dealings; honest to the backbone, and with all a heart as tender as a woman's. Fiery, if you like, but I don't believe in a man who has not got a temper. In fine it was a privilege to have received two years and more under such a chief. I believe I am a better man from knowing him.[12]

There were many others who felt similarly. Jackson had the ability to inspire confidence and loyalty.

JOHN WALTER AND THE (FIRST) RETURN OF JACKSON

The Board's natural first choice for Acting Chief Manager was Ewen Cameron, but as with McLean before him he begged to be excused on the grounds that his continued presence in Shanghai was more important to the Hongkong Bank. The Board then turned to John Walter who had first come to the Bank in 1868 from Dent and Co. and who had had, despite McLean's dictum that good bankers don't come from merchant houses, a distinguished career as Manager Yokohama, and during Cameron's last leave, Acting Manager in Shanghai.

John Walter's name is attached to three semi-annual reports – for the half-years ending June and December 1886 and June 1887. During this period total assets fell and then merely recovered their former position, loans declined in amount, net earnings (after China loan profits – see Table 9.4) declined drastically, and the dividend rate could no longer be maintained at £4 per annum. More serious, the reserves fell by $1.1 million to $3.9 million, wiping out the Reserve for Equalization of Dividends. Only deposits continued to increase. The capital/assets ratio remained between 10% and 11%.

Thomas Jackson then returned from leave, net earnings recovered – although not to their 1885 levels, nor was the dividend restored to £4. At the end of 1888 the reserves were back to $4.3 million and the Bank was in general ready to face Jackson's second and presumably final departure, this time openly stated as for the London Office.

1886 and the fall of silver

The fault was not with Walter.

For the first time a Chairman of the Hongkong Bank, M. Grote, referred to a 'silver crisis', for the exchange had fallen from 3s:4d to 3s:0½d, or 8.8%, in the first six months of 1886 – the decline actually did not begin before April and the likely extent of the fall was not immediately apparent. As the Bank had to lay in funds 'for the season' to finance the export of tea and silk, they were caught uncovered. The Chairman stated:

we had started the half year exceedingly well; none of us could foresee the silver calamity. Mr John Walter, who has taken charge of the chief management in the meantime, on the departure of Mr Thomas Jackson, has had to go through very hard times indeed. We have to thank him and Mr Cameron in Shanghai in particular, for the very able manner in which they have steered the Bank through what may be called a Silver Crisis with a comparatively favourable result.

The Bank had also to write off the Manila loss from the previous year and there were other less important problems, including a fraud in Yokohama. The dividend of £2 was paid by drawing down the Reserve for Equalization of Dividends by $300,000 – which was, after all, the purpose for which it was designed.

Despite high published earnings as a result of China loan operations in the second half of 1886, the Board, in order to pay out the $547,000 required to meet even the reduced dividend of £1:10s had to withdraw the remainder of the Reserve for Equalization of Dividends. The situation in Manila continued to give concern and the Manager, C.I. Barnes, was summoned to Hong Kong for discussions with the directors. Several unresolved problems, including Martin Dyce and Co.'s failure in the Netherlands East Indies, the Jurado and Co. case (to be considered below), and losses in Singapore forced the Board to establish a published Contingency Fund of $500,000.

The Hongkong Bank on a gold basis

The suddenness of the decline in exchanges focused public attention on the Bank's sterling deposits, and correspondence in the *North-China Herald* revealed an excusable confusion, which could, nevertheless, damage the Bank. J.W. Maclellan, the journal's knowledgeable editor, was able to support the discussion with a sound explanatory leader.[13]

The concern may be briefly stated. The Chairman announced that the Bank obtained deposits in London to an amount equal to about one-third of total deposits. Were these deposits, worried shareholders were apparently asking, being written down? Their line of reasoning was as follows – if the Bank accepts a deposit liability of £100 at say 4s:0d, that is $500 on its books. If the exchange falls to 3s:6d, then the $500 is worth only £87.50. Accordingly the sum of £12.50 should be written off by subtracting the dollar equivalent at 3s:6d, $71.40, from the Bank's assets and the identical amount from reserves. The actual sum to be written off, if this approach had been correct, would have been $1.5 million.[14]

As long as the average shareholder expected silver to rise again, the problem as thus stated appeared of interest only to short-term shareholders or speculators, but with the realization that silver might continue its downward course, many more of the public became concerned.

The principle of the 'even keel' is that such calculations become irrelevant. The above argument presumably assumes that the funds acquired by deposits in London are used to buy exchange on China; that the funds are then utilized in China but that, when the exchange falls, an adjustment must be made by subtracting a sufficient amount from assets and reserves.

In fact the key to the Bank's operations was to be found in noting the difference between 'bills receivable', which arise from the finance of exports from China, and 'bills payable', which are for import finance. Exports were financed by bills at three to four months' usance; imports, as has already been stated, in increasing percentages by telegraphic transfers. As the finance of outward business increased at the same time the method of finance was changing, the total value of TTs which had to be paid in sterling before 'bills receivable' fell due also increased significantly; hence the Bank's need for funds in London.

While shipments from China are generally drawn against 4 months' sight, the proceeds of imports are usually remitted by telegraphic transfer. The London deposits of the Hongkong and Shanghai Bank are used to pay the telegraphic transfers while the 4 months' drafts against exports are maturing . . .

The sterling deposits therefore never really leave London or New York, and a rise or fall in the exchange does not affect them, except so far as striking a balance is concerned.[15]

A second correspondent put it another way:

The principle of banking is to *turn over money*, and *not bury it in the East* . . . The London deposits may come out to the East half-a-dozen times in the course of the year, and be returned at a profit or loss as the case may be . . . and looking at the very large proportion of 'Bills Receivable' in the half-yearly reports for some years back, it is evident the Bank has been working on a gold basis.[16]

The Editor added that not only do the London deposits never leave London but they are inadequate for the Bank's purposes, an assertion which McLean would certainly have endorsed and the Bank's correspondence with the London and County Bank would affirm. And he concluded:

In other words, the Bank has for years been working on a gold basis and has been holding more gold than the liabilities it has incurred in that metal, having long ago converted some of its superfluous silver into gold, which it now employs in what is called, in the cant of Lombard Street, 'liquid securities'.[17]

The Hongkong Bank's sterling operations were funded in sterling; a high proportion of its capital was invested in sterling securities; and its silver operations were funded in silver, covered by silver investments.

The third meeting, August 1887 – losses in Manila

As early as February 1887 Charles S. Addis, the Bank's Agent in Peking, was writing to his father about the Bank's loss of five lacs of dollars in Manila: 'The Bank never was in a sounder financial position. We have done well everywhere except that thrice accursed Manila. I am very proud to be in a bank that can drop $5,00,000 [five lacs] in six months and hardly feel it.'[18]

Not everyone was equally sanguine, and, with further Manila losses to be considered, the meeting in August 1887, the month before Jackson's return from leave, was the first since 1875 that might be described as 'disputative', although the questioning came entirely from Robert Fraser–Smith the controversial editor of the *Hongkong Telegraph*. There were two major problems: (i) the further losses in Manila and (ii) accusations in the *Chinese Times* of Tientsin that the Chairman and/or his company, Melchers and Co., had been selling Bank shares on the basis of insider information.[19]

As in the case of the Hongkong Bank's three 'bug–bears' of the early 1870s, the Board underestimated the gravity of the situation. They had declared that the first sum of $500,000 set aside mainly to meet Manila losses would be sufficient; the Chairman now announced a further $600,000 would have to be found. Was this the end of the problem? Fraser–Smith forced the Chairman to respond definitely 'Yes', although Grote confessed that he was really unable to foresee the future with the desired degree of assurance.

The explanation of the Bank's problems was two-fold. First, there were continuing commercial difficulties: negotiations with Macleod and Co. (who were connected with another Bank constituent, Smith, Bell and Co.) relative to steamers the Bank had financed in 1879 on an 'amply secured' basis (presumably against shares which had depreciated), the failure of Baer and Suhm, and, to climax it all, the failure of the long-established Peele, Hubbell and Co. in March 1887. A week later the Bank's Manila Agent resigned and joined the partnership of Warner, Blodgett and Co. on the coincidental death of Blodgett. The firm then became known as Warner, Barnes and Co. and today is an important constituent of the Bank in the Philippines.

For the commercial difficulties the Board added $150,000 to contingencies, but the second factor involved in the Bank's difficulties was the change in the basis of the Philippine currency, and for this $450,000 had to be set aside.

In 1877 the Spanish Government had begun a series of attempts to secure a separate currency for the Philippines by forbidding the import of Mexican dollars and thus, by the concurrent circulation of gold in the Islands and silver dollars in Spain, maintain an exchange rate independent of the declining gold value of silver. This would make uncovered exchange operations on London relatively safe. In fact Mexican dollars were smuggled into the Islands; gold, being undervalued, was exported, and the reversal of Spanish policy came with the demonetization of the Carolus dollar in Spain, thus preventing the arbitrage in silver coin necessary to maintain the higher exchange value of the otherwise silver-based Philippine unit of account. As the directors put it at the August 1887 meeting of shareholders:

The Philippine currency has until quite recently been regarded as resting on a Gold basis, and the Bank's funds employed in the Island have been provided by drawings on London. The Spanish Government, however, in the early part of the year made the Carolus Dollar (it had previously circulated alike in Spain and the Philippines) uncurrent in Spain, and the result was a sudden heavy fall in the Sterling value of the Philippine dollar, against which the Bank had no opportunity of safeguarding itself . . . [Safeguarding] has been impossible because the paralysis of trade in the Philippines made it utterly impossible to keep covered against this loss.

The Manila branch had a net oversold position in London of £95,000.

At this point the Chairman of the Hongkong Bank, M. Grote, turned to the accusation made in the *Chinese Times*. The charge was all the more of interest since it was widely believed that the paper received a subsidy from or had other close connections with Jardine Matheson, whose senior Hong Kong partner, John Bell-Irving, sat on the same board of directors with Grote.[20] Bell-Irving denied the connection at this meeting. The Editor of the *Chinese Times*, however, was Alexander Michie, Jardine's agent in Tientsin and the north, and a somewhat bitter critic of the Hongkong Bank apparently for personal reasons, both historical – he claimed a grievance – and current – he objected to the successful competition of the Hongkong Bank's capable Agents, E. Guy Hillier and Charles S. Addis in Peking, and their senior, Alexander Leith, in Tientsin.[21]

Michie's remarks were anti-Semitic, referring to a gambling ring of Indian and Hamburg Jews. The directors at a Board meeting had already commiserated with Grote. He now took this opportunity of publicly denying the charges on behalf of himself and Melchers and Co. The Hon. P. Ryrie, who was the Bank's auditor, moved a motion of condolence for Grote which Fraser-Smith changed to a hearty vote of thanks:

I am so thoroughly convinced of the probity of Mr Grote and also of the able manner in which he has been discharging his duties as Chairman of the Board, that I think we should bestow upon him a very hearty vote of thanks. This will show the people of Shanghai and of other places that, whatever they may think, we at least have confidence in Mr Grote, and that altho' mistakes may have been made by the Board in the management of the Bank's affairs, they have at least acted honestly.

This was gracious, but it is not clear where the Board had erred. The problem with the Manila exchange was not one in the normal course of business but was the consequence of a sovereign act. The commercial difficulties were long-standing; Barnes had been appointed Manila Agent with very little experience in 1875, before Jackson was Chief Manager. Over the intervening years Barnes had made the Bank virtually indispensable to British business in the Philippines.[22] Withdrawal, despite harassment from the courts and the risks inherent in financing sugar, was not considered; frequent inspections had noted problems but no catastrophe. In fact, had it not been for the unfortunate timing, the business losses could have been absorbed without discussion at a general meeting. But with the focus on the Philippines all aspects of the business were exposed.

Michie remained unrepentant and in another attack, in the form of an 'apology', used his paper for his personal vendetta with the Bank.[23]

The general meeting remained uninformed of losses in Singapore and Batavia. The Board had long been watching W.G. Greig's management in the former port and at this time asked for his resignation. The problem in Batavia came before the Board in July, but it also was long-standing. With the failure in 1884 of Martin Dyce and Co. the Board had, on the advice of Noble and the support of Jackson – but against the strong warnings of McLean – appointed the former Martin Dyce agent, A. Maccoll, as the Bank's first Agent.[24] He had not done well and the climax came with news of $30,000 lost.

There was one extraordinary, if esoteric, source of $142,000 profit to the Bank, probably in the first half of 1887, arising from the United States decision to redeem the U.S. Trade Dollar coin at its apparent but incorrect 'face value' of one U.S. dollar. This silver coin had been minted in the early 1870s as a rival to the Mexican dollar, and although intended originally to be a legal tender coin, it had in fact been demonetized in 1876 and was after that year only receivable in the U.S. for its silver content. The standard U.S. silver dollar coin, minted under the terms of the Bland–Allison Act, was lighter than the Trade Dollar coin but was legal tender for a U.S. dollar unit of account. With the depreciation of silver, the lighter standard silver dollar, linked as it was to a gold unit of account, came to be worth more in terms of the U.S. dollar unit of account than the heavier Trade Dollar.

The ordinary citizen may be excused, perhaps, for not following the course of events. Those who held Trade Dollars objected to the refusal of the U.S. Treasury to accept them 'at face value'. In this the Treasury acted correctly; special legislation was required which would, in effect, give holders of the coin a windfall gain.

The Trade Dollar's excessive weight had not been adequately covered by the premium over Mexican dollars at which it was quoted in the East, and in consequence it came to be melted for bullion. One reason for the reluctance of the U.S. Treasury to redeem the coin at its 'face value' was that it did not know the number which had survived, especially the number overseas.[25] A.M. Townsend, as the Bank's New York Agent, gave the Government the apparently reassuring figure of between two and three million, and the Congress, acting under various political pressures, enacted the necessary legislation in February 1887.[26] The Board's estimate of profit suggests that the Bank must have been holding some 620,000 Trade Dollars, as the coin's silver content was worth approximately 77 cents in terms of the gold-based U.S. dollar unit of account.

There is the suggestion in this story that the Bank was possessed of expert information and the ability to act thereon.

The year was nevertheless dominated by the Bank's problems. Jackson was en route to Japan when news of the Batavia problem reached him. He wrote to the Board in July to ask whether he should continue to Yokohama or come direct to Hong Kong. By a vote of 3–2 the Board requested him to return immediately to Head Office.

Whatever reservations Jackson may have had about returning to Hong Kong – and Addis pictured the 'struggle' – Jackson's wife and family were settled in Chislehurst, Kent – the stream of adverse information must have decided him. As Addis put it after Jackson's July visit of inspection to the Peking agency, his duty to corporation and shareholders came first.[27]

Jackson at the helm, 1887–1888

McLean once more had predicted correctly. In November 1886 he had written to John Walter, 'I am very sorry for you as the outside public will put [the losses] down to your management, however I shall keep them right as far as I can.'[28] In April 1887 a group of London shareholders wrote that Jackson, Cameron, and Walter should remain in the East and that McLean, who had just resigned as London Manager effective in 1888, should stay in London.[29] 'I believe [McLean wrote to Walter] the petition is being got up by the shareholders as they think if no change is made the shares will go up and they will get rid of their shares. They don't care two straws as to anything else.'[30]

The petition was nevertheless representative of opinion and puts several matters in clearer perspective. Although Jackson was 'on leave' and Walter still only Acting Chief Manager, it was always possible – as the £8,000 gift would seem to have indicated – that Jackson would not return. Before leaving Hong Kong Jackson had informed the Board that McLean might wish to resign and that, if he did so while Jackson was on leave, he would wish for private reasons to take over the London Office. The Board had agreed.

Jackson in fact decided to remain in London, but McLean recommended that, before settling down to the London managership, Jackson should tour the branches and agencies – 'Jackson says he wants my berth. If he is to have it then I think he should go out and inspect . . .'[31] McLean accordingly resigned in January 1887 with effect in March 1888. William Kaye, the former Shanghai manager of the Chartered Bank and McLean's able and long-serving Sub-Manager, resigned effective December 31, 1887, with a gratuity of £1,250.

When Jackson, in consequence of these events, asked for instructions from the Board in January 1887, he was told to return to Head Office, inspecting the Bank's offices en route. The minute does not state whether the return to Head Office was part of McLean's recommendation or for the purpose of taking over again. Perhaps the Board itself was unsure. In any case, the events of the next six months decided both the Board and Jackson. McLean would postpone his retirement and Jackson would return as Chief Manager.

This account would seem confirmed not only by Addis's letter quoted above, but also by McLean's sudden visit to Chislehurst in September when 'some idiot' leaked the new arrangements to Mrs Jackson prematurely.[32]

Not surprisingly, Jackson could not set matters to rights immediately. At the end of 1887 the Bank's Contingency Fund stood at $950,000, all of which was allocated to meet specific contingencies. The failure of Martin Dyce and Co. had proved unexpectedly expensive due to the misinvoicing and falling price of the sugar which creditors controlled as security; losses in Singapore were an additional $240,000.

Nevertheless the Bank's business was expanding, published profits were not less than in mid-1887 and the Board voted to recommend both a £1:10s dividend and an allocation of $100,000 to reserves. This would only be possible, however, by revaluing the Bank's sterling securities, held on the books at 3s:3d, to 3s:2d (exchange being at 3s:1½d). The Bank had not before realized this form of exchange profit, and it marked the focus of the directors, following the fall in the value of Hongkong Bank shares in the second half of 1887, on stability in the thin market for Bank shares.

On the eve of the general meeting however news came of a possible adverse judgement – and the assurance of additional legal fees – in the Jurado case. It is to the credit of the Board that under conflicting pressures they rewrote their report and transferred the $100,000 openly to contingency rather than reserve account. But they did maintain the dividend.

The August 1888 meeting passed quietly, but the Chairman, John Bell-Irving of Jardine, Matheson and Co., had again to reassure shareholders of the Bank's practice of taking over the branch accounts at the rate of the day and absorbing exchange losses as they occurred – the dollar had fallen to 3s:0d. He also confirmed that the Bank's utilization of assets had improved with the fall in the cash/assets ratio and increase in the loan/deposit ratio. Jackson had, in fact, reported to the Board in July 1888 that Head Office loans at $12.6 million had reached an all-time high. Reserves were increased for the first time in three years, that is, since August 1885, shares rose slightly, and the market/book ratios improved.

Walter meanwhile had not 'lost face' in that, as far as the public were concerned, he had only been acting while 'TJ' was on leave. Walter agreed to take a Sub-Manager's post in London and then, on the return of TJ to London, to return East. Offered the choice of Chief Manager or Manager Shanghai, he accepted the latter and served there from 1889 to 1891. He then became Inspector of Branches until 1898 when he succeeded Noble as Junior Manager London. On retiring in 1902, he served on the London Consultative Committee for four years and died in January 1907.

The Bank, 1886–1888 – another viewpoint

In the previous survey of the Hongkong Bank's performance consideration of certain questions which would nevertheless assist in an understanding of the Bank's operations were postponed. In this section there will be an examination of the allocation of Bank capital, of the profitability of the branches and agencies, the composition of charges, and the relative efficiency of its operations.

As will be noted further below, the information is unfortunately not all from the same year, but the picture is in general accurate for the period 1886–1888, that is, for the Hongkong Bank at the end of Thomas Jackson's first administration.

The various branches and agencies of the Bank held accounts with each other according to their banking requirements, and profits made from operating any such account went to the branch or agency which had opened it. Similarly overdrafts bore interest and other services were charged for. The allocation of capital to a branch (Table 9.8) resulted, therefore, in funds on which the branch did not have to pay interest; but branch profits contributed to overall profits from which dividends were paid.

A branch's sources of funds in order of increasing cost would be (i) assigned capital, (ii) note issue, if permitted, (iii) current accounts, (iv) savings accounts, (v) fixed deposits, and (vi) overdrafts and credits granted by Head Office or other branches. The rules relating capital to banking activity would be in principle the same for a branch as for the Bank; indeed, the branches were for all practical purposes – very much in the Scottish tradition – 'banks', and the Hongkong and Shanghai Bank was correctly likened by Treasury officials to a collection of banks operating under one overall direction.

McLean would often in his letters advise branch managers, sometimes in pressing terms, but he would not take responsibility for the consequences. Managers would cite his letters in explaining their losses, but never, McLean pointed out, when explaining their profits. In other correspondence he might urge a manager not to assist another branch on his own account, but only on 'their account' and on 'their' instructions.

This is background to an understanding of the importance not only to overall profitability of the Bank but also to control of the independent – under general

Table 9.8 *The Hongkong and Shanghai Banking Corporation*
Allocation of capital, June 1888

(in thousands of dollars)

Shanghai	2,000[a]
Yokohama	1,500
Manila	1,000
Singapore	1,000
Special Reserve:	
$250,000 sterling paper, London	1,415[b]
50 lacs of rupee paper domiciled	
in London, Bombay and Calcutta	2,196[c]
Bank Premises:	
at branches	453
at Head Office	354
Balance: working capital at HO	1,472
Total = paid-up capital + Reserve Fund	11,400

Notes:
[a] Shanghai capital was first set by the Board at $3 million but the
  Manager, Ewen Cameron, reported that he had some $2 million in
  idle balances. The Board accordingly shifted $1 million to Head
  Office working capital as shown.
[b] interest credited to London P&L account.
[c] interest credited to P&L a/c of domicile.

Board regulations and ultimate instructions from the Chief Manager – managers,
and the importance therefore of their individual profit returns and the amount of
their charges.

Table 9.8 states the allocation of the Bank's capital, defined as the paid-up
capital plus the Reserve Fund, as of mid-1888. The assignment of the Special
Reserve is in a sense arbitrary and is designed, as explained earlier, to cut the
branch's costs and so permit lower charges to other branches for overdrafts and
services. The Board wrote down the value of buildings in the Premises Account,
and this practice permitted the branches to calculate net profits without charging
their account rent for that portion of the buildings used by Bank offices or
residences.

Table 9.9 shows profits and charges; unfortunately the figures for 1888 are not
as complete as for the half-year chosen, but the basic allocation of capital to the
major branches would have been the same; the change is in the size of the special
reserve and in adjustments to premises accounts.

The organization of Table 9.9 indicates the grouping of agencies under their
own 'head office' or branch, with Batavia reporting directly to Hong Kong. In
interpreting these figures, the reader should bear in mind that accounting

Table 9.9 *The Hongkong and Shanghai Banking Corporation*
Charges and profits, July–December 1887
(in thousands of dollars)

Branch	Charges		Net profit
Hong Kong (Head Office)		185.8	+ 334.0
New York	18.9		+ 1.7
Saigon	6.7		− 3.5
San Francisco	17.6		+ 58.0
Amoy	8.1		+ 13.4
Bombay	17.9		+ 33.2
Calcutta	15.2		− 36.4
Foochow	9.4		− 19.0
Lyons	11.3		− 10.9
Hong Kong office	80.7		+ 297.5[a]
Shanghai		80.6	+ 200.0
Peking	4.9		− 3.5
Tientsin	12.8		+ 18.8
Hankow	8.5		− 10.6
Shanghai office	54.4		+ 195.3[a]
Yokohama		42.5	+ 100.0
Hiogo	10.9		− 6.7
Yokohama office	31.6		+ 106.7[a]
Singapore		34.6	+ 78.0
Penang	9.8		+ 4.2
Singapore office	24.8		+ 73.8
Manila		26.7	+ 12.2
Iloilo	6.9		+ 9.1
Manila office	19.8[b]		+ 3.1
Batavia		16.1	+ 16.7
London		63.9	not listed[d]
Total:			+ 741.0
Less contingencies[c] = published profit			+ 598.7

Notes:
[a] a residual figure: branch returns less net profits attributed to the agencies listed.
[b] of which $6,038 or 30% were legal expenses.
[c] includes $100,000 for Jurado case, Manila.
[d] London profits were minimal due to method of crediting profits from operations
   for tax purposes.
Source: attachment to the Board Minute Book for 1888.

practices relative to allocation of profits of a particular transaction could be arbitrary, especially if tax questions arose, and that the figures for any one year would contain exceptional but unstated items. The legal expenses in Manila, for example, are 30% of the total charges, and the deduction for contingency account of $100,000 is a further allowance for this item in the coming half-year.

On the other side, high profits from San Francisco reflect involvement with the Nevada Bank of San Francisco's heavy speculations in wheat, for which the Hongkong Bank handled a portion of the exchange – and the background for which lies outside this history. Profits in Shanghai were due in large part to the China loans.

The purpose of this unusual compilation from the Board's minutes was to examine the costs of the Bank's operations, and the result indicated that, as a percentage of gross profits less losses, the Hongkong Bank's 'charges' were significantly smaller, the Board were informed and minuted, than those of other Eastern exchange banks – 42% as compared with 55% for the Chartered Mercantile Bank and 56% for the Chartered Bank.

Another glimpse of the Hongkong Bank at work is provided by a detailed breakdown of 'charges', but again, unfortunately, for a different period, this time for the full year of 1886. Allowing for exceptional items, the figures should not, however, be significantly different from those to be expected in the years considered above.

The figures in Table 9.10 should not prove surprising. The exceptional Philippine legal fees have already been noted and are due to the number of losses under dispute, the Jurado case, and the efforts to put the Bank in Manila on a proper legal basis. Salaries at 73.5% of total charges appear reasonable and the high City of London rent is as expected. Indeed, the figures seem to illustrate an almost routine series of international operations.

Postscript

G.E. Noble became Chief Manager of the Hongkong Bank on January 1, 1889. Jackson, however, attended the February meeting, which discussed the accounts which bore his name. It was the last meeting he attended before his return to Europe and his replacement of David McLean as London Manager, and shareholders would again note an improvement in the Bank's position.

Net earnings were high, again due to profits from China loans and, on this occasion, the Manila Railway Loan. The Board was able to set aside $212,432 from current earnings to Reserves while maintaining the dividend; the uneven amount being a consequence of another precedent-setting decision to revalue sterling and rupee securities and transfer the difference of $87,568 to Reserves, which, with the allocation from current earnings, made a total of $300,000 (see

Table 9.10 *The Hongkong and Shanghai Banking Corporation*
Charges for 1886

(in thousands of dollars)

Branch	Salaries	R&T	P&S	Legal	Post	Other	Total
Hong Kong							
Head Office[a]	100.4	11.0	3.5	1.5	7.0	10.0	133.4
New York	26.9	4.4	0.5	0.1	0.9	1.6	34.4
Saigon	11.3	1.7	0.3	0.0	0.0	1.3	14.6
San Francisco	26.5	4.3	0.0	0.0	0.4	1.8	33.0
Amoy	11.5	2.2	0.0	0.0	0.0	2.3	16.0
Bombay	26.0	5.2	0.6	0.0	0.0	2.7	34.5
Calcutta	22.8	5.1	2.0	0.0	0.0	2.1	32.0
Foochow	10.7	3.4	0.4	0.0	0.0	2.0	16.5
Lyons	15.6	3.2	0.6	0.0	1.0	1.0	21.4
Shanghai							
Shanghai branch	81.0	8.0	1.0	1.6	0.0	9.1	100.7
Peking	6.8	1.2	0.0	0.0	0.0	2.6	10.6
Tientsin	17.5	3.9	0.0	0.0	0.0	3.1	24.5
Hankow	14.0	2.4	0.0	0.0	0.0	1.3	17.7
Yokohama							
Yokohama branch	45.6	6.8	1.0	0.3	2.9	5.1	61.7
Hiogo	18.2	2.7	0.5	0.2	0.6	2.3	24.5
Singapore							
Singapore branch	38.8	5.3	0.1	0.0	0.0	3.7	47.9
Penang	12.4	2.8	0.0	0.2	0.0	2.6	18.0
Manila							
Manila branch	25.8	6.9	0.4	7.0	0.0	5.3	45.4
Iloilo	8.8	1.9	0.0	2.2	0.0	1.2	14.1
Batavia	20.8	3.0	0.3	0.0	0.0	3.2	27.3
London	37.6	13.9	2.8	0.2	1.6	3.7	59.8

Salaries = salaries and wages	578,840	73.5%
R&T = rent and taxes	99,372	12.6
P&S = printing and stationery	14,215	1.8
Legal = legal expenses	13,364	1.7
of which 69% in the Philippines		
Post = 'postages'	14,968	1.9
Other items	67,149	8.5
Total charges	787,908	100.0

[a] Head Office refers to the Hong Kong office's operations as a whole, that is, both as a Hong Kong branch and as head office responsible for the Bank's reserves.

Tables 9.4A–B). Such unrealized gains from revaluations would later be transferred directly to inner reserves. The business of the Bank continued to show growth; only share prices did not respond.

The Bank had opened an agency in Bangkok, the capital of the Kingdom of Siam, and established merchant agents in Sandakan in the territory of the British North Borneo Company.

William Kaye became a director of the London and Argentine Bank. David McLean's activities will be noted in subsequent chapters.

Compared to Jackson's previous departure, this time it was relatively low key. H.N. Mody moved a vote of thanks to the Chief Manager which was carried with loud applause and cheers, but Jackson is recorded as responding with a brief, 'I thank you very much.' On December 27 at his last Board meeting as Chief Manager, the Chairman, W.H. Forbes, stated he was pleased that the Bank would not lose his services as he would leave shortly to take up the position of Manager London branch.

This Jackson did. But he did not long remain. His departure marked only the end of his first, though interrupted, administration of the Hongkong Bank as Chief Manager. There was much more to come.

10

THE BOARD, POLICY, AND GOVERNMENT, 1876–1888

. . . the more Englishmen the better.

David McLean to Thomas Jackson, 1877

The developments described in the last two chapters took place while Thomas Jackson was Chief Manager, but Jackson managed the Bank under the direction of a Board of Directors, and they, in turn, were subject not only to the provisions of the Hongkong Bank Ordinance but also to the interpretations placed upon its provisions by British Colonial and Treasury officials and Hong Kong Government officials. The fate of the Bank was also subject to political developments throughout the region in which the Bank operated.

The Board of the Hongkong Bank were to learn early that they must watch carefully not only the credit-worthiness of their constituents but also who was elected to the California Legislature in Sacramento, what were the effective legal trends in Madrid, and how the preconceptions of the British Treasury might best be circumvented in the interests of Hong Kong and Far Eastern banking.

The Bank's accounts state clearly that this was a period of growth, but growth primarily within a basic geographical framework which may be described as (i) the open ports of China and Japan, (ii) Hong Kong's trading area, Hong Kong as the 'hub' – Saigon, Manila, Batavia, and (iii) agencies established primarily for exchange operations. Although the Bank were to resist miscellaneous opportunities to extend their operations, there was expansion, the most important being (i) into North China, first to Tientsin then to the imperial capital, Peking, and (ii) the Straits Settlements, first in Singapore and then Penang. The Board remained aware of its regional role and its limitations.

The Bank operated under a 'charter', an ordinance of incorporation, which was due to expire on August 13, 1887. The renewal after 21 years was handled without controversy. It was the Bank in its public functions which introduced subjects of controversy – the note issue, especially the one-dollar issue, the savings bank, the handling of public monies, and especially the problem, mistakenly applied, of the extraterritorial competence of the Hong Kong legislature and, therefore, of the legal existence of the Hongkong Bank outside the Colony.

Hong Kong was a small outpost of an Empire on which, in a phrase popularized by her one-time Treasurer, R. Montgomery Martin, the sun never set. The Bank's attempts to advise and assist had therefore to be considered not on the merits of the proposals alone but in the context of (i) the persistent currency problems of the region and (ii) the Imperial precedents, against a background of suspicion of any proposal which, while in the public interest, would nevertheless benefit the shareholders of a private company, of the Hongkong Bank.

The Imperial authorities in London, much like their counterparts in the Ch'ing capital of Peking, had a set of regulations and precedents which they administered on an Empire-wide basis. Exceptions to their application had to be proved in despatches (or memorials), read by a critical bureaucracy and often rejected. Writing some sixty years earlier on Indian government, James Mill had stated 'that no government . . . can be good government, but a government upon the spot'. It was quite unrealistic to expect intelligent decisions on day-to-day matters of governance to be made by men removed by 'half the circumference of the globe'.[1]

The Hongkong Bank's Board of Directors were in Hong Kong. The interaction of their expertise with that of government administrators could lead to policy proposals sound in themselves but inconsistent with the Imperial model.

On the other hand, the pressures of powerful private citizens in small colonies needed a check, provided impartially if not always wisely by monitors of the Colonial Office and Treasury. Men on the scene may be confused by the rush of events, the manager and directors of private banking corporations affected by their duty to shareholders, or government officials in a small territory temporarily overawed by the collective opinion of the business community expressed through the directors of the Hongkong Bank, reinforced by their concurrent roles as members of the Hong Kong General Chamber of Commerce.

The solution was for a dialogue between practitioners in the field and those with access to a broader range of experience in London. This at times proved frustrating. There existed in the bureaucracy a rather simplistic view of the 'profit motive' and therefore a tendency to react with grave suspicion to a proposal from the private sector which, while beneficial to the community, was also advantageous to the shareholder. This attitude, coupled with the theoretical preconceptions and perhaps social ('upper-class') prejudices of Imperial officials, resulted in disputes and correspondence while Hong Kong officials and bankers defended themselves against policies designed on the basis of experience in, as it happened, Honduras and Malta.

The political philosopher who would consider India unprepared to undertake sound government through 'enlightened public opinion', would find in Hong

Kong a Colony too small, too self-interested a constituency; in both cases the Imperial response was a 'regime of experts'. And those experts were in London. To paraphrase John Stuart Mill:

the whole Government of [the Empire] is carried on in writing. All the orders given, and all the acts of the executive officers, are reported in writing, and the whole of the original correspondence is sent to the Home Government; so that there is no single act done in [the Empire], the whole of the reasons for which are not placed on record.[2]

A problem arises, however, if someone loses the file.

The Hongkong Bank Ordinance had been modelled, on the recommendation of the Treasury, on that of the Asiatic Banking Corporation. The relevant correspondence, although originating in the Treasury, was 'private' and apparently only in the Colonial Office files. The reasons for certain provisions of the ordinance were, therefore, not known in the Treasury and were matters of speculation among officials until, in 1887, their attention was drawn to the missing correspondence by R. Meade of the Colonial Office. But Meade confessed he did not have a copy of the Asiatic's charter in his files. He then speculated on its contents, it apparently not being practical to canter up to Chancery Lane or otherwise search about for the original.[3]

This is an example of acknowledged confusion, but the minutes also contain summary memorandums which are objectively inaccurate. In discussing the provisions necessary to secure the Hongkong Bank's note issue, for example, the fact that the Bank's shareholders had unlimited liability relative to that note issue went unnoticed, and when the Bank reminded the Colonial Office, both parties neglected to take into consideration the impact of the 1882 charter amendments.

Expertise is not equivalent to omniscience, and on the crucial question of the Bank's legal personality outside Hong Kong, the experts were initially wrong; the Bank suffered from a costly uncertainty which was wholly avoidable in the context of the knowledge of the time. The question of extraterritoriality was at first misunderstood by the experts consulted in London and inconsistently interpreted.[4]

Through the disputes of these years runs, like a *leitmotiv*, the question of the one dollar note issue. What should have been a minor side issue to be decided locally became a great principle of monetary regulation, souring relations, distorting or delaying decisions on sometimes unrelated matters.

But underlying all this was a sense of inevitability.

Eventually the Treasury would, under the weight of evidence, revise its view or seek new expert opinion. The Bank had in the end what it sought and what the communities it served required. Throughout it remained the Government's banker; even while apparently exasperated officials were providing amusing asides in the minutes – for example, 'the Bank is a slippery customer' – the Bank was serving Government requirements somewhere in the East.

Thus despite controversy and delays, a relationship of mutual assistance tempered by mutual distance developed.

The account of these events has been divided into two chapters. The first deals with the composition of the Board and its policies – development of the Bank, the founding of the Hong Kong Savings Bank, the Bank's building policy and related matters. The second, Chapter 11, considers the charter revisions rendered necessary either as a consequence of Board policies or from the changing regulations of Government, or on occasion, the interaction of both.

THE BOARD OF DIRECTORS

When Thomas Jackson first took over as Acting Chief Manager in February 1876, the Board of Directors had seven members, of whom only one, A. McIver of the P&O, came from the United Kingdom.

Jardine's remained unrepresented and their election to the Board was still unexpected. In December 1874 A.F. Heard had written to his brother that Jardine Matheson had failed to negotiate the China loan which the Heards and the Bank, the latter successfully, were all seeking. He then added cryptically, 'There is no question of Whittall's [of Jardine's] joining the Bank'.[5] But two years later, in January 1877, there was a breakthrough – the Hon. William Keswick, taipan of Jardine, Matheson and Co., was elected a director of the Hongkong Bank. The same month a German member, J.F. Cordes of the ailing Wm Pustau and Co., resigned, and Edward Tobin restored the membership of Gilman and Co.

Not only was the search for 'English' directors, stressed more than a year previously, beginning to prove successful, but with the presence of Keswick the Bank now had the opportunity to become, without any qualification, the 'local' bank. It had indeed done well enough in its early years without Jardine, Matheson and Co., and their reluctance, whatever motives may legitimately be ascribed, could be explained, both by their concern for the speculative consequences of the general Companies Ordinance and a local bank to fuel speculation in their shares and by their unwillingness to associate with competitors in the opium trade with India. Now it was clear that no merchant house could itself finance its operations; Jardine's needed the Hongkong Bank. Furthermore, Jardine's had withdrawn from competition in the Indian opium business. It was a mutual 'reconciliation' though there were to be rough times ahead.

By the end of 1888 the Board, with Jardine's Bell-Irving as Chairman, had thirteen members of whom seven were 'Englishmen'. The American, German, and Jewish/Indian interests remained fully represented, managing a regional banking institution whose executive staff were, almost without exception,

British. This was to prove, for the times, an effective combination.

The purpose of the following sections is to examine the Board's structure, role, and membership more carefully.

Membership of the Board of Directors (see Table 10.1 and Appendix)

Nomination and election

'With regard to strengthening the board the more Englishmen the better . . .', McLean wrote to Jackson in May 1877, 'I don't know Birley's man but if he is a decent fellow by all means ask him.'[6] It would be unwise to conclude from this that either McLean's or Jackson's opinions on the composition of the Board were conclusive, but H.L. Dalrymple of Birley and Co. was elected in February 1878.

The Board however seemed reluctant to expand. Not until 1882 did the Board approve a net addition, this time with the election of Alexander P. McEwen of Holliday, Wise and Co., perhaps balancing the simultaneous election of M.E. Sassoon of E.D. Sassoon and Co. This second Sassoon company, based in Shanghai, represented the separate interests of a younger son and not increased influence for D. Sassoon, Sons and Co. on the Board. In 1884 C.D. Bottomley of Douglas Lapraik and Co. was elected, a net addition; three years later representatives of the Borneo Company, Ltd and Gibb, Livingston and Co. were elected with a new German representative, L. Poesnecker of Arnhold, Karberg and Co.

Membership was characterized by continuity and the restoration of old ties, broken in the mid-1870s. The independent E.R. Belilios, who had done so much as a critical conscience for the Board, retired in 1882. The second Sassoon firm was undoubtedly a consequence of shareholding, although there are no records to support this. The family relationships of all the Sassoon representatives should be noted – Gubbay, Moses, and Levy were Sassoon in-laws – but, as noted above, the two companies operated independently and had differentiated banking interests. It may be that the 1887 election of Poesnecker was a late decision to restore the German 'quota' ten years after the resignation of J.F. Cordes.

One conclusion can be safely made from the records – Board members were elected on the basis of the firms they represented. Although there might be minor gaps, perhaps due to the delayed arrival of a new senior partner, a firm once represented on the Board remained on the Board while its status permitted.

When Cordes resigned, he nominated his successor von Pustau, but he found no seconder. The company, Wm Pustau and Co., failed within two years and presumably those present knew of its difficulties.

The case of Gilman and Co. would appear to have been more confused. A. McConachie of Gilman and Co. had been 'elected' in January 1888, some four years after the resignation of W.S. Young the previous representative.

Table 10.1 *The Hongkong and Shanghai Banking Corporation Companies represented on the Board of Directors, 1876–1888*

	From-To[a]
On the Board in 1876	
Siemssen and Co.	1864–1914
D. Sassoon, Sons and Co.	1864–1956
P&O SN Co.	(1864–67), 1875–87
Russell and Co.	1866–1891
Wm Pustau and Co.	1867-January 1877
Melchers and Co.	1871–1914
Year of Joining or Rejoining	
1877	
Gilman and Co.	(1864–74), 1877–84
Jardine, Matheson and Co.	1877-present
1878	
Birley and Co.	(1871–74), 1878–91
1882	
Holliday, Wise and Co.	1882–96
E.D. Sassoon and Co.	1882–85, 1887–1920
1884	
Douglas Lapraik[b] and Co.	1884–93
1886	
Gibb, Livingston and Co.	(1868–70), 1886–90
1888	
Borneo Company, Ltd	(1864–66, 1875), 1888–90
Arnhold, Karberg and Co.	1888–1914

Notes:
[a] Discontinuities of one year or less are not taken into account. For membership periods beginning after 1888 see Table 13.2 etc.
[b] The uncle of this Douglas Lapraik was a founder of the Bank.

Unfortunately, the Board had supposed that Bottomley had resigned, thus leaving a vacancy; this was an error, and McConachie had to be told the election was invalid. A year later when Bottomley in fact resigned, McConachie resubmitted his name, this time to be told that the Board preferred to choose replacements from the same firm, turning to J.E. Davies of Douglas Lapraik and Co. (McConachie was eventually elected in 1890.)

From time to time the Board did act favourably on letters requesting election, as indeed in the case of E.R. Belilios, but in the post-1876 period such applications were accepted, if at all, in terms of 'the next vacancy' for which no presently represented firm was competing.

This began to give the Board a 'closed' look, accentuated by the custom of elections being made by the Board during the year, which elections were

consequently without prior shareholder approval. General Meetings were asked
to confirm previous decisions, that is, shareholders were voting for confirmation
of a 'sitting member', and names were proposed by a director, even if seconded by
a non-director.

While no one suggested this was illegal or even unusual, some considered it too
'cosy', and Fraser-Smith of the *Hongkong Telegraph* at the February 1888
meeting, although not objecting to any present or proposed director, stood on
principle.

> I beg to give notice that at the next meeting I shall oppose – and I think I can legally oppose
> – the elections of directors being proposed by directors. It is a matter for the shareholders.
> I hope that in Hong Kong this sort of thing will be washed out – and it will not be before it
> is time. Directors should be proposed and seconded by shareholders, not by the Board.

No such opposition proved necessary. In August 1888 the confirmation of
N.A. Siebs as director to replace H. Hoppius, both of Siemssen's, was proposed
and seconded by non-directors.

The Chairman and Deputy Chairman

The principle of seniority generally prevailed in the election by the Board of its
Chairman and Deputy Chairman (see Table 10.2).

Two years after his first election to the Board, William Keswick was elected
Deputy Chairman and in February 1880 became the first Chairman of the Bank
from the princely hong of Jardine Matheson. This fast rise to prominence, given
leaves and resignations, was nevertheless well within the rules of seniority.

By 1887 Jardine's representative, then J. Bell-Irving, was Deputy Chairman as
a result of M. Grote's departure at mid-year and the consequent assumption of
the chair by C.D. Bottomley. In 1888 Bell-Irving became Chairman. But this
succession had not been based strictly on seniority. When Grote succeeded
McIver as Chairman in mid-1886, Hoppius became Deputy Chairman by
seniority and should have continued in that position in 1887, becoming Chairman
again in 1888. But in February 1887 H. Hoppius stepped aside on the grounds
that a German, Grote, would be Chairman for eighteen months and should not be
succeeded by another German. Instead Bottomley was elected, Grote left in
September, and Bottomley took extended leave in 1888. Thus the next ranking,
Bell-Irving of Jardine Matheson, took over.

There is need to explain the apparent visibility of Jardine Matheson in view of
the firm's overwhelming importance and the inferences which might otherwise
be made. It is also pleasant to record the statesmanship of Hoppius who served
the Bank from the crisis of August 1874, with breaks for leave, until 1894 when he
left Hong Kong a short time before his death from cholera. He was Chairman of
the Hongkong Bank in 1877/78 and again in 1893/94.

While the rotation of these key Board positions was essential if the Bank were

Table 10.2 *The Hongkong and Shanghai Banking Corporation Chairmen and Deputy Chairmen, 1876–1888*

1876/77	*1881/82*	*1885/86*
E.R. Belilios	A. McIver	F.D. Sassoon
Adolf von André	H.L. Dalrymple	A. McIver
1877/78	*1882/83*	*1886/87*
H. Hoppius	H.L. Dalrymple	A. McIver (to June)
F.D. Sassoon	H. de C. Forbes	M. Grote (Chairman from June)
1878/79	*1883/84*	H. Hoppius (Deputy from June)
F.D. Sassoon	W. Reiners (to Dec.)	*1887/88*
W.H. Forbes	A.P. McEwen (fr. Dec.)	M. Grote (to September)
1879/80	W.S. Young[a] (Deputy)	C.D. Bottomley (Chairman from September)
W.H. Forbes	*1884/85*	John Bell-Irving
Wm Keswick	A.P. McEwen	
1880/81	F.D. Sassoon	*1888/89*
Wm Keswick	[a]Young was Deputy the	John Bell-Irving
A. McIver	entire year.	W.H. Forbes

Chairmen: from United Kingdom, 7; from Germany, 3; from the United States 2; other British, 3 occasions.

to remain independent of any leading hong and yet be representative of the major economic interests, a 'local bank' to a majority of interests, there could be lack of leadership in a crisis. This was the protest of shareholders at a later time, but it could be remedied, with dangers of its own, by the presence of a strong Chief Manager. And such a person the Board then had in Thomas Jackson.

The chairmanship of the Bank remained international, with Americans, Germans, and the Sassoon interests sharing the rotation with the 'Englishmen'. And there were at last sufficient 'Englishmen' on the Board to give it credibility as a British bank.

The Board, the Chief Manager, and management

There is little mention in the Board minutes of Thomas Jackson. There is no need; he is present and he is writing the minutes. A measure of his influence may be assumed from the references to him, recommendations from him, and discussions of his views which are recorded when he is absent, as in 1886–1887 and from 1889. The assessment of his role *vis-à-vis* the Board's is difficult to make. It must, however, be attempted if only to evaluate the reasons for the Bank's difficulties when Jackson left, even temporarily, the helm.

The period began with the elimination by the Board of Directors of their standing sub-committee and the resolve to hold weekly meetings of the full

Board. This practice was continued, with directors being given assignments from time to time to check specified accounts.

The Board was non-executive; the chief executive officer of the Bank, the Chief Manager, was not a member of the Board. Virtually all communications from the Hongkong Bank as a corporation, whether written by the direction of the Board or not, were signed by the Chief Manager. Only three exceptions come to mind, (i) the Chairman's report and the accounts, (ii) legal documents requiring the signature of the Board (in the absence of a 'Secretary'), and (iii) key letters on the charter written to the Governor, in contrast to those written to the Colonial Secretary.

Nevertheless, the public were very much aware of the directors, and newspaper editorials directed criticism of operational failures at the Board or the Chairman. There was certainly speculation in shares in the East, and there is evidence that members of the Board were not always discreet in their handling of information relative to the Bank's profitability. Ewen Cameron, the Shanghai Manager, suggested that the fall in the value of Bank shares after the publication of the quite reasonable results for the half year ending June 30, 1888, was a reaction to unreal profit expectations. These, he claimed, had been fuelled by leaks from members of the Board projecting profits on the basis of monthly 'exchange profit' figures to which they had access as members of the Board and which, he warned, were not a sound basis for the purpose of estimating semi-annual results.

The Board were aware of their public position. The minutes indicate clearly that serious discussion of problem accounts took place and questions asked of the Chief Manager when losses occurred.

An apparently serious argument between Jackson and Jardine's representative, F.B. Johnson, took place in 1883 over the former's failure to anticipate the losses from Vogel and Co. Jackson, who wrote the minutes, accused Johnson of addressing him in an aggressive way and showing hostile intention towards him. Johnson denied the charge, asserted his right to ask such questions, and complained of words the Chief Manager had used towards him. Both appealed to the Board, there was a discussion, and the matter was dropped.

The Chief Manager was considered as the principal servant of the company, however favoured, however highly regarded. As Jackson came more into the eye of the public and was cheered at General Meetings, there is no sign that this basic position was modified, but subtle changes in relationships are difficult to detect from the sources.

The Board, for example, remained in firm control of personnel policy, although it is clear that Jackson made key proposals on behalf of the staff – this subject will be considered separately in Chapter 15. Furthermore the Board continued its practice of reaching past the Chief Manager, as it were, to call managers to Hong Kong for questioning by a sub-committee, or even to take advantage of the presence of a sub-manager when members were concerned with the performance of his manager – as with E.H. Oxley who was questioned on W.G. Greig's policies in Singapore, or with H. Lamond questioned on events in Manila.

The Board acted in this way infrequently – the cases of Greig from Singapore and Barnes from Manila were the most important, but the right and precedents were there. In other cases, acting on information received from sometimes anonymous sources, the Board would direct that a specially appointed inspector be sent to the agency to report – as in the case of the alleged intemperance of A.E. Cope in Saigon. Cope was cleared for the time being, but his performance in Manila and his medical report in London confirmed that there was a problem.

The appointments of E. Morel as Manager in Lyons and A. Maccoll in Batavia were to prove costly, and they were done against the advice of David McLean in London, but with the advice of Jackson and, in the latter case, of G.E. Noble.

The Board then had independent sources of information, but they might well conflict. There were also the branch and agency and Head Office accounts themselves. The question of conflict of interest and the vital secrecy of the Bank's exchange position had not yet become of such importance that the Board denied itself the right, or duty, of keeping informed on such matters.

The directors were members of firms which had their own network of communications. Reports on performance of Bank agents might come from this source, bypassing the Chief Manager. The need for a full-time, travelling inspector on the staff of the Bank had long been recognized, but, as stated earlier in this history, no one was appointed until the temporary appointment of G.R. Johnston in 1885; later that year G.E. Noble was appointed Inspector of Branches. Their reports might be directed to the Chief Manager, but they were immediately available to the Board. And finally, there was the London Committee – and David McLean.

The role of London

David McLean was in a most unusual position. A servant of the Bank he had been virtually called on by name by shareholders to inspect the Bank and tell them what by inference no one else would state, the truth. Twice offered the chief managership, he had twice refused and had returned to London. Without his report and the public's acceptance of its integrity, the future of the Bank could well have been in doubt.

But he was not the Chief Manager, and he was distant from Head Office and the Board. He was close, however, to the London Committee, to A.H. Phillpotts, director of the London and County Bank, to E.F. Duncanson of Messrs T. and A.

Gibb, and to Albert Deacon, partner of E. and A. Deacon. These were the London 'friends' of important Eastern constituents of the Bank – Gibb, Livingston and Co. were, from time to time, represented on the Board; Deacon had been tea taster for Augustine Heard and Co., and his own company represented the Bank in Canton until 1909.

McLean was also realistic. His four volumes of private letters written from Shanghai and the five volumes which he wrote as London Manager, mainly to Thomas Jackson but also to other managers and agents in the East, are forthright, containing specific advice and criticism. But they are tempered with the frequent reminder that he is only offering advice and accepts no executive responsibility. The decision must be made by the manager on the spot. His criticisms are outspoken, his advice to Jackson, especially in the early years, is 'fatherly' as might be expected – Jackson, as noted in Chapter 6, had taken up the chief managership with McLean's support. On the other hand, McLean accepted throughout that Jackson was the chief.

As Manager in London McLean had specific insights of great value to managers in the East. His feel for the markets and movements in exchange, and his evaluation of the many firms with which the Bank dealt were an essential input into the Bank's success. Not that McLean was always right. His advice was certainly not always accepted, and on the question of the Bank's operations with India there was always a difference of opinion, with Jackson's overriding.

In this role of adviser McLean received information from the London Committee and its members individually. When the matter was serious, the Committee might communicate directly with the Board in Hong Kong. This was done sufficiently infrequently to make it a matter of importance when such a communication was received. Jackson was called on, for example, to explain why he was buying bills on firms against the advice from the London Committee. He explained he had stopped once the advice had been received.

There was a considerable exchange of views between the Board and the London Committee in 1882 over the proposed increase in capital. Although the Committee did not attempt to dictate to the Board, it is clear they disagreed both with the timing and with the price placed on the new shares. The communications from both McLean and the Committee were informational inputs of great value to the decision-making process in Hong Kong. But the decisions, right or wrong, were made at Board level.

The London Committee protested in November 1887 against the volume of business the Hongkong Bank's San Francisco agency was doing with the Bank of Nevada, then involved in wheat speculations. McLean had tried to discourage the Committee; his own opinion, correct as it turned out, was that Harries was fully covered and that the operations were profitable. The Committee, however, saw these transactions together with the losses in Manila as detrimental to the credit of the Bank. There is reference to the situation in the Board minutes, but no record of the action, if any, taken.

The London Committee played a valuable role as a 'presence' in London and was given public credibility by the presence on the Committee of a director of the Hongkong Bank's 'clearer', the London and County Bank. The Committee provided the Hongkong Bank's Manager in London with valuable information and acted as the ultimate, independent adviser and critic. The relationship appears to have been one of mutual acceptance. The Committee's opinions were received with respect and, if critical, with concern, but the Board never permitted itself to be overruled solely on advice from London nor did it provide the Committee with sufficient information to permit it to second-guess the Board's decisions.

The London Committee had nevertheless a dangerous potential. Its members were well-known in the City and their names appeared prominently on the standard advertisements the Bank placed in key newspapers. Using their names required the Bank to heed their advice.

The Board in Hong Kong had definite views on the London Committee's composition and resisted suggestions from McLean for expansion of membership. Hints of availability from retired Hongkong Bank directors in the United Kingdom were positively discouraged, although, judging from the McLean correspondence, men like von André and F.D. Sassoon, the latter who was by then head of D. Sassoon, Sons and Co., remained actively interested as shareholders in the Bank and commented on policy directly to the London Manager. A London Committee, prominently advertised and consisting of leading members of 'London friends' of Eastern partnerships, retired (but still very active) ex-Hongkong Bank directors – F.D. Sassoon died, for example, in 1917 – could have been seen as a threat to the Hong Kong direction of the Bank. To appreciate the Board's concern, the context must be remembered. There were 50% of the shares of the Hongkong Bank registered in London, London was the political and economic capital of an Empire, and there was a precedent in the history of other exchange banks initially operating from colonial head offices. Whether consciously or not, the Board acted cautiously.

Until McLean accepted an invitation to join the Committee in 1889 after his retirement, the composition remained unchanged. Perhaps this was one reason for the workability of the relationship and the Committee's consequent value to the Board of Directors in Hong Kong.

Charity

The attitude to joint-stock companies which stressed the real role of the shareholder, the responsibility of the directors, and the role of the staff as 'servants' was consistent with a low profile on charitable contributions. The company had been incorporated for specified purposes; perform these successfully and dividends would be paid; the recipients of the dividends would make the appropriate charitable contributions. The closer the shareholder was involved with the company, the more 'local' the company, the less should be its role, by this philosophy, in charity. A paid manager should not be permitted to give away shareholders' money.

This theoretical position understood, the humanitarian pressures on the direction of a bank operating in a world of crisis can be placed in perspective. The Hongkong Bank did make limited charitable contributions, but they were kept firmly under the control of the Board as not being, by any definition, part of general banking business. The list is brief and the contributions relatively small, but the directors and Chief Manager gave from their personal funds, and Jackson in particular had a reputation for generosity.

The most common grants fall into two categories, funds to relieve those caught in natural disasters and funds for jubilees and public celebrations.

Among those in the first category were:

China Famine Fund, 1878 $1,000; Java Disaster Fund, 1883 [$?]; Irish Famine Fund, 1880 $500; Kwangtung Inundation Fund, 1885 $750

The celebrations include:

Bombay Exhibition, 1884 $5,000; Penang Centenary, 1886 $500; Colonial & India Exhibition, $2,500; Queen's Jubilee, 1887 $1,000

The Board made the grant for the Bombay Exhibition on the condition that this sum was 'general'. Several such queries from the Board, and no doubt from other company boards, must have led local managers to agree on a sum in advance and inform their chief executives that 'everyone else' was giving the specified amount – a satisfactory arrangement for all.

The Board also authorized grants to such organizations as the Berlin Foundling Hospital, the Diocesan Home and Orphanage (which has developed into the Diocesan Boys' School) in Hong Kong, the Chinese College of Foochow, and many others. The records are not clear but imply, by the citing of exceptions, that some at least of the grants approved constituted authorization for annual subscriptions.

The Board and the expansion of the Hongkong Bank

The Board of Directors in a minute dated November 1879 stated that the Board 'deprecate any extension of the Bank's business, but . . .'

This comment, made in connection with the decision to open in New York, characterized their policy in this period. In the context of the problems of staff development and the limitations of the Bank's capital base, the policy was a sound one.

Indeed, agencies opened previously had not as yet fully developed and continued to present problems. The Managers in Singapore, Saigon, and Manila did not immediately develop a routine of business which was in itself both profitable and safe, and these are matters reflected in the minutes of the Board.

The Board seemed less at home with problems outside the open ports of China and Japan, despite their own marginal interests in Hong Kong's southern trading area, resisting, for example, suggestions to enter local banking business in India.

Another way of describing the Bank's proper area of operations would be in terms of access to information; the expertise of the Board and the London Committee and the experience of the Bank's own staff were China and Japan oriented. The Sassoons were an obvious exception and they, as constituents and directors, would certainly have encouraged the Bank's exchange operations in India. There is continuous evidence that the Bank, both the Board and the Chief Manager, remained cautious relative to involvement in local Indian finance.

Yet another criterion would be the ability of the Bank's principal Far Eastern constituents, including the firms represented on the Board, to provide business. British firms in India already had their banking connections, and the partners in Bombay or Calcutta might not have the authority to share the business with a new bank. Batavia was over-banked with Dutch financial houses; Saigon had its Banque de l'Indo-Chine. The Bank's success in Hong Kong, Shanghai, and Yokohama depended on the decision-making authority of the Bank's local supporters. Where their constituents' authority ended, the Bank's profitability ceased.

An alternative banking activity would be 'native business', but here again the Bank was China-biased. Where there was a Chinese compradore, the Bank could operate in the local financial markets and deal with native firms – although the Bank's managers in Singapore and Colombo would, after several dangerous mistakes, learn to deal with the chettiars over the next half century. In general, attempts to change the position suddenly, to take on Indian business, for example, without background, would inevitably lead to difficulties.

Therefore it is not surprising that the Board turned down invitations to open in Colombo on at least three occasions, succumbing only in 1892 when other factors were at work. There was discussion of an agency in Madras, but the Board never accepted the necessity for essentially India-initiated operations, and the argument for Madras would be based on the triangular trade finance involving chettiars in Southern India and in Ceylon and with London. With the Bank opened in Rangoon and a year later in Colombo, a Madras agency would eventually be missed, but that was all in the future.

By the above criteria, Bangkok might be considered marginally within the

Bank's region; there was a Far East trade component and a Chinese business community. There was also a Government sympathetic to controlled Western influence. The rumour of an exclusive French financial operation, the immediate threat of action by the Chartered Bank, and the growth of the Bank's own business through merchant agents were the deciding factors. The Hongkong Bank opened in Siam in 1888.

In China the Bank moved north, establishing agencies in Tientsin and Peking and entering tentatively into Formosa (Taiwan) by appointing Russell and Co. their agents in the Treaty Port of Tamsui in 1885; the first fully Bank-staffed office, however, was in Taipei in 1983. Surprisingly, despite the growing volume of business as witnessed by the successful request of their new merchant agent (Messrs Deacon and Co.) for a $1,000 fixed fee in addition to commission, the Hongkong Bank did not open in Canton until 1909.

Nor did the Bank open in Macau. From the first it had dealings with the Portuguese territory 64 kilometres west across the Pearl River Estuary, and a loan to the Macau Government was sanctioned by Lisbon in 1876. In 1886 the Board of Directors agreed to a loan of up to $200,000 for harbour improvement, but there is no evidence the matter went further.

There is no record of a permanent Bank agency there. In April 1887, however Gershom Stewart wrote from Macau to his close friend Charles Addis in Peking. 'I am over here doing a little agency business to try to get customs revenue for the Hongkong Bank . . . [The agency] is not doing a roaring business at present . . .'[7] This explanation is reasonable; an agreement between China and Portugal had just been concluded whereby the former recognized the long-standing claim that Macau was territory under Portuguese sovereignty, while Portugal in return agreed to grant facilities in connection with the collection of the Chinese customs revenues.[8]

There is no other reference to the 'agency', and it must be assumed that Stewart was soon withdrawn and not replaced. If the Bank's Canton business was insufficient to justify a Bank-staffed agency, there would have been even less chance for Macau. By the time the colony had grown, the Portuguese had established their own Banco Nacional Ultramarino and exclusion policies which prevented the Hongkong Bank returning until 1972.

Nevertheless Macau Government archives confirm that during the period covered in this chapter, the Hongkong Bank served the Macau authorities – but from Hong Kong.[9]

In considering Korea, the uncertain international status of the country and the lack of clear banking opportunities persuaded the Board not to open. And the Board for the same reasons declined consideration of a proposed £400,000, 25-year loan to the Korean Government in 1885.

The first tentative consideration of a branch in Borneo, specifically in

Table 10.3 *The Hongkong and Shanghai Banking Corporation*
New branches and agencies, 1875–1892

1875 Manila[a]–	1884 Batavia[a]–
1875 San Francisco[a]–	1885 Peking[c]–1955[e]
	(1886 Tamsui[d])
1877 Singapore[b]–	1887 Macau[c]–1887[e]
1880 New York[b]–	1888 Bangkok[b]–
1881 Lyons[c]–1954	
1881 Tientsin[c]–1955	1889 Hamburg[c]–
1883 Iloilo[c]–1982	1891 Rangoon[b]–1963
1884 Penang[c]–	1891 Nagasaki[b]–1930[e]
	1892 Colombo[b]–

Notes: offices operating in 1985 except as noted.
[a] replacing failed 'merchant agents'.
[b] business growth, replacing 'merchant agents'.
[c] de novo.
[d] Russell and Co., merchant agents.
[e] a representative office or branch has been reestablished, see Volume
    IV.

Sandakan, then the capital of British North Borneo (now the Malaysian State of Sabah), was made in December 1888, but nothing would come of this until after World War II.

The Board were not particularly responsive to offers of specific business outside the Bank's main area of operations. Thus they would turn down a request in 1887 to lend 23 lacs of rupees at $5\frac{1}{2}\%$ to the Rangoon Municipal Council, although they did take note that the appeal came from Rangoon's then most prominent citizen, R. Rowett, a former Chairman (1871/72) of the Hongkong Bank.

The Straits Settlements[a]

An apparently obvious but actually quite new development was the Hongkong Bank's role in Batavia and the Straits Settlements. The former was forced on the Bank by the failure of its merchant agents, and the importance of its sugar trade to, *inter alios*, the Bank's Hong Kong constituents persuaded the Bank to remain despite the over-banked position and Dutch dominance. The important policy problems arose in the Straits Settlements and until 1884 this meant Singapore.

[a] This section is indebted to W. Evan Nelson for information and references in his 'The Hongkong and Shanghai Banking Corporation Factor in the Progress toward a Straits Settlements Government Note Issue, 1881–1889', in King, ed. *Eastern Banking*, pp. 155–79.

Singapore

Ewen Cameron uttered the appropriate caution when he wrote to the Board in November 1876, minuted as follows: 'Mr Cameron deprecated opening a branch at Singapore so long as the Bank's funds could be fully used in China as at present, but when the case altered, he would like to see a branch opened at Singapore.'

The Chinese arrived in Singapore with the British, but, when the Malay States came under British influence, there was immigration of Chinese into the tin-producing areas. Certainly with the remittance business, with the entrepôt activities involving the Far East-Netherlands East Indies and Borneo trade, there was justification for a Bank agency in Singapore, and H. Cope took over from the Bank's merchant agents, Boustead's, in 1877.

However, the Board from the first decided on a branch, a decision which was to involve them in four years of negotiation with the various British authorities. In the end the Bank opened a branch and issued notes. These negotiations are significant in the rationalizing of the extraterritorial argument and affected the Bank's charter; they will, therefore, be discussed in Chapter 11. The Hongkong Bank also became involved in local finance and in the initial years lost considerable sums from clean advances to British companies, for which Cope was dismissed. By 1885 the branch was profitable and the Bank had already opened in Penang.

Penang

The Board of Directors did not extend the Bank's branch network without commercial consideration. In the case of Penang there were two factors, one immediate, one potential. The Chartered Bank and the Chartered Mercantile Bank had both established themselves there successfully and had sizeable note issues. In addition the Hongkong Bank had been approached personally by Major J.F.A. McNair, then administering the Government of the Penang Settlement, with the warning that if the banks did not provide facilities in the Native States, there was a distinct possibility of a government note issue. Penang was seen as a springboard to the development of banking in Malaya, and the Bank accordingly sought authority for a branch in Penang and an agency in Perak.

The move to Penang proved sound in itself; the plan to establish an agency in neighbouring Perak was premature. Desirable as banks might be for Perak, it was not a brilliant banking prospect. In 1889 the Chartered Bank could only be induced to move there if the Government granted it a number of 'compensations' for the losses it expected to sustain in the 'public service', a policy which would be accepted many years later when banks were reluctant to move into the less-developed East-coast states. Six years later the Chartered Bank decided that in Perak, 'apart from the convenience to the Government, there is no field for banking operations,' and closed down its agency.[10]

The intentions of the Hongkong and Shanghai Bank were therefore probably predicated largely on McNair's advice which whetted the Bank's desire to defend the principle of a private note issue against government expansion into that field. The only thing that could conceivably make a bank profitable in Perak was the right of issuing notes there, and this the Bank may have hoped to gain. Certainly the Chartered Bank, when it opened in Taiping, began agitation immediately for this right.[11]

Initially it seemed as if the Hongkong Bank's intended move into Perak would prove successful. Cecil C. Smith, who was the Officer Administering the Straits Government in Governor Weld's absence and who had served as Colonial Secretary in Hong Kong, regarded the Bank highly. Indeed, it had been during his temporary administration of Hong Kong that the Hongkong Bank had become in 1872 the Colony's banker. Smith had typically given an enthusiastic endorsement to the Bank's proposed branch in Penang, citing in particular, 'The fact of there being unlimited liability as regards the note issue of the Corporation has brought it into special favour at the present time, while its sound position justifies the confidence which is liberally extended to it.'[12]

Expansion to Penang, however, was considered routine, for it was part of the Colony of the Straits Settlements. The Chartered and Chartered Mercantile Banks already had branches there, issuing nearly Straits $1,600,000 between them. Permission to open duly arrived from London in August, including the privilege of issuing notes.[13]

Requesting an agency in Perak was a different and unprecedented matter. Indeed, Smith's endorsement of the Hongkong Bank was part of an overall policy initiative on the entire subject of currency in the Native States, which would also, he assumed, pave the way for the Bank's application. In a despatch to the Secretary of State he stated, 'The time has arrived for a decision to be given on a subject pressed by the Residents of the Native States, namely the means to be adopted for giving Banking facilities in those countries.'[14] He reiterated the hardship a total lack of these facilities caused European entrepreneurs, and then spoke of the uncertain situation in which perhaps some $1,500,000 in banknotes circulated without authority or regulation in the States. These unsound conditions made it 'worthy of consideration whether the Government of each Native State should establish a State Bank, or whether . . . Banks now established in the Colony should be authorized to open Branch Banks in the Native States'. Though admitting that state banks would meet 'with the favour of Sir F[rederick] Weld', Smith argued that they would be expensive and useless. Depositors would still use the Singapore banks which could offer higher interest rates. Since opinion in the Straits remained unreconciled to a state note issue which might serve the Peninsula as well, he saw no reason why the Government should not:

... facilitate the opening of a Branch of such a Bank as the Hongkong and Shanghai Bank. It should refuse to allow a note issue from such a Branch, but it should continue to permit the circulation of notes from Banks in the Colony ... (I have particularized the Hongkong and Shanghai Bank solely because that Bank alone at present of the Eastern Banks has an unlimited liability as regards its note issue.)[15]

Smith's initiative was meant to forward the interests of the Hongkong Bank. Instead, he opened up a veritable Pandora's box of controversy, during which government departments were at loggerheads and Imperial policy in utter confusion. His timing had not been ideal. Smith wrote his despatch in June of 1884. On May 3 the Oriental Bank Corporation had stopped payment.

The Hongkong Bank did not open in the Malay States until 1910. This significant expansion into the Malayan area undertaken by the Board in Jackson's first administration was, then, confined to Singapore and Penang.

Nevertheless as Table 10.3 indicates, the Bank opened nine branches or agencies within the years 1876–1888. Of these two, Tientsin and Peking, marked development in China. Iloilo was forced by the potential competition in the sugar business from the Chartered Bank. Batavia was the consequence of the failure of the Bank's agents, and Bangkok, which like Singapore marked the potential development of a new area, was forced by the growth of business and the danger of competition.

The accounts show that the Bank's capital was fully employed – and indeed additional capital would be sought in 1890. Chapter 15 will suggest that the Bank's staff was also fully but thinly deployed. Growth came from within the region; the Bank's capital was fully deployed in the East.

THE BOARD AND GOVERNMENT

The Hong Kong Savings Bank, 1884

The Victorian Age of self-help and thrift reached Hong Kong in the early 1880s in the form of attempts by the Hong Kong Post Office to form a Savings Bank. The Postmaster General claimed that Hong Kong was a sort of Clapham Junction for ships and that he was consequently overworked, but by 1884 he had agreed to operate such a bank – for two days a week.[16] A bill to authorize a postal savings bank was introduced into the Hong Kong Legislative Council and then withdrawn after the second reading.

The reason for this abrupt reversal of government plans was simply explained. The Hongkong and Shanghai Banking Corporation had agreed to operate a savings bank; it would be open daily and pay interest at the rate of $3\frac{1}{2}\%$. For the Postmaster General this was extremely good news, and he reported:

This offer [of the Hongkong Bank] was accepted. Its main advantage is that the Bank is open every day, instead of two days a week only, and that depositors who have $100 to credit at once open a banking account and increase their deposits indefinitely. Against this may be set the fact that the deposits are not secured by the Government, but this would seem to have been no obstacle to the success of a Savings Bank at Shanghai, and need not be here.[17]

This would appear non-controversial. Indeed, in 1881 the Hongkong Bank had pursued, with Board sanction, a similar course in Shanghai. The Municipal Council had gladly withdrawn its own scheme, and there had been no comment from the British Treasury.

[The Hongkong Bank] had successfully opened a Savings Bank at Shanghai, where, without any of our elaborate machinery of Ordinances etc, Savings to the amount of about £13,000 were received in a short time from shipmasters, mates, engineers, pilots, etc., in a word, from the most notoriously extravagant and improvident class of foreigners we have out here.[18]

The advantages of a postal savings bank were four-fold: (i) free mailing privileges were granted both to the bank and to savers, (ii) no stamp duty was payable, (iii) unused stamps could be saved and submitted in sums of a dollar for credit to the savings account, and (iv) the savings were effectively guaranteed by the Government. All but the last of these advantages the Hong Kong Government attempted to pass on to 'any' local bank willing to operate a savings bank under agreed regulations, and an enabling ordinance, No. 10 of 1884, was accordingly passed, assented to by the Governor, and sent to the Colonial Office.[19]

As it happened, and as was expected, only the Hongkong Bank submitted proposed rules in their new role as managers of a prospective Savings Bank. These included provisions for free postage from any British post office in China or Hong Kong and exemption from stamp duty. And, in accordance with the ordinance, the regulations were approved and the establishment of the Hong Kong Savings Bank proclaimed in the *Government Gazette* with the comment that 'the assets of the Hongkong and Shanghai Banking Corporation will form a direct security for the repayment of sums deposited in the above Bank'.

Unfortunately the Colonial Office first read about the ordinance in the *London and China Telegraph*, and Lord Derby demanded a report from Governor Bowen. By a slip of the pen the newspaper, the source of the information, was referred to in Derby's despatch as the 'Hongkong and China Telegraph'. Even more unfortunately Governor Bowen, assuming the paper cited was Robert Fraser-Smith's contentious *Hongkong Telegraph* about which he held strong opinions, decided to defend himself not only by pointing out that his report had in fact been in the Colonial Office all the time but also by offering some unsolicited comment.

It has been surmised here that it may be a mistake arising out of the notorious habit of some gentlemen of the permanent Department, viz, of frequently taking action on unverified rumours published in obscure local newspapers and of, at the same time, ignoring the Statute law of the Colony (as the Attorney General pointed out on former occasions) together with other official instruments and documents emanating from responsible authorities. This strange habit has, from time to time, not unnaturally produced much mischief and irritation in the Colonies.[20]

The 'obscure' journal was authoritative and well-established, but as it had been misnamed in the original despatch, one Colonial Office minute wisely suggested that the very name 'Telegraph' had 'rubbed the Governor the wrong way'. Fraser-Smith did not restrict himself to criticisms of the Hongkong Bank, and the *Hongkong Telegraph* had become known in the Colonial Office as the 'tabooed paper, which the Hongkong Government do not allow us to see here now'.[21]

The Secretary of State required the Governor to withdraw his critique of the permanent staff and address the issues.[22]

By the time these communications had travelled back and forth via Suez, the Colonial Office had reached the conclusion that the whole ordinance was designed to enable the Hongkong Bank to obtain cheap deposits. They objected, naturally, to the remission of stamp duty and to the apparent Government sanction of a privately owned savings bank, where the deposits of the poorest of the community would find their way. The Hongkong Bank, the Treasury argued, was naturally (and, by inference, quite properly) motivated by profit; if it failed, would not the Government be under pressure to repay the savings bank depositors?[23] It was the same as the cry against the one-dollar note issue.

The only hesitation among senior Colonial Office officials appears to have been caused by the expressed reluctance of R. Meade to interfere with the plans 'of this choleric old gentleman', Governor Bowen, but braver hearts prevailed.[24] On the initiative of the Colonial Office and with the agreement of the Treasury Her Majesty was advised to disallow the ordinance in May of 1885.

The Government, however, had no authority to close the newly established 'Hong Kong Savings Bank' or impede its operations. In consequence the Hongkong and Shanghai Bank published its own regulations, omitting reference to the security of the assets and to stamp duty, but referring to free mail privileges. These had been incorporated into the Hong Kong postal regulations and the disallowance of the ordinance did not affect them. They fell into disuse after World War II and were finally omitted from the regulations in 1957, although they had continued to feature prominently in the Savings Bank 'pass books'.[25]

The Hong Kong Savings Bank was operated as a department of the Hongkong Bank whose activities were covered by its own ordinance of incorporation; the Savings Bank was moreover specially referred to in the comprehensive revision of the ordinance in 1929 (para. 3c).

The purpose of the Savings Bank and its connection with the Post Office did not in fact change as a consequence of the Imperial veto. Small-savers could still paste ten ten-cent stamps on a special sheet and mail it postage free to the Bank for the one-dollar minimum credit as originally envisaged. Reporting on this aspect of the Savings Bank's first year of operation, the Postmaster General commented:

It can hardly be said that it was hoped to introduce more thrifty habits amongst a certain class of our young fellow-citizens, but it was felt that at least the attempt should be made. Whether, however, pocket-money is not a Hong Kong institution, or whether other attractions are too strong, certain it is that the ten-cent system of saving does not seem to take hold of the young here as the penny system does in England. Only $65 has been collected since the Bank was opened . . . [compared to £200 a week in England].[26]

And yet the Savings Bank would grow and serve the lower wage-earning group at a time when banking facilities were not that well understood nor cheques so widely accepted. From the first direct deposits were more encouraging, with $50,000 credited in the first seven months of operation.[27]

On one point, however, the Hongkong Bank would talk back. The National Debt Office had charged that the Hongkong Bank and the Savings Bank were identical 'with the single difference that Depositors in the Savings Bank Branch would receive a lower rate of interest on their deposits than the ordinary customers of the Banking Corporation'.[28] Governor Bowen, on a protest from the Hongkong Bank, informed the Secretary of State that the Bank paid $3\frac{1}{2}\%$ on savings accounts as against 2% on current accounts; 5% was only paid for twelve-month fixed deposits.

What had appeared as a community service in Hong Kong, undertaken at the Government's request, had set off automatic responses in London. 'I was [wrote the Hong Kong Treasurer], though willing to attempt the Bank myself, profoundly thankful to have so prosperous an institution as the Hongkong and Shanghai Bank to relieve me of it.'[29] The Treasury and Colonial Office, bound by precedent and Imperial responsibilities, were not.

Hong Kong Government deposits

The current account of the Hong Kong Government was wholly in the hands of the Hongkong and Shanghai Bank. The Colonial Treasurer, A. Lister, had audited the 1882 accounts of the Bank in the temporary absence of one of the elected auditors and wrote of the Bank's soundness in official correspondence.[30] Government current account business was granted on the basis of tender, although there was some evaluation, and Lister expressed the view that only the Hongkong Bank had the staff available to undertake the work required.[31]

There were, however, problems of which the Bank itself may not have been fully aware, but which are an illustration again of the tendency for the Imperial authorities to base their instructions on precedents based on experience elsewhere.

The Colonial Office attempted to ensure, from London, that (i) the Government Treasury was operating soundly, (ii) the current account was kept in a chartered bank following a successful tender, (iii) fixed deposits were distributed, subject to equal rates being offered, (iv) the soundness of the depository banks was unquestioned, and (v) surplus balances were remitted to the United Kingdom to be invested in consols and other first class securities. From time to time the implementation of these policies affected the Hongkong Bank.

First, however, the Hong Kong Government had no physical 'treasury' and was, exceptionally, permitted to do a daily business with the bank holding its current account, although the Colonial Office urged the Hong Kong Government to put its extra cash in a chest and lock it in the Bank's vaults. This in fact was not carried through; but in any case the Government's banker had to be an institution with a large staff, and hence in fact only the Hongkong Bank could really fulfil the tasks required.[32] As long as this remained true and subject to its offering competitive rates, the Hongkong Bank would remain the Government's banker.

In quantitative terms sums up to $200,000 on current account and $400,000 on fixed deposit were involved, both sums varying considerably in response to Government requirements – on occasion there was on deposit less than 50% of the figures quoted.

In 1882/83 the Hong Kong Government became concerned with the safety of both the Oriental and the Chartered Mercantile banks, in which large fixed deposits were held. This concern was intensified with the worsening of Franco-Chinese relations and the withdrawal of sycee from the Colony. The Government was faced with a classic dilemma – how to safeguard government funds without being accused of undermining confidence in the banks.[33] The correspondence is clear that the Hongkong Bank and Chartered Bank were considered secure, and accordingly deposits were withdrawn from the Oriental and Chartered Mercantile gradually and after several weeks notice as they matured.[34]

When the Oriental failed, the Government deposited funds with the New Oriental, despite the fact that it was not chartered. The Colonial Office, although it refused permission for the Mauritius Government to use the New Oriental, does not appear to have interfered in Hong Kong.[35]

The bulk of the correspondence, however, deals with the question of the maximum balance the Government required in the Colony and the amount which was required to be remitted to London. The problem arose because the Colony was beginning for the first time to generate a budget surplus, but it was complicated by the plans for large public works and for concern over the rate of the exchange. The Secretary of State decided the maximum should be $200,000, an amount proportional to that proved satisfactory in the Straits Settlements; the

Treasurer of Hong Kong attempted in long despatches to prove this calculation irrelevant, confusing the issue with the question of subsidiary coinage and Thomas Jackson's estimate of the Colony's requirements, but frequently reasserting that his maximum balance requirement was $350,000.[36]

For the history of the British Empire it is necessary to conclude that much correspondence was written at cross-purposes on the basis of minutes prepared by officials too often misinformed, without adequate files and lacking the necessary background to interpret those files, available. For the history of the Hongkong Bank it is sufficient to conclude that to the extent permitted the Bank provided facilities and advice to the Hong Kong Government, which in the long-run proved satisfactory. Elsewhere the Bank also handled government business; as the local bank it had staff in the East; as a silver-based bank it could use the funds deposited. But in the larger questions of Imperial policy, the Bank at this time had no voice.

THE BUILDINGS OF THE HONGKONG BANK

There is yet another development of Jackson's first administration to be considered, the new office building – 'Lucky Jackson's palatial money palace' at No. 1, Queen's Road.[37] Those who hold the belief that bank buildings planned in prosperity are bound to be completed in more difficult times will find little support from this story. But as with so many head offices of growing enterprises, 'Jackson's Folly' became all too soon inadequate for the Hongkong Bank's operations. The remedy is a story for Volume III.

The Board and the Bank buildings[b]

There is insufficient information in the archives to provide a definitive statement on policy, but general observations may be useful.

The Hongkong Bank acquired property by actual purchase, taking advantage perhaps of the withdrawal of a company or bank as in the case of its enlarged Hong Kong property, or as the consequence of a reclamation or other special consideration. Alternatively, the Bank might find itself in possession of property as a result of a debtor firm failing; the Bank's Iloilo premises, for example, were on the books of the failed Peele Hubbell at $22,000, and the Bank was resolving

---

b On the occasion of the April 7 formal opening of the Bank's 1986 Headquarters, a well-illustrated history of previous buildings on One, Queen's Road Central, was published by the Bank. The book, *One Queen's Road Central: the Headquarters of HongkongBank since 1864*, by Ian Lambot and Gillian Chambers, can be recommended as a supplement to Christopher Yip's study of the Bank's four major buildings (cited in note 38). The account presented here can consequently be brief.

Table 10.4 *The Hongkong and Shanghai Banking Corporation*
Bank premises account, 1889

(in thousands of dollars)

Place	Standing in the Bank's books at		Valued at	Rent per annum
Hong Kong		marine lot 104	425.0[c]	
		reclamation[a]	139.0	
		inland lot 580[b]	50.0	
	418.9		614.0	
Shanghai	130.0		130.0	
Yokohama	83.9		100.0	4.2
Kobe	15.1		50.0	1.8
Singapore	19.7		35.0	0.8
Saigon	8.2		7.5	0.5
Hankow	19.1		26.5	2.1
Tientsin	54.6		54.5	2.9
Bombay	48.9		50.0	2.9
Amoy	28.6		35.0	2.0
Manila	100.9		102.0	0.6
Total	928.0		1204.5	28.0

Notes:
[a] value of right to reclaim land in front of lot.
[b] St John's Place.
[c] of which the building $200,000.

the problem of the firm's indebtedness by paying its account $1,800 per annum in rent. There were other chance occurrences. The Board authorized the purchase of property in Hankow in anticipation of future needs, their intention being to rent out the existing building in the meantime. Unfortunately, the Agent, W.G. Greig, was not informed and forced the Board's hand by having the building knocked down.

Although the Bank did not open in Canton until 1909 it very early owned property on Shameen, the former sandbank which foreigners had built up into their settlement. Destruction caused in the 'Shameen Incident' in 1883 resulted in a Bank claim of $15,000 against the Chinese Government. The compensation paid for all foreign claims totalled Canton Ts 143,400 (=$200,000) and was included in the Hongkong Bank's 1884 'C' Loan, negotiated initially through the Hong Kong compradore.

There is record of property dealings in other ports, but they are scattered and primarily of interest in reconstructing the early plans of those cities.

In 1889 when the Board agreed (as will be described in Chapter 11) to place security for the note issue in the hands of trustees, they hoped that the deeds of Bank property would be acceptable and accordingly had a statement of the Bank Property Account made up (Table 10.4). The practice of writing down the property had resulted in a total value of $1,204,500 being on the Bank's books at $928,000.

The Board kept firm control over property decisions, but acted on the advice of managers in the field and once the decision was made appeared to have delegated the details and execution of plans. They took advantage of opportunities, but accepted the need for adequate space and recognized that the junior staff required 'Mess' accommodation. As was noted in the case of the Shanghai office in 1875, the Board's timing was not always perfect, but buildings take time from conception to completion and the fortunes of the Bank can change. Even with the successful 1886 Head Office, further embellishments planned for 1887 were postponed; it was no more a year for embellishments than 1983.

The Head Office building of 1886

Until the beginning of 1883 the Hongkong Bank occupied Wardley House, rented from D. Sassoon, Sons and Co. in 1864 and purchased for $60,000 in 1866. The decision of the Chartered Mercantile Bank to downgrade its Far Eastern operations enabled the Bank to purchase their building, which was fortuitously next door, for the sum of $80,000 in 1881. This gave the Hongkong Bank a frontage on Queen's Road and the Praya (now Des Voeux Road) of 125 feet and a length of 225 feet along Wardley Road to the east.

Wardley House itself bordered Queen's Road on one side, the major east to west traffic artery, and the harbour on the other. Just to the east was the City Hall. So even though fifteen years of growth and change had made a new Head Office necessary, the Wardley House site retained its excellence.

The Board had also purchased St John's Place for $45,000 as a residence for the Chief Manager and for other officers, but the Head Office building was always to possess residential facilities, so that the traditional dual purpose building so common in early nineteenth-century London was preserved.

The decision to rebuild the Head Office was taken in 1881 and in the following year the Board concluded an agreement with the P&O for the temporary use of their old building until completion of the Bank's new Head Office building. The original estimate for the building was $250,000, the final cost $300,000 or an overrun of 20%.

Some five years after occupation the Bank had to spend an additional $35,000 to replace timbers and supports destroyed by white ants. Unfortunately the contract was insufficiently specific on matters of quality to permit recourse to the contractors. This put the cost of the building some 34% in excess of estimate.

As Christopher Yip described the plans in his essay on 'Four Major Buildings' in the Bank's architectural history, the successful Bird and Palmer design merged two buildings into one.[38] On the main Queen's Road side there was a domed structure wrapped in a screen of gigantic Corinthian columns; on the harbour side, there was a Victorianized 'compradoric' building much like the other buildings that lined the waterfront. In essence, part of the building reflected bank design as it had developed in England, while the other part responded to the local building tradition that had adapted European architecture to the climatic and social requirements of the South China coast.

The basement floor was done in native granite, while the floors above were of brick with granite facing and granite columns. The interior had teak woodwork and tiled passages and basement floors. Such modern conveniences as gas lighting and an electric bell system for communication were installed, along with fire extinguishers for safety. The bank furniture was designed by the architects and made in Hong Kong, while residential furnishings were turned over to the firm of Hall and Holtz in Shanghai.[39]

The *China Mail* described the banking hall in the year of its opening:

We will pass in from Queen's Road entrance. The large main door is gained by ascending two small flights of steps, which land us on a level with the verandah formed by the colonnade that runs round the whole building. Passing in at the main door we find ourselves in the bank proper – an immense hall which might be considered as a building apart from the rest. It is roofed by a large octagonal dome, the apex of which is 100 feet above the floor. This dome rests on arches supported by eight massive Corinthian pillars of polished red Aberdeen granite, and is lighted by a series of circular windows filled with stained glass.

The bank building is cut into two halves by a corridor which runs the whole length of the structure from Queen's Road to the Praya. On the right hand side is the general office for Europeans, while on the other side is the compradore's office, where the Chinese will do business.

These offices have each broad counters in front of them, bending inwards at the centre of the passage so as to give more space for moving out and in to the Bank. They have doors opening on the verandah, and on the left or Chinese side the verandah will be utilised for the money-counting stalls.[40]

The other portion of the building that faced the harbour was designed, as noted above, in a Victorianized 'compradoric' that better suited the social requirements of the European staff and the climatic conditions of the South China coast. 'Compradoric' refers to the hybrid architecture that developed on the South China coast during the nineteenth century to reconcile the desire for a proper Western building in a radically different setting. These buildings had to retain a European character while adapting to the lifestyle of a predominantly male merchant culture. The buildings also had to respond to the worst weather conditions of the region without the use of the elaborate mechanical systems common to buildings of the late nineteenth century.

The ground floor was bifurcated by a corridor that led from the banking hall to the compradoric Praya side with its ground floor offices and strongrooms:

Regaining the centre corridor, we will now pass from the bank proper to the adjoining offices, which form the ground floor of a three-storey building.

The first rooms we come to are two large rooms, or safes, 28 feet by 20 feet, one on each side of the corridor. On the right hand side of the corridor the next room we come to is the Correspondents' room, 36 ft by 20 ft, which is connected with the General Office by a passage running along the back of the strongroom. From the Correspondents' room we enter the Sub-manager's room, which is of somewhat smaller dimensions, being only 24 feet by 26. It recedes from the line of the corridor, forming a small open passage, which can be utilised as an ante-room to the Manager's room. From the Sub-manager's room we pass to the Manager's room – a large room, 36 by 24, looking out on the Praya verandah. To the Manager's room there is also an entrance for brokers and merchants from the small passage just mentioned.

Before passing from the ground floor we may visit the rooms on the other side of the corridor, the most of which are devoted to Chinese officials. Opposite to the Manager's room is a room of corresponding size, where will be held the meetings of the Directors and which is accordingly called the Board room. Facing the Sub-manager's room is the grand staircase leading to the mess rooms of the junior clerks on the second floor while at the back of this staircase are spacious lavatories for the European clerks.

Retracing our steps still further we come to the Stationery room, having behind it the Head Compradore's room, which communicates with the Chinese side of the General Office or Bank. The only other room on the left side is the strongroom previously mentioned which faces the one on the European side. On the Chinese side there is also a lift running from the kitchen on the basement floor to the topmost floor of the building, also a back staircase leading to the upper floors and a staircase leading to the basement floor.[41]

The upper stories continued the tradition of residential quarters and dining facilities for the foreign staff of the Bank.

We reach the grand staircase leading to the first floor, where are the mess rooms of the junior clerks. This floor is divided into two equal parts by a wide passage that runs from end to end.

On the one side is a large dining room 33 feet by 24 ft 6 in, looking out on the Praya. There are also two storerooms, 18 feet by 10 feet, three bathrooms, and two bedrooms, 20 feet by 18 feet, looking out on the dome of the general office. On the other side of the passage there is, opposite the dining room, a drawing room of similar size, looking out on the Praya, with a billiard room adjoining, 36 feet 6 in by 24 feet. The centre of this side is taken up with a large bedroom, 24 feet 6 in by 20 feet, with a linen dressing room in front and three other bathrooms, while at the further end are two other bedrooms, looking out on the dome of the Bank.

Ascending now to the topmost or second floor we find this floor almost entirely taken up with bedrooms of various sizes, ranging from 21 ft by 18 ft to 25 ft by 24 ft and 27 ft by 18 ft. This part of the building is yet a good way from being complete, but judging from the plan, the rooms ought to be airy and comfortable. A wide corridor as on the other floors runs along the centre. There are also a number of bathrooms on this storey, which, like the others, are supplied with cold and hot water.[42]

The new Head Office building was a triumphant visual comment on Jackson's contribution to the prosperity of the Hongkong Bank. The timing was excellent; the building was completed a year before the first adverse report marred the memory of the early Jackson years. But whether flourishing or not, the Hongkong Bank needed these facilities; they were to be overshadowed by the Shanghai building of 1923 and eventually by those of Hong Kong successor buildings. Thus whatever wit or circumstance suggested to the popular mind, the 1886 Head Office building was never fairly known – white ants excepted – as 'Jackson's Folly'.

APPENDIX: MEMBERS OF THE HONGKONG BANK
BOARD OF DIRECTORS, 1876–1888

From:
February 1876

E.R. Belilios		Chairman
Adolf von André	Melchers and Co.	Deputy Chairman
J.F. Cordes	Wm Pustau and Co.	
H. Hoppius	Siemssen and Co.	
F.D. Sassoon	D. Sassoon, Sons and Co.	
A. McIver	P&O SN Co.	
S.W. Pomeroy	Russell and Co.	
7 members		

J.F. Cordes	Wm Pustau and Co.	(resigned Jan. 1877)
Edward Tobin	Gilman and Co.	(elected Jan. 1877)
William Keswick	Jardine, Matheson and Co.	(elected Jan. 1877)

February 1877

H. Hoppius	Siemssen and Co.	Chairman, 1877/78
F.D. Sassoon	D. Sassoon, Sons and Co.	Deputy Chairman, 1877/78
Adolf von André	Melchers and Co.	
A. McIver	P&O SN Co.	
S.W. Pomeroy	Russell and Co.	
Edward Tobin	Gilman and Co.	
William Keswick	Jardine, Matheson and Co.	
E.R. Belilios		
8 members		

S.W. Pomeroy	Russell and Co.	(resigned March 1877)
W.H. Forbes	Russell and Co.	(elected March 1877)
Adolf von André	Melchers and Co.	(resigned March 1877)
Wilhelm Reiners	Melchers and Co.	(elected March 1877)
Edward Tobin (died)	Gilman and Co.	(last meeting 31 Jan. 1878)
H.L. Dalrymple	Birley and Co.	(elected Feb. 1878)
A. McIver	P&O SN Co.	(on extended leave)
A. Lind	P&O SN Co.	(elected Jan. 1878)

February 1878

F.D. Sassoon	D. Sassoon, Sons and Co.	Chairman, 1878/79
W.H. Forbes	Russell and Co.	Deputy Chairman, 1878/79
E.R. Belilios		
William Keswick	Jardine, Matheson and Co.	
Wilhelm Reiners	Melchers and Co.	
H.L. Dalrymple	Birley and Co.	
A. Lind	P&O SN Co.	
H. Hoppius	Siemssen and Co.	
(A. McIver on extended leave)		
8 members + 1 on extended leave		

APPENDIX TO CHAPTER 10 (*cont.*)

W.S. Young	Gilman and Co.	(elected Feb. 1878)
H.L. Dalrymple	Birley and Co.	(Leave of absence June 1878)
Adam Lind	P&O SN Co.	(resigned, leaving HK, Nov. 1878)
A. McIver	P&O SN Co.	(returned from leave)

February 1879

Wm H. Forbes	Russell and Co.	Chairman, 1879/80
William Keswick	Jardine, Matheson and Co.	Deputy Chairman, 1879/80
E.R. Belilios		
Wilhelm Reiners	Melchers and Co.	
H.L. Dalrymple	Birley and Co.	
H. Hoppius	Siemssen and Co.	
W.S. Young	Gilman and Co.	
A. McIver	P&O SN Co.	
F.D. Sassoon	D. Sassoon, Sons and Co.	
9 members		
Wm H. Forbes	Russell and Co.	(resigned, leaving HK, Feb. 1880)

February 1880

William Keswick	Jardine, Matheson and Co.	Chairman, 1880/81
Alexander McIver	P&O SN Co.	Deputy Chairman, 1880/81
E.R. Belilios		
Wilhelm Reiners	Melchers and Co.	
H.L. Dalrymple	Birley and Co.	
H. Hoppius	Siemssen and Co.	
W.S. Young	Gilman and Co.	
F.D. Sassoon	D. Sassoon, Sons and Co.	
8 members		
W. Reiners	Melchers and Co.	(resigned March 1881)
Adolf von André	Melchers and Co.	(elected March 1881)
H. de C. Forbes	Russell and Co.	(elected April 1880)

February 1881

Alexander McIver	P&O SN Co.	Chairman, 1881/82
H.L. Dalrymple	Birley and Co.	Deputy Chairman, 1881/82
E.R. Belilios		
H. Hoppius	Siemssen and Co.	
W.S. Young	Gilman and Co.	
F.D. Sassoon	D. Sassoon, Sons and Co.	
Adolf von André	Melchers and Co.	
H. de C. Forbes	Russell and Co.	
9 members		
Adolf von André	Melchers and Co.	(resigned March 1881)
W. Reiners	Melchers and Co.	(elected March 1881)
Wm Keswick	Jardine, Matheson and Co.	(resigned April 1881)
F.B. Johnson	Jardine, Matheson and Co.	(elected April 1881)

APPENDIX TO CHAPTER 10 (*cont.*)

February 1882

H.L. Dalrymple	Birley and Co.	Chairman, 1882/83
H. de C. Forbes	Russell and Co.	Deputy Chairman, to March 1882
W. Reiners	Melchers and Co.	Deputy Chairman
		from March 1882/83
E.R. Belilios		(retired at meeting by not seeking reelection)
H. Hoppius	Siemssen and Co.	
W.S. Young	Gilman and Co.	
F.D. Sassoon	D. Sassoon, Sons and Co.	
F. Bulkeley Johnson	Jardine, Matheson and Co.	
Alexander McIver	P&O SN Co.	
Alexander P. McEwen	Holliday, Wise and Co.	(confirmed at meeting)
Meyer Elias Sassoon	E.D. Sassoon and Co.	(confirmed at meeting)

    11 less Belilios = 10 members

H de C. Forbes	Russell and Co.	(resigned March 1882)
C. Vincent Smith	Russell and Co.	(elected March 1882)

February 1883

W. Reiners	Melchers and Co.	Chairman, to Dec. 1883
W.S. Young	Gilman and Co.	Deputy Chairman, 1883/84
H. Hoppius	Siemssen and Co.	
F.D. Sassoon	D. Sassoon, Sons and Co.	
F.B. Johnson	Jardine, Matheson and Co.	
Alexander McIver	P&O SN Co.	
Alexander P. McEwen	Holliday, Wise and Co.	Chairman, from Dec. 1884
Meyer Elias Sassoon	E.D. Sassoon and Co.	
C. Vincent Smith	Russell and Co.	
H.L. Dalrymple	Birley and Co.	

    10 members

H. Hoppius	Siemssen and Co.	(resigned March 1883)
Albert Gultzow	Siemssen and Co.	(elected March 1883)
C. Vincent Smith	Russell and Co.	(resigned May 1883)
W.H. Forbes	Russell and Co.	(elected May 1883)
W. Reiners	Melchers and Co.	(resigned Dec. 1883)
M. Grote	Melchers and Co.	(elected Dec. 1883)

February 1884

Alexander P. McEwen	Holliday, Wise and Co.	Chairman, 1884/85
F.D. Sassoon	D. Sassoon, Sons and Co.	Deputy Chairman, 1884/85
F.B. Johnson	Jardine, Matheson and Co.	
W.S. Young	Gilman and Co.	
Alexander McIver	P&O SN Co.	
Meyer Elias Sassoon	E.D. Sassoon and Co.	
H.L. Dalrymple	Birley and Co.	
Albert Gultzow	Siemssen and Co.	
W. H. Forbes	Russell and Co.	
M. Grote	Melchers and Co.	

    10 members

APPENDIX TO CHAPTER 10 (*cont.*)

W.S. Young	Gilman and Co.	(resigned Feb. 1884)
F.B. Johnson	Jardine, Matheson and Co.	(resigned March 1884)
Wm Keswick	Jardine, Matheson and Co.	(elected March 1884)
C.D. Bottomley	Douglas Lapraik and Co.	(elected March 1884)
A. Gultzow	Siemssen and Co.	(resigned July 1884)
H. Hoppius	Siemssen and Co.	(elected July 1884)
Meyer Elias Sassoon	E.D. Sassoon and Co.	(resigned Feb. 1885)
E.E. Sassoon	E.D. Sassoon and Co.	(elected Feb. 1885)

February 1885

F.D. Sassoon	D. Sassoon, Sons and Co.	Chairman, 1885/86
A. McIver	P&O SN Co.	Deputy Chairman, 1885/86
Alexander P. McEwen	Holliday, Wise and Co.	
F.B. Johnson	Jardine, Matheson and Co.	
H.L. Dalrymple	Birley and Co.	
W.H. Forbes	Russell and Co.	
M. Grote	Melchers and Co.	
Wm Keswick	Jardine, Matheson and Co.	
C.D. Bottomley	Douglas Lapraik and Co.	
H. Hoppius	Siemssen and Co.	
E.E. Sassoon	E.D. Sassoon and Co.	
11 members		

E.E. Sassoon	E.D. Sassoon and Co.	(resigned Nov. 1885)
W.H. Forbes	Russell and Co.	(resigned Dec. 1885)
E.H.M. Huntington	Russell and Co.	(elected Dec. 1885)

February 1886

A. McIver	P&O SN Co.	Chairman, to June? 1886
M. Grote	Melchers and Co.	Deputy Chairman, 1886 then Acting Chairman, 1886/87
Alexander P. McEwen	Holliday, Wise and Co.	
F.B. Johnson	Jardine, Matheson and Co.	
H.L. Dalrymple	Birley and Co.	
Wm Keswick	Jardine, Matheson and Co.	
C.D. Bottomley	Douglas Lapraik and Co.	
H. Hoppius	Siemssen and Co.	
E.H.M. Huntington	Russell and Co.	
F.D. Sassoon	D. Sassoon, Sons and Co.	
10 members		

Wm Keswick	Jardine, Matheson and Co.	(resigned May 1886)
J. Bell-Irving	Jardine, Matheson and Co.	(elected May 1886)
W.H.F. Darby	Gibb, Livingston and Co.	(elected June 1886)

(F.D. Sassoon offered to resign in November due to ill health; not accepted)

February 1887

See explanation under February 1888.

M. Grote	Melchers and Co.	Chairman, to Sept. 1887
C.D. Bottomley	Douglas Lapraik and Co.	Deputy Chairman, 1887 Chairman, from Sept. 1887/88

APPENDIX TO CHAPTER 10·(*cont.*)

A. McIver	P&O SN Co.	
A. P. McEwen	Holliday, Wise and Co.	
H.L. Dalrymple	Birley and Co.	
H. Hoppius	Siemssen and Co.	
E.H.M. Huntington	Russell and Co.	
F.D. Sassoon	D. Sassoon, Sons and Co.	
J. Bell-Irving	Jardine, Matheson and Co.	Deputy Chairman from Sept. 1887
W.H.F. Darby	Gibb, Livingston and Co.	
10 members		

A. McIver	P&O SN Co.	(resigned April 1887)
J.S. Moses	E.D. Sassoon and Co.	(elected May 1887)
E.H.M. Huntington	Russell and Co.	(resigned July 1887)
W.H. Forbes	Russell and Co.	(elected July 1887)
M. Grote	Melchers and Co.	(resigned Sept. 1887)
S.C. Michaelsen	Melchers and Co.	(elected Sept. 1887)
F.D. Sassoon	D. Sassoon, Sons and Co.	(resigned Dec. 1887)
E.A. Solomon	D. Sassoon, Sons and Co.	(elected)
W.H.F. Darby	Gibb, Livingston and Co.	(resigned Jan. 1888)
B. Layton	Gibb, Livingston and Co.	(elected)
W.G. Brodie	Borneo Company, Ltd	(elected)
L. Poesnecker	Arnhold, Karberg and Co.	(elected)

February 1888
Hoppius is next for Chairman after Bottomley, but due to Grote having been Chairman (or Acting Chairman) 'for 18 months' (due to McIver's leave), Hoppius suggests the next Chairman should be British.

A. McConachie of Gilman and Co. 'elected' in error as it was thought Bottomley had resigned; the election was declared invalid – see text.

John Bell-Irving	Jardine, Matheson and Co.	Chairman, 1888/89
W.H. Forbes	Russell and Co.	Deputy Chairman, 1888/89
H. Hoppius	Siemssen and Co.	
A.P. McEwen	Holliday, Wise and Co.	
H.L. Dalrymple	Birley and Co.	
J.S. Moses	E.D. Sassoon and Co.	
S.C. Michaelsen	Melchers and Co.	
E.A. Solomon	D. Sassoon, Sons and Co.	
B. Layton	Gibb, Livingston and Co.	
W.G. Brodie	Borneo Company, Ltd.	
L. Poesnecker	Arnhold, Karberg and Co.	
C.D. Bottomley	Douglas Lapraik and Co. (on extended leave)	
11 members + 1 on leave		

H. Hoppius	Siemssen and Co.	(retired April 1888)
N.A. Siebs	Siemssen and Co.	(elected April 1888)
A.P. McEwen	Holliday, Wise and Co.	(resigned August 1888)
J.F. Holliday	Holliday, Wise and Co.	(elected August 1888)

APPENDIX TO CHAPTER 10 (*cont.*)

December 31, 1888

John Bell-Irving	Jardine, Matheson and Co.	Chairman, 1888/89
W.H. Forbes	Russell and Co.	Deputy Chairman, 1888/89
H.L. Dalrymple	Birley and Co.	
J.S. Moses	E.D. Sassoon and Co.	
S.C. Michaelsen	Melchers and Co.	
E.A. Solomon	D. Sassoon, Sons and Co.	
B. Layton	Gibb, Livingston and Co.	
W.G. Brodie	Borneo Company, Ltd	
L. Poesnecker	Arnhold, Karberg and Co.	
C.D. Bottomley	Douglas Lapraik and Co. (on extended leave)	
N.A. Siebs	Siemssen and Co.	
J.F. Holliday	Holliday, Wise and Co.	
12 members		

11

THE BANK AND ITS ORDINANCES –
REVISION AND RENEWAL, 1882–1890

When, after long negotiations, the Hongkong Bank was incorporated in 1866 and its revised Deed of Settlement accepted in 1867, no doubt directors took note that their charter had a time limit of 21 years and perhaps assumed that until 1887 their contacts with the British Treasury would be of little significance. And then, provided the Bank were reasonably prosperous, there would be a formal submission for renewal and the Bank would be chartered by ordinance for a further period of time.

Strangely, in view of the problems which arose, the renewal of the Bank's charter was accomplished without controversy. A last minute cable informed the Governor that Her Majesty had not been advised to disallow the ordinance. The Bank was rechartered on a schedule which some might legitimately regard as a 'cliff-hanger', but about which apparently no one in Hong Kong was at all concerned. The foreordained atmosphere which surrounded the early years of the Hongkong Bank prevailed once again.

There had, however, been stormy times in the fifteen years preceding the charter renewal. The Bank was aware of the problems, but they are concerns which feature primarily in the archives of government; the Bank might be delayed or even temporarily frustrated, but in the main its directors had other concerns.

The areas of contention were (i) extraterritoriality and the establishment of branches, (ii) the one-dollar note issue, (iii) the holding of reserves against the note issue, and (iv) the privileges which had been granted and then partially withdrawn in connection with the Hong Kong Savings Bank.

At one stage, the Treasury would have preferred to rewrite the Bank's ordinance of incorporation, but the delays and frustrations of inter-departmental communication would eventually force officials to permit partial decisions and piecemeal legislation. Indeed a fully revised ordinance was not enacted until 1929 and in 1936 the Chief Manager, V.M. Grayburn, was still writing to Government about an expansion of the one-dollar note issue.

The Savings Bank problem, which arose in 1884, while representative of the type of problem the Hongkong Bank faced in its relations with Government, is separate from the sequence of charter revisions and has, therefore, been considered in Chapter 10. The other issues are interlinked and involved the Bank and Government in trade-offs which partially satisfied the Treasury's prevailing theories while doing the least damage to the continuity of the Bank's business.

THE SINGAPORE BRANCH, THE NOTE ISSUE, AND THE ORDINANCE OF 1882

The Hongkong Bank took over from its Singapore merchant agent in 1877 and, recognizing that it needed Treasury authority to establish a branch, instructed H. Cope to open an agency, pending approval for the branch. Whatever other differences existed between a branch and agency, it seemed clear that only a branch could issue notes. The Bank, with the encouragement of Cope, wished to issue notes and in consequence precipitated a series of problems previously bypassed.

Using the very strict criterion that a branch is an office of a bank assigned its own capital, the Hongkong Bank had in effect opened branches in Shanghai, Yokohama, Manila, and London. As efforts by the Bank to have branches approved elsewhere had either been ignored by the Treasury or rebuffed on the grounds that the Treasury could not by its intervention remedy the inability of the Hong Kong legislature, being colonial, to enact legislation which would imply an extraterritorial capacity, the Bank established 'agencies'. And if the situation were particularly delicate, the 'agent' would be said to be acting, for this particular purpose, under the fiction that he merely represented Head Office.

In consequence of the Board's uncertainty of its authority, the distinction between branch and agency had been, to use a non-technical term, fudged. Thus agencies such as Amoy and Hankow issued notes and there were others which undertook full banking business with or without a note issue (see Table 11.1). When, however, the Bank wished to issue banknotes in Singapore, the Board was informed by Cope that the distinction would be enforced; to issue notes the Bank had to establish a branch; to establish a branch the Bank needed Treasury approval. The problem could no longer be bypassed.

The status of the Bank's agency in Singapore was changed to branch in 1881. In the intervening period the various authorities had worked on two major problems: (i) how, consistent with its ordinance of incorporation and Colonial Office policy, the Bank might best be permitted to establish a branch and (ii) how, given the Treasury objection to the Bank's one-dollar note issue, the Bank's request for permission to issue banknotes in Singapore might be granted in return for the Bank's agreement on other currency matters. The Bank had authority to issue notes from an authorized branch, but this authority could only be exercised according to the laws and regulations of the territory in which the branch was situated. In the case of Singapore specific permission from the Treasury was required.

Accordingly David McLean, the Bank's London Manager, petitioned the Lords Commissioners of the Treasury on December 13, 1877, citing section 4 of the ordinance of incorporation, and arguing, *inter alia*, that:

> the transactions between the Agency at Singapore and the head office at Hong Kong and the agencies at Amoy and Manila are very numerous and important, and in order fully to develop the Company's business, it is deemed desirable by the Court of Directors that there should be a Bank or branch Bank at Singapore instead of the present agency . . .

and requesting permission to open a branch.[1]

The authorization for the branch

Although the Treasury was reluctant to grant further privileges to the Bank while it enjoyed, as the Treasury put it, the monopoly of a small-note issue in Hong Kong, the desirability of the Bank's operating in the Straits Settlements was never in dispute. The Bank's preference for a branch was acceptable to the authorities provided the right way could be found to effect it.

The problem was to avoid appearing to give the Hong Kong legislature extraterritorial jurisdiction by simply accepting the Hongkong Bank as a corporation capable of existence in Singapore. The first proposal was for the Straits Settlement Legislative Council to enact a parallel ordinance effective for the Bank's operations in the Straits Settlements, and this procedure the Treasury advised in 1878.[2]

But anticipating the resolution to the extraterritorial problem embodied in Hong Kong Ordinance No. 29 of 1889 (see below), the Treasury subsequently concluded that a special Singapore ordinance would be inappropriate. Taking the logical position, described in Chapter 4, that a lack of competence to permit entailed also a lack of competence to prohibit, the Treasury revised its advice on the basis of international and intercolonial law, that corporate status created in one country will be recognized in other countries provided its presence (i) does not 'infringe the instrument of its foundation' and (ii) does not contravene the laws of the locality.[3]

And in another memo the Treasury added, 'in the absence of restrictive Banking legislation in the Straits Settlements, there would appear to be no absolute necessity in this case for a Straits ordinance'.[4]

Under the terms of the Hongkong Bank Ordinance (section 4), the Bank had to obtain permission from the Treasury to open a branch in, among other specified places, Singapore. The effectiveness of this provision rested not with its enactment by the Hong Kong Legislative Council but (i) by the fact that the

Treasury could instruct Singapore not to permit the branch and (ii) the gatekeeper function whereby some act of the Bank, disapproved of by the Treasury, could lead to Treasury refusal to approve other requests from the Bank, as for example the renewal of the charter, unless corrective measures were taken.

Thus, whether under section 4 or otherwise, the Bank needed Treasury approval to open a branch in Singapore. McLean's petition has been cited, and the required approval was granted in 1881 as the consequence of bargaining between the Bank and the authorities over matters concerning the currency, and to these issues this history now must turn.

The one-dollar note issue

The Treasury did not soon forget its defeat in the matter of the issue by the Hongkong Bank of one-dollar notes in 1872. The Bank acted in good faith, and no one suggested otherwise; it was Governor Kennedy who bore the brunt of Treasury criticism. But in view of the overwhelming support the Bank had received, the Treasury had backed down.[5]

The question of Hong Kong's currency could not, however, be neglected, and underlying much of the correspondence on this complex subject was the theme that, once the system had been reformed, the Hongkong Bank must be induced to withdraw its one-dollar note issue. The need for the Bank to obtain Treasury approval for the Singapore branch was the lever the Treasury had needed – the approval would be given in return for the Bank's formal undertaking to withdraw the offending notes whenever the Hong Kong Government was ready to introduce its own. To this the Bank's Board of Directors agreed in November 1880, but the correspondence was not forwarded to the Treasury for another nine months, with consequent delays and consideration of side-issues while the Hongkong Bank awaited the outcome.[6]

Once the position had been established that approval of the branch was connected with the note issue, important related problems were introduced.

First, although the Bank's shareholders had an unlimited liability for the note issue, the way in which this might be enforced was clumsy, and note-holders could well be deprived of their funds for some considerable period; they would appear to have been given no effective priority.

Secondly, the Bank was required by its charter to hold a one-third specie reserve at its Head Office against the note issue. Since prudence, even in the absence of local legislation, required a one-third reserve at the office of issue, the Bank was in the position of holding a reserve against its note issue in two places in a total amount far in excess of the amount intended by the authorities. The Bank sought relief in the form of revision of its charter, and this the Colonial Office saw as a particularly suitable moment to make the Treasury's point relative to the one-dollar note issue.[7]

Unfortunately these matters were not discussed between the Bank, the Hong Kong Government, the Colonial Office, the Treasury, and the Government of the Straits Settlements with the primary purpose of granting the Hongkong Bank's requests: (i) permission to open a branch in Singapore, (ii) permission to issue notes in the Straits Settlements, and (iii) a modification of the specie-reserve requirement. On the contrary, the whole atmosphere was clouded by the Treasury's obsession relative to the one-dollar note issue. Underlying it all were the faint beginnings of a movement, pressed particularly by the Straits Settlements authorities, for a government as opposed to a private-sector issue.

In August 1881, John Winton, the Bank's Singapore Agent, wrote pleadingly to the Colonial Secretary of the Straits Settlements reciting recent events, the Bank's immediate compliance with the requirements, and concluding, 'Here the matter rests.'[8] Eventually all official parties recognized that these long-term discussions, however important, were unfairly − perhaps improperly − delaying decisions on a private corporation's straightforward requests.[9]

Accordingly the Treasury approved the Hongkong Bank's opening of a Singapore branch.[10] The currency issues were then settled (i) by the passage in Singapore of an act which dealt not with the opening of a branch *per se* but with the method of registration and the right to issue notes and (ii) by the passage in Hong Kong of Ordinance No. 21 of 1882 which revised the Bank's charter to take account of the specie reserve and the unlimited liability problems.

Plans for an overall revision of the Bank's charter were, the Treasury thought, postponed until the renewal of the original ordinance as required by its own provisions on or before August 14, 1887; plans for currency reform including a 100% specie-backed Hong Kong Government one-dollar note issue were, the Treasury thought, under active consideration. On both these counts the Treasury would again be frustrated, but this did not affect the corporate constitution of the Hongkong Bank.

Hong Kong Ordinance No. 21 of 1882; Straits Ordinance No. X of 1881

The Straits ordinance is first in time, but the main issues are best considered in the context of the Hongkong and Shanghai Bank Ordinance Amendment Ordinance promulgated on December 13, 1882.

The Hong Kong ordinance[11]
On the question of the one-dollar note issue, the right of the Governor to permit the Bank to issue notes of a denomination less than $5 was withdrawn; the existing one-dollar note issue of $226,000 was permitted to remain, subject to

their 'unconditional withdrawal from circulation should the Government of the Colony decide to issue Small Notes of lower denomination than $5 . . .' Hereafter Hong Kong would be frustrated by the failure of currency reform and the inability of the Hongkong Bank, consequent to the provisions of the ordinance, to meet the community's needs for small-denomination currency.

The Bank's original ordinance provided that its notes were to be payable at the office of issue and at the Head Office in Hong Kong. The key amendment in the ordinance of 1882 brought the Hongkong Bank's position more into line with those of other chartered banks: banknotes were henceforth redeemable at the office of issue and also at the principal office in the territory of issue – each Settlement of the Straits Settlements being considered a separate territory for this purpose. Thus a note issued from Singapore was no longer by right redeemable at the Head Office in Hong Kong, but a note issued in Tientsin could be redeemed in Shanghai.

From this it followed that (i) the specie reserve was to be held at the 'establishment' of issue equivalent to one-third the total value of notes issued and circulating from that establishment and (ii) notes could only be reissued from the original office of issue. Thus a Singapore-issued note taken to Penang and encashed (at the rate of the day for sight bills on Singapore) had to be sent back by the Bank to Singapore to be reissued; it could not be paid out over the counter in Penang.

The total limit to notes in circulation remained an amount equal to the paid-up capital of the Bank.

Of the Eastern exchange banks, the Hongkong Bank was the only one whose shareholders had unlimited liability for the note issue. And yet in the event of winding up, the note-holders received no priority; indeed, if the practical consequences of unlimited liability are questioned, the note-holders may have had no advantage at all over other creditors. The ordinance of 1882 improved on this by granting the right of immediate payout to note-holders. The unlimited liability provision would come into force only if the Bank proved unable to pay off all creditors; then, to the extent that the Bank's assets had been used to pay off note-holders, the general creditors were entitled to an additional sum from the shareholders up to this amount.

The provisions of this ordinance were obviously sound, improving the position of the Bank and the public. As for the one-dollar issue, the Bank had already agreed to limit the issue. The 'concession' it made in return for the Singapore permission and modification of the specie-backing requirements more than compensated for the contentious privilege of a small-note issue which would, in any case, most certainly have been withdrawn on renewal of the charter in 1887.

The Straits ordinance

The correct legal interpretation of the Bank's position outside the Colony of Hong Kong was that it was a legal corporation in any area where its presence was not forbidden and where it complied with local regulations relative to registration. The Straits Ordinance, No. X of 24 November 1881, set out the regulations under which the Hongkong Bank could operate in the Straits Settlements: for example it had to file copies with the Registrar of Companies of its Hong Kong ordinance and amendments together with the Deed of Settlement as revised.

The Hongkong Bank was obligated to register in this way in each Settlement where it established an agency or branch, as, for example, in Penang in 1884.

The remainder of the ordinance anticipated the provisions of the Hong Kong ordinance so far as the Bank's note issuing activities were concerned. This was a consequence of the additional problems involved in formulating the Hong Kong ordinance; the Colonial Office had in fact agreed to the principles involved in both ordinances, but working out the details had delayed enactment of the more important Hong Kong ordinance.

This whole exercise would seem to have sifted through the conflicting concepts of extraterritoriality and reached a consistent solution. Unfortunately, this was not so; the question of extraterritoriality would arise again in the period to 1889. A confusion, addressed but not finally agreed, would develop from the supposed difference between establishing a branch in those places specifically referred to in section 4 of the Bank's original ordinance and in those places not so mentioned. But the matter is better considered below.

The Bank, in keeping with its usual practice, had been operating in Singapore since 1877; it even shared with the Chartered Mercantile the Treasury business. On the matter of the note issue, however, not even the Hongkong Bank would act prematurely. The Bank waited until permission was granted and first issued its notes in Singapore from December 1, 1881.

Penang and the Malay States

Under the provisions of its Straits Settlements ordinance the Hongkong Bank was empowered to open in the other Settlements, subject to stated registration procedures. In 1884 the Bank sought and obtained Treasury approval for opening a branch in Penang, including the right to issue banknotes.[12] No new principles were involved.

Unfortunately, the efforts of the Officer Administering the Government of the Straits Settlements, Cecil C. Smith, to facilitate the Hongkong Bank's entry into Perak with note-issuing privileges were not only ill-timed but reintroduced the extraterritoriality question, specifically the distinction between those places cited in the Hongkong Bank's charter and all other places – Singapore and Penang were mentioned, the Malay States were not. And to ensure the point was understood, the Treasury added, 'It does not appear to my Lords that the Native States can be described as in Penang or Singapore.'[13]

With this issue raised once again the Colonial Office undertook further research and concluded that the Hongkong Bank, with agencies in Lyons, Manila, and San Francisco, evidently supposed they were not in fact restricted. They asked the Treasury for a legal opinion, coinciding with the Bank's own appeal for reconsideration. This led to the Treasury's obtaining a new and favourable interpretation of the international law on the subject.

Postscript, 1883–1884

The problem with the arrangements completed in 1882 was that Hong Kong and Singapore were still without an adequate supply of one-dollar notes, the Bank's issue having been frozen at $226,000 for issue in Hong Kong only, although they were also circulating in the neighbouring districts of China. Neither the Singapore nor the Hong Kong Governments were prepared to handle the issue of such notes, and in 1883 David McLean in London, acting on behalf of the Bank, submitted a formal petition to the Secretary of State for permission to issue one-dollar notes in Singapore.[14]

In 1884 the Hongkong Bank submitted a proposal to the Hong Kong authorities whereby it would issue additional one-dollar notes against a 100% reserve managed under rigorous conditions.

That is to say, the Bank [wrote Thomas Jackson] would earmark and deposit in a separate vault, the keys of which would be kept by the Colonial Treasurer, a special reserve of Mexican Dollars, equal to the full extent of its one dollar notes in circulation.

This reserve would be, in case of a suspension of payment, inalienable to any other purpose than that of paying the Notes.[15]

Unfortunately, although this solution commended itself to Governor G.F. Bowen and had the support of the Finance Committee – among whose nine members were the Hongkong Bank's auditor, Chief Manager, Deputy Chairman, and a second director – the ordinance of 1882 had stripped the Bank of the right to issue additional one-dollar notes under any circumstances, and new legislation would have to be passed, rescinding in part the but recently passed amendment ordinance.[16]

For some time the relevant discussions seemed to have missed this point, but eventually even with the facts before them the Colonial Office officials minuted on the basis of a *non sequitur*: the Hongkong Bank was a private institution designed to make a profit; hence the Bank would not issue the one-dollar notes even under these stringent conditions unless they would make a profit from the issue; therefore, the issue of one-dollar notes was profitable. From this they concluded that there was no reason why, if the need for such notes were so great, the Hong Kong Government should not undertake the issue and make the profit.[17]

Furthermore, the officials continued, even if sanctioned would the Hongkong Bank's one-dollar issue be all that secure? Surely on winding up, the claims of all note-holders would have to be considered. Although the one-dollar note-holders would eventually be paid in full, they would 'at any rate be kept waiting'. The risk of panic would not, it was thought, be removed altogether.

Lord Derby, the Secretary of State for the Colonies, regretted that the Hong Kong Government 'have not seen their way simply to accept the proposal for a government issue'.[18]

Treasury reception of the Bank's proposal was even less kind. But a new element was shaping policy. In 1884 the Oriental Bank Corporation had failed, and Governor Gordon of Ceylon had agreed to guarantee that bank's note issue – as had the Hongkong Bank, the Chartered, and the Chartered Mercantile in Singapore. The Governor's action, taken without reference to the Colonial Office was, however, subsequently endorsed by the Secretary of State, and the Treasury were suspicious of any scheme for note issue which might involve the appearance of government involvement and hence possible ultimate financial responsibility.[19]

The matter was referred to counsel quoting the Bank's original ordinance but neglecting to refer to the amendments made in 1882. These were forwarded after the original opinion was rendered.[20] The opinion was unfavourable – creditors would rank *pari pasu*, in contradiction to an opinion rendered in 1889 concerning the efficacy of the Bank's hypothecation of securities against the note issue. In consequence, the Lords saw no merit in the Bank's plan and concluded, without explanation, that the special reserve proposal was 'ingeniously contrived to secure a maximum of advantage for the Bank and a maximum of disadvantage for the Government'.[21]

It is clear, however, that the target of Treasury criticism was not the Hongkong Bank but the Secretary of State for the Colonies. Objecting to the Bank's proposal was punishment for Derby's sanctioning the Governor of Ceylon's guarantee of the Oriental Bank note issue. The Treasury not unreasonably saw the principle behind the guarantee as applicable to a bank failure in any colony and thus as a conclusive argument against any private note issue in any Crown Colony. The Treasury concluded:

... and My Lords are in consequence resolved not to assent to any extension of existing note privileges in such Colonies.

They may add that in their opinion it is incumbent on the Secretary of State to avail himself of every legitimate opportunity for carrying out the policy which he has inaugurated, and to substitute a state issue for private issues in Colonies which are not self-governing.[22]

And with these thoughts, the Bank's proposal and the requirements of Hong Kong and the Straits Settlements became caught in the cross-fire of inter-departmental arguments for and against colonial government note issues.

THE RENEWAL OF THE CHARTER, ORDINANCE NO. 15 OF 1887

The purpose of incorporation by a charter of limited duration was to enable all relevant parties, but especially the Government, to review the situation. It was a convenient time to cause the terms of the charter to conform with changed regulations or practices, to consolidate amendments, or to impose new limitations. Given the contentious nature of much of the Bank's recent relations with the Treasury, one might have expected full advantage to be taken of the end, in August 1887, of the Bank's first 21 years.

In fact, nothing of the kind happened. The granting of the necessary ordinance was a non-event.

Initial approaches

The Hongkong Bank was well-prepared. In February 1886 the Board of Directors made arrangements for an extraordinary meeting of shareholders to follow on the regular semi-annual General Meeting. Accordingly the Chairman proposed:

That the Court of Directors be authorized to apply for and accept a Renewed or Supplemental Ordinance to renew or supplement the Hongkong and Shanghai Bank Ordinance of 1866, and for the extension of the time for which the said Ordinance was passed, for a further term of 21 years or for such other period as may be by such renewed ordinance provided.

Approval was unanimous, and the necessary second meeting, held on March 17, confirmed the resolution.

Apparently the Colonial Office also anticipated that an early introduction of the subject was necessary. The Treasury had previously intimated that the charter and amendments needed to be consolidated.[23] But when the topic was broached in 1881 the Treasury considered it too early. By the time the documents were actually laid before the Treasury, it was too late.

The Secretary of State for the Colonies suggested to the Treasury that, 'as the term in which the Bank is authorized to carry on business is rapidly running out', the Hongkong Bank be invited to submit its proposals for the terms under which its charter might be renewed. After the controversies of the previous six years, this was more than the Treasury could take.

My Lords are unwilling to increase the number of questions connected with the currency and banking arrangements of the small settlement of Hong Kong which are and have been for years under consideration, and they view with apprehension the proposed invitation to the Bank to submit its general views on the intricate subjects at least five years before the expiration of the ordinance under which it carries on business.

They think further that when the time comes the Bank may safely be trusted to look after its own interests and propose amendments which it thinks necessary without an invitation of the unlimited character which the Secretary of State appears to contemplate.[24]

The reader of the Treasury and Colonial Office files cannot help but sympathize with My Lords of the Treasury, but the fact is that the bulk of the correspondence emanates from the bureaucracy; the Bank, with due allowance for the language of the time, kept to the point. Contrary to Treasury expectations, the Bank did not propose amendments; the Treasury's opinion on the ordinance prolonging the Bank's life would come first in the form of comments on an ordinance actually passed by the Hong Kong Legislative Council.

The never fully resolved problem of extraterritoriality was not an issue that the Hongkong Bank would voluntarily revive, but events in Manila forced the Bank to reapproach Government. Although the moment of charter renewal was not used either by Government or the Bank as an opportunity for resolving potential problems, yet even as the final stages of the relevant ordinance were being processed, the Bank had initiated correspondence which would force a revision of the terms of that ordinance – after much discussion and in 1889. The extraterritorial problem, real or imagined, could not be avoided.

The granting of the renewed charter

The next reference to the Hongkong Bank's charter renewal after the 1881/82 exchange between the Treasury and the Colonial Office appears in the explanatory correspondence accompanying the actual Ordinance, No. 15 of 1887, as passed by the Hong Kong Legislative Council. The ordinance provided for the extension of the life of the corporation for a further 21 years from August 14 under the terms of the original charter as amended; it also contained, as required by the Royal Instructions, a clause suspending the operation of these provisions until news of Her Majesty's pleasure not to disallow the ordinance had been received in Hong Kong.

The text was received in the Colonial Office on June 11, 1887, and time was, therefore, short. However, the Colonial Office did not appear concerned. The minutes summarize the history of the affair and recall that the Colonial Office had been willing to discuss the matter in 1881 but that the Treasury had in 1882 urged delay. The amending ordinance of 1882 had in fact covered the only subjects still in dispute with the Bank, and the minutes accordingly conclude with the unusual note that 'it appears to me we have nothing to say as to the present ordinance'.[25]

The ordinance was then sent to the Treasury where it was received on July 28. While they had no objection, the Treasury did point out that, given the fact the original ordinance would expire on August 14 at which point and in the absence of confirmation of the renewing ordinance the Hongkong and Shanghai Bank would cease to exist, the Treasury had been given little time had it found objections.[26]

This response was received at the Colonial Office on August 10. There were but four days of life left for the Bank. Fortunately the telegraph was in working order, and the Government of Hong Kong received the following – sent at 2:00 p.m. August 13 – say 10:00 p.m. Hong Kong time, that is with two hours to spare:

'DARAXLES 166 ADDABLE 15 CONFIRMED'

which being interpreted is, 'Referring to your despatch No. 166, Ordinance No. 15 is confirmed'.[27]

The Hongkong and Shanghai Banking Corporation was authorized to conduct banking business for another 21 years.

JURADO, MANILA, AND ORDINANCE NO. 29 OF 1889

DEVELOPMENTS IN THE PHILIPPINE ISLANDS

Despite the uncertainty existing over the Hongkong Bank's ability under Ordinance No. 5 of 1866 (and, subsequently, No. 15 of 1887) to establish itself outside Hong Kong, it seemed as if the prediction of the Colonial Office official in 1872 had been soundly based – the Government in Hong Kong, even with the requisite power, would never interfere with the Bank wherever it went.[28]

Indeed by 1887 the question of extraterritoriality appeared of little practical moment. If the Bank had not received authorization for its expansion in the open ports of China and Japan, there had been no objections; even during periods of controversy with the Treasury the Bank's unilateral actions had not adversely affected the outcome. Agencies in India had been set up with the knowledge of the Treasury and the approval of the Indian Government, the Bank's operations in London had never been questioned, and the branches in Singapore and Penang had been established only after a thorough consideration of all the circumstances.

These operations had, however, two characteristics which made them less controversial – (i) the locations involved were specifically referred to in section 4 of the incorporating ordinance and (ii) with the exception of the open ports (where the British had extraterritorial jurisdiction), no foreign country was involved. It was on the question of Saigon that the Treasury had, in fact, first refused to act.

Thus the question as to the ultimate limits of the Bank's right to claim a corporate existence was still left open to debate.

The Board of Directors was not unaware of the potential problem. When W.H. Harries and C.I. Barnes were first sent to San Francisco and Manila respectively, they were instructed to advertise under their own names as special agents for the Bank. But this nice distinction was soon lost sight of, and in the Philippines, particularly, the operations of the Hongkong Bank were those of a regular branch or branch bank.

The issue of the Bank's status could equally well have been raised in the United States or Batavia. In fact, it was raised in Manila at the instigation of Jurado and Co., a constituent against which the Bank had brought an action in 1885. Consequently the whole question of the Bank's rights under its ordinance had to be reconsidered. After some confusion and change of position, the Imperial authorities agreed to a clarifying amendment which, whether necessary or not, was incorporated in Ordinance No. 29 of 1889 and ended all discussion. Indeed, it may be said that only with this ordinance was the history of the Hongkong Bank's incorporation process complete.

The Bank's status in the Philippines

Although the original ordinance accepted the principle of extraterritoriality, it attempted to duplicate as closely as possible the provisions of a standard Imperial charter. Therefore, in reciting that 'nothing herein contained shall restrict the said Company . . .' it then distinguished between branches in enumerated locations which would require the consent of the Treasury and agencies for 'exchange, deposit, and remittance' which did not require such consent. This created two problems for the Bank: (i) the Treasury throughout the period to 1888 refused, except in the case of the Straits Settlements, to acknowledge its capacity under the ordinance and (ii) the Bank did not confine the activities of its 'agencies' to exchange, deposit, and remittance, but, in Manila and Iloilo at least, conducted a full banking business.

The discussions arising from the intra-governmental and Bank correspondence from 1887–1889 reached agreement on the proposition that whatever impediment the Bank suffered from the original ordinance it could be corrected by amending the relevant clause in section 4 to read that nothing therein should be deemed to restrict the company, with Treasury consent, from establishing branches or agencies 'at any place out of the Colony in conformity with the law of such place'.

To establish a branch the Bank had to obtain two approvals, one from the British Treasury and one from the relevant authorities (if so required) in the host country. The first was unnecessary except as a matter of Imperial policy, but it had the key function of eliminating any argument that the Bank was not a properly constituted corporation under British law, a provision incorporated in British commercial treaties and the legal basis for such a company to register in the foreign country.

These preliminaries were important because, although the whole controversy over the Bank's authority to open branches in non-specified territories – specifically in the Philippines – led to an emergency revision of its ordinance, the Bank had in fact been deficient in not having registered as required by Philippine law. When it attempted to do so during the Jurado controversy, it was barred by the Manila courts, but these were overruled by Madrid. The Hongkong Bank was actually registered and recognized in the Philippines some months before the passage of the special amending ordinance of 1889.

The Bank's status as a corporation properly constituted under British law had been recognized by the highest Spanish courts before the passage of the ordinance which satisfied the British Treasury. The specific crisis was apparently the consequence of a particular political and legal situation in Manila at the time, aggravated by Jurado and Co.'s knowledge of the rejection of the Bank's earlier efforts, in 1872–1873, to eliminate the alleged deficiencies in its charter.

The security of the note issue – a new problem

By 1889 the British Treasury had a new concern and its enthusiasm for an amending ordinance was not wholly disinterested. Just as in the Singapore case the Treasury was obsessed with the question of the one-dollar note issue, so now they were concerned with the consequences of the failure of the Oriental Bank in 1884 and the guarantee of the Oriental's 'private' note issue agreed by the Governor of Ceylon. In every Crown Colony where a banknote issue was permitted, there now existed, as the result of the policy of the Secretary of State for the Colonies, a *de facto* contingent liability of Government – and therefore a possible claim on the taxpayers – to meet the obligations of a private-sector corporation over which neither the Colonial Government nor the Treasury exercised any effective control, charters and regulations notwithstanding.

The Treasury solution was to have the issuing banks hypothecate securities as a special reserve for the note issue. This new measure could only be enforced, however, either when the bank's charter came up for renewal or through its voluntary agreement, legally executed. This latter was likely only if the bank wished a favour from the Government. The Treasury waited; the Hongkong Bank's crisis in Manila provided the opportunity.

This direct interference with the Bank's activities was not inconsistent with the Treasury's policy of withdrawing from the pretence of supervising the activities of chartered banks, a policy consequent on the 1880 discussions on colonial chartered banking. The lack of any supervision, especially with reference to the opening of agencies and branches, made it all the more important that the politically necessary ultimate responsibility of the Government for the note issue be minimized by protective provisions which were legally certain and which did not require supervision of banking operations *per se*.

Thus although Ordinance No. 29 of 1889 dealt exclusively with the extraterritoriality question, the Treasury consented to advise in favour of its confirmation only on receipt of an agreement that the Hongkong Bank would hypothecate securities to the value of one-third of its paid-up capital as security for the note issue. The Treasury was once again taking advantage of its 'gate-keeper' function to impose a new regulation on the Bank in return for what must be called, despite any question of real necessity, the grant of a distinct advantage. There is after all much to be gained in banking from the elimination of uncertainty.

The Jurado case and events in the Philippines[29]

How long the Bank might have continued to operate in an atmosphere of constitutional uncertainty is impossible to tell. Perhaps if Bank agencies had operated only as agencies in the narrow definition contained in the charter, no problem would have arisen. But the Bank was operating a branch bank in the Philippines under the style of 'agency' and it was doing so without specific sanction in its charter. Given time this would be challenged.

The actual case involving a Philippine company, Jurado and Co., and their London friends, was prolonged, only in part dealing with the issues being considered in this chapter. Nevertheless, its importance to the Bank is sufficiently great to warrant an extended exposition. Parts of the story are, therefore, a digression from the main theme.

The narrative makes clear that the Bank's immediate problem, its right to a corporate personality in the Philippines, was solved when the Bank had complied with the registration requirements of the Philippine Government. The ordinance of 1889 proved unnecessary. The Bank was not to know this when the crisis loomed in the early months of that year, and, in appealing to the British authorities, the Bank had aroused new interest in the whole matter; it was too late to withdraw.

The next section will, therefore, deal with the events leading up to the passage of the ordinance; in this section, the Jurado case is described.

The basic features of the original case

The saga began on March 14, 1885, when the then Manager, Barnes, acting as agent of the Hongkong and Shanghai Banking Corporation and holding their power of attorney, filed a petition in the Court of First Instance of the District of Tondo, Manila, that the firm of Jurado and Co. be declared insolvent.

Exactly ten years later to the day the Audiencia, the Supreme Court in the Philippine Islands, decided the bankruptcy case in the Bank's favour, the bankruptcy was published in May 1895 and confirmed on appeal by the Supreme Court in Madrid in July of the following year. Much had happened in between and a little more was to happen afterwards.

The background is reasonably straightforward. In 1883 the Hongkong Bank financed the purchase and shipment of goods by the London firm of M.R. Jurado and Co. Drafts for the value of the merchandise were accepted first by Don Ricardo Regidor y Jurado, a partner of the firm in London, and later by Jurado and Co. in Manila, who took possession of the goods.

Subsequently Regidor obtained from the Bank in Manila a credit for $20,000 for three years at 8% by selling two houses of his in Manila to the Bank for the sum of over $40,000 under a covenant to re-convey the same should a better price be offered by another buyer. The latter figure included two mortgages, one in favour of Obras Pias and the other in favour of a Don Gonzalo Tuason. In February 1884 Don Ricardo received another credit, for $10,000, by selling a third house on the same terms, and in March his firm endorsed to the Bank ten promissory notes for $5,000 each, for a total $50,000.

Between August 1 and October 31, the invoices for merchandise received by the firm as consignment on commission totalled over $70,000, but the deposits which the firm had agreed to make in the Bank were not made, and Barnes received information that goods stored in Jurado's warehouses were being withdrawn. Barnes then protested the notes and drafts endorsed by Jurado and Co., by then matured, and filed an action of voluntary jurisdiction in order to obtain the return of a corresponding amount of merchandise.

In the immediate subsequent proceedings it developed that the Bank was not the only creditor, the houses had been over-valued, the maker of the $50,000 in promissory notes a silent partner, and the value of the goods stored in the warehouses worth little more than a third of the amount placed on them as security. Thereupon Barnes petitioned that Jurado be declared bankrupt and he, on behalf of the Bank, and a certain Don Pedro Gruet independently instituted criminal proceedings for embezzlement.

Jurado questions the personality of the Bank

At this point the case becomes relevant to the extraterritoriality question. Jurado's lawyers pleaded that the Bank had no personality in the Philippines and claimed damages; in January 1887, despite the fact that the Bank had been paying Philippine taxes since 1872, judgement was given by the Audiencia against the Bank on the grounds of lack of status, the Bank's lawyer was refused the right to appear in court, and the company, which denied failure to pay, had reserved the right of action for damages.

The Hongkong Bank reacted, as it had to do, on two fronts: it attempted to protect itself in Manila and to have its status as a corporation accepted in the Philippines through representations in Madrid. The success of the first became dependent on the second, and thus, until June 1889 when the Bank became registered in Manila, it was in a difficult position.

In early 1888 it even seemed that the case might be settled out of Court if the Hongkong Bank would pay Regidor $108,000. The Board of Directors in Hong Kong at first agreed in principle and negotiations were held, but two members of the Board, the Deputy Chairman, W.H. Forbes (of Russell and Co.), and H.L. Dalrymple (of Birley and Co.), after a visit to Manila, recommended no compromise even at the risk of closing the branch, and it was at this time that the Bank decided to take the main case, the bankruptcy of Jurado and Co., to Madrid. In consequence the Board of Directors set aside a further $100,000 to contingencies rather than to the reserves (see Chapter 9).

From this point until the final settlement in 1903 the Bank suffered harassment. In October 1888, for example, the Bank's Manager, G.H. Townsend (East in 1878), was placed under house arrest on the charge, subsequently proved unsubstantiated and withdrawn, that he had been signing cheques in Manila dated from Hong Kong in order to avoid taxation. The Bank's success in securing Townsend's release in November was an indication that justice could be obtained and that the eventual outcome of the overall case would be successful.

The next threat to the Hongkong Bank was the seizure of its funds, and indeed in March 1889 G.H. Townsend cabled that Jurado and Co. had embargoed $330,000 with respect to debts claimed and that a further $500,000 might be claimed for damages.

The Bank had already asked the Banco de Castilla, Madrid, to request approval of the Spanish Government for the establishment of the Bank's agencies in Manila and Iloilo retroactively. Fortuitously, the relatively junior Harry Lamond (East in 1883), who was the officer in Manila most familiar with the details of the case, had recently reached London on emergency sick leave. The Board took advantage of the situation to send him on to Madrid where he stood by to assist the Bank's counsel there. The expense the Board was willing to incur measured the importance they attached to the case.

But it was clear that Jurado and Co. were desperate and that the Bank should be fully prepared. The Board sought the cooperation of the Chartered Bank and the British Consul.

With the former there was cooperation, but the Consul was placed in a difficult position.

His first response to the Bank's appeal was to call on the Governor-General of the Philippines together with legal advisers who made the case that the embargo was illegal, no evidence of indebtedness having been presented by Jurado and Co. The Governor-General agreed to take up the matter privately with the President of the Audiencia.

The Consul had been reinforced in his resolve to assist the Bank by a petition from British merchants:

. . . calling [his] attention to the serious consequences which were likely to arise to all commercial interests here, and to British interests in particular, through what they considered the illegal actions of the Spanish Courts against the Bank, and this letter [the Consul informed the Foreign Secretary in London] I sent to the Governor-General.[30]

But at this point history intervened.

British Government doubts on the Bank's status

Regidor came to the Consul's private residence and presented him with the opinion that the Bank had no right to exist in Manila, the story of the disallowed ordinance of 1872, and the conclusion that the Bank was in every way *ultra vires*.

While this did not alter the facts of the claims and counter-claims in Manila, it did undermine the determination of the Consul, who was apparently faced with the need to assist a British corporation, not on its legal merits, but because of the danger its closure would cause to British interests in the Philippines.

The Consul continued his account of events in the following terms:

I confess, My Lord, that this information quite bewildered me. It appeared to me utterly inexplicable how an Institution of the high commercial standing and respectability of the Hongkong and Shanghai Banking Corporation could act deliberately in direct contravention of its statutes, and of the express orders of Her Majesty's Secretary of State for the Colonies. Further the agent here [G.H. Townsend] was kept in the dark and did not know of the prohibition, nor did his legal Adviser, Dr Godinez; and it is I trust needless to say that had I been aware of it I would have taken no step with the local Spanish authorities on behalf of the Bank without first soliciting Your Lordship's instructions.[31]

In view of a possible further embargo on the Bank's funds, the Consul requested urgent instructions, adding, however:

. . . that whether or not any plausible reasons can be produced for having started [the branch of the Hongkong Bank] here without the necessary official sanction, it has, as a matter of fact, been in actual operation for the last 15 years, and has conducted business on so large a scale that its outstandings must be enormous. Were therefore the sudden necessity to arise for it to close its doors immense loss, not only to the Bank but to British Commerce generally, must ensue. In view of this contingency, and having consulted with several of the leading Merchants here whose interests would be greatly prejudiced were the Branch withdrawn, I have ventured to give the following advice to Mr Townsend, the Agent . . .[32]

(i) to apply afresh to HM Government for permission to open in the Philippines, and if successful to (ii) ascertain the requirements under Spanish law for establishing a branch in the Philippines, and (iii) after fulfilling these requirements ensure that the permission is retroactive. These were the steps which the Bank was taking, and it would be successful, although not, as it turned out, in the same order.

As the whole process started with a London firm, it is not surprising that in April 1889 M.R. Jurado and Co. also appealed to the Foreign Office, claiming it was the Hongkong Bank that had instituted the proceedings and had insisted on pressing them. As a consequence the Foreign Office had second thoughts and in May instructed the Ambassador in Madrid to suspend action relative to the Bank. The Foreign Office subsequently observed that the matter could be allowed to rest as the cases were proceeding in the normal way through the courts of Spain, and the British authorities could meanwhile pursue the basic question of the authority of the Bank and how the *status quo* might be regularized.[33]

The Bank would now, as it had earlier in the years of its formation, push through the formalities of the various departments on the grounds that it was a going concern and that vital financial and economic interests – and not only those of the Bank – were at stake.

The Spanish solution

The intervention by the Foreign Office on the Bank's behalf in Manila had been in terms of the 1883 British Commercial Treaty with Spain, with no mention of the Bank's supposed equivocal position relative to British law. The Spanish authorities thus proceeded independently of the events which led to the amended charter; they eventually authorized the Bank's registration.

In May 1889 the Supreme Court in Manila signed an order for the registration of the Bank, and, after some further delay, the Bank was in fact registered in June. Also in June the Supreme Court in Madrid gave a favourable verdict as to the question of the Bank's personality. There had been a brief 'Catch-22' situation, described by the Bank's London Manager, David McLean, in a letter to the Foreign Office, whereby the Bank found it impossible to register as a corporation in Manila because, since it was not yet a corporation, it had no personality to achieve the deed. But the Bank was duly registered.[34]

The Madrid Embassy made a summary report to the Foreign Office on the state of the cases pending, noting that the Bank had won a criminal case in which it had been charged with defrauding the revenue by using unstamped cheques.[35] At the same time the case for the bankruptcy of Jurado and Co. was proceeding satisfactorily.

Postscript on the Jurado case

All was not over.

In 1891 a new embargo, this time for $900,000, was made on the Bank without notice, and all the branch's available cash, $290,000, was sealed but not removed. François de Bovis, then the Hongkong Bank's Chief Manager, again had to request government assistance, this time from the strong position of a revised charter and legal registration in Manila. The Officer Administering the Government cabled the Colonial Office:

Position in Manila most serious. Hongkong Bank seized illegally by petty judge. Local authorities powerless. Madrid instructions apparently ignored. Unless prompt assistance is rendered by Her Majesty's Minister for Foreign Affairs or by Fleet mischief may be incalculable.[36]

In a subsequent letter the Officer Administering the (Hong Kong) Government added the interesting speculation that the new embargo (otherwise inexplicable) might be in retaliation for recent anti-gambling legislation which had specifically banned Manila lottery tickets in the Colony.[37]

The Foreign Office instructed both the Consul in Manila and the Ambassador in Madrid to seek a final solution to the affair. In consequence the action by a Manila judge was ruled illegal and he was removed, but the tie-up of the Bank's cash still totalled $620,000, on all of which interest was being lost – and, incalculable, customers being inconvenienced. Early in 1892 the first embargo was removed, but subsequently reimposed, and at the Bank's August 20, 1892, meeting of shareholders the Chairman, after advising that $3 million would have to be withdrawn from the Reserve Fund to meet general losses, turned to the Manila situation.

I must say that it seems very hard on us that our property should be thus locked up, no one can dispute our ability to pay the amount, and we have never attempted, and never should attempt to escape our liabilities under the Laws of Spain or of any other country where we have carried on our Banking business . . .

By the end of 1892 the Bank had apparently won its cases in Madrid and the embargoes on its funds were lifted in April 1893, although appeals kept the matter before the courts until August 1894 when the funds were actually in the possession of the Bank. H.R. Coombs (East in 1880), then the Bank's Manager in Manila, urged a generous payment to their lawyer, Icaza, and to various other advisers and procurators, otherwise the case might have dragged on. Icaza himself died in 1896.

In January 1895 recognizing presumably that the case was turning against them, Regidor went to Hong Kong but, on the advice of Coombs, the Board refused to compromise, and the definitive judgement of bankruptcy was issued in March and confirmed in August 1896. In the interim, judgement was brought against the Bank locally for $10,700 and, when the Bank refused to pay pending the outcome of an appeal, an attempt was made by the authorities to force open the Bank's treasury door. This was stopped by order of the Governor-General, and the decision on appeal was ultimately favourable.

For the sake of completeness it should be recorded that an effort by Jurado and Co. to impose a further embargo on the Bank's funds in 1900 was unsuccessful, but that the Board in 1903 approved the recommendation of the then Manager, H.D.C. Jones (East in 1884), that the Bank accept Regidor's offer to forgo all further action against the Bank on payment *ex gratia* of Mex$25,000, provided that such an agreement was in accordance with American law. A minute in 1904 records that the case had been settled without any possibility of resuscitation largely through the efforts of Jones.

Thus the 'notorious' Jurado case was concluded, but not without credit first being given to both the Chartered Bank and the Banco Español-Filipino (subsequently the Bank of the Philippine Islands) for their assistance, which had included guarantees, physical facilities, and, in the case of the former, actual business cooperation.

To the Chartered Bank of India, Australia and China the Board of the Hongkong Bank wrote a formal letter of appreciation. The author of their history noted, 'The Chartered Bank and the Hongkong Bank were on better terms in Manila than anywhere else in the East . . .'[38] The Hongkong Bank had reason to be thankful this was so.

THE 1889 ORDINANCE AND RELATED ISSUES

Negotiations for the 1889 ordinance

In January 1887 the Hongkong Bank's Board of Directors had been informed that the Jurado case was moving against them on the grounds that the Bank, with no personality recognized in Manila, was unable to plead its case. This was the proximate cause of the Bank's renewed attempt to clarify the provisions of its charter, which the Board itself supposed restricted their operations. The courts in Madrid were to conclude otherwise, but that would take time.

The initial communication, signed by four directors of the Hongkong Bank to the Secretary of State for the Colonies, was dated May 17, 1887. The argument was based mainly on the Philippine situation. The directors acknowledged the adverse history of similar requests in the early 1870s but asked for a reconsideration.

We desire especially to call your attention to the exceptional position of British Commerce in the Philippine Islands and the urgent need there exists that we should be allowed to establish a branch in those Islands . . . The trade of Manila now amounts to about $33,000,000 annually, the greater portion of which is in British hands . . . the expansion of our operations directly and greatly assists the extension of British commerce . . . We desire especially to call your attention to the exceptional position of British Commerce in the Philippine Islands . . . the commerce of the Port [Manila] which is chiefly in British hands would suffer . . .[39]

The first to sign this patriotic appeal in support of British merchants and commerce was the Hongkong Bank's German Chairman, M. Grote of Melchers and Co.

In the context of past Treasury opinion, the Bank had prepared a thorough, if defective, case. It must have come somewhat as a surprise for them to discover that there was no official opposition to the proposal for an amending ordinance. There was some consideration of the exact wording and nature of the required supervision, but the Treasury's first communication on the subject was one of full acceptance in principle. The item of contention was the apparently unrelated question of security for the note issue. These two threads in the discussion, although not as distinct as might at first be supposed, are considered separately.

Extraterritoriality[a]

In the initial Treasury response the question of extraterritoriality was effectively laid to rest.

A Colonial Ordinance has no doubt force only within the limits of the Colony; but by international law and intercolonial law the Corporate status of an institution created by the laws of one country or Colony will be recognized in other Countries and Colonies provided that the company in establishing itself outside its country of origin does not infringe the instrument of its foundation, and provided that when so established it does not contravene the laws of the locality.[40]

The phrase 'infringe the instrument of its foundation' was no doubt a reference to the persistent belief that the Bank was somehow able without violation of its charter to open with Treasury approval in the places named in section 4 but not elsewhere. By this interpretation opening in Manila with or without Treasury approval could be considered as 'infringing the instrument of its foundation', consequently placing the Bank outside the provisions of the commercial treaty with Spain. The doctrine of extraterritoriality, however, forces the conclusion that the Bank on the contrary could establish itself in the unnamed places without Treasury approval and its opening in Manila was not an infringement of the provisions of its charter.

In their joint letter to the Colonial Secretary of April 22, 1889, the Hongkong Bank's Chairman, W.H. Forbes, and Chief Manager, G.E. Noble, indeed took the precaution to refer to the purpose of the proposed ordinance as 'removing doubts' with respect to the powers of the Bank.[41]

---

[a] This section is dependent for its underlying thesis on P. Wesley-Smith's essay on 'The Hongkong Bank and the Extraterritorial Problem, 1865–1890', in King, ed. *Eastern Banking*, pp. 66–76.

However this may be, the Treasury had at last acknowledged in connection with foreign countries what it had earlier stated with reference to colonies, in particular to the Straits Settlements, that the lack of extraterritorial jurisdiction of the Hong Kong legislature was irrelevant to the question of the Bank's personality outside Hong Kong.

The problem was simply to remedy what the Bank considered a doubt, and the Treasury accepted as a defect, as to the ability of the Bank to establish itself in places not named in the ordinance. Contrary to the views expressed in 1873, the Treasury now agreed that the 'defect' could be remedied by an amendment to the ordinance of incorporation.

This decided, the Treasury addressed itself to the question of policy, whether, that is, 'it is expedient to make the concession to the Bank, and if so whether that concession should be made dependent upon conditions'.[42]

The responsibility of Government and the question of regulation

Following the full Parliamentary consideration of chartered banking in 1880, the trend of Treasury policy had been to withdraw from interference in the affairs of colonial banks.[43]

Their Lordships admit that there is much to be said in favour of leaving Banks entirely unfettered. The responsibilities which restriction involve may be serious and difficult, and it may be urged that the Banks themselves are the best judges of their own requirements.[44]

At one point in the inter-departmental correspondence an attempt was made to balance (i) the advantages of spreading the risks by a broad expansion of a bank against (ii) the dangers of ill-advised activities by a branch too distant to control. The Colonial Office was concerned with the impact a bank failure would have in the colony of its main activity.

It was the note issue, however, which became the key desideratum. In a private letter R.H. Meade, Assistant Under-Secretary in the Colonial Office, expressed his opinions to Hamilton of the Treasury in these terms:

My opinion, *ceteris paribus*, would be to leave these Banks perfectly unfettered, considering that they are more likely to understand their own business than we are. But the note-circulation complicates matters . . .

On the whole I think I should give permission. But we want something, and this would be a means of purchasing it.

Might we not say to the Bank, If you establish Branches at places where we can know nothing of your proceedings, you may, by reckless trading at such Branches, endanger the stability of the note circulation within the Colony. If, therefore, we give you leave to set up these branches, you must secure your note circulation in the manner which has been proposed to the Colonial Bank in the West Indies . . .[45]

Nor did Meade wish the Treasury to abdicate their right to authorize the new branches.

If the Treasury wipe their hands of all responsibility, I think the Secretary of State must go in, in their place, at any rate as long as the Bank Note circulation is unsecured; but *I much prefer to leave the Treasury in*. We could not trust Colonial Governments. The Bank Managers are generally members of the Legislative Council, and of great influence.[46]

Events were overtaking the leisurely progress of the discussion. In April 1889 the situation in Manila took a further turn for the worse. The Governor of Hong Kong, Sir William Des Voeux, cabled the Colonial Office to request assistance from the British Embassy in Madrid. But the Bank had meanwhile considered a more direct solution. At the Bank's expense the Governor again cabled the Colonial Office stating the Bank's request for a declaratory ordinance to the effect that:

Nothing in the herein before recited ordinances shall be read or construed as in any way prohibiting or restraining or as having been intended in any way to restrain or prohibit the said company from establishing Banks branch Banks or agencies at ports towns cities or places not specifically mentioned in the said ordinances.[47]

The Governor himself urged approval and concluded, 'time of great importance'.

The delay in London had not been due to any disagreement. Officials were waiting to settle a similar question of the note issue relative to the Anglo-Egyptian Bank in Malta, thus setting a precedent which could be cited in the correspondence with Hong Kong, and possibly vice versa. Confronted with the urgent request of Des Voeux some immediate response was required. 'Of course [Meade minuted] we cannot do what is asked. It would be giving away the only sop we have to offer towards securing the note issue which we and the Treasury are endeavouring to arrange.'[48] But the Colonial Office did send out the draft ordinance without waiting for a settlement of the Maltese affair.

With the legal victories in Madrid and Manila in June the pressure was lessened, nevertheless the Hong Kong authorities pressed ahead and Ordinance No. 29 of 1889, which was passed by the Legislative Council in December and accepted by an Extraordinary Meeting of the Bank's shareholders on January 16, became effective by Proclamation No. 1 published in the *Hongkong Government Gazette* of January 25, 1890, and was sent to London for confirmation.

The Treasury were not completely pleased. The Treasury observed that the ordinance required the prior consent of the Treasury before the Bank could exercise its 'new' privileges. With the note issue secured (see below), the Treasury reverted to its basic policy: 'My Lords have, as you are aware, been careful to divest Themselves of interference in the affairs of Banking Companies.'[49]

The Secretary of State for the Colonies nevertheless defended the ordinance in terms of Meade's private letter cited above and added that such a provision would keep Colonial Office policy 'in concert' with that of the Treasury.[50]

The Bank now had its amending ordinance, but what price did it pay and why?

Securing the note issue

In guaranteeing the note issue of the Oriental Bank, the Governor of Ceylon had taken an action which in effect changed the political character of banknotes. Hitherto, it might be argued, a banknote was merely a bill payable by a private-sector corporation to bearer on demand; it had no legal tender status, its use was entirely optional, and the consequences were a matter of concern only to the note-holder and the issuing bank. This, at least, was the official Treasury position. Governments may not have taken quite so disinterested a view, and the Colonial Regulations were formulated to contain just those provisions necessary to protect the note-holder within the context of the bank's operating charter and without the necessity of further Government intervention in the private sector.

When the Oriental Bank failed it was immediately clear that unless the bearer notes were guaranteed, there would be disturbances which would immediately damage the economy and could develop into a situation of potentially serious political consequence. The note-holders, as already pointed out, expected 'someone', presumably the Government, to protect them immediately – charters, economic and political theories, etc. notwithstanding.

This was the beginning of a general move towards colonial government note issues. Just as Government were held responsible for a sound coinage with disappointing results, so they were soon to be equally responsible for the paper money. A sound currency and a state issue were in the future; in the interim, banknotes had to be recognized as having a public character. They were still not legal tender, but they were an essential part of the money supply; they could no longer be treated simply as ordinary private-sector bank liabilities.[b] Without them the economy would function inefficiently.

Government could not now be satisfied with setting up the rules of issue; as a political reality it had to guarantee the issue. To protect itself – and the taxpayers – the obvious remedy was to have note issuing banks hypothecate securities to the total amount of the note issue, setting aside specified assets, that is for a particular class of priority creditor, the note-holder.

Accordingly the Hongkong Bank was requested, as a condition for approval of the unrelated amending ordinance, to agree to hypothecation of securities equal in value to the whole of their note issue, an amount in excess of $5 million. On learning of the Government's new requirements, the Hongkong Bank accepted the principle, and presented a counter-suggestion. The Treasury modified its position and the Hongkong Bank accepted the new terms in a letter dated September 29, 1889.[51]

[b] Commercial bank demand deposits would, with the increasing use of the cheque, pass through the same evolution. Current accounts were not part of the 'legal tender' system, but as a political matter, they must be protected today, either by deposit insurance or, as in Hong Kong, by raiding secret public funds.

Table 11.1 *The Hongkong and Shanghai Banking Corporation*
Note issue, April 1889

(in dollars)

Hong Kong	3,023,437		
Singapore	1,367,150		
Penang	633,920		
Amoy	113,124	of which	%
Foochow	39,259	Hong Kong	52.2
Shanghai	507,000	Straits	34.5
Hankow	1,860	China	11.7
Tientsin	17,571	Japan	1.5
Kobe	60,462		
Yokohama	26,055		
	5,791,838[a]		

Note:
[a] The total is as given in the source; the figures actually add up to
$5,789,838.
Source: G.E. Noble, Chief Manager, to Colonial Secretary, 8 June
1889, CO 129/241, f. 622, or T. 1/8504[c].

McLean had argued that the Bank differed from other note-issuing banks in
that the shareholders had an unlimited liability for the note issue which in 1889
stood at $5.8 million (see Table 11.1). The Bank's 1882 amending ordinance had
already given note-holders priority as creditors.[52]

As McLean pointed out, any sign of trouble and the Bank's note-holders
would very early cease to hold them, at least in any quantity. There were two
problems with this argument. First, it begged the question. If the Bank were in
disrepute such that note-holders would demand redemption in cash, this act
would precipitate a crisis, probably assuring the Bank's ultimate failure and the
need for Government to act relative to the note issue as yet unredeemed.

But would the note-holders be able to assess the Bank's position? The second
problem was, therefore, that with the Bank's operations spread widely over the
East, the difficulties of a remote branch might bring down the Bank before local
note-holders in Hong Kong or the Straits Settlements were aware of developments. Indeed, this is the reason, as mentioned earlier, that granting the privilege
of opening branches virtually without restriction and a full security for the note
issue were provisions linked together in the minds of Treasury and Colonial
Office officials.

McLean argued further that the Bank's note issue varied considerably because
of seasonal factors. This was especially true at Chinese New Year when cash was
required, or in any time of trade crisis. McLean cited this as the reason for the
Bank's relatively high cash holdings.

He also argued the Bank's record, noting that it had come to the rescue at Singapore when the Oriental failed, accepting the Oriental's banknotes, thereby taking on itself any cost of delays in repayment. This relieved the ordinary citizen of this particular consequence of the Oriental's failure.[c]

The Treasury accepted the argument relative to unlimited liability; this contentious clause at last gave the Bank an advantage.[53] The need now was to bargain on the actual amount and then, over a long period of time, dispute the nature of the securities to be pledged. What was at stake was the interest differential from alternative uses of funds, estimated as 3% on the type of security acceptable as a note reserve against 10% on funds lent in the normal course of the Bank's business. This would constitute an opportunity cost of $400,000 in consequence of the required purchase of securities acceptable to the Crown Agents.[54]

The Bank offered $2 million. The Government, however, settled for $2.5 million or one-third the paid-up capital of $7.5 million – the latter figure being equal by statute to the Bank's maximum permitted note issue. The Government requirement was fixed, regardless of the size of the issue at any one time. In this way the problem of supervision was minimized – there was no need to monitor the Bank's constantly changing note issue. The Bank formally agreed in a letter from David McLean in September 1889.[55]

The desired ordinance was authorized, enacted, and promulgated, but the Treasury did not immediately approve the Bank's consequent list of established agencies and branches. The reasons for this are considered briefly below.

The approval of branches and the securing of the note issue

The Bank's past
Following the promulgation of Ordinance 29 of 1889, confirmation of which had been granted as a matter of urgency before passage of the legislation, the Hongkong Bank's constitutional future appeared assured. The Bank had, however, a past. Accordingly the Bank, when reporting that the securities required against the note issue had then been turned over, submitted a list of 25 branches and agencies to be approved in retrospect.

The Treasury professed to be disturbed.

It is evident to this Board [the Treasury] that the Bank has systematically violated the instruments by which it was incorporated.

[c] This was true, but the action taken by the Manager, W.G. Greig, was severely criticized at the time by McLean and commented on adversely by the directors. In 1884, the Bank's perception was perhaps clouded by their long competition with the Oriental. The Hongkong Bank's Board of Directors had not yet fully appreciated the public nature of their note issue; as with Government, their man at the scene most certainly had.

... I am to state that [the Lords Commissioners of the Treasury] feel precluded from giving such consent without receiving explanations of the Bank's past proceedings, and a distinct assurance from the Bank that the provisions of the Ordinance of 1889 will not be neglected like those of the 1866 ordinance.[56]

In the Colonial Office minutes there was some recrimination. The impact of the Treasury's anger at the Bank was softened by the fact that the Colonial Office confessed – whether for 'diplomatic' reasons or not is difficult to ascertain – to having failed to keep the Treasury fully informed during the negotiations of the extent of the Bank's 'violation'. Since another branch of the Treasury did business with the Bank in most of the agencies and branches listed, the lack of communication throughout is apparent.

The fact is that the Colonial Office was aware of the Bank's activities and, according to Meade, 'undertook to give them a general whitewashing as soon as they secured their note issue', a statement which totally undermined any adverse action the Treasury might wish to take - and there are in the files several very pompous memorandums.[d]

The Bank's Board of Directors never accepted that they had violated the 'instruments by which [the Bank] was incorporated'. The Bank had asked for permission and did not receive a reply, the minutes – of which the Bank was undoubtedly made aware at some point during the abortive negotiations for an amending ordinance in 1872 and 1873 – had concluded that the Treasury had no authority to give it. Subsequently, the Treasury had acted favourably in the case of Singapore.

The 'restrictions' in the original ordinance could only have affected (i) agencies in India – for which the Bank received full permission – and (ii) branches. And the Bank did not admit to having opened branches, except Shanghai, London, and Yokohama, which were in existence before the original ordinance, and Singapore – for which, as noted, permission had been granted.

The Bank's request for the ordinance of 1889 was 'to remove doubts' and neither the Treasury nor the Colonial Office were themselves certain of either the law or how to handle the complex situation which had developed.

In fairness the Colonial Office letter to the Bank was relatively mild and referred to 'apparent' disregard of the provisions of the ordinance, suggesting that the directors distinguish branches from agencies in the list submitted and give assurance for the future.[58]

There was much, therefore, which the Bank could dispute, but wisely the Bank did not do so. G.E. Noble, then in London on sick leave, wrote personally to R.H. Meade to say that the wording of the Bank's official letter to the Colonial Office,

---

[d] The Treasury even had the India Office files searched for activities of the Bank and would have moved into the Bombay and Calcutta files but for the plea of a subordinate that they had not been indexed – another point which John Stuart Mill had overlooked.[57]

Table 11.2 *The Hongkong and Shanghai Banking Corporation*
Branches and agencies
(as submitted to the Colonial Office, July 1890)

Branches	Existing agencies		Proposed agencies
London	New York	Bangkok	Colombo
Singapore	San Francisco	Manila	Borneo
Hong Kong	Hamburg	Iloilo	Rangoon
Shanghai	Lyons	Saigon	Sourabaya
Yokohama	Bombay	Amoy	Vancouver
	Calcutta	Foochow	Peking
	Penang	Hankow	
	Batavia	Tientsin	
		Hiogo	

signed by the London Manager, Ewen Cameron, had been suggested to him by Hamilton of the Treasury. The letter admitted nothing but 'haste'; it did, however, express regret if the Bank had acted in any way incorrectly, made promises for the future, and submitted a revised list broken down into agencies and branches.

I note [wrote Cameron] with much regret that the Treasury consider that we have been guilty of irregularities in the past, and while admitting that we acted hastily in opening Branches and Agencies without first obtaining the necessary permission in writing from the Lords Commissioners, I can only assure you that we exceedingly regret having committed any breach of the Bank's ordinance and that we faithfully undertake to rigidly observe the provisions contained in the new ordinance (No. 29 of 1889) in the future.[59]

The list of existing and proposed branches and agencies was appended (see Table 11.2), but in the absence of any clear definition of an agency, the list is stated on the basis of a definition by administrative control. It was obviously in the Bank's interest to minimize the number of branches it admitted to having opened. By the note-issuing definition, Penang, Amoy, Foochow, Hankow, Tientsin, and Hiogo were branches; by the capital definition Manila was a branch.

Peking was a special case. The agency was not listed as such; the Bank preferred to pretend that a member of its Tientsin staff was resident in the Imperial capital for an indefinite period. This, in view of Chinese official opinion, was wiser.

The proposed agencies were presumably added to preclude trouble with the Treasury later. Borneo, actually Sandakan, was then being actively considered, the others had been discussed, and a fully operating Vancouver office was to wait until the founding of the Hongkong Bank of Canada in 1982.

But it would be a further two months before the Treasury authorized the list. Another problem had developed.

'Eligible securities' – definition and location

The Bank's original submission of securities to be lodged against the note issue included title deeds of the Bank premises in Hong Kong, a mortgage on the property of the Land Investment Company and debentures of the China Merchants' Steam Navigation Company. The Treasury considered that these were insufficiently marketable; the CMSNCo debentures, the Treasury noted, had not been guaranteed by the Chinese Government. They did agree to accept Chinese Government silver securities, the D Loan of 1884 and the F Loan of 1888, which their experts concluded were high ranking among second-class securities.[60]

Thus the value of the acceptable securities deposited fell short of the $2.5 million required. 'Accordingly', wrote the Treasury, 'until this condition is fulfilled to the satisfaction of My Lords, They will feel precluded from according their required consent to the extended operations of the Bank.'[61]

Those involved in the setting up of this 'trust fund' to secure the notes were unclear as to what securities would be eligible and where and how the fund was to operate. But, equally certain, all involved wished to push the matter through to completion. The Bank therefore replied almost immediately that they were prepared to substitute Indian Government 4% rupee notes, an offer which was acceptable. As far as the Bank was concerned all arrangements had been completed by August 25.[62]

A new problem now arose: the Chinese Government securities were better realized in Hong Kong and should be kept there; the Indian securities should be in London. The Colonial Office and the Treasury needed to work out arrangements whereby the Bank would be allowed to substitute say a Chinese bond for further rupee paper while assuring themselves that the reserve of at least $2.5 million was maintained throughout. This occupied the time until mid-September.[63]

Then on September 22, 1890, all was in place, and the Treasury sent to the Hongkong Bank the official permission to be where they were and open where they would, as listed in Ewen Cameron's letter of two months previous. The Hongkong and Shanghai Banking Corporation was now at last properly incorporated, established in all places by Treasury consent.[64]

The legitimate concern of the Imperial authorities was the transformation of the Hongkong Bank from a Hong Kong and Shanghai based operation, financing through small agencies regional trade among the Treaty Ports of China and Japan, to a fully regional bank, the ramifications of whose operations extended to

India, London, the United States, and the Continent of Europe. The Bank's constituents in Hong Kong could no longer judge its overall position; of the note-holders a majority knew nothing of the Bank except its popular reputation. As Sir Robert Hart in Peking well knew after his experience with the Oriental Bank, reputations could outlive reality.

The Bank on the other hand had proved itself basically sound and had become essential for the finance of British commerce. The Imperial authorities had, therefore, to reconcile the changed scope of the Bank's operations with their responsibility to the colonial governments and the note-holders in the geographically separated areas in which the Bank operated.

The solution was to require the Bank to seek from the Treasury as 'gate-keeper' permission for any further expansion and, in the meantime, to secure the note issue, which alone of the Bank's activities was now recognized to be in some degree a public responsibility.

The Bank at no stage disagreed with the principles expressed and indeed showed little concern with the delays and recriminations which were the result of inter-departmental confusion in London. In the end all obtained what they required, and the writers of minutes, with their misinformation, their failures to research the background, and their occasional amusing comments can be forgotten. In the end the Imperial system had produced an acceptable and rational solution which permitted the Hongkong Bank to develop within the region, prepared to meet the more severe tests of the years immediately ahead.

12

INTERREGNUM, 1889–1893

Truly Joss take care this bank.
— Shanghai compradore, 1892

Imperial China was in 1889 at last opening to apparently unrestricted modernization.

The Middle Kingdom had been and indeed remained subject to periodic 'openings', during which the incautious could catch glimpses of the unlimited market waiting to be criss-crossed by railways. The 1889 opening was sparked by a reported loan proposal to the Hongkong Bank's Tientsin agency for the Tungchow Railway and fuelled by a series of memorials acknowledging the importance of railways and making various proposals which were climaxed by an Imperial edict of August 27, 1889, ordering the construction of the Peking-Hankow (Lu-Han) line.[1]

These manifestations of China's 'self-strengthening movement', accompanied by evidence that such conservative officials as Chang Chih-tung and Weng T'ung-ho were supportive of change and that the young Kuang-hsu Emperor might be won over to reform, caught Europe at a particularly opportune time.[2] The impact of these events, which carefully considered might have been recognized as tentative, coinciding with a series of reinforcing but unrelated events, committed Western finance to a short but intensive period of unfounded optimism followed by loss and confusion. For the Hongkong and Shanghai Banking Corporation the problems thus created were compounded by management disruption which witnessed, for example, seven changes in the effective leadership within three and a half years culminating in the return of Thomas Jackson as acting Chief Manager in April 1893.

The year 1889 also witnessed the founding of the China Association in London by 'Old China Hands' almost in a fit of nostalgia. Although the Association's first year was marked by corporate inactivity, there being 'nothing to do', as Sir Thomas Sutherland, chairman of the P&O and founder of the Hongkong Bank, put it in his best after-dinner style, there was much to add about the activities of individual members of the Association:

Personal, individual, and internal efforts . . . had been all-powerful in carrying an atmosphere of civilization into the benighted country of China [laughter] and not only into that country but also into other countries which stood almost as much in need of Chinese civilization as Great Britain did Herself. [Renewed laughter and cheers]. What had they not done? Why they had started a Bank of Persia [laughter] which at no distant date was destined to revolutionize the history of that country [cheers].

He had heard of another undertaking of an important character, not by any means disassociated from that body to which he was addressing himself. He alluded to a most important, and, in the future, he was quite sure, a most valuable factor in the progress of the country and China herself. He need scarcely say he meant the China Trust . . . [It would] establish a universal system of Railways throughout the length and breadth of China . . .[3]

The 'Bank of Persia' was the Royally chartered Imperial Bank of Persia, later the British Bank of the Middle East, which since 1960 has been a member of the Hongkong Bank Group. William Keswick, sometime Chairman of the Hongkong Bank, was its first chairman, and David McLean, retired London Manager of the Bank, was also on the board. This is sufficient to explain why Sutherland introduced the topic at a China Association dinner. There would be further links – F.D. Sassoon, a long-time Hongkong Bank director, represented his family's interests in the new bank which served an area from which his grandfather had left for Bombay; Thomas Jackson, retired finally from the Hongkong Bank and in London, would take over the chairmanship – but the Imperial Bank of Persia's history is told elsewhere.[a] And although the Imperial Bank cannot be said to have revolutionized Persia, it successfully provided needed facilities.

The history of the Trust and Loan Company of China, Japan and the Straits, which Sutherland referred to as the 'China Trust', on the other hand, is more immediately relevant but less satisfactory, the shares of its successor company (the Bank of China, Japan and the Straits) trading at *minus* £1:10s within four years.[b] It will serve as an introduction to this chapter on the Hongkong Bank's 'interregnum', the period during which the Bank attempted unsuccessfully to find a new leader; one who, in a period of financial disorder, would prove capable of commanding the confidence not only of those shareholders and constituents based on the China coast but also of those in London who were becoming increasingly influential in the fortunes of Hong Kong's 'local' Bank.

---

[a] A commissioned history of the Imperial Bank of Persia/British Bank of the Middle East has been published: Geoffrey Jones, *Banking and Empire in Iran. The History of The British Bank of the Middle East*, Volume I (Cambridge, 1986); Volume II is entitled *Banking and Oil* (Cambridge, 1987).

[b] Subscribed capital was only partly paid up, and shareholders feared being required to pay a further call to meet the company's liabilities, hence their willingness to pay others to take their shares.[4]

THE SETTING

THE EXCHANGES AND INVESTMENT IN THE EAST

The rise and fall of silver

Attempts to reverse the consequences of the decision by the Latin Monetary Union suspending the unlimited coinage of silver met apparent success with the passage by the U.S. Congress of the Sherman Silver Purchase Act of 1890, requiring the U.S. Treasury to purchase up to 4.5 million ounces of silver per month (if offered) at a price reflecting the old 16:1 ratio. After the sharp decline in value from 1886, silver had in fact stabilized in the twelve months from mid-1888, and the unusually heavy demand for silver coinage in Britain in 1889 coupled with the success of the silver lobby in America forced a reversal of the market's downward trend beginning in September 1889 and reaching a climax a year later at prices which had not prevailed for some thirteen years (see Table 12.1).

The fall from the September 1890 peak was at first seen as a natural process of the market seeking a new level pending further successes of the Bimetallic League (to which the Bank subscribed modestly), but the decline was in fact to accelerate dramatically, passing previous lows by mid-1892. Reinforced by the repeal of the Sherman Act and the closure of the Indian mints to the free coinage of silver in 1893, the decline continued virtually uninterrupted through the end of the century.

The continued fall of silver, beyond anticipated minor adjustments in 1891, was totally unexpected. This is the key to an understanding of the decisions of 1889–1890 and their unexpected consequences.

The 'China Trust'

Exchange followed silver, but those working on 'an even keel', matching sources and uses of funds by monetary area, need not have been particularly concerned. And yet the 'even keel', while reflecting sound management in an exchange bank, would not appeal to those seeking investment opportunities in a China on the eve of modernization. If China were to take the cultural risk inherent in railway construction, could she also be expected to take the exchange risk of say sterling or mark denominated investment funds? Investment in China's development therefore involved an exchange risk which for the first time in over a decade seemed, even to the most hardened Old China Hands, fully justified. Not that the subscribers to the 'China Trust' necessarily expected silver to remain at mid-1890 highs but rather they had supposed any loss from a decline in the gold price

Table 12.1 *The price of silver and the Hong Kong exchange,*
1888–1893

Year	d/ounce of silver	$ = x s/d^a	% change in 6 months
1872 June	60.0	4/6	–
1877 October	54.6	3/11$\frac{1}{8}$	–
1888 June	42.2	3/0	−4.0
1888 Dec.	42.9	3/0$\frac{1}{2}$	1.4
1889 June	42.2	3/0$\frac{1}{2}$	0.0
1889 Dec.	44.4	3/1$\frac{1}{2}$	2.7
1890 June	49.0	3/4$\frac{3}{8}$	7.7
(1890 September	54.6	3/10$\frac{7}{8}$)	
1890 Dec.	49.5	3/5	1.5
1891 June	46.0	3/2$\frac{1}{2}$	−6.1
1891 Dec.	44.3	3/1	−3.9
1892 June	41.1	2/10$\frac{3}{8}$	−7.1
1892 Dec.	39.2	2/8$\frac{3}{4}$	−4.7
1893 June	38.8	2/6	−8.4
1902 Dec.	22.6	1/7	–

Note:
[a] rate quoted in HSBC semi-annual reports. For other years, see
    Tables 8.2, 9.2, and 13.1.

of silver would be modest and adequately covered by the interest rate differential.

This optimistic view was undoubtedly encouraged by the publicized and apparently intimate connection of the Hongkong Bank with the China Trust and by the composition of its board of directors.

In the East shares were offered through the offices of the Hongkong Bank. In January 1890 the *North-China Herald* described an all too familiar Shanghai scene:

A copy of the detailed prospectus of the Trust and Loan Company of China, Japan and the Straits, Limited, has at last reached Shanghai, and it is well for the comfort of the officials of the Hongkong Bank here that it did not reach Shanghai before. There was eagerness enough displayed to make application for shares on the skeleton prospectus that was telegraphed out from home; but if this full document had been in the possession of Shanghai, the rush to subscribe would have overwhelmed the bank.[5]

Alexander Michie, whose efforts on behalf of Jardine, Matheson and Co., had met with little practical success, was writing words of warning in his *Chinese Times*, based on considerable and relevant experience: 'It is three years since we were told in a somewhat oracular and even menacing manner that China was awakening; but of a genuine awakening it is difficult to perceive any certain symptoms.'[6] Though Michie wrote from the key centre of Tientsin, his voice was drowned.

The glowing predictions of the Trust Company's prospectus were, after all, supported by a board of directors presided over by the senior partner of Matheson and Co. and former Chairman of the Hongkong Bank, William Keswick, and composed of recognized Eastern experts, including the hard-headed and experienced David McLean. In China the Trust was to be represented by Russell and Co., who attempted to recruit *inter alia* Hongkong Bank staff for the new company. Charles S. Addis, who had served as the Bank's agent in Peking itself, was offered the position of Shanghai representative; in Hong Kong a local committee could boast the experience of Hongkong Bank directors, including H. Hoppius, and the Hongkong Bank were prominently declared as the Trust's bankers.[7] Both Keswick and McLean were members of the Bank's London Committee. It was not unreasonable – but dangerously inaccurate – to see the 'China Trust' as the 'merchant banking' arm of the conservative, successful Hongkong and Shanghai Banking Corporation and to measure its likelihood of success by the record of the Bank.

The new investment company was established as a 'Trust', a form of incorporation then particularly popular in England, with broadly defined purposes and permissive articles.[8] The prospectus proclaimed that China now required investment in 'all kinds of public works, railroads, telegraphs, docks, waterworks, etc, etc, in short [in] all means of communication and [in] all auxiliaries of commerce and industry'. The company was empowered to negotiate and issue public and private loans in China and the Far East. With a nominal capital of £1 million of which only the premium and a fraction of the subscribed capital was called-up, the Trust's investments were to be financed by debentures and fixed deposits, the major part denominated in sterling, the funds from which would be 'sent out East' to be employed in medium- and long-term investments.[9]

From the first there were difficulties. Shanghai and Hong Kong were enjoying a period of share and real estate speculation, whereas China's modernization, although hopefully about to begin, had not, as Michie warned, taken a specific investment form. The Trust therefore lent against mortgages and made advances on shares with funds transferred to the East at increasingly high exchange rates. The Trust's first report was in consequence of these speculative activities financially satisfactory, and unwanted calls on shareholders were not seen even as a possibility.

There was already, however, an undercurrent of organizational problems. The cooperation of the Hongkong Bank had been won only with the understanding that the Bank would handle the Trust's exchange requirements, the Trust itself undertaking not to operate in foreign exchange. This was essential if a conflict of interest were to be avoided and Keswick and McLean were to be members of both the Bank's London Committee and the Trust's board of directors;

Hoppius's position in Hong Kong was the same in reverse. Although F.D. Sassoon was on the Trust's board of directors, there was the threat of competition from another branch of the family in the Imperial and Foreign Investment and Agency Corporation, also established in 1889. This corporation, with Sassoons and Hongkong Bankers among the founding shareholders was wound up in 1892 without creating the major public excitement the China Trust was to enjoy.[c]

Meanwhile a complex set of factors led to the defection of Russell and Co., at that time the Trust's agents in China, involving the establishment in 1891 of the National Bank of China Ltd and the resignation of W.H. Forbes from the Hongkong Bank Board.

In January 1891 the China Trust changed its name to the Bank of China, Japan and the Straits Ltd, sought and obtained additional capital at a premium but renewed its agreement that, except in India, it would not compete with the Hongkong Bank in the Eastern exchange business.[11] Subsequent statements suggest that the change of name was at least partly based on the directors' intention to stay closer to banking, but the company's assets had already been committed and the directors could only watch helplessly as the exchanges fell with silver. The 8% dividend declared in early 1892 on the basis of the bank's second year of operations was questioned by the auditors as being based on the January 1891 exchange rate of 3s:5d, thus indicating a particularly sanguine expectation concerning the course of exchange.

The choice of the high exchange rate did however permit the holders of 'Founder's shares' to receive a dividend and thus recoup their investment before the fall.

In March 1893 the directors announced that they had faced up to developments and had written off all their reserves by revaluing their Eastern assets at an exchange of three shillings, but even as they spoke the rate was 2s:9d and falling.[12]

Financial history is replete with stories of disaster caused by dishonesty and incompetence. The point to the history of the Trust, then the Bank of China, Japan and the Straits, is that the decisions were made openly by men with a wide range of Eastern experience. Having recouped some at least of their original investment by the dubious means described above, they stayed with their company and tried to save what was left. In late 1893 the 'Bank of China' informed the Hongkong Bank they intended to operate in Far Eastern exchange, thus requiring both institutions to reexamine their relationship. Reluctantly Keswick and McLean decided that despite their long association with the Hongkong Bank, they would in honour have to remain with their troubled 'Bank

---

[c] Founder shares were held by Reuben David Sassoon, Meyer Elias Sassoon, Paul Chater, Ewen Cameron, Thomas Jackson, David McLean, and Albert Deacon; of its £2 million subscribed capital £671,490 (£10 per share) was paid up.[10]

of China' and leave the London Committee (see Chapter 13). In December 1894 after a restructuring, the one-time 'China Trust' was renamed once again; it would be simply the 'Bank of China and Japan Ltd'; its directors included William Keswick, David McLean, F.D. Sassoon, E. Iveson, and Adolf von André.[13]

The Old China Hands had been misled. They were not China experts; they were merchants who had been directors of the Hongkong Bank. The Bank's success was based on a set of principles directly opposed to those of the China Trust – the proven loyalty of constituents, the finance of a diverse China trade with profit based on the turnover of funds, and the principle of the even keel. But surely, the promoters had argued, China must change. Not only must China change but the Emperor himself had expressed his interest; the West must come to China's assistance – and now is the time. These premises proved false, and the turn in the exchanges compounded the problem.

CHANGES IN THE BANKING COMMUNITY

Failures and new institutions

The investors in the China Trust were not alone in failing to assess correctly developments in the East. In June 1892 the New Oriental Bank Corporation, Ltd, suspended payment and was not again to open its doors.[14] The Comptoir d'Escompte de Paris failed as a result of copper speculations in France and was reconstituted as the Comptoir National d'Escompte de Paris; henceforth the principal French banking role in the East would be played, surprisingly in view of its original colonial orientation, by the Banque de l'Indo-Chine. The Chartered Mercantile Bank of India, London and China was weakened but would have survived the turmoil of the period 1889–1893 had it not fallen victim to an embezzlement which forced a reorganization (involving the loss of its charter) and its consequent re-incorporation in 1892 under the Companies Acts as The Mercantile Bank of India, Ltd. The Chartered Bank of India, Australia and China and the Agra Bank remained strong competitors throughout.

The Hongkong Bank faced two new institutions, the Deutsch-Asiatische Bank and the National Bank of China, Ltd. The former, founded in 1889 with its head office in Shanghai and a board of directors in Berlin, made no significant impact in the period covered by this chapter. It will be considered in detail in Volume II where its history becomes intimately linked with that of the Hongkong Bank.

W.H. Forbes, Russell and Co., and the National Bank of China

The National Bank of China, Ltd, was briefly known as the Banking Corporation of China, a creature of the share speculation of the 1890–1891 boom. The latter's registration in February 1891 coincided with that of the Bank of China, Ltd, and both were reorganized in April into the National Bank of China, Ltd, with the express purpose of 'securing the cooperation of Russell and Co.', who were to be the bank's permanent secretaries.[15] The bank was registered in England with capital expressed in sterling; the bank's purposes were stated in the same broad terms as that of the 'China Trust', but its head office was in Hong Kong with a committee, eliminated in 1893, in Shanghai.

The name 'national bank' would not have suggested to contemporaries a special national, in the sense of 'official', status; parallels would be the National Bank of India, National Bank of Turkey, National Bank of Scotland, etc. The National Bank of China was, however, the consequence of Chinese merchant agitation for a Western-style exchange bank with primarily Chinese interests. This was partially achieved – there were Chinese on the board of directors; G.W.F. Playfair, the chief manager, had Chinese experience and language ability; and the shareholders included the Howqua family, descendants of the great Cohong merchant of the Canton trade days Wu Ch'ung-yueh (1810–1863) and whose relations with Russell and Co. were of long standing. Prominent among this bank's founders were W.H. Forbes, as recently as 1889/90 the Chairman of the Hongkong Bank, and H. de C. Forbes, sometime Deputy Chairman of the Bank. Also listed was the well-known C.J. Dudgeon; in England the best-known founder would probably have been Charles B. Stuart Wortley.

Russell and Co.'s sponsorship of the rival National Bank of China was not unanimously supported by the company's partners. S.W. Pomeroy, a former director of the Hongkong Bank, recognized that the National Bank would be seen as a rival of the Hongkong Bank and that his partners' act would appear surprisingly antagonistic for a firm so long represented on the latter's Board of Directors – the precise charge actually levelled, presumably by de Bovis, against W.H. Forbes, leading, as noted below, to his resignation from the Board of the Hongkong Bank in March 1891.[16]

The rashness of Old China Hands was not limited to Scotsmen in London.

During the rise in silver, Russell and Co.'s New York partner, apparently with informed, perhaps inside opinion as to the provisions and likelihood of passage by Congress of the Sherman Silver Purchase Act, speculated successfully by buying silver forward. That is, he contracted to buy silver and, putting up no cash, further contracted to pay for the silver at some later date at an agreed price which he correctly expected to be less than the market or spot price at the time the contract would become due. This was speculation since he was not covered and had no purpose for the silver – other than the expectation that he could immediately sell with a profit arising from the difference between the buying and anticipated higher selling price, which latter he expected to result from passage of the Sherman Silver Purchase Act.

So far so good. He then, according to Pomeroy, lost his head, contracting for enormous sales of forward exchange against purchases of silver. Or to parallel the description above, he continued to buy increasing amounts of silver forward at five shillings a tael in contracts, principally with the Hongkong Bank, which were due from May 1891 onwards. The price of silver by this time had declined to 4s:2d a tael (= 3s per dollar); consequently, Russell and Co. had then to find the difference of 10d per tael in cash, difficult at any time, but especially difficult when other assets could not be sold in Shanghai except on a declining market. This put the Hongkong Bank in a position, as Pomeroy expressed it, to 'smash us up in the hope that the National Bank would be killed also'.[17] Or, less dramatically, the Hongkong Bank could and in the event did refuse accommodation. The Bank instead demanded settlement.

In June 1891 Russell and Co. failed. The Hongkong Bank minutes for the next two years detail the assistance the directors offered, after careful consideration, to other long-standing constituents. The failure of Russell and Co. is merely noted. Pomeroy had been correct.[d]

The National Bank of China, unlike the abortive Shanghai attempts in 1872 and 1882, nevertheless survived. The Chinese shareholders were determined that 'their' bank should not be abandoned, and indeed it remained a credible though modest member of the Hong Kong financial scene until the first decade of this century, being reorganized under the Kadoorie interests in 1905 and fading away in voluntary liquidation in 1911.[19]

Its early history is reminiscent of that of the Hongkong Bank – born in a period of speculation, beginning operations in the aftermath of a boom and confronted with the failure of its sponsoring institution – but this cannot be said to necessarily constitute a formula for success. In the troubled 1890s the superior resources and established constituency of the Hongkong Bank were too strong for poorly capitalized competitors. The Hongkong Bank survived, although this too was not inevitable.

Salvaged from the wreckage of Russell and Co. on the China coast were the British interests in the firm represented by R. Shewan and C.A. Tomes, whose subsequent partnership was first represented on the Hongkong Bank's Board in 1895.

TRADE

Although the Hongkong Bank's income during the first years of the 'Interregnum' must have been to a great extent the consequence of (i) advances on shares

---

[d] The Hongkong Bank however moved to assist Frank B. Forbes in Paris to protect the outside shareholders of the Kechang Filature Association in Shanghai from the effects of his cousin's bankruptcy – F.B. Forbes had at this time no interest in Russell and Co. The correspondence shows Ewen Cameron in London and John Walter in Shanghai to have been particularly cooperative.[18]

and (ii) relations, direct or indirect, with the Chinese Government, the Bank's regular business remained the finance of trade. The value of China's imports and exports in 1893, HkTs 268 million, was some 36% over that of 1889 – or 21% over that of the more flourishing year of 1888. These percentages mask a fall in the cotton trade and considerable though irregular fluctuations in almost all other commodities. Nor was there any significant change in the composition of trade, although the small net decline in tea exports – in the context of considerable fluctuation – was part of a trend, more significant in the longer term.

Meanwhile in Japan economic development implied the growth of foreign trade, and the average annual total of imports and exports for the period 1888–1893 at Yen 356 million was some 140% of the average annual total of the previous five years. The special relationship of the Yokohama Specie Bank with the finance of the export trade limited the benefit that these increases would bring to the foreign exchange banks, although to the extent Japanese trade operated through foreign merchant agents or required facilities in, for example, the silk city of Lyons, the Hongkong Bank became involved.

The Hongkong Bank's normal operations were to be affected not by the value of the trade which, as has been shown, was increasing, but by the consequences of business failures which resulted from speculation not only in commodities but also in the share and property markets.

THE HONGKONG BANK'S BOARD OF DIRECTORS – PROBLEMS AND POLICIES

BOARD OF DIRECTORS – COMPOSITION

Although in general there was little change in the company composition of the Board, changes in membership being due mainly to retirement or leave, the resignation of W.G. Brodie of the Borneo Company without replacement permitted the Board to nominate the twice disappointed A. McConachie and thus reinstate the representation of Gilman and Co. (see Table 12.2). In the Jardine succession, J.J. Keswick, a younger brother of William, was succeeded by his cousin John Bell-Irving; John was in turn succeeded by his younger brother James J. Bell-Irving.[20]

A request from the long-established China-coast firm of Adamson, Bell and Co. in 1889 that they be represented on the Board was only 'formally acknowledged'; the company failed in May 1891 and presumably the Board had knowledge of its weakness.

More significant was the resignation of W.H. Forbes in March 1891, foreshadowing the failure of Russell and Co. in June. That he should have expected to remain on the Board given his role in the founding of the National

Table 12.2 *The Hongkong and Shanghai Banking Corporation*
Board of Directors, 1889–1893

February 1889

W.H. Forbes	Russell and Co.	Chairman, 1889/90
H.L. Dalrymple	Birley and Co.	Deputy Chairman, 1889/90
J.S. Moses	E.D. Sassoon and Co.	
S.C. Michaelsen	Melchers and Co.	
E.A. Solomon	D. Sassoon, Sons and Co.	
B. Layton	Gibb, Livingston and Co.	
W.G. Brodie	Borneo Company, Ltd	
L. Poesnecker	Arnhold, Karberg and Co.	
C.D. Bottomley	Douglas Lapraik and Co.	
N.A. Siebs	Siemssen and Co.	
J.F. Holliday	Holliday, Wise and Co.	
John Bell-Irving	Jardine, Matheson and Co.	

12 members

Resigned: C.D. Bottomley (Feb.)　　　Elected: T.E. Davies (March)
　　　　　J. Bell-Irving (April)　　　　　　J.J. Keswick
　　　　　J.F. Holliday (Nov.)　　　　　　A.P. McEwen
　　　　　N.A. Siebs (Dec.)　　　　　　　H. Hoppius
　　　　　E.A. Solomon (Jan. 1890)　　　David Reuben Sassoon

February 1890

H.L. Dalrymple	Birley and Co.	Chairman, 1890/91
J.S. Moses	E.D. Sassoon and Co.	Deputy Chairman, 1890/91
S.C. Michaelsen	Melchers and Co.	
B. Layton	Gibb, Livingston and Co.	
W.G. Brodie	Borneo Company, Ltd.	
L. Poesnecker	Arnhold, Karberg and Co.	
T.E. Davies	Douglas Lapraik and Co.	
J.J. Keswick	Jardine, Matheson and Co.	
A.P. McEwen	Holliday, Wise and Co.	
H. Hoppius	Siemssen and Co.	
D.R. Sassoon	D. Sassoon, Sons and Co.	
W.H. Forbes	Russell and Co.	

12 members

Resigned: W.G. Brodie　　　　　　　　Elected: A. McConachie (Gilman)
　　　　　(March; Borneo Co.)
　　　　　B. Layton (April)
　　　　　A.P. McEwen (Aug.)　　　　　　C.J. Holliday (Feb. 1891)

February 1891

J.S. Moses	E.D. Sassoon and Co.	Chairman, 1891/92
S.C. Michaelsen	Melchers and Co.	Deputy Chairman, 1891/92
L. Poesnecker	Arnhold, Karberg and Co.	
T.E. Davies	Douglas Lapraik and Co.	
J.J. Keswick	Jardine, Matheson and Co.	
H. Hoppius	Siemssen and Co.	
D.R. Sassoon	D. Sassoon, Sons and Co.	
W.H. Forbes	Russell and Co.	

Table 12.2 (*cont.*)

A. McConachie	Gilman and Co.
C.J. Holliday	Holliday, Wise and Co.
H.L. Dalrymple	Birley and Co.
11 members	

Resigned: W.H. Forbes (March)   Elected: E.L. Woodin (July P&O)
       H.L. Dalrymple (Aug.)
       E.L. Woodin (Oct., ineligible)

February 1892

S.C. Michaelsen	Melchers and Co.	(to May) Chairman, 1892
T.E. Davies	Douglas Lapraik and Co.	(from May) Chairman, 1892/93
H. Hoppius	Siemssen and Co.	Deputy Chairman, 1892/93
L. Poesnecker	Arnhold, Karberg and Co.	
J.J. Keswick	Jardine, Matheson and Co.	
D.R. Sassoon	D. Sassoon, Sons and Co.	
A. McConachie	Gilman and Co.	
C.J. Holliday	Holliday, Wise and Co.	
J.S. Moses	E.D. Sassoon and Co.	
9 members		

Resigned: S.C. Michaelsen (May)   Elected: C. Jantzen
       J.J. Keswick   J.J. Bell-Irving
       L. Poesnecker   J. Kramer
       A. McConachie (Sept.)   G. Slade
       T.E. Davies
         (Dec., d. March 1893)   J. Lapraik

February 1893

H. Hoppius	Siemssen and Co.	Chairman, 1893/94
C.J. Holliday	Holliday, Wise and Co.	Deputy Chairman, 1893/94
D.R. Sassoon	D. Sassoon, Sons and Co.	
J.S. Moses	E.D. Sassoon and Co.	
Carl Jantzen	Melchers and Co.	
J.J. Bell-Irving	Jardine, Matheson and Co.	
Julius Kramer	Arnhold, Karberg and Co.	
Gerald Slade	Gilman and Co.	
John S. Lapraik	Douglas Lapraik and Co.	
9 members		

To June 30 1893

Resigned: J.J. Bell-Irving (April)   Elected: J.J. Keswick
       G. Slade   A. McConachie
                          H.H. Joseph (May P&O)

Bank of China is difficult to explain, except that it would be consistent with the initial view of that bank as an investment company; Forbes could then be seen as leaving the 'China Trust' for a rival investment bank rather than as setting up a rival exchange bank in opposition to the Hongkong Bank with which Russell and Co. had been closely associated virtually since its founding.

Forbes's departure was not a happy one, and the Board minutes record a letter dated March 10, 1891, which suggests a dispute, the nature of which has already been considered, between Forbes and the Chief Manager, François de Bovis.

With reference to what passed between us the other day [Forbes wrote de Bovis], and in case my disclaimer of any hostility to the Bank should not be satisfactory, I now beg to place my resignation of the position of Director of the Bank in the hands of the Court of Directors.

The Board, after mature consideration, accepted Forbes's offer of resignation. There is a tradition in the Forbes family that it was Thomas Jackson who had engineered his removal from the Board and that there was an anti-American element in the decision, but Jackson at the time was the Hongkong Bank's London Manager and, given Russell and Co.'s ill-advised silver operations and sponsorship of the National Bank, the event is in any case self-explanatory.

With the departure of Russell and Co. American membership on the Board of Directors of the Bank was ended for a period of 90 years, renewed only in 1980 by the election of three directors from the board of Marine Midland Banks, Inc. The Hongkong Bank retained its German connections until 1914 and was thus able to confront the competition of the Deutsch-Asiatische Bank from a position of considerable strength; American banking competition, which came only in the first decade of this century, was successfully contained in the inter-war period by the aggressive operations of what was by then still the 'local bank' although very much also a 'British bank'.

The case of E.L. Woodin of the P&O was particularly unfortunate. Elected to the Board in July 1891 he left the Colony almost immediately. By October an irregularity in the P&O accounts kept with the Bank had been found which disturbed long-standing relations with that company. The matter was eventually settled, Woodin having rendered himself ineligible to retain his directorship, and the P&O was again represented on the Board with the election of H.H. Joseph in May 1893.

TWO SHAREHOLDER CRITICISMS

Two issues, general in nature – although prompted by a specific situation – were raised at the semi-annual meeting by shareholders: (i) the seniority system whereby the chairmanship of the Hongkong Bank was based on rotation and (ii) the lack of information in the published accounts.

The election of the Chairman

The debate on the method of selecting the Chairman was not particularly edifying, possibly because Mr Wicking had just finished implying that the Chairman was guilty of improper dealings in Bank shares.

Mr Wicking: I am of the opinion, Mr Chairman, that the mode of electing the Chairman of the Bank is not very satisfactory. I think it should be done either at a general meeting or by the Board of Directors themselves by ballot. I think the system of appointng a Chairman simply by rotation is a very unsatisfactory one.

Chairman [J.S. Moses]: That is a matter of opinion. The directors think otherwise, and according to the Deed of Settlement it lies with the directors to appoint their own Chairman. That being so, what does it matter what you think about it?

                                                          22 August 1891 meeting.

But Moses perhaps unconsciously stated the main issue. Was he the Chairman of the Hongkong and Shanghai Banking Corporation or the Chairman of the Board of Directors, the latter considered as virtually a private affair of concern to no one but the directors themselves, a matter quite rightly arranged for their own convenience? The answer is complex. The chief executive officer of the Bank was the Chief Manager, but the Chairman, who was not a banker, had to speak for the Bank and preside at the semi-annual shareholders' meetings. His failure to handle the meeting could reflect on the credibility of the report. It was a problem not then properly understood and certainly not fully resolved until 1969 when an executive board was authorized with the chief executive officer as Chairman.[21]

In any case, an examination of Tables 12.2 and 12.3 will confirm that seniority prevailed and that, in addition, the Bank continued for a time its tradition of leadership without reference to national origins.

The adequacy of the semi-annual statement of accounts

The second issue, lack of information, was not any better handled. The complaint was made at the August 1889 meeting by the contentious editor of the *Hongkong Telegraph*, R. Fraser-Smith, who declined to arrange a seconder and thus ensured his own ineffectiveness.

Fraser-Smith: I say that no professional accountant would pass the statement of accounts. It is a skeleton; it is not a statement of accounts. . . . The gross earnings, expenses and working, these are the items which the shareholders wish to know – not this thing. . . .

Chairman: [W.H. Forbes]: If the shareholders think that the statement is not sufficient, let them come forward and say so.

Fraser-Smith: Well, I say so now as a shareholder.

Chairman: You must get someone to support you.

Fraser-Smith: I want no support. I am simply stating my opinion.

Chairman: Yes, but if you are going to propose anything you must get some one to second it.

Fraser-Smith: What I say is this . . .'

Table 12.3 *The Hongkong and Shanghai Banking Corporation Chairmen and Deputy Chairmen, 1889–1893*

1889/90		*1893 (Jan)/94*	
W.H. Forbes	Russell and Co.	H. Hoppius	Siemssen and Co.
H.L. Dalrymple	Birley and Co.	C.J. Holliday	Holliday, Wise and Co.
1890/91			
H.L. Dalrymple	Birley and Co.	*Chairmen:*	
J.S. Moses	E.D. Sassoon and Co.	British (from U.K.)	2
1891/2		British (other)	1
J.S. Moses	E.D. Sassoon and Co.	American	1
S.C. Michaelsen	Melchers and Co.	German	2
1892 (Feb.-May)		*Deputy Chairmen:*	
S.C. Michaelsen	Melchers and Co.	British (from U.K.)	3
T.E. Davies	Douglas Lapraik and Co.	British (other)	1
		American	0
1892 (May-Dec.)		German	2
T.E. Davies	Douglas Lapraik and Co.		
H. Hoppius	Siemssen and Co.		

Fraser-Smith in consequence made little impact. Interestingly, when a Shanghai shareholder wrote for information on the Bank's expenses, the Board instructed the Chief Manager to respond suitably, the inference being that he would be provided with at least part of what he required.

Secrecy was to be a continuing issue. At times the Bank's managers argued that the Board was not sufficiently secret, but the simplicity of accounts which would later disguise hidden reserves was the consequence of custom and shareholder acceptance. In fact, the presentation of the accounts did change in this period, providing in particular separate information on the Bank's gold and silver assets and liabilities, including details of the securities held in special reserves. When contingencies impinged on the ability of the Bank to pay the expected level of dividends or would, if kept confidential, give an excessively unfavourable view of the Bank's basic earning ability, a contingency account was included in the published statement. All this was undoubtedly in response to pressure from fixed-deposit customers and shareholders in London. The Board was more responsive than Forbes's approach to the unreasonable Fraser-Smith would suggest, but the charge of secrecy would be made again.

THE PROBLEM OF THE SUCCESSION – THE CHIEF MANAGERSHIP IN
THE INTERREGNUM

The 'interregnum', the period between Jackson's first administration and his management of the Bank from 1893 through 1901, was naturally not seen as such

Table 12.4 *The Hongkong and Shanghai Banking Corporation*
Principal Managers, 1889–1893

	Chief Manager	London Manager	Shanghai Manager
1889 January	G.E. Noble	D. McLean	E. Cameron
May			John Walter
June		T. Jackson	
1890 March	J.P. Wade Gard'ner[a]		
April		E. Cameron[b]	
May	T. Jackson[a]		
1891 February	F. de Bovis		
April			J.P. Wade Gard'ner
May		T. Jackson	
1892 April	J. Walter[a]		
June	F. de Bovis		
1893 April	T. Jackson	E. Cameron[b]	

Notes:
[a] acting.
[b] London junior joint-Manager to acting senior.

by contemporaries. Had all gone well Jackson would not have returned in 1887, and until end-1893 his return to Hong Kong was always on an 'acting' basis. The Board on each occasion thought they had found a viable solution, but financial crises and sickness compounded by the time taken in transport from London gave rise to six changes in this period. It would be well to understand how these came about before considering the chronology of the Bank and its fortunes in the troubled years 1889 to 1893 (see Table 12.4).

The London succession

First it should be said that the impact of events on the management of the London Office was negligible. Jackson took over from McLean on June 1, 1889, after handing over to Noble in Hong Kong and taking a short leave. After some delay, in part resulting from his connection with the 'China Trust', McLean's services were retained and continuity maintained through his appointment to the London Consultative Committee. At Cameron's suggestion and with Jackson's concurrence, the Board had agreed that both Jackson and Cameron should sign as 'manager' although, as far as the Board was concerned, Jackson was senior and responsible. Jackson's command of exchange was undoubtedly valuable to the London Office, but his absence in Hong Kong for nine months in 1890/91 meant simply that the equally capable Cameron was in charge without public ceremony.

The problem was in Hong Kong.

The Board's plan and its frustration

The intention of the Board in 1888 was that G.E. Noble should remain Chief Manager until he wished to retire, at which time François de Bovis would take over. Accordingly de Bovis was in Hong Kong as Sub-Manager. Two events frustrated this straightforward plan. First, problems in Lyons, which will be considered below, forced the Board to send the French de Bovis to take charge there. Thus he was absent when the second problem arose; Noble became ill and in March 1890 required emergency sick leave.

The Chairman's proposed solution to the immediate problem was to recommend the appointment of the then Sub-Manager of the Hong Kong office, J.P. Wade Gard'ner (East in 1873), as Acting Chief Manager. Jackson had apparently been consulted by cable and had replied, 'Cannot suggest better arrangement.' The Chairman, H.L. Dalrymple, apparently met with opposition on the Board, other directors favouring, inevitably, inviting Thomas Jackson to become *acting* Chief Manager pending – and this is important – the settlement of affairs in Lyons and the return of de Bovis. The London Committee, in response to the Board's query, cabled their concern that Jackson's sudden departure for Hong Kong would arouse the suspicion that all was not well with the Bank. Despite this warning, when the vote was taken, only Forbes stood with Dalrymple in favour of Gard'ner.

Even then the decision was not clear-cut. On March 29 the Board instructed London, 'Directors opinion unaltered [in favour of Jackson] but leave matter to the discretion of the London Committee. If Committee think least cause of suspicion or injury to Bank's credit possible then by no means let Jackson come. Reply at once.' The London Committee approved Jackson's departure and he left via Brindisi on April 14.

In the meantime Wade Gard'ner was appointed Acting Chief Manager.

When these decisions were made there was no question but that Noble would return after six-months' absence. The Board minuted the directors' extreme regret at the necessity which obliged Mr Noble to take six months' furlough and in token of their appreciation voted him $10,000.

But Noble was not to return. In June there was some criticism of Noble's handling of Head Office overdrafts, and in July the Board asked for a confidential medical report. As the latter was unfavourable, the question of Noble's handling of the Bank's affairs was never formally considered independently; the medical report was sufficient to cause Noble to cancel his already booked return passage; and the Board granted him a further year's leave. Jackson was to stay until de Bovis could return to become Acting Chief Manager – again pending Noble's eventual recovery.

Jackson's last Board meeting was on January 29; de Bovis took over as Acting Chief Manager on February 1, 1891.

By mid-1891 the Board had ascertained that Noble could not return to Hong Kong and they accordingly, as originally planned, offered de Bovis a substantive appointment as Chief Manager for five years retroactively from January 1891 to January 1896. The succession had apparently been solved. There was no hesitation, no debate on the wisdom of attempting to retain Jackson in the East. The fact is that although the problems then facing the Bank had their origins in Noble's administration, the Bank remained in crisis and the Board may well have had reservations about Jackson's omniscience. Indeed Jackson wrote from London 'conveying his deepest regret for the losses recently experienced'.

The appointment of de Bovis as Chief Manager

With the appointment of de Bovis the Board had attempted to pass the chief managership of the Hongkong Bank on to the next generation. Born in 1853 in Tahiti of a French father and English mother, Louis François David de Bovis was thirteen years younger than Jackson and twenty years younger than McLean.[22]

De Bovis was not the first to be intended as Jackson's successor, and the Board's decision should be seen in its historical context.

Assuming that Jackson would not have returned from that first leave in 1886 had all gone well, the Board's first choice of a successor had been Ewen Cameron. When he refused, they turned to John Walter – both of Jackson's seniority. Jackson had been appointed Chief Manager at a particularly young age, and therefore the selection of the 'same generation' as intended successors was not unreasonable.

The first 'actual' successor, that is, an Eastern staff member appointed Chief Manager with Jackson Manager in London, was George E. Noble. He was actually a few months senior in the service of the Hongkong Bank to Thomas Jackson and his selection for the burdensome task in 1889 would seem more a desire on the part of the Board to give him the title for a few years rather than a long-term management decision. Otherwise Noble was a reasonable choice; his career had provided a sound background, very similar indeed to that of Jackson's eventual successor, J.R.M. Smith (East in 1882). Although he was for a long time Agent in Bombay, Noble was brought to Hong Kong in 1882 as Sub-Manager and in 1886 was appointed Inspector. His knowledge of the Bank's world-wide operations must therefore have been unique. But he was of the Jackson generation.

Having decided that the responsibility was to be passed, the Board had to determine who was available. Since de Bovis became the heir expectant in 1889 and since the Board left no analysis of their decision, an examination of de Bovis's career in relation to those senior and immediately junior to him may explain the Board's action.

After Cameron and Walter there were W.H. Harries, A.M. Townsend, Alexander Leith, and Andrew Veitch (East in 1871), all of whom, while senior to de Bovis, had been for a time with him in the London Office before coming East. Harries and Townsend had become American specialists, and Harries, although highly respected and on occasion called on to inspect the Bank world-wide, had probably already let it be known he preferred to remain close to the Golden Gate. Leith had been responsible for early loan contacts with Chinese officials in Foochow but had not done well in Calcutta and was in 1889 Agent in Tientsin, the office opened by de Bovis in 1881. Veitch had been for many years Accountant Shanghai; he was Sub-Manager in Hong Kong from 1886 while de Bovis was Manager Bombay. On leave in 1889 Veitch was first appointed a full Agent when he was assigned Calcutta probably in 1890.

Two London juniors came East with de Bovis in 1872 – R.H. Cook and John MacNab. Cook would appear to have done an unusually long (for the period) apprenticeship in Yokohama; his first appointment was to Saigon as Agent in 1881; during the 1880s he moved to Amoy and Hiogo, retiring in 1904 as Agent Hiogo and second (after Harries) in seniority on the Eastern staff.

John MacNab on the other hand received his first appointment, as Accountant in the new Singapore agency, in 1876 and became Accountant Manila in 1881. He was then assigned to open and manage the new Iloilo sub-agency in 1883, at which post he remained until his retirement, in early 1897, as sixth in seniority on the Eastern staff.[e] Cook and MacNab served the Bank in small agencies; the Addis diaries picture Cook as a mild, homely man doing his particular assignment well, the doyen eventually of the Port he had made home. MacNab is amusingly portrayed as 'Jock MacPerritch' in Walter Young's (Chartered Bank) *A Merry Banker in the Far East*.[23]

Cook and MacNab had their essential role, but they were not candidates for the post of Chief Manager.

Edward Morriss came to the Hongkong Bank in 1872 from Jackson's old Agra and Masterman's Bank and was a very successful Manager in Calcutta. Then in 1883 he was transferred to become Manager in Yokohama. The change presented problems and by 1886 there were reports he was in poor health; he had often been in financial difficulties and McLean noted that his son's going East would relieve the strain. Percy de C. Morriss left London in 1889 but his father died in Yokohama in 1890. Of the same Hongkong Bank seniority as Cook and MacNab, Edward Morriss was for different reasons not a likely candidate for Chief Manager.

---

[e] The Eastern staff list excluded those who had returned permanently to Europe and thus would not in the relevant years include Cameron, Walter, or de Bovis. Harries in San Francisco was, however, included on the Eastern staff until his retirement in 1912 at the age of 70.

Of those immediately junior, Edward Cope had been adversely noticed and was now refused a return to the East on medical grounds. H.M. Bevis (East in 1875), the Sub-Manager Shanghai, and A.W. Maitland (employed in the East, 1876), the Chief Accountant, had sound records but were not as yet sufficiently experienced; E.H. Oxley and Charles B. Rickett had followed the small port route and were insufficiently broad in their background; the case of M.M. Tompkins, the Accountant in San Francisco, was, as noted in Chapter 7, a special one.

This leaves J.P. Wade Gard'ner, who was considered a possible successor to Noble in 1890 and who in fact served as Acting Chief Manager during the period of Jackson's passage to Hong Kong (Table 12.4). The Board could hardly have offered him a substantive appointment solely on the grounds of de Bovis's absence, at Board request, to handle the emergency situation in Lyons. He had replaced the unsuccessful W.G. Greig as Manager Singapore in 1887 and had not as yet proved himself when he was called to Hong Kong to replace de Bovis as Sub-Manager on the latter's departure for Lyons. Wade Gard'ner's day would come and he would be appointed Manager Shanghai and then New York. But his career would not have made him a likely candidate when Jackson made his recommendation to the Board in 1888.

As for de Bovis he had served his first days in the East under both Jackson in Hong Kong and Cameron in Shanghai, the latter involving him in contacts with Chinese officials in Tientsin in 1874 and 1875. He was appointed Accountant in Calcutta in 1877, returning to Hong Kong as Sub-Manager in February 1880. The following year he opened the Bank's office in Tientsin where he remained as the first Agent. In 1883 he returned to Hong Kong as acting Sub-Manager for Noble and in October he was involved in negotiations with the Canton Viceroy which resulted in the 1884 'A' and 'B' Loans for a total two million Canton taels (= $2,789,400).

On the failure of merchant/banker Hu Kwang-yung, de Bovis was sent to Peking to determine whom the Bank should contact in the event of any failure in loan repayment; he also had discussions with the British Minister, Sir Harry Parkes, relative to the sufficiency of the Imperial edicts authorizing the Hongkong Bank's China loans. Both missions were successful, and the 1884 loans were signed by Jackson in August.

Also in 1884 de Bovis left Hong Kong on leave, en route acting for six months as Manager of the Bank's New York agency, relieving A.M. Townsend; in 1885, after leave, de Bovis was appointed Manager Bombay. His success in that key position resulted in his being brought back to Head Office as Sub-Manager in 1888 under conditions already described.

Here was a balanced career in sensitive and difficult positions, in each case successfully undertaken.

De Bovis was then the logical successor as Chief Manager. He was a reasoned and defensible choice. And yet in May 1893 Jackson was once again back in Hong

Kong and de Bovis had returned to Europe, at first 'on leave' and then as substantive Manager Lyons. What had happened?

Frustration again and the reappointment of Jackson

It is true that the Bank experienced serious difficulties throughout 1892, but the Board – and Jackson – resisted all attempts by the London shareholders to engineer the latter's return. On July 9, 1892, the Board wired the London Committee, 'The Directors are quite positive de Bovis is not to be held responsible for loss of Compradore and other losses caused chiefly by shrinkage of securities everywhere. Repeat we have great confidence in his management . . .' But they added that the Bank's credit was the first consideration and they enquired whether Jackson was willing to come. De Bovis, they added, was willing to do all possible to assist. On July 12, London wired simply, 'Jackson unwilling to go.'

Jackson had played it correctly throughout. When a shareholders' intended requisition had come to his attention, he had immediately written to de Bovis stating his disapproval; he then requested his friends to ensure that the petition was withdrawn. Jackson's reply of July 12, supplemented by a letter which was considered by the Board on August 15, apparently ended the matter. There is certainly no further reference in the minutes to the question of de Bovis's replacement.

And then, apparently without warning, de Bovis asked for twelve months' leave from March 1893. At this point Jackson was invited by the Board to act in his place.

There would be criticism later of de Bovis, but at the time the Board were probably correct in their favourable assessment of de Bovis's management. But were there private pressures which are unminuted or was there an early reassessment of their Chief Manager's record which is reflected in de Bovis's 'sudden' request for twelve months' leave? Certainly the record invites such speculation, but it is speculation and there is a simpler explanation.

Twice in the crisis year of 1892 de Bovis sought and obtained 'local' leave. He was absent two months from early April, and John Walter, then the Bank's Inspector, was requested formally to take charge. De Bovis was absent when the Bank's compradore absconded. A second but shorter leave was granted de Bovis in December although no formal appointment of an 'acting chief manager' is recorded. The assumption is reasonable that health – whether purely physical or induced by the strain of the assignment – was the proximate cause of these requests. And this would appear supported by the immediacy of de Bovis's March 1893 request for an extended leave of twelve months.

Had de Bovis been in disgrace or affairs reached a critical point the Board would undoubtedly at this point have turned immediately to Jackson. In fact there is evidence that they again requested John Walter to take over as Acting Chief Manager. Only *after* receiving Walter's cable to the effect that 'it would not suit him to be at Head Office after September' did the Chairman cable Jackson, 'De Bovis applied 12 months leave. Directors invite you coming out take Chiefmanagership during his absence if convenient.'

This time there was before Jackson no suggestion of criticism of de Bovis, no suggestion that only he, Jackson, could save the Bank. The Board had made a straightforward offer. Nevertheless here was again evidence that the Bank needed him in Hong Kong, and London replied, 'Jackson willing proceed Hong Kong at once if sufficient remuneration offered. Please state terms.' To the Chief Manager's salary of $20,000 per annum [@2/6 = £2,500] the Board offered to add £3,000, which Jackson agreed to accept and to leave on the next English mail via Brindisi. He took over, as previously noted, on April 28, 1893, for an initial period of twelve months.

This at least is the reading from Hong Kong. In London Jackson may have been developing doubts as to the competence of de Bovis's management. There is a record of serious disagreement over the removal of Charles Addis from Calcutta in 1892. When Jackson later asked Addis's view of de Bovis, Addis called him an 'unscrupulous dog'; Jackson agreed and subsequently was said to have used the term himself.[24] De Bovis had faced an almost impossible task and with hindsight one may conclude he had made mistakes. But his departure from Hong Kong was initially marked, not unlike Victor Kresser's, James Greig's, and G.E. Noble's, by the Board's sincere best wishes.

In any case, the interregnum had ended. At the August 1893 meeting the Chairman was already able to assure shareholders that Jackson had taken over the Chief Managership and that de Bovis would, after a short vacation, become Agent in Lyons. In fact Jackson would remain until early 1902 and de Bovis took charge once again in Lyons until 1922 when he retired. The change was not at once final; should Jackson decide to retire, the Board informed de Bovis, he would have the option to return as Chief Manager during the period of his initial appointment, that is, until 1896. The sense obtained from the records is, however, that the arrangement actually reached was satisfactory to all. As Cameron wrote to Jackson, 'You never did enjoy the London Office.' As for de Bovis, he was at home and highly respected in Lyons where he remained Manager until his retirement.

THE BOARD AND LONDON

The London Consultative (Advisory) Committee[f]

When David McLean retired as the Bank's London Manager in 1889 he was offered and accepted a place on the London Consultative Committee. It would be the first change in the composition of the Committee since its inception in 1875 and the first time that a former officer of the Bank would be a member. There were, however, two delays; the first was caused by the Board of Directors' concern to ensure that the appointment would meet with the approval of Jackson as the new London Manager and subsequently the question of McLean's role as director of the China Trust should that company undertake exchange business.[25] As noted, the Trust and its successor bank agreed that, subject to giving the Hongkong Bank six months' notice, it would not compete in the Far Eastern exchanges.

William Keswick, whose importance in the history of the Hongkong Bank and role in Jardine Matheson was supplemented by his chairmanship of both the Imperial Bank of Persia and the 'China Trust' and his presidency of the China Association, became a new member of the London Committee in 1890.

In September 1891 on the death of E.H. Phillpotts, an original member of the Bank's London Committee, the Hongkong Bank requested the board of the London and County Bank to nominate another of their colleagues as his successor; they chose William A. Jones. Meanwhile the key 'arrangement' with the London clearing bank would remain. This included advances to the extent of £750,000 on accepted bills, subject to a 5% margin, with shipping documents attached.[26]

The role of the London Committee remained apparently unchanged. However with Jackson and Cameron in London and with McLean and Keswick on the Committee there was change, the potential of which was not fully realized due in part to the return of Jackson to Hong Kong, in part to the awareness of the Board of Directors and their determination to keep the control of the Bank in the East.

As originally conceived, the Committee was one of Bank 'outsiders'; they were experts with a role in the City who could advise a distant Board of Directors on affairs in London. But the Committee had come to include two men, Keswick and McLean, who knew the Bank as well and its history perhaps better than anyone in Hong Kong. If their influence were to dominate the Committee's advice, the Bank's directors would lose the independent assessment of

---

[f] The early title of the Committee was 'London Advisory'; this changed without notice to 'London Consultative'; post-1945 the term 'advisory' is once again used officially.

representatives of the City. And more than this: if those on the Committee with Hong Kong connections liaised with returned senior managers then in London, possibly in association with vocal London shareholders, the balance of authority might shift to London. Given the dominant role of London in world finance, those in London might become impatient with direction from a colony; the Committee could attempt to usurp the role of the Board, the London Manager that of the Chief Manager – especially a new chief manager.

In World War II with Hong Kong occupied by the Japanese, this is precisely what happened. The London Committee was by Order in Council granted the powers of the Board of Directors, and the London Manager, who had long before been designated the Committee's *ex officio* Chairman, was appointed Acting Chief Manager; thus Arthur Morse became the first Chief Manager to act also as Chairman of the Hongkong Bank (see Volume IV).

The purpose of this glance at a future of admittedly very different circumstances under a wartime fiat is merely to recall the ease with which the change was in fact effected. As already noted, the early history of the then existing London-based Eastern banks proved the danger; the new 'national banks', of which the Imperial Bank of Persia and the Deutsch-Asiatische Bank are examples, were then establishing their 'head offices' overseas, but their boards and therefore control remained in Europe. With such questions as increasing the Bank's capital or checking the withdrawal of sterling fixed deposits dominating Board considerations, the Hongkong Bank's Hong Kong based Board of Directors was increasingly dependent on London advice; could it avoid London instructions?

There are two parts to this question: first, the role of senior returned staff – McLean, Jackson, and Cameron; secondly, the role of the London Committee.

The 1889–1893 interregnum, especially during periods in which only an Acting Chief Manager directed affairs in Hong Kong, forced on the successful former Chief Manager, Thomas Jackson, an unusual role. This, it is clear, he did not intentionally abuse. From 1875 to 1889 David McLean's private correspondence contained strongly worded, forceful advice to managers in the East, advice, nevertheless, which was not necessarily followed; Jackson had been very obviously in charge.[27] But if Jackson now wrote such letters, there might be different results, and there is indirect evidence – in the absence of Jackson's correspondence – that he and Cameron did on occasion 'strongly advise' a resentful de Bovis and with unfortunate results.

The increasing role of London during the interregnum came quite legitimately and, in the end, without detriment to the dominance of Hong Kong. There was the question of the succession itself; in this Jackson was directly consulted, but his presence or absence from London became an issue which concerned the London Committee and on which their advice was sought. The directors also needed advice on the question of increasing the capital of the Bank in 1890, on the impact in London of such Bank crises as the 1892 defalcation of the compradore, and on the number of Bank shares to be permitted registration in London.

The fall in silver and its impact on the highly publicized Trust and Loan Company, the problems of Eastern exchange banks in 1892, the Australian banking crisis in 1893, and the specific position of the Hongkong Bank led to a drain of sterling deposits from London Office, particularly serious in early 1893. To stem this flow was a priority consideration for the Board; the problem was partly educational, explaining the 'even keel' again, but explanations had to be supplemented by policy, and here the advice of the London Committee, including those who had in the Trust Company abandoned the even keel, was almost of binding force on Hong Kong.

The London Committee was the Hongkong Bank's link with the City. Its members were listed, with their primary affiliations, on the Bank's advertisements. If the Board in Hongkong disregarded the strong advice of the Committee it could be seen as defying the London and County Bank and experienced City merchants. Just as the Hongkong Bank would ask McLean and Keswick to leave the Committee in 1893 to avoid an association between the Hongkong Bank and the ill-fated 'China Trust' and its successors, so the London and County Bank, for example, could ask their representative to leave the Hongkong Bank's Committee, with serious consequences to City confidence in the Bank. All parties recognized the position. If the Hongkong Bank appeared to be in difficulty, the Board in Hong Kong could not safely disregard the strong advice of its London Committee.

As the subsequent sections will document, the Hongkong Bank Board's acceptance of advice was never capitulation. They were later able to resist, for example, Cameron's recommendation that the Bank's published accounts be denominated in sterling. When Jackson's management of the Bank was in London's view most needed, London's status was not changed; it was Jackson who returned to Hong Kong – as did Arthur Morse in 1946. The Hongkong Bank remained always the 'local' bank.

London, the Board, and the Baring crisis, 1890

Once the role was reversed.

In November 1890 the Hongkong and Shanghai Bank, responding to a request by the Governor of the Bank of England, William Lidderdale, subscribed to the guarantee of an advance of over £17 million made by the Bank of England to pay off the liabilities of Baring Bros pending the realization of their assets over a period initially set at three years. The Hongkong Bank thus became liable for a payment of up to £250,000 – compared to the London and County's £750,000 and Antony Gibbs' (acquired by the Hongkong Bank in 1980) £200,000; even the reconstituted Mercantile Bank of India was liable for £25,000 by a revised agreement of April 1893. Baring's had met its liabilities by early January 1895, and the guarantors were never called upon.[28]

The Hongkong Bank's decision was made in London by the London Manager, Ewen Cameron, acting on the advice of the London Committee.

Jackson was in Hong Kong as Acting Chief Manager. The Bank's Board of Directors were only informed at their meeting on November 20.

The need for secrecy and the immediacy of the crisis prevented consultation with Hong Kong, but the Bank's ability to respond to the request of the Governor of the Bank of England was not thereby impaired. The Hongkong Bank was considered, and considered itself, part of the City banking community. It could and did act decisively in a unique situation without reference to Hong Kong.

In 1981/82 this might well have been considered a significant precedent relevant to the Bank's attempt to acquire the Royal Bank of Scotland Group (see Volume IV).

Or possibly the Bank's London initiative was obscured by the Chairman's explanation at the February 1891 semi-annual meeting: 'Invitations were made to the leading banks in London to participate in a guarantee to the Bank of England and in this your directors at once agreed to share.'

This is not quite how it happened.

THE ROLE OF THE BOARD OF DIRECTORS

The uncertainty of the management and the constantly changing role of Thomas Jackson undoubtedly placed an unusual burden on the Board of Directors, increasing their direct involvement in the working of the Bank. As Jackson must take the credit for the Bank's turnaround in 1876 so the Board must now be credited with 'seeing the Bank through' the interregnum. Having achieved this, the directors turned again to Jackson; this and the nature of the crisis were to eventually erode the force of their direct involvement in the Bank and remove them from any significant executive role. But that is a matter for Chapter 13 and for Volume II.

As the following sections will detail, the Board were directly involved in decisions relative to the statement of the accounts and dividend policy, even to the point of 'raiding' the Officers Good Service Fund. The decision to increase the Bank's capital had to be made by the Board, and they had also to face the strain on the Bank's resources when it became clear that, if London confidence were to be retained, the dividend could no longer be 'passed'.

New agencies

The 'geographical' policy of the Board remained unchanged and the new agencies have been listed in Table 10.3. The opportunity to open in Mauritius in 1892 was passed on the ground that its isolation would make supervision difficult and that its connection with the China trade was marginal.

Tentative consideration given in October 1889 to the establishment of an agency in Sandakan, British North Borneo, was not pursued beyond sending H.E.R. 'Harry' Hunter (East in 1882) to make a survey.[g] But although the directors had no objection to setting up an agency, if it could be done cheaply, in the end even the merchant agency was not continued. As McLean warned, the Borneo trading companies did not wish to deal through a rival merchant.[29] Tentative proposals by the British North Borneo (Chartered) Company to establish their own bank had similarly made no progress; there was simply not the business, and the Hongkong Bank directors had no illusions that shareholders wished them to follow the flag or service each outpost of Empire – unless it were a business proposition.

Control and inspection

As was made dramatically clear by the inability of Edmond Morel, in 1889 the Bank's Lyons Agent, to repay his self-granted overdraft, the problem of inspection and control had not been solved. An agent with a power of attorney could commit the Bank with literally a stroke of the pen.

One obvious solution was to recruit the 'right sort of officer', and this resolved itself into a hardening of the Bank's 'through London Office only' policy.

There are two instances of this firm policy. First, there was the Board refusal in 1893 to appoint a locally employed Iloilo clerk, and secondly, there was the case of E.M. Bishop, first referred to in 1892 as a seventeen-year-old assistant to the Calcutta Manager, Charles Addis, and who is in 1897 found on the 'Eastern Staff' list.[30] Unlike earlier Eastern recruits, A.W. Maitland or F.W. Mitchell, Jr, for example (see Appendix Table to Chapter 7), Bishop was not trained in the East but went to London with Addis's recommendation and was thereafter handled in the usual way. But this did not solve the Board's immediate problems.

There was no effective way, apparently, to control unauthorized overdrafts granted by agents or managers. There were also advances against inadequate security granted by agents to members of their staff; these practices were once again forbidden. With the more frequent inspections by formally appointed inspectors and by senior officers instructed to inspect en route, these practices

---

[g] This is the first special reference to Hunter, an officer who would become Sub-Manager to J.R.M. Smith in 1902, acting Chief Manager during Smith's leave, and a successful Shanghai Manager during the revolution of 1911.

and the problems created were brought more frequently to the Board's attention. Certainly the failure of staff to practice sound personal financial habits would seem to have affected careers. J.P. Wade Gard'ner as Shanghai Manager requested a year's leave at full pay to enable him to pay off sums owed the Bank; the Board, in order to avoid a precedent, granted leave at the usual half-pay and an *ex gratia* provision of $5,000 for the debt repayment.

In the interregnum and with Noble's assumption of the chief managership there was no official 'inspector of branches' during a critical period of the Bank's history. In mid-1890, however, W.H. Harries, the respected San Francisco Agent, was instructed to inspect the branches on a world-wide basis. John Walter and Thomas Jackson inspected en route to and from Europe, but Walter was only designated 'inspector of branches' on his retirement from the Shanghai managership in 1893.

A Committee of the Board inspected Head Office loans and special committees considered particularly difficult accounts. One inspection report contained too many key names to circulate, but was made available to directors in the Chief Manager's office. As old constituents failed and heavy losses were incurred, the directors no doubt had difficult decisions to make, but they appear to have remained firm in their determination to write off losses in the half-year they occurred, a policy marred in its implementation by adjustments which will be considered below.

Buildings

As for the Bank's buildings, despite difficult times the Board appears to have followed a consistent policy, repairing as necessary, authorizing the installation of electric lighting, and buying previously rented property when the occasion allowed. Aside from expenses with the Head Office building previously noted, there were developments in Singapore, where in 1890 the Bank bought its present site on Collyer Quay opposite the Singapore Club at a cost of £23,000 and the following year sanctioned a further £15–20,000 for a new Bank building.

In 1890 the Board agreed to a new building project in flourishing Hiogo, to the purchase of Cloudlands (for $29,000) and the building of staff summer quarters on Hong Kong's 'Peak' (on doctor's advice), to strengthening the existing building in Tientsin, and to purchasing rented property in Peking for Ts8,000 and the 5.5 acre site in Penang for $3,900.

In September 1889 the Hongkong Bank had decided to accept the Government's offer of a marine lot in front of its Head Office site. In return the Bank agreed to meet the cost of the lot's reclamation as part of the Praya development project. It would eventually become part of a public open space, Statue Square, where in 1906 Sir Thomas Jackson, Bart, would make his final return – as a statue.

PERFORMANCE

The performance of the Hongkong Bank in the years 1889 to mid-1893 was determined broadly by two factors, (i) the rise of silver to September 1890 with its subsequent decline and (ii) the boom in shares and real estate on the China coast followed by a collapse virtually coincident with the fall of silver prices, thus undermining the value of the Bank's security. Underlying these trends was a gradual but dangerously irregular growth in trade, marred by business failures among the Bank's weakened constituents.

These general conditions were reinforced or countered by factors special to the Hongkong Bank, including the earnings from loans and advances to the Government of China and Imperial officials, the variations in the fortunes of the Jurado case in Manila, the behaviour of the Lyons Agent in 1889, the increase in the Bank's capital approved in 1890, the defalcation of the Bank's Hong Kong compradore in 1892, and the effects on the confidence of London shareholders and fixed-deposit customers caused by the general problems of Eastern banks in 1892 and the failure of Australian banks in 1893.

The figures are set out in Tables 12.5 to 12.7. The upward trends were not all reversed on the same date; deposits and notes, for example, continued to grow through December 1891. But the half-year ending December 31, 1890, with its high net earnings and extraordinary dividend payout of $1.2 million – or $2 million for the year, £5:10s per fully paid-up share – is in clear contrast to the June 1891 results which indicate a performance requiring the transfer of $1.47 million to a published contingency fund and the reduction of the dividend to the basic rate of £1:10s per half-year. It is equally clear that the eventual turnaround, hinted at in the 1895 figures appended to Tables 12.6 and 12.7, came after mid-1893 and thus belongs to the following chapter.

The narrative is best divided at the end of 1890.

RIDING THE UPSWING, 1889–1890

The best half-year, but for . . .

When the Board first examined the accounts for the first half of 1889 they showed a record net profit of just over $1 million. By the middle of July public expectations had driven up Bank share prices on the Hong Kong market to a premium of 195% and they were up to £54:10s in London. Shanghai profits were $325,000, Head Office $300,000, and Yokohama and Singapore $150,000 each. Despite a decline in bill business, the growth in income from loans and advances enabled a potentially good showing for this first period of Noble's management. Meanwhile the favourable trend in the Jurado case was a relief to the directors and the public, while the share markets had not as yet shown signs of weakening.

On July 18 the Board met to consider a cable from London informing them that Edmond Morel had overdrawn his account – the final figure was found later to be Fr1,294,000 (= $330,000). Against this the only security was 50 Hongkong Bank shares. The Board decided to write off the entire amount, approximately one-third of the half-year's profits, and the published accounts accordingly show net profits at $712,000.

W.H. Forbes, as Chairman of the Bank, explained the situation at the semi-annual meeting in August, but at least one shareholder, Fraser-Smith, refused to accept this quietly. His criticism could be separated into three categories: first, the lack of judgement in selecting Morel as Agent in the first place; secondly, the lack of control and previous heavy losses which indicated poor supervision by the Board of Directors; and thirdly, the lack of information in the semi-annual published accounts – this last has been considered in an earlier section.

There is no question but that the appointment of Morel had been a surprising one. McLean had advised strongly against it and had been ignored.[31] Nor was Fraser-Smith speaking with hindsight. He asked the directors, 'how it was possible that a notorious gambler like Mr. Morel, a gentleman whose reputation in China is perfectly well known as a gambler, should have had the opportunity to defraud the shareholders of this bank of the large sum of $330,000'.

Morel had been manager of the Shanghai branch of the Comptoir d'Escompte de Paris in 1865 and had been succeeded by Hermann Wallich, who records certain of Morel's dubious operations.[32] Nevertheless his career does not seem to have suffered; he had already been at one point awarded the Legion of Honour.[33]

The opportunity to misappropriate went, as it were, with the job. The Lyons agency Accountant, C.S. Haden, Jr, had warned London of Morel's overdraft early in 1889; it was reduced from over FrF1 million to FrF435,000 by May. But Morel had been speculating on the Bourse and lost further, eventually forcing the July announcement. Even with these facts Jackson in London warned the Board to say as little as possible about the case, and the Bank apparently never referred to the matter as other than an 'overdraft'. The Bank of France inspector was not so delicate; he referred to Morel's overdraft as an embezzlement.[34]

Fraser-Smith used the opportunity to remind the Board of other losses and he concluded, 'There is no other bank on the face of God's earth the shareholders of which would have tolerated such management.' Forbes did not reply with particular effectiveness, but many another bank had simply not reported such losses until accumulated errors brought it down. It was ironic that Fraser-Smith should choose that moment to complain about lack of information.

G.H. Burnett, the London Office Accountant, was sent to Lyons to investigate; Morel was dismissed and the Lyons office inspected more regularly – although this would probably not have prevented the loss. The blame for the failure to properly assess Morel before appointment was never stated, but

Table 12.5A *The Hongkong and Shanghai Banking Corporation*
Key indicators, 1889–1893
(in millions of dollars)   (in thousands of dollars)

Year	Assets	Deposits and notes	Reserve Fund	Net earnings	To Reserves	To Dividend	Rate $1 = xs/d$
1888 Dec.	114.6	82.4	4.300	864	300	590	3/0½
1889 June	120.0	89.0	4.400	712	100	@£1.5 = 592	3/0½
1889 Dec.	125.9	95.3	4.600	1049	200	£2.0^c = 768	3/1½
1890 June	134.3	99.6	5.482^a	1109	200	£2.5^d = 892	3/4¾
1890 Dec.	149.7	109.3	6.807^a	1567	300	£3.0^e = 1185	3/5
1891 June	157.9	117.7	6.300^a	907	− 1291^b	£1.5^f = 725	3/2½
1891 Dec.	153.8	120.4	6.300	706	0	£1.5 = 778	3/1
1892 June	138.8	107.3	3.300	733	− 3000	£1.0^g = 558	2/10⅜
1892 Dec.	129.5	99.7	3.600	897	300	£1.0 586	2/8¾
1893 June	130.3	89.9	3.900	998	300	£1.0 640	2/6

Shareholders' funds (1888 Dec.) = \$12,109,000 million (@ 3/0½ = £1,842,000).
Shareholders' funds (1893 June) = \$14,269,000 million (@ 2/6 = £1,784,000).

Notes:

(i) 12.5A is taken directly from figures as they stand in the published accounts with the exception that the figures for the Reserve Fund are given as approved at the shareholders meeting.

(ii) Allocations to the Reserve Fund are explained in Table 12.5B.

^{a} Including the premium received from new shares, see Table 12.5B.

^{b} \$1,470,000 were transferred to a published contingencies account, see Table 12.5B and explanations.

^{c} £1:10s plus bonus of ten shillings.

^{d} £1:10s plus bonus of £1:00.

^{e} £1:10s plus bonus of £1:10s; pro-rata on partly paid-up new shares.

^{f} £1:10s; new shares pro-rated.

^{g} New dividend rate is £1:00.

Rate: the rate as shown in the semi-annual reports.

Jackson may well have been involved. Morel, however, rose again and reappeared as a broker in Shanghai. The Hongkong Bank, despite Morel's personal plea before a committee of the Board in Hong Kong, refused to do business with him.

Further success, a capital increase, and the seeds of later problems

The successful operations in the second half of 1889, marred only by the failure of the Saigon compradore and consequent writing off of \$15,000 from the Saigon profits, led to the Board's decision to grant a dividend bonus of ten shillings, for a total payment of £2 for the half-year, against the advice of Noble, the Chief Manager. The exchange was rising, net earnings were at a record level, and all indicators were favourable. The directors argued that failure to offset the rise in

Table 12.5B *The Hongkong and Shanghai Banking Corporation
Reserve and contingency appropriations, 1889–1893*
(in thousands of dollars)

	(i) From P&L A/c	(ii) To Reserve Fund	(iii) To Premium Account	(iv) From Reserve Fund	(v) Reserve Fund + Premium	(vi) To published contingencies
Balance at:						
1888 Dec.					4,300	
Subsequently:						
1889 June	100	100			4,400	
1889 Dec.	200	200			4,600	–
1890 June	200	200	682		4,800 + 682	–
1890 Dec.	300	300	1,025		5,100 + 1,707	–
1891 June	179	0	784	1,291	3,809 + 2,491	1,470
1891 Dec.	0	0			6,300	–
1892 June	124	0		3,000	3,300	3,124
1892 Dec.	300	300			3,600	–
1893 June	300	300			3,900	–

Notes:
  (i) This should read: 'P&L Account but treating published "contingencies" as a
   separate account'. This column differs from the 'To reserve' column in Table
   12.5A in two ways: first, column 'i' above includes only net allocations from
   Profit and Loss Account as defined; secondly, column 'i' above notes by
   definition allocations within P&L Account to published contingencies. In June
   1891 and June 1892 funds were actually first transferred from the Reserve Fund
   (see col. iv above) to the P&L A/c and then designated for 'contingencies'.
 (ii) Amounts from P&L A/c actually transferred to the Reserve Fund.
(iii) The Premium each half year was first transferred to the Reserve Fund as a
   separate item and then combined, as shown in (v) above.
 (iv) The sums taken from the Reserve Fund for published contingencies.
  (v) The balance in the Reserve Fund at the conclusion of the transactions listed.
   While the premiums on the new shares were being paid in, the Reserve Fund
   proper and the Premium Account were separate items, as shown above.
 (vi) The published contingencies were an exceptional item in the P&L Account and
   appear in the accounts only twice, as shown.
Source: Table 12.5A and semi-annual statements of account.

exchange by paying out a bonus dividend would lead to great dissatisfaction
among the China shareholders. As a matter of expediency, they considered it wise
to grant the bonus.

  This is the first such statement in the minutes. It reflects a change in the
relations of the corporation to its shareholders. Local small shareholders had
always expected a steady return, as McLean had observed in 1870. The

Table 12.5C *The Hongkong and Shanghai Banking Corporation Dividends, 1889–1893*

Year	Interim £ = $ @		Final £ = $ @		Bonus £ = $		Total £ = $		Total payout £ = $ (millions)		Payout ratio %	Total dividend as % of Book value £ $ (per cent)	
1889	1:10 3/0½	9.86	1:10 3/1½	9.60	0:10	3.20[c]	3:10	22.66	0.21	1.36	72	10.8	10.9
1890[a]	1:10 3/4⅜	8.92	1:10 3/5	8.78	2:10	14.72[d]	5:10	32.42	0.35	2.08	78	14.9	15.0
1891[b]	1:10 3/2½	9.35	1:10 3/1	9.73			3:00	10.08	0.24	1.50	93	9.4	9.2
1892	1:00 2/10⅜	6.98	1:00 2/8¾	7.33			2:00	14.31	0.16	1.14	70	8.4	8.2
1893	1:00 2/6	8.00	1:00 2/3	8.89			2:00	16.89	0.16	1.35	64	9.8	9.3

Notes:

Bold face = $ equivalent

[a] Figures include pro rata dividends etc. on 20,000 new shares.

[b] Figures for the first-half are on 60,000 + pro rata on new shares; for second-half and after on 80,000.

[c] Bonus is at same rate of exchange as final dividend.

[d] The sum of two bonuses, the first £1:00 at 3/4⅜ = $5.94; the second £1:10 at 3/5 = $8.78.

Source: Tables 12.1 and 12.5A.

Table 12.6 *The Hongkong and Shanghai Banking Corporaion*
Earnings and share prices, 1889–1893

Year	(i) $ 000 Net earnings	(ii) £ Dividend/ share	(iii) $ Book value	(iv) £ Book value	(v) Share price Shanghai	(vi) London	(vii) $ M/B ratio	(viii) £ M/B ratio	(ix) Rate $1 = xs/d
1888 Dec.	864	£1.5	202	30.7	320	52	1.58	1.69	3/0½
1889 June	712	£1.5	204	40.0	363	54	1.78	1.35	3/0½
1889 Dec.	1,049	£2.0	208	32.5	368	58	1.77	1.78	3/1½
1890 June	1,109	£2.5	211	35.6	336	57	1.59	1.60	3/4⅜
1890 Dec.	1,567	£3.0	216	36.9	395	68	1.83	1.84	3/5
1891 June	907	£1.5	208	33.4	334	55	1.61	1.65	3/2½
1891 Dec.	706	£1.5	207	31.9	330	49	1.59	1.54	3/1
1892 June	733	£1.0	170	24.4	234	34	1.38	1.39	2/10⅜
1892 Dec.	897	£1.0	174	23.7	266	36	1.53	1.52	2/8¾
1893 June	998	£1.0	178	22.3	253	30	1.42	1.35	2/6
1895 June	1,634	£1.5	201	21.4	358	44	1.78	2.06	2/1⅝

Notes:
(i) Net earnings in thousands of Hong Kong dollars from Table 12.5A.
(ii) Dividends declared in pounds sterling, see Table 12.5.
(iii) Book value = shareholders' funds, i.e. paid-up capital + reserves (including amounts paid in from net earnings) + retained profits, divided by the number of shares outstanding.
(iv) Column (iii) converted into pounds sterling at rate of semi-annual report.
(v) Shanghai shares were quoted at so much percent premium, which is added to the par value of shares, i.e. $125; the dates are mid-July and mid-January.
(vi) London prices for shares on the London register.
(vii) Equivalent to (v) divided by (iii).
(viii) Equivalent to (vi) divided by (iv).
(ix) The rate used in the semi-annual Hongkong Bank accounts.

431

Table 12.7 *The Hongkong and Shanghai Banking Corporation*
Cash, selected balance sheet items, and ratios^a, 1889–1893

(in millions of dollars)

Year	Assets	Index[b]	Cash and Bullion	Cash/A ratio	Net earn.	E as % of A	Deposits + notes	Loans etc.	Loan/D ratio	Bills rec.	BR index[c]	Bills pay	BP index[c]	Rate $1 = xs/d
1888 Dec.	114.6	96	9.15	0.08	0.864	0.75	82.36	52.16	0.63	48.5	102	19.6	108	3/0½
1889 June	120.0	100	10.89	0.09	0.712	0.59	88.99	56.73	0.64	47.6	100	18.2	100	3/0½
1889 Dec.	125.9	105	13.77	0.11	1.049	0.83	95.32	55.62	0.58	51.2	108	17.3	95	3/1½
1890 June	134.3	112	18.91	0.14	1.109	0.83	99.58	63.88	0.64	46.9	99	19.8	109	3/4⅜
1890 Dec.	149.7	125	24.10	0.16	1.567	1.05	109.30	61.23	0.56	57.9	122	22.6	124	3/5
1891 June	157.9	132	29.96	0.19	0.907	0.57	117.66	62.70	0.53	60.0	126	21.4	118	3/2½
1891 Dec.	153.8	128	29.66	0.19	0.706	0.46	120.37	56.68	0.47	62.0	130	16.0	88	3/1
1892 June	138.8	116	17.25	0.12	0.733	0.53	107.25	54.84	0.51	63.9	134	14.3	79	2/10⅞
1892 Dec.	129.5	108	16.33	0.13	0.897	0.69	99.74	44.14	0.44	61.4	129	15.3	84	2/8¾
1893 June	130.3	109	19.59	0.15	0.998	0.77	99.58	46.98	0.47	55.5	117	15.8	87	2/6
1895 June	167.1	139	51.39	0.27	1.678	0.98	129.35	47.65	0.37	60.0	126	20.8	114	2/1⅝

Notes:

E = earnings D = deposits + notes.
A = assets.
Loans etc. = bills discounted, loans and credits.
Bills pay = BP = bills payable, incl. 'drafts on London Bankers and short sight drawings on our London Office against bills receivable and bullion shipments'.

a Ratios affected by China loan operations.
b Index of total assets, June 1889 = 100.
c June 1889 = 100.
Bills rec. = BR = bills receivable

432

Hongkong Bank was, however, no longer a local association owned by those whose long-run interests were those of Hong Kong and thus of Hong Kong's local bank. Many shareholders were holding Bank shares not as constituents involved in the fortunes of the Bank at several levels but simply as investors who had selected Bank shares on some objective financial criterion. The Board now had a responsibility to maintain a stable market; they were responsible to shareholders for the capital value of their investment. The Morel affair brought discredit on the Board not only because of people's concern in the Bank's operations *per se* but because of the immediate impact the news caused on share prices. In January 1890 Noble hoped to bring the Reserve Fund at least to $5 million where the total published reserves had stood before the withdrawals of 1886–1887; he accordingly urged the transfer of $400,000 to reserves, but the Board would agree only to $200,000; it then approved the bonus at a cost of $192,000.

By the end of 1889 all government approvals had been given for the Bank's amended ordinance, as described in the previous chapter. With the constitutional problem solved, the Bank's currency issue on an approved basis, and the management succession apparently solved, the Board had now to face again the capital problem created by success.

As J.J. Keswick pointed out, shareholders' funds as a percentage of deposits and notes in circulation were dangerously low. Although the Bank's business, including its deposit liabilities, had grown since 1885 the Reserve Fund had not yet returned to the $5 million level and the capital/deposit (+ notes) ratio was 11% as compared with the 16% prevailing in 1882 when the directors had last recommended a capital increase. The capital/assets ratio was a reasonable 10.6%.

There was no question but that Keswick was correct, but neither the Chief Manager nor the London Committee were at first convinced that Keswick's remedy, a further increase in capital, was a satisfactory answer – the arguments were virtually the same as those of 1882 (see Chapter 9).

With exchange rising and the increased confidence of investors overseas, this was an excellent opportunity to offer shares at a considerable premium, but the Chief Manager expressed doubts on two points, (i) could China-Coast investors find the funds to subscribe to additional shares offered at a premium, and (ii) could the Bank sustain the dividend level at £3 per annum on the increased capital? In London the argument was again advanced that with sterling fixed deposits exceeding £4.3 million, there was evidence the Bank could obtain the funds it needed without the inflexibility of an increased capital.

The Board agreed in February 1890 to ask the Governor's permission for the Bank's capital to be increased from $7.5 million to the maximum of $10 million authorized by the ordinance of incorporation by a rights issue at a price of £42:10s on the basis of one share for every three shares held; the Governor's approval was proclaimed on February 20. This decision was endorsed by shareholders at a special meeting on May 31, 1890, and final payment was to be due on March 31, 1891.

The dire predictions made by the critics of the proposal proved correct, but the consequences to the Bank had the capital not been increased at this particular time would have been particularly serious. The new capital was to be needed immediately, not as the basis of the Bank's continued growth but for its survival. Growth would come later. By June 1892 the dollar book value of a Bank share, despite the premium paid on new shares, was 18% below that of December 1889; with the fall in exchange the problem was compounded in London where the book value in sterling had fallen 25%. The losses incurred in 1891–1892 were obvious enough in terms of dollars, but they were sufficient, in terms of sterling, to create an overall decline in shareholders' funds from £2.67 million in June 1891 when the new capital and bonus had been paid up to £1.94 million in June 1892, thus wiping out the entire bonus received on the issue of the new shares and part of the newly subscribed and paid-up capital. Had such losses fallen on the Bank as it stood in 1890 it would not likely have survived in the general atmosphere of distrust of Eastern banks. The withdrawal of London funds alone would have put its survival in doubt, even though the capital/assets ratio had fallen by less than 1% to 9.8% (see Table 12.8).

Such events were not to be foreseen. In January 1890 G.E. Noble's caution was understandable. Can we, he asked, maintain the dividend at £1:10s per half-year, representing a payout of eight lacs against an average net profit over the past ten years (including income from the China loans) of 7.8 lacs? In the event the dividend had to be cut back to £1 in June 1892 and, with the falling rate of exchange, even this required a payout of 7.6 lacs in June 1894 – the annual regular dividend returned to £3 only in 1899.

Noble's second question was even more interesting. Could Hong Kong shareholders find the money to pay for the new shares and their premium? At this point approximately 50% of the shares were registered in the East and 50% in London; if the Eastern shareholders could not afford to buy the new issue, the only remedy would be to issue more shares to the London register, possibly upsetting the balance of ownership. This, it was generally feared, would change the nature of the Bank, with the possibility of the Head Office being forced to London.

At the Board's February 1890 meeting A.P. McEwen recommended increasing the proportion of shares in London to relieve Hong Kong. He acknowledged that London shareholders could use such a move to the detriment of the Bank but he thought it highly unlikely that they would. At the same time the London Committee, undoubtedly urged by Jackson, who felt strongly on the matter, recommended against the move.

Table 12.8 The Hongkong and Shanghai Banking Corporation
The capital increase of 1890/91

	Authorized = Paid-up capital	Reserve Funds	Shareholders' funds	C/A ratio	Book value	Share price	M/B ratio	Exchange rate $1 = xs/d
	in millions of dollars				$			
60,000 shares								
Dec. 1889	7.50	4.60	12.49	10.6	208.2	368.0	1.77	3/1½
80,000 shares								
June 1891	10.00	6.30	16.66	10.5	208.3	334.0	1.60	3/2½
June 1892	10.00	3.30	13.62	9.8	170.3	234.0	1.37	2/10⅜
	in millions of pounds				£			
60,000 shares								
Dec. 1889	1.17	0.72	1.95		32.5	58.0[a]	1.78	3/1½
80,000 shares								
June 1891	1.60	1.01	2.67		33.4	55.0[a]	1.65	3/2½
June 1892	1.43	0.47	1.95		24.4	34.0[a]	1.39	2/10⅜

Note:
[a] This is the London price in pounds sterling.
C/A = Capital/assets.
Source: see Tables 12.5A and 12.6.

435

In the financial crisis that followed, however, some relief to Hong Kong became essential. As early as May 1890 two hard-pressed constituents, John S. Lapraik and G.S. Coxon, were urging the Bank to register as many as 50,000 shares in London. The Bank resisted until late 1892 when it agreed formally to permit the transfer of Hong Kong registered shares – but only those against which the Bank had lent funds – to be re-registered in London. The Hong Kong and Shanghai share markets could absorb no more; if the Bank were to be repaid advances secured on its shares, it had to permit their sale in London. The limit on the London register was accordingly increased to 44,000 or 55% of the 80,000 then outstanding, but the dire consequences did not follow. McEwen had been correct.

Although at first arguing that an increase in London fixed deposits would meet the Bank's needs, in early February the London Committee cabled the Board its agreement on the need to increase the capital and recommended a price of £45. The Board's decision to issue at £42:10s was dictated precisely because they recognized the limitations of the Eastern share markets and were unwilling as yet to increase the proportion of shares registered in London.

As the Hongkong Bank had been lending heavily against shares, Noble had gained a feel for the market and could estimate the capacity of local stock exchanges to absorb the new issue. The expectations were favourable, in great part because the Hongkong Bank had created a bull market by fuelling share promotion. Many of the companies were speculative mining ventures in Southeast Asia. The Bank had created a market for its shares, but had also prepared for the crisis which was to have such an impact on the Bank's shareholders' funds.

A mid-1890 internal investigation during the market boom by Dalrymple as Chairman, Wade Gard'ner as Sub-Manager, and Thomas Jackson as Acting Chief Manager revealed that Noble had initially set sound credit limits for brokers, but that beginning in August and September 1889 he had under pressure permitted these limits to be exceeded. The system then prevailing had been unsound: a broker (i) received the shares from the seller, (ii) drew on his account with the Bank and paid the seller, but (iii) did not pay in against the following sale – instead the broker held the shares for the buyer at the high 'fictitious' price then prevailing. As the Bank attempted to insist the broker reduce his overdraft, the broker in turn had to seek payment from the buyer or place the shares on the market. As this would undermine the price of the shares, the broker put pressure on the Bank to increase his advance – and it was to this pressure that Noble apparently yielded.

When a series of adverse factors began to influence the market, however, prices could not be sustained, and the Bank's advances very quickly became inadequately secured. Attempts to call them in inevitably triggered further problems. As noted above, in riding the upswing the Bank was setting the stage for its role in the financial crisis of 1891–1892.

1890

The results of operations in the first-half of 1890 inspired the editor of the *North-China Herald* to write glowingly of 'the Bank': '. . . as in England when people talk of "the Bank" they mean the old lady in Threadneedle Street, so in China whenever we talk of "the Bank" further description is unnecessary, and it is known at once that we mean the Hongkong and Shanghai Bank.'[35]

His praise was for directors and managers. His admiration was for the high level of declared profits, which he assumed, incorrectly, were but half of actual net profits, large amounts having supposedly been put away into an unnecessarily high contingencies account, which 'unnecessary' portion would have constituted the Bank's 'hidden' or 'inner' reserves. The payout ratio for 1890 was 78%, and the unpublished contingencies were not significantly greater than the amounts actually required against specific accounts.

Once again the Bank's success was attributed to 'the courtesy and geniality of its managers, the forbearance where necessary, and the readiness to oblige, that have always characterized its officers from the highest down'.

There was reason to write in this vein. The Board without dissension had voted a bonus dividend of £1 a share, the cost of which had, it is true, been virtually offset by the rise in exchange; it could be argued that the 'bonus' did little more than restore the value of the dividend in dollars. A total half-year dividend of £2:10s had been declared only twice before, in 1882 and 1885, and the *North-China Herald* was correct in supposing that the Bank intended an even higher dividend at the end of the year.

But the Bank had in fact written off $1.2 million before declaring a net profit of $1.1 million. Of this write-off 1.5 lacs of dollars were the result of revaluing sterling investments from a rate of 3s:1d to 3s:4d. A further 2 lacs were due to defalcations and swindles and only $355,000 was transferred to contingency account. Thomas Jackson had inspected Singapore en route to Hong Kong and had been concerned with the outstanding advances to the chettiars, the local money-lenders, especially in the wake of the collapse of several mining ventures in the Malay Peninsula. The Manila capital was written down in view of the continued problems with Jurado and Co., and there were bad debts in Bombay, Yokohama, and on Head Office books.

Press reports were correct in supposing the Bank had realized capital gains in the sale of rupee securities. And the directors had resisted any temptation to take over unrealized gains on their remaining rupee paper. In all it was a conservative handling of the accounts, based on the exceptionally heavy gross earnings of

$871,000 by Head Office. The one deficiency, in the opinion of the Shanghai editor, was the failure of the Bank's directors to reward the staff. This omission the directors corrected in March 1891 with the announcement that a bonus, equivalent to 10% of salary, or $62,500 had been voted. A further $50,000 had been transferred to the Officers Good Service Fund, but this was not made public at the time. Other announcements were equally favourable. The dividend was continued at £1:10s (£3 per annum), which would require a payout (on the assumption of all shares fully paid and exchange at 3s:5d) of $1.4 million. The transfer to the Reserve Fund was $300,000, and a further $100,000 was written off the Building Account.

The large Head Office profits were partly due to realized gains on the sale of investments but the main extraordinary source would appear to have been profits on exchange. Thomas Jackson was given public credit for this at the March 1891 meeting, but the Board had voted their New York Agent, A.M. Townsend, £1,000, presumably in addition to any general staff bonus, for 'work during fluctuations in silver in which the Bank benefited'.

It was the climax. The Chairman, H.L. Dalrymple, noted that Jackson had already left and de Bovis was now in charge until Noble's expected return in the Autumn. With Jackson in London, de Bovis, like John Walter before him, would preside over the fall.

COLLAPSE AND REASSURANCE, 1891–JUNE 1893

Flushed with success the directors voted themselves an increase in their semi-annual fees from the total $10,000 to $18,000 effective in 1891. It would be the first increase since the incorporation of the Bank in 1866. The June results however were such that the directors decided this would not be well received. Not until 1895 did the Bank recover sufficiently for the directors to consider an increase appropriate, and then only to $15,000.

The first losses, January–June 1891

Four major failures set the tone of the recession which now characterized the markets of the East. In April 1891 B. and A. Hormusjee, associated with the Hongkong Bank since its founding and their first agents in Bombay, failed with losses to the Bank estimated at £65,000. In May Adamson Bell suspended payment, affecting the Bank in Shanghai, Yokohama, and London. Russell and Co. failed in June. Nor had the Bank been successful in the Straits Settlements. The failure of Dickson and Co. and Browne and Co. in Penang, the continuing problem with the chettiars in Singapore, and the fall out from mining speculations caused the Bank to set aside $377,000.

The Bank sold rupee securities, realizing a capital gain, and transferred the proceeds to a Contingency Account. To some extent the Bank's manoeuvrability had been limited by the requirement to set aside acceptable securities, equal to one-third of its paid-up capital, against the note issue, and the requirements of 'eligibility' were more stringent than expected. With the increase of the Bank's capital to $10 million, reached at the end of March 1891, a further assignment – much to the Bank's chagrin – of securities worth $83,333 had to be made. The Bank's concern to improve its London image by increasing its special reserve with the Bank of England further limited its ability to use funds for its regular and exchange business, but visible strength in London was seen as basic to the Bank's position.

The 'net' profits of the Bank in the first six months of 1891, after taking account of a $200,000 loss in Singapore, were only $907,000 compared with the previous half-year's net earnings of $1.8 million. Expected losses were only partially covered by the unpublished Contingencies Account, and the Board resolved to set aside $1.47 million in a published Contingencies Account. At the same time they determined to continue the payment of the then standard half-yearly £1:10s dividend at a cost of $725,000. To accomplish all this the Board had no choice but to transfer $1,290,000 from the Reserve Fund and allocate as shown in Table 12.5B, despite the fact that the fall in exchange provided a small margin for capital gain on sterling securities, the value of which had previously been written down as the exchange rose.

As noted, the dividend at the standard rate of £1:10s for the half-year had to be maintained. The Board could not risk the impact on share prices and on depositors' confidence which passing the dividend would, given the depressed atmosphere in Hong Kong, have undoubtedly caused. Dividends were not being paid out of current earnings, properly defined; they had been transferred to contingencies. Dividends were being paid from the Hongkong Bank's Reserve Fund – in the same half-year that the Fund received its last credit from the bonus on the new capital. Here was a further element of inflexibility in the decisions available to management.

At this point the Bank's Chairman, J.S. Moses, announced to shareholders that G.E. Noble had been considered too ill to return to Hong Kong and that de Bovis had been confirmed as Chief Manager. It was not an auspicious beginning, but those at the August 1891 meeting applauded loudly. Moses was also able to announce the favourable inspection report by Harries, a name which would be familiar to the shareholders present. Otherwise the Chairman could do nothing more than assure shareholders that their problems were common to all Eastern banks, that the Board had written off the losses, that the Bank had unrealized capital gains, and that the earning capacity of the Bank was apparently unimpaired.

Trade depression, 1891–1892, and the flight of the compradore

In the quiet of a monastery in the distant mountains of Kwangtung, Lo Hok Pang, who had a short time before 'swayed the sceptre of authority in the Compradore's department of "Lucky" Jackson's palatial money shop on Queen's Road Central', that is to say, the compradore of the Hongkong Bank, died probably in late 1892. He left a widow and six children in Whampoa and a debt of $1,292,000 to the Hongkong Bank.[36] The compradore had 'gone Canton, more far', absconded, in March 1892; his nephew and head shroff, Lo Yuk, left Hong Kong with $12,000 unaccounted for in May.[37]

To cover this and the other business losses after a year of reduced earnings, the directors withdrew $3 million from the Reserve Fund, which consequently stood at $3.3 million. The additional shareholders' funds acquired by the share issue of 1890 had been all but lost (see Table 12.8); the Bank had to begin again.

For a time it had appeared as if the Bank, after writing off its losses in June 1891, might have stabilized its position until general economic conditions improved. But the losses had continued. The compradore had for a time been able to prevent his own collapse, but as the Bank called in its loans and scrutinized his credits more carefully the day of crisis could not long be postponed. When it came the impact on the Bank was serious, but the worst of the crisis was over and the earning power of the Bank recovered sufficiently to lend credibility to a favourable assessment of its recovery. With the outbreak of the Sino-Japanese War in 1894 and the defeat of China the following year, the East Asian situation and the position of the Hongkong Bank were to change significantly.

July–December 1891

As evidence that the Bank was not paralysed, the directors authorized the opening of a small agency in Nagasaki and sent J.R.M. Smith to test out the prospects in Rangoon. A doubtful advance of Ts200,000 to the Pingtu (P'ing-hsiang) Mines, which was guaranteed on a personal basis by Li Hung-chang, had been repaid, and the directors felt sufficiently buoyant to confirm their approval for construction of a new building in Singapore.

Then came heavy losses in Java, the defalcation of the newly elected director, E.L. Woodin, losses in Bombay for which David Jackson (East in 1878), the young brother of Thomas Jackson, was reprimanded, and in early 1892 losses in Hiogo and Penang for which last mentioned P.E. Cameron (East in 1880) was reprimanded. Meanwhile a serious problem was developing in Hong Kong with various long-standing accounts, and at the last moment the Board decided to write off some $260,000. When all these losses had been deducted from the early estimates of 'net' profits, that is, net of 'normal' trading losses, the estimated figure had to be reduced from $1.1 million to the published $705,500. The

11 The Hong Kong Waterfront, circa 1890, with the Hongkong Bank on the left.

12 Hongkong Bank Office, Hong Kong, 1886 building from the harbour.

13 Hongkong Bank Office, Hong Kong, 1886 building, a corner view from
Queen's Road.

14 Hongkong Bank banknotes.

The notes illustrate variations in the Chinese name of the Bank; the one-tael note is a reissue from the days of the 'Company Limited'; all show handwritten signatures validating the notes.

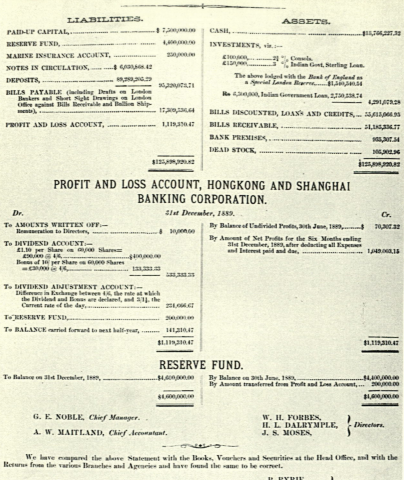

ABSTRACT OF ASSETS AND LIABILITIES, HONGKONG AND SHANGHAI BANKING CORPORATION.

31st December, 1889.

LIABILITIES.

PAID-UP CAPITAL,	$ 7,500,000.00
RESERVE FUND,	4,400,000.00
MARINE INSURANCE ACCOUNT,	250,000.00
NOTES IN CIRCULATION, ... $ 6,030,868.42	
DEPOSITS, ...$ 89,289,205.29	95,320,073.71
BILLS PAYABLE (including Drafts on London Bankers and Short Sight Drawings on London Office against Bills Receivable and Bullion Shipments),	17,309,536.64
PROFIT AND LOSS ACCOUNT,	1,119,310.47
	$125,898,920.82

ASSETS.

CASH,	$13,766,227.32
INVESTMENTS, viz.:—	
£100,000,......2¾ % Consols.	
£150,000,.........3 % Indian Govt. Sterling Loan.	
The above lodged with the *Bank of England* as a *Special London Reserve*....$1,540,540.54	
Rs 5,500,000, Indian Government Loan, 2,750,538.74	
	4,291,079.28
BILLS DISCOUNTED, LOANS AND CREDITS, ... 55,615,066.95	
BILLS RECEIVABLE,	51,185,336.77
BANK PREMISES,	935,307.54
DEAD STOCK,	105,902.96
	$125,898,920.82

PROFIT AND LOSS ACCOUNT, HONGKONG AND SHANGHAI BANKING CORPORATION.

Dr.   *31st December, 1889.*   Cr.

To AMOUNTS WRITTEN OFF:—	
Remuneration to Directors, ...$ 10,000.00	
To DIVIDEND ACCOUNT:—	
£1.10 per Share on 60,000 Shares=	
£90,000 @ 4/6,...............$400,000.00	
Bonus of 10/ per Share on 60,000 Shares	
=£30,000 @ 4/6,.................. 133,333.33	
	533,333.33
To DIVIDEND ADJUSTMENT ACCOUNT:—	
Difference in Exchange between 4/6, the rate at which the Dividend and Bonus are declared, and 3/11, the Current rate of the day,...................... 234,666.67	
To RESERVE FUND,	200,000.00
To BALANCE carried forward to next half-year, ... 141,310.47	
	$1,119,310.47

By Balance of Undivided Profits, 30th June, 1889,.........$ 70,307.32	
By Amount of Net Profits for the Six Months ending 31st December, 1889, after deducting all Expenses and Interest paid and due,	1,049,003.15
	$1,119,310.47

RESERVE FUND.

To Balance on 31st December, 1889,	$4,600,000.00	By Balance on 30th June, 1889,	$4,400,000.00
		By Amount transferred from Profit and Loss Account, ...	200,000.00
	$4,600,000.00		**$4,600,000.00**

G. E. NOBLE, *Chief Manager.*
A. W. MAITLAND, *Chief Accountant.*

W. H. FORBES,
H. L. DALRYMPLE,   } *Directors.*
J. S. MOSES,

We have compared the above Statement with the Books, Vouchers and Securities at the Head Office, and with the Returns from the various Branches and Agencies and have found the same to be correct.

P. RYRIE,
F. HENDERSON,   } *Auditors.*

HONGKONG, *6th February, 1890.*

15 Abstract of Assets and Liabilities, December 31, 1889.
Note the details of the Bank's investments, the Dividend Adjustment Account, and the healthy state of the Reserve Fund.

ABSTRACT OF ASSETS AND LIABILITIES, HONGKONG & SHANGHAI BANKING CORPORATION,

31st December, 1898.

LIABILITIES.		ASSETS.	
PAID-UP CAPITAL	$10,000,000.00	CASH	$25,259,491.05
RESERVE FUND	9,000,000.00	COIN lodged with the Hongkong Government against Note Circulation in excess of $10,000,000	3,250,000.00
MARINE INSURANCE ACCOUNT	250,000.00	BULLION IN HAND AND IN TRANSIT ..	3,952,081.33
NOTES IN CIRCULATION :—		INDIAN AND COLONIAL SECURITIES ..	4,907,751.93
Authorised Issue against Securities deposited with the Crown Agents for the Colonies $10,000,000.00		INVESTMENTS, viz.:—	
Additional Issue authorised by Hongkong Ordinance No. 6 of 1898, against Coin lodged with the Hongkong Government .. 2,503,537.57		£250,000 .. .. 2¾ % Consols. Lodged with the *Bank of England* as a *Special London Reserve* .. $1,900,000.00	
	12,503,537.57	£475,500 .. Consols and other Sterling Securities.. .. .. 4,856,170.21	
CURRENT {Silver $55,835,768.57			6,756,170.21
ACCOUNTS, {Gold £1,219,604 12s.9d. = 12,455,841.72		BILLS DISCOUNTED, LOANS AND CREDITS	64,366,272.16
	68,291,610.29	BILLS RECEIVABLE..	72,505,741.14
FIXED {Silver $32,107,804.64		BANK PREMISES	757,648.84
DEPOSITS. {Gold £2,997,056 15s.7d.=30,617,411.94			
	62,725,216.58		
BILLS PAYABLE (including Drafts on London Bankers and Short Sight Drawings on London Office against Bills Receivable and Bullion Shipments)	14,592,602.56		
PROFIT AND LOSS ACCOUNT	4,392,189.66		
Liability on Bills of Exchange re-discounted, £4,646,959 8s. 7d. of which up to this date £3,708,805 7s. 9d. have run off.			
	$181,755,156.66		$181,755,156.66

GENERAL PROFIT AND LOSS ACCOUNT, HONGKONG & SHANGHAI BANKING CORPORATION,

31st December, 1898.

Dr.   **Cr.**

To AMOUNTS WRITTEN OFF :—			By Balance of Undivided Profits, 30th June, 1898	$376,916.76
Remuneration to Directors	$15,000.00		„ Amount of Net Profits for the Six Months ending 31st December, 1898, after making provision for bad and	
„ DIVIDEND ACCOUNT :—			doubtful debts, deducting all Ex-	
£1 10/ per Share on 80,000 Shares= £120,000 @ 4/6 .. .. .. $533,333.33			penses and Interest paid and due .. 4,015,272.90	
Bonus of £1 per Share on 80,000 Shares= £80,000 @ 4/6 .. .. 355,555.55				4,392,189.66
	888,888.88			
„ DIVIDEND ADJUSTMENT ACCOUNT :—				
Difference in Exchange between 4/6, the rate at which the Dividend and Bonus are declared, and 1/11¾, the current rate of the day	1,153,664.32			
„ TRANSFER TO RESERVE FUND	1,000,000.00			
„ TRANSFER TO BANK PREMISES ACCOUNT	500,000.00			
„ BALANCE carried forward to next half-year	834,636.46			
	$4,392,189.66			$4,392,189.66

RESERVE FUND.

To Balance	$10,000,000.00	By Balance, 30th June, 1898	$9,000,000.00
		„ Transfer from Profit and Loss Account ..	1,000,000.00
	$10,000,000.00		$10,000,000.00

T. JACKSON, *Chief Manager.*

J. C. PETER, *Acting Chief Accountant.*

J. J. BELL-IRVING,
R. M. GRAY,   } *Directors.*
R. SHEWAN,

We have compared the above Statement with the Books, Vouchers and Securities at the Head Office, and with the Returns from the various Branches and Agencies, and have found the same to be correct.

F. HENDERSON, } *Auditors.*
C. S. SHARP,

Hongkong, 31st *January*, 1899.

16 Abstract of Assets and Liabilities, December 31, 1898.
In this year Jackson achieved his goal of a Reserve Fund equal in value to Paid-up Capital; in addition to the transfer of $1 million to the Reserve Fund, note that $0.5 million was written off Premises Account.

17 Hongkong Bank Office, Shanghai, 1892.

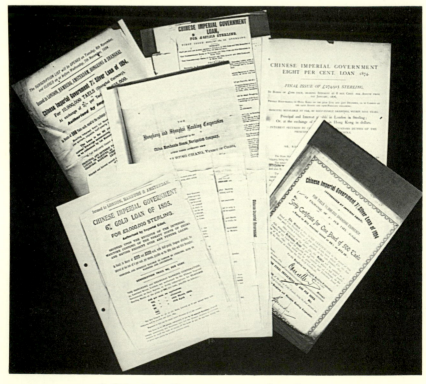

18 China Loan Prospectuses, etc, 1874–1895.

19 A Foreign Staff Group in Hong Kong, 1886.
(Left to right, back row) H. M. Thomsett, A. G. Stephen,
W. H. Gaskell, W. H. Wallace; (second row) D. H. Mackintosh, Ewen
Cameron, G. E. Noble, V. A. Caesar Hawkins, H. M. Bevis, T. McC.
Browne; (front row) J. P. Wade Gard'ner, Gershom Stewart,
C. S. Addis, T. Jackson, H. R. Coombs – from the private collection of
Sir Michael Jackson, Bart.

20 Foreign Staff, Hong Kong, on eve of Sir Thomas Jackson's retirement, 1902.
(Left to right, back row) H. W. Fraser, R. E. N. Padfield, A. Sharp, O. J. Barnes,
W. Inglis, L. J. C. Anderson, A. Boyd, R. C. Edwards, E. M. Knox, H. E. Morris
(temporary staff); (middle row) H. C. Sandford, A. B. Lowson, P. A. Barlow,
B. C. M. Johnston, A. H. Barlow, E. E. Deacon, R. T. Wright, G. H. Ardron,
W. C. D. Turner, E. D. Sanders; (front row) J. C. Peter, J. R. M. Smith,
Sir Thomas Jackson, V. A. Caesar Hawkins, C. W. May.

Hongkong & Shanghai Banking Corporation.

ABSTRACT OF ASSETS AND LIABILITIES.
31st December, 1901.

LIABILITIES.

PAID-UP CAPITAL	$10,000,000.00
STERLING RESERVE FUND	10,000,000.00
SILVER RESERVE FUND	3,750,000.00
MARINE INSURANCE ACCOUNT	250,000.00

NOTES IN CIRCULATION:—
Authorised Issue against Securities deposited with the Crown Agents for the Colonies ... $10,000,000.00
Additional Issue authorised by Hongkong Ordinance No. 19 of 1900, against Coin lodged with the Hongkong Government ... 3,006,761.37 = 13,006,761.37

CURRENT ACCOUNTS { Silver $84,438,654.24 / Gold £2,275,728 3/9 = 24,512,736.38 } = 108,951,390.62

FIXED DEPOSITS { Silver $41,052,600.47 / Gold £3,687,660 3/3 = 39,768,041.28 } = 80,820,641.75

BILLS PAYABLE (including Drafts on London Bankers and Short Sight Drawings on London Office against Bills Receivable and Bullion Shipments) ... 18,175,305.05

PROFIT AND LOSS ACCOUNT ... 3,879,090.77

Liability on Bills of Exchange re-discounted, £5,270,363 5s. 11d., of which up to this date £3,620,356 have run off.

$248,833,189.56

ASSETS.

CASH	$37,545,408.13
COIN lodged with the Hongkong Government against Note Circulation in excess of $10,000,000	5,360,000.00
BULLION IN HAND AND IN TRANSIT	14,309,998.96
INDIAN GOVERNMENT RUPEE PAPER	2,009,196.29
CONSOLS, COLONIAL & OTHER SECURITIES	8,386,462.30

STERLING RESERVE FUND INVESTMENTS, viz.:—

£250,000 .... 2¾% Consols, Lodged with the Bank of England as a Special London Reserve, at 90 £225,000 $1,000,000.00

£267,500 2¾% Consols, £255,000 2¾% National War Loan } at 90 £470,250 4,702,500.00

£355,500 .... Other Sterling Securities standing in the books at .... £339,750 3,397,500.00 = 10,000,000.00

BILLS DISCOUNTED, LOANS AND CREDITS...	74,711,466.41
BILLS RECEIVABLE	95,780,452.12
BANK PREMISES	730,205.35

$248,833,189.56

GENERAL PROFIT AND LOSS ACCOUNT.
31st December, 1901.

Dr.

To AMOUNTS WRITTEN OFF:—
Remuneration to Directors ... $15,000.00

„ DIVIDEND ACCOUNT:—
£1. 10/ per Share on 80,000 Shares—£120,000 @ 4/6, ... $533,333.33
„ BONUS of 10/- per share on 80,000 Shares = £40,000 @ 4/6 ... 177,777.78 = 711,111.11

„ DIVIDEND ADJUSTMENT ACCOUNT:—
Difference in Exchange between 4/6, the rate at which the Dividend and Bonus are declared, and 1/10¼, the current rate of the day ... 1,014,731.59
„ TRANSFER TO SILVER RESERVE FUND 500,000.00
„ TRANSFER TO BANK PREMISES ACCOUNT 200,000.00
„ BALANCE carried forward to next half-year ... 1,438,248.07

$3,879,090.77

Cr.

By Balance of Undivided Profits, 30th June, 1901 ... $1,485,715.99

„ Amount of Net Profits for the Six Months ending 31st December, 1901, after making provision for bad and doubtful debts, deducting all Expenses and Interest paid and due 2,393,374.78 = $3,879,090.77

$3,879,090.77

STERLING RESERVE FUND.

To Balance	$10,000,000.00	By Balance 30th June, 1901 (invested in Sterling Securities.)	$10,000,000.00
	$10,000,000.00		**$10,000,000.00**

SILVER RESERVE FUND.

To Balance	$4,250,000.00	By Balance 30th June, 1901	$3,750,000.00
		„ Transfer from Profit and Loss Account	500,000.00
	$4,250,000.00		**$4,250,000.00**

T. JACKSON, *Chief Manager.*

J. C. PETER, *Chief Accountant.*

R. SHEWAN,
J. J. BELL IRVING, } *Directors.*
N. A. SIEBS,

We have compared the above Statement with the Books, Vouchers and Securities at the Head Office, and with the Returns from the various Branches and Agencies, and have found the same to be correct.

HONGKONG, *4th February*, 1902.

F. HENDERSON,
C. S. SHARP, } *Auditors.*

---

21 Abstracts of Assets and Liabilities, December 1901.
Note the 'even keel' policy – building up a new Silver Reserve Fund in addition to the Sterling Reserve Fund; note also the details of both sterling and silver investments; the Hong Kong dollar was 1s/10¼d and falling.

tentative stability of earnings in the depression was at least partly the result of lower interest rates on deposits.

The net earnings figures are not comparable. In most years the directors wrote off losses and published the figures net; in others, especially when large sums had to be taken from reserves, the Board gave profits gross of major losses and then credited these sums to a published Contingency Account. Another source of incomparability arises from the practice of allowing for losses recognized after the end of the half-year but before the finalization of the accounts. Earnings for the half-years ending June and December 1891 (and even June 1892) were virtually the same, but the published accounts show a $200,000 difference.

The directors were nevertheless determined to maintain the dividend at £1:10s. To achieve this without withdrawing funds from the reserves, the directors wrote up the value of their rupee securities to market, say 105. This unusual step might be justified by noting that although the gain had not been realized by December 31, the securities were sold in February 1892 at an average price of $105\frac{1}{8}$, before the directors finalized their report. They were aware that their write-up was conservative. The sale and the consequent purchase of consols was, as it happened, a sound long-run decision, especially in view of the subsequent history of the Indian exchanges.

The last minute write-offs of doubtful Hong Kong accounts were still not provided for, and the directors decided to 'sacrifice' $130,000 from the Officers Good Service Fund (see Chapter 15). At the same time, the Board resolved formally that 'at no distant period' they intended this sum should be 'replaced for the benefit of the Staff'. The Bank might have to scrape, but the Board maintained both the dividend and its conservative write-off policy. The handling of the Staff Fund, payments into which had only recently been augmented, the Board considered a matter wholly discretionary with themselves, and indeed the Fund had no contractual restrictions nor had shareholders been informed officially of its existence. But this use of the Fund as an embryo 'hidden reserve' was unique; as commitments to the staff became more formal, the Bank was to develop other ways to meet financial emergencies.

This time Charles Addis, writing from Calcutta, did not view the situation with the same sanguine calm as in 1889 when he had expressed himself proud of a Bank which could transcend such losses as it had sustained in Lyons. Writing to his older brother George, by then retired from the Chartered Mercantile Bank, he complained:

The staff were sacrificed to pay last half-year's dividend. The Officers Good Service Fund was pillaged and only $95,000 remain. Of course the Directors say they will pay it back again, but will they be able?
Dear old Jackson, how I wish we had him back . . .[38]

He added, all too optimistically as it turned out, 'The latest is that our Hong Kong compradore has absconded with $500,000. Truly the Hongkong Bank seems to have struck a streak of bad luck.'

January–June, 1892
No questions were asked at the August 1892 meeting; the position was startlingly clear.

The compradore, the man who like his father before him, had managed the Chinese business of the Hong Kong office, had absconded at a cost to the Bank of $1,300,000. The transfer to Contingencies Account totalled just over $3 million, and shareholders present would no doubt have recognized that, having accounted for the compradore's deficit, the bulk of the remainder arose from further losses in Hong Kong resulting from advances on shares. And a dividend had to be paid, even if it were at the reduced rate of £1 (or £2 per annum); there was, therefore, no alternative but to transfer $3 million from the reserves, 48% of the total remaining in the Fund. It was a bitter blow.

The Bank had been in the practice of granting clean advances to Chinese customers on the guarantee of the compradore. De Bovis had determined this practice was unsound, especially as Lo Hok Pang was engaged in business for himself and had close connections with at least four Chinese 'native banks', which fell with him. For nine months de Bovis tightened up, renewing credits only against trade bills, thus depriving the compradore of the credit he required to keep his own affairs afloat. Failing to obtain credit elsewhere and unable to meet his debts, the compradore had failed. The Bank's losses arose from the outstanding clean credits which were not paid on maturity.

The Hongkong Bank had granted advances to customers against a total of 30,587 Trust and Loan Company (Bank of China, Japan and the Straits) shares, which were by now virtually worthless. But the consequences of general depreciation of shares on the market had worked itself out, and the Bank could expect a revival of its fortunes, if only confidence in its operations continued. The suspension of the New Oriental Bank in July 1892 had caused a run on the Hongkong Bank's Calcutta agency; there was potential trouble in other cities.[39]

The directors' task both before and after the mid-1892 meeting was to restore the image of the Bank.

The handling of the crisis, 1892

The Board began poorly.

Decisions affecting London
When news of the compradore's disappearance came before the Board, losses were first estimated at five lacs of dollars and the London Consultative

Committee were so advised by cable. Almost immediately the Board recognized that the losses would exceed ten lacs; the Chief Manager – possibly John Walter or perhaps there was confusion in the transfer back to de Bovis, who had been on leave – advised the London Committee of the new figure by sea mail. This not only angered London but it also made those interested in the Bank feel that poor management was proven.

At the time deposits were being withdrawn as the ordinary result of the lower interest rates offered. This reflected a conscious policy consequent to the shortage of profitable uses for the Bank's funds, but with bad news the withdrawal appeared to have been caused by those possibly with inside information and the trend intensified; interest rates were increased again, but the potentially dangerous trend continued through the early months of 1893.

Bank share prices were already falling and to prevent an early crisis the Board were induced by the London Committee to publish an assurance that a dividend would be paid. The Board complied in terms which were at least temporarily satisfying.

The Board supplemented this by responding in detail to a Mr MacWatt, a London shareholder, in a letter dated July 28 and signed, most exceptionally, by the Chairman and Deputy Chairman of the Hongkong Bank rather than by the Chief Manager. MacWatt had warned of further withdrawals of sterling fixed deposits:

With regard to the possibilities of withdrawal of deposits in Europe consequent to the probable diminished confidence of depositors in Eastern Banking institutions, we may say that not only have we prepared for present withdrawals, but we are steadily preparing for any future possible withdrawals and, in addition to this, to check outgoings our London office has raised the rate from 4% to $4\frac{1}{2}\%$.

With regard to other points mentioned by you, we would say that it is our policy to keep in London large sterling investments as security against deposits, but we do not speculate in either silver or gold, so working exchange that we keep on an even keel with regard to either metal.

Our deposits in London are utilized strictly for the payment of outward remittances pending the arrival of inward bills purchased on this side.

Yours faithfully, the Hongkong and Shanghai Bank,
T.E. Davies, *Chairman*; H. Hoppius, *Vice-Chairman [sic]*

Reassurance in Hong Kong

At the August 1892 meeting itself the Chairman, T.E. Davies, attempted to reassure shareholders and constituents by (i) noting the high quality of the management and praising the performance of de Bovis, 'a thoroughly good man of business, holding the soundest Banking views', (ii) reporting on the just completed tour of inspection by John Walter (as the Chairman had done previously with the report of Harries), (iii) listing the Bank's sterling investments and stressing their growth, and (iv) reminding them of the method of the Bank's employment of funds under the 'even keel' policy. Gold funds, he reminded the proprietors, were not sent East. This was an important point in view of the fate of the Bank of China, Japan and the Straits, the New Oriental, and the well-known problems of the Chartered Mercantile.

In July the Board had advised the London Manager, Thomas Jackson, that, 'in times when Eastern Finance seems to be distrusted in London . . . we should err on the right side by being more conservative in our outward business, limiting purchases to very good constituents, and insisting on New York and Hamburg following the same policy.'

This was followed up in September by a general circular setting out a more conservative basis for the business, noting that this was already the practice in Head Office and was circulated so that other branches and agencies could be guided accordingly. The circular stated, *inter alia*, that no advances should be made against Bank shares, although very temporary accommodation could be given against such shares up to their par value of $125.

The Bank's problems with their compradores resulted in a survey of agreements being undertaken; furthermore, in 1892 the Board for the first time played a major role in the selection of the Bank's third Hong Kong compradore, Lau Wai Chün, and announced their decision to the August meeting. The selection of a compradore had not before been a Board decision; the first compradore was not mentioned in the minutes until his death in 1877, and then only in connection with the succession of his son, the now notorious Lo Hok Pang.

The Board's choice, Lau Wai Chün, was declared bankrupt with severe loss to the Bank in 1906; it was, as the promoters of the Hongkong Bank had known well, the system which needed reform. This would not be achieved until after the Second World War.[40]

Changes in the accounts

The end-1892 'Abstract of Assets and Liabilities', to give the published accounts their proper title, was cast to show separately the Bank's silver and gold position. The purpose was to give a more complete picture to London constituents and shareholders in a period when, for perhaps the first time, the majority did not rule out the possibility of silver continuing to depreciate to an unpredictably low level. Confidence in the Hongkong Bank might be maintained by reassurance in its management, but confidence in Eastern banks *per se* required not only a theoretical understanding of the system but a quantitative statement of the actual position.

On December 31, 1892, for example, the Bank's sterling deposits were published as £4.9 million or 36% of total deposit liabilities. The sterling investments were listed under 'Assets' and totalled £896,000. The Chairman of the March 1893 meeting, H. Hoppius – news of the death of the Bank's

Chairman, T.E. Davies, was received on the morning of the meeting – was careful to explain that the funds representing the difference between sterling assets and sterling deposits, 'the surplus of sterling deposits over sterling securities', was used in London for the payment of telegraphic transfers, bullion, outward remittances, etc., pending the arrival of bills afloat. David McLean had once complained during a London Office liquidity crisis, bills on the water are no good to me; to overcome this difficulty the sterling deposits were needed.

The new accounts were clearly a step forward in assisting the public to understand the Bank's position. The London deposit holders could now see how the Bank stood.

Unfortunately, they did not like what they saw.

THE HONGKONG BANK AND GOVERNMENT

In the midst of these problems the Hongkong Bank became involved in two continuing issues with Government, (i) the close relations of the Bank with the Hong Kong Government and the size of government balances and (ii) the nature and size of the security for the Bank's note issue.

Government balances

The first was basically a controversy between the Hong Kong Government and the Colonial Office and Treasury over the maximum balances which ought to be held in the Colony's banks, a controversy complicated by the financing of the Praya reclamation. The 'best minds' of England were assigned to the Imperial Treasury and these worked out the exact value of the demand and fixed deposits the Hong Kong authorities should keep on hand, bank by bank. The Treasurer of Hong Kong, A. Lister, argued, on the basis of his practical experience, that the balances permitted by the Lords of the Treasury were manifestly insufficient, and on the margins of his long memorandums Treasury officials wrote testy comments.[41]

These are considerations for historians of Britain's past Imperial grandeur.

The Hongkong Bank became involved because the ultimate Treasury solution was to limit the funds the Government could place on deposit, insisting that any excess be placed, literally, in a chest. Whenever the permitted bank balance was exceeded, the Treasurer was to take the chest down to the Bank, draw out the excess, place it in the chest and carry it back – under the tropical sun and through the tropical rain, as Lister dramatically protested – to the Government Treasury, where facilities to store it were inadequate.[42]

Lister felt this would be insulting to the Bank. There is no evidence the policy was ever implemented.

Eventually the Treasury revised its estimates upward from $200,000 to $350,000 but protested that not all the additional funds should go to the Hongkong Bank despite Lister's enumeration of the valuable services the Bank rendered his department and Government in general. The Treasury determined however that the Hongkong Bank should have a sum not exceeding $125,000, and the Chartered Bank, the New Oriental Bank, and the Chartered Mercantile only $75,000 each.[43]

At this point the New Oriental suspended payment and the Chartered Mercantile had to be reorganized. In March 1893, therefore, the Hongkong Bank's maximum was raised to $200,000 and the Chartered Bank's to $150,000, pending a reassessment of the stability of the reorganized Mercantile Bank of India.[44]

There is nothing in the correspondence to suggest that Government was concerned with the Hongkong Bank's stability. The problem was one of general policy, the spreading of risk, and the Treasury's preference for investment of surplus Colonial funds through London. The Treasury remained less than enthusiastic about the dependence of the Hong Kong Government on the Hongkong Bank's facilities, but it had to recognize the relative position of the Bank in the Colony. Thus in its period of crisis the Bank was able to retain augmented Government balances.

The note issue

As stated above, with the increase of the Hongkong Bank's capital from $7.5 to $10 million the Bank was required to deposit additional securities equivalent in value to one-third the capital increase, say, $833,333, against the note issue whether or not the note issue itself increased to the limit of $10 million now permitted. This arrangement had in fact been suggested by the Bank to prevent the necessity of constant change in the securities deposited, but it now looked less attractive and the Bank requested a change. As the maximum authorized note issue would soon be reached, it was perhaps fortunate for the Bank that the Treasury refused.[45]

Despite the fixed one-third arrangement, with the fluctuation of the silver exchanges the question of the adequacy of the security lodged with the Trustees became a matter of routine concern. The advantage of a specific, permanent sum had been lost.

The Bank's main concern, however, was that all this involved a further tie-up of funds at a time when the directors needed as much flexibility as possible. Accordingly, Jackson in London wrote to the Colonial Office in August 1891 requesting that this additional security not be required on the grounds that the present note issue was only $6.2 million and would not exceed the previously authorized maximum of $7.5 million for 'many years'. When the note issue in fact exceeded the limit, Jackson asserted, the Bank would immediately notify the Government and deposit the additional security in full.[46] The Secretary of State recommended approval; the Treasury refused.[47]

Even the Colonial Office considered this refusal 'very churlish'.[48] Further correspondence revealed that the Treasury's decision was based on lack of faith in the integrity of the Bank. Referring once again, inaccurately, to the Bank's alleged illegal opening of branches, the Treasury declined to sanction a system whereby the adequacy of the security depended upon note-issue figures supplied by the Bank.[49]

The possibility of amending the Bank's ordinance to permanently limit the Bank's right to issue notes to the previous limit of $7.5 million was considered by Government but fortunately not proceeded with.[50]

In April 1892 Thomas Jackson was instructed by Head Office to make a new approach. This time he was to argue that the securities were in fact a poor backing for the note issue since, in the event of a run on the Bank, these funds would not be available for the encashment of the notes presented. The Bank therefore requested the Treasury to agree to release the securities; the Bank would instead hold a 50% reserve in cash, of which half would be under the direct physical control of the Colonial Treasurer. Jackson argued cogently that the notes were not legal tender and that there was no 'Bank of England' as lender of last resort in Hong Kong; hence the Bank had to have a high proportion of cash on hand. To be required to set aside securities in addition endangered the Bank and made more likely that disaster which the various regulations were designed to prevent.[51]

Unfortunately, this missed the point. The policy of insisting on the lodging of securities was not intended for the immediate protection of the note holders but of the Government. The policy had been designed to meet the Ceylon precedent whereby the Colonial authorities might find it politically expedient to take emergency responsibility for the note issue; they would be covered from loss by the previous hypothecation of securities by the issuing bank with trustees in London and/or in the place of issue.

Jackson failed to point out that the problem faced by the Board of Directors was the survival of the Bank. The Government's policy was designed to meet a situation in which the Bank had already suspended payment.

As the note issue reached $9.7 million by mid-1893, the question was moot. But the Bank would continue to be subject to inaccurate criticism in Government minutes. Of these minutes the Bank was probably unaware and consequently could not counter. On balance and with the present exception, they probably had little impact on the ultimate decision.

1893: DE BOVIS AND JACKSON

Support for de Bovis

At the March 1893 meeting a shareholder, J.D. Humphreys, took the opportunity in seconding adoption of the accounts to include François de Bovis in his general statement of support. 'I feel sure the shareholders join with me in passing a vote of thanks to the directors and the chief manager for the skill and care with which they have piloted the bank through the troublous times we have just gone through. (Applause)'

The second-half of 1892 had been one of initial recovery. In fact earnings were lower than in previous half-years but could be stated in the accounts without the subtracting of large provisions for expected losses. Not all accounts were in satisfactory condition, especially in Hong Kong, but these were no longer a source of real concern. And the directors were able to pay a £1 dividend despite the further 4.7% fall in exchange and still transfer $300,000 to begin once again the building up of the Reserve Fund.

But de Bovis had sought and been granted leave; he would not return. At his last Board meeting the directors recorded 'their appreciation of the able services rendered by Mr de Bovis as Chief Manager during a very trying period in the Bank's history and the hope that he would enjoy his holiday'.

Restatement of policy – and a reevaluation of de Bovis

When de Bovis left Hong Kong, the Bank had not exactly been 'turned around'; there would be further problems for Jackson to solve before the Bank recovered its former financial position. But stability had been achieved and as Hoppius, the Chairman, expressed it:

The nature of the business we transact is the best and most legitimate banking which can be found anywhere [applause] and consists mainly of buying homeward and outward bills against goods, while our advances on merchandise in the East are only temporary pending clearances.

Back, that is, to basics. There is no mention here of China loans or being the Government banker. When the turnaround was complete, there would be time to remind the financial community and governments of the Hongkong Bank's other activities. This was a time of caution and waiting.

Inevitably at such a time, even as praise is given the Chief Manager, there is a reevaluation of his role. These had been difficult times, but in 1882 Jackson had seen the Bank through a Chinese credit crisis in Hong Kong virtually without loss – partly perhaps by unloading bad accounts on the luckless Oriental Bank. De Bovis was not in charge when the initial boom was fuelled, but he had the task of forcing restraint; the only basis for criticism, therefore, is whether his handling was sufficiently sure. For several months he tightened up on the Bank's compradore and, it might be argued, he should have known the consequences. Instead he was on leave when Lo absconded. And if this major problem had not been handled with sufficient skill, had de Bovis been 'big' enough to deal with the leaders of Hong Kong's financial community in their crisis?

It may be that although de Bovis was always in the technical sense 'right', he was not always wise. Jackson was a leader in the community; he was also a leader of the team. His team did not always play well with de Bovis in control. But to assess this loss of spirit in terms of dollars is not at this time possible – or fair.

In effect de Bovis, by asking for twelve months' leave before the Bank's turnaround was assured, had resigned. That he had done as well as any, except Jackson, it would inevitably and without possibility of proof be asserted. Because he was right, because he saw the Bank through, de Bovis's management of the Bank must, given the times in which he operated, be judged successful. But it had been too much for him. He was, after twenty years in the East, ready for French provincial life in Lyons.

Before de Bovis is forgotten, there is one further test to apply. Kind words had been said before to departing managers; what was said of de Bovis *after* his departure? In August 1893 at the meeting announcing his reassignment to Lyons, J.D. Humphreys once again seconded the motion: 'The Bank has been exceedingly carefully and well-managed throughout the whole time, not only here under Mr de Bovis but at home under Mr Thomas Jackson, assisted there by an old and experienced staff . . .'

The Australian banking crisis and the continued fall of silver

Then in April 1893 the Commercial Bank of Australia and the English, Scottish and Australian Chartered Bank suspended payment, followed by the suspension of the Australia Joint Stock Bank and the London Chartered Bank of Australia.[52] The Australian banking crisis had other origins, but its impact on general confidence in overseas banking would hinder Jackson's early efforts on his return to Hong Kong.

The mid-1893 accounts show a 13% fall in sterling deposits, reflecting the failure of depositors to renew when fixed deposits became due. At the May 18 meeting, for example, the Board noted that 60% of deposits falling due or £140,000 had not been renewed; on May 25, 72% or £55,000, and the drain continued.

Then in June the Indian mints were shut to the free coinage of silver with the Bank having silver worth £171,000 en route. The Hong Kong exchanges fell 8.4% in the half year; the rate with India initially fell 20%, although there was an upward adjustment to a net 12%. Trade was disrupted and the Hongkong Bank had a new set of problems. These are subjects for the following chapter – for the account of Jackson's second administration.

Despite further adjustment of Hong Kong accounts and further write-offs, net earnings as published rose to $998,000, the dividend of £1, now requiring a payout of $640,000 at an exchange rate of 2s:6d, was maintained, and a further $300,000 transferred to reserves. Shareholders' funds were now $14.3 million, 18% above the end-1888 level, but the new capital was included in this figure; shareholders' funds in sterling showed a decline due to the fall in the exchanges. The capital/assets ratio had slipped to 9.1%.

The Bank had, however, survived and, providing the outflow of sterling deposits could be checked or an alternative source of gold funds could be discovered, its earning power was unimpaired and would grow with the recovery of trade then underway.

China, as it happened, proved not to have been ready for modernization; consequently the construction of railways and factories did not take place as anticipated by, among others, the promoters of the Trust and Loan Company of China, Japan and the Straits.

As if to round out the period, the Bank of China, Japan and the Straits in May 1893 notified the Bank that it intended to operate in the Eastern exchanges; from a trust investment company it had become a rival bank, but, as it turned out, an ineffective one. So controversial was its background and so catastrophic its record that William Keswick and David McLean, the Hongkong Bank's first Shanghai Manager, had been asked to leave the London Committee, quietly, before the Bank of China's 1893 results were published. This was indeed the end of an era.

13

THE BANK COMES OF AGE: JACKSON'S SECOND ADMINISTRATION, 1893–1902

> I look at this as realization of hopes entertained for years, but until the present beyond our reach.
>
> Sir Thomas Jackson in the Board Minutes, January 1899

With its reserves at a minimum, confidence in overseas banking shattered by the Australian banking crisis, and the benefits of the 1890 rights issue virtually dissipated, the Hongkong Bank was in no condition to face the twin challenges of financing China's ever-expected modernization and overcoming threatened competition.

Fortunately, it did not have to – not yet.

There was growth in trade, but the expectations of the late 1880s had been shattered, and the hopes for a fundamental policy change within China following that country's defeat by the Japanese in 1895 were dashed by the overthrow of the reformers in 1898 and the Boxer Uprising of 1900. The competition of the new exchange banks, although always a potential factor in the Hongkong Bank's profitability, was not in the 1890s a real threat; as the Bank's Chairman stated, the Hongkong Bank and the Chartered remained dominant; only in the 1900s would the situation be modified.

The Hongkong Bank had nine successful years, from April 1893 to early 1902 under the chief managership of (Sir) Thomas Jackson. By the end of 1901, his last full year in office, there had been an 82% growth in published shareholders' funds; with paid-up capital of $10 million there were reserves of $14.25 million, of which £1 million (= $10 million), a 'second capital', were in sterling. Jackson could step down knowing that the Bank had not only weathered an eventful decade but that it had also become a financial institution of international stature and was already playing the leading role in consortiums and railway finance, advising governments on currency and banking policies, while retaining the confidence of Eastern governments and continuing its basic role of financing the Eastern trade.

Jackson would later be quoted as saying, 'Nothing is too big, nothing is too small for the Hongkong Bank.' While participating in the issue of two China indemnity loans totalling £32 million, the Bank would accept ten ten-cent stamps on a special card for a $1.00 credit to a 'Savings Bank' account.

The Hongkong Bank had issued and underwritten China loans before; the

Bank had been from the first both a 'local' bank and an 'exchange' bank; it was also a merchant bank. In this decade of the 1890s there would be a subtle change. London had already shown its importance; now more than 50% of the shares were registered there and the bulk of the Bank's reserves were in sterling. Then too the older generation of negotiators – Ewen Cameron and John Walter – had transferred to London, even as the Chinese had increased the effectiveness of their London Legation. The Chinese too had become capable of operating financially in London, but they insisted on negotiations in China.

The London focus never became overwhelming; Jackson remained in Hong Kong with his Board of Directors.

The Bank from 1895 certainly to 1914 had two focuses: (i) Hong Kong, the centre of final decision making, of allocation of capital resources and which also provided what the directors still referred to as 'the legitimate business' of the Bank and (ii) London, where Sir Ewen Cameron and later Sir Charles Addis would preside over the Bank as merchant bank, as leader of the China consortiums and of the British Group, and as promoter of and banker for the British and Chinese Corporation, Ltd.

In this chapter the concern is with the Bank as corporation; discussion of the post-1895 loan and consortium operations, of the Bank's branches, and of its role in currency reform is left for Volume II. In the later years of Jackson's second administration, the profits of its merchant banking operations will feed in; they will prove important to an understanding of the Bank's growth. Nevertheless the details can be told later.

In this period, after all the profits of the major loans had been accounted for, the source of the Hongkong Bank's new-found strength rested in its commercial banking operations. There were two factors which alone accounted for success in 1893–1901, one independent of, the other dependent on the genius of Jackson. After 1893/94 this would be the first extended period the Hongkong Bank was free of serious business losses; its earning potential could be fully realized. This may fairly be said to be due both to the nature of the times and to the judgement of the Bank's managers throughout the network.

The decade was also one of considerable silver and exchange fluctuations, of sudden requirements and drastic changes in direction. If many factors and many people contributed to the success of the Bank as a commercial bank, as a 'local bank', if wise banking decisions virtually eliminated serious losses, then the exchange profits, the basis of the Bank's growth, were sustained throughout at an unusually high level by the master in exchange, Thomas Jackson. He foresaw the requirements and moved the bullion; he understood the trends and acted with them.

At an early point his hand had been forced. The 'even keel' which depended on sterling deposits to cover sterling trade finance became impractical as London distrust of Eastern banks resulted in an unwillingness to renew fixed deposits.

Jackson had to move the Bank's funds to London while sterling continued to appreciate in terms of the dollar.

As the Bank grew, Jackson also prevented the dissipation of that growth. In 1898 he achieved his goal; the Bank's reserves of $10 million were for the first time in its history equal to its subscribed and paid-up capital. The Bank was solidly based not only in the silver area but, with £1 million in sterling securities, it was once again on an 'even keel'. Perhaps the Chairman of the Bank exaggerated when he said that the Bank, from the point of view of its own business, was 'indifferent' to the course taken by the price of silver, but it is true that the Bank operated from a position of financial strength both in the East and in London. The Bank was thus capable of operating across the gold/silver line both within the East and between the East and a Europe and United States now working on a gold basis.

BACKGROUND TO GROWTH

Events, 1893–1901

Jackson's administration began as the Australian banking crisis of 1893 developed; within two months of his return the Indian mints had been closed to the free coinage of silver and that same year the United States repealed the Sherman Silver Purchase Act. Silver fell 17.6% in 1893; it fell 10% in the second six months of the year alone (see Table 13.1).

In 1894 there began the First Sino-Japanese War, ending in China's defeat in 1895. The consequent Treaty of Shimonoseki resulted in economic concessions to Japan which, through the most-favoured-nation clause, were automatically extended to the other Treaty Powers. The Chinese were also obligated to pay an indemnity which, as it happened, provided the basis for Japan's decision to go on a gold exchange standard.

The Hongkong Bank assisted China in financing its struggle; when Japan prevailed, the Bank sought to create an international consortium to finance the entire indemnity. In this the Bank failed, a partial loan being made by French and Russian interests. But the Hongkong Bank, in cooperation with the Deutsch-Asiatische Bank, did successfully manage the second and third indemnity loans of 1896 and 1898; the Bank was also to make loans for productive purposes to both China and Japan.

Silver, which rose in price in response to China's demands for war finance, fell from mid-1896 as Japan declared for gold. Also in 1896 William Jennings Bryan urged the cause of bimetallism against 'sound-money' Republicans, and in an eloquent address proclaimed that they should not crucify his people upon a Cross of Gold. The American electorate did not respond. The silver party were defeated.

Plague and famine disturbed the Indian economy; the threat to the supply of

Table 13.1 *The price of silver and the Hong Kong exchange,*
1893–1901

Year	d/ounce of silver	Hong Kong on London $\$ = x$ s/d[a]	% change in 6 months
1872 June	60.0	4/6	–
1877 Oct.	54.6	$3/11\frac{1}{8}$	–
1892 Dec.	39.2	$2/8\frac{3}{4}$	− 4.7
1893 June	38.8	2/6	− 8.4
1893 Dec.	32.3	2/3	− 10.0
1894 June	28.9	$2/1\frac{1}{4}$	− 6.5
1894 Dec.	28.5	2/0	− 5.0
1895 June	30.7	$2/1\frac{5}{8}$	6.8
1895 Dec.	30.7	$2/1\frac{5}{8}$	0.0
1896 June	31.6	$2/2\frac{1}{2}$	3.4
1896 Dec.	30.0	$2/1\frac{3}{8}$	− 4.2
1897 June	27.8	$1/11\frac{3}{4}$	− 6.4
1897 Dec.	27.8	$1/11\frac{5}{8}$	− 0.5
1898 June	27.5	1/11	− 2.6
1898 Dec.	27.6	$1/11\frac{1}{2}$	2.2
1899 June	28.0	$1/11\frac{5}{8}$	0.5
1899 Dec.	27.3	$1/11\frac{3}{8}$	− 1.1
1900 June	28.6	$1/11\frac{7}{8}$	2.1
1900 Dec.	29.9	2/1	4.7
1901 June	27.6	$1/11\frac{7}{16}$	− 6.3
1901 Dec.	25.8	$1/10\frac{1}{4}$	− 5.5
1902 June	24.4	$1/8\frac{1}{2}$	− 7.9
1893 (June)–1901 (December)			− 26.7
1872 (June)–1901 (December)			− 59.3

Note:
[a] rate quoted in HSBC semi-annual reports. For earlier rates, see
   Tables 8.2, 9.2, and 12.1.

dollar coins in the East was met at the urging of the Hongkong Bank and the
Chartered Bank by the minting of a British dollar; in 1899 the Boer War marked
an end of cheap money in the London market, and consols fell as interest rates
rose, affecting the Bank's reserve investments. Silver rose slightly and fluctuated
in 1900, as demand for silver developed both in India and Japan, despite their
choice of gold as a standard. Silver then resumed its fall.

   There was investment in China; mines were tentatively developed, railway
mileage extended. But plans for major development could not be implemented
through a free market influenced solely by economic forces while the cost of
money was high. The unrest in China and the disruption of the capital markets in

Europe invited political intervention. Into all this the Bank would interject an element of economic sanity, but in this chapter, the concern is with the impact on the Bank's growth narrowly defined.

Trade – an underlying factor in the Bank's growth

The base for trade had expanded. China's defeat in war brought the opening of such important secondary trading centres as Shasi, Soochow, and Hangchow; in 1897 came the opening of the West River; and earlier Treaty Ports, Newchwang in Manchuria with its port of Yingkow, and new railways were beginning to realize their potential. The development of the plantation economy and of tin mining in Southeast Asia was marked by Dutch exploitation of the East Indies while the British sponsored economic penetration into the Malay States. Siam was brought into the trade orbit; the French developed Indo-China.

This extension was matched by the increase in population at the old-established ports of Shanghai, Tientsin, Hong Kong, Singapore, and the centres of foreign residence in Japan. Hong Kong, for example, grew some 26% to a colony of 300,000; Shanghai too was growing into the metropolis it was soon to become, but there were still residences along Shanghai's Bund.

These developments are reflected first in the overall increase in the value of trade and secondly in the development of new patterns of Eastern inter-port trading, with new products matching new industrial developments and, in some cases, the fading of traditional trade – especially in China. To give some measure of this growth, without attempting a thorough discussion, may still be useful.

The overall trade figures for China show little disturbance during the Sino-Japanese War, but the impact of the Boxer Uprising was greater. Indeed, to reflect the trend 1902 figures must be used: in the ten years from 1893 total imports and exports as stated in revised Maritime Customs estimates rose 122% from HkTs242 million to HkTs539 million. The fall in the value of black tea exports in response to South Asian competition was offset by the growth of green tea and red brick tea. Raw silk exports doubled as the industry was encouraged in the Canton Delta. The growth of raw cotton exports became particularly important after 1903 although there had been indications of change; vegetable oil export, while still small, more than doubled in the period. As for imports it was still too early for significant capital goods imports; opium stayed relatively stable at HkTs30–32 million, but the import of cigarettes was beginning. The upward trend was due to the significant increase, percentage-wise, of many imports rather than as yet a radical change in composition.

There was a 50% increase in the shipping tonnage entering Hong Kong, although the percentage of British tonnage declined from 74% of the total in 1893 to 59% in 1902. This is reflected in figures for the China trade in general.

Japan's trade had more than tripled, and total imports plus exports in 1901 were Yen 508 million, sufficient to stress all the more the apparent opportunities supposedly being lost in China. If Japan had developed so far, then how much more was China's potential, and the stage was set for the political pressures to which that country would be subjected.

Further south Singapore trade was $19 million in 1892 and $39.5 million in 1901, an increase of 108%. The production and export of primary products, especially sugar, was being promoted throughout Southeast Asia, where the Hongkong Bank had offices and supplementary merchant agencies. The Netherlands Indies, the Philippines, and Siam all contributed to the corporation's high level of net profits.

And all this required larger overheads, houses and docks, eventually electric power, tramways, promotions of local enterprise, secondary industries. This was the base of the Hongkong Bank's growth, but was not the full explanation.

Banking

The Deutsch-Asiatische Bank had been established in 1889 with a head office in Shanghai; it would cooperate with the Hongkong Bank at the merchant banking level, compete in commercial and exchange banking. Its impact in this latter field was slight even in the finance of German trade to the Far East. In the general growth of business, it was not a significant rival.

The Yokohama Specie Bank was however a more important competitor, having a privileged relationship with certain of the Japanese trading firms. Nevertheless sufficient trade was done through foreign agents, either in Japan or overseas, that the Hongkong Bank's Japan business grew throughout.

The last few years of the century witnessed severe exchange fluctuations against a change in trading methods – the Eastern import trade was no longer on a consignment basis and the extended use of telegraphic transfers had reduced the exchange banks' interest income as usance bills were less in demand. The Crédit Lyonnais withdrew from India in 1899 after a three-year attempt to compete with the established exchange banks, and the Agra Bank, becoming unprofitable, was wound up in 1900. The reconstituted Chartered Mercantile, the Mercantile Bank of India, Ltd, prospered but remained small; it had returned to Shanghai in 1894 but only with an agent working in the offices of Jardine, Matheson and Co. Jardine's role had been agreed after consultation with the Hongkong Bank.

As a consequence of these events, the failure of the National Bank of China to capture the Chinese business and the slow impact of the French and German banks, the finance of Far Eastern trade continued to be dominated by the Hongkong Bank and the Chartered Bank. In 1902 the Chartered's capital plus reserves totalled only some 65% of the Hongkong Bank's; the same proportion held for total assets.

A greater threat was seen in the Russo-Chinese Bank with its finance of the tea trade from central China and its operations in Manchuria. The Hongkong Bank, however, was not prepared as yet to establish itself, except through merchant agents, north of the Great Wall of China; unlike a government-sponsored bank, for example, the Banque de l'Indo-Chine pressured in 1899 to open unprofitable branches in Canton and Hankow, the Hongkong Bank was still its own master.

The United States, which had virtually withdrawn from banking in the East with the collapse of Russell and Co., showed a renewed interest with the establishment of American rule in the Philippines. At the February 1902 meeting of the Hongkong Bank's proprietors (shareholders), the Chairman, Robert Shewan, referred specifically (and inevitably) to 'Our American cousins' and 'though it comes in the form of competition with which we shall have to reckon, we cordially greet the advent of the Guaranty Trust Co. and the International Bank of America [International Banking Corporation], for we know there is ample room for all'. The impact would not be felt until the 1950s.

The first successful modern-style Chinese exchange bank was the Imperial Bank of China (Chung-kuo t'ung-shang yin-hang), whose European manager was, as has been stated earlier, A.W. Maitland, the retired Manager of the Hongkong Bank's Tientsin branch. Founded in 1896 through the efforts of Sheng Hsuan-huai, the Imperial Bank never realized its purposes; first, it failed to float a Ts7 million internal loan, and, secondly, it never achieved the status of the Government's principal bankers. The bank was Chinese in the sense that all shareholders had to be Chinese; its regulations were ostensibly those of the Hongkong Bank. It was China's first Western-style bank, but it could not yet compete with the 'Customs' or Haikwan banks in the receipt of government funds or the Shansi banks in their transmission, and an official Chinese bank, the Hu-pu (Board of Revenue) Bank, would be chartered in 1904. The Imperial survived several reorganizations to become the Commercial Bank of China.[1]

THE BOARD AND THE LONDON COMMITTEE

The directors and Thomas Jackson

With the departure and death of Heinrich Hoppius in 1894 no director remained who had been on the Board when Jackson was first appointed Chief Manager. Old companies had failed or for other reasons their representatives had disappeared from the Board – John Lapraik had died in 1893. Five companies were represented for the first time during the period 1893–1902 (see Tables 13.2– 4). Of the founding companies three remained – Siemssen and Co., D. Sassoon, Sons and Co., and Gilman and Co. – although only Sassoon's had been represented continuously.

Jardine Matheson's respected taipan, William Keswick, had returned to

London and the Hongkong Bank's Board had offered him a seat on the London Committee. The firm was represented on the Bank's Board by J.J. Keswick and J.J. Bell–Irving alternating.

Whatever theory one might hold on the role of managers in joint-stock companies, it became clear that, as the Bank's successes continued, the role of Jackson and his colleagues in that success seemed less and less dependent on the Board of Directors. Such was Jackson's eventual reputation that new directors must have appeared 'new boys' and, in matters of banking, deferred to his experience and judgement. Certainly Jackson's high-principled concepts of commercial morality were of key importance at a time when the Bank was prospering, 'inner reserves' were being created, and opportunities for the misuse of 'insider information' by directors considerable. The directors apparently accepted this leadership, recognizing the special responsibilities of a bank and the role of the Hongkong Bank in serving the entire community. The conflicts which apparently impaired the management of certain other local companies at this time did not touch the Hongkong Bank.

But the Chairman of the Hongkong Bank had his day. At the semi-annual meeting his speech did much to explain the Bank's position, supplementing the admittedly limited information in the 'abstract' of accounts which shareholders and the public were provided. The Chairman's speech in addition to expressing views on silver, on the course of the rupee, and preparing shareholders for the impact of competition and consequent loss of profits which did not in the event occur, began including comments – albeit reluctantly – on broader topics, on war and peace, which affected the Bank. On the more routine level, the Chairman stated the reasons for the Board's recommendations on the allocation of funds credited to the Profit and Loss Account, informed shareholders of awards to staff, and spoke words of praise, always well received, for the Chief Manager.

The Board had found a Chief Manager who could manage. The minutes of Board meetings, never a wholly reliable gauge, became briefer until in the majority of instances they only list the accounts examined by the directors. A hasty conclusion would be that the Board were playing an increasingly diminished role in the management of the Bank. This alone would justify the title to Part II, 'the Age of Jackson', but the situation is more complex.

The Board of Directors considered the semi-annual accounts, noting the profitability of branches, deciding on the allocation of funds from the Profit and Loss Account, and agreeing on the Chairman's speech. In 1901 the other topics considered by the Board were: the appointment of directors and the noting of their absences, staff assignments and terms of service, including several inconsistent decisions on marriage, all decisions relative to property, contributions to charities and related non-banking matters, extraordinary claims arising out of, for example, the Boxer Uprising, the appointment of a new merchant agent, and routinely the examination of accounts laid before the meeting.

Comparing this list to the more active Board of say 1892 leads to the tentative conclusion that the directors had withdrawn from banking but remained active in decisions which would be common to any corporation – personnel, property, and shareholder relations.

The key suggestion here is that the directors, who were not in any case bankers, had withdrawn from *banking* decisions in the presence of a brilliant banker-manager. The Hongkong Bank was no longer the directors' bank, but the shareholders'; the latter were interested in performance, and thus the directors' primary responsibility had been achieved with the appointment of successful managers. Control was maintained through checking the accounts, sanctioning staff assignments, and presenting the Bank to the shareholders at their meeting.

Or is this apparent change merely the consequence of particular circumstances?

First, there was Jackson's special position. Not only was he senior to all the directors in his association with the Bank, but he had returned with a considerable show of reluctance only at the urgent request of the directors. He had to be encouraged to stay; he would be doing the directors and the Bank a favour by agreeing to remain.

This interpretation is consistent with the 'encouragement' offered, an agreement which enabled him to share in the profits of the Corporation. Specifically, it was decided in July 1893 that, in consideration for his agreeing to remain in Hong Kong as Chief Manager, he would receive a bonus equal to $2\frac{10}{2}\%$ of net amounts paid out in dividends or transferred to reserves. This would be in lieu of the £3,000 bonus referred to in Chapter 12 as the inducement for his fourth coming.

Although this profit sharing was not a particularly exciting offer when the Bank was in crisis, the agreement in the bonanza year of 1898, for example, would result in a bonus of $126,000, equivalent at the rate of the day to £12,337 for a total remuneration of say $152,000 or £15,000, the latter being three times the straight salary that would be offered J.R.M. Smith in 1902.[a] However, in 1895 the Board – and possibly Jackson – thought it prudent to put a floor of £5,000 on

---

[a] This assumes that the Chief Manager's bonus was convertible into sterling at the rate of the day and that his regular salary in 1898 of $20,000 a year was converted, by decision of the Board relative to salaries (see Chapter 15), into pounds one-half at the rate of 3/4 and one-half at 1/11½ to the dollar, or £2,562. This latter sum incidentally cost the Bank (£2,562 converted back into dollars at the rate of the day) $26,000.

In the more 'normal' year of 1901, Jackson's bonus was $105,646, and thus his total remuneration, calculated as before, was £13,825.

When Charles Addis was offered the chief managership of the Royal Bank of Scotland in 1910, the salary offered was the same as Smith's, £5,000 per annum, a normal figure for a 'small bank'. A managing director or 'chief manager' of a major clearing bank would have received as much as £10,000.

his remuneration, presumably in fear of a further decline in the exchange. This is all consistent with a decision that, once having obtained his services, he ought to be allowed to 'get on with the job'.

An examination of the Board minutes suggests a second 'special factor' in the decision relative to Jackson's remuneration. In the final years of Jackson's administration the Bank was in a period of prosperity; it was not that the directors no longer concerned themselves with serious problems, it was rather that there were no serious problems. The absence of major failures with consequent losses to the Bank eliminated many potential agenda items, the drain of London deposits which threatened the working of the Bank's 'even keel' policy had ceased, the vexed question of interest rates, which the Board was considering as late as 1900, had been resolved. Matters which, in time of crisis required Board consideration, in a Bank flush with funds could be handled routinely at the discretion of the responsible manager.

The actual strength of Jackson's position *vis-à-vis* the Board could only be judged finally if the unminuted discussions were available. The minutes themselves reflect apparent inconsistencies in the handling of major items – one China loan may be fully discussed, another only referred to, if at all, after allotment. There is no reference in the minutes to the process whereby the Bank in 1898 joined with Jardine, Matheson and Co. in founding the British and Chinese Corporation – nor for that matter had there been any reference to Ewen Cameron's earlier (1880s) but less formal agreement with Jardine's in Shanghai relative to cooperation in matters of China loan business negotiated in Tientsin/Peking (see Chapter 14).

The relationship of the Board with Jackson must be placed in perspective. The Board frequently noted developments and instructed that the manager concerned use his discretion, even when considerable sums were involved. On the other hand, the Board wished to see building plans and have what they most certainly did not refer to as a 'ball park figure', but in the end, whether it was Cameron underwriting a £16 million loan or a more junior manager redecorating the premises, the Board would not second-guess the man they, after all, had placed in charge.

And, finally, was this relationship between Board and its Chief Manager unique?

The major British joint-stock banks had no uniform pattern, but it is clear that in one way or another directors participated in the day-to-day banking decisions. In the Hongkong Bank the directors, being constituents and representing competing firms, could not and did not. Until late in the decade a sub-committee of directors was concerned with remaining problem accounts, but these latter eventually disappeared; the directors could withdraw in the period of prosperity. Thus, although Jackson's management made the evolution possible, the 'withdrawal' of the directors was a consequence of long-standing factors fully recognized in Hong Kong and independent of the Chief Manager's capabilities.

Kingsmill (Chapter 7) had argued that the company's servants were not 'partners' and should not be treated as such. Jackson's responsibilities made him virtually the managing partner, and the Board rewarded him accordingly.

Nothing in all this changed the provisions of the articles of association or the charter of incorporation. The directors' responsibilities remained and were, it might be said, retrieved briefly with the appointment of a new Chief Manager or were held in reserve for a period of crisis. The Board was basically non-executive, but Chief Managers were careful to keep it informed and recognized the ultimate source of their authority.

There is nevertheless the temptation to conclude that the Hongkong Bank was by 1901 in the hands of its 'servants'. The Board kept a watching brief, more intensely perhaps on a change-over in management, but it nevertheless denied itself access to customer and exchange accounts and was removed, except as noted above, from the day-to-day activities. Even its appointments came on the recommendation of management and the requests for leave and other applications to the Board would become a formality. But while Jackson was Chief Manager, his special position overshadowed all other factors; any final judgement is therefore premature.

The Board – its composition and Chairmen

By comparison with the larger British joint-stock banks, the Board of the Hongkong Bank remained small with only ten or eleven members – in 1898, however, the Chartered Bank's board had only nine members. The members represented the leading British and German firms; the strong representation of Sassoon interests probably reflected the shareholdings of the two separate companies represented as well as their continuing importance in the India/Hong Kong trade. This historic trade did not, despite dire predictions, diminish as a consequence of the appreciation of India's currency following the adoption of a gold exchange standard.

One notable absence was Butterfield and Swire, despite the banking relationship developed in the sugar and other activities of the firm. The senior Swire did not approve of his managers becoming prominent in the community or becoming too close to Jardine Matheson.[2] And the decision was made in England. Similarly the presence on the Board of representatives of any company incorporated in England would depend very much on the individual and on the reactions of his managers at home. Thus the Borneo Company and the P&O were periodically represented, but for relatively short periods of time.

The strength of the Hongkong Bank had been based on its role as a local bank

Table 13.2 *The Hongkong and Shanghai Banking Corporation Companies represented on the Board of Directors, 1889–1902*

Arnhold, Karberg and Co.	1888–1914
Birley and Co.	1871–74, 1878–91
Borneo Company, Ltd	1864–66, 1875, 1888–90
Bradley and Co.	**1896–1902**
Carlowitz and Co.	**1897–1914**
Gibb, Livingston and Co.	1868–70, 1886–90
Gilman and Co.	1864–74, 1877–84, **1890–1930**
Holliday, Wise and Co.	1868–74, **1882–96**
Jardine, Matheson and Co.	**1877–present**
Dodwell, Carlill and Co.	**1895–98**
Douglas Lapraik and Co.	1884–93
Melchers and Co.	**1871–1914**
P&O SN Co.	1864–67, 1875–87, 1891, **1893–95**
Reiss and Co.	**1893–1923**
Russell and Co.	1866–91
Siemssen and Co.	**1864–1914**
D. Sassoon, Sons and Co.	**1864–1956**
E.D. Sassoon and Co.	1882–85, **1887–1922**
Shewan, Tomes and Co.	**1895–1911**

Notes:
Bold face indicates (i) new companies or (ii) years operating in the period 1893–1902. For subsequent years, i.e. for periods of representation not *beginning* in 1889–1902, see Tables in Volumes III and IV.

with its directors being partners in leading Hong Kong hongs of several nationalities. The Board in the 1890s changed in two respects: first, there were representatives of new or reorganized companies; secondly, and more significant, there were representatives of partnerships whose head offices remained in Shanghai or were in Europe. This in itself gave the Hongkong Bank a broader-based constituency, and, with the strength of the Bank and the strong remaining influence of Hong Kong based directors, did not suggest the need for a move to London.

Coupled with these new developments was the further expansion of the agency-house system. The Bank, in inviting, for example, Shewan, Tomes and Co.'s senior partner to the Board, would also be encouraging the business of those firms for which Shewan Tomes were either agents or general managers, including China Light and Power, China Merchants' Steam Navigation Company, Green Island Cement, China Provident Loan and Mortgage Company, and many others.

Shewan, Tomes and Co. is an example of a 'successor' company, formed in

Table 13.3 *The Hongkong and Shanghai Banking Corporation*
Boards of Directors, 1893–1902

June 1893

H. Hoppius	Siemssen and Co.	Chairman, 1893/94
C.J. Holliday	Holliday, Wise and Co.	Deputy Chairman, 1893/94
D.R. Sassoon	D. Sassoon, Sons and Co.	
J.S. Moses	E.D. Sassoon and Co.	
Carl Jantzen	Melchers and Co.	
J.J. Keswick	Jardine, Matheson and Co.	
Julius Kramer	Arnhold, Karberg and Co.	
A. McConachie	Gilman and Co.	
John S. Lapraik	Douglas Lapraik and Co.	
H.H. Joseph	P&O SN Co.	
10 members		

Dies: John S. Lapraik (July)   Elected: R.M. Gray (Reiss & Co.)

February 1894

C.J. Holliday	Holliday, Wise and Co.	Chairman, 1894/95
J.S. Moses	E.D. Sassoon and Co.	Deputy Chairman, 1894/95
D.R. Sassoon	D. Sassoon, Sons and Co.	
Carl Jantzen	Melchers and Co.	
J.J. Keswick	Jardine, Matheson and Co.	
Julius Kramer	Arnhold, Karberg and Co.	
A. McConachie	Gilman and Co.	
H.H. Joseph	P&O SN Co.	
R.M. Gray	Reiss and Co.	
H. Hoppius	Siemssen and Co.	
10 members		

Resigns: Carl Jantzen (March)   Elected: S.C. Michaelsen
Dies: H. Hoppius (December)   N.A. Siebs
Resigns: H.H. Joseph (at the meeting)

February 1895

J.S. Moses	E.D. Sassoon and Co.	Chairman, 1895 (to April)
Julius Kramer	Arnhold, Karberg and Co.	Chairman, 1895/96
A. McConachie	Gilman and Co.	Deputy Chairman (from April)
D.R. Sassoon	D. Sassoon, Sons and Co.	
J.J. Keswick	Jardine, Matheson and Co.	
R.M. Gray	Reiss and Co.	
S.C. Michaelsen	Melchers and Co.	
N.A. Siebs	Siemssen and Co.	
C.J. Holliday	Holliday, Wise and Co.	
9 members		

Resigns: J.J. Keswick (April)   Elected: J.J. Bell-Irving
         J.S. Moses (April)   M.D. Ezekiel
         C.J. Holliday (June)   G.B. Dodwell (Dodwell)
                                              R.G. Shewan (Shewan, Tomes)

Table 13.3 *(cont.)*

February 1896

A. McConachie	Gilman and Co.	Chairman, 1896/97
S.C. Michaelsen	Melchers and Co.	Deputy Chairman, 1896/97
D.R. Sassoon	D. Sassoon, Sons and Co.	
R.M. Gray	Reiss and Co.	
N.A. Siebs	Siemssen and Co.	
J.J. Bell-Irving	Jardine, Matheson and Co.	
M.D. Ezekiel	E.D. Sassoon and Co.	
G.B. Dodwell	Dodwell and Co.	
R.G. Shewan	Shewan, Tomes and Co.	
Julius Kramer	Arnhold, Karberg and Co.	
10 members		

Resigns: (October)   Elected: A. Ross (Holliday, Wise)
   (October)   R.L. Richardson (Bradley)
   J. Kramer (November)   C. Beurmann
   A. Ross (December)

February 1897

S.C. Michaelsen	Melchers and Co.	Chairman, 1897 (to Dec.)
J.J. Bell-Irving	Jardine, Matheson and Co.	Dep. Chair., Chair., 1897/98
D.R. Sassoon	D. Sassoon, Sons and Co.	
R.M. Gray	Reiss and Co.	
N.A. Siebs	Siemssen and Co.	
M.D. Ezekiel	E.D. Sassoon and Co.	
G.B. Dodwell	Dodwell and Co.	
R.G. Shewan	Shewan, Tomes and Co.	
R.L. Richardson	Bradley and Co.	
C. Beurmann	Arnhold, Karberg and Co.	
A. McConachie	Gilman and Co.	
11 members		

Resigns: M.D. Ezekiel (February)   Elected: A.J. Raymond
             G.D. Böning (Carlowitz)
   D.R. Sassoon (March)   D. Gubbay
   A. McConachie (April)   G. Slade
Dies: G. Slade (November)
Resigns: S.C. Michaelsen (December)   A. Haupt (January 1898)

February 1898

J.J. Bell-Irving	Jardine, Matheson and Co.	Chairman, 1898/99
R.M. Gray	Reiss and Co.	Deputy Chairman, 1898/99
N.A. Siebs	Siemssen and Co.	
G.B. Dodwell	Dodwell and Co.	
R.G. Shewan	Shewan, Tomes and Co.	
R.L. Richardson	Bradley and Co.	
C. Beurmann	Arnhold, Karberg and Co.	
A.J. Raymond	E.D. Sassoon and Co.	
G.D. Böning	Carlowitz and Co.	

Table 13.3 (*cont.*)

D. Gubbay	D. Sassoon, Sons and Co.
A. Haupt	Melchers and Co.
11 members	

Resigns: G.D. Boning (April)   Elected: P. Sachse

                                           A. McConachie (Gilman)

         G.B. Dodwell (May)

         R.L. Richardson (October)   R.H. Hill

February 1899

R.M. Gray	Reiss and Co.	Chairman, 1899/1900
N.A. Siebs	Siemssen and Co.	Deputy Chairman, 1899/1900
R.G. Shewan	Shewan, Tomes and Co.	
C. Beurmann	Arnhold, Karberg and Co.	
A.J. Raymond	E.D. Sassoon and Co.	
D. Gubbay	D. Sassoon, Sons and Co.	
A. Haupt	Melchers and Co.	
P. Sachse	Carlowitz and Co.	
A. McConachie	Gilman and Co.	
R.H. Hill	Bradley and Co.	
J.J. Bell-Irving	Jardine, Matheson and Co.	
11 members		

Resigns C. Beurmann (March)   Elected: E. Goetz

         D. Gubbay (April)   E. Shellim

         J.J. Bell-Irving   J.J. Keswick (May)

         E. Shellim (October)   D.M. Moses

         R.H. Hill (December)   R.L. Richardson (January)

February 1900

N.A. Siebs	Siemssen and Co.	Chairman, 1900/01
R.G. Shewan	Shewan, Tomes and Co.	Deputy Chairman, 1900/01
A.J. Raymond	E.D. Sassoon and Co.	
A. Haupt	Melchers and Co.	
P. Sachse	Carlowitz and Co.	
A. McConachie	Gilman and Co.	
E. Goetz	Arnhold, Karberg and Co.	
J.J. Keswick	Jardine, Matheson and Co.	
D.M. Moses	D. Sassoon, Sons and Co.	
R.L. Richardson	Bradley and Co.	
R.M. Gray	Reiss and Co.	
11 members		

Resigns: A. McConachie (April)   Elected: G.W. Slade

         E. Goetz (November)   P. Witkowsky

February 1901

R.G. Shewan	Shewan, Tomes and Co.	Chairman, 1901/02
J.J. Keswick	Jardine, Matheson and Co.	Deputy Chairman, 1901/02

Table 13.3 (*cont.*)

A.J. Raymond	E.D. Sassoon and Co.
P. Sachse	Carlowitz and Co.
A. Haupt	Melchers and Co.
D.M. Moses	D. Sassoon, Sons and Co.
R.L. Richardson	Bradley and Co.
R.M. Gray	Reiss and Co.
G.W. Slade	Gilman and Co.
P. Witkowski	Arnhold, Karberg and Co.
N.A. Siebs	Siemssen and Co.
11 members	

Resigns: R.M. Gray (March)	Elected: H.E. Tomkins
P. Sachse (April)	H. Schubart
J.J. Keswick (May)	J.J. Bell-Irving
P. Witkowski (December)	E. Goetz

February 1902

R.G. Shewan	Shewan, Tomes and Co.	Chairman, 1902/03
J.J. Bell-Irving	Jardine, Matheson and Co.	Deputy Chairman, 1902/03
A.J. Raymond	E.D. Sassoon and Co.	
A. Haupt	Melchers and Co.	
D.M. Moses	D. Sassoon, Sons and Co.	
R.L. Richardson	Bradley and Co.	
G.W. Slade	Gilman and Co.	
N.A. Siebs	Siemssen and Co.	
H.E. Tomkins	Reiss and Co.	
H. Schubart	Carlowitz and Co.	
E. Goetz	Arnhold, Karberg and Co.	
11 members		

1895, having taken over the China-coast business of Russell and Co., with whom both Robert G. Shewan and Charles A. Tomes had been associated, the former since he joined the firm in London in 1888. Dodwell, Carlill and Co. had been formed by two partners and had taken over the business of the failed Adamson, Bell and Co.; the company registered with limited liability as Dodwell and Co. in 1899.

Bradley and Co. was originally a Swatow company, specializing in coal, shipping, and general imports, and had only recently come to Hong Kong. Reiss and Co. began in Manchester in the late eighteenth century as Reiss Bros and first came to China in 1849 when it established in Shanghai. Carlowitz and Co. and E.D. Sassoon also had their head offices in Shanghai, whereas D. Sassoon, Sons and Co., Holliday, Wise and Co., and Gibb, Livingston and Co., for example, had English head offices.[3]

The Hongkong Bank secured its German position by inviting Carlowitz and

Co. to join the Board. The company had been founded in Canton as early as 1846 by two merchants originally from Leipzig, and, after establishing the Hong Kong branch in 1866, set up their head office in Shanghai in 1877 – which may explain why they were not represented on the Board at that time. From this base they extended to Tientsin and became successful in China loan business, particularly in association with the Warschauer Group. By 1895 the firm was involved in a railway deal with Krupp to be financed by the Deutsch-Asiatische Bank, which in accordance with an existing agreement offered participation to the Hongkong Bank. These activities and associations no doubt influenced the Board's decision in 1897 to invite a representative, G.D. Böning, to become a director.[4] The decision proved wise; Carlowitz and Co. became leading importers of armaments and dies, supplementing their business in Manchester goods by obtaining British manufacturing agencies as well as by handling German exports, including acting as sole agent in China for Krupp interests.

With three other German firms already on the Board – Siemssen's, Arnhold, Karberg and Co., and Melchers and Co. – the Hongkong Bank was in a strong position relative to the Deutsch-Asiatische Bank in the finance of normal trade.

Changes in the personal composition of the Board, while obviously reflecting the introduction of five new companies as well as the departure of Holliday, Wise and Co., Douglas Lapraik and Co., Dodwell's, and the P&O, were due mainly to the retirement, transfer, or departure on long leave of the directors concerned. In one case the minutes specifically record that a director was being replaced while he remained on leave – E. Goetz by P. Witkowsky of Arnhold, Karberg in 1900/01; this was becoming a general practice.

The Board also recorded the death in 1894 of Heinrich Hoppius, a victim of the cholera: 'a man of the highest integrity and exceptional capacity, esteemed by everyone who knew him . . . over twenty years a director of the Bank, three times its chairman and with the keenest interest in its affairs'. The Board similarly noted the death of John S. Lapraik, who had been connected with the Bank since its foundation and whose uncle, Douglas Lapraik, had been on the founding committee. G. Slade of Gilman and Co. died in 1897, having just replaced McConachie, who, once on the Board, had proved to be a director much respected by his colleagues.

The chairmanship of the Board and, therefore, of the Hongkong Bank continued in general to pass by seniority. D.R. Sassoon was, however, passed over, presumably at his own request. An examination of Table 13.4 will indicate, however, that the pattern was broken with respect to Jardine, Matheson and that, for the first time since the days of the 'Company Limited', there was a director, the highly regarded Robert G. Shewan, who was elected for two years in succession and was thus Chairman from 1901 to 1903.[5]

Table 13.4 *The Hongkong and Shanghai Banking Corporation*
Chairmen and Deputy Chairmen, 1893–1903

1893/94		*1898 (January)/99*	
H. Hoppius	Siemssen	J.J. Bell-Irving	Jardine Matheson
C.J. Holliday	Holliday Wise	R.M. Gray	Reiss (February)
1894/95		*1899/1900*	
C.J. Holliday	Holliday Wise	R.M. Gray	Reiss
J.S. Moses	E.D. Sassoon	N.A. Siebs	Siemssen
1895 to April		*1900/01*	
J.S. Moses	E.D. Sassoon	N.A. Siebs	Siemssen
Julius Kramer	Arnhold Karberg	R.G. Shewan	Shewan Tomes
1895 (April)/1896		*1901/02*	
Julius Kramer	Arnhold Karberg	R.G. Shewan	Shewan Tomes
A. McConachie	Gilman	J.J. Keswick	Jardine Matheson
1896/97		*1902/03*	
A. McConachie	Gilman	R.G. Shewan	Shewan Tomes
S.C. Michaelsen	Melchers	J.J. Bell-Irving	Jardine Matheson
1897/1898 (December)			
S.C. Michaelsen	Melchers		
J.J. Bell-Irving	Jardine Matheson		

One activity of the Board remained unchanged – its control of charitable donations. Table 13.5 reflects the continuity of policy.

The London Committee – membership and role

The Board of Directors in Hong Kong from time to time changed their conception of the London Committee, but it was always important. The first committee provided links with the Bank's 'clearer', the London and County Bank, and with knowledgeable Eastern houses. In the period dealt with in the present chapter, the connection with the London and County continued, the P&O became represented – although the chairman, Sir Thomas Sutherland himself, did not accept, and the Bank's increased interest in Chinese railway finance was reflected in the appointment of Carl Meyer, formerly of N.M. Rothschild and Co. and sometime chairman of the Pekin Syndicate. Meyer was also a director of the Bank of Egypt and closely associated with such South African mining activities as de Beers Consolidated as chairman of their London Committee; he was close to Cecil Rhodes. Originally from Hamburg, Meyer had served as personal private secretary to Lord Rothschild; he was made a baronet and his son served in the British Forces, but this would not protect him from anti-

Table 13.5 *The Hongkong and Shanghai Banking Corporation Charitable donations as listed in the minutes, 1889–1902*

A. *Charity*

1890:	Alice Memorial Hospital	$250
1892:	Cholera Fund, Hamburg	$125
	'Bokhara' Fund (P&O ship)	$200
1895:	Plague Committee	$500
	New English Church, Hiogo	$250
1899:	San Juan de Dio Hospital, Manila	$1000
	Treaty Port Chaplaincy Fund	$300[a]
	Tientsin Community Church	$500
	Tropical School of Medicine	$50
	Tung Wah Hospital and Plague Hospital Fund	$1000
	A German widow in Japan[b]	$1000
	Indian Famine Fund	Rs2500[c]
1900:	St George's Hospital Nursing Fund, Bombay:	
	building	Rs1000
	annual	Rs200
	Indian Famine, donation in India	Rs5000
	donation in Hong Kong	$1500
	Raffles Institution, Singapore	$100
1901:	Scotch Church, Penang	$500
	Shanghai Seamen's Church and Mission Society	Ts500
	The Hongkew Coffee Shop	Ts500

B. *Other non-business*

1895:	Bi-metallic League		£250
1896:	Bi-metallic League		£100
	Manila Patriotic Fund	max.	$1500
1899:	Boer War Mansion House Fund (London Office)		£250
	ditto other branches total		£500
1901	Memorials for Queen Victoria		
	in India	max.	Rs2000
	London		£105
	Hong Kong		$2500

Notes:

[a] annual 'at the pleasure of the directors'.

[b] Mrs Grunwald put the proceeds of her life insurance policy into her late husband's firm, which failed, and she was penniless.

[c] for some reason not sent, see under 1900.

Semitic and anti-German prejudice in the hysterical period prior to and during the Great War (see Table 13.6).

As previously noted, the first change in the London Committee had come with the appointment in 1889 of William Keswick (see Chapter 12). The same year David McLean had been the first former officer of the Bank on the Committee.

Table 13.6 *The Hongkong and Shanghai Banking Corporation*
London Consultative Committee, membership, 1875–1919

A.H. Phillpotts	Director, London & County Bank	1875–1891
E.F. Duncanson	Messrs T.A. Gibb and Co.	1875–1899
Albert Deacon	Messrs E. and A. Deacon	1875–1895
David McLean[a]	former London Manager, HSBC	
	Director, Trust and Loan Company of China etc.	1889–1894
William Keswick[a]	Matheson and Co.	
	Chairman, Imperial Bank of Persia	
	Chairman, Trust and Loan Company of China etc.	1889–1894
William A. Jones	Director, London & County Bank	1891–1905
F.D. Barnes	Director, P&O SN Co.	1895–1899
G.E. Noble	retired, HSBC Chief Manager	1898–1901
Carl Meyer[b]	Chairman, Pekin Syndicate	1899–1916
William G. Rathbone	Director, P&O SN Co.	1900–1919
John Walter	retired, HSBC staff	1902–1906
Sir Thomas Jackson (Chairman)	retired, HSBC Chief Manager	
	Director, London & County Bank	1903–1915
Sir Ewen Cameron	retired, London Manager HSBC	1906–1908
J.R.M. Smith	retired, HSBC Chief Manager	1912–1918
Henry Keswick	Matheson and Co.	1912–1919
A.M. Townsend[c]	retired, London Manager HSBC	1915–1933

Notes:

[a] Resigned in view of the poor standing of the Trust and Loan Company of China, later Bank of China, Japan and the Straits.

[b] Later Sir Carl Meyer, Bart.

[c] With the death of Rathbone and the retirement of Keswick, Townsend was for a short time the only member of the Committee pending its reorganization in 1919, see Volumes II and III.

Both were also directors of the unfortunate Trust and Loan Company, and the Hongkong Bank, still struggling to regain the confidence of the City, did not wish there to be any link between the two organizations when the former's expected unfavourable 1893 report was published.

There is no question where Keswick's and McLean's sympathies lay – Keswick in fact came personally to see Ewen Cameron, the Bank's London Manager, to explain that he couldn't in honour leave the Bank of China although 'his sympathies are entirely with us'. Cameron was sympathetic and as a gesture promised Keswick to 'keep his seat open for him'. Only one new appointment was consequently made at that time, although there was not, in fact, a fixed membership, and Matheson and Co. was not represented again until 1912. McLean submitted his understanding of the situation in February 1894. The resignations were not publicly announced; the names simply did not appear in the Hongkong Bank's usual advertisements.

When due to ill health G.E. Noble retired from the junior manager's position in the London Office, he requested appointment to the Committee, explaining to the Board that many British banks followed such a custom. The Board agreed and at one point stated the desirability of there being two Bank-connected appointees. In any case John Walter succeeded after the death of Noble in 1901, but resigned in favour of Sir Ewen Cameron. Cameron's poor health forced his retirement in 1905; he recovered unexpectedly although temporarily in early 1906.

With the chairmanship of Sir Thomas Jackson in 1903 the nature of the Committee was changed; this will be considered in Volume II.

During the second Jackson administration the Committee worked closely with Ewen Cameron advising on the Bank's Chinese and Japanese loans and their reception on the London market. Cameron also consulted them on reserve investment policy, and the Board of Directors' instructions to Cameron to use his discretion were undoubtedly given with the knowledge that he would consult the Committee.

As with the Board itself the Committee's work is more fully documented in times of crisis, and there were urgent calls from the Committee in 1893 for the Board to clarify its dividend policy as early as possible in view of the non-renewal of sterling fixed deposits and the consequent drain of sterling funds from the Bank. The Committee were also consulted in the matter of London deposit interest rates; the Committee, one may reasonably assume, continued to provide routine 'opinions' on constituents.

Perhaps much if not all of this could have been done by an enhanced London Office staff, but the fact is that the Hongkong Bank still needed independent support in the City. The Board was not yet ready to do without its expert advice, even if this were regularly channelled for and to management. In 1895 the fee paid each member of the London Committee was raised from £200 to £300 per annum, putting them on a 'par with the directors' as far as remuneration was concerned; in this period there was apparently no question of their usurping the prerogatives of the Board.

PERFORMANCE, 1893–1897

The basic earning power of the Bank had remained unimpaired throughout the crisis, and, with the compradore's defalcation written off, the Bank had been able to begin the reconstruction of its reserves with semi-annual transfers of $300,000, increased eventually to $2 million per annum from July 1897 to June 1899. Net earnings, reflecting the absence of business losses and the high rate of exchange profits, rose to some $4.5 million per annum by 1898, permitting the directors to increase the dividend from £2:10s per annum to a regular £3 and to vote a year-end bonus of ten shillings – in 1898 exceptionally the bonus was £1.00 (see Tables 13.7A and B).

Behind this was Jackson's goal of establishing the Bank in so firm a position that its survival would never again rest upon such random devices as raiding the Officers Good Service Fund. This explains the extraordinary figures for December 1898, and a first consideration of his second administration should focus on the events leading to that particular half-year. At that point the Bank might be said to have come of age. From 1898 through his last full year in 1901, Jackson managed the resources which the Bank, with the support of the directors and the forbearance of the shareholders, had been able to accumulate.

The period from 1893 to 1898 was not, however, a simple recovery; it was recovery and growth to a level at which the Bank might safely operate. The year 1898 was a reexamination of the position and consequent ordering of accounts, including an extraordinary dividend payout which, taken by itself, would be inexplicable except perhaps as evidence of an erratic policy.

The history will follow these divisions, considering first the development of the Bank to the key year of 1898.

The pressures of 1893

As successive Chairmen had been careful to explain the Bank used its sterling funds to finance its sterling business. Its Eastern business was financed by silver liabilities. But the fall of silver, the Bank's loss of reserves in 1892, and the Australian banking crisis of 1893 all combined to cause a loss of London confidence with a consequent non-renewal of sterling fixed deposits, a source of funds on which the Bank had depended if it were to maintain its 'even keel'. The drain continued into 1894 and reduced the Bank's sterling deposits as shown in the published semi-annual accounts from £4.9 million at the end of October 1892 to £2.9 million eighteen months later.

To offset the drain, which was not of a kind correctable by an adjustment of the interest rate, the Bank in the second half of 1893 curtailed business in the East and remitted to London, building on already overbought sterling and rupee positions. This is reflected in the accounts by the drop in bills discounted (see 'Loans etc.' in Table 13.9) and a rise of $7 million in 'bills receivable'. The Bank was forced to move funds to London as exchange, Hong Kong on London, was falling (see Table 13.1); the Bank was not so much renouncing the even keel but adjusting its basis by taking a larger position in sterling. This adjustment was necessary for the finance of outward business on a new basis and was undertaken at a time favourable, given the continuing fall in exchange, to the overall position of the Bank.

If the Bank's policy were to be independent in London, then it needed additional sterling reserves. The Bank was always exposed to exchange fluctuations by an assignment of its capital to territories operating on a different standard, for example, Europe, the Philippines, and India – and later Japan, Siam, and the Straits Settlements. However, even in these cases timing could be of vital importance, and here Jackson's judgement became important. There was nothing automatic about the 'even keel'.

The increase in sterling reserves represented a transfer of capital from Head Office to London. The interest from the investments was assigned to London Office, which was consequently instructed to lower the interest charged on inter-branch overdrafts, thus giving branches access to cheaper funds and enabling them to take up opportunities they had been passing by due to the cost of their London overdrafts. That this was more a corrective device than a factor distorting the use of funds by the inter-branch use of non-market rates of interest is consequent to the difficulty of allocating overheads precisely and of securing a manager's cooperation in operating at a loss for 'global' or 'imperial' reasons. The Board's capital and investment decisions had many ramifications.

This level of action was neither immediate in its public impact nor fully understood at the time. Decisions on dividends, on the contrary, seemed to be a clear statement of a firm's situation, and with Bank shares in London having fallen to £25 on July 4, 1893, the Board of Directors in Hong Kong and the Committee in London entered into an emergency discussion.

The first step was to assure London shareholders that a semi-annual dividend of at least £1:00 (= £80,000 or $640,000 at 2s:6d) would be paid for the first-half of 1893. This had an immediate impact on the market, with shares trading at £27 the following day (see Table 13.8).

The next problem was to determine the actual dividend and the consequent availability of funds from Profit and Loss Account for transfer to the Bank's reserves. A dividend in lieu of an allocation to correct the depleted reserve position would not have been well-received in London; the mix was important. Unfortunately, the Bank's earning power had not yet recovered, there were still losses to provide for, and net profits at just under $1 million were but two-thirds of the level reached in the second six months of 1890. The proper course of action was not immediately obvious.

The Bank's holdings of consols, listed as London special reserves, were on the books at 95 and an exchange of 2s:10⅛d, whereas the exchange for the end-June accounts was 2s:6d; thus taking over these securities at the rate of the day would result in the significant addition to profit of $240,000, thereby enabling the directors to recommend a dividend plus a significant transfer to reserves. The Chairman, Heinrich Hoppius, convinced the Board that the Special Reserve should not be revalued, but kept – and so noted publicly – at the old rate so that:

The London shareholder in particular can see we do not write down [the rate of exchange for] our securities to help pay our dividend . . . The above profit of $241,818 being left in special reserve would have a very good effect in London where items of this kind are carefully looked into.

Table 13.7A *The Hongkong and Shanghai Banking Corporation Key indicators, 1893–1901*

(in millions unless otherwise stated)

Year	Assets $	= £	Reserves[a] (i)	+ (ii)	Net earnings	To Reserve	To dividend		Rate $1 = *x*s/d
1893 June	130.3	16.3	3.9		1.00	0.30	£1	0.64	2/6
1893 Dec.	134.0	15.1	4.2		1.12	0.30	£1	0.71	2/3
1894 June	139.3	14.7	4.5		1.14	0.30	£1	0.76	2/1¼
1894 Dec.	153.2	15.3	5.0		1.68	0.50	£1¼	1.00	2/0
1895 June	167.1	17.8	5.5		1.63	0.50	£1¼	0.94	2/1⅝
1895 Dec.	187.1	20.0	5.75		1.20	0.25	£1¼	0.94	2/1⅝
1896 June	203.4	22.4	6.0		1.16	0.25	£1¼	0.91	2/2½
1896 Dec.	184.1	19.8	6.5		1.46	0.50	£1¼	0.95	2/1⅜
1897 June	178.3	17.8	7.0		1.53	0.50	£1¼	1.01	1/11¾
1897 Dec.	169.4	16.6	8.0		2.13	1.00	£1¼	1.02	1/11⅝
1898 June	221.9	21.3	9.0		2.39	1.00	£1¼	1.04	1/11
1898 Dec.	181.8	17.8	**10.0**		**4.02**	**1.00**	**£2½**[b]	**2.04**	1/11½
1899 June	202.6	20.0	11.0		2.61	1.00	£1½	1.22	1/11⅝
1899 Dec.	208.3	20.4	11.5		2.16	0.50	£2[b]	1.64	1/11⅜
1900 June	220.5	21.6	10.0	2.0	2.48	0.50	£1½	1.21	1/11⅞
1900 Dec.	211.5	22.1	10.0	3.0	2.24	1.00	£2[b]	1.54	2/1
1901 June	222.0	21.8	10.0	3.75	2.07	0.75	£1½	1.23	1/11$\frac{7}{16}$
1901 Dec.	248.8	23.1	10.0	4.25	2.39	0.50	£2[b]	1.73	1/10¼
1902 June	271.4	23.2	10.0	4.75	2.12	0.50	£1½	1.41	1/8½

Shareholders' funds (1893 June) = $14,269,000 (@2/6 = £1,784,000)
Shareholders' funds (1901 Dec.) = $25,938,000 (@1/10¼ = £2,405,000)

Notes:

[a] The figure for the Reserve Fund *includes* the amount transferred at the end of the period as approved by the shareholders at the subsequent meeting. That is, for December 1897, the Reserves show $8.0 million, which includes the $1.0 million transferred on December 31, 1897.

The Reserves from June 1900 reflect the decision to indicate whether the reserves had been invested in sterling or silver securities; (i) is the amount in sterling, i.e. the 'Sterling Reserve Fund' and (ii) is the 'Silver Reserve Fund'. Total reserves as published are (i) + (ii).

[b] The dividend is at a new rate of £1:10s plus the bonus. For details see Table 13.7B.

Table 13.7B *The Hongkong and Shanghai Banking Corporation Dividends, 1893–1901*

Year	Interim		+	Final		+	Bonus[a]		=	Total		Total payout		Payout ratio	Total dividend as % of Book value	
	£ = $	@		£ = $	@		£ = $			£ = $		£ = $ (millions)		%	£	$ (per cent)
1893	1:00 2/6	**8.00**		1:00 2/3	**8.89**					2:00	**16.89**	0.16	**1.35**	63.7	9.8	**9.3**
1894	1:00 2/1¼	**9.50**		1:05 2/0	**12.50**					2:05	**22.00**	0.18	**1.76**	62.4	11.7	**11.4**
1895	1:05 2/1⅝	**11.71**		1:05 2/1⅝	**11.71**					2:10	**23.42**	0.20	**1.87**	66.1	11.5	**11.5**
1896	1:05 2/2½	**11.32**		1:05 2/1⅜	**11.82**					2:10	**23.14**	0.20	**1.85**	70.6	11.1	**10.9**
1897	1:05 1/11¾	**12.63**		1:05 1/11⅝	**12.70**					2:10	**25.33**	0.20	**2.03**	55.5	11.0	**10.9**
1898	1:05 1/11	**13.04**		1:05 1/11½	**15.32**		1:00	**10.21**		3:15	**38.57**	0.30	**3.09**	48.0	14.5	**14.6**
1899	1:10 1/11⅝	**15.24**		1:10 1/11⅜	**15.40**		0:10	**5.13**		3:10	**35.77**	0.28	**2.86**	60.0	12.7	**12.6**
1900	1:10 1/11⅞	**15.08**		1:10 2/1	**14.40**		0:10	**4.80**		3:10	**34.28**	0.28	**2.74**	58.3	10.9	**11.1**
1901	1:10 1/11⁷⁄₁₆	**15.36**		1:10 1/10¼	**16.18**		0:10	**5.39**		3:10	**36.93**	0.28	**2.96**	66.4	11.6	**11.4**

Notes:
Bold face = $ equivalent
[a] Bonus is at same rate of exchange as final dividend.
Source: Tables 13.1 and 13.6.

The difficulty with this conservative policy was that the Bank would have been able to pay but one lac of dollars into the reserves, whereas London, noting the probable and consequent decline in the price of shares, urged that at least two lacs be transferred.

After consulting with Hoppius, Thomas Jackson wired his calculation of the trade offs: (i) if we leave Special London Reserve at 2s:10⅜d and 95, the Bank can pay from Profit and Loss Account a £1:00 dividend, put one lac to reserves, and carry $75,000 forward; (ii) if we lower the rate to 2s:8d, we can pay £1:00, plus 2 lacs to reserves, plus $100,000 carry over; (iii) if we lower the rate to 2s:6d, we can pay £1:00, plus 3 lacs to reserves, plus $115,000 carry over.

The second choice had no rationale.

The London Consultative Committee, supported by the manager of the London and County Bank, whom they had consulted, considered the listing of the Hongkong Bank's consols at 95 sufficient evidence of a conservative policy and urged writing down the rate at which the investments were valued to the rate of the day, 2s:6d, and transferring $300,000 to reserves (see Table 13.7A).

And the directors, 'deeming it of the first importance to do whatever would promote the credit of the Bank', decided to act upon the suggestion of the London Committee.

Net earnings for the second-half of 1893 improved some 12%, but losses in Calcutta and Colombo prevented the Bank from as yet realizing its potential. The increase nevertheless permitted the Bank not only to repeat the mid-year allocation of a £1:00 dividend – at the lower rate of 2s:3d, thus costing an additional $70,000 – but also to write off $100,000 from Bank Premises Account and repay $50,000 of the $130,000 to the Officers Good Service Fund.

The period of growth

The increased cost of the £1:00 dividend caused by the fall in exchange more than offset the increase in published net earnings. The payout ratio varied from 55.5% to 70.6% (see Table 13.7B). For the first six months of 1894 (and for the last time) the pattern of a £1:00 dividend and an allocation of $300,000 to reserves was maintained.

Exchange had been unsettled, falling at one point to 1s:11¼d compared to the end-June rate of 2s:1¼d, and the drain of the Bank's sterling deposits continued. With recovery in the East, however, silver deposits improved and the Bank was in a strong cash position. During the half-year the directors had agreed to pay the Hong Kong Government $60,000 for reclaiming the land in front of the Bank, which sum had been written off. The reclamation was part of the new Praya scheme and the land was potentially of great value, but the Bank would eventually dedicate it to public use as part of Statue Square, thus giving rise to one of Hong

Table 13.8. *The Hongkong and Shanghai Banking Corporation*
Earnings and share prices, 1893–1902

Year	(i) Net earnings ($ millions)	(ii) £ Dividend/share	(iii) Book value $	(iv) Book value £	(v) Share price Shanghai	(vi) Share price London	(vii) M/B ratio $	(viii) M/B ratio £	(ix) Rate $1 = xs/d
1892 Dec.	0.90	£1	174	23.7	266	36	1.53	1.52	2/8¾
1893 June	1.00	£1	178	22.3	253	30	1.41	1.35	2/6
1893 Dec.	1.12	£1	182	20.5	248	28	1.34	1.39	2/3
1894 June	1.14	£1	186	19.6	250	28	1.34	1.43	2/1¼
1894 Dec.	1.68	£1¼	192	19.2	252	31	1.29	1.61	2/0
1895 June	1.63	£1¼	201	21.4	358	44	1.78	2.06	2/1⅝
1895 Dec.	1.20	£1¼	204	21.8	356	40	1.75	1.83	2/1⅝
1896 June	1.16	£1¼	207	22.8	360	43	1.74	1.89	2/2½
1896 Dec.	1.46	£1¼	213	22.5	353	42	1.66	1.87	2/1⅜
1897 June	1.53	£1¼	219	21.7	359	44	1.64	2.03	1/11¾
1897 Dec.	2.13	£1¼	232	22.8	345	42	1.49	1.84	1/11⅝
1898 June	2.39	£1¼	245	23.5	376	47	1.53	2.00	1/11
1898 Dec.	4.02	£2½	264	25.8	428	54	1.62	2.09	1/11½
1899 June	2.61	£1½	278	27.3	500	60	1.80	2.20	1/11⅝
1899 Dec.	2.16	£2	284	27.7	556	61	1.96	2.20	1/11⅜
1900 June	2.48	£1½	300	29.8	500	49	1.67	1.64	1/11⅞
1900 Dec.	2.24	£2	308	32.1	556	61	1.81	1.90	2/1
1901 June	2.07	£1½	319	31.1	606	62	1.90	1.99	1/11 7/16
1901 Dec.	2.39	£2	324	30.1	620	64	1.91	2.13	1/10¼
1902 June	2.12	£1½	330	28.2	600	63	1.82	2.23	1/8½

Notes:

(i) Net earnings in millions of Hong Kong dollars from Table 13.7A.
(ii) Dividends declared in pounds sterling, see Table 13.7A.
(iii) Book value = shareholders' funds, i.e. paid-up capital + reserves (including amounts paid in from net earnings) + retained profits, divided by 80,000, the number of shares outstanding.
(iv) Column (iii) converted into pounds sterling at rate of semi-annual report.
(v) Shanghai shares were quoted at so much per cent premium, which is added to the par value of shares, i.e. $125; the dates are mid-July and mid-January.
(vi) London prices for shares on the London register.
(vii) Equivalent to (v) divided by (iii).
(viii) Equivalent to (vi) divided by (iv).
(ix) The rate used in the semi-annual Hongkong Bank accounts.

Table 13.9 *The Hongkong and Shanghai Banking Corporation Cash, selected balance sheet items, and ratios[a], 1893–1901*

(in millions of dollars)

Year	Assets	Index[b]	Cash and bullion	C/A ratio	Net earnings	E as % of A	Deposits + notes	Loans etc.	Loan/D ratio	Bills rec.	BR index[c]	Bills pay	BP index[c]	Rate $1 = xs/d
1892 Dec.	129.5	99	16.33	0.13	0.90	0.69	99.74	44.14	0.44	61.37	111	15.27	97	$2/8\frac{3}{4}$
1893 June	130.3	100	19.59	0.15	1.00	0.77	99.58	46.98	0.47	55.52	100	15.81	100	$2/6$
1893 Dec.	134.0	103	21.73	0.16	1.12	0.84	99.47	40.63	0.41	63.03	114	19.14	121	$2/3$
1894 June	139.3	107	26.29	0.19	1.14	0.82	102.08	45.37	0.44	59.02	106	21.52	136	$2/1\frac{1}{4}$
1894 Dec.	153.2	118	42.77	0.28	1.68	1.10	114.28	44.22	0.39	57.53	104	22.33	141	$2/0$
1895 June	167.1	128	51.39	0.31	1.63	0.98	129.35	47.65	0.37	60.04	108	20.77	131	$2/1\frac{5}{8}$
1895 Dec.	187.1	144	38.07	0.20	1.20	0.64	152.65	53.86	0.35	84.04	151	17.23	109	$2/1\frac{5}{8}$
1896 June	203.4	156	58.28	0.29	1.16	0.57	171.08	61.11	0.36	71.73	129	14.83	94	$2/2\frac{1}{2}$
1896 Dec.	184.1	141	28.29	0.15	1.46	0.79	151.08	63.57	0.42	80.22	144	15.02	95	$2/1\frac{3}{8}$
1897 June	178.3	137	27.75	0.16	1.53	0.86	147.26	65.27	0.44	72.96	131	12.47	79	$1/11\frac{3}{4}$
1897 Dec.	169.4	130	24.69	0.15	2.13	1.26	130.93	61.26	0.47	69.85	126	18.75	119	$1/11\frac{5}{8}$
1898 June	221.9	132	45.08	0.20	2.39	1.08	183.70	87.55	0.48	76.29	137	17.29	109	$1/11$
1898 Dec.	181.8	139	32.46[d]	0.18	4.02	2.21	143.52	64.37	0.45	72.51	131	14.59	92	$1/11\frac{1}{2}$
1899 June	202.6	155	44.65[d]	0.22	2.61	1.29	165.68	63.81	0.39	78.27	141	13.22	84	$1/11\frac{5}{8}$
1899 Dec.	208.3	160	39.73[d]	0.19	2.16	1.04	169.19	59.71	0.35	90.91	164	14.74	93	$1/11\frac{3}{8}$
1900 June	220.5	169	37.73[d]	0.17	2.48	1.12	170.07	74.60	0.44	90.18	162	25.25	160	$1/11\frac{7}{8}$
1900 Dec.	211.5	162	51.84[d]	0.25	2.24	1.06	163.26	71.24	0.44	68.55	123	21.99	139	$2/1$
1901 June	222.0	170	52.97[d]	0.24	2.07	0.93	179.10	75.43	0.42	74.76	135	16.12	102	$1/11\frac{7}{16}$
1901 Dec.	248.8	191	57.22[d]	0.23	2.39	0.96	202.78	74.71	0.37	95.78	173	18.18	115	$1/10\frac{1}{4}$
1902 June	271.4	208	60.20[d]	0.22	2.12	0.78	215.13	88.50	0.41	99.32	179	28.17	178	$1/8\frac{1}{2}$

Notes:

[a] Ratios affected by China loan operations.

[b] Index of total assets, June 1893 = 100. June 1893 = 100.

[c] Loans etc. = bills discounted, loans and credits. Bills pay = BP = bills payable, incl. 'drafts on London Bankers and short sight drawings on our London Office against Bills receivable and bullion shipments'.

[d] Includes coin lodged against 'excess' note issue on a dollar for dollar basis. For effects, see Table 13.11.

E = earnings D = deposits + notes.

A = assets. Bills Rec. = BR = bills receivable.

478

Kong's most persistent myths – that the Hongkong Bank had, somehow, the right to a 'view to the sea' (see Volume IV).

The fall in silver had caused a flow of gold from the East to London, contributing to the low cost of funds there. This, in turn, was responsible for the rise in the price of gilt-edged securities, and the Bank's reserves were on its books at considerably less than the market price, a development which, when realized, would be a further source of strength.

Despite the Bank's previous problems, there was no difficulty when in 1894 as the result of a successful tender the Imperial Treasury signed a further agreement with the Hongkong Bank for conducting the financial business of the Treasury Chest in China at an interest of 6%, with the condition that the Bank supply the Government with silver dollars at the rate of the day in the 'Consular ports'. The agreement was as usual extended to include Japan.[6]

Indeed, the Bank's position was such that the directors were under strong pressure to increase the dividend. After considering the end-1894 results they could resist no longer, and the dividend was increased to £1:5s, which remained the standard rate through June 1898. Share prices responded but the rise was at first inhibited by the uncertainty of the Sino-Japanese War, with a later cautious rise due, in part, to the profits the Bank received from the issue of loans for the Chinese Government.

With net profits of $1.86 million despite small losses in Bombay and Colombo, the constraints which had limited the directors' allocation decisions were in part removed. Not only could they raise the dividend, they could allocate $500,000 to the reserves and write off sums from dead stock and premises accounts. But before passing the published statement the Board had declared a 10% salary bonus to staff costing $90,000 and an additional bonus to specified managers of $12,500.

This improved position and dividend having been announced, a shareholder, Robert Shewan, proposed at the February 1895 semi-annual meeting that the fees to directors be increased from $20,000 to $30,000 per annum; this was not quite as much as the increase the directors had intended in 1891, but still the first since the Bank's incorporation. No vote is recorded, but the higher fees are indicated in the next 'abstract' of accounts.

By the end of 1894 the Bank was committed to the issue of a Kuping tael 10 million, 7% Chinese Government Loan (= ShTs 10.9 million), issued in silver at par or in London, Hamburg, and Amsterdam (through Hope and Co.) in sterling at 98, with exchange at an arbitrarily high rate of 3s:0d (thereby approximately offsetting the discount), and repayment of interest and principal at the rate of the day. The Bank would receive a 2% commission from the proceeds. In January 1895 the Bank agreed to issue the Chinese Government 6% Gold Loan for £3 million at 96½ in London, Hamburg, and Amsterdam, also on a 2% commission basis.[7]

The second loan was not an initial success and the Bank itself held a high proportion of the bonds, which were eventually sold on a rising market. In February the Bank permitted the Canton authorities to delay repayment on the £750,000, 1885 loan, the Bank 'advancing' the sums in arrears at 7%. Government loan business, which had featured so prominently in the Bank's performance from 1875, was again active and would help explain the Bank's improving position through the remainder of the decade.

Loan commissions totalling $430,000 virtually doubled Shanghai's profits in the first half of 1895, and although the general level of profits had declined slightly, the Bank was again able to pay a dividend of £1:5s – at the improved rate of 2s:1$\frac{5}{8}$d – and transfer $500,000 to reserves. Profits from Head Office exchange operations exceeded $1 million, and this item would grow as Jackson's hand became more certain in the face of continuous fluctuations. The directors awarded bonuses to those directly involved in the loan negotiations and noted particularly 'the very great services E.G. Hillier (the Bank's Peking Agent) has rendered to the Bank in connection with recent loans'.

Shareholder pressure for a further increase in the dividend was countered by the argument that the course of silver was uncertain and the directors were unwilling to commit the Bank to a high level of sterling dividends, a reminder of the anomalous position in which this silver-based bank found itself. At the same time here was further evidence that the directors understood the need for a stable dividend policy, as confirmed by the statement of A. McConachie at the February 1896 semi-annual meeting. The directors, he said, 'aim at uniformity of dividend'. The dividend, he noted, represented a return of 18$\frac{3}{4}$% on the par value of the shares, $125; it represented, however, only 6$\frac{1}{4}$% per annum on the London share price of £40, and apparently some thought this return too low or, alternatively, that the price of the shares had been bid up too high, presumably with the expectation of a higher dividend.

Earnings fell for two successive half-years and the allocation to reserves was reduced to $250,000. The Bank was facing competition; it also held funds in excess of what could be profitably used, and interest rate adjustments were attempted. Analysis of the apparently erratic changes in both cash holdings and deposit liabilities is, however, confused by unusual and temporary requirements resulting from loans and related indemnity operations on behalf of the Chinese Government.

Following the defeat of China in 1895 there was considerable activity in the financing of the indemnity, but the results of this, as far as the Hongkong Bank's balance sheet was concerned, would appear later, and the fall in exchange profits and consequent overall earnings of $1.16 million were impressive only in the context of the difficult times; they did not permit any dramatic change in the Bank's semi-annual allocations. Nevertheless the Bank's position was improving

– there was an excess of $1.7 million in the difference between the Bank's investments on the books and at market price, while Contingencies Account showed an excess of $0.9 million. These figures were not released, but the former at least could be calculated.

The China loans and inner reserves[b]

A bank may legitimately understate the value of its shareholders' funds (i) by announced conservative valuation policies relative to its securities held against the Reserve Fund (as noted above) and (ii) through so-called 'inner reserves', that is, accounts which are unappropriated but which are not listed under 'capital accounts'; they are included instead under some general liabilities item. The former method understates the 'footings', that is, the total assets or the total liabilities plus capital accounts; the latter method in itself does not affect the company's footings, rather it understates capital account and overstates liabilities by an equal amount.

Joint-stock companies often held inner reserves. The practice lost general support in the early 1930s, but British joint-stock banks continued to hold inner reserves, a practice specifically permitted under the 1948 Companies Act (Schedule Eight banks), but the practice began to lose popularity in the early 1970s with the rise of a crisis in the secondary banking market.

One explanation of the need for inner reserves arose from the difference between legally acceptable and generally acceptable policy. One acceptable purpose of reserves was the equalization of dividends but their actual use for this purpose was taken as a reflection on the ability of management. Banks traditionally held inner reserves to support their position in times of financial crisis, a purpose all the more necessary in Hong Kong, where, as the directors pointed out, there was no Bank of England.

It may be assumed that a bank which had to raid an appropriated fund, for example, the Officers Good Service Fund, had no 'inner reserves'. The Hongkong Bank's position in the early 1890s was such that its shareholders' funds had to be fully revealed.

By the end of 1896, however, profits from China loans, including the just completed Second Indemnity Loan of £16 million, exceeded $1 million. After transferring $328,000 of this to general Profit and Loss Account, the balance was 'unappropriated'; it thus became an 'inner reserve'. This new policy was publicly

---

[b] To avoid repetition the details of the post Sino-Japanese War loans and the various negotiations and alliances which preceded them are reserved for Volume II. This chapter details the consequences of activities the details of which will be considered later. From the point of view of Jackson's administration the end-date for the period is 1902; other historical factors suggest a cut-off at 1895.

announced by the Bank's Chairman, A. McConachie, at the February 1897 meeting:

I am glad to say that we have a large portion of the profit upon the loans we recently participated in still unappropriated; some will go to enrich future profit and loss accounts, and will help us maintain a steady dividend in bad times as well as in good ones – that is the goal we are aiming at, and we are confident of realizing it. (Applause)

Since these unappropriated funds were largely incorporated into the published accounts as a result of the success of 1898, the best explanation of the Board's decision is in terms of Jackson's desire to establish the reserves on a safe basis at a level equal to paid-up capital, that is, $10 million. To pay into reserves at the rate of $500,000 or, as in December 1897 and June 1898, $1 million without raising the dividend required a policy which, while hardly secret in view of the frank statements on the Bank's affairs by successive Chairmen, at least did not flaunt the Bank's new-found wealth in precise terms in its published accounts. Share prices rose to £54 by the end of 1898 and the improved market/book ratio reflected the market's assessment of the Bank's true position.

In August 1897 the Bank's Chairman, S.C. Michaelsen, confirmed the policy of 'unappropriated' profits and described how the Bank had made the accounts 'comfortable', presumably referring to the growing differential between the market price of the London securities and their value in the Bank's accounts. After a brief rise, probably due to China's urgent demand for silver during the war with Japan, the price of silver fell significantly with, *inter alia*, Japan's announced intention to go on a gold basis. In June 1896 the rate had been 2s:2½d; in mid-1897 it was 1s:11¾d and would continue to fall through 1899. This led the Chairman to stress once again that the Bank's sterling liabilities were never permitted to exceed its sterling assets, so that the fall in silver was in this sense a matter of indifference to them. However, this position had been achieved with some difficulty, and the Bank admitted shortcomings in providing constituents with their legitimate, trade related, exchange requirements.

By the end of 1897 the profits of the Bank had improved to such an extent that $1 million – equivalent to the entire net earnings in the half-year ending June 1893 – could be transferred to the Reserve Fund, while a further $100,000 could be written off 'dead stock'. And this was done without, in the Chairman's word, 'trenching' into the unappropriated profits previously referred to; the 'inner reserves' were very much a subject for public comment. The proceeds from the 1897 $4 million, 5% Loan to Japan had resulted in an addition of £13,633 to the profits of the Bank's Yokohoma branch. Exchange profits again exceeded $1 million at Head Office, and the extensive movements of silver bullion – yen coins to Japan, sycee silver to the newly opened West River ports, including Wuchow, and to the ports of the Yangtze helped raise the Bank's half-year net earnings to over $2 million for the first time in its history.

This last point was in itself a good omen for the extraordinary year of 1898.

THE HONGKONG BANK IN 1898

The consequences of the years through 1898 were formalized in the discussions prior to and substantiated at the semi-annual meeting the following February. And events up to the last moment could obviously affect the final outcome. Before considering the disposition of the Bank's end–December 1898 resources, the realization of hopes until then beyond reach, this section will recite the principal events of the year and then review the Board's policies from 1893. Finally, there must be a statement of the Bank's position and the allocations which would set the stage for Jackson's final years.

Developments in 1898

There were no losses in the first half of the year, business was favourable, the Head Office profits on exchange in excess of $1 million, and the Bank's net profits stated at $2.4 million. The main event had been the floating, in joint account with 'our German friends', the Deutsch-Asiatische Bank, of the Third Indemnity Loan for £16 million which had been underwritten at $4\frac{1}{2}\%$ and 90. Despite the inscription of the Bank of England, public subscription was only £1.46 million, the Japanese took £2 million, and the underwriting syndicate, including the Bank, were left with the balance. The Chairman at the August meeting noted that the profits on this loan had not been appropriated, but he was surely premature; the net profits of £220,971 were not available until November.

Since the Bank found itself with a large holding of the Third Indemnity Loan, it attempted to have these bonds accepted, as in the case of previous China loans, as part of the required security for the note issue. The Colonial Office assumed correctly that the purpose behind this was to provide the Bank with greater liquidity by releasing other more marketable securities from the Note Security Fund. Noting the poor public response to the loan, the Treasury supported the Colonial Office in refusing permission to the Bank on this and future China loans, a position subsequently modified.[8]

In 1898 the Bank as agent for the British and Chinese Corporation signed a preliminary agreement in connection with the Shanghai-Nanking Railway, but the financial impact of this came later.

In fact, the situation was such that Jackson felt justified in taking a five weeks' leave at the end of April, and the Bank was left in the charge of the Hong Kong Sub-Manager, V.A. Caesar Hawkins (East in 1882). Interestingly, in view of future developments, Jackson informed the Board on his return that he was well satisfied with Hawkins's management.

From the net profits the directors granted bonuses to managers, especially those involved in the China loans, totalling $22,500, credited the Officers Good Service Fund with $50,000, and after other deductions published net profits as

$2.4 million. This permitted the usual dividend of £1:5s, the transfer of $1 million to reserves, and the writing off of $250,000 from Premises Account.

The rise in the market value of the Bank's shares must have been due in part not only to the performance reflected in the mid-year accounts, but to the assurance of the Chairman that there were funds on hand to sustain the rate of growth and achieve the long-sought goal of having a Reserve Fund equal in value to the capital account. If the Bank had the funds, why did the Board not accomplish its purposes at the August meeting? First, the profits of the Indemnity Loan had not in fact been finalized and, secondly, the mid-year accounts had come to be treated to some extent as 'interim'; later the mid-year meeting would be eliminated.

Banknotes – the 'excess' issue problem

Problems come with success, and in meeting the requirements of trade in the Straits Settlements, South China, and Hong Kong the Bank exceeded its authorized note issue of $10 million (equivalent in value to the Bank's paid-up capital) for a period between January and May 1898, the adjustment of which in June caused 'inconvenience' to normal trade. The ultimate solution was to enact legislation in Hong Kong and the Straits Settlements whereby the Bank was permitted to issue notes in excess of its authorized issue against the deposit with the Colonial Treasury of an equal amount of specie.

The long-standing controversy as to the desirability of a government note issue in the Straits Settlements had been apparently concluded in September 1897 with the passage of an ordinance which would have permitted the concurrent circulation of banknotes and government notes. Governor Sir Charles B.H. Mitchell, however, was manoeuvring for an exclusive government issue, and the Bank was involved in disputes related to banknotes, the introduction of a British dollar coin, and a proposal for a gold standard for the Straits Settlements (see Volume II).

In 1896, Mitchell had noted that the Hongkong Bank had exceeded what appeared from the documents available to be its authorized limit of $7.5 million. He was technically correct. The $10 million was legally effective only when the Bank had informed Government that the additional capital had been fully paid up and a Proclamation to this effect had been issued. The Bank had omitted to notify Government in 1891 and consequently there had been no Proclamation; but the defect was remedied in early 1897, the Straits Government informed, and all was in order once again.[9]

Then in May 1898, studying the banknote figures for Hong Kong and the Straits, the Officer Administering the Government, F.A. Swettenham, noted that the Hongkong Bank had $11,856,532 in circulation on January 31, 1898, and that

Table 13.10 *The Hongkong and Shanghai Banking Corporation*
Note issue, December 31, 1894, and 1897/98

(in dollars)

December 31, 1894

Hong Kong	4,577,737	Hiogo	925
Amoy	26,204	Straits Settlements	4,362,000
Bangkok	475,000	Tientsin	6,000
Foochow	5,434	Yokohama	4,750
Hankow	570	Shanghai	496,035

Source: HSBC Board of Directors, Minutes.

Information is not always available for the distribution of notes at the end of every year. The above totals $9,954,705, which leaves little room for growth. In 1896 the average note issue of the Hongkong Bank in the Straits Settlements was $4,024,297. The figures below presumably include all 'other' note issues under 'Hong Kong'. The increase due to Chinese New Year can be clearly seen (see letter of Gray below).

	December 31, 1897	January 31	28 February 1898
'Hong Kong'	5,947,463	8,126,528	7,676,009
Straits	3,449,191	3,730,004	4,138,079
Total	9,396,654	11,856,532	11,814,088

Source: Singapore National Archives, SSLCP 1898, p. C548.

this unauthorized excess had been continued, contrary to the Bank's charter. 'The penalty contemplated by Hongkong law, section 27, seems to be the cancellation of the Incorporation of the Company,' wrote Swettenham to the Secretary of State, misreading the ordinance, but he added, magnanimously, 'In this Colony I think it will be sufficient to deprive the Company of the privilege they have abused by withdrawing from them their note circulation in the Straits Settlements circle' – he accordingly recommended that the enabling clause in the relevant Straits ordinance (No. X of 1881) be repealed.[10]

Instead he was instructed to pass new legislation authorizing an 'excess' banknote issue. The Hongkong Bank had outmanoeuvred him.

Aware of its over-issue the Bank had refrained from reissuing banknotes paid into its Hong Kong Office, and, by the date of the semi-annual accounts, June 30, 1898, the total issue had been brought to within the legal limit. The Deputy (temporarily Acting) Chairman of the Bank, R.M. Gray, then wrote to the Colonial Office apologetically, but explained the reasons and recommended a remedy.

We had to pay notes for the large requirements preceding the China New Year settlements which was unavoidable without creating a crisis. In other years large disbursements for the China New Year speedily returned to us, but from January to June this year the insufficiency of our Note Issue here has been a constant source of anxiety and worry to us as it certainly will continue to be until it is placed upon a more elastic basis than the existing one . . . [See Table 13.10]

... we would draw your attention to the change which has been gradually going on in the appreciation in which Bank notes are held by the Chinese.

The old system of making large payments in chopped dollars and fragmentary silver has been largely if not entirely discarded, and the Chinese traders have not now the same supply of skilled and expert shroffs as they formerly had.

The Chinese fully appreciate the relief which they enjoy from the old and cumbersome form of dealing in silver in which they suffered greatly from delay and squeezing in the shroffage and further from the point of view of portability there is no comparison between the two as a circulating medium (so much is this acknowledged that notes are now at 1% premium in Canton).

Our over-issue has been forced upon us by economic changes which the progress of Western ideas amongst the Chinese render stronger every day, and it will be a great blow to the whole trade of Southern China if we are compelled to inflict upon it as a permanency the grave inconvenience of a contracted currency.[11]

These were appealing arguments, fully supported by the General Chamber of Commerce, by other banks, and by the community at large. In the case of the Hongkong Bank's 'excess issue', the arguments were considered favourably by the Colonial Office and the Treasury primarily, it would seem, because the proposed remedy was expected to be temporary. 'When the Straits Government commence issuing their notes,' Gray continued, 'we will withdraw our circulation from Singapore and Penang, the position here will be relieved . . .'[12]

Jackson was then authorized by the Board to seek approval for a temporary 'excess' issue, backed 100% by coin or bullion deposited by the Bank with the Colonial Treasury.

The wording of the Bank's ordinances was peremptory; the Acting Governor, Major-General W. Black, could not accept the Bank's offer without supplementary legislation, which, being on a reserved subject, would require authority from London. As the Bank's proposal was so obviously in the public interest and without any apparent profit to the Bank, General Black expedited the matter by cabling the Colonial Office.[13]

Recognizing that the problem arose from delays first in implementing the Straits Settlements ordinance and then in supplying the necessary government notes, neither the Treasury nor the Colonial Office had objections and authorized the necessary legislation at first on a year to year basis.[14] The Bank's proposals were incorporated in Ordinance No. 6 of 1898, amended due to poor drafting by Ordinance No. 1 of 1899, extended by Ordinance No. 17 of 1899, and then again by Ordinance No. 19 of 1900 for a period to August 1908, the year in which the Hongkong Bank's charter itself terminated and by which time, the Colonial Office expected, a Hong Kong Government note issue might be initiated.[15]

Parallel legislation was eventually passed by the Straits Settlements (Ordinance No. III of 1899) but not before Swettenham attempted to incorporate extraneous additional conditions. These he was instructed to remove in favour of the simpler Hong Kong ordinance.[16]

The important 1900 legislation was handled for the Bank by H.M. Bevis as Acting Chief Manager, but not without an unsuccessful effort to have the 100% backing requirement modified to conform with the 'authorized issue' system.[17] Such a change would have provided the Bank with an income to offset the cost of issue. Interestingly, the Mercantile's Hong Kong manager, John Thorburn, was a member of the Hong Kong Legislative Council which approved the ordinance.[18]

One alternative to an 'excess' issue by the Hongkong Bank was the re-granting of note-issuing authority to the Mercantile Bank of India Limited as successor to the Chartered Mercantile.[19] But the chimera of a government note issue threw the balance against this approach, since the Colonial Office hoped that the excess issue would be temporary and therefore inappropriate for a bank not already involved. The Chartered Bank made no offer, although their manager, T.H. Whitehead, supported the Hongkong Bank's proposals in the Chamber of Commerce. The National Bank of China's small issue of $450,000 could not, under the terms of Ordinance No. 2 of 1895, be expanded and was apparently not accepted by the Government, the bank being incorporated under the Companies Acts rather than by charter.[c]

As the Hong Kong Government was not, it developed, prepared to undertake the task of note issue, the problem proved to be long run, and the expected solution – the withdrawal of the Bank's note issue in the Straits Settlements in favour of the newly authorized government issue – did not occur speedily enough to permit the Hongkong Bank to transfer its note issue to meet Hong Kong/South China requirements within the limits set by the 'authorized issue'. In 1903 there were still $2.86 million Hongkong Bank banknotes in circulation from its Singapore and Penang offices and, as Gray and later H.M. Bevis foresaw, the increasing demand for banknotes in the China area continued; the 'excess' issue remained a permanent feature of the Hong Kong currency system.[22]

In fact, the authorized note issue, then $10 million, with its part-coin, part-securities backing, and the elastic excess issue with 100% backing in coin or bullion became the long-run solution to the contentious problem of the 'profit of issue' and the note-issuing role of a private corporation. This judgement however remained subject to realization of the always pending Hong Kong Government

---

c The question was subject to considerable correspondence over a period from 1894 at least to 1900, and it is clear that the Government was reluctant to concede either an increase in the National Bank of China's note issue or permit its notes to be received at the Treasury, although the latter may have been relaxed.[20]

Until 1895 any bank could *issue* notes in Hong Kong, but the Government itself would *accept* only those of chartered banks. With the increased popularity of banknotes, non-chartered and foreign banks were tempted to issue in the Colony. This proliferation, with its consequent dangers to the stability of the currency, led the Government to pass the ordinance which actually restricted the right of issue to specifically authorized banks.[21]

Table 13.11 *The Hongkong and Shanghai Banking Corporation*
Cash and demand liabilities, 1898–1901

(in millions of dollars)·

Year	(i) Assets	(ii) Cash and bullion	(iii) C/A ratio	(iv) Deposits	(v) Authorized + excess notes	(vi) Excess note reserve	(vii) Adjusted C/A ratio
1898 Dec.	181.8	32.5	0.18	131.0	10.0 + 2.5	3.3	0.16
1899 June	202.6	44.7	0.22	152.1	10.0 + 3.6	5.0	0.20
1899 Dec.	208.3	39.7	0.19	156.5	10.0 + 2.6	5.0	0.17
1900 June	220.5	37.7	0.17	158.7	10.0 + 1.4	6.1	0.14
1900 Dec.	211.5	51.8	0.24	150.7	10.0 + 2.5	3.0	0.23
1901 June	222.0	53.0	0.24	166.5	10.0 + 2.6	4.0	0.22
1901 Dec.	248.8	57.2	0.23	189.8	10.0 + 3.0	5.4	0.21
1902 June	271.4	60.2	0.22	200.51	10.0 + 4.62	5.5	0.20

Note:
(i)–(iii) from Table 13.8; (iv) is 'deposits and notes' from Table 13.8 less the note issue; (v) highlights the excess note issue against which a minimum deposit of coin is required on a 100% reserve basis; (vi) is the actual reserve lodged against the excess note issue; (vii) is the adjusted cash/assets ratio, determined by subtracting the excess note issue reserve (vi) from cash and bullion (ii) and dividing the result by assets (i).

legal tender note issue, which (excluding the eventual limited legal tender issues of one dollar, ten cent, five cent, and one cent denomination notes) never came.

This would not solve all Hong Kong's currency problems but it was a partial solution, partially satisfactory, for a time.

By the end of 1898 the 'excess' note issue was $2.5 million against a deposit of $3.25 million with the Colonial Treasury, providing a margin for expansion. This situation, however, had an impact on the Bank's cash holding policy and could give a slight distortion to the cash/assets ratio as a comment on the Bank's utilization of funds; therefore a special table has been provided to permit analysis (see Table 13.11).

Those familiar with Scottish banking may be bemused. When the 'authorized' note issue of Scottish banks was limited, under the Scottish Bank Act of 1845, to the average outstanding during the year preceding May 1, 1845, the banks were permitted an 'excess issue' subject to the provision that a 100% cover in gold or silver be deposited in mutually agreed offices of the bank concerned. This precedent does not appear to have been considered during the discussions relative to the Hongkong Bank's position. The temporary nature of the original ordinances rather suggests the tradition of suspending the Bank Act in crises. England rather than Scotland was the model.[23]

Policies and accounts

The accounts of the Hongkong Bank as published for the proprietors (shareholders) at the semi-annual meetings were 'abstracts'. Their interpretation has many problems.

The Corporation's balance sheet as of say December 31 could not, in fact, be a statement of the position on that day. Communication problems forced branches to close their books up to two months earlier, leading to last minute adjustments between January and the semi-annual meeting if the position changed drastically or if sudden losses occurred. Each branch had its own Profit and Loss Account and wired in profits, the amount of which was open to subsequent negotiation between the branch manager and the Chief Manager. The contribution of a branch to the Corporation's profits depended upon (i) the manager's estimate of contingencies, (ii) the rate of exchange he considered appropriate, and (iii) the inter-branch arrangements relative to interest rates, booking of profits etc., as negotiated with the Chief Manager. There is no evidence to suppose that the process involved was purposely erratic or arbitrary, but there were subjective elements.

The agency accounts for Amoy, Foochow, Saigon, Bangkok, and San Francisco appeared as part of Head Office accounts; Lyons, Hamburg, New York, and London were also handled through Head Office books; the other China branches were consolidated in Shanghai, Japanese branches in Yokohama, the Straits Settlements in Singapore, Iloilo with Manila, and Sourabaya with Batavia. Colombo, Bombay, and Calcutta (with Rangoon) reported separately.

The Board received the net profit figures from these sources and any special explanations. Particularly poor performances were noted and the manager censured; in the 1890s the Board was reviving the custom of rewarding managers who had made significant contributions to net profits, although there is the suggestion that Jackson also recommended a bonus to an able manager in a less desirable post, for example, Henry Hewat as Manager of Saigon, where profits were hardly spectacular.

The balance carried forward from the previous half-year's Profit and Loss Account was then added to the net total; this total the Board allocated and minuted in detail. The directors made these decisions after hearing, but not always following, the recommendation of the Chief Manager. Exceptionally, for the important allocations at the end of 1898 a prior discussion had taken place with a small sub-committee.

There were in a sense two categories of allocation: (i) allocations before determining published profit and (ii) allocations which would be proposed in the 'abstract' of accounts and would require the approval of the proprietors. The first included those items which might be considered as proper charges against profits in any case, for example, the bonus to salaries of the staff, the Chief Manager's remuneration (which could not be calculated until the amounts to dividends etc. had been agreed), and contingencies; the second included dividends, write-offs on Premises Account and 'dead stock', and published Contingency Account in times of great difficulty.

The Board's declared policy was to write off 'non-interest bearing accounts', specifically bank premises and dead stock. The latter was eliminated, and the former was written down whenever the directors felt in a position to do so in anticipation of major building expenditure, while building was in progress, or afterwards. In this they were following the practice of the time. The consequence of this policy was to provide the branches with interest-free premises, thus overstating the return on capital and the profitability of the branch, but there is no indication that this was sufficient to have any real impact on Bank policy.

The Marine Insurance Account appears on the published abstract and to this fund was credited amounts which would have been required as premiums by commercial insurance companies. When the Account reached $250,000, any further premiums were paid instead into the Officers Good Service Fund. In 1892 the Bank had lost heavily by the sinking of the P&O's SS *Bokhara*, and the Marine Insurance Account had been drawn down. This proved to be only temporary, however, as salvage attempts were highly successful, and the Account was quickly restored.[d]

The position of the Hongkong Bank until the mid-1890s was such that there was little purpose in hiding its reserves; the directors' main task, if confidence in the Bank was to be maintained, was to ensure that the public knew the precise reserve position. Indeed, as silver fell, the Board recognized that it needed to provide additional information as to the division between sterling and silver both as to assets and liabilities. This was in response to Ewen Cameron's impractical suggestion that the accounts be actually kept and published in sterling. The further explanations provided in the accounts and by the Chairman at the annual meeting were designed to reassure depositors and shareholders, particularly those in Europe, that the Bank was on an 'even keel'.

Thomas Jackson and the directors were agreed on the necessity of building up reserves from the low point of 1892. But the dividend had already been cut to £1 and there was natural pressure for a higher figure to be reinstated. To offset this pressure the directors set publicly stated goals for their Reserve Fund policy: first merely to rebuild, then to equal the capital. At the end of the first stage the semi-annual dividend had to be raised to £1:5s; at the end of the second, in 1898, to

d   The community of Hong Kong were less fortunate; all but three of the Colony's cricket team were drowned, including G.S. Purvis of the Hongkong Bank. They had been playing in an interport match in Shanghai.[24]

£1:10s, with the expectation of a virtually certain 'bonus' of ten shillings at the end of each year.

But all this achieved, could the directors continue the policy of building the reserves? Higher dividends had never been explicitly promised, but there had been the suggestion that once the present goal had been achieved, the shareholders would have their reward. And, as has been stated, they did. But profits continued, business increased, and the Bank needed ever increasing margins in a world of uncertain silver movements, of increasingly complex events which affected the position of the Bank, whether it be the distant Fashoda Affair on the Upper Nile (which in 1898 affected the price of consols and so of the Bank's London investment policy) or the more immediate physical threat to the Tientsin branch during the Boxer troubles, the battleships in Manila Bay, or the long-term concern over exclusive rights in Manchuria.

These contradictory pressures undoubtedly influenced the directors to permit the evolution of practices which understated either both published profits and shareholders' funds or simply the latter. This was facilitated by the fact that the Bank's sterling securities had been bought at a low price and that in the crises all potential losses had, they supposed, been allowed for. The appreciation of the securities and the failure of the 'losses' to actually be realized, resulted by the end of 1898 in an understatement of securities by as much as $1.5 million and an overstatement of contingencies by $1 million.

At the same time the Bank made 'extraordinary' (in the sense of 'extra ordinary') profits through its participation in the China and Japan loans. When this happened in 1875 the exceptional profits were needed immediately to enable the Bank to pay its first dividend in four half-years. In 1895–1898 this was not the problem; it is not surprising, therefore, that given general accounting practices of the time, there should be for the first time in the history of the Bank unappropriated profits. Although all this was to be adjusted at the end of 1898, the policy had been announced: the Bank would have unappropriated profits available for equalization of dividends.

The then generally accepted principle of hidden shareholders' funds had been stated publicly and tacitly agreed; the years to 1898 provided the embryo source of such funds; the particularly good year of 1898 provided the opportunity to reach Jackson's goal, award shareholders for their patience, and begin a new reserve policy.

Profit and Loss – December 31, 1898

By the end of December 1898 the promises of the Hongkong Bank's Chairman, J.J. Bell-Irving, at the August meeting had been accomplished, despite momentary hesitations by the directors. London office had purchased sufficient securities so that their total value, even when the newly purchased consols had been written down to 90 with exchange at 2s:0d, was £1 million (= $10 million).

The interest from these investments was assigned to London; London's overdraft rates could consequently be reduced, and those branches which were largely overdrawn on London, for example, Yokohama, could become more profitable and their business encouraged.

And it was at this point that Jackson declared this to be the realization of hopes entertained for years.

By writing down to 90 Jackson hoped that the Bank would be able to ignore all market price fluctuations; the sterling reserve would stand at £1 million. In fact, the high cost of funds in the immediate pre-Great War period eventually forced the writing down of these reserves to 70. But that was for the future; attention could now be paid to rebuilding the silver reserves under Head Office control.

The immediate problem which next confronted the Board of Directors was the allocation of 1898 year-end Profit and Loss Account which totalled $6.3 million or the equivalent of 63% of the value of the Bank's paid-up capital. Of this $3.7 million was listed as net profit from the current half-year; part of this was, however, non-recurrent income, the current profits from major public loans, including the Third Indemnity Loan. Head Office alone returned a net profit of $1.5 million, including profits (gross) from exchange operations exceeding $1.9 million. Major contributors to these startling results were Shanghai and Yokohama $700,000 each, Manila $300,000, and Singapore $250,000.

Unappropriated profits of some $2.3 million were then added to the current figures and a further $377,000 had been carried forward from the end-June accounts.

For the first time the minutes record that three directors – Bell-Irving, as Chairman, McConachie, and Gray – considered the allocation problem with the Chief Manager before the main meeting. As usual there was a division between pre- and post-publication allocation. In the former category the Board took the following decisions:

 (i) the Provident Fund was put on a sterling basis at a cost of $352,000;
 (ii) a sum of $250,000 was transferred to the Officers Good Service Fund;
(iii) staff were awarded a 20% bonus costing $200,000;
(iv) specified managers were awarded additional bonuses totalling $20,000;
 (v) under the agreement the Chief Manager was awarded $76,000; and
(vi) $1 million was transferred to Contingencies Account.

This left a balance of $4.4 million which the directors published as the total credit to the Profit and Loss Account. From this they recommended to the proprietors appropriations as follows:

 (i) remuneration of directors, $15,000;
 (ii) dividend at the rate of £1:10s plus a bonus of £1 @ 1s:11½d, the latter a consequence of the extraordinary profits from the major loans, the whole costing $2.04 million;

(iii) transfer to reserves, $1 million;
(iv) transfer to Bank Premises Account $500,000;
(v) balance to be carried forward $835,000.

The Bank as seen in February 1899

A first glance at the accounts for December 1898 is confusing – in what has been referred to as a brilliant half-year deposits and loans both declined approximately 25%, whereas the various ratios were favourable mainly because they reflected the addition of unappropriated profits into this particular half-year's results. As the Chairman explained at the semi-annual meeting, the decline in deposits was a consequence of the previous holding of government loan funds on current account, and hence the uneconomic cash/assets ratio in June 1898, while the draw down of loan-connected deposits resulted in a loss of liquid funds available for lending on the London market.

Because deposits are netted out, the dramatic movements in the several categories cannot be noted from the published accounts. The Chairman, however, reported that while gold current accounts fell $5.4 million (to a total of £1.2 million), gold fixed accounts showed a slight increase; meanwhile silver deposits increased by $934,000.

There is opportunity for endless rearrangement of the accounts, but the principles are clear. The Hongkong Bank remained a local bank not only in Hong Kong and Shanghai but in the Treaty Ports and the Straits Settlements. The source of funds was current and fixed deposits both in the East and in London as demand required; the Bank's profits from this source depended on the adjustment of interest rates to regulate the flow of funds.

In London, however, the Bank's position had in a sense improved despite the comparatively low level of total deposits, a level which would have been considered a major problem had it prevailed in the period from the late 1880s to early 1890s when the Bank's outward business was financed by sterling fixed deposits. In 1898, however, the directors no longer had to watch weekly cables detailing the percentage of non-renewals. The Bank had £1 million of its own assets as a London reserve, one quarter of which, or £250,000, was a Special Reserve of $2\frac{3}{4}$% consols carried on the Bank's books at 95 converted into dollars at the rate of 2s:6d; the consols were held at the Bank of England. In addition there were the newly purchased consols, totalling £522,500 which had, as previously noted, been written down to 90 and 2s:0d.[e] The Hongkong Bank also held other first class sterling securities – Indian sterling loans, railway debenture bonds,

---

[e] The only reason for the two systems of valuation was that the Special Reserve had long stood on the books at 95 and 2/6 and writing it down would have proved too costly given the other demands on the funds available. Thus until 1901, when the anomaly was corrected, only the newly acquired consols were on the books at 90 and 2/0.

colonial stocks and bonds, a Greek guaranteed loan, and London County Council bonds – carried at cost, a figure slightly less than the then market value, and at an exchange of 2s:od.

The interest earned from these investments minimized the Bank's dependence on London opinion; the magnitude of the reserves on the other hand ensured respect.

In the East the silver basis of its accounts, its access to local sources of funds, and its familiarity with the silver bullion market all combined to provide the Hongkong Bank with a key advantage over competitors. The Bank was in a position to advance monetary silver to the Chinese Government against the issue of publicly subscribed bonds, a high proportion of the funds for which would be deposited to the credit of the Bank's London Office. To the extent these London funds were not required for the use of the borrowing government in gold, the Bank could operate in the silver bullion market. The abstract of accounts began, indeed, to indicate bullion holding separately, and the Bank's role in effecting the availability of bullion for monetary purposes became a key responsibility, ensuring the smooth operation of the exchanges and, therefore, of the Eastern trade itself.

Not only was the Bank once again on an even keel but it had surplus resources which could be safely moved to meet specific requirements.

Other aspects of the Bank were seen to be equally well provided for. During the 1890s considerable building and purchase of previously rented property had been completed and Premises Account now stood on the books at $257,000 compared to the cost price of over $2 million.

This was the favourable report with which shareholders were provided and which pushed up share prices and sent the London market/book ratio to a high 2.2. But there were other matters which were equally of importance for the future of the Bank.

The directors had taken advantage of the high current earnings and the existence of unappropriated profits (i) to write down the London investments to a safe level, (ii) to put certain accounts in order, accounts which were basically a Board responsibility, the Provident Fund and the Officers Good Service Fund, and (iii) to restore inner reserves by the transfer, noted above, of $1 million to a contingencies account which was already overstated by approximately the same amount.[f]

The seen and the unseen plus the announcement that the Chief Manager had agreed to another term of office – until May 1902 – all combined to place the Bank in the strongest of positions. As the Hongkong Bank's Chairman, R.M. Gray,

---

[f] A contingenices account which bears no relation either to specific expected losses or to any 'average' loss – except in the vaguest terms of eventual but wholly unforeseen crisis – is a form of inner reserves.

stated at the August 1899 meeting, 'A bank wants three things, viz: good character, good management and solid resources of its own. In the absence of any one of these, pronounced success would be impossible. [Applause]' In the event the Hongkong Bank had earned all three; it would use well its enhanced resources.

SIR THOMAS JACKSON AND THE BANK, 1899–1902

In the three remaining full years of Jackson's administration, which began auspiciously with his receiving a knighthood and ended with a baronetcy, the Hongkong Bank's total assets would increase 37% to $249 million and shareholders' funds 14% to $26 million – in sterling only 8.6% to £2.4 million as exchange had fallen to 1s:10¼d. The decline in trade due to the Boxer Uprising, which also caused the sharp drop in share prices shown for June 1900 (see Table 13.8), robbed Jackson of the opportunity for increasing published reserves by a further 50%, but by December 1901 they stood at $14.25 million. Jackson was able to steady earnings sufficiently to fulfil the Bank Chairman's promise that semi-annual dividends would be maintained at £1:10s (£3:00 per annum), and there was sufficient also to justify a bonus of ten shillings at the end of each year.

Not that all the credit should go to Jackson. In 1900 he took six months' leave in Europe and in his absence the Bank was administered by H.M. Bevis, previously successful as Manager in Shanghai and Manager Yokohama. The year was a difficult one for several reasons, not the least being the rise in the sterling exchange to 2s:1d in parallel with the increasing gold price of silver – from 27.3d to 29.9d a fine ounce (see Table 13.1). Although Caesar Hawkins again acted for Jackson during a six weeks' leave in 1899, he was due for leave himself in 1900 and, either for this reason or because a good Sub-Manager was not necessarily a sound Chief Manager and exchange operator, he was not appointed Acting Chief Manager for the longer period.

Bank premises

The directors continued to invest in property as required for the business of the Bank.

Major alterations were made in the Shanghai office in 1899 and the neighbouring land was purchased in 1901, thus preparing the way for eventual expansion. There was a new building in Rangoon and the Saigon property was bought in 1899 which was subsequently rebuilt. The following year the Board increased their holdings on the Peak in Hong Kong, buying property which Jackson had personally rented and furnished for his own use. 'Cliffs', near the junior mess 'Cloudlands', was also purchased. The Board approved expenditure of Yen200,000 for a new building in Hiogo, and military action in Tientsin required significant reconstruction there.

Finally, in 1901 the Board recorded their unanimous opinion that the site on their reclaimed land in front of the Head Office should, together with similar land in front of the City Hall, be an open space for all time even though they did not feel justified in entering into an agreement which would be binding on their successors. That decision once made public and the land set aside, however, political considerations would make reconsideration a practical impossibility, and central Hong Kong had its open space which, despite the usual threats of progress, has been maintained for public use.

There was a write-off of $250,000 from the Premises Account in June 1899 and of $200,000 in 1901, but, given its other priorities, the Board could not maintain the policy consistently, and this account stood at $730,000 on the December balance sheet at the end of the Jackson era.

Valuation of investments

The Bank's ability to cope with sudden changes in the capital value of its securities and the often simultaneous but unrelated changes in the exchanges while continuing to pay out a dividend equal to between 58% and 66% of published earnings, a dividend moreover set in terms of sterling for a bank whose accounts were kept in a silver unit of account – all this required a particularly flexible policy relative to the valuation of its sterling security holdings. There were two variables, the sterling price at which the security was to be carried on the accounts and the rate of exchange at which it was to be converted into a dollar value.

As the Bank moved from crisis to crisis generalizations seem inappropriate. Nevertheless it is reasonable to state that the Bank appears to have valued its reserve securities initially at cost or market whichever were the lower, but that (i) if prices were falling the price might be written down below market in anticipation of a further decline and (ii) if prices then rose, the security would not necessarily be written up to market.

The Bank's reserves were noted in the accounts at a certain rate and the Board, as stated above, was loath to change the rate even though it caused a serious understatement of market value in terms of the dollar unit of account. Many banks had followed a contrary policy, waiting for a more favourable rate which never came; the Hongkong Bank seemed to prefer to anticipate disaster, make excessive provisions, and then delay reevaluation in the Bank's favour until forced to do so by some other priority consideration.

The rationale for this was simply that it was wise to write down when funds were available for the purpose rather than wait for the market to force the writing down – this might occur when funds were needed to cover adverse changes in the exchange or other losses. Underlying the policy was the need to ensure, to the extent possible, the availability of funds for the payment of a regular dividend.

In the light of these comments, the policies described in the 'course of events' below will seem more reasonable.

The course of events

The Boer War began in 1899 causing a rise in London interest rates as the British Government increased its borrowing and the flow of gold from South African mines was interrupted; this in turn increased the cost of discounting and impinged on the Bank's profits. Commissions on a £2.3 million Chinese railway loan and a 4% £10 million loan to Japan, the latter in participation with Parr's Bank, the Chartered Bank, and the Yokohama Specie Bank, accounted for 34% of the second half-year's net earnings and made possible a year-end dividend bonus despite a fall in profits on exchange operations, the need to write down certain investments, and the adverse impact of the cost of funds.

At the same time the Bank reported a year without losses and both branch and Head Office set aside funds to general, that is, unallocated, contingencies, the balance in Head Office exceeding $2.3 million by the end of the year.

The Bank's previous decision to write down its consols to 90 had now been justified by the fall in the price. At the same time London Office, in consultation with the London Committee, recommended a switch from $2\frac{3}{4}\%$ consols to $2\frac{1}{2}\%$ consols to offset an expected decline in the premium on the former as the 1903 date for their scheduled conversion approached. The book profit realized in this transaction was used to write down the new investments. As usual in such cases the Hong Kong Board instructed Cameron to act at his discretion. Thus a conservative investment policy did not permit neglect, and the Bank actively managed its London portfolio to its advantage. With the rise in security prices in 1900 the Bank could register an unrealized capital gain of $1.5 million.

The rise in exchange, Hong Kong on London, during 1900 was due in part to the demand for silver bullion for coinage in India, despite the link of the Indian currency with gold, and the requirements of the Allied Forces in North China. Although the bullion transactions brought profit to the Bank, the uncertainties suggested moderation in mid-1900, but with profits of $1.7 million carried forward an allocation of $1 million to the newly designated silver reserves and a ten shilling bonus in addition to the now regular £1:10s dividend was possible at year-end. The staff received a 10% bonus.

The position at the end of 1901 was particularly strong. The abstract of accounts was well-received, all consols now stood at 90, a bonus of 15% had been paid to the staff, the Contingencies Account (unpublished) stood at $2 million and the difference between current and book value of investments was nearly $3.5 million, and $1.4 million was carried forward for the next half-year when a new Chief Manager, J.R.M. Smith, would be responsible.

These figures may have been estimated by the market, explaining why the price of shares had reached £64, which compared to a par of £28:2s:6d (@4s:6d, the 'par rate') indicated a premium of 127% or with a par of £11:10s:3¼d (@1s:10¼d, the 'rate of the day') a premium of 455%. The Shanghai premium of approximately 400% suggests the impact of share quotas on London and Eastern registers, preventing arbitrage in a situation where demand for Eastern registered shares was apparently out of phase with London.

As Jackson left Hong Kong he confided to his successor that there was something extra available to see him through. In a personal letter to Jackson after his departure R.T. Wright, who kept the books, wrote that he had shown Smith the April 1902 figures for the 'third' or 'hidden' reserves; they totalled $8,921,843.91.[25] Unfortunately Wright's detailed memo on the subject has not survived but the sum was composed of unappropriated funds in both Head Office and branch contingency accounts, surpluses on exchange accounts, and presumably the understatement in the investment account. Of the 'hidden' reserves, excluding published unappropriated carryovers from the Profit and Loss Account, $5.6 million can be identified; the balance remains truly 'hidden'. Property worth $4.8 million was carried on the books at $0.5 million, but that was normal accounting practice.

The ability of the Bank to build reserves may reflect the good sense of the shareholders in a risky environment which nevertheless promised future development. Capitalization of reserves by a 'bonus' or capitalization issue was never considered. The only alternative policy consistent with the growth of the Bank would have been high dividend payouts over a larger capital obtained by a rights issue. Shareholders could have forced this through by requisition, but there were two practical considerations: first, proprietors do not disturb a successful management, and, secondly, the Hong Kong headquarters meant effective leadership control by a few shareholders from the major hongs based in Hong Kong itself. The Bank's main Hong Kong share registers have not survived, but it is safe to assume on the basis of the Shanghai registers that there were many very small holders, including Bank staff, who would accept the policy of the merchant and community leaders represented on the Board.

Sir Thomas Jackson had been Chief Manager of the Hongkong and Shanghai Banking Corporation for nearly 26 years, excluding the period of the Interregnum (see Chapter 12). The February 1902 semi-annual meeting was, therefore, a time for remembering and for eulogizing. Robert Shewan, the Hongkong Bank's Chairman, quoted Addison, ''Tis not in mortals to command success', and added, 'but looking at Sir Thomas Jackson I may say we much doubt it.'

The Board had voted him an honorarium of $100,000 (say £8,500) and appointed him Chairman of the London Consultative Committee at a salary of £1,500 a year. His services were not yet at an end, but he was not to return to Hong Kong. Once he had left the Colony, the Board, as already noted, agreed to commission a statue – 'a permanent memorial of old T.J. in our midst'.

But for the Hongkong Bank the Age of Jackson had ended. There was a new Chief Manager, J.R.M. Smith. Who he was and what he did are subjects for Volume II of this history. Before that, however, the story must return almost to 1876 and consider (i) the Hongkong Bank in China and (ii) the stories of Hongkong Bankers, including something more personal about the redoubtable Sir Thomas Jackson, Bart.

14

THE HONGKONG BANK IN CHINA, 1874–1895

> The Hongkong Bank shows itself of a more obliging disposition, and understands China better . . .
>
> (Sir) Robert Hart, Inspector-General, Imperial Maritime Customs, 1878

A successful bank with its main offices in Hong Kong and Shanghai, its Board of Directors composed of partners in the principal trading firms of the Far East, with branches on the China coast and the Yangtze must surely be assumed to 'understand China'.[1] But 'China' is not a simple concept. Nor, after examination, is it clear what 'understanding China' consists of or whether, after accepting some definition of the concept, the Hongkong Bank could really be expected to have achieved what perhaps no other person or institution has achieved – except in self-delusion.

Contrary to the practice in India, for many years it was unusual to have Chinese on the boards of public companies in East Asia. There were notable exceptions, but before the 1930s such elections, except in a company organized by Chinese interests, would be explained by special circumstances. The first Chinese director of the Hongkong Bank was elected in 1972. Although in its early years the Hongkong Bank recruited executive staff in the East, these men, as those coming later through London Office, had no knowledge of Eastern cultures or people. Their Eastern backgrounds, if any, were 'family'; even then it would be second-hand from relatives rarely seen after early childhood and confined almost entirely to the life of the Treaty Ports. Nor was a knowledge of Eastern cultures particularly encouraged, although in the Hongkong Bank there were periodic efforts to consider programs for learning Chinese.

The opportunities for a young 'expatriate' to break out of the confines of the Treaty Ports might exist later for those in firms whose activities required a presence in the interior of China; before the new treaty provisions of 1895, however, these opportunities were limited, and for a young banker, with office duties at a restricted number of Treaty Ports and practically no local leave – except for inter-port sports or reasons of health – they were even fewer.

There were several reasons for this perhaps surprising state of affairs. Confining the discussion to the Hongkong and Shanghai Bank, a list of China branches opened before 1895 provides an indication of their limited geographical scope – they were on the edge of China (see Table 14.1). Of the Bank's branches

Table 14.1 *The Hongkong and Shanghai Banking Corporation*
Branches and agencies in China, 1865–1949
(with dates of opening)

		(a)				
Shanghai	1865	19	Hongkew	1909[b]	Dairen	1919[d]
Foochow	1867	1	Canton	1909	Chefoo	1926
Hankow	1868	2	(Taipei	1909)[c]	Mukden	1926
Amoy	1873	2	Tsingtao	1914	Swatow	1937
Tientsin	1881	3	Harbin	1915	Chungking	1943
Peking	1885	2			Nanking	1947

Notes:
(a) Eastern staff numbers in 1895.
[b] authorized 1906.
[c] Japanese ruled, reported to Yokohama.
[d] date a Hongkong Bank staff member assisted the merchant agents; the agency opened in 1922.

and agencies, only those in Peking, Tientsin, and Hankow were in areas where the business language was Chinese, that is, 'Mandarin' or *kuo-yu*. Elsewhere the Shanghai, Fukienese, or Cantonese dialect dominated, and mastery of these in a service where transfers were relatively frequent and destinations uncertain was impractical.

The Hongkong Bank nevertheless had a considerable and very valuable relationship with Chinese constituents in the normal course of business; the Bank had close banking relations with several leading Chinese officials, and it dominated the Chinese Government loan business – not on the basis of political interference, but in the market.

Robert Hart, despite his long-standing preference for the Oriental Bank, considered the Hongkong Bank 'obliging'; the Bank, he said, 'understands China', and certainly many Chinese officials, bankers, and merchants did their major foreign-style banking business with that 'focus of wealth' they referred to as 'Wayfoong' (*hui-feng*).

The Hongkong Bank had no official status in China. Unlike the Imperial Bank of Persia (now the British Bank of the Middle East), which was the national bank of that Empire and served the country through a branch network and the issue of currency, the Hongkong Bank was an exchange bank designed to finance foreign trade; its banknotes were nowhere legal tender. The founders also, admittedly, referred to their new creation as a 'local bank', by which they were referring to its intended role in the finance of enterprises in the Treaty Ports, within the British or other foreign concessions. There was never any thought so impractical as the Bank serving the local communities of China as a retail bank.

The Board of Directors followed a conservative policy with reference to the establishment of new agencies. The offices listed in Table 14.1 were supplemented by the presence of merchant agents in the lesser ports, but even without this list the Table reflects the Bank's focus on trade finance. In the early history of the Bank agencies were established to provide facilities for foreign trade.

The major policy break came in 1881 with the establishment of a Tientsin agency, followed in 1885 with a sub-agency in Peking, both intended to further the Bank's contacts with senior Ch'ing Government officials, especially the Tientsin-based Viceroy of Chihli, Li Hung-chang. The Bank's branch and agency policy, however, did not change radically after this, even when its financing of major railway and mining enterprises seemed to involve it beyond traditional geographical confines. In the period through 1918 the Bank opened a Shanghai sub-agency across Soochow Creek in Hongkew, a surprisingly delayed agency in Canton, an office long-sought by German interests in Tsingtau – ironically only weeks before the outbreak of the Great War – and only one branch in developing Manchuria. The bean trade took the Bank to Manchuria, embroidery exports encouraged its eventual Swatow investment, but the desire to be in the Republican capital motivated the establishment of a Nanking agency, in 1947 the last to be opened before the establishment of the People's Republic.

In 1895 of a total Eastern staff of 140 only 29 were assigned to offices in China; a further 22 were in Hong Kong. Of these only seven men or 5% of the total were in cities where Mandarin was the language of business. There were 23 branches and agencies to which Eastern staff could be assigned, and of these only six were in China – three in Mandarin speaking areas. Such statistics were bound to have had an effect on policy, even the policy of a bank which was admittedly focused on China.

Of the Hongkong Bank's $10 million capital in 1893, some $4 million was designated 'reserve'; of the balance $3 million was assigned to Shanghai for use there and in the agencies under its control – Hankow, Tientsin, and Peking. Amoy and Foochow worked under Head Office. This compares with the $2.5 million assigned to Yokohama and the $1 million each to Manila and Singapore. Shanghai's profits (including its subordinate agencies of Peking, Tientsin, and Hankow) for the relatively non-controversial second half-year of 1894 were $575,000 or say 30% of the total $1.86 million for the Bank as a whole, before various adjustments; this compares to Yokohama's $500,000 and Singapore's $200,000.[a] The profits of Head Office, which included earnings from business with China, especially with the southern agencies of Amoy and Foochow, was $534,000. This understates the contribution of China to the earnings of the

---

[a] Net earnings as published for the six months were slightly less at $1.68 million, see Table 13.7.

Hongkong Bank, since a high percentage of transactions credited to other branches was due to business to or from China.

Nor can the importance of China to the Hongkong Bank be assessed by the number of branches/agencies in China or the number of Eastern staff assigned to them. The restrictions placed on foreigners by the 'unequal treaties' forced business beyond the Treaty Ports into Chinese hands; thus, as was intended by the Imperial Government, the presence of foreigners – their banks and merchant firms – was long confined to small areas along the coast and the Yangtze River. The impact of the Bank's business, however, went far beyond these narrow limits. Moreover, it was the need to service the China trade, a term including Hong Kong, by which the establishment of agencies in Southeast Asia, India, Europe, and the United States was justified. The Philippines and Japan had been opened consistent with the early definition of the Bank's sphere of operations and continued to be viewed in their own context, but the Board remained reluctant to open agencies unconnected with the China trade – as in the case of Colombo.

Despite limitations at various levels, few agencies, limited staff, lack of intimate, personal knowledge of the Chinese scene, the Bank developed its China-oriented business, and the purpose of this chapter is to consider the nature of that business and how it was operated.

The role of the compradore and his staff is basic to this discussion. As described in the first section the compradoric system was flawed; it was essential yet, considered as a system, it was unsatisfactory. There were, therefore, efforts to find an alternative, usually based on schemes to encourage staff to master Chinese. In this common frustration of business on the China coast the Hongkong Bank shared, and the discussion of the Bank's move north to Tientsin and Peking as well as efforts to find alternatives to the compradoric system will be considered in the next section, following which there is an outline of the Bank's loan business with the Chinese authorities.

THE BANK'S CHINA BUSINESS AND THE COMPRADORIC SYSTEM

THE HONGKONG BANK IN THE TREATY PORTS

Trade finance

The domestic banking system of China was highly developed, but the units were small and their sources of funds limited. The Hongkong Bank and the other exchange banks injected funds into this system; the local banks were quite capable of intermediating between foreign sources of funds and Chinese merchants and/or, through the specialized Shansi banks, transmitting the funds to any place required in the interior.

The cash shops (*ch'ien-p'u*) played a less important role in the wholesale operations being considered in this section. The local banks received deposits and made local loans – they could also remit to neighbouring towns; their funds were supplemented by loans from the Shansi banks which had branches in more than a single region and played a role in the movement of Imperial revenues.

Thus even with the limitations which the Chinese, through the 'unequal treaties' and the Treaty-Port system, imposed on foreign economic intercourse, the scope for the development of business was considerable. The extent of the local banking system in Hong Kong, for example, provides a glimpse of the complex and developed Chinese banking system to which the foreign exchange banks could direct funds. There were in 1886 some twenty Chinese banks. They did not have branches but transacted business outside Hong Kong through agents. Of these twenty banks, six had a capital of $5–10,000, and dealt mainly in exchange and 'cash' notes; fourteen had a capital from $30–60,000 and were administered by a manager and assistant, with share profits at some 15% per annum on capital, borrowing funds at 8% and lending to merchants at 10–15%, with an annual turnover of say $150,000 on the average.[2] As noted above, these local banking systems were interconnected by the specialized remittance banks, especially the Shansi banks, operating virtually throughout China.

Through the business connections of the Bank's compradore or through the compradore of one of the Bank's constituents funds were made available directly to Chinese traders – 'hundreds of millions of taels', as Ewen Cameron, the Bank's Shanghai Manager, put it. 'For the last 25 years the Bank has been doing a very large business with Chinese in Shanghai amounting, I should say, to hundreds of millions of taels, and we have never met with a defaulting Chinaman.'[3] These funds enabled Chinese merchants to finance the purchase of export crops in the interior, the import of goods for shipment from the coast to the markets beyond, and to engage themselves in intra-regional trade. Alternatively funds could be made available to Chinese financial intermediaries, the so-called 'native banks', who would in turn channel the funds to the ultimate Chinese borrower.

The Hongkong Bank's agencies in the smaller ports – Amoy, Foochow, Hankow – were subordinate either to Hong Kong or, in the case of Hankow, to Shanghai. Their funds came mainly from Shanghai/Hong Kong office overdrafts, although of Hankow agency's total liabilities in April 1875 half came from current accounts. These latter varied from the small accounts of such local foreign activities as represented by the 'drama society' to the larger deposits of the Treaty Port's 'municipal council', Chinese officials, merchant hongs, and local foreign-sponsored companies, especially insurance and utilities, in which the Hongkong Bank had invested.[4]

The large holding of cash, Ts557,187 out of total assets of Ts678,914, in the Hankow agency indicates the role of the Bank in the advancing of so-called 'packing credits'. Finance for the export of, for example, tea from Foochow was covered by credits opened by the responsible branch and the security for advances on tea shipped was the tea itself – inadequate though this might prove in the event of a serious fall in the market. The Bank, however, made funds available either directly or through local banks (*ch'ien-chuang* or *hui-tui kuan*) to merchants dealing with the up-country suppliers. These advances permitted Chinese merchants to finance the processing and shipment of the export crop to the port; these were the 'packing credits' which extended the role of the Bank far beyond the confines of the foreign settlements into the interior of China.

Hankow's holding of cash reveals another risk inherent in the system. The silver funds were 'uncovered', and the Bank ran a risk in terms of sterling. This risk was demonstrated in the sudden fall of the exchanges during the crucial months of April and May, in the early part of the tea 'season' of 1886 (see Chapter 9).

Figure 5, designed by Robert P. Gardella for his study of the export of Taiwan tea through Amoy and, in Figure 6, from the interior of Fukien Province to the Treaty Ports, shows the flow of funds from the Hongkong Bank to the middleman and/or the foreign firm, and from the latter's compradore on to the tea manufactory, the tea buyer, and eventually to the tea farmer. Gardella indicates that an alternative source of funds was the native banks, but Hongkong Bank records suggest that some portion even of these latter funds came from the Bank in the form of clean or 'chop' loans [*ch'e-p'iao*].[5]

The provision of funds to 'middlemen' is shown on the Bank's accounts by overdrafts secured by shares quoted on the Hong Kong or Shanghai markets. Jardine's Foochow compradore, 'Alum' (as listed in the accounts), provided security including, typically, Hongkong Bank shares and shares of the Shanghai Steam Navigation Company and the Yangtze Valley Insurance Company. Other borrowers offered a more varied list of shares, but the principle was the same.[6] In the Bank's early years these Foochow advances especially were of sufficient importance to be subjects for discussion by the Board of Directors, with such cryptic references as '5 lacs to teamen in Foochow' agreed in February 1878.

The Bank financed the silk trade in similar fashion, especially through Jardine Matheson in the Canton Delta region; in Japan the Bank advanced funds to the Mitsui Bank on the security of silk stored in godowns. Sugar from the Philippines and the Netherlands East Indies was another crop financed by the exchange banks through merchants and their up-country agents with all the market risks involved.

Whatever the particular form the financing took there was a common element – neither the foreign trader nor the exchange banks had access to the producer nor could they have direct knowledge of the situation in the area in which the products were grown and processed. Although the banks were shielded by the

Figure 5 Methods of financing tea exports in late 19th-century Taiwan.

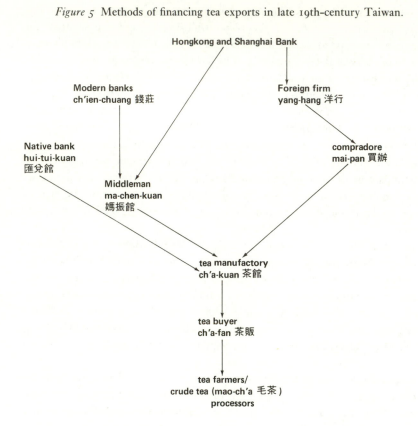

Note: the arrows indicate flow of funds.

Source: Robert P. Gardella, Jr. 'Fukien's Tea Industry and Trade in Ch'ing and Republican China: the developmental consequences of a traditional commodity export', p. 143.

risks taken by the foreign merchant and by the security (if required) deposited, the business was risky, and the Hongkong Bank's Profit and Loss Account reflects this fact.

The techniques of trade finance changed over the years covered in this chapter – the Suez Canal, the telegraph, and above all the growing exchange risk as silver depreciated in terms of gold had their impact. The changes were particularly marked in the finance of imports. After the renewed decline in silver in the mid-1890s exchange and price were settled in China, and the Hongkong Bank financed imports by selling telegraphic transfers on London, a procedure which minimized the Bank's interest income which had arisen from the allowance included in the rate quoted for finance bills.

Figure 6 Tea marketing and finance in Mainland Fukien.

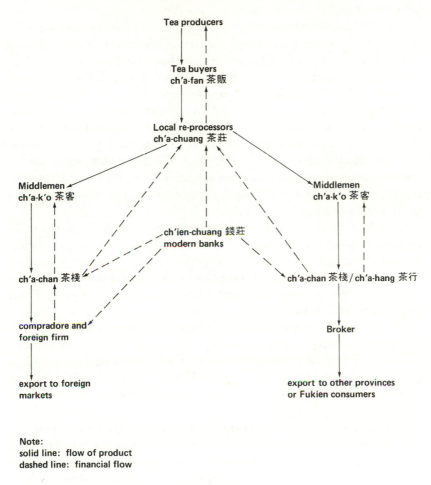

Note:
solid line: flow of product
dashed line: financial flow

Source: Robert P Gardella, Jr. 'Fukien's Tea Industry and Trade in Ch'ing and Republican China', p. 147. The table is adapted from Nanshi chōsa shiryō, <u>Fukkensho no chagyō</u>, p. 56, and 'Fukkenshō chagyō no kenkyū, p. 222.

Finance of local companies

Although shareholders and directors of the Hongkong Bank were resolved not to repeat the errors of local company finance which brought about the Bank's problems in 1874/75, the demand for assistance from the Bank was soon renewed as optimism returned to the China coast. The earlier problems could be explained away – failure was consequent on poor management, a misestimate of public demand, or an inability to obtain adequate supplies of raw materials, for example, sugar for the Hong Kong refinery. The new companies promised to avoid these difficulties and they came to the Hongkong Bank for funds.

The published accounts of public companies indicate that they had borrowed from the Bank; a glance at the assets on occasion reveals that the overdraft granted was greater than the value of the materials on hand; the Bank must have been financing fixed capital investment. Or, to put it another way, the Bank had tied up its funds. The 1882 accounts of the Companie du Gaz de la Concession Française, Shanghai, listed a Hongkong Bank loan of Ts9,810 against a paid-up capital of Ts50,000 and reserves of Ts12,226, but the value of the materials in stock and used for the manufacture of the gas was less than Ts7,000.[7] By the late 1900s the Bank's loans to public companies had grown sufficiently that the Board, virtually retired from active consideration of the Bank's actual banking activities, required the Chief Manager to submit a list of such loans granted in Hong Kong and Shanghai (see Volume II).

Growth of the Bank's loans to public companies during the period under present consideration was limited by the restrictions of the 'unequal treaties'. Until the Treaty of Shimonoseki in 1895 the right of foreigners to establish modern factories in China was challenged by the Imperial authorities. Although small foreign enterprises were financed, the Bank's main support was to Treaty Port utilities and docks.

The future of China was seen as dependent on the encouragement of Chinese enterprise, including enterprises initiated with official sanction. In financing these developments the Hongkong Bank again found itself dealing through its compradores, especially Wu Mao-ting in Tientsin. All this is reflected in the consequences of the Bank's move to the north and will be considered later in this chapter.

From the above discussion it should be clear that the impact of the Hongkong Bank on the economy of China is not to be measured by its few branches, small staff, and limited geographical presence. The Bank was the major factor in the finance of trade and supported the establishment of overhead investments in the Treaty Ports. In doing so it violated certain customs of British commercial banking; on the other hand the Bank acted as a true financial intermediary.

The Bank's sources of funds were the deposits of its constituents, including the major hongs operating on the China coast, the public companies, the various foreign governmental units, the British consular and diplomatic funds (and similar funds of other countries), limited Chinese officials funds, and the savings of great and small on the China coast. The Bank dealt with constituents who were primarily merchants, but merchants who nevertheless saw the need for enterprises which required fixed investment. The merchants no less than the Bank needed to remain liquid.

The impasse was solved, with risk, by the merchants' promoting public companies and by the Bank's financing the purchase of shares as well as agreeing to limited overdraft facilities which proved in fact to be injections of long-term capital. The merchants had however invested some of their own funds. They therefore turned again to the Bank to finance their trade using these shares as security. The whole structure was subject to collapse when the Bank made credit too readily available for speculative purposes. The Bank's chop loans to the local banks were one particular source of danger since the end-use could not be controlled, and the Bank's funds might be forcing up prices in the share market both by loans on margin directly to constituents and indirectly through the local banks. When the situation was recognized the Bank might find it difficult to withdraw without endangering the entire financial structure.

Jackson's and Cameron's calling in of chop loans in late 1883 was a factor forcing the great merchant-investor Hsü Jun into bankruptcy, bringing down the Bank's friend Hu Kwang-yung, and endangering the financial stability of the China Merchants' Steam Navigation Company with which the Bank would become increasingly involved in the years to come.[8]

So serious were the consequences of the 1883 collapse that Kwang-Ching Liu has suggested the events set back China's self-development; a new generation of entrepreneurs had to be found.[9] This may be so, but the new generation fared little better. The pattern of company promotion, real estate speculation, and collapse after the over-extension of credit – a pattern not unique to the China coast – was repeated in 1891. As Noble had been too generous so de Bovis may have been too severe (see Chapter 12). In 1910 the pattern was repeated, although in each case there were, naturally, distinguishing features.

The analysis so far permits another significant conclusion. In the context of falling exchanges only a truly silver-based bank could participate safely in the finance of China's modernization. The qualifying 'truly' has been added to exclude banks, the Deutsch-Asiatische Bank for example, whose accounts were in silver but whose source of funds remained the gold-based financial institutions which sponsored them. Even where the funds were raised in terms of sterling, the Chinese needed silver. Laying down the funds in China could be done effectively and in large quantities only by a silver-based bank.

These factors explain the growing predominance of the Hongkong Bank in the finance of China trade and development.

THE COMPRADORIC SYSTEM – ITS ROLE AND DEFECTS

The Hongkong Bank as a silver bank was able to play a major role in the finance not only of trade but of early industrial enterprise. Nevertheless the facts stated earlier in the chapter relative to the Eastern staff and their lack of Chinese background knowledge raise the question of how these bankers managed the

Bank's affairs to effect the impact described. They were shrewd, able men who gained experience on the China coast, but they needed a point of contact, a personal intermediary to effect the financial intermediation. They found it in the compradore.

Local managers might have contact directly with officials; certainly the Bank's move north to Tientsin and Peking brought the Bank into close contact with key 'modernizers'. The managers were apparently no longer wholly dependent on compradores, and yet even in the direct contacts the compradores provided introductions, interpretation, and continuity. Furthermore the compradores extended the contacts by their own industrial investment in cooperation with the officials.

This dependence on the compradore may appear ironic in view of the prediction in the Bank's initial Prospectus relative to the 'almost certain disappearance of the existing Compradoric system (so far as money is concerned)' (see Appendix to Chapter 2). The promoters' expectations, however, proved correct: the Hong Kong Mint, it is true, was unsuccessful, but the Hongkong Bank rationalized both the form and availability of funds. Within the context of a policy which determined Hong Kong should have the same currency as that of China and that the ordering of China's currency was not a task which could be performed by foreign banks, the Hongkong Bank's provision of banknotes, current accounts with chequing facilities, and savings banks eliminated the arbitrary role of the compradore in matters relative to monetary payment.

The role of the compradore did not remain unchanged throughout the period under consideration, nor was the role of the compradore the same in each hong or even, in the case of the Hongkong Bank at least, in every office of the corporation. The importance of the compradore within a firm varied from one of a subordinate under specific instructions to one of a virtual equal 'partner' in or co-manager of the business.

The role of the compradore in modern Chinese history has been the subject of many studies, and the discussion here is confined, as closely as possible, to the system as it affected the Hongkong Bank, its business, and its staff.[10] The present section describes the 'compradoric system' as it evolved in the late nineteenth century. This general section will be followed by specific examples of the system as it functioned in the Hongkong Bank.

The compradoric system

The elimination of the compradore's arbitrary role over monetary payments did not result in a general approval of the system by foreign merchants and bankers. Before considering the reasons for this, however, an acceptable definition of 'compradore' (*mai-pan*) must be provided. W.F. Spalding, a prolific writer on

Eastern banking and exchange and a member of the 'Home Staff' of the Hongkong Bank, has described the compradore's duties thus:

> To transact business for the bank with other Chinese, to look after all monetary affairs connected therewith – such as the receipt and payment of money and the collection of drafts and notes; to offer advice to the bank regarding the condition of local markets; to compile commercial information as to the standing of Chinese and to recommend, control and guarantee the Chinese staff of the Bank.[b]

The compradore was a salaried employee of the foreign firm. On the other hand he worked on his own account, personally guaranteed transactions between his firm and others, and guaranteed the Chinese employees. This dual role as employee and independent businessman caused problems under British law – as applied extraterritorially in China; it caused confusion in practice. This mattered little in periods of good business; in financial panics the compradore's dual role, his probable over-extension, and consequent inability to honour his guarantees would compound a firm's problems – the more so if that firm were a bank.

The first objection to the compradoric system was therefore the unreasonable degree of reliance placed on the guarantee *of* the compradore – and, by extension, on the guarantees and/or security provided *by* the compradore. The Hongkong Bank, as other firms, attempted to secure as compradore a man who would have the right contacts to introduce sound business and sufficient financial standing to be able to provide his own guarantee. Usually a manager had to compromise: the compradore might be a younger son of a 'great man', as in the case of Yap Ho Chiu in Amoy; he might have the contacts but be too dependent on potential bank customers for his guarantee; on occasion the titular compradore might have become too grand to do the day-to-day work, as in the case of Chan Lim Pak (Ch'en Lien-pai) in Canton; alternatively, the compradore might be largely dependent on one man who stood behind him, as Sir Robert Ho Tung stood behind the Bank's compradores in Hong Kong.[12]

Whatever the actual position, the compradore, no more than the Bank itself, could easily manage the withdrawal of facilities required in periods of financial crisis.

The compradore was part of the Chinese business community, often guaranteed by its members – and therefore dependent on them, and subject to the same business vicissitudes.[13] In a boom the compradore was tempted to become involved on his own account; in crisis he might find himself over-extended and, as de Bovis learned in 1892, tightening up might provoke the failure of the compradore. There is much in the literature attesting to the integrity of the Chinese businessman and indeed of the compradore; Ewen Cameron, the Bank's Shanghai Manager, spoke of it in handsome terms on his departure from the

---

[b] Although writing in the 1920s Spalding would have checked his statements with Sir Charles Addis who had served the Bank in China between 1882 and 1904.[11]

Settlement in 1889. But there were times when integrity was inadequate for the generation of sufficient cash flow, nor could integrity alone stem the consequences of a crisis of confidence.[14] Such times would cost the Bank dearly.

The Board of Directors in Hong Kong attempted to control the credit extended to, for example, native banks through chop loans guaranteed by the compradore. These could on occasion reach sums in excess of $1 million for bills outstanding, and managers were expected to explain, when there was a sudden increase in clean advances, the purposes for which the credit was being extended, as, for example, the finance of rice exports to Japan.

The few books which survive from the Shanghai branch of this period indicate a close relationship between the Hongkong Bank and the local banks, the former holding fixed deposits possibly against other transactions. There is also record of official fixed deposits, the majority of them obtained through the compradore.

The task of withdrawal once over-extension had taken place was a difficult one. Thus the Chairman at a semi-annual meeting thought it important to inform shareholders that in the crisis of 1882 Jackson had been able to withdraw funds from the Hong Kong market without losing a single Chinese customer; it would be a point of criticism that a decade later de Bovis, in attempting to cut back on advances to the Bank's Hong Kong compradore, brought about his collapse – with serious consequences to the Bank. As the Shanghai market became more developed, the interaction between Chinese and foreign business interests forced the Hongkong Bank to play a more systematic role, as seen from its actions in 1910 (Volume II). But there was always the feeling that the Bank was operating, as it were, once removed, and there was continued frustration.

The second objection arose from just this exclusiveness of the system – the compradore stood between the firm and the 'limitless' Chinese market. If only the foreign merchant or banker could establish first-hand contact with his Chinese counterpart wherever and whoever that might be, foreign trade would prosper – that was part of the dream of the China market. The foreigner saw himself restricted by the unequal treaties his government had been induced to sign with a China which, even in defeat or military disadvantage, nevertheless seemed somehow to maintain the initiative. He saw himself further restricted by having to deal with the compradore, with, that is, one Chinese businessman on whom the foreigner's success was so greatly dependent. This second objection was as unreasonable as the first was sound. The consideration which the Hongkong Bank's management – and no doubt others – gave to eliminating or modifying the system and the Hongkong Bank's failure to achieve any progress in this matter until after World War II are indications that the system served a purpose.

The Bank did not actually depend on 'one man' – the Bank had a compradore in each office, employed independently of each other mainly on local considerations. This must be understood in the context of the 'Cantonization' of the Treaty Ports; many compradores were nevertheless of Cantonese origins. Furthermore, a compradore in a particular branch or agency was usually (but not always) related or came from the same area as other compradores in the relevant businesses; they and their merchant contacts in the interior formed a business community into which the Bank was thereby introduced.

As shown earlier in the chapter, the foreign exchange banker was brought into contact with the China market in perhaps the only way practical at the time. Funds were made available through the intermediation of the compradore directly to Chinese traders or to Chinese financial intermediaries, in either case to finance the purchase of raw materials in the interior or the import of goods for shipment from the coast to the markets beyond.

Could this trade have been undertaken by other methods?

An apparently obvious solution would have been for the Hongkong Bank to train 'China experts', or at least insist on its staff learning Chinese. These efforts will be described below, but even had they been successful, they would not have given the foreigner access to the necessary connections nor to the credit information which is essential to sound banking. There were instances when Chinese customers, with a sufficient knowledge of English, wished to do business directly with the Eastern staff manager – without going through the compradore and hence without either the compradore's guarantee or the payment of the commission to the compradore for that guarantee. To this the compradore himself objected; his salary was nominal, although legally significant; he lived on his commissions.[c]

The lack of local information also forced managers to depend on the compradore for the introduction of Chinese staff and for their guarantee. This practice had, however, exceptions, especially during the inter-war period and in the larger branches. In Shanghai, for example, there was a 'compradore's department', which supplied shroffs where necessary in, for example, the savings bank, the current accounts department, etc. These were certainly the compradore's men, guaranteed by him. There were also miscellaneous Chinese employees, engineers, detectives, and guards, and here the relationship with the compradore is not so clear or absolute. As the book-keeping tasks grew the Shanghai branch used a second team, a Chinese team, which came in after the Portuguese staff had concluded the day's work. They would seem to have been independent of the compradore.

The Chinese staff were, however, all employees of the Hongkong Bank and paid by the Bank, their names (or in early days, their status by function) entered

---

[c] Alexander Michie asked Addis, when Sub-Manager Shanghai, to permit the English speaking Chinese representative of the 'Wan Wei Ching Co.' to deal directly with the Agent rather than with the compradore. The outcome of the case is not stated.[15]

in the charges book. For most of them, whether actually guaranteed by the compradore or not, the compradore was the Chinese manager.

The early Hongkong Bank managers and the early compradores grew up in the firm together, and a personal relationship was established. By the 1890s many of the compradores were the products of Anglo-Chinese education and spoke 'proper' as opposed to pidgin English. In contrast there remained compradores who used an interpreter to deal with the manager, and there would seem to have been little social contact between certain managers and their compradores. The 'system' had its infinite variations; the essence was contact between two communities; the guarantees were a further essential element.

The compradore was not only an essential interface between foreign banker and the Chinese merchant community, he was also a factor in the introduction of Western-type enterprise into China, often working with key officials in the establishment of factories or in the management of shipping and railways. This relationship, which had such potential for China's modernization, would later be criticized, especially by those who in any case opposed the capitalist system. The role of the compradore on the wider stage of Chinese history has been severely but unfairly judged on the basis of political and nationalist dogma. Consideration of these issues, however, lies beyond the scope of a corporation history; the story must turn now to accounts of individual compradores set against this brief description of the compradoric system.

The compradores of the Hongkong Bank, 1874–1895

Although the compradore was a man of considerable importance in a foreign company, information relative to his background, education, other business interests and, most important, his family or clan relationship with other compradores is difficult to locate and 'scrappy' when found. The history of the Hongkong Bank's compradores in this period suffers from this defect, and there is no file in the Archives with which to fill in the already published notes on compradores. But there are a few insights, and considerable detailed research has been done on the background of the Bank's Hong Kong compradores.[d]

Shanghai

The Hongkong Bank's first Shanghai compradore, Wang Huai-shan or Wah Sam, was from Chekiang Province and has been referred to in Chapter 7; he was succeeded, probably in 1875 by Hsi Cheng-fu, known in the Bank as Chin Foo. Described by Yen-P'ing Hao as a wealthy native banker from Chekiang, he

---

[d] Information on the Hong Kong compradores is based on Carl Smith's 'Compradores of The Hongkong Bank', in King, ed. *Eastern Banking* (London, 1983), pp. 93–111.

remained until his death in 1905 when he was succeeded by his son, Hsi Li-kung.[16] The Board authorized a gratuity to Chin Foo's widow of Ts10,000 in appreciation of his long and faithful service. However, there is evidence that Wah Sam remained involved in the Bank's affairs at least into the 1880s, and it is to him that in 1884 the Board presented an honorarium of $10,000 at Ewen Cameron's request for his 'loyalty and foresight' in the handling of a financial crisis without loss to the Bank. Cameron stated that he had earned no salary for ten years; the Shanghai Charges Account indicates a salary was paid to the 'compradore' throughout, hence the suggestion that Wang stood behind Hsi Cheng-fu, the latter being the 'compradore' in the usual sense, but Wang playing a guarantee role.

The Shanghai situation illustrates (i) the need for a compradore with the appropriate business background, (ii) the low salary, Ts120 per month and the consequent dependence on commissions, reinforcing the compradore's insistence on an exclusive role in the matter of Chinese business, but (iii) the possible existence of overlaps, of 'senior' compradores and the sharing of the position in some way peculiar to each situation.

Hong Kong

The Bank's first compradore in Hong Kong, Lo Pak Sheung, came from Whampoa, whereas the usual origin of Hong Kong compradores was in the Heung Shan (now Chung Shan) district near Macau.[17] That he performed the required services satisfactorily can only be assumed, in the absence of specific commentary, from the facts that he survived three changes in the chief managership of the Bank and that his son, Lo Hok Pang, succeeded him on his death in 1877. The elder Lo was one of the founders of the Tung Wah Hospital and compradores were always represented on their board.

Lo Hok Pang, as noted in Chapter 12, absconded in March 1892 with debts to the Bank totalling nearly $1.3 million against which his guarantees were inadequate. Indeed, the guarantee system was not designed to cover all the commitments made by the compradore, the expectation was rather that the compradore's security would be sufficient to cover losses in the normal course of business.

The Lo's, father and son, had outside business interests, although the Hongkong Bank attempted in its agreement with Lo Hok Pang to insist – as it had done with James Greig as successor to Victor Kresser – that he devote his full time to the business of the Bank and not be engaged in outside ventures. This proved difficult to enforce. Lo Pak Sheung's Will lists shares in several Hong Kong firms and investments in a native bank, a gold dealer's shop, a trading firm and a ship chartering office. He had also invested in an early Chinese newspaper, the *Universal Circulating Herald*.

In 1885, the son also invested in a Chinese newspaper, the *Hong Kong Uet Po* (Hong Kong-Canton news), losing heavily. Criticism of the Ch'ing rulers of China led, in this period, to the establishment of Western-style journalism reflected in such short-lived Chinese newspapers in the Treaty Ports and Hong Kong, an example of compradore involvement in the still muted calls for reform and modernization. But Lo Hok Pang had also become involved in the Oriental Sugar Company, the successor to Wahee Smith and Co., one of the Hongkong Bank's early 'bug-bears', and eventually in 1880 the refinery was sold to Jardine's China Sugar Refinery. During the boom of 1889–1890 Lo became involved in at least four local banks, advancing on finance bills which were unpaid when the crash came.

The first Hong Kong compradore is mentioned in the Board minutes only at the time of his death, and then only in connection with his son's succession and security. The second compradore becomes a subject of Board concern only in March 1892, but the selection of the third compradore is fully recorded.

Lau Wai Chün, a Vancouver-educated native of Heung Shan, came from Tsing Shan near Macau. He was apparently well-established in Hong Kong and may have come to the Bank from E.D. Sassoon and Co. where he had been the (or possibly 'a') compradore, in which case his acceptance is understandable – J.S. Moses of that firm had, after all, only just retired from the chairmanship of the Hongkong Bank and remained on the Board. That he was adequately secured is a comment on the interlocking, mutually supporting positions compradores would take, because two of Lau's principal guarantors were his brother, the compradore of the Mercantile Bank of India in Hong Kong, and Mok Kon Sang. The senior Mok family member was Mok Cho Chuen, the compradore for Butterfield and Swire. Lau's involvement in the Wei Sing lottery was to be his eventual downfall in 1906, but that complex story can be told in its appropriate historical sequence.

Amoy

The Bank's first compradore in Amoy was Yap Ho Chiu, the eighth son of a retired Ch'ing official, known in the family tradition as 'Yap Ta-jen'. Apparently Yap 'Ta-jen' had had a connection with the Foochow Arsenal and knew some English, which suggests one reason why the Bank would have contacted him for assistance. Yap Ho Chiu was succeeded as compradore by his son Hong Siong, the last compradore. As Hong Siong became older, much of the actual compradorial work was done by his son Siong Lin, until, with the revolution, Siong Lin left Amoy to become, eventually, Business Manager of the Hongkong Bank's Brunei office (see Volume IV). There he was succeeded by his nephew Tony Yap Chai Ping. Dates are unavailable, but this family history covers years of change, Hokien migration to the Nanyang, and the continued role of the Yap family in the Hongkong Bank under radically changed conditions.[e]

The Yap 'dynasty' is worth further consideration. The Bank would appear to have approached Yap 'Ta-jen' who in turn recommended his eighth son, remaining the 'great man' behind the compradore. At one point the Hongkong Bank had been in difficulty and Yap 'Ta-jen', on the instigation of his son, Ho Chiu the compradore, saved the situation by having his coolies ostentatiously carry baskets of silver coins to the Bank for deposit. Unfortunately no date is given, but there could easily have been a run on the Bank during some anti-foreign crisis or during the banking failures of 1893; even a local run could have been serious for the Bank's reputation since cash could not be replenished from Hong Kong immediately.

Yap Ho Chiu, the first compradore, was succeeded by his son (and Tony Yap's grandfather), Yap Hong Siong, a great merchant, landholder, and entrepreneur. In the first capacity he was involved in the finance of the tea trade, in the second he held considerable land in Fukien Province, both in the country and in Amoy itself, and in the last he was chairman of the Amoy Electric Company, one of the founders and life-director of the Amoy Canning Corporation, director of the local water supply company, and owner of two local banks (*ch'ien-chuang*). Educated in the Amoy American school, he spoke what was described as 'Victorian' English, correct and formal. As chairman of the Chinese Chamber of Commerce and a wealthy businessman, he was also a public benefactor, setting up stalls where tea was served gratis to travellers, providing coffins for the poor, and initiating other charitable work.

Other compradores

One of the more widely known of the Hongkong Bank's compradores was Wu Mao-ting, the Jim Pah or 'Jim Crow' of the early Shanghai branch (see Chapter 7). As Tientsin compradore he was close to the modernizing projects of Li Hung-chang and was the principal or managing director of the Imperial Chinese Railways, whose accounts were with the Hongkong Bank.

According to Chang Nan, Wu Mao-ting, whom he refers to as Wu Tiao-ch'ing, had been born in Wei-yuan, Anhui, the same town as Li Hung-chang, a potentially important tie in traditional China; he was also the brother-in-law of Hu Yü-fen.[18] Wu was involved in other projects; he was, for example, a director of the Tientsin Gas Company; there are also references in the Tientsin branch correspondence to the 'Jim Pah Cotton Mills'. His alleged anti-German attitudes

---

[e] The information in this section was provided by Tony Yap Chai Ping. He does not know the name of his great-great grandfather, and efforts to locate him in the several Ch'ing biographical collections have proved unsuccessful.

caused some concern to the Bank in London in connection with their cooperation with the Deutsch-Asiatische Bank, but the complaints were misconceived.

In Hankow the Cantonese Tang Kee Shang (Teng Chi-ch'ang) had been compradore since the opening of the branch in 1868 and, according to Arnold Wright, had been involved on behalf of the Bank in important financial negotiations with the Government; at some point he had also become a director of the government cotton mills at Wuchang. When Charles Addis was Manager in Hankow in 1896, he referred to Tang Kee Shang, the compradore, and how he had appreciated a letter from the former Manager, A.M. Townsend. The reference is patronizing, Addis recording that Tang had shown the accompanying picture 'with pride' to his parents.[19]

In 1889 the Hongkong Bank's Saigon compradore had, in the usual way, guaranteed the shroff, who absconded, involving the Bank in losses of $25,000 which the compradore was unable to pay. The Agent, H.R. Coombs, noting that the compradore had done good work for ten years, recommended that the Board write off the losses – 'Do not press the compradore as he is without means.' The role of the compradore varied from port to port; in some cases, he was virtually a commission agent with sound connections but with limited resources of his own. In this case the Board even approved his continued employment, requiring only that he obtain further security for the future. Both the compradore and the Agent wrote to the Board expressing gratitude for their handling of the affair.

As in China the Bank's compradores were well-established within the system and the generations succeeded each other, so in Singapore the Bank was well-served by the long-established See family who had settled in Malacca and moved to Singapore in 1828. See Tiong Wah, who succeeded his uncle See Ewe Boon as compradore in 1909, was the sixth generation in the Straits, a J.P., a municipal commissioner, and president of the Chinese Chamber of Commerce. His father, See Ewe Lay, founder of the *Lat Pau*, had been compradore to 1890.[20]

The Bank, in common with other foreign firms, had Chinese compradores in the Netherlands East Indies, the Straits Settlements, and the Philippines. In other areas a related system was customary. The 'guarantee shroff' of Ceylon, for example, bears full comparison with the compradore; there the Bank made funds available to the local market through the chettiars usually on the guarantee of the guarantee shroff. The essence of the system is the use of a well-connected local businessman to introduce and guarantee business from the local firms and to handle the details of contacts with the local government, including those representations and payments which were advised as necessary for business success. A Tientsin compradore, for example, paid off the Thieves Guild to ensure the safe landing of silver bullion, and they, accordingly, sent a man to the jetty with a signal to indicate the shipment should not be interfered with – or so it has been reported.

Relations with the compradore – and other Chinese

The Hongkong Bank was not without its China experts, of which Charles Addis was one, but in his record of guests entertained in his Shanghai Bank residence there is no reference to a Chinese. Except at the most formal, commemorative events, the two societies did not mix – except perhaps in Peking. In November 1898 Addis, then Sub-Manager Shanghai, attended the Taotai's Ball in honour of the birthday of the Empress Dowager; this is a lone reference to such an event and for this reason is recorded.

As retired Bankers who remember China in the 1920s recall, the compradore seemed to a young junior as someone entitled to great respect but with whom, except in the most unusual circumstances, they had no contact. Except for a rare formal dinner, hosted by the compradore, there was no social contact until the late 1930s, on the eve of the Japanese invasion.

And yet there are tempting vignettes . . .

David McLean thought highly of Wah Sam, and there are occasional references to him in his later correspondence with Ewen Cameron and John Walter, McLean's successors as Shanghai Manager. Usually it is over a personal item being purchased, but at one point McLean urges Wah Sam to visit England, at another he approves the Board's gift of 1884.[f] In 1884 there is correspondence with reference to Wah Sam's holdings of China loan bonds, in which he had bought heavily. Wah Sam was also interested in the London-incorporated Shanghai Waterworks and supported a move to have McLean intervene at a London shareholders meeting.

At a totally different level is the record of contacts found in the report of a mission regarding the opium trade with India, a mission undertaken in 1881 by Ma Chien-chung, a key financial official in the entourage of Viceroy Li Hung-chang.[g]

Ewen Cameron, described as an 'old acquaintance' of Ma's and who was then Manager of the Bank in Shanghai, entertained both Ma and his subordinate, Wu Kuang-p'ei, to drinks. The Hongkong Bank was prepared to lend China up to £20 million for railways, Cameron informed him. 'Our Bank is well aware', Cameron continued, 'that the Chinese are far more trustworthy than the

---

[f] On May 18, 1877, for example, McLean wrote to Jackson, 'I think you will be pleased with the purchase [of the gold ring] and I am sure Wah Sam will be. We picked up the stone and had it set.' On November 14, 1884 he wrote to Walter in Shanghai, 'Tell Wah Sam to come to England, a trip would do him good. Tell him also that the Tea arrived all right for which thanks.'[21]

[g] Ma himself was French educated and, with the *licencier en droit* and considerable experience, might fairly be termed an expert in financial affairs; he carried letters of introduction from Li to the Governor-General of India and the Governor of Hong Kong. His mission was connected with the problem of limiting through taxation the import of the drug into China, and in India he met with opposition from the Sassoon interests, whose Hong Kong representatives were members of the Board of the Bank.[22]

Japanese. And we all know that railways are for China what should be most useful with no harm at all . . .'[23]

In Hong Kong Jackson came to see Ma and, in one report, invited him on a boating trip, an invitation he did not accept. E. Morris looked after the two Chinese envoys in Calcutta, G.E. Noble in Bombay.

Ma Chien-chung himself provides an explanation for these invitations which, by Treaty Port social standards, would seem exceptional. On his trip south from Shanghai he had the opportunity for leisurely discussions with a fellow-passenger, William Keswick, taipan of Jardine, Matheson and Co., and Chairman in 1880/81 of the Hongkong Bank. Having praised the mercantile ability of the Chinese, Keswick is reported to have advised – as translated into Chinese and back to English (through Japanese) – as follows:

Actually, your country not only does not know how to help commerce, but also rather obstructs it in various ways. If you thus still want to be wealthy and powerful, it would be just like seeking a fish on a tree.

But, one thing to be noted here is that Chinese merchants are not learned. Many of them are rather vulgar. The *literati* do not want to make friends with them. We Westerners in China have also, so far as I know, never invited Chinese merchants to a public dinner. Really I think that, if Chinese merchants become more literate and well-mannered, the *literati* will not despise them and Westerners will be willing to mix with them. Then people will tend more to struggle for money in the market than to struggle for prestige in the court.

Is this not to be one way of seeking wealth and power?[h]

This theme was followed up by Ma after his visit to Penang where the leading Chinese merchants, unable to speak either ordinary Chinese, *kuan-yu*, or sufficient English, had to call on the British Assistant Protector of Chinese, E. Karl, who spoke both Cantonese and Fukienese, to act as interpreter, presumably into English or French. Another British official, entertaining Ma at tiffin, commented that all the wealthy merchants in Penang were Chinese and that although they were too vulgar to be befriended they had been able to build up family fortunes owing to their trustworthiness.[i]

These entrepreneurs were among the constituents of the Bank, served through the compradore. They were one basis for the Bank's success in the Malay Peninsula.

---

h Messrs Ma and Banno between them appear to have added a certain quality to the translation; it is doubtful that Keswick's normal conversation sounded quite so like a Legge version of the Chinese classics.[24]

i Ma Chien-chung replied that perhaps more Anglo-Chinese colleges (*Hua-Ying shu-yuan*) should be set up in order to free them from vulgarity. This policy has had brilliant consequences. Indeed, George Addis had written to his brother, Charles, from Penang as early as September 1874, that he was on the school board; 'there are 500 boys of whom 350 approximately are Chinese. Very creditable in dictation, writing . . .' (PP.MS. 14/70).

The Hongkong Bank and China – *tentative conclusions*

The Hongkong Bank, wrote Sir Robert Hart, 'understands China'. How can this now be interpreted?

The understanding did not come from social gatherings, from mutual cultural interests, or close friendships among junior members of the Bank and Chinese constituents. The race course was a base of mutual interest, but Chinese and foreigners did not usually have access to the same stands. The gentleman Britisher with his basic schoolboy knowledge of his classics could not mix socially with the untutored Chinese merchant; the Chinese official/scholar would not mix with the barbarian foreigner. The lines became formalized; later the returned Chinese student, skilled in the art of rugger, would still find himself barred from the European football club. The barriers continued long after the initial causes had been eliminated; in a period of Nationalism, this was a major source of social and, from this, political friction.

These generalizations would not apply to early intercourse in Peking. The references to personal relationships between managers and compradores are limited, but there are suggestions of close business friendships which could not extend to the purely social level nor, at that time, were either side particularly desirous that they should. The two societies had their own standards and there was no common ground for a meeting.

The understanding must be considered therefore in a narrower business context. It must also be examined at the managerial level where business contact was possible. The Hongkong Bank Manager and his compradore worked close at hand; contractually there should have been and in fact there must have been a continuous exchange of information. This was supplemented by the Bank managers' and compradores' contacts with their constituents both formally in the office and daily at the respective clubs to which they belonged. The Hongkong Bank Manager 'understood' China the way nineteenth-century managers understood their business in general – by long experience and on-the-job training, which included close association with key sources of information.

In this process the managers learned business on the China coast and obtained their experience in the context of its special requirements. There was no reason not to be 'obliging'. There was no one in London to gainsay their deviations from 'normal' commercial banking practice, except in those instances where the fortunes of the Bank were concerned and support from London was essential.

Sir Robert Hart's main concern was, however, the Bank's attitude towards the financial requirements of the Imperial Government. From a social and political analysis of life on the China coast it is difficult to see immediately how the Hongkong Banker and the Imperial official ever came into contact. The two apparently did not meet socially; the Imperial officials tended, in theory, to deal only with what in pre-Treaty days would have been seen as the political 'headman'. Indeed, throughout this period, official communications from the Bank, for example a complaint relative to a delay in a government loan repayment, would be transmitted through the British Legation. Although Addis's early experience in Peking would prove something of an exception, his official contacts were unusual and tentative.

The official contacts came through intermediaries, for example Hu Kwang-yung for Tso Tsung-t'ang in Shanghai, and through the compradores. The subsequent association of the latter with officials in government-sponsored enterprises suggests a continuity of contact at the compradorial level. That bankers and officials had formal meetings on occasion is a matter of record, that loan negotiations were carried out often over extended periods of time and often with attention to minor detail is recorded indirectly – there are no minutes of negotiating sessions. Nevertheless if the occasional references are brought together, they form a record, albeit without detail, of meetings sufficiently frequent, sufficiently relevant to business to form a record of personal contact between banker and official, supplementing the relations established through compradores.

The Hongkong Bank was based on the China coast; there was a continuity of presence, the Chief Manager was in Hong Kong, the Shanghai Manager had virtually equal relevant authority, and the directors were familiar with the problems through similar dealings with their own compradores and with officials. Ch'ing Dynasty collections of memorials from officials to their superiors and to the Throne suggest that a process of education was resulting from these contacts. The increasing understanding which Chinese officials showed in their comments on Western lending practices, while sometimes not wholly correct, suggest that the meetings in China and, later, through the Chinese Legation in London, were making possible the adjustments necessary for doing business with the foreign banks and especially with the Hongkong Bank.[25] The latter at the same time was prepared to encourage this adjustment by meeting the special requirements dictated by the needs of the Chinese fiscal system. There were mutual adjustments, although the pace was forced when Chinese requirements for borrowed funds increased dramatically with the imposition of an indemnity at the conclusion of the First Sino-Japanese War.

The increasing knowledge of Western business methods which can be noted in Chinese official communications during the period through 1895 has been generally observed by historians. Nor did the Chinese restrict their business to the Bank. Nevertheless the majority of the major loans and the bulk of China's business was done through the Hongkong Bank. Hart explained this in terms of an 'obliging' Bank's 'understanding'. A more precise explanation would appear to require comment on the Bank's continuity in China, its ability to understand China's requirements on the basis of close associations through compradores and intermediaries, and, essential to a full appreciation of the situation, its capacity and ability as a silver bank for fulfilling China's official banking requirements as close as possible to China's particular (but changing) practices.

These conclusions can be tested against the events described in the remainder of this chapter. The Hongkong Bank's involvement in China loans was of greater importance in the period after 1895, but by then the international scene had changed and China's requirements had become greater in a changed domestic political scene. These new factors will require consideration in Volume II.

FROM THE SOUTHERN TREATY PORTS TO NORTH CHINA

We were due to reach Hong Kong in the early morning [April 1909], and I was up on deck soon after dawn to see our entry through the Lyemoon Pass, which was so narrow that tigers would swim across the strait . . . this was the start of what I vaingloriously considered my 'career' – the Golden East, the Head Office of the Hongkong Bank – I might be sent anywhere – turn to the right and I'd be in Manila – what about Siam and the Frenchness of Indo China – straight north to Shanghai, the mart for all North China, even perhaps to Peking. 'PEKING' . . . there would be a city for adventure and wonder.

H.E. Muriel, autobiography[26]

The establishment of the Bank's Peking agency

China's first public loan, the Foochow Loan of 1874, was negotiated in that southern Treaty Port far from the Imperial capital. Through Tso Tsung-t'ang's agent, the wealthy merchant-banker Hu Kwang-yung, the Hongkong Bank's Shanghai Manager, Ewen Cameron, established contact with the world of Chinese provincial authorities, but the prize, as David McLean was pointing out from London, must surely lie in Peking.

The executive authority of the Imperial regime was, however, vested in the regional Viceroys, in provincial governors and in officials with a wider-based authority, Li Hung-chang for example, with direct access to the central authorities.

Furthermore Peking was not a Treaty Port. It was not open for foreign settlement, much less for exchange banking. The Hongkong Bank decided therefore to establish in Tientsin, where they could, by accommodating Li Hung-chang in his important position as Superintendent of Trade for the North, become his banker and from there have access to the Imperial capital. The Bank wished to be ready when China was ready – not simply for emergency provincial military or flood rehabilitation loans but for the loans which would develop China's railways and industries.

The move to Tientsin came in 1881, but Peking was as far away as ever. Bank representatives made occasional visits, but Cameron wanted a representative in the capital.

Cameron's choice was a dramatic departure from the Board's policy. In 1883 he selected the twenty-six year old Edward Guy Hillier (1857–1924), a Cambridge University graduate, schooled in the Chinese language, connected with a scholarly family with a tradition of service in the East, but a man, already in the East and without banking experience. Cameron, however, knew his man. E.G. Hillier was the posthumous son of Charles B. Hillier (died 1856), who left business in 1842 to become a clerk and eventually Chief Magistrate of the Colony of Hong Kong; in 1856 he had been appointed HBM Consul in Siam. E.G. Hillier's mother was the daughter of the famous China missionary Dr W.H. Medhurst. After graduating from Cambridge E.G. Hillier had been tutor to young Buchanan-Jardine, had come East as secretary to the Governor of British North Borneo, had taken up employment with Jardine, Matheson and Co. in Hong Kong and, with their introduction, was brought into the Hongkong Bank in 1883.

After initial training in Shanghai, Hillier was assigned to Tientsin, but in June 1885 he was sent to Peking with a letter of introduction from Alexander Leith, the Hongkong Bank's Tientsin Agent, to Nicholas O'Conor, the British chargé d'affaires.[27] He was instructed to establish a representation of the Bank in the capital.

Jardine Matheson had already established the Tung Yuen Lung 'bank' in Peking – it became the Ewo (I-ho) Bank in 1889. In fact it was not a bank in the ordinary sense, but was designed to provide a 'presence' in the capital, and Jardine's representative, Alexander Michie, remained based in Tientsin although he was a frequent traveller to Peking. However the actual setting up of a true bank agency, staffed by a foreigner, was a matter for caution.

Cameron apparently took the step without the prior approval of the Board of Directors in Hong Kong. Ten days after Hillier had been sent to Peking, correspondence from Cameron was presented to the Board stating that he had found it necessary to send Hillier from Tientsin to Peking where he was instructed to remain for the time being. The minutes reflect no decision by the Board to open the 'agency' at this time, and Cameron reported a week later that Hillier's presence in Peking was still only 'tentative', and that he was 'holding down expenses'. He added that he anticipated that the office would become permanent.

Although the Bank's representation in Peking was often referred to as an 'agency', it was not formally established as such until 1891. In the interim the situation in Peking remained ambiguous. The salary to be paid to the Peking

Agent was not fixed as it was elsewhere. And local business was for a short time arranged as if it had been initiated in one of the Treaty Ports, but certainly within the first year the acting Agent, Charles Addis, had his own supply of Peking-dated cheques and stationery.

By November 1885 problems had arisen leading to the temporary suspension of the 'agency's' activities. J.J. Keswick referred to the Bank's 'fiascos' in Peking, noting that it seemed to have endangered the existence of Jardine's Tung Yuen Lung Bank.[28] The 'agency' had been unfortunately established in the district where the native banks were located, and, presumably at the instance of the local native banks, Chinese officials had threatened the agency through the Bank's compradore. Cameron suggested that the opposition would be lessened if the 'agency' took up new quarters in a building leased from the Catholic fathers near the Legation Quarter. This was arranged in July 1886 and the Board ruled that in the meantime only the Agent (Hillier) and one shroff were to remain in Peking.

Guy Hillier had established the sub-agency in 1885 but the following year was granted leave and replaced temporarily by Charles Addis. The contrast in the interests and subsequent careers of these two men is illustrative of the career dilemma, the choice between specialization (with early promotion but limited career development potential) and the general service – and in this case, the stigma of being considered a 'China expert' rather than a banker.

As Addis boarded the ship in Hong Kong for Shanghai in 1886 a Chinese lad came up shyly from the background to bid him farewell. 'Who will teach me [English] now that you are gone?' he said.[29] This was part of the problem. For the effective financing of China's modernization Chinese merchant/compradore, Hongkong Banker, and Imperial official had to plan together. In the period of the Ch'ing Dynasty, however, if Chinese merchants and British bankers were to sit down together with Chinese officials, the first apparently had to be educated, the second had to learn Chinese, and the third . . . would remain exactly as they were. China was the Middle Kingdom; Chinese officials would set the tone.

Nor was China yet committed to the modernization which was behind the Bank's plans. Cameron lived in Shanghai; his Chinese associates were among those sympathetic to development. The Bank had contact with provincial authorities with practical problems, the reformers and the modernizers would surely soon prevail. In any case, the Bank had to be ready. This then is an account of the Hongkong Bank's early efforts in direct communication. If it resolves virtually into the personal history of one man, Charles Addis, this is a consequence of the source; much basic work had been done by Hillier and it was Hillier who would carry on to his death in 1924, twenty years after Addis had left the East.

Banker or China expert

In 1980 the officer on the Hongkong Bank's 'China desk' was a university graduate with a degree in Chinese. But, he was anxious to assert, he was a banker, not a China specialist.

In 1886 before Addis left Hong Kong for the North, Thomas Jackson reminded him, 'You have chosen a commercial and not a scholarly career.'[30] His first instincts appeared literary. Writing to his father shortly after his arrival in May 1886, Addis described his reactions – the fulfilment out of time of H.E. Muriel's youthful dream:

At three in the afternoon I drew reins under the walls of Peking. What a thrill of wonder and delight went through me as I saw for the first time these frowning walls and decaying towers. Under the Chinese city wall we rode and down by the moat to the gate that leads into the Tartar City where the Imperial pleasure parks were green with Spring and the palace roofs flashed yellow in the sun.[31]

And to his friend Dudley Mills in Hong Kong:

I have not yet recovered from the effect of the first view of the great city from its walls. It was for me profoundly impressive.
    And this evening I have just returned from a ride through the 'Forbidden City' over the Marble Bridge from the centre of which the lotus lake and royal parks studded with pavilions richly decorated, offered a scene to be remembered. Everywhere the Imperial Yellow was shining like gold in the sunlight. I thought of Poe's lines –

>   Banners, yellow, glorious, golden,
>   O'er its roof did float and flow,
>   This – all this – was in the olden
>   Time long ago.[32]

And yet on completing his leave in 1889 Addis refused the offer to return to the Peking agency, stating quite frankly to Ewen Cameron, who had in a sense promoted the idea of Addis as China expert:

I did not think it feasible for a business man to gain more than a smattering of Chinese and to retain his business habits. I told him directly that for myself I had no desire to make it a speciality; that I preferred to take my chance and that I should be sorry if I found that my slight knowledge of Chinese were to keep me out of the general line of promotion.[33]

Addis at his own request returned to the ranks and became a junior in the Tientsin office. In that same year he gave up the study of Chinese; he made the decision. He would be a banker.

Guy Hillier, with one brother in the service of China's Imperial Maritime Customs and another in the British consular service, returned to Peking; he would remain there, virtually blind with glaucoma but fully in control, until his death in 1924. In 1893 he requested a transfer so that he might become competent in banking practices, but the Board of Directors voted him an increase in salary. Management encouraged him in his choice, and thus as the Hongkong Bank's

China expert he remained to negotiate the great China loans with officials in Peking and ironically, with the Bank's London Manager, Sir Charles Addis, whose China expertise was to serve him as a banker, not rule his career. They had made their choice and their careers reflect the contrast.

When Hillier died, no one in the Bank's service was judged qualified to succeed him. The Bank sought an expert from the outside, seconding first G.E. Hubbard and then W.C. Cassels from the British Foreign Service. Hillier, although Peking Agent throughout, developed his high degree of expertise on the job – he had not come East as a banker, he travelled in China, and his home was truly Peking; even had this appeared attractive to a young Hongkong Bank junior, the opportunity was never there, and Hillier's self-acquired skills were not transferable.

Addis and the study of Chinese

In Hong Kong, Shanghai, and the older Treaty Ports it could be argued there was no need to study Chinese; the compradoric system was adequate. As Addis put it in a letter to his Hong Kong friend, Dudley Mills, 'If a man shows any interest in the Chinese or attempts to do business with them except through the recognized compradoric channel, he is set down either as bad or mad. You and I were the latter, I believe.'[34]

North of the Yangtze and west of Shanghai they spoke Mandarin. If the Bank were to become intimate with the officials or deal with constituents at least in parallel with the compradore some of its officers should have an understanding of the language. Certainly in other countries of operation there were Bank officers who made the attempt in the normal course of business. Whatever had been different in China must now change.

At a cost of £3:3s a term of ten weeks per scholar, Robert K. Douglas, Professor of Chinese in King's College, London, a pale, nervous looking man who, reported Addis, had been for a long time in the East, undertook to teach Hongkong Bank juniors the Chinese language (Mandarin). There were six who began. There was Addis's life-long friend, Gershom Stewart, later a member of Parliament, H.M. Thomsett, H. Lamond, T.McC. Browne, and Jamieson (who did not go East); G.H. Burnett, the London Office's veteran Accountant, took them down on May 12, 1882, for the first of their twice weekly lessons.[35]

Four days later Addis records in his diary, 'We are still hammering away.'[36]

Douglas, scholar that he was, insisted they each have a dictionary costing five guineas – the equivalent of $3\frac{1}{2}$ weeks' salary. Burnett was not prepared to sanction the expenditure of £31:10s; the drop-out rate would seem to support his decision. It also reflected the lack of commitment of the Bank to the necessity of Chinese studies. Addis studied one hour every night except Wednesday and by May 23 he

had become sufficiently curious to enter into correspondence with Sir
Rutherford Alcock about Sir Thomas Wade's already well-known introduction
to Chinese, *Tzu Erh Chi*.[37]

Few stayed the course. One developed a secret disease and left the Bank. 'At
the Chinese class,' Addis wrote in his diary at the end of the year, 'I am first (no
wonder; all the original members have gone save Thomsett).' In mid-January
1883 Douglas reported personally to Burnett on the great progress Addis and
Thomsett were making, and Burnett proposed the two be placed in a senior class;
Douglas was then introduced to McLean and Kaye and it was agreed that
progress in Chinese would affect salaries and priority on being sent East.[38] There
is no evidence that this resolution was ever put into effect – presumably the
exigencies of the service would not permit it.

Addis's first posting in the East, in March 1883, was to Singapore, where his
brother George was manager of the Chartered Mercantile Bank. 'Malay is much
spoken here,' he wrote, 'I must get a teacher and begin at once.'[39] When he was
later assigned to Rangoon, Addis began learning Burmese.

Fortunately for his Chinese studies, he was transferred to Hong Kong in
November and became close friends with J.H. Stewart Lockhart, the Registrar
General, later Colonial Secretary, and a student of Chinese. In Hong Kong too he
made a lifelong friend with Dudley Mills of the Engineers, an eccentric but eager
student of things Chinese. The two took local leave to explore Swatow.

Addis began studying Cantonese with a tutor, An Yeung Wai:

For two years morning after morning we have sat together – teacher and scholar. An old
man with huge goggle spectacles but as keen in his wits as many a younger. . . . He always
spends the whole of Sunday forenoon with me. He comes after breakfast and with tobacco
and those little Chinese covered cups of tea we talk over our different customs or he tells
me story after story of China's old heroes and I sometimes tell him a story of our Land – he
listens rather incredulously, though too polite to express his incredulity – and somehow I
think we always finish up with the belief strengthened that folks with [pig]tails are very like
those without and that a strong chain of human sympathy binds together the children of
one father.[40]

Addis also attended a weekly meeting under the chairmanship of the redoubtable
Dr John Chalmers (1825–1900), the great missionary, successor in Hong Kong to
James Legge, and Sinologue of dictionary fame, to discuss the classics.

We meet every Tuesday night at 9 o'clock at Chalmers' house and there seated round a
large table with paper and pencil beside us, while the centre of the table is littered with
dictionaries and the works of different authorities. . . . I enjoy it very much. . . . It does
one good after days of small talk and small things to breathe even for so short a time a loftier
and purer atmosphere.[41]

While Addis was studying Cantonese and literary Chinese in Hong Kong,
Hillier, as has been described, had opened in Peking and there problems had
developed. Cameron decided to withdraw Hillier temporarily and he had

approached Thomas Jackson to release Addis, whose interest in the language had been recognized. Jackson, who apparently already entertained high expectations for Addis as a banker, at first refused. But on April 19, 1886, Addis was released and sent north to Peking to relieve Hillier as acting Agent – rather like sending someone to Berlin because he had studied French was Addis's realistic assessment.

On the advice of Lockhart, Addis left his cat behind. The study of Chinese was generally thought the sure road to insanity; carrying a yowling cat through China would, he wrote to his sister, prove the argument.[42] Behind the humour in a family letter there was the slightly defensive attitude of someone doing the right thing but worried at the inevitable reaction of one's peers. Addis's fellow bankers in the mess might find his Chinese useful when the servant couldn't be made to understand, but still, learning Chinese suggested something peculiar.[43]

Addis's first reaction to his new assignment, however, was one of unqualified enthusiasm.

No doubt it was a lucky chance that brought me here and I may bless my stars that ever I took a fancy to Chinese study. Only that could have raised me over the heads of 30 or 40 seniors and sent me at a jump from a humble clerk to Acting Agent at Peking. My salary was $175 per mensem. Now including allowances I get $380.86 per mensem. I have a fine house, stables, servants, mule and cart (the carriage of Peking) coal and oil (heavy items during the severe winter) newspapers, furniture, house and table linen all supplied by the Bank. I was in charge of an Agency at 25 years of age, the youngest agent in China.[44]

All very true, but, as the specialist would someday realize, although the initial reward is fast, afterwards there could only be in-place salary increments. There was no career pathway from the Peking agency to the chief managership.

The Bank also paid for Addis's language teachers; it was Cameron's idea that he would have time in Peking to devote to study. Addis began in the great Hongkong Bank tradition by ordering 1 case Melvins beer, 5 doz breakfast claret, 2 doz after dinner claret, 1 doz whisky, 1 doz champagne (quarto), 1 doz champagne (pinto), and 1 campbed with mosquito curtains.[45]

It is clear that Addis entertained not only a fascinating range of diplomats and others among the few foreign residents – Alexander Michie, Jardine's agent, was an occasional guest – but that he made the breakthrough to the Chinese. 'February 25, 1887: Entertained a lot of my Chinese friends here a few days ago and filled them up with champagne and good cheer.'[46] Addis gave a speech in Chinese which had been prepared with the help of his teacher.

Writing to his father in August he described an occasion on which the dinner was 'getting cold while two secretarys discuss who should be the first to enter my dining room'.[47]

Marquis Tseng Chi-tse (1839–1890), sometime Chinese minister to the Court of St James, returned to Peking late in 1886. In London he had had contacts with the Bank, and McLean thought the relationship established would be useful, but contacts with foreigners were made cautiously in the capital. Tseng was appointed to serve in the Tsungli Yamen (the Chinese alternative to a Foreign Ministry), was a junior vice-president of the Board of War, a senior vice-president of the Board of Revenue, and on the Board of Admiralty. Addis could record, with pardonable pride – for he was still a young man – that not only had he dined several times with Tseng but also:

> Marquis Tseng dined at my table, the only private table, I believe, he ever sat at in China. He called on me and I on him on more than one occasion, in fact I was several times at his house. I met him out many times. I sat by his couch during his last illness.[48]

Furthermore, Addis wrote, 'I knew pretty well two or three of Li Hung-chang's office officials. I met several of the petty court officials at Peking.'

On such occasions the compradore, one is tempted to assume, was not present. Addis had his teachers and it is they, rather than the compradore, a nephew of Wu Mao-ting in Tientsin, who would assist the young foreign banker at his entertainments.

In his diary, April 13, 1888, Addis recorded, 'The gold shop people gave me a grand entertainment in the Chinese city at 1:00 p.m. A splendid feast, afterwards to Chinese theatre.'

Charles Addis had broken out of Treaty Port society, but not in a Treaty Port. Even then, as Addis was later to recall, his teacher would not, if possible, appear to recognize him in the street and Tseng's association with foreigners was viewed with suspicion.[49] But there was quiet socializing and familiarization; Guy Hillier had made the initial contacts, and the presence in the British Legation of Hillier's brother, Walter C. Hillier, as Chinese Secretary must certainly have encouraged acceptance. The contacts he made were still restricted, but they were a nucleus on which Addis, Henry Hewat, and Hillier again could build.[j]

The Chinese Court, however, still preferred to deal at the provincial level, and negotiations would be carried out in Tientsin, but the Peking foothold was important, the Hongkong Bank was there, discreet but visible, and it already provided minimal banking services through the compradore. Indeed, there is evidence of some political influence, for Addis may have successfully warned Peking officials of the banking and concession schemes of the notorious 'Count' Mitkiewicz, with whom Li Hung-chang had become too closely involved (see below).[50]

---

[j] Hewat (East in 1880) impressed Addis with his knowledge of Chinese and after experience in Tientsin was appointed acting Agent, Peking, in 1887. Surprisingly Hewat developed an intense dislike for Peking and spent the major part of his later career in Saigon.

The business of the Peking agency

To break out socially, to meet Chinese officials might be seen as first tentative steps to business without the compradore. Addis could be more flexible in the new agency, but its purpose was not to undermine the compradoric system but rather to establish relations at a higher level, the actual business to continue through the compradore. The system was not, after all, without its merits; the foreigners objected to its exclusiveness, to being cut off from all else in China. This, Addis hoped, he was in the process of breaking down.

Addis attempted to negotiate a loan; more accurately, one might say he 'dabbled'. The Chinese officials with whom he mainly dealt were apparently junior, and they were unable to provide security; Shanghai office, presumably Cameron, was concerned with just this problem, and Addis was left to complain that he was helpless between the two extremes.[51] But serious major loan negotiations were not to be carried through in such an informal or haphazard way. Feelers might be made, tentative discussions held; and this technique Hillier would perfect. But the final stages would be more open; they would still return to Tientsin. Only after 1895 would they move to Peking and London.

The Peking agency did prove useful for a loan which had been negotiated, and Addis recalls how bullion was stored in the Bank building pending completion of the agreements and the advance of the funds to the authorities in the capital. This was in itself a service which only the Hongkong Bank could provide, although as bankers they would lay down funds for loans successfully negotiated, for example, by Jardine's.

Although routine business was handled by the compradore, there is a direct business letter to Scottish-educated Chiang Chiou Ying in terms which suggest a day – then far-off – when the Hongkong Bank would deal directly with constituents of all nationalities.

I beg to acknowledge the receipt of your favour of 29th ultimo giving cover to a Chinese draft of Ts1,553 Sung Chiang silver. In accordance with your instructions I now beg to hand you a deposit receipt for the equivalent, viz Kung-fa Ts1,484 pure silver having interest at rate of 5% per annum.
With my best regards to yourself and Captain Lew Buah,[k]
I am, Yours faithfully, C.S. Addis, Acting Agent.[53]

Addis considered his main function in Peking was representative. His contacts with the Embassy provided him with information on Chinese affairs which he presumably compiled and forwarded to his immediate superior, Alexander Leith

---

[k] Lew Buah, who with Chiang had been exiled to Kalgan by the Chinese authorities, had been educated in Aberdeen (Scotland) and would in defiance of death appear from time to time in Addis's Peking office/home.[52]

in Tientsin, and also to Shanghai. He also employed Chinese 'agents' to obtain information and thus keep him in touch directly with minor officials.[54]

The Peking office also undertook regular banking business for foreigners, indeed to such an extent that Addis placed a large order for various forms to facilitate his work. He transmitted funds for various relief and charitable contributions. In short, the Hongkong Bank became bankers to the foreign community.

As success in working with the Chinese gold dealers had brought trouble to Hillier from the native bankers in the first year of the agency, so the possibility of the agency's success with foreigners brought a reaction from the manager of the Chartered Mercantile Bank in Shanghai. He protested to the acting British Consul-General that either the Hongkong Bank should be prohibited from establishing its agency or other banks should be notified that similar facilities would be afforded them.

It is obvious that power to trade or even a blind acquiescence cannot in justice be extended to any one British Bank in particular and I beg therefore that either prompt steps be taken to prohibit the Hongkong Bank remaining longer in Peking for purposes of dealings in Bullion and other operations, or a notification be given us that we are entitled to proceed there and open operations at once under cover of the British authorities.[55]

He pointed out further that the Hongkong Bank had established its agency 'for the purpose of trade', and that, as Peking was not a Treaty Port, foreigners were prohibited from trading there. He complained specifically that the Hongkong Bank had completed bullion operations in Peking which had considerably interfered with the Chartered Mercantile Bank's business.

This was the 'Treaty system' in reverse – a British bank attempting to secure from British authorities the limitation of a rival's activities in China. The acting Consul-General replied that he had no information, but he correctly observed that the allowance of privileges in excess of treaty right by Chinese officials was 'rather a matter for congratulation than complaint'.[56] Though granted at first to individuals, such rights might in course of time be extended. He advised the manager of the Chartered Mercantile that if his bank wished to open an office in Peking, he would be willing to communicate this information to the Legation.

The Mercantile was correct, however, in its assessment of the importance of the gold bullion business; it covered the costs at least of the Hongkong Bank's Peking agency. And here too were the limitations of Addis's independence; the bullion business brought him into conflict with the Guild and after the posting of Wu Mao-ting's nephew as the new compradore, a reorganization took place through which Addis lost direct contact with his Chinese customers.[57]

The Peking agency buildings, a digression

Treaty Port architecture was basically European with modifications in 'compradoric' style to meet climatic and other requirements. In Peking there were further modifications, although the Bank had, after its first unfortunate experience, to settle in the Legation Quarter. 'Our task [explained Addis] is to keep quiet . . . and so my office is completely hidden from the street and I hang out no sign. Some mouldy censor going past would find employment for a week in laying before the Emperor how his laws were trampled or defied.'[58] And he provided a description in a letter to his sister, Janie:

A wall hides the house from the street. At the gate is the Porter's Lodge, then a small courtyard and then the house. It is built in the form of a square with a courtyard in the centre, each side forms two rooms.

The front side serves, divided into four, for the Chinese cashiers. The East side forms two bedrooms and bathroom. The West has one room for my office, the other is my study and a lobby is in between. South is the drawing room, a lobby, and the dining room off which opens a pantry and a kitchen at the back. The dining room and drawing room look out on to what I hope will soon deserve the name of a garden. Beyond that is a wall which shuts out the stables and Chinese Quarters.[59]

Here the young acting Agent of the Hongkong Bank entertained. In his daring parties he brought two hitherto separate societies together – the foreign diplomatic community and the missionaries; it was perhaps too much to expect him to follow up this social revolution with entertainment bringing Westerner and Chinese together. And there is no evidence he attempted the task. His entertainment of Chinese was, as far as the sources permit a conclusion, of them alone.

The office/home behind the walls soon become too small and Hillier bought the land adjacent, but in a tragic fire in March 1900, before the catastrophe of the Boxers' Siege of the Legations, the whole was burned down – only the Chubb safe surviving.

The Peking agency, the Chinese-language program, and the compradores – conclusions

The Hongkong Bank had been the first foreign bank to establish an agency in Tientsin; it had now successfully established itself in Peking. De Bovis had been succeeded in Tientsin by Leith, who had previously dealt successfully with provincial officials in Foochow. Hillier and Addis in Peking were in turn relieved by Henry Hewat, another Chinese-speaking junior with considerable experience in the Tientsin branch; direct communication with the Chinese could now be developed.

But it was not to prove so simple. In 1889 Addis returned briefly to Peking to relieve Hewat who was suffering from ill-health; he was, in the cliché of the time, 'seedy'. On Hewat's return from Chefoo, Addis had in his turn become seedy – with dysentery. Addis was taken to the Western Hills where he rested before returning by boat down the river to Tientsin.[60]

In the end, however, Hillier returned permanently to Peking, Addis gave up serious Chinese language study, and in 1891 Hewat was assigned as Agent in Saigon, where he remained, except for a brief assignment back to Tientsin in 1900/01, with much success until his retirement on health grounds in 1906. As for Addis's fellow Chinese-language student in London, H.M. Thomsett, his career with the Bank was mainly in Hong Kong and Singapore; he began a long sick leave in 1893 culminating in his retirement several years later.

Gershom Stewart's efforts with Chinese may have been aborted by his January 1883 departure from London for Hong Kong, three months before Addis. There is no mention of his continuing the study with Addis in Hong Kong. Nevertheless, his assignment as 'agent' in Macau, given that his mission was to establish contact with officials in connection with collecting the customs revenues, may have depended on his having acquaintance, albeit passing, with Chinese. Indeed, he even wrote advice to Addis on how best to learn the language.[61] If this is correct, it is the only other specific reference to a young banker being assigned on the basis of his knowledge of the Chinese language. Bank personnel records listed language ability and this information may have had an unmeasured influence.

Of Addis's other fellow-students, Lamond spent his brief Hongkong Bank career in Hong Kong and Manila. T.McC. Browne was briefly in Tientsin and was Agent, Hankow, but his main contribution was his managership of the Bangkok agency.

On his leave in 1888, Addis visited the Bank's language class in King's College; five juniors were present and Addis read Chinese sentences to them.[62] This is but a random reference. Addis was to make several efforts to formalize the study of Chinese in the context of the Bank's increasing operations in the North and dealings with officials, and although these apparently made little impact in the Bank's history, they merit further consideration in Volume II.[63]

The fact is that Bank business continued to be undertaken directly with the foreign community in the ordinary way and through the compradore with Chinese constituents. The delicate negotiations with Chinese officials would require the experience of Hillier in Peking and Addis as Sub-Manager in Shanghai; in London there was Ewen Cameron and later Charles Addis dealing directly with the Chinese Minister. A knowledge of Chinese would be a convenience in an emergency or in a casual meeting, or perhaps even at an official gathering, but it was not essential to a career in banking.

The move north to Tientsin and Peking had accomplished the purposes of the Hongkong Bank. It was positioned for its merchant banking operations, for its increasingly close dealings with Customs and other funds, and for its important political contacts. Activities and relationships in the North, either in Tientsin or Peking, did not, however, change the basic business patterns of the foreign and Chinese communities, nor did they affect the key role of the compradore.

Ironically, perhaps, it was in Peking that the most serious defalcation of a Hongkong Bank compradore would eventually occur.

THE CHINA LOANS[1]

Our [Tientsin] agent is not to join in any movement that would give the Viceroy the slightest offense.

Board of Directors, August 1894

Of the major public loans issued on behalf of the Imperial Government of China between 1874 and the end of the Sino–Japanese War in 1895, all but the 1885 Chartered Bank 8% Dollar Loan for Canton Ts1 million (= £244,000), the 1885 6% Baring Loan for £1.5 million, the 1887 5½% Warschauer Loan for Marks 5 million (= £250,000), the 1894 6% German Loan for £1 million, and the 1894 6% Cassel Loan for £1 million were issued by the Hongkong and Shanghai Banking Corporation (see Table 14.2). The Bank also lent directly to the China Merchants' Steam Navigation Company and, through such intermediaries as Jardine, Matheson and Co., in smaller amounts for the development or reconstruction projects of various regional officials, especially those of the Chihli Viceroy and Northern Superintendent of Trade, Li Hung-chang.

The Hongkong Bank had become the banker to the Imperial Maritime Customs and held the accounts of various officials and customs banks. As noted earlier in this chapter, the Bank made funds available by loan and overdraft for fixed investment, often on the initiative of the Shanghai or Tientsin Managers before a more sceptical Board could veto the project.

The Bank's major role came, however, in its willingness to manage, as agent of the Imperial Government, various public loans either in silver or gold (sterling). The Bank and the Chinese Government had no mutual long-run obligation; the Bank's role was based on the terms of each loan contract and the Chinese retained their right to seek financial assistance as they chose. The dominance of the Hongkong Bank was consequent on the commercial advantages it offered.

The Hongkong Bank undertook Treasury Chest business in the East; the Bank

---

[1] This section is based on D.J.S. King's research report 'China's Early Loans, 1874–95, and the Role of the Hongkong and Shanghai Banking Corporation', now in the Group Archives.[64]

were bankers to the British Government. This business had been obtained in the usual way by successful tender. The Bank's activities with the Chinese authorities were undertaken, therefore, as a commercial bank operating in the private sector. The Bank did not operate as an agent of British foreign policy. Chinese procedures often forced the Hongkong Bank to communicate through the Legation, a requirement as much deplored in the Foreign Office as it was by the Bank's Board of Directors, but all parties were clear that no obligations were created thereby. The transactions described in this chapter were 'commercial'; they were for the most part undertaken by the Hongkong Bank because it alone could handle the business, it alone could lay down sufficient silver funds, it alone could afford to tie up its resources in the East.

The China loan business came to the Bank not only because the Bank was often the only practical choice. Once more reference must be made to Sir Robert Hart's judgement that the Bank was obliging and 'understood' China. Through discussions with officials and compradores the Bank's Hong Kong, Foochow, Shanghai, Tientsin, and Peking – and later Hankow – agents came to appreciate the reasons for China's way of doing business; here and in London the senior managers attempted to advise the Chinese on more economical ways of borrowing.

The Bank operated as an interface between two differing financial systems, making it possible for the parties to understand each other.

The London-based banks and the concession seekers did not understand the problem; if they had, they would have been unable to adjust. By the time their correspondence had passed back and forth to Europe, the prospective consortium would have fallen apart and/or the Chinese would have turned elsewhere – to the Hongkong Bank.

Only a bank based on China could over time achieve the necessary relationship; the Hongkong Bank's predominance in China was based not on Government support – there was none; the Bank's role was based on the experience, knowledge, and consequent flexibility of its managers as supported by its Chief Manager and Board of Directors in Hong Kong.

Interface

Before considering in historical sequence the Hongkong Bank's role as agent for the Chinese Government, an example of its interface operations will illustrate the problems facing those who sought to participate seriously in the loan business. The following relates to the so-called 'A' and 'B' Loans of 1884 (see Table 14.2).

At the request of the Viceroy of the Liang Kwang provinces and with the authority of the Emperor granted by edict, the Hongkong Bank advanced the sum of Canton taels 2 million against the issue of two public loans repayable by the Chinese at $7\frac{1}{2}$ *li* per tael per lunar month according to the Chinese calendar over a period of three years for one loan and six years for the other.

The Hongkong Bank thereupon issued the loans for public subscription in Hong Kong to an amount of \$1,394,700 each in bearer bonds of \$500 at 8% and par. Since the public subscribed to only 15% of the total and only 5% at par – and since the Board of Directors then decided not to issue below par – the balance, or 95%, was held by the Bank and gradually sold as the market permitted.

The references above concern the Chinese Imperial Government 'A' Loan (for three years) and 'B' Loan (for six years) issued to the public in October 1884. These were silver loans, that is, they were denominated in a unit of account payable by a fixed quantity of silver. The loans were denominated in Canton taels but converted, for ease of dealing, by the Hongkong Bank into dollars at the standard rate of Canton Ts717 = \$1,000; the rate of interest payable by the Chinese authorities to the Bank can be recalculated, allowing for intercalary months, as 9.3% per annum, Western calendar.

The Hongkong Bank acted as agents of the Chinese Government but, in fact, by advancing the full amount before issue, had taken the loan 'firm' and accepted the risk that the public would not subscribe – as proved to be the case. The Bank's profit derived from the 1.3% interest rate differential over the life of the loan, less expenses. Profit in European markets usually derived from a commission deducted from the proceeds of a loan issued at a discount. The Chinese Government, however, would not agree to this procedure; the Hongkong Bank adjusted accordingly. The actual income from the loan as a whole would depend on the Bank's ability to sell off its holdings, and this, as successive Chairmen reported at semi-annual meetings, it was in general able to do.

The Hongkong Bank had received a request to meet specific requirements of the Chinese Government. The Bank met this request as stated, even though it was not possible to issue a loan to the public on these terms. The Bank did not insist on the Chinese changing their terms to suit the Bank or the public; the Bank, however, understood China – even if the public did not. The Bank also understood both the Hong Kong and Shanghai markets and, note well, the London market; accordingly, having met the terms of the borrower, the Bank translated not only the terms but also the approach to meet the requirements of the lender.

The Bank acted as an interface between the financial systems of East and West.

There was a further factor in the Hongkong Bank's operation. Its source of funds was in the silver-using area, its accounts were denominated in a silver unit of account, and it financed trade between silver-using and gold-using territories, requiring funds in each. The Bank was therefore in a position to advance silver funds against loans not yet issued.

An account of the principles and explanations behind these activities is the purpose of the remainder of this section; the details of the loans are left to a separate study.

The borrower

The potentially prosperous Chinese Empire was subjected to a series of revolts, attacks, and natural disasters which strained a relatively inflexible and decentralized fiscal system. The Taiping Rebellion (1851–1865) and its suppression had devastated rich agricultural areas and had come close to toppling the dynasty, while the Nien-fei rebels, active in North China (1853–1868), and problems with the Moslems in the Northwest (1862–1878) kept pressure on government resources. From the outside the Japanese threat against Formosa (Taiwan) in 1874, the Sino-French War (1883–1885), and the Sino-Japanese War a decade later (1894–1895), all required special financing which, as it happened, only foreign sources and foreign intermediation with Chinese sources could provide. The erratic behaviour of the Yellow River, 'China's Sorrow', added a further strain on the country's resources, both financial and administrative.

At the same time continued foreign presence in the region had led to a series of concessions within the traditional Imperial system permitting settlement and trading at frontier points, expanded to a series of so-called Treaty Ports or 'open ports'. Here foreigners were able to live under conditions of extraterritoriality; their missionary zeal, both religious and economic, led conservatively inclined Chinese leaders to consider costly development projects and to weigh their advantages against the financial problems their construction would bring, the foreign interference which the new technology would require, and the consequent dangers not only to the Ch'ing administration but to the very foundations of the Chinese political system.

The urgency of the requirements for defence, military, and disaster finance forced the Chinese Government to give such matters priority, while the foreigners remained always hopeful that development projects, especially railway construction, would eventually receive attention. The former, besides straining the fabric of the political system, were unproductive and purely financial; loans for such purposes could exhaust the country's credit-worthiness before initiation of development projects. The latter involved not only finance, but the supply of expertise, equipment – even labour in the early phases – and were the subject, on the part of foreigners, of misplaced expectations, false starts, and international rivalry.

Imperial policy was considered and sanctioned by the Emperor advised by central boards operating in Peking; initiative for such policies and their eventual execution usually came from Imperially appointed officials in provincial or regional executive positions. The fiscal system was also provincially based but centrally supervised, with Imperially sponsored projects being financed by the allocation of provincially raised funds. Where such procedures involved the transfer of funds raised, or supposed to be raised, in one province for use by a governor or other official in another province, usually for an Imperial or regional project, problems and delays could arise. The reallocation might, for example, be ordered on unrealistic assumptions as to the availability of funds; officials facing provincial responsibilities and pressures might attempt to delay implementation of instructions requiring the transfer of resources out of their province, in the hope perhaps of an eventual Imperial reassessment of the original instructions.

The provincial authorities had local responsibilities which might require financing in excess of available funds. If so, their ability to find additional sources of funds was limited. The administration was not capable of a thorough reorganization, hence the tendency to seek *ad hoc* solutions, among them borrowing from foreigners. Domestic borrowing was difficult given the repayment record of the Government; additional taxes, *likin* or transit duties for example, were possible but caused political repercussions, and contributions from the gentry, forced or voluntary, with or without official recognition in the form of honorary rank, had an eventual limit.

Control – provincial and central borrowing
Early borrowing by provincial authorities, acting on their own responsibility and repaying from funds within their own control, was arranged, often through compradores, with such trading hongs as Jardine, Matheson and Co., Augustine Heard and Co., and others. The potential political dangers of this unsupervised activity, should repayment not be made or debts repudiated by successors in office, led to the promulgation in 1868 of an Imperial edict or rescript requiring the Emperor's sanction of a foreign loan, which would in normal practice be granted only after consideration of the loan by the central boards and later also by the Tsungli Yamen.

To the extent this requirement was observed, the foreign borrowings became national responsibilities and could be assessed as sovereign-risk loans by potential lenders. They are referred to in this study as Imperial loans, as if by a central Chinese Government in the Western sense; loans guaranteed by Chinese authorities without Imperial sanction were provincial or local loans and carried additional risks.

The apparent willingness of foreigners to lend was a continual temptation to hard-pressed authorities. Control was maintained (i) by the requirement of the Imperial edict, (ii) by the need to commit funds not immediately under the control of the borrowing officials or agency for repayment, and (iii) by the inherent reluctance of the Chinese authorities to borrow from foreigners, a reluctance reinforced by the threat of impeachment by conservative censors or other officials.[65]

The Chinese position was reinforced by the attitude of the foreign lenders, including the Hongkong Bank and the London Stock Exchange, and their diplomatic and consular representatives. These were aware of the dangers of unrestricted provincial borrowing and were anxious to enhance the role of the central authorities along Western lines, if only to facilitate immediate enforcement of treaties and the rights and privileges these had bestowed. Imperial control was facilitated by the insistence of the London Stock Exchange, supported by those expecting to float any portion of the loan in London, that the Imperially required edict, properly transmitted through the appropriate legation according to Chinese procedures, be obtained and its contents made public.

The role of the foreign-staffed Chinese Imperial Maritime Customs in foreign borrowing throughout this period was crucial, although it fell short of the expectations of its Inspector General, Sir Robert Hart. Hart hoped that his office would at least act as a clearing-house for foreign borrowing, but in this he was disappointed. Not until 1894 were the financial requirements of the Government placed temporarily in his hands. Nevertheless, the influence of the Customs, although indirect, was there – it is best considered from the point of view of the lender.

Small provincial borrowing was secured on the seal of office of one or more of the relevant officials; on occasion specific provincial revenues were pledged as security. This procedure was unsatisfactory for larger loans, especially if they were to be publicly issued, since they could be repudiated by the central authority as unauthorized and there was no sure way of enforcing repayment. This is not to suggest that the record of repayment was poor; on the contrary, there were few instances of repudiation; but the risk, given all the circumstances, was high and wholly unacceptable to the ordinary lender.

Marquis Tseng Chi-tse, the former Chinese minister to the Court of St James, put the position this way to Thomas Jackson, the Hongkong Bank's Chief Manager: (i) for loans up to five lacs, it is safe to lend on the basis of a departmental seal, but the Bank should advise the Tsungli Yamen of the transaction, (ii) for loans from say five to ten lacs, it would be sufficient for the loan to be made to a provincial governor or viceroy sealed in his capacity appropriate for the loan – governors might have more than one responsibility, for example, Governor of Chihli, Superintendent of Trade, member of the Board of Admiralty – provided the activity for which the loan was made had received authorization in the form of an Imperial edict, and (iii) loans over ten lacs should be specifically approved by a public edict of the Emperor, officially communicated through the Legation.[66]

Charles Addis in a memorandum dated sometime in 1886/87, while he was in

Peking as Agent, summarizes what he refers to as the opinion of Li Hung-chang. On the whole Li would appear to have agreed closely with Tseng. However Li also referred to a category of three lacs or less which could be made to a governor provided (i) a memorial had been sent and a secret edict received authorizing the *work* for which the loan was to be made – even if the edict did not refer specifically to financing by borrowing and (ii) that the loan agreement state the purpose of the loan and how repayment was to be made, that is, whether direct from the borrowing authority or from the Imperial boards concerned.[67]

The internal bureaucratic restraints went far to control Chinese borrowing in the smaller categories, and the need for Imperial sanction of the project facilitated foreign assessment of the risk. The Chinese fiscal system was capable of repaying such borrowings under these conditions, although the diplomatic consequences of default when dealing with the troublesome foreigners may have been partially responsible for the excellent repayment record.

China could still have wrecked its finances by major uncontrolled borrowing, given military necessity and the political position of certain powerful viceroys. It is here that the Imperial Maritime Customs played an important though interestingly indirect role. The Customs were, as an exception, centrally administered by Robert Hart in Peking. Hart instructed his commissioners at the Treaty Ports that, in accordance with the Imperial edict, they should not sanction the pledging of local Customs revenues for the security of loans unless these loans had been centrally authorized. This procedure safeguarded China's credit; without the authorizing edict and Hart's instructions consequent to it, an essential element in any proposed public offering, the security of the Customs revenues, became unavailable.[68] This public exposure, this very open and fairly prolonged procedure, permitted an examination of the proposals and a reconsideration of the desirability of the loan itself. But the knowledge of this procedure would itself make the provincial governor or viceroy cautious; he would tend to proceed only in accordance with the rules, and he would have to justify his negotiations with the foreigners.

Technicalities

Chinese authorities were not used to borrowing for public purposes at interest; they were used to contributions, disguised as loans or otherwise.

In the period to 1895 the Chinese as borrowers were able to demand that lenders meet their terms. Since these terms were often unusual in the London capital market sense, if they had to be explained by correspondence to shifting groups of marginally interested capitalists or to banks whose European directorate had established rules of conduct, there would be either delays or refusals. The Hongkong Bank was able to assess the position after lengthy negotiations and restate the terms; hence, as has been stated, its success.

Specifically, the Chinese Government would not at first agree to a loan being issued at a discount. This forced the lender to obtain his profit by means which were unconventional by Western standards and, from time to time, subject to criticism: (i) by setting agreed but obviously unreal exchange rates and/or (ii) by issuing the loan at a nominal interest rate lower than that obtaining in the agreement with the Chinese authorities. These devices were in lieu of and often less than the usual commission.

The Chinese Government required a guarantee that the funds would be delivered; usually they insisted on an advance, as the funds were urgently required – or became so during the usual lengthy negotiations. Since the Hongkong Bank had accepted the advice of its clearing bank, the London and County Bank, only to act as agents for the loans, it technically was issuing on commission. In fact since the advance made no provision for repayment should the public issue fail, the Hongkong Bank in making the advance had in effect taken the loan firm. This increased the risk to the Bank and had to be reflected in the interest rate or exchange rate differential.

The currency of China was on a silver basis; if the loan were denominated in a unit of account repayable in silver, the Chinese took no exchange risk. This meant, however, that for practical purposes the bulk of the public subscriptions must come from those in a silver-using area or, alternatively, the rate of interest must be high enough to cover the exchange risk as assessed by the lenders. The Hongkong Bank assessed – though not necessarily correctly – the chances of floating a silver loan in the East or its likely reception in London, and they could by reason of their strong position in the East virtually veto this means of finance.

The alternative was for China to authorize a gold loan, that is, a loan repayable in sterling or, in one instance, German marks. In this case China took the exchange risk but had the facilities of the London market and probably more favourable terms. China would not, however, send its officials to London, as other borrowing nations did, to conduct the negotiations. Banks with branches in China had, therefore, a special advantage; special missions of European-based banks had first to return to Europe and discuss their findings and their agents were difficult to control and communicate with; on the other hand, China-based concession hunters found it difficult to find a reliable executor to pick up the 'concessions' on the terms they had supposedly obtained. The Hongkong Bank with its Head Office in the East was again in a key position to act as an essential intermediary between China and Western investors and those Chinese investors who were willing to lend to their government but only through the buffer of extraterritoriality the Hongkong Bank provided.[m]

---

[m] Chinese merchants bought Imperial silver loan bonds issued by the Hongkong Bank in Shanghai and Hong Kong and used them as security against mercantile advances from the Bank.

There were other difficulties. The Chinese preferred short-term to long-term borrowing; they preferred many specific loans to one large loan; they were biased against the annuity-type repayment arrangement; and they preferred to repay annually instead of semi-annually. The foreign investor preferred large loans with semi-annual repayment; the Stock Exchange was likely to react more favourably to a loan the terms of which were comprehensible.

All this made the issue more complex and, be it noted, more expensive.

Finally, the Chinese authorities did nothing to explain the Empire's finances to the West; thus European borrowers had virtually no information on China's ability to repay. Nor, indeed, did they have any knowledge of that key factor in sovereign-risk lending, the willingness of the borrower to repay. These were additional factors increasing the cost of borrowing.

Offsetting this were (i) the flexibility of the Chinese in negotiations once the issues had been clarified; there was a willingness to change over time and in this the Hongkong Bank played an informal role, (ii) the pressures of cost when the loans increased in size, and (iii) the particular role of the Maritime Customs, a matter which will be considered below.

The lenders

Expectations and realities in China

Potential lenders to China (the Hongkong Bank excepted) generally suffered from the almost missionary, and certainly self-destructive, urge to tell the Chinese (i) what they should borrow for and (ii) how they should go about borrowing.[69] On both subjects, however, the Chinese had very firm ideas. Promoters operating in China were more flexible but could not produce the funds when the agreement, often on unusually favourable terms to the Chinese, was signed. Still others found that, even when negotiating in good faith, by the time the negotiations had been concluded the situation in Europe had changed and their principals in London or Berlin had deserted them.

The Hongkong Bank remained in Hong Kong, Foochow, Shanghai, Tientsin, Peking, and Hankow. There was an office and a Consultative Committee in London. Ewen Cameron, Thomas Jackson, François de Bovis, Alexander Leith, and even the young Charles Addis advised the Chinese Government, but at a point they stopped; they acted as instructed and they received the commission. In London the experienced David McLean attempted to carry out the Chinese Government's requirements; if he could not, he so informed Hong Kong. In 1889 he retired, to be replaced by the veteran Ewen Cameron. The Bank's agents on the China coast, indeed Chinese officials themselves, knew the Bank's capabilities in London. With the development of the Chinese Legation there, the Bank and China could work together in the world's capital market, but the principal negotiations were still conducted in China and the terms reflected the fact.

There was a development over time in the China loan operations, although this, like many generalizations, is subject to exceptions.

In the years immediately following the First Sino-British War the merchant houses made small loans to provincial authorities; then, with borrowing under Imperial control from 1868, there were larger direct loans from major hongs and even from the cautious Oriental Bank Corporation.[70] This was a period of abortive schemes put forward cold by foreign merchants for large, comprehensive loan programs at exorbitant cost. The Chinese avoided the temptation; more rational alternatives proved available, and in 1874 there was the first of the Imperial public loans, issued by the Hongkong Bank and very much designed to meet Chinese requirements.

There was criticism that even these early loans were wasting China's credit; the time had come to put China's external finances on a sound footing preparatory to major productive loans connected, hopefully, with contracts for construction. This approach also saw the beginning of national rivalries, and groups from Germany came to examine possibilities in China itself; the concession hunters were also at work with their impossible promises and vast schemes.

A more acceptable development was the concept of syndicates or other associations, for example the premature attempt in 1885 by the Deutsche Bank to interest N.M. Rothschild and the Hongkong Bank in joint operations.

The Chinese, however, were not yet committed either to railways or Western development *per se*. There were divided counsels which ranged from a policy of limited modernization for 'self-strengthening', to acceptance of Western technology consistent with retaining Chinese traditional political and ethical values (the policies of Chang Chih-tung for example), to a latent nationalism, especially among the younger merchants longest in contact with the West.

Instead, therefore, of major syndicates floating vast development loans, foreign interests had to be content with manoeuvring for position and making small loans as inducements to the Nei-wu-fu (Imperial Household), to minor departments and to provincial officials. These loans were not necessarily unproductive, but they fell short of foreign expectations and were explained to doubtful principals in terms of securing one's position in China, ensuring an opportunity to be in at the beginning of China's modernization; the small loans were made pending the 'opening of China' and the 'big loan'.

Robert Hart's early preference for the Oriental Bank Corporation has been noted (see Chapter 8); he was unsuccessful in interesting them in 'small' loans, and in any case they failed in 1884, before the Government sought larger loans. Even the larger hongs did not have the funds to commit against indefinite future expectations; in the 1880s Jardine Matheson reached an agreement with the

Hongkong Bank, the latter made funds available for relending to the Chinese, Jardine's agent in Tientsin and Peking, Alexander Michie, always claiming to be on the verge of a breakthrough, always blaming failure on the machinations of rivals, including the Hongkong Bank.

The Hongkong Bank in London

That the Hongkong Bank understood China and was ready to accommodate her was not inevitable, but given the pragmatic approach of the Bank's management it is perhaps not surprising. That the Bank could issue small silver loans on the China coast surprised no one. What was surprising, what certainly surprised Baring and Rothschild, was the ability of the Bank to handle the issue of the loans in London. The Bank's performance in London on behalf of the Chinese Government was exceptional.

When the Hongkong Bank first undertook the issue of a public China loan in 1874, David McLean, with his years of Shanghai experience, was already in London. The London Consultative Committee had not as yet been appointed, but he had access to the advice of the London and County Bank. The loan was for £627,615, still 'small' by international standards, and not all this was to be placed or subscribed for in London. By the time the Bank was ready to issue further loans they had teamed up with a broker familiar from long residence with the situation in China, Panmure Gordon of Panmure Gordon and Co., and this association was to further the Bank's capabilities in the City, so much so that they were able to compete against Baring Brothers, who had become interested in a China loan in 1885, and turn down the invitation to join a proposed consortium made by N.M. Rothschild and the Deutsche Bank the same year.[n]

Not that the Bank always correctly assessed the market; it did not. But it had sufficient resources of its own to in effect underwrite its own issues; later it would organize underwriting syndicates to minimize its risk.

As the principal agent for the Chinese authorities, the Hongkong Bank was concerned with China's credit. This necessitated at least three courses of action. First, the Bank ensured that China repaid on schedule – or appeared to do so. If China were late, the Bank made arrangements with the authorities for a temporary advance against the payment of principal and/or interest then due.[72] Secondly, the Bank acted to maintain an orderly market on issue, so there was no adverse reaction if stags unloaded or the loan was not fully subscribed. This was essential if the Chinese Government were ever again to borrow on the open

---

[n] Harry Panmure Gordon (1837–1902), educated at Harrow, Oxford, and Bonn, commanded a unit in the 'Ever Victorious Army' suppressing the Taipings, hence he knew Li Hung-chang. It is difficult to imagine a better match for the Hongkong Bank's purposes. Ewen Cameron's son, E.A. Cameron, became a partner of the firm in 1905.[71]

market – and called, as might reasonably be expected, on the Hongkong Bank to assist them.

The lending public, however, were made aware of two conditions for a secure China loan, (i) the Imperial edict and (ii) the security of the Imperial Maritime Customs. The Hongkong Bank's third task, therefore, was to ensure that these window-dressing conditions were met where the loan was of sufficient size to warrant it. In a sense, if the edict were obtained, all the resources of China were committed, as Sir Robert Hart in vain attempted to assert, but there was a feeling of added safety if the security of the Customs were specified.[73]

This is understandable. The finances of China defied simple explanation and statistical evidence was lacking. The foreign-staffed Imperial Maritime Customs, however, compiled trade statistics and the related revenues could be accurately estimated. The actual duties, however, were not collected by the foreign staff or by the Imperial Maritime Customs service; they were paid instead to the Haikwan, or Customs, banks, which were wholly Chinese institutions. Nor should the security of a loan be confused with the intended source of repayment; these were not necessarily the same. The actual advantage of Customs security lay not in the revenues paid, but in the revenues to be paid – that is, the Chinese authorities, when properly authorized, placed in the possession of the Hongkong Bank as their agents, Customs bonds which could be used, in the event of a loan default, in payment of Customs duties. This ultimate remedy was never utilized.

The security of the Customs did not, therefore, ensure prompt repayment of a loan, since the funds for this purpose might comprise a mixed package of various revenues in various proportions from several jurisdictions. In 1875 a repayment had been delayed owing to a miscalculation on the part of the Chinese authorities responsible, but, as they agreed with Alexander Leith, the Bank's Foochow Agent, to make up the deficiency without delay, the Hongkong Bank, as the servicing bank, paid out the sums due to the public without comment. The failure of Hu Kwang-yung, Tso Tsung-t'ang's representative in Shanghai, in May 1884 was preceded by difficulties with his banking interests and related complications; repayments of the 1881 Kansu Loan were delayed and in February 1884 portions of the 1878 Loan were in default. De Bovis had been sent to Peking to make representations; he was now instructed to approach Sir Harry Parkes, himself a heavy subscriber to the Hongkong Bank's China loans, to present the problem to the Tsungli Yamen.[74]

This action brought a focus on the attitude of the British Foreign Office towards the intervention of British representatives in support of private business ventures. That the edict authorizing the loans should be transmitted through the Legation, thus appearing to the uninformed investor to involve British authorities in the affair, was exceptional enough, but in June 1884, at the formal request of Thomas Jackson, Parkes intervened by approaching the Tsungli

Yamen on the matter of loan repayment. For this he was sharply criticized by Childers, the Parliamentary Under-Secretary of State and an outspoken opponent of any government entanglement in private affairs. However, J. Pauncefote, the Assistant Under-Secretary of State for Foreign Affairs and former Attorney General of Hong Kong at the time of the Bank's founding – and a large holder of Hongkong Bank shares – defended Parkes' action on the grounds that:

> Diplomatic intervention in China is a necessity in many cases where it would not be resorted to elsewhere and established no claim whatsoever on the part of the private parties interested against HMG. This arises out of the peculiar conditions of our intercourse with China, and I would strongly deprecate any restriction being placed on the existing practice.[75]

Pauncefote noted that the Hongkong Bank was acting merely as the agent of the Chinese Government to pay off the drawn bonds of the loan and that they had not received the full amount at the appointed date through the negligence of the provincial authorities. The Bank could only approach the Tsungli Yamen through the Legation. At the same time Pauncefote agreed that Parkes should be informed privately of the grounds on which his 'intervention' had been approved and that it should be suggested to him that he warn all parties on whose behalf he might take such action that it implied no obligation on the part of the British Government to pursue the matter further if the Chinese Government should repudiate their engagements.[76]

Despite the passive nature of British representation, it was enough to ensure credibility with potential investors in London. There would be criticism of the lack of diplomatic aggressiveness with the advent of German investment interests in China, but that was a separate, although not wholly unrelated problem.

Thus despite the esoteric nature of Chinese politics and finance, there was a basis for her foreign credit. To preserve this and provide her requirements was a task set itself by the Hongkong Bank; it was one which proved profitable; in 1874/75 and again in 1894/95 the income from the loans would prove particularly important, but throughout the period the loans were an important factor in the growth of the Hongkong Bank.

The Hongkong Bank's public China loans (Table 14.2)

During the period 1874 when the first public loan was signed to 1895 at the end of the Sino-Japanese War, the Hongkong and Shanghai Banking Corporation issued loans with a value at the rate of the day of some £12 million equivalent, approximately 35% of which were issued in silver and the balance in sterling. An additional £4 million, of which half was raised to finance the Sino-Japanese War,

Table 14.2 The Hongkong and Shanghai Banking Corporation
China: public loans, 1874–1895

(in millions)

	(i)	(ii)	(iii) Ts	(iv) Ts	(iv) $	(v) £	(vi)		(vii)	(viii)
I. Formosa Crisis										
Foochow Loan	1874									
1st tranche	1875					0.300	8%	95		a
2nd tranche	1875					0.275	8%	99		
Total		g	2.00^m		2.4	0.628^s			10	
II. Northwest Campaigns										
Kansu Loan	1877	g^m	5.00^n	5.6^q		1.604	8%	98	7	b
Kansu Loan	1878	s	1.75^n	1.9^q		[0.490]	8%	100	5.3	c
Kansu Loan	1881	s	4.00^o	4.4^q		[1.115]	8%	103¾	5.8	d
III. Sino-French War										
'A' and 'B'	1884	s	2.00^p		2.8	[0.513]	8%	100	3/6^u	c
'C' Loan	1884	s	1.14^p		1.6	[0.277]	8%	100	8	c
Foochow Loan	1885	g	[4.00]^q	–		1.000	7%	98	10	h
Canton Loan^k	1885	g	–	–		0.505	7%	98	10	c
6% Loan	1885	g	[3.00]^o			0.757	6%	98	10	c
IV. China Merchants' Steam Navigation Co.										
Loan	1885	g	[1.29]^q	–		0.300	7%	105	10	e
V. Kwangtung Authorities (for Peking)										
'D' Loan	1886	s	0.30^p		0.4	[0.061]	7%	105	9.7	d
'E' Loan	1886	s	0.70^r	0.8^q		[0.069]	7%	105	30.5	g
VI. Yellow River Conservancy										
'F' Loan	1888	s	1.00^r	1.1^q		[0.229]	–^{v}		5	n.a.
VII. Sino-Japanese War										
7% Silver Loan	1894	s	10.00^r	10.9^q		[1.635]	7%	100^t	20	f
6% Gold Loan	1895	g	–	–		3.000	6%	96½	20	f

548

Source: D.J.S. King, 'China's early loans, 1874–1895', Group Archives.

Table 14.2.

Column headings

(i) year of issue, (ii) gold or silver, (iii) nominal amount in taels millions, (iv) dollar or Shanghai tael equivalent in millions, (v) sterling or (sterling equivalent) in millions, (vi) nominal rate of interest and price of issue to the public, (vii) period of loan in years, (viii) source of profit.

Note: equivalent values are in [ ]. Rates of exchange are as in agreements; where equivalents are not stated in the agreements, the nearest Hongkong Bank semi-annual rate is used for consistency.

Notes in the Table

Sources of profit:

a. Exchange rate differential between that at which issued and the actual rate of the day.

b. Differential between rate of interest paid by the Chinese to the Bank and the rate paid by the Bank to the public, plus source 'a'.

c. Interest differential.

d. Premium at issue and interest differential.

e. Commission and exchange differential.

f. Commission only.

g. Premium on issue and commission.

h. There was a loss on issue due to Bank paying Chinese 100 firm but issuing loan to public at 98.

Other:

k Actually issued with the above Foochow Loan as series B.

l A silver loan to the Chinese, gold to the public; exchange guaranteed for a 5% commission by Telge and Co.

m Yang-p'ing Taels.

n Haikwan Taels.

o Kansu taels: 4 million = ShTs4.384m.

p Canton taels.

q Shanghai taels.

r Kuping (or Treasury) taels: 700,000 = ShTs767,200; 1m = ShTs1.096m.

s Including $52,000 not publicly issued.

t Advertised at 98 but effectively at 100 due to arbitrary exchange and interest calculations.

u 'A' Loan, 3 years; 'B' Loan 6 years, each for Ts1 million.

v Not formally issued to the public.

was issued by other banks. Although smaller loans were raised privately for minor economic development projects, including mines and railways, China's major foreign borrowing was for military purposes, defence, civil war, and foreign war.

An apparent exception was the loan to the China Merchants' Steam Navigation Company (CMSNCo), a company to which the Bank was already extending credit in the form of overdrafts. The purpose to which these last mentioned funds were put appears, however, to have been the refunding of previous foreign borrowings, a refunding necessitated in turn by the shortage of working capital consequent on the losses by private investors in 1883, Hsü Jun's borrowing for personal purposes from the CMSNCo of which he was a director, and the inability of Government to support the company or replace needed funds during the Sino-French War.[77]

The Hongkong Bank's 'D' and 'E' Loans to the Kwangtung authorities, which were Imperially sanctioned and denominated in Kuping (or Treasury) taels, were presumably intended for use by the Imperial Household department (Nei-wu-fu), probably for the finance of the Kaiping mines.

In 1895 Sir Robert Hart wrote to Campbell, his London Office manager, to urge Ewen Cameron that the loan agreements should be kept simple and that he should 'confine himself to the indispensable requirements, avoiding what is sentimental, unnecessary or merely technical'.[78] It was a hopeless wish, and it is difficult to write of the Bank's experience in the handling of loans in any summary way. Each loan had its different problem; each was accordingly handled in a distinctive way. However, from the viewpoint of the Hongkong Bank's history, the essential point is that the Bank was able to continue its role as interface although confronting continually changing requirements in both China and London against a background, both political and financial, of increasing complexity.

There is no record of how the day-to-day negotiations were conducted, but it is clear that the Bank's compradore was often involved and that the Chinese used '*wei-yuan*' or agents, of whom Hu Kwang-yung and his 'Shanghai Forwarding Office' would have been a particularly institutionalized example.[79] As suggested above, this procedure would explain how complex negotiations could be accomplished given the language qualifications of the principals and the social situation in the Treaty Ports at the time.

That the compradore was an intermediary not only between the Bank and the Chinese business and banking community but also with the world of officials is evidenced in a letter from the Bank's compradore Lo Hok Pang to Jackson in 1886. This letter informed Jackson that the Governor of Kwangtung had received an Imperial edict, given in response to the representation of the Hu-pu (Board of Revenue) in answer to a petition from the Viceroy of the Liang Kwang provinces and dated on the 13th day of the 6th moon in the 12th year of the Kwang-Hsu Emperor, authorizing Jackson to be designated an official of the 3rd rank with a new blue button. 'At first,' he added in a postscript, 'it was proposed to give you 4th rank but through my exertion and mediation I now obtained for you a third rank button which is the position of a provincial judge.'[80]

Lo Hok Pang was himself of the rank of *tao-t'ai*. Chinese merchants purchased their rank, thereby facilitating their communication with the officials, and cooperative foreigners were, in the long tradition of 'managing the barbarians', encouraged in their service to the Empire by the award of rank from the Emperor of the Middle Kingdom.

The Hongkong Bank has been criticized for (i) incorporating unrealistic exchange rates in the loan agreements and (ii) issuing to the public at a nominal interest rate different from that which it received from the Chinese authorities. The need to proceed in this way arose from the particular demands of the Chinese and these were alternative methods of obtaining the commission which was normally included in the discount at which the funds were paid over to the borrower. Both parties were aware of the procedure and its consequences: the Chinese were enabled to receive the loan at par and the Hongkong Bank to obtain a return for the risks and expenses involved. A study of the terms for loans listed in Table 14.2 would confirm that, as both sides became more familiar with normal procedures, these peculiarities were minimized. The 1895 loans, for example, were issued to the public at a discount and a sum less than the nominal amount was paid to the Chinese, the Bank being remunerated by a commission deducted up-front.

The Chinese Government preferred a silver loan, but the decision to issue in gold or silver depended (i) on lenders' expectations on the course of exchange and (ii) on expectations as to the willingness of the several markets to accept any China loan and, if so, to what extent and in what currency. The Eastern capital markets had a limited capacity; this capacity might be increased and supplemented, however, if the loan, even if issued in the East were denominated in sterling. The CMSNCo's loan, for example, was issued in the East but denominated in sterling.

The Chinese authorities might be unwilling to accept an exchange risk and yet a loan might be too large for the East; thus the 1877 Kansu Loan was issued by the Hongkong Bank in gold in London but the exchange risk was underwritten at 5% commission by the German firm of Telge and Co. in Shanghai. During the Sino-Japanese War there was general concern for the fate of silver, and the Chinese could borrow in gold on considerably better terms; they chose, however, given their preference for fixed amounts, to borrow as much as the market could absorb in silver.

The 1874 Foochow Loan was a gold loan denominated in sterling, but the first tranche (or 'portion') was issued in Shanghai and Hong Kong, with allotments made from the Hong Kong quota to friends in London. When loans were actually issued in London, the Hongkong Bank had to ensure proper listing with the Stock Exchange, select an appropriate broker, Panmure Gordon and Co., and make related decisions on underwriting and syndication. Although certain of these matters are minuted by the Board in Hong Kong, there is no consistent pattern; the experienced London managers must have played a major role, but to what extent they brought in the London Consultative Committee as a committee is not recorded.

As China developed a sound record, in part due, as previously noted, to the precautions taken by the Hongkong Bank, China's credit rating had improved. The Bank had ensured on time repayment of interest and principal to the public and had managed the market so that bonds remained at issue price or above. These developments were offset in the market, however, by the risks created by fluctuations in exchange, the negative impact caused by the non-productive purposes of the loans, and finally by the extent of China's borrowings during the Sino-Japanese War (see Table 14.3). Although certain of the earlier smaller loans were in fact secured by revenues other than those of the Maritime Customs, later agreements become more specific and a clause establishing priority of repayment in the event of a shortfall was introduced.

The 6% 1895 Gold Loan for £3 million was the largest the Hongkong Bank had attempted to issue and China's circumstances at the time were not favourable. The Bank was therefore in a strong position to insist on terms which would be well-received on the London market, including explicit statements relative to the ranking of the loan in connection with the security of the Customs revenues. At first the Bank urged that China agree not to borrow again in London for a period of twelve months, but on Hart's objection this requirement was withdrawn. The expectation of China's defeat and consequent need to borrow to meet anticipated indemnity demands would result in the need to approach the London market again; the Bank was concerned that public anticipation of such events would depress the price of the current issues and cause the Bank additional problems.

Borrowing in connection with the Sino-Japanese War had for a short time in 1894 been centralized with Sir Robert Hart, and he had approached the Bank. Unfortunately the Bank decided it could not float the full £5 million requested. The Chinese Government withdrew its confidence in Hart and reverted to *ad hoc* measures.

In fact, as already suggested, the Bank faced problems. With its 7% Silver Loan it had to deliver silver to Tientsin under threat that it might be seized as contraband of war. The problems in London were, perhaps, less dramatic, but they were significant. Faced with resistance in the market, the Bank agreed, with the reluctant permission of the directors who were concerned at the tie-up of funds, that, in the event of non-subscription, it would take up £150,000 of the

Table 14.3 *Chinese loan financing during the Sino-Japanese War, 1894–1895*

Loan:	Manager:	Amount in £:
Chinese Domestic Loan		unlimited
Ch. Imp. Gov. 7% Silver Loan	Hongkong Bank	(1,635,000)
Ch. Imp. Gov. 6% Sterling Loan	Hongkong Bank	3,000,000
6% 'German' Loan	National Bank für	
	Deutschland	1,000,000
6% 'Cassel' Loan	Chartered Bank	1,000,000

loan at 97 (issue price was 96½); the Bank's brokers, Panmure Gordon and Co., agreed to take £100,000. The public in fact subscribed to only £1,030,000 and the balance had to be taken up by the underwriters and the Bank. To regain the use of its funds, the Bank organized a syndicate to take a portion of its holdings at 95½, and by May of 1895 the price had risen to 103¼.

The Bank had also offered the shares at its branch in Hamburg and through Hope and Co. in Amsterdam. Its own profit was a straight 2% commission or £60,000, against which must be noted the loss incurred in selling to the syndicate.

But the complexity of *ad hoc* arrangements which characterized the first Bank issues of Imperial Chinese Government loans had been replaced by a capability of dealing on behalf of that government on the London market, even at the most unfavourable of times. This led to two developments: (i) the eventual support by the Foreign Office of the Hongkong Bank in the post 1895 period and (ii) the self-confidence of the Bank which made it extremely reluctant to operate with other British financial institutions on a basis of equality, at least until virtually required to do so as the price of further official support.

The Hongkong Bank, Jardine Matheson, and Baring

In 1874 the Hongkong Bank attempted to include a clause in its loan agreement with the Foochow authorities which would have required the Chinese to give the Bank priority in any future loan, with the hope of being appointed the Government's agent in Europe. These were early dreams shared by the Oriental Bank Corporation and by many of the merchant taipans – A.F. Heard, for example; such proposals were in general discussion. The Chinese, however, never lost control and kept their options, for the most part, open.

The Bank achieved virtually the same position by meeting China's requirements in open competition. That is to say, the Hongkong Bank came to dominate the loan market by its greater 'understanding' of China's real requirements and its superior ability to carry them out. Having achieved the dominant position, the Bank was reluctant to yield any of its gains. Indeed, when the loans were small and prospects for modernization slight, the great private banks in London showed little effective interest. Baring's when approached on behalf of Russell and Co. in 1874, simply suggested that it was a matter for 'one of the local banks in China'.[81]

In 1885, however, the Hongkong Bank and Baring's found themselves in competition. Jardine Matheson through Alexander Michie in Peking had made their own arrangements for a £1.5 million loan to a central government department known as the 'Peking Field Force' (*Shen-chi-ying*). As Jardine's considered this an industrial loan, it did not necessarily come within the informal agreement between Jardine's and the Bank's Shanghai Manager relating to financial loans, but end-use was hard to control and the loan was probably financial. In any case Jardine's expected to interest their London friends, Matheson and Co., in the financing. When the latter proved not interested, Jardine's turned not to the Hongkong Bank as suggested by Matheson's but first to the Chartered Bank where James Whittall, the Jardine partner who had long before opposed the formation of the Hongkong Bank, was a director; when that bank also proved uninterested, Jardine's approached Baring's.

Baring's were aware that the Hongkong Bank was also involved in negotiations for an issue of the London market, the 6% Gold Loan of 1885 for £757,000 on behalf of the Viceroy of the Liang Kwang provinces, and suggested that the Bank combine its loan with Jardine's under an extraordinary arrangement which would have left the Bank's role unpublicized. The developments in this surprising story are related below.

On June 11, 1885, Baring Bros wrote to Matheson's noting that the Hongkong Bank intended to issue its loan at once and suggested that, if possible, they should cooperate with the Bank to avoid opposition.[82] They also noted that they had already arranged to transfer the proceeds of the Jardine Matheson loan through the Hongkong Bank. The next day David McLean called at Matheson's at the request of Ewen Cameron, then Shanghai Manager, to see if some arrangement could be reached by which the Hongkong Bank could issue the Jardine loan.[83] He left with the understanding that nothing could be done.

However that afternoon Matheson sent for him to meet with Baring who proposed that the Hongkong Bank allow Baring's to issue the Bank's loan along with Jardine's, and without mention of the Hongkong Bank's name. In exchange Baring's offered to issue the Bank's loan without commission.

This would have reduced the Hongkong Bank to a mere agent of a London merchant bank and was totally unacceptable. McLean described it to Jackson as an attempt to supplant the Hongkong Bank in the China loan business. At the same time he did not feel competent to reject the offer (which would have saved the Bank the expenses of the issue) without referring it to Jackson.

From this point McLean was in a race to make sure that Baring's could not issue the Jardine loan before the Hongkong Bank was ready with its own. If the two loans were issued together, McLean was confident that the Bank's regular customers would buy bonds of the Hongkong Bank loan in preference to the one issued by Baring's.

Baring's was willing to delay the issue of its loan until Jackson responded to their proposal, presumably because they believed that the Hongkong Bank would not be ready to issue its loan for some time. This delay in fact allowed the Bank time to forward to London the remaining information required for its prospectus.

The relationship of the Hongkong Bank with Jardine Matheson was always close but with the ever-present merchant banking aspirations of the latter creating an atmosphere of tension in a context of potential conflict of interest. McLean pointed out that it seemed extraordinary that William Keswick should sit on the Board of Directors of the Hongkong Bank – receiving privileged information about the Bank's loan negotiations (if in fact he did) – and then step in and arrange a loan without offering to allow the Bank to issue it. He had heard that Jardine's were paying Baring's a 2% commission (covering all expenses, including advertising, brokerage, etc.), and he felt the Bank would have been glad to bring out the Jardine loan at that price. He suspected Jardine's hoped to oust the Bank from the China loan business.

However, the rivalry was never absolute. The Hongkong Bank was willing to facilitate the transfer of the proceeds of the Baring's loan to China. And right until the end there was a chance that some more equitable overall arrangement could be reached.

On June 16 McLean received Jackson's reply rejecting Baring's one-sided proposal. He passed the information on to Matheson's and was told that Matheson's would wire to let him know what Baring's had decided. McLean further told Matheson's that the Bank was ready to issue its loan at a moment's notice; he reported to Jackson that Baring's and Matheson's had thought the Bank was not ready.

The first intimation he had that Baring's had decided to issue the Jardine loan came a week later when a broker showed him a copy of their prospectus at 2:15 p.m. Matheson did not inform him of Baring's decision till 4 p.m., by which time however McLean was already preparing to mail the Bank's prospectus and by that evening's post 5,000 copies were sent out. The envelopes had all been addressed the week before.

Both loans were in the event heavily oversubscribed and Baring's closed its subscription book before the date in its prospectus. The *Bullionist* attributed the success of the issues partly to the lack of good securities offering yields of 5 to 6% and to the low cost of money.[84] This does not imply however that the race to bring out the loans together was unnecessary. In addition to the matter of prestige, many of the applications for bonds were made by so-called 'stags', who had no intention of holding the bonds, but who anticipated that the bonds would soon be at a premium and hoped to sell them at a profit. It was in the interests of the Bank to see that it could secure for its loan as many bona-fide subscribers as possible, thus minimizing the possibility of 'dumping' should the market for the loan weaken.

National consortiums and the Hongkong Bank

The ability of the Hongkong Bank to handle China's interests was limited by the very obvious fact that it was a private corporation acting primarily in the interests of shareholders; its commercial nature also restricted its size. Nevertheless its success suggested to visionary promoters China's need for a national bank, perhaps along the lines much earlier proposed by Robert Montgomery Martin and his Imperial Bank of China (1864/65) or by the successful Imperial Bank of Persia.[85]

In 1887 'Count Eugene de Mitkiewicz', actually the emigrant son of a Polish postmaster and a convicted swindler, arrived from the United States with promises of railway finance, development projects, and a central bank, which were in whole or in part believed.[86] Many foreigners had held high expectations relative to China's post-Sino-French War development plans; they had been frustrated and the American schemes were tentatively welcomed by some not too closely connected with the Hongkong Bank. Alexander Michie wrote in his *Chinese Times* (Tientsin) that the directors of the Hongkong Bank would:

. . . see with pleasure and not with jealousy the establishment of a properly conducted national bank of China. Such an institution they hold would work in harmony with and would be beneficial to their own corporation without competition between the two or clashing of interests.[87]

This may have been inspired by Ewen Cameron's sympathetic reaction as communicated to Addis, then in Tientsin, who was friendly with Michie.[88] And although Michie, who still harboured resentment against the Bank, was possibly writing tongue-in-cheek, he foreshadowed a problem, the creation of 'national' banks which the Hongkong Bank and the traditional exchange banks were to face in India, Siam, the Philippines – and, post-World War II, in all territories with the striking exception of Hong Kong.

The multi-million dollar schemes of the 'Count', despite support from the Chinese officials who approved the low interest rates promised on the non-existing funds, came to nothing; Mitkiewicz was unable even to raise the $10,000 necessary to keep his alleged concessions alive. The prospects of an American take-over of China development were thought to be sufficiently real during the period of promotion, however, to affect the Bank's share prices and to alert McLean to make investigations in London.

Table 14.4 *China: public loans managed by foreign banks other than HSBC,*
1874–1895

Title	Manager	Amount millions	£ millions	Years	Issued to public
1885					
(8%) Dollar Loan	Chartered Bank	Canton Ts 1	$(0.25)^a$	3	100
CIG 6% Loan	Baring Brothers	(Haikwan Ts 5.5)	1.50	10	98
1887					
CIG 5½% Loan	Warschauer Group	Marks 5	(0.25)	15	–
1894/95					
6% German Loan	National Bank für Deutschland	(HkTs 6.1)	1.00	20	104½
CIG 6% Gold Loan	Ernest Cassel	(HkTs 6.1)	1.00	20	106
		Total	3.90		

Notes:
[a] Since the loan was issued to the public in May, the exchange rate on 30 June 1885
has been adopted for conversion.
CIG Chinese Imperial Government
( ) = equivalent to the face value of the loan in the currency named.

The Bank's real competition in terms of relatively sound schemes in realistic
terms would come, in McLean's view, from the established firm of
N.M. Rothschild and Sons in London and their associates in Paris and
Frankfurt.[89] He was partially correct although competition came first from other
financial groups. In 1887, for example, the Warschauer Group, of which Jacob
S.H. Stern and the Berliner Handels-Gesellschaft were members, concluded a
China loan for 5 million Marks (= $1.6 million), and Maximilian von Brandt, the
German Minister in Peking, had been actively encouraging German participa-
tion in Chinese development through appeals to the Deutsche Bank and the
Disconto-Gesellschaft (DG). A list of China's public loans, other than those
managed by the Hongkong Bank, is found in Table 14.4.

Believing that the Hongkong Bank, although able to handle small issues on the
London market, would need to join with others for large development loans,
Lord Rothschild attempted to bring together the Germans under Adolph von
Hansemann of the DG and the Hongkong Bank into a syndicate to be presided
over by Rothschild's in association, perhaps, with Rothschild frères in Paris. The
assumption of these negotiations was that the Chinese wished to borrow and

would, therefore, have to conform to the requirements of the European markets.

Rothschild assumed that the Germans were about to be successful in loan and railway concession negotiations and wished to secure part of the business for British interests in London; the Germans wished to share in the prestige the Hongkong Bank had built up over the years with the Chinese authorities and in any case needed the London market.

On all counts the great financier proved wrong, and the proposals, which would prove acceptable by 1895, were premature. The Hongkong Bank had no incentive to join a syndicate.

McLean and the Hongkong Bank directors did not suppose German groups would be able to manage a major loan nor did they fear German competition. Thus, despite the leadership of Rothschild and the approaches of Hermann Wallich of the Deutsche Bank and von Hansemann of the DG, McLean took a cautious approach, referred back to Hong Kong, and was instructed that the Bank were interested only if they took the lead in all the negotiations and participated to the extent of 50%. The German proposal had been one-third each for the Bank, the German Group, and Rothschilds. The Bank's demands were unacceptable to both the Germans and the Rothschilds.[90]

In consequence negotiations were broken off, and the Germans began a series of missions and discussions which led in 1889 to the founding of the Deutsche-Asiatische Bank with head office in Shanghai and the Konsortium für Asiatische Geschäfte. With the former the Hongkong Bank established a varying relationship in the period from 1895 to 1917 when China entered the Great War.

The Hongkong Bank acted purely as a commercial private-sector institution. The British Foreign Office was in principle anxious to avoid appearing to support specific companies or become involved in their transactions. British officials in the East were anxious to avoid intervention of any kind at any level. This was tempered in China by the need to act as a 'post office', forwarding communications between the Tsungli Yamen and the Bank; at the same time London was warning the Peking Legation of its concern that China might become enmeshed in high-interest, non-productive loans, eventually borrowing to repay previous loans until there was financial collapse – 'another Constantinople' was one comparison.

Nevertheless, as already stated, the British diplomatic authorities did find themselves involved by the very fact of acting as a channel of communications, more or less narrowly defined according to the predelictions of the British minister. The peculiar circumstances of China forced this minimal participation, but the basic policy remained one described as 'holding (or 'keeping') the ring'. The more active involvement of the German representatives was seen by the Foreign Office (but not by the British press) as counterproductive.

The Hongkong Bank served the Chinese authorities; it acted in the interests of its constituents and shareholders. Except by equally business-like criteria, as when handling British and Hong Kong Government funds, the Bank did not take action primarily motivated by concern for the policy or interests of the United Kingdom; it was not, in fact, ever pressured to do so. The events of 1895–1920 require this statement here.

The British Government recognized that the Bank was British and should be encouraged; it also recognized that it was managed by those with considerable expertise and should be consulted. But the consequent relations were very carefully defined and monitored – almost one might say with suspicion – by the Colonial Office, the Treasury, and the Foreign Office.

Miscellaneous loans and basic principles

In all this discussion of high finance there is the danger of forgetting certain basic principles. The Hongkong and Shanghai Banking Corporation was basically an exchange bank. In strict business terms the development of China promised profits to the Bank from three sources: (i) commissions on loans which the Bank introduced, (ii) fees for servicing the loans, and use of funds deposited relative to loan servicing, and (iii) income from the finance of the resulting trade. Of these three, the last mentioned, being continuous and certain (if prevailing opinion proved correct), was the more important. From this it followed that there were limits to the Bank's willingness to advance funds for minor development projects; the Bank would assist in issuing a public loan and advance funds temporarily against its success, but the lock-up of funds was opposed to sound exchange banking principles.

From this it followed that the Hongkong Bank was interested in finance for its own sake. Although it is correct to note that representatives of the Far East's leading hongs, who were in turn agents for a wide range of suppliers and manufacturers, were represented on the Board, the Bank had matured. It would no longer be a source of finance for industrial schemes sponsored by directors because they were directors. The diffusion of ownership prevented pressure on the basis of shareholdings; the Bank would serve the financial requirements of its constituents, but on a basis the Bank's management itself would determine.

These positions and attitudes differentiated the Hongkong Bank from the German and French financial institutions. Business connections or a 'national interest' imposed upon them required their financing a project mainly to secure business for Home industries rather than on the basis of the banking merits or the financial aspects of the project itself. The Hongkong Bank would attempt to monopolize the financial aspects of a total operation, but, preferring a separation of finance and the details of the project, it would be willing to cooperate with others for this purpose.

This enabled the Hongkong Bank to finance international trade in a later period of growing national rivalries. It also made it possible for the Bank to finance trade and development projects through the would-be supplier/manager, Jardine, Matheson and Co. for example.

The loans issued through the Hongkong Bank (see Table 14.2) were, as has been said, for the most part advanced for admittedly unproductive purposes. The hope throughout was that at some point China would begin the development process and that it would require heavy financing. The Hongkong Bank was interested to position itself to undertake the task; Jardine, Matheson and Co. were, for example, anxious to obtain the contracts for the actual construction work involved. They too were anxious to be in position.

During the 1880s, probably from 1881, the Hongkong Bank and Jardine's were operating in the North under an understanding which never, apparently, came before the Board of Directors. Ewen Cameron and J.J. Keswick agreed that they would not compete. This requires clarification since it may not be immediately clear how a bank and a mercantile agency house would compete. Jardine's had never completely abandoned their banking aspirations – although Matheson and Co. would at times seem to have been reluctant to indulge them. The Bank and Jardine's did find themselves competing on loans, since the Bank would not tie the borrower to any conditions, thus depriving Jardine Matheson of the leverage they required to obtain the contracts for supplies and management which alone made the transaction worthwhile for them. If Jardine's could obtain the funds from the Bank, it could make small loans, gain goodwill, and eventually make the industrial loan which would include provision of materials through Jardine's agency.

The Bank/Jardine understanding therefore involved the non-intervention of the Bank in small loans to government departments, especially in the Tientsin-Peking area. Instead the Bank would finance Jardine's requirements at 7% (as opposed to the usual 6%). Jardine's would, through its agent Alexander Michie and subsequently J. Spence and H. Mandl, specialize in contacts with the Nei-wu-fu and other government departments on the assumption that this would position them when, for example, railway projects were promoted. The Hongkong Bank's representatives in the North would, in the normal course of business, facilitate Jardine's operations while being free to negotiate its own major financial operations.

This dichotomy of interests is perhaps seen in its clearest form in the establishment in 1889 of the Trust and Loan Co. of China, Japan and the Straits. The China Trust was not seen by the Hongkong Bank as a competitor – once it had agreed not to engage in exchange operations. Indeed, it was promoted, if not by, then through the Bank and the two were seen as complementary. The fate of this venture confirmed the wisdom of the Hongkong Bank's overall approach to banking.

When the Trust or its successor bank failed to achieve its purposes and devolved into a competitor exchange bank, the Hongkong Bank naturally withdrew its cooperation. The need to join finance with long-term development projects, however, remained. The precedent was found in the Cameron/Keswick understanding which was in a sense institutionalized when in 1898 Jardine, Matheson and Co. and the Hongkong and Shanghai Banking Corporation promoted the formation of the British and Chinese Corporation, a subject for consideration in Volume II.

The Cameron/Keswick understanding, although based on sound theoretical distinctions, was difficult to enforce, especially when it had not been formally sanctioned. The Chinese naturally objected to being confronted with collusion and may have purposely led the local representatives, Hillier and Michie, to suppose that the understanding was not being faithfully pursued. So frequent were Michie's complaints to Shanghai and so frequent were Cameron's denials that Keswick considered the complaints as being just 'one of (Michie's) hobbies', and at another time added that he could not 'conceive how Michie allows himself to get carried away with the haphazard gossip he gets from the Chinese entourage in any matter in which he can suspect the Hongkong Bank to be interested ever so remotely. Michie cannot help believing the very worst with regard to other institutions.'[91]

Nevertheless there were problems. First, the Hongkong Bank, realizing that Jardine's would pass on the Bank-supplied funds at a high rate of interest, itself charged what Keswick referred to as a 'very full rate'; secondly, the Bank was not always able to provide Jardine's sudden requirements for sycee to meet loan commitments, and its normal charges for shipment were a subject of dispute; but, thirdly, there was one instance where the Chinese may well have outsmarted Jardine's efforts to gain administrative control of the Kaiping mines by borrowing funds from the Hongkong Bank through the Canton 'Hoppo' or Customs Superintendent – the so-called 'E' Loan.[92]

Aside from the Bank's relations with Jardine's in the North, the Bank's special relationship with Li Hung-chang must have been important – as witness the statement at the head of this section. The Tientsin Manager had authority to permit overdrafts up to Ts300,000 against Li's official seal, and the Chinese companies sponsored by Li did a major part of their banking business with the Hongkong Bank. During the period 1889–1891 there were many proposals, including the finance of railway construction, which proved abortive.[93] There were, nevertheless, other business relations with the Viceroy, but it is not always clear which of the many proposals were actually sanctioned and, if sanctioned, actually carried through.

It is certain, however, that the Hongkong Bank entertained Li Hung-chang on his London visit in 1896. It is almost equally certain that, despite Board disapproval, which had come too late, the Tientsin branch advanced Ts1 million for five years in 1891 for the construction of cotton mills against security inadequate to permit a public issue. A loan of Ts150,000 had already been approved in 1890 for the Tientsin Arsenal and there were additional advances to finance railway construction (see Volume II).

The Hongkong Bank was sympathetic to the cause of modernization in China, but their main role in 1874–1895 was to supply funds for non-productive purposes at China's insistence. The success of the Bank was due both to its willingness to meet the requirements of its principal customer and its awareness of the limitations of commercial and exchange banking in the British tradition.

The Bank kept clear of major concessionary schemes. On the financial side, other than a flexible understanding with Jardine Matheson, the Bank avoided entangling alliances and kept itself independent of the great private banking houses in the City.

Nevertheless, as the Bank's poorly documented relationship with Li Hung-chang confirms, its resources were available to finance legitimate schemes within the limitations set by the Board's proper concern over the 'lock-up' of funds. The Bank channelled funds through the compradores, the native banking system, and the great trading hongs to facilitate both trade and production; undoubtedly some of these funds were used for fixed construction, but there are no figures. Certainly the Bank showed a flexibility which was evidence that its Board and management, whatever their individual lack of knowledge of the language, the social customs, or the Confucian classics might be, 'understood China'.

All this would place the Bank in a strong position when the world of China changed. The double impact of the defeat by Japan and the chaos rendered by the Boxers would change basic relationships, but the Hongkong Bank stood by its principles and remained prepared to play a constructive role in a China of political weakness and growing nationalism though the former was always offset by China's consistently tenacious bargaining ability.

15

HONGKONG BANKERS IN THE AGE OF JACKSON

If you get into the Hongkong Bank, you will be very lucky. It is about the best institution in the East.

George Addis, Chartered Mercantile Bank, 1880

SIR THOMAS JACKSON, BART, KCMG (1841–1915)

The genius of Thomas Jackson lay in his combination of talents. He combined a brilliance in foreign exchange and silver dealings with an ability to inspire men and win their loyalty. As Sir Newton J. Stabb (Chief Manager 1910–1920) expressed it on Jackson's death, 'It was he who welded the Staff into "a service", and so long as he was at the helm – there was always a fine esprit de corps among the men.'[1]

Jackson as legend

Here was the making of a legend – Lucky Jackson, who turned the Bank around in 1876 and returned, Arthur-like, whenever the Bank needed him to turn it around once again. There was old 'TJ', whom juniors revered and contemporaries admired. After he left Hong Kong, his successor's performance was measured against that of an idealized Jackson; staff morale was compared with that which supposedly existed in the golden days of the Bank's youth and Jackson's management. When something unfortunate occurred – as was bound to happen, a junior was misassigned, another was refused permission to marry or treated with supposed lack of consideration, a senior was not given sufficient support in a crisis – his colleagues looked back to a past when TJ was Chief Manager and the Bank was one great family.

Jackson had become a legend even before he left Hong Kong in 1902. Not all the staff knew him intimately or had been directly influenced by his personality. The closeness which had developed in the early 1880s could not be continued, even by the Eastern staff of 1900. He had become a symbol of the Bank's success. Then for London juniors in the early years of this century he was, like the retired headmaster, 'great' for reasons unknown – and every year at the annual dinner he sang 'The Wearin' o' the Green'.

563

Jackson and the Bank as 'family'
Yet it is true, under Jackson's management the Bank had prospered greatly; under Jackson's leadership and with his example there had developed a spirit, a morality of service, and a pride in an institution which he came to personify in his lifetime. The legend was a reality; of all the Bank's Chief Managers only Sir Arthur Morse (1941–1952) can claim to share with Jackson the fact of having become a legend not only in his own lifetime but also while still on active duty.

The Bank never really lost that feeling of family which Jackson created, and Charles Addis, with his twelve brothers and sisters and his thirteen children – and others like him (only with smaller figures) – would have understood the complexity of the concept 'family'. Paternalism was not an unacceptable concept *per se*. The resulting personal attention could however be erratic. For example there was a clearly stated rule – 'no one with less than ten years in the East will be permitted to marry' – but this was not always systematically enforced. There were apparently *ad hoc* decisions which permitted three to marry but forbade a fourth. When resignations occur there are gratuities, but the amounts, viewed from this distance and with the information available, defy rationalization. Staff schemes are carefully enacted and then, when the Bank is in crisis, the family are required to make sacrifices.

And yet the overall record is difficult to fault. Jackson set an example in commercial morality, not only to his staff but to the community, including, one should add, certain of the directors. His devotion to the Hongkong Bank was noted and accepted; it set the standard. When he recommended a bonus for the staff, the directors knew they had earned it, the shareholders applauded the award.

As for his profit-sharing contract of service and the gratuities bestowed on him by the Board of Directors on his two retirements, 1886 and 1902, these were an indirect comment on his integrity. The Board had decreed with the departure of Victor Kresser that Chief Managers should not engage in outside ventures; Jackson did not. Indeed, knowing that even legitimate personal activities on the market would be noted, he bought in concert with McLean and Burnett, the London Accountant (usually under Burnett's name), and there must have been insider knowledge. Later, in the absence of nominee companies, he appears to have curtailed his activities and took little advantage of his financial skills to forward his own fortune. The Board and with them the shareholders took note.

Memories of Jackson
Writing at the age of 90, A.M. Townsend recalled the first encounter with Jackson in Yokohama. This story has been told in Chapter 7.[2]

The immediately favourable response to Jackson's personality is similarly found in the correspondence and diaries of Charles Addis, who was, quite frankly, his disciple. 'Only a good man can be a good banker. Any mean or dirty trick is not less fatal to business than to a man's private character.'³ Sir Thomas Jackson himself summarized his work at the First Annual Dinner of the Bank in 1908:

I do claim for the Hongkong Bank that in the past our ideals have been high. We have tried with all our might to ennoble the art of banking. I have tried always, and I have succeeded, I think, in making my principal friends among the junior members of the staff. Rubbing the old file against the young flints brings out the best qualities of both and provides a fire of intellect which has been gratifying to us all.⁴

By the time Jackson retired from the East in 1902, the Hongkong Bank was the financial power behind what has been referred to as Britain's 'informal Empire' in the East; Jackson had been knighted in 1899 for services to British commerce in the East; he was now made a baronet. If some, including Jackson himself, considered these honours were really for the Bank, it was but a quibble; he was responsible for the Bank.

Unfortunately, the major part of the material concerning him which has survived – outside the formal official letters in the Public Record Office – consists of letters of congratulations for this or that award, speeches and addresses upon public occasions, and obituaries. None of these provide a balanced picture.

Even with the limited sources an image does emerge.

He had a temper. This is attested to by Addis – 'Fiery, if you like, but I don't believe in a man who has not got a temper.'⁵ His daughter recalls that he once came to meet their ship on arrival in Hong Kong. A ship's officer pushed a Chinese woman roughly out of his way and found Jackson 'shaking him like a puppy' while voicing sharp criticism.⁶ A Parsee broker, H.N. Mody, named his horse 'TJ' because 'my friend is a bobbery beast with a very bad temper'.

He was certainly hospitable – too hospitable if David McLean's strictures to his young chief are to be taken seriously, stories of Jackson's entertaining had reached his critical Scots ears in London.

Your brother [David Jackson] and [G.H.] Townsend go out by this mail, and I told them both to try and save money at once. I also told your Brother to tell you to do the same. I hear you have been entertaining all Hongkong with dancing parties almost weekly. Save your coin is my advice. You will find the dollars useful when you come Home.⁷

There are references to his hospitality from people as far apart as Lord Charles Beresford, whom the Bank assisted throughout his China visit in 1902, and Ma Chien-chung on a mission from Li Hung-chang designed to curtail the activities of the opium interests which had representatives on the Bank's Board of Directors (see Chapter 14).

Although Jackson's first 'mistress', first 'love' was the Hongkong Bank, he was concerned with people and their welfare. The Townsend encounter with him in

Yokohama is evidence of this. In July 1890 the junior members of the staff in Hong Kong wrote to thank him for 'what you have done for the benefit of the junior mess and staff generally since your return to Hong Kong', specifically, the providing of a sanatorium at the Peak, the payment by the Bank of the passages of men going home on furlough, and the additional allowance to juniors joining the Eastern staff from London Office.

The juniors were wise enough to request Jackson to convey their appreciation also to the Board of Directors.

A local journalist wrote:

As Chief Manager, the relations of Sir Thomas with the members of the Bank Staff were not merely cordial; they might be termed affectionate. He took the keenest interest in their welfare and amusements and was ever ready with a joke or, when necessary, with encouragements and advice.[8]

Nor were his thoughts only with the staff – there is a story which, by its nature, suggests it is not exceptional. As told by Arthur Hamilton, Viscount Lee of Fareham (1868–1947) – who later as military attache to the United States was made an 'honorary Rough Rider' and who gave Chequers to the British nation – he was in his early twenties stationed in Hong Kong and had, for no good reason, placed himself in serious debt warranting, if discovered, dismissal from the Army. A letter from Jackson summoned him to the Chief Manager's office of the Hongkong Bank – this, the young man thought, is really the end.

'Well, my boy,' said Jackson cheerfully, 'You are looking very seedy. When is your leave due? You should go on a trip to Japan.'

'Oh, sir,' the youngster replied, 'don't you know?'

'Oh, yes,' Jackson replied, 'I know all about that – but no sensible man ever makes a fool of himself twice in the same way, so take this note to the Chief Accountant – he will put your overdraft right and settle everything else – there'll be enough over to take you to Japan. Cut along now – ask for leave and forget all about it.'

Lord Lee concluded the story thus:

[Thomas Jackson] in five minutes took me from hell to heaven and I've never owed a penny since, and in the course of my career I've met scores of men who as young chaps were saved by him in the same way. So long as I live I shall look upon him as the best man I have ever known.[9]

The tributes

Among the many tributes Jackson received on his departure was one from the Gonsalves family, signed first by Constancio Jaoquim, the author of the brief diary quoted in Chapter 7. 'Especially do we recall with glowing hearts your liberal devotedness in averting the impending and gloomy consequences of that unfortunate event of December 1887 which caused us so much concern, anxiety and fear' – the nature of which the records now available fail to reveal.

There was also an address from the Chinese Community presented by (Sir Robert) Ho Tung.

Of the very extensive business which [the Bank] controls in the farther East by far the largest proportion is that with China and the Chinese . . . in fostering the good works of all classes of charitable and religious institutions in Hong Kong, without discrimination, your private munificence has long been recognized and, without doubt, will find living monuments amongst those who gratefully cherish the name and the memory of a universal benefactor.

The address made note of the 'very cordial relations that ever existed between yourself and the Chinese merchants and traders of Hong Kong'.

As Chief Manager of the Hongkong Bank in Hong Kong it was obvious that Jackson would be well-known. Sir Henry Blake, Governor of Hong Kong, intending only a concluding hyperbole, said:

Who does not know T.J.? I believe, ladies and gentlemen, that if letters were dropped in the post at St Petersburg, Berlin, Paris, London, San Francisco, Santa Fe and the little post office in the Straits of Magellan addressed 'T.J. China' they would find their way into the Hongkong & Shanghai Bank in Queen's Road.

Someone, moreover, tried it; today the Hongkong Bank's Archives possess the card addressed and delivered safely to 'T.J. China'.

Jackson and Government

There are some who hold the view that behind the façade of governors, executive and legislative councils, and their civil servants, the real power is exercised by others – bankers, perhaps; this certainly appears to have been an opinion widely held in the Treasury and Colonial Office. Bankers are in any case likely candidates for an alleged hidden government.

The Hongkong Bank's record of community involvement is mixed. The Board of Directors did not, as a matter of general policy, approve of the Bank's servants becoming engaged in formal public service. There were exceptions, often in the interests of the Bank or because of matters related to money and banking, for example, during a currency crisis. Only the Chief Manager in Hong Kong and the local managers and agents in Shanghai and the outports were of sufficient stature to permit significant public involvement, but the extent of such involvement was affected not only by the Board's injunctions, but also by the pressure of business – a man who ran an exchange position was not available for meetings during business hours.

The Bank would comment publicly and privately on the currency, but further involvement depended on the man and his time – and on the Board.

Jackson is again exceptional in the extent of his public involvement. He began simply as a Justice of the Peace in 1876; in 1884 he was nominated by the Hong Kong General Chamber of Commerce as their first representative on the Legislative Council, resigning on his first retirement to England in 1886. He was chairman of the Chamber in 1900. He served on the Retrenchment Committee of 1894, the Queen's Statue Committee of 1896, and the Insanitary Properties Commission. He was for ten years chairman of the Victoria Recreation Club. As with most bankers, he often served as honorary treasurer for worthwhile funds, for example the Irish Famine Relief Fund in 1880, the Queen's Diamond Jubilee Committee in 1897, the Indian Famine Relief Fund, the Typhoon Fund in 1900, and the Queen's Memorial Fund Committee in 1901. His advice was sought on currency matters, a subject considered in Volume II.

Jackson was a Conservative in politics and concerned with the welfare of the forces, especially the Royal Navy, whose officers he entertained hospitably when in port. He was Irish, but he was British in a British Colony; he objected strongly when, on a particularly contentious subject, the Hong Kong General Chamber of Commerce communicated with the American rather than the British minister in Peking. On China, Jackson supported a policy which would ensure China's sovereignty with trade open to all nations.

In this spirit he accepted Germans and Americans on the Board of Directors, but his staff was British and the Hongkong Bank's traditions can be found only in those of British exchange banks. As far as the records indicate, he would never turn rabidly on the Germans in the decade prior to the Great War, but there is no reason to suppose he disagreed with de Bovis in his 'smashing' of the American Russell and Co., which, while represented on the Board, attempted to manage an American-inspired, Chinese-promoted rival bank (see Chapter 12).

As late as 1906 when the Peak Preservation Ordinance was passed, Murray Stewart, the younger brother of Gershom Stewart – both Stewarts had earlier left the Bank to become brokers – wrote to Jackson giving him credit for having laid the groundwork, adding, 'Deep Water Bay is mainly now patronized by "military" men and women, none of whom know, much less reflect, that if it had not been for you a cement factory would have flourished on the links.' Jackson was apparently an early environmentalist!

Jackson and the succession

Despite all these tributes at the professional, personal, and public service levels, there is still the possibility that Jackson's contribution was flawed. Consider the record of his would-be successors. John Walter, G.E. Noble, and François de Bovis were unsuccessful; had Jackson created a one-man bank organized in such a manner that the succession would prove traumatic if not impossible?

The evidence defends Jackson. Walter's lack of success was a misfortune universally accepted as not of his making, Noble had a serious illness, and the 'failure' of de Bovis is debatable and complex. In the end he may have felt the burden too much for him. And when Jackson finally retired, J.R.M. Smith was able to carry on successfully.

Jackson could not have run a one-man bank even had that been his objective –

or failing. It is not simply that there was (Sir) Ewen Cameron in equally important Shanghai, succeeded by John Walter, J.P. Wade Gard'ner and H.M. Bevis, all of whom could by poor decisions – especially in exchange – ruin the Bank. The position can be put rather more positively. Jackson and the older managers successfully 'trained', if so formal a term is not premature, a succeeding generation of bankers, including C.S. Addis, J.R.M. Smith, N.J. Stabb, A.G. Stephen, and many others. By the time Jackson left Hong Kong the Chief Managers up to and including A.C. Hynes in 1929 had felt his influence, and V.M. Grayburn had met him while a junior in London.

Managers and agents indeed prided themselves on their independence, to a point; they held the Bank's power of attorney and they could and did take actions which 'paid the dividends' or caused the losses. There were, however, general rules and regulations within which they exercised this discretionary authority. Jackson could, as Chief Manager and with the Board's approval, control by appointment, transfer, and dismissal. But on specific subjects not reserved for Head Office approval, that is, for general banking and exchange decisions Jackson (and McLean in London) could only advise – or admonish after the fact.

Jackson could and did inspire; this was his greatest contribution, especially in an age when communication was difficult and personal contact necessarily limited. Like the Emperor himself Jackson could only personally command his own head office, and while he did manage the imperial allocation of surplus funds among the several branches and agencies, the executive function was delegated to the viceroy or manager in the provinces. But from Jackson as from the ideal Confucian emperor there emanated a virtue – a standard of morality and conduct – which was the essential element of Jackson's success.

It was this personal element that was so difficult for the new Chief Manager to continue; no doubt the staff looked on him as a 'new boy' to be tested against the former chief idealized. No doubt, it would be too easy – at least until the 1902 departure when all accepted he was really leaving Hong Kong not to return – to see as the solution of any problem the return of Jackson. These misconceptions were not operative; the reasons for Jackson's earlier returns have already been more objectively described in this history.

Sir Thomas Jackson's record as Chief Manager, described in Chapters 8 through 13, cannot be gainsaid, his public reputation is fully attested. Of his private life there is little information, except the testimony of his daughters, and the knowledge that Lady Jackson accepted the priorities in his life and suffered the separations, undertook the entertaining, and was, in the spirit of the times, the true 'Bank wife'. Jackson was capable of leaving his office behind – as he left his home, his face changed and he 'switched on' to the Bank. Thus with all his work, there was family life, kindly remembered.

TERMS OF SERVICE

By 1901 the Eastern staff was triple its 1876 strength with 157 men assigned to 24 branches and agencies. Equally important was the fact that the number of juniors in the Shanghai and Hong Kong offices had increased from eight each to eighteen or nineteen. This was not yet a size preventing reasonably intimate social intercourse, but the working relationships were becoming more distant and there were juniors in 1901 whose work and, indeed, whose potential cannot have been known personally to the Chief Manager or Manager Shanghai; the number of offices and the overall number of staff required some development of regulations.

Such a development would, unfortunately for the historian, remove certain personnel matters from the agenda of the Board of Directors and thus, in the absence of other records, from later knowledge. But enough continued to exercise the Board's attention to permit the conclusion that, just as the diversity of the Bank's business in the several offices required independence in decision-making, so the variety of problems facing the staff as yet defied full systemization.

The junior who joined London Office with prospects of coming East as a bank clerk was joining a 'service' – although he never signed a formal agreement. Even his first posting might be unstated, or the nominal 'Hong Kong' become, in an emergency, a surprise disembarkation in Colombo or a reembarkation in Hong Kong for a port farther north. But as he came East he recognized immediately as the ship progressed from port to port that he had joined a service, a family, which would entertain him en route, house him on arrival, transfer him, promote him, and finally, if his health held and his personal finances did not get too far out of hand, retire him with his provident fund and usually a gratuity of uncertain amount.

Within this apparently 'all-found' system there was room for ambition. Perhaps at the first port in the East the junior might be entertained at the house of the local manager, a house which would, given the background of the vast majority, appear from its spaciousness as 'palatial'. He would seek to learn the road to that house, combined hopefully with visions of himself mastering the finances of the East. (He would also learn that in the Eastern climate, the spaciousness was not the luxury it first appeared.) For the less ambitious there was the prospect of a small agency, quietly located in a minor port, carrying out banking arrangements already made for the most part by the responsible branch.

For both, however, there would be problems.

Marriage

The Board of Directors determined very early in the history of the Bank that two could not live as cheaply as one, not if one were a lady. On the other hand six, seven, or eighteen juniors could live very cheaply in a bachelors' mess. Then too a transfer might be ordered by the next mail steamer, and a bachelor could travel light. A plea that a prospective bride was sufficiently wealthy to supply the furniture for the new home was seen, in one specific case, as a further impediment since it increased the cost of transportation.

A Bank junior, however grandly titled as a full member of the Eastern staff, was a clerk. The best contemporary euphemism was 'banker's assistant'. As a clerk he was relatively highly paid and the life-style, with its sports, servants, and even a pony – a griffin for a griffin – was almost unintelligible to the humble bank clerk in a High Street branch of a Scottish clearing bank. A more practical point is that the junior's salary not only permitted this level of living but was sufficient to enable him, after a few years in the East, to pay off debts almost inevitably incurred during penurious London junior days.

Having said as much there are two cautions. Corporation life is dictated by the custom of the corporation and by one's peers. The level of living in the East, no matter how modestly or cautiously pursued, left little room for extras. The essentials of life were virtually provided in kind; if they were not, allowances were awarded; the salary was for maintaining the style and for beginning a lifetime of saving in a world before corporation pension schemes. Secondly, the clerk was worth no more; he was competing against the potential local clerk and he had only custom and perceived 'integrity' to recommend him, although until the early 1950s this would prove enough. Nevertheless, he was in no bargaining position.

In brief, a young bank clerk in the East could not afford to marry.

As impecuniousness has not always acted as an impediment to marriage, the Bank set rules – no marriage without permission and this would rarely be granted until the clerk had an appointment in the Bank, until, that is, he were appointed 'Accountant'.

Even in the early days of the Jackson Era a clerk was not usually an Accountant within the five years of his first tour, and thus he could not normally get married on his first Home leave. The pressures would mount during his second tour – an engagement previously made would prove too long, a rare daughter or nurse living in the port or a young lady out with the 'fishing fleet' would offer a possible solution – with the permission of the Board of Directors.

But the Eastern staff expanded faster than the number of senior positions (see Table 15.1). In 1886 a junior received two salary increments – after two and four years' service. Soon after this, it was argued, a man, if any good at all, would be appointed Accountant or agent; as the staff grew, this was less likely, and additional increments were permitted. Finally in 1897 full recognition of the new situation was given by authorization of a new salary increment – $25 per month after ten years' service. The Board minuted their acknowledgement that the previous judgement was no longer valid – even a good man would not become an Accountant within ten years.

It was not until 1898, however, that the next logical step was taken and Eastern

Table 15.1 *The Hongkong and Shanghai Banking Corporation Growth and advancement, 1876–1902, of the Eastern staff*

Year	Agencies	Branches & appointments		Staff				Normal wait for appointment	
		no.	+	no.	+	New	End	seniority	no. of years
1876	12	19		44	1	3	2	1873	3
1877	13	22	2	47	4	4	1	1873	4
1878	13	22	0	52	5	6	1	1873	5
1879	14	23	1	50	−2	3	5	1873	6
1880	14	24	1	59	9	10	1	1873	7
1881	15	26	2	61	2	4	2	1874	7
1882	15	26	0	64	3	7	4	1875	7
1883	16	27	1	68	4	9	5	1878	5
1884	18	29	2	78	10	14	4	1878	6
1885	19	30	1	87	9	10	1	1880	5
1886	19	31	1	94	7	9	2	1880	6
1887	19	31	0	96	2	5	3	1880	7
1888	20	32	1	94	−2	5	7	1880	8
1889	20	34	2	106	12	16	4	1882	7
1890	20	35	1	109	3	11	8	1882	8
1891	22	39	4	108	9	13	4	1884	7
1892	23	38	1	119	6	13	7	1884	8
1893	23	40	2	122	3	3	0	1884	9
1894	23	41	1	133	11	17	6	1884	10
1895	23	42	1	140	7	7	0	1884	11
1896	24	42	0	145	5	11	6	1885	11
1897	24	42	0	151	6	8	2	1886	11
1898	24	42	0	152	1	13	12	1886	12
1899	24	42	0	156	4	10	6	1886	13
1900	24	42	0	156	0	7	7	1886	14
1901	24	42	0	157	1	11	10	1886	15
1902	24	42	0	162	5	15	10	1888	14

Notes: This table refers to the Eastern staff only; 'end' indicates the number of people leaving the East permanently – taking an appointment in London Office, Lyons or Hamburg. An 'appointment' refers to sub-accountant's and all senior posts. New staff refers to juniors arriving in the East or, in rare cases, to Eastern staff hired in the East. The year chosen as the basis for the normal wait is that in which say three or four of that seniority receive appointments, thus barring the unusual case, e.g. Lamond and Addis (1883) in 1886.

staff still in the status of 'clerks' were permitted to marry. But for the reasons stated the Board's general opinion remained that this should not be permitted until after ten years of service.

There is little question but that Jackson had begun to filter through requests to the Board. Immediately upon announcement of the new policy, two 'juniors' or 'clerks' of over ten years' service were permitted to marry.

As Jackson or perhaps a local manager could dissuade a young man from applying to the Board and thus having the matter considered in the minutes – although he could not absolutely prevent it – the evidence is insufficient to quantify the impact of the Board's regulation or to judge whether the Bank should be better known as the 'Heart and Soul Breaking Corporation', as at least one retiree has suggested. The Board minutes provide examples, even in cases of five years' service, where the Board made exceptions for a man whose intended bride had an income; there were also cases favourably considered where the 'clerk' was considered a sound man with say at least eight years' service.

Did the Board use this authority to prevent a member of the Eastern staff from marrying a foreigner? Since society in a Treaty Port was provincial and the Bank was concerned that the bride, of whatever nationality, be of the proper social class, there was not the later tendency to consider all foreigners undesirable. Indeed, there were American wives, and Bank staff married French in Indo-China and Dutch in the Netherlands East Indies. A.G. Stephen (East in 1885), a future Chief Manager, had not been appointed an Accountant in his first ten years; he was given permission to marry a Spanish-Italian lady in Bombay – she was talented musically, but talent was often regarded with suspicion. Stephen was one of four Chief Managers to have had a foreign (defined to exclude Irish) wife.

There is no record of a request being denied on the grounds that the proposed bride was native to the country in which the officer was serving. In one case a junior is noted as wishing to marry an 'Armenian lady' in Penang; Thomas Jackson stated he saw no way to ask the directors to depart from their seniority rule. The young man was neither an Accountant nor had he been in the Bank ten years. But the background of the lady is mentioned.

The directors, it should be noted in fairness, had taken the same position only some sixteen months earlier, even though the young lady was English with £450 per annum. However, the young man appealed on grounds that the 'matter had gone so far'. That he stayed with the Bank is known, the result of his appeal, which is not minuted, may therefore be assumed to have been favourable.

The ten-year rule would often be appealed against. Although some such rule would be standard with all career firms in the East, it remained contentious. For some it created a distress which must have affected the morale of the organization; others made a virtue of a regulation which could, after all, only be justified on a cost/benefit basis.

The bachelors' mess then became a virtue in itself, a continuation of life on the Bank's playing fields at New Beckenham, which in turn was a continuation of life, at least for the English (as opposed to Scottish) juniors, in a public school. The bachelor parties, the after-dinner 'scrums' on the floor of the manager's home in white tie, all part of the English gentleman's tradition, it is true, but perpetuated by the public school-like conditions of life in the junior mess, first at Beaconsfield House, across Queen's Road on a bluff overlooking the Bank, and then high in Hong Kong's Peak district at Cloudlands.

As the service grew larger the managers might not know personally every junior. This suggested two developments: (i) increased 'discipline' in the office, a discipline coming not from self-motivation of the ambitious, mature clerk, in close contact with an inspired leader, but a discipline enforced downwards by a Sub-Manager on a group of youngsters and (ii) vertical familiarity replaced by greater knowledge of one's peers; the junior who was later Manager Tientsin would well remember the character and hopefully the merits of the Manager Manila with whom he was then transacting business. Or, even more important, a Chief Manager might find that many of the managerial posts were filled with his contemporaries, men whose measure he took while a junior at Cloudlands. A.H. Barlow, a junior in Hong Kong in 1895, would as Chief Manager in 1925 find that his fellow juniors had become the agents in Bangkok, Penang, San Francisco, Lyons, Amoy, Tientsin, Manila, Harbin, and Nagasaki. But, as Table 15.2 suggests, there was no fixed pattern; N.J. Stabb, for example, became Chief Manager at an early age, J.R.M. Smith, A.G. Stephen, and V.M. Grayburn were not long in Hong Kong as juniors.

The Hongkong Bank actually only had an official junior mess in Hong Kong and Tientsin. Elsewhere a new junior might live temporarily with the manager's family and then find a chummery or private mess he could join. Most found setting up bachelor's quarters marginally too expensive, even with the housing allowance. Even in Shanghai the juniors were on their own; it was the Hong Kong mess at Cloudlands and later the senior mess in the Bank's Head Office building which set the tone and are remembered.

There were alternatives to marriage. Addis comments in his diary on the faithfulness of a manager's Chinese mistress and his care for their two children. There was a growing demand for schools for Eurasian children in the East and the consequences were not all happy. Of his Calcutta Manager, Andrew Veitch, Addis wrote,

A kindly man within his limits; honest after a fashion, fond of his wife and the three charming children she bore him. There was some trouble about his two half-caste boys but he never neglected them. They were properly educated and when I left China seemed likely to do well. The Chinese mistress died.[10]

Another alternative was a briefer relationship. There were also alternatives to sex, sports was one, drink another, neither a wholly satisfactory substitute. All this merely confirms the social consequences of the ten-year rule. This constraint was not peculiar to the Bank and had indeed come to be part of expatriate life in the East – of all regulations it was the most controversial, enforced (with numerous exceptions) only as a sad necessity.

Recruitment in London

London becomes the only 'gate'

In the early years the Bank certainly recruited in London for juniors especially marked for training before being sent East. But the Bank also hired a London staff the members of which might, if the circumstances proved suitable, be sent East – at first there was no firm rule. Similarly the Bank hired 'Eastern Staff' in the East. By the late 1880s certainly, the division, though not totally unbridgeable, had been established in London as between London or 'Home' staff and juniors for the East.

With the refusal to transfer the local Shanghai employed B. Ruttonjee in 1884 or Figuera in Iloilo in 1893 to the Eastern staff, the Board of Directors confirmed that entry to the Bank's executive staff could be made only through London Office. Addis, impressed with E.M. Bishop (East in 1897), his young Calcutta assistant, locally employed during the crisis of 1892, encouraged him to go to London; A.M. Townsend in New York recommended the Newfoundlander Newton J. Stabb (East in 1891) and later the Staten Islander A.G. Kellogg (East in 1906) to London. The rule was applied almost universally, but there is no record of any but a British subject of European ancestry – Kellogg (American), de Bovis (French), and F.T. Koelle (German) excepted – actually applying.

The exceptions were (i) local citizens for European branches: E. Morel in Lyons, who was responsible for defrauding the Bank in 1889, and J. Brüssel in Hamburg, (ii) a Chinese language student, E.G. Hillier, employed by Cameron in Shanghai and long-time Agent in Peking, and (iii) seniors taken over from a failed firm – A. Maccoll from Martin, Dyce and Co. in Batavia and M.C. Kirkpatrick from the New Oriental Bank. These were all special cases and did not undermine the Bank's London policy.

The growing role of sport

The record of those hired in the East, the 'Eastern juniors' of Chapter 7, was, as noted there, mixed. Jackson wanted 'gentleman clerks' and David McLean sought them out, complaining that English school boys (as opposed to Scots with their banking experience) were 'very deficient in writing and in figures. Their time at school seems to be spent in playing football and other games.'[11] Later this preoccupation with sport, even in the judgement of the Scottish Cameron and Addis, would be considered an asset. McLean himself sent his son to Harrow.

The beginnings were, however, in this period. A scratch Rugby football match

Table 15.2 *The Hongkong and Shanghai Banking Corporation*
Juniors in Hong Kong with later Chief Managers – and their positions when he *was*
Chief Manager

1891 Sir Newton Stabb

Hong Kong, 1903	*1915*	*1920*
1894 R.C. Edwards	Agent, Nagasaki	Agent, Nagasaki
1895 D. Forbes	Act. Agent, Canton	Agent, Canton
1895 E.E. Deacon	Acct, Yokohama	Sub-Manager, Yokohama
1896 F.A. Rickard	Acct, Bombay	Acct, Bombay
1899 W.C.D. Turner	Acct, Shanghai	leave, Dalney (Dairen)
1899 H.C. Sandford	Act. Chief Acct, HK	leave, Chief Acct
1899 A. Ross	Agent, Dalny (Dairen)	leave, Acct, Batavia
1900 H.A. MacIntyre	Act. Acct, Tientsin	Act. Sub-Manager, Shanghai
1901 R.E.N. Padfield	London but Acct Hamburg	Hamburg, London
1901 W. Inglis	Act. Acct, San Francisco	ti/c, San Francisco
1902 O.J. Barnes	#2 jr, Shanghai	Acct, Shanghai
1902 A. Boyd	#1 jr, Batavia	Acct, Batavia
1902 L.N. Murphy	#3 jr, Hong Kong	Acct, Calcutta
1903 J.M. Forrester	#2 jr, Bombay	Act. Acct, Rangoon
1903 W.D. McCullagh	#1 jr, Singapore	ti/c, Iloilo
1903 A.S. Henchman	#1 jr, Manila	Acct, Manila

1885 A.G. Stephen

Hong Kong, 1889–1890	*1921*
1886 R.T. Wright	Manager, Yokohama
1889 G.H. Stitt	Manager, Shanghai

1891 A.H. Barlow

Hong Kong, 1895	*1925*	*1927*
1894 R.C. Edwards	Agent, Bangkok	Agent, Bangkok, died Feb.
1894 J. McArthur	Act. Manager, HK	
1895 E.E. Deacon	Agent, Penang	Agent, Penang
1895 J.R. Gillingham	Agent, San Francisco	Agent, San Francisco
1898		
1896 C.C. Barlow	Manager, Lyons	Manager, Lyons
1900		
1898 L.J.C. Anderson	Agent, Amoy	Agent, Saigon
1899 B.C.M. Johnston	leave, Agent, Tientsin	Sub-Manager, Shanghai
1901		
1894 J. Kennedy	Manager, Manila	
1901 R.E.N. Padfield	London but Acct Hamburg	Sub-Manager, London
1901 E.M. Knox	Agent, Harbin	Agent, Harbin
1901 H.A. Courtney	Act. Agent, Nagasaki	leave, A. Agent Nagasaki

Table 15.2 (*cont.*)

1897 A.C. Hynes

Hong Kong, 1904	*1929*
1895 E.E. Deacon	Agent, Penang
1895 J.R. Gillingham	Agent, San Francisco
1901 R.E.N. Padfield	Act. Manager, London
1901 H.A. Courtney	Agent, Amoy
1902 A. Boyd	Agent, Colombo
1902 L.N. Murphy	Act. Manager, HK
1903 A.S. Henchman	Sub-Manager, Shanghai

1905	
1902 R.C. Allen	leave, Agent, Peking
1904 F.H. Pentycross	Agent, Hankow
1905 M.A. Murray	Agent, Sourabaya

1906	
1899 B.C.M. Johnston	Act. Manager, Shanghai
1905 A.C. Putley	Sub-Agent, Sungei Patani

1907	
1900 G.W. Wood	Sub-Agent, Chefoo
1907 T.M. Knott	Act. Agent, Canton

1908	
1899 H.D. Sharpin	Manager, Singapore
1902 H.C. Joass	Sub-Manager, Singapore
1907 A.C. Leith	Act. Agent, Tokyo
1908 W. Hay	Acct, Singapore

Act. = acting   Acct = Accountant   jr = junior, i.e. without appointment
ti/c = temporarily in charge
The purpose of this table is to indicate the distribution of Eastern staff who were in Hong Kong's junior mess with the future Chief Manager.
 J.R.M. Smith was in Shanghai as a junior; V.M. Grayburn was in Singapore and Shanghai.

---

was played against the Chartered Bank in 1887; the following year a full match card was organized with G.C. Murray (East in 1889) as the 'skipper' – he would become Agent Iloilo and die on leave in 1915. The initiative seems to have come, however, from W.S. Edwardson, subsequently the London Office Accountant, and the London Office staff were always involved. The games moved from Chislehurst to Leytonstone and finally in the late 1890s joined with the cricketers to form a joint sports club using a field at New Beckenham.[12]

 At its meeting on December 17, 1898, the Board of Directors were addressed by the Staff London Office Athletic Club requesting an annual subsidy of £50 per annum to support it. The Board granted £100; they did not see their way to an annual grant. The following year a new request was made, and the Board agreed to a second grant of £100, which was intended to be final. Meanwhile the teams were training in London and the basis of the Bank's athletic prowess had begun.

A November 4, 1900, despatch from Paris, however, was headlined 'English Footballers Beaten in France' and recounted how a combined XV from the London and Westminster and the Hongkong banks had been defeated by the Racing Club de France, 25 to 18, before 6,000 spectators.

The entrance requirements

To join the team – and the Bank – a young lad needed a recommendation, but this was not too difficult to obtain, and it was the combination of written examination and interview which determined the final decision. George Addis, on Home leave from the Chartered Mercantile in Penang, wrote to his younger brother Charles in January 1880 to prepare for the Hongkong Bank exams: 'I would strongly advise you to work up arithmetic, especially calculations of interest on odd amounts and at odd rates. For example on £232:8s:4d @ $1\frac{7}{8}$ for 46 days.'[a] Had the Bank in fact asked such questions there might have been even fewer juniors to train for the East. Such things were not learned on the playing fields of British public schools.

On the list of the Bank's Eastern staff there were many names familiar in the East – de St Croix from the Channel Islands, Harries, Vacher, Morriss, Addis, and many others some of which suggest family relationships, although these are not always possible to establish (but see Table 15.3). The performance of sons does not appear particularly brilliant, but then there would be little opportunity for a father in the East with a young family to be able to assess, or for the son to assess, the qualifications possessed and required. The record more often reflects a serious health problem. P. de C. Morriss (East in 1889) and H.R. Cook (East in 1906) were sent East to meet a family financial crisis – not always a sound reason; H. Burnett (East in 1899) had a first tour in San Francisco and Yokohama, married early and without permission, and did not settle down in Calcutta; G.H.W. Sexton (East in 1896), Mrs G.E. Noble's nephew, came from an Anglo-Indian family; he left the Bank for the Catholic priesthood; Noble's son, J.F.S. Noble, left the Bank during his first Home leave. Apparently, no generalization would be valid.

After two to three years in London Office at a salary from £60 to £100 a year the junior might well be in debt; he *had* to go East. In 1881 Addis, for example, lived on £130 per annum, the difference being made up by a gift of £10 from older brother George and a loan from his brother-in-law. Even then his frugality led to illness; later as London Manager he would be instrumental in providing a subsidized midday meal to the juniors, and then to the Bank's entire London staff, in a world still innocent of luncheon vouchers.

---

[a] 'P.S. Do you know decimals? You can't do without them in a Bank.'[13]

Table 15.3 *The Hongkong and Shanghai Banking Corporation*
Known family relationships of 1864–1902 Bank staff[+]

Name & years of service	Highest position	Relationship
John Grigor, 1864–1871	Manager, Yokohama	
James M. Grigor, 1871–d1885	Agent, Bombay	brother
W.H. Vacher, 1865–1875	Manager, London	
H.H. Vacher, 1881–1890	Accountant, Yokohama	son
G.E. Noble, 1866-1897	Chief Manager	
G.H.N. Sexton, 1896–1903	Junior, Bombay	wife's nephew
J.F.S. Noble, 1897–1901	Junior, Hong Kong	son
Thomas Jackson, 1866–1902	Chief Manager	
David Jackson, 1878–d1903	Manager, Yokohama	brother
A.H. Dare, 1880–1892	Sub-Manager, Yokohama	an in-law
(Dr William Hartigan[a]	Bank Doctor, Hong Kong then London	brother-in-law)
T.McC. Browne, 1882–1905[b]	Manager, Bangkok	'near relative'
V.A.C. Hawkins, 1882–1907	Manager, Yokohama	cousin
R.H. Lloyd, 1940–1970	Head Office (books)	great grandson
G.H. Burnett, 1866–1899	London Office Accountant	
H. Burnett, 1899–1907	Junior, Calcutta	son
Ewen Cameron, 1867–1905	Manager, London	
A.M. Townsend, 1870–1911	Manager, London	brothers-in-law
*N.J. Stabb, 1891–d1931	Chief Manager, Manager London	son-in-law
Herbert Cope, 1867–1879	Manager, Singapore	
A.E. Cope, 1873–1891	Agent, Saigon	brother
John Walter, 1868–1902	Manager, Shanghai[c]	
N.A. Walter, 1886	Junior, Shanghai	nephew
James Greig[d], 1869–1876	Chief Manager	
W.G. Greig[d], 1870–1888	Manager, Singapore	brother
H.A. Greig, 1925–1954	Manager, Colombo	grandson
*H.E.R. Hunter, 1882–1912	Manager, Shanghai	cousin
William Nicholls, 1868–1913	London Office	
W.S. Nicholls, 1892–1927	Agent, Rangoon	son
W.H. Harries, 1870–1912	Manager, San Francisco	
H.E. Harries, 1893–d1898	Junior, Yokohama	nephew
Alexander Leith, 1871–1891	Agent, Tientsin	
A.C. Leith, 1907–1940	Sub-Manager, Shanghai	son

Table 15.3 (*cont.*)

G.M. Lind, 1871–1902	London Office	
J.H. Lind, 1901–1935	Manager, Hamburg	son
Edward Morriss, 1872–d1890	Manager, Yokohama	
P. de C. Morriss, 1889–1923	Sub-Manager, Singapore	son
François de Bovis, 1872–1922	Chief Manager	
Raymond de Bovis, 1891–?	Acting Accountant, New York	brother
Paul de Bovis, d1914	unknown	brother?
R.H. Cook, 1873–d1904	Agent, Kobe (Hiogo)	
H.R. Cook, 1906 (2 weeks)	Junior, Hong Kong	son
H.M. Bevis, 1875–d1906	Manager, Shanghai[c]	
*H.B. Pike, 1890–1916	Agent, Penang	nephew
H.E.R. Hunter, 1882–1912	Manager, Shanghai[c]	
C.W. May, 1888–1912	Agent, Nagasaki	brother-in-law
G.H. Cautherley, 1926–1960	Agent, Kuala Belait	nephew
*W.R. McCallum, 1889–1920	Agent, Colombo	brother-in-law
Charles S. Addis, 1883–1922	Manager, London	
A.S Adamson, 1919–1952	Manager, Hong Kong	nephew
W.S. Addis, 1955–1987	Senior Manager, Head Office	grandson
R.A. Adamson, 1958–1973	Kota Kinabulu	grand-nephew
Gershom Stewart, 1883–1889	Junior, Hong Kong[e]	
Murray Stewart, 1890–1900	Junior, Hong Kong	brother
J.D. Taylor, 1884–1911	Agent, Hankow	
J.McG. Taylor, 1925–1955	Manager, Djakarta	son
S.A. Gray, 1919–1955	Manager, London	nephew
J.M. Gray, 1956–	Executive Director	grand-nephew
W.R. McCallum, 1889–1920	Agent, Colombo	
J.J. French, 1915–1948	Manager, Bangkok	son-in-law
F.J. French, 1962–	General Manager, Head Office	grandson
W.K. Dods, 1889–1922	Agent, Calcutta	
C.H. Dods, 1905–1909	Junior, Manila	cousin
N.J. Stabb, 1891–d1931[f]	Chief Manager	
G.W. Stabb, 1930–1960	Agent, Kuala Belait	cousin
N.J. Stabb, 1935–d1942	Junior, Shanghai	son
A.H. Barlow, 1891–1927	Chief Manager	
B.D.G. Barlow, 1934–d1936	Junior, Dairen	son

Table 15.3 (*cont.*)

S. Gilmore, 1898–1903	Junior, Shanghai	
A.H.G. Gilmore, 1898–d1906	Junior, Tientsin	cousin
H.B. Pike, 1890–1916	Agent, Penang	
D. Pike, 1931–1962	Asst. Manager, Tokyo	son
M.J. Pike, 1971–	Senior Manager, Hongkong Egyptian Bank	grandson

Notes:

+ Excludes those who did not go East, e.g. R.A. Butt, killed in action.
* See below in the list for his relations serving in the Bank.
a Not a member of the Bank staff.
b Thought to have been born in Ireland near Carlingford.
c Also Acting Chief Manager.
d In a second family connection, the Greigs' younger brother, John, married a sister of Harry Hunter, see Vol. III.
e Temporarily in Macau as 'Agent'.
f Manager, London Office, 1920–1931.
Source: Compiled by Catherine E. King from diaries, letters, directories, Bank records – especially after 1890, and oral history. Please note: this list may not be complete.

But all would be mended once one went East. Unfortunately not all were successful; some failed to pass the physical examination of Dr George Thin, a former Shanghai doctor, half-brother of Alexander Michie, and also doctor for the Chartered Mercantile and the Imperial Bank of Persia.

I can assure [McLean wrote to Jackson] we take no end of trouble in selecting Candidates. Just to show you, since you wired for the last two men, we have had eight fellows examined. Some of them passed our exam all right, but failed to pass Dr Thin. Others failed to do our questions and had to go.[14]

For the young man who had borrowed against a career in the East, this was a serious blow. Often they would try again; sometimes they would succeed. One junior whose health needed improvement was urged to take a sea voyage and return to try again. He did; he travelled to South Africa, took a liking to the place, and decided not to return.

The fortunate left for the East with an advance of £50 – which became a gratuity in 1890 – and £20 travelling money, part of which was spent, in the absence of reliable 'station reports', on the purchase of inappropriate tropical gear, which was later discarded, and the farewell party. The usual route was via Suez on the P&O. To save time, most staff members did not leave by P&O directly from England, rather they travelled across Europe by train to a Mediterranean port, at first Brindisi, later Marseilles, to pick up their ship for the East.

Leave, Home and local

Home or long leave
For the five-year tour the conventional wisdom was that the first year was of one of financial recovery, the next three of saving for and the fifth planning for the next leave. The Bank's initial policy was one year's leave on half pay after five years in the East – with exceptions for particularly valuable managers.

In 1885 with the fall in silver Jackson represented to the Board that some could not afford a full year under these conditions; they were permitted to take six months at full pay; two of these months were used up en route via Suez. By 1894 too many were taking this option, causing, as Jackson explained, a shortage of staff in summer and a surplus in winter. The terms were further modified to permit a year's leave, the first half of which was on full pay, the second half on half-pay, which concession the Chief Manager took as additional proof of the directors' consideration for the staff of the Bank. P&O first class sea passages or equivalent had been paid by the Bank since 1890.

One major justification of the long leave was the return to a temperate climate; staff would have to justify tropical detours. Addis visited his sister in Australia, another his brother in Java – arguing that the brother managed a plantation at a high altitude. Almost without exception the travel was without stopover, the short time the ship was in port providing the only experience elsewhere in the Orient. Some, it is true, returned via Canada or the United States – Addis met the Jacksons and W.B. Thomson of the Bank in Yosemite Valley and, returning to San Francisco, found Edward Cope and his wife with other China-coast people. Despite this extraordinary gathering, the generalization stands.

Having set the pattern, there were variations, each of which the Board considered individually. A.M. Townsend in New York preferred and obtained an annual summer leave. Those who were ill were often awarded early passage and special leave conditions, one junior being instructed to winter in Cairo.

Local leave
Many of today's retirees in the Hongkong Bank recall that local leave, that is, leave within the five-year tour and without passage payment, was rare and usually granted only for reasons of health or to enable participation in inter-port sport. Whatever the Hongkong Bank's actual policy may have been, the records, personal diaries, and letters extant suggest that local leave was taken, on perhaps an erratic basis, in the period now under consideration.

There were always 'long weekends', coinciding with bank holidays – good for shooting, a trip by houseboat, a visit to a neighbouring island or, more often, for paper chases, riding and inter-hong or commercial vs services sporting events; there were holidays for the races.

A glance through the China-coast newspapers suggests that a surprising number of people died a few days out at sea; this was a reflection of doctors' tendency to prescribe a sea voyage as a cure for general 'seediness', a condition which covered practically anything. Some reported local leave may actually have been sick leave on a doctor's advice. A trip to Japan from the Treaty Ports was possible, or to Colombo from Calcutta, but the most usual way to escape the hot weather was to visit a Hill Station or a seaside resort – for example, Kuling in the Lu Han mountains of central China, the Western Hills from Peking, Chefoo and its beaches for North China, Darjeeling from Calcutta, and Buijtenzorg from Batavia. Wives and children would go for extended periods, the husbands would join them for at most two weeks.

Career patterns and salaries

In 1876 Eastern staff with appointments as Accountants, agents, or managers had seniorities ranging from three to eleven years. With the exception of the ill-fated C.H. Beveridge there were no 'clerks' with more than four years' service.

The growth of the staff, despite deaths and resignations, (i) affected the length of time it would take to obtain a promotion and (ii) is reflected by the increasing seniority of those with an 'appointment', that is, a Board of Directors appointment to a position of sub-accountant or above (see Table 15.1). Thus in 1883 the 'normal wait' for an appointment had dropped from seven to five years, would stay within the range five to eight years until 1892 and then begin to increase until 1901 when a young man coming East would have to wait fifteen years for an appointment.

Finally, in 1900 all appointees had more than ten years' service, with managers in the twenty-year range. The youngest appointee had twelve years' service, but fifteen was a more normal figure.

There must be a change of approach in a service in which career opportunities change so significantly over a twenty-five year period. Much would depend on the method of promotion and the perceived fairness, and it is here, perhaps, that Noble and de Bovis might be faulted. With an increasing number of staff waiting for appointments to a position only slightly more responsible than the non-differentiated section chief, it would have been very difficult not to move to a system of promotion based primarily on seniority. Addis noted this tendency, which he ascribed to G.E. Noble, then newly appointed Chief Manager. Under de Bovis there was a sense of favouritism also at work; Addis became further concerned – not only for himself but for the Bank. At least one of de Bovis's appointments proved disastrous and the officer in question, L.C. Balfour (East in 1878), resigned early.

It is not necessary to examine the merits of each case to acknowledge that the service had changed from a small intimate group, all of whom were known to the Chief Manager, to a hierarchical service in which the majority had to serve, possibly without special commendation or encouragement, for ten or more years before recognition, before rising from the designation 'junior' or, in the world at large, 'clerk'.

The slow road to an appointment could be quickened by an early retirement for reasons of health, by a death, or by a forced retirement of a superior. This last could result from a dramatically poor performance in a senior position, by early recognition of unsuitability, from becoming financially entangled personally, or from observed 'intemperateness'.

The London junior who came East with the Bank probably thought in terms of a lifetime career, but there were dropouts. The obvious categories have been listed, but there was also the 'golden handshake' – the Hongkong Bank was not committed to see an officer through to retirement, although the record is mixed.

Fred W. Barff with 40 years' service in the East was in 1920 the senior member of then 259-strong Eastern staff; he was technically a junior; unfortunately there is no record of what duties he actually performed those last years. With seniority dating from 1880, he had been Agent in Foochow in 1885 – a significant responsibility for a first-tour junior. Although after Home leave he returned to departmental assignments in Shanghai and then Hong Kong, he was appointed Accountant Calcutta in 1890. He was, it seemed, still well within the time frame for a successful career. Unfortunately his performance proved unsatisfactory and he was placed on probation, returning from leave to Shanghai. This time his performance was reported wholly satisfactory and his probation was ended; he was even permitted to marry, but he would never again receive an 'appointment'. He remained at the departmental level, receiving, after approval by the Board of Directors, special increments for long service. His extraordinary length of service was at least partly the consequence of staff shortages in the East during World War I.

This case was exceptional. A.B. Anderson, the first Agent in Nagasaki, was asked to retire on the grounds that he could never again be appointed an agent and he was too old for a junior position. He died in Peking en route Home in 1897. That there are not more clear cases of this kind is the consequence of unsatisfactory performance often being accompanied by other problems which dominate that Board's decision.

Nevertheless, as the statistics cited earlier clearly show, promotion was slow despite the dropouts, and the periodic salary increments would be little compensation to the ambitious. There were occasions when fairly senior staff, Accountants or managers, left the Bank to accept new challenges – H.R. Coombs, for example, resigned with the good wishes of the Board in 1899 after nineteen years in the East, including the position of Manager Manila, to head the Anglo-

Egyptian Bank; A.W. Maitland, an Eastern junior, retired in 1895 and subsequently accepted managership of the new Imperial Bank of China; the relatively junior Harry Lamond (the son of David McLean's Oriental Bank senior in Hong Kong, 1862–1864) was sent to New York after some six years in Manila and there succumbed to an offer to be a branch manager for the Anglo-Argentine Bank; others were seconded – in this period A.M. Bruce, with thirteen years' seniority, was seconded in 1900 for service with the Imperial Chinese Railways. V.A. Caesar Hawkins, disappointed in the post-Jackson Era, left the Bank in 1907, and was later a director and member of the finance committee of the Imperial Bank of Persia, of which Sir Thomas Jackson was then Chairman.

For those with less experience there was the temptation to move to other companies with better prospects, tempered by the recognition of the consequences of losing the seniority they had gained in the Hongkong Bank, the firm of their first choice. Addis was approached by his uncle in Shanghai to become Russell and Co.'s special agent in Tientsin – possibly something parallel to Michie's duties with Jardine, Matheson and Co. – or to join the new Trust and Loan Company, and as he reviewed his present prospects, there was some reason to consider the offers. Gershom Stewart, whom Addis thought to be a potential chief manager, did resign to join a brokerage firm, despite the Board's offer of a salary increment; his younger brother Murray Stewart (East in 1890) would join him later. Three other juniors resigned to become brokers in the stock boom in 1889 – 1890, but two later obtained permission to rejoin the Bank, although without retaining their original seniority.

While it is true that, even if one reached the position of agent, one might remain in a small port for the remainder of one's career, this should have been expected (see Table 15.4). The Bank's area of operation was known, and within it the great opportunities were Hong Kong, Shanghai, Yokohama, Manila, Singapore, and New York – San Francisco being blocked until the retirement of Harries; the Indian offices, although important, were in a different world. At the most this totalled eight posts in a service totalling 157 Eastern staff in 1901.

There is the tradition that the amiable, moderately competent officer would be 'shunted' to manage an agency in a small port. The evidence here is that these posts were important and valued; the ability of the man assigned naturally varied, but the list includes a majority of sound reputation.

Writing of his experience in 1896 while E.H. Oxley was on leave, Charles Addis stated: 'Life in Hankow – small place can be demoralizing and difficult to keep intellectually alive. Three years is all one should stay in a Treaty Port.'

Oxley came East in 1874 and after a varied career, including Accountant Calcutta, was appointed Agent Hankow in 1887 where he remained, apart for Home leaves, until his retirement in 1903. Nor was this unusual – as Table 15.4 indicates. Alexander Leith, G.H. Townsend, W.N. Dow, and Anderson are

Table 15.4 *The Hongkong and Shanghai Banking Corporation*
Long-term final assignments in smaller agencies, 1880–1900

		years
Hankow	Oxley, E.H. (1887–1903)	17
Tientsin	Leith, A. (1885–1891) health	7
Tientsin	Mackintosh, D.H. (1897–1913)	17
Foochow	Rickett, C.B. (1889–1903)	15
Amoy	Broadbent, J.F. (1888–1900)	13
Hiogo	Cook, R.H. (1888–1892; 1897–1904) died	13
Saigon	Hewat, H. (1892–1905)[a]	14
Calcutta	Cameron, P.E. (1895–1904)	10
Bombay	Townsend, G.H. (1893–1899) died	7
Iloilo	MacNab, J. (1883–1896)	14
Batavia	Kirkpatrick, M.C. (1887–1909)	23
Sourabaya	Drysdale, W. (1896–1918)[b]	22
Penang	Dow, W.N. (1892–1897) health	6
Bangkok	Browne, T.McC. (1892–1904)	13
Nagasaki	Anderson, A.B. (1891–1897) terminated	7
Colombo	Wilson, R. (1893–1903)	11
and, for information:		
San Francisco	W.H. Harries (1875–1912)	38
Lyons	F. de Bovis (1893–1922)	30

Notes:
[a] Hewat was briefly Agent Tientsin, 1900–1901
[b] Drysdale was briefly Agent Batavia, 1903.

listed despite their relatively shorter periods, as the assignments were their last for the reasons stated. A.M. Townsend was just over twenty years in New York (1880–1901), but went on to be first junior, then senior Manager in London until his retirement in 1911.

A mid-career problem

If a young man came East at the age of say 23, he might marry at age 33; he would then from the age of 40 face the problem of separation. Although there were school facilities in India, especially at the Hill Stations, it was customary to send one's children back to England for their education, and the wife was torn between staying with her husband or following her children. Mid-tour visits were not even thought of.

The ideal solution was for the husband to find a 'berth' in England at just that crucial moment and avoid the separation. George Addis was offered the sub-managership of the Bank of Liverpool in 1886 at £1,000 a year. He accepted, writing to Charles, 'My Eastern life is closed.'[15] Charles Addis too felt the pull of Britain; certainly his wife Eba did – in 1897 she wrote, 'Our great desire is to *settle* at home.' When George died of cancer in 1901, Charles Addis applied for his position; he was unsuccessful.[16] Addis was eventually fortunate; as will be told in Volume II, the timing of Cameron's illness at the moment Addis was on Home leave caused the new Chief Manager J.R.M. Smith to assign him to London Office.

These were not isolated cases. As early as 1889 A.M. Townsend, the Bank's New York Manager, was reported anxious to return to Britain. George Addis told his brother Charles that Townsend 'has been laying tracks for settling at home and altho' unsuccessful as yet in finding a post to suit him', he hoped soon to be able to leave 'Yankeeland'.[17] There are many references to wives too ill to return to the East, Eastern staff husbands requesting additional time to remain with them, and always the break up of the family looming as the reality of Eastern life. The 'stiff-upper lip' is a false caricature of all too-human men struggling unsuccessfully with a system neither they nor their employers seemed capable of either understanding or changing.

Local staffs

The refusal to promote local staff to executive rank and the resulting three-tier system (see Chapter 7) combined to restrict local employees to their original office. A very few Portuguese appear to have been transferred from Hong Kong to Shanghai or Yokohama in the first years of the Bank, but not subsequently. If any local staff moved on their own account, for example, from Iloilo to Manila, no record exists for this period, but such a move would not be impossible.

For them the career pattern was dictated by the caste or hierarchical system local to the office. This would hold true for all foreign companies in the East. The first regional officers in the Mercantile Bank were appointed in the immediate pre-World War II period, those in the Hongkong Bank not until the 1950s. This development will be examined in Volume IV.

In London the problem of a career in a single branch office could also cause discontent, and there were domestic banks for comparison. The solution was mainly in extending the range of salaries, thus permitting additional increments. J.F. Broadbent and T.S. Baker were the last of the London Office staff (defined as those who joined without expectations of going East) to be in fact sent East (in 1878 and 1883 respectively) until transfers from Home to Eastern staff took place in the straitened periods at the end of each World War; no other system appeared feasible.

Salaries and fringe benefits

Charles Addis, the Bank's Agent in Peking, wrote in his diary: 'I have a fine house, stables, servants, mule and cart (the carriage of Peking), coal and oil (heavy items during the severe winter), newspapers, furniture, house and table linen etc., all supplied by the Bank.'¹⁸ The matter of salary must then be surely something of little importance. Addis, however, was in an unusual position for a man of 25, and even he would find it difficult but not impossible to save, given the expenses of his position – the cost of establishing (or perhaps, in the Peking of the time, hiding) the corporate image. Certainly, it is safe to conclude, the salary was but part of a package; salary and fringe benefits must be considered together.

Salaries

The reluctance to change the basic salary scale is a fact of history – instead add allowances, change the exchange rate, provide in kind, pay non-market interest rates on staff accounts; for exchange rates can be changed, allowances eliminated, ratios rearranged, but a basic salary once raised can never be moved down again. Furthermore allowances, gratuities, and final payments are often geared to basic salary. In the 1930s the Hongkong Bank *did* lower salaries, but the cut was a percentage and 'temporary' and caused such soul searching and heart rending that, for all practical purposes, 'fiddling' with remuneration rather than reassessing salary scales would appear the preferred, although not the only policy.

The Hongkong Banker started then with a basic salary. By 1897 when a salary review was actually undertaken by a sub-committee of the Board, the scale for juniors ranged from $150 per month to $300 in six increments of $25 payable after each two years of service, the last being on commencement of the twelfth year – indicating the new realization of the time it took even a good man to be appointed an Accountant.

There were salary scales, first adjusted in 1886: for juniors, $150 with two increments of $25 after two and four years of service; by 1897 there were the further increments noted above; Accountants $350–400, agents $600, managers $1,000 to $1,250, and the Chief Manager $1,666; $500 for the Chief Accountant and Sub-Manager Hong Kong office. The point on the scale depended on the agency or branch, which were graded in order of responsibility: (i) Shanghai, (ii) Yokohama, Singapore, Batavia, Bombay, and Calcutta, and Sub-Manager Hong Kong Office, (iii) Sub-Manager, Shanghai, (iv) Tientsin, Hiogo, Foochow, Amoy, Penang, Iloilo, and Peking. Saigon was eventually recognized as a hardship post for a junior, and an extra allowance made.

An acting agent received half his own pay and half the pay of the man he was acting for; it therefore paid the Bank to refrain from substantiating a man in a post too quickly, and the 'acting' became a virtual sub-grade in the pay scale. Even John Walter, when he was 'acting' Chief Manager on the departure of Jackson in 1886, received not the full entitlement of $20,000 but only $16,000 per annum, that is, one-half Jackson's pay and one-half his own salary as Manager Yokohama.

On the other hand there was the long-established manager pressing for a transfer to a post graded at a higher level; often he could not or should not be moved, and the Board would make him an additional allowance rather than increase the grading of the post itself. In 1892 J.F. Broadbent sought an increase in salary for long service; the Board granted his request on this basis. There was thus no absolute policy.

The Hongkong Bank kept its accounts in a silver unit of account, its salaries in the East were quoted in dollars, and they were apparently credited in outports at par. The impact on the Eastern staff of the decline in the gold value of silver was mixed. There is evidence that the price of locally produced items, including services, did not change significantly during the period, and, in any case, a large portion of the requirements of life were 'found', that is, they were paid in kind. For these items the rate of exchange was of little concern.

The member of the Eastern staff was probably remitting funds to Britain either for support of his family or to save for retirement. These remittances were affected by changes in the rate of exchange, the impact of which caused considerable dissatisfaction. The Board's solution was to make the remedy appropriate to the problem – the salary was not changed but only the rate of exchange at which it could be remitted. To complete the logic, no one could claim to remit his entire salary, so the Board fixed an arbitrary percentage – from 1886 the staff member could remit 25% of his salary at the preferential rate of 3s:9d and the balance at the rate of the day; from October 1897 the percentage was 50% at 3s:4d, thus partially offsetting the continued depreciation of silver. As this was strictly *ex gratia* it could be readjusted by simple decision of the Board.

Not all the staff were assigned to Hong Kong and China. The Board accordingly set rates for Japan and India on the same principles.

In 1899 in its general readjustment of accounts, the Board put the Provident Fund on a sterling basis, which solved that particular concern and will be considered in the discussion of retirement. The Board supplemented these provisions by allowing a special rate of interest on staff accounts, but this arrangement was at one point cancelled, creating considerable concern.

The Eastern staff, as a consequence of these changes, were intended to be on the whole as well off as before. The Bank, on the other hand, was not; staff 'salaries' had in fact been increased. On the assumption that the manager with $1,000 per month would transfer half his salary to London at 3s:4d against the rate of the day at 1s:9½d, his salary after 1897 would in fact cost the Bank $17,163 per annum instead of the $12,000; and there would be additional charges on the Provident Fund, since the total contribution was paid in sterling as a percentage of the sterling equivalent of a dollar salary calculated at the two exchange rates on a 50/50 basis – in 1899 the Board estimated this would cost the Bank, at the then rate of exchange, some $27,000 annually.

By this logic the Portuguese staff salaries ought not to require adjustment since they would retire in the East and, as suggested before, the cost of living in the East had not changed significantly. But their salaries were adjudged low even by contemporary standards and in 1898 the Board agreed to increases of $5 or $10 for clerks receiving under $170 per month with gratuities from time to time for those above this level.

Adjustments in London were made the same year as part of a career package. There the Accountant had received £750 a year and the sub-accountant £400; no other member of London Office could receive more than £350. The Board raised the sub-accountant to £500 and gave management discretion to pay department heads and 'other deserving officers' up to £450. Thomas Jackson declared that this had placed the London staff in a 'satisfactory condition'.

Other benefits

Members of the Eastern staff received bonuses (i) as a result of a decision by the Board to grant a bonus of usually 10% on salaries, (ii) a grant before declared profits to specified managers for their contribution to profits, (iii) a grant from the net profits of a major loan to those involved in the negotiations, or (iv) a specific award for some particular duty, for example, a bonus to J.R.M. Smith for handling the Shanghai books while still a first-tour junior.

From the net profits before publication the Board authorized the allocation of a total $6,000 to managers in Shanghai, Yokohama, and Saigon for their contribution to the second-half 1886 profits.

In 1898 gratuities to staff involved in negotiating the £16 million Third Indemnity China loan totalled £9,450, with Ewen Cameron receiving £3,000, E.G. Hillier £2,500, Julius Brüssel £1,500, and others lesser amounts – including £500 for G.H. Burnett on the London staff. Cameron as London Manager was authorized to give smaller gratuities to other London and Hamburg staff. These were proportionately large amounts; Brüssel, who had a few months previously been refused an increment, had been reminded of a possible gratuity which, in the event, was equivalent to 100% of his salary.

Normally the Hongkong Bank provided a Bank house only for the branch or agency manager, although when the opportunity arose a house might also be purchased or rented for the 'number two', the sub-manager or Accountant. F.T. Koelle as a junior in Batavia experienced the sequence – living with the Manager, M.C. Kirkpatrick, on his first arrival, moving to a hotel, and finally moving into a house with others. First, he provides a description of the manager's home at the time of his arrival in 1898:

The Manager's house I found to be a large stone bungalow (the Bank's property) raised a few feet from the ground, with large rooms, spacious airy verandahs, plants and flowers, marble floors and elegant and comfortable furniture. The houses are all built on very much the same lines, & certainly seem adapted to the climate. The House is lighted throughout with electric light, in the drawing room, on the piano, verandahs, bathrooms and outhouses, and the floors are marble. . . .

On 17th September I cleared out of the Kirkpatricks . . . across the Koningsplein to the Grand Hotel Java or, as it is called by the natives 'Ruma Makan Java' (Java Eating House). I had the choice of two rooms & chose one with a larger bathroom & clear of smells. There are several English fellows & we live in a row of rooms on each side of the entrance drive to the Hotel, very like the sergeants' quarters at Fort Canning, Singapore. The road is narrow, though quiet, and the atmosphere is rather stagnant & close. . . .

Our motives for [a second] change were the wish to learn Dutch, and economy. By chance we heard of the very place, and it suits to a T. Really the only fault we can find with it is that it is too cheap; as the few men we have confided in, except Kirkpatrick, think that we must be 'pigging it' at the price which is F 75 each month, besides light, while I was paying F 120 in the 'Hotel Java'. We have a charming little pavilion with rather small rooms, a verandah in which we breakfast, a sitting room where I am writing, and a bedroom each, besides a storeroom, kitchen, and bathroom of our own. The only meal we have with the family is dinner, which has so far been a great success. None of them [parents and three children] can speak anything but Dutch & Malay, so we are bound to plunge and flounder about in Dutch, French, Malay & German.[19]

Financial problems and expense accounts

There were no family passages – and no school fees – paid. With late marriage and often early retirement forced in part by poor health, the burden of educating the family was a heavy one. A Hong Kong magistrate found at the end he could not afford to send his son to college, he offered him to the Bank in 1900 as the exchanges, which the lad was never to understand, continued to decline, the consequences of which were brief but fond memories of P.G. Wodehouse.[20]

E. Morriss had a long career as Agent Calcutta and Manager Yokohama, but he had been unable to save and had run up overdrafts which came from time to time to the directors' attention. In 1888 they increased his salary, adjusted the rate of interest on his overdraft, paid a gratuity of £1,000 and urged McLean to send out his son Percy, then in London Office, to help relieve the father's financial burden. The following year the son came East, but his father died in November 1890; the directors granted the widow £3,000.

The reference to the overdraft is significant because the directors ruled from time to time that no staff overdrafts and no loans to staff without adequate security should be permitted. The rule was strangely unenforceable.

The expense account is the child of progressive income tax. In the Age of Jackson Bank agents and managers were expected to entertain from their salaries, and their houses, servants, and carriages provided in kind were designed to make such representation possible. In a later period special functions could, with permission, be debited to charges account, but the records are insufficient to determine whether this practice had already been authorized. Special assignments, such as inspecting branches, called for 'allowances', but it is significant that John Walter, on leaving his position as Shanghai Manager, offered in 1892 to act as inspector at a lower salary, say $10,000 as opposed to $15,000, on the grounds that he would not be involved in entertaining. The Board, however, agreed that his salary should not be reduced below $1,000 per month.

Charles Addis as a very junior Agent in Peking had a salary of $350 a month; he was specifically assigned what he refers to as an 'expense account' of $50 per month.

As already noted, Home leave was granted on changing terms; there appears to have been local leave, but without a declared policy and certainly without 'entitlements'. Sick leave was granted on a doctor's recommendation and took the form either of a local trip to a Hill Station or inter-port sea voyage or of a trip Home to a temperate climate pending medical approval to return under *ad hoc* financial arrangements.

Medical

There were more formal methods of providing for the health of staff, although sports were coming to be considered basic. In larger offices there was a company doctor, paid a fixed fee on a per head basis. This provision was first granted in June 1880 at the request of W.G. Greig, Agent in Hankow, and the Board ordered similar provisions for all agencies. Ten years later the medical fees per annum were fixed at $750 for ten men, rising to $1,000 for twenty. Fees for families and for hospitalization do not appear to have been included. Saigon in 1899 was an exception since the doctors were military or naval officers on brief tours of duty and their high fees of $25 per visit had to be considered against the Bank's individual officer's allowance of $100 per annum; the Board asked the Agent, H. Hewat, to offer an alternative scheme – which is not minuted.

Not everything could be encompassed routinely. In 1880 M.A. Carvalho, a 'very old and valuable clerk' in Shanghai, was provided $300 to pay for an eye operation – the normal medical allowance for Portuguese staff was $25 per annum. Alexander Leith, after many years of negotiating the Bank's China loans, lost his mind, and in granting an allowance to his wife the directors added £10 per month for his care in a suitable mental home – recovery was not expected. Happily within two years he was well again and walking abroad 'without a keeper'. For E.G. Hillier's glaucoma and virtual blindness there was no cure, but he had his exceptional memory and the Board authorized a secretary.

In 1890 E.J. Pereira, the pioneer Portuguese officer sent in 1866 from Hong Kong to Yokohama, suffered a paralytic stroke; the Bank paid the fee at the German hospital, the cost of passage home, and a pension at half-pay, minuting their recognition that, should he die, his widow would need continued support.

In London G.M. Lind, who joined the Bank in 1871, had his foot amputated and the Board authorized a payment of £50 to cover the operation. These are small matters perhaps, but they still remained the responsibility of the Board of Directors. They were not matters of routine banking which had been delegated to management. Thus the minutes cover the increase in capital, the Bank's accounts, the great problem constituents – and the minutiae of individual problems. 'Nothing', said Jackson, 'is too great and nothing too small for the Hongkong Bank.' In that day of paternalism there were many on both the Eastern and local staffs who had reason to be pleased this was so.

Too often, however, the consequence of illness was early retirement or death. In its first 35 years, the Hongkong Bank witnessed the death of sixteen of its Eastern staff in the East, ten of senior level and six juniors, whose service varied from six months to six years. Many more left the East for reasons of health. Widows of local staff too might need assistance. The Board's response to these problems will be considered below.

Pensions and retirement gratuities

Although the Hongkong Bank enjoyed prosperous periods, the Board of Directors may be excused for taking a short-run view during most of the Bank's history until the mid-1890s. If there were 'extra' funds unallocated, prudence suggested building the reserves and the shareholders had some legitimate claims. As Table 13.5 confirms, as far as the minutes reveal, the Board's record with charity is restrained (see also Table 10.2 in Volume II). In the spirit of the times, charity was a matter for private companies and individuals, not corporations. Jackson was noted and praised for his private munificence, but the Bank's role was narrowly defined.

Against this background the Board's treatment of staff is both understandable and relatively generous, although pragmatic. The payment of adequate and competitive salaries was the duty of the Board; not so clear was its obligation to those who had left the Bank's service or to their widows. The Board kept such matters strictly under its own control; it was not a banking matter to be delegated to a Chief Manager no matter how revered.

As with other personnel matters, the best procedure is to state the basic policy and then consider the nature of the many exceptions.

There is no evidence in the records of any policy on the age of retirement or on the length of expected service in the East. 'Retirement' is virtually not mentioned as such; indeed, until the late 1970s officers requested permission to 'resign'. Since in the earlier days gratuities were awarded at the discretion of the Board, the officer tended to resign on stated grounds of ill-health. In the inter-war period, 30 years would appear normal, but in the nineteenth century a member of the Eastern staff would be under no obligation except to serve out his current five-year tour, although the expectation was for steady employment until one had no further need to work or one was unable to work in the East. In practice this meant that many left, as suggested above, for 'health' reasons and 25–30 years would be long service; some of the Eastern staff served longer, Harries served 42 years; for ten years he was actually the senior member of the staff – but then the climate by the Golden Gate is particularly invigorating.

There were no pension funds. The sources of income potentially available to a retiring staff member were (i) his Provident Fund, (ii) the departing gratuity, and (iii) his own savings. The last depended very much on assignments, on the success of personal investments, and on the age distribution of the family. The discussion below is limited to the Provident Fund and the gratuity.

The practice of providing a retirement gratuity forced, in a sense, the development of a Provident Fund, if the Board were not to be faced with an *ad hoc* decision with each retirement. Eastern and Portuguese staff were expected to contribute 5% of their salaries, the Board 5%. In 1891 this latter was raised to 10% by drawing from the Officers Good Service Fund, which was, presumably, sufficiently well funded. The Provident Fund was deposited at a favourable rate of interest and, in 1899, put on a sterling basis – this last provision for the Eastern staff only. The Fund was not, however, inviolate; when in serious personal financial difficulties members could be authorized to draw on it, with the result that on retirement there could be difficulties.

The Board's flexibility came from the Officers Good Service Fund (OGSF), the origins of which lay in the Officer Guarantee Fund, an enforced contribution arising from the crisis of 1874/75. In 1880 this contribution was stopped, the balance of the fund was paid into the newly established OGSF which was in turn to be fuelled by the credit of the value of insurance premiums which the Bank would otherwise have paid into their Marine Insurance Fund. Once the latter had reached a maximum of $250,000, further premiums, plus any bonus received from an outside insurance company as a result of premiums and interest at 5% in the Marine Insurance Fund would be paid into the OGSF, which was itself guaranteed a 5% rate of interest.

The OGSF itself was at first not permitted to exceed $150,000 but in 1890 G.E. Noble persuaded the Board to increase the limit to $300,000. As it turned out the Bank was soon to be in crisis and in 1892 the Board 'sacrificed' or, as Addis preferred, 'pillaged' the OGSF, repaying in full only in early 1899 from the profits of the previous half-year. Also in 1892 the Board, after 'mature deliberation', by which one may assume that the Board recognized the unsound nature of their policy, invested $100,000 of the Fund in the debentures of a company in difficulties and with which the Bank was heavily involved.

The purpose of the OGSF as originally stated by the Board of Directors was (i) to pay a gratuity to officers forced for health reasons to retire early or (ii) to provide a pension – an interesting distinction – to their widows. As practice evolved, the Board's decisions were less nicely defined, and the OGSF became a supplement to the Provident Fund as a reward for good service – regardless of length of service – rather than as compensation for lost opportunity.

Before touching the OGSF the Board attempted to make sums available from current operating funds. Thus if an officer returned Home on leave after five years and died say two months later, the Board would usually make the balance of his leave pay, which they would inevitably note as 'due to him', payable to the widow. They would only then, after noting any balance in the Provident Fund, consider the case for further assistance on the basis, very often, of a request from his family. If the staff member had been found merely unfit to return, he himself would have sought the gratuity and the Chief Manager would present the relevant facts to the Board. This policy conserved the OGSF but it also reflected the theoretical approach of the directors who considered themselves bound to account carefully for funds not expended in the course of business.

Examples will confirm, perhaps, that the directors acted pragmatically.

After John Moffat (East in 1881) died unexpectedly in Vancouver in 1892 en route Home on sick leave, the Board were told that the Bank had realized his securities leaving him a credit balance of $332, and there were three unmarried sisters partially dependent on him. He would have been entitled to six months' leave on full pay. In view of the very high opinion directors entertained of Mr Moffat and in appreciation of services rendered the Bank, they voted the sisters twelve months' full pay equivalent, or $6,000 instead of $3,000. But the grant was worded in terms of services rendered, thus enabling payment to be made from working funds. The OGSF was, as it happened, at a low point.

Similarly on the sudden death of Andrew Veitch in Yokohama in 1893, the directors voted six months' *salary* for his children.

In cases of prolonged illness, as in the case of Harry Thomsett, doomed to lie paralysed in England for many years to come, the Board continued sick leave, usually at half-pay up to the point when further service was out of the question; they then might make a terminal grant from the OGSF and in the case of Thomsett they also appear to have continued a 'pension' to Mrs Thomsett.

A simpler case would be the retirement of A.W. Maitland after twenty years' service; the Board voted him £2,000 in 1895 from the recently partially restored OGSF. John MacNab (East in 1872), Agent in Iloilo, was granted £1,250 after 25 years, but then his service had been marred by his failure to prevent a fraud by a local clerk. A younger man with only eight years in the East died after returning to the United Kingdom in 1897, and his mother was voted £250 on the assurance of Jackson that he was 'a good man'.

When the former Chief Manager G.E. Noble retired for reasons of health from London Office in 1897 the matter was one for individual consideration and he was voted a gratuity of £3,500 after 32 years' service.

The Board could also be flexible. J.M. MacLachlan (East in 1889), former assistant at Foochow, had retired to California for his delicate lungs and had been receiving a payment of US$70 (gold) per month. He then requested a loan of US$2,500 to enable him to buy into a ranch partnership, but the Board was not yet ready to become involved in domestic California ventures and instead capitalized the monthly payments by granting a single gratuity of US$2,500.

When Murray Stewart resigned in Hong Kong to join his brother as a broker after only ten years' service, he was granted $2,000 on the basis of the Chief Manager's testimony.

The OGSF could also be used as a payment to soften the blow of 'requested' resignation. Despite the tradition that before Personnel Departments and mid-career reassessments the Bank carried Eastern staff through to the end, there were in fact golden handshakes. That they were relatively few is consistent with the tradition that the Bank had a need for experienced 'Eastern staff' to undertake relatively routine work – and to be paid accordingly. Neither of these factors are likely to be operative today.

The Board looked after its Eastern staff consistent with the customs of the time, for the majority of directors were, after all, senior executives of their own companies, well aware of the standards. But what of the Portuguese and 'local' staffs?

When the Hongkong Bank commenced business in 1865 it recruited Portuguese staff as local clerks, and perhaps for a time it was thought that the differentiation between Eastern staff and local staff would not become sharply defined. This is reflected in Gonsalves' diary quoted in Chapter 7; it is also reflected in the fact that even the few records extant provide evidence that the Bank paid the passages of at least two Portuguese staff, one to Shanghai and one to Yokohama.

In the 1890s the oldest of the local staff in the East and, indeed, in London were past work, and the Board had on occasion to deal with the resulting problems. In 1898 Pereira, as previously noted, was brought back from Yokohama. M.A. Carvalho of the Shanghai office had returned to Macau for a long retirement; he died in 1913, the Bank having paid him $800 a year since 1879. Another clerk had served in Hong Kong for 29 years and was retired, but, being in financial difficulties, his Provident Fund already drawn down to meet debts, the Board granted him $50 per month, and when he died in 1901 the allowance – it was not technically a pension being paid at the pleasure of the directors – was continued to the widow.

There is evidence that personal financial trouble for Hong Kong residents often had its beginning with share speculation.

The 'native' staff were apparently the responsibility of the compradore or guarantee shroff, but the Board nevertheless considered isolated cases; these men were after all employees of the Bank and treated as such.

On the deaths of Teo Chow Sick in 1900 and Lim Tiang Moh in 1901, both shroffs in Singapore since the branch had opened there, the widows appealed and were granted, doubtless on the recommendation of the Singapore Manager, allowances of $50 per month for five years. Lim had been ill for some time and the Bank had previously granted him leave on full pay. And in Bombay P. Sorabjee, described as an old servant of the Bank almost since the start of the agency, died leaving a widow and seven children; his salary had been Rs 105 per month and his Provident Fund was $365. He was voted a gratuity of Rs1,500. There were other cases which the local family system could not handle and which the Bank considered. The gratuities would seem to have become standardized at about eighteen months' salary.

In London G.H. Burnett, the Bank's London Office Accountant, who began as the Accountant in the Bank's then small office in 1866, a man who had once tried service in the East and who worked on the China loans, was often ill and was due for retirement. All the Eastern staff would remember him; as London juniors they learned a little from him and from his department heads; he sometimes went to see them off from Charing Cross. In 1899 he still had family responsibilities, and so the Board voted him full pay for the balance of the year and then £500 per annum.

In other cases, for example that of George Mackie, who in 1894 had completed 22 years with the Bank in London, the Board had taken the position that, as they had no pension fund, they could not vote an open-ended gratuity in this way; they voted Mackie £250 a year taking into consideration his previous salary of £350 and knowledge of his continuing responsibilities for a wife and young family. The fact is the Board were cautious, and much depended on the prosperity of the Bank itself.

There were other cases, including some, perhaps, which were handled without reference to the Board.

The Hongkong Bank began business when attitudes were shaped by the master-servant relationships and by the distinction between partners and clerks in private companies. These attitudes dominated personnel thinking. After some thirty-five years this had changed little. Terms of service had improved, it is true; the Board, guided by a sympathetic Chief Manager, were reasonable – when the position of the Bank permitted. But local staffs were on minimal, if competitive, conditions and the Eastern staff, unlike those in other banks, came East without a contractual agreement. They did not as yet have to. The Bank even with its growth remained a family and with Jackson at the helm they felt, correctly as it turned out, that anything formal was either impractical or unnecessary.

THE DEPARTURE OF THE EARLY MANAGERS

As an encouragement to Charles Addis then working as a London Office junior, his brother George wrote from Penang, 'There are good men in [the Hongkong Bank] abroad, but *not many* . . .'[21]

The key to the Hongkong Bank's turnaround in the late 1870s was the underlying loyal constituency of the Bank and their business, supplemented by the profits from loans to the Chinese authorities. All this could, however, be offset by business and exchange losses. The actual success of the Bank depended on the quality of its officers as bankers and their management of the Bank's resources. The potential was there, but it could be and, at one time or another, almost was in danger.

After Jackson himself the most important of the Bank's managers were Ewen Cameron in Shanghai, John Walter in Yokohama, and David McLean in London.[b] San Francisco was in the very competent hands of W.H. Harries, New York was dominated until 1901 by A.M. Townsend. The Indian agencies were capably managed by G.E. Noble and Edward Morriss, but the Bank would have problems with Manila's C.I. Barnes and Singapore's Herbert Cope.

There were competent men just below this level either simply in support or preparing for future leadership. William Kaye as Sub-Manager in London remained through 1887, retiring to open the way for the return of the Eastern managers, but G.H. Burnett would remain until 1899; Henry C. Smith was Chief Accountant in Hong Kong until his death in 1882, M.M. Tompkins stayed with Harries in San Francisco, Alexander Leith had done good work in Foochow and would take over in Tientsin until his illness in 1891 – that completes the early list.

Of the remaining seniors no others made a mark in the Bank's history, either because of early death or poor health or because in the test of running an agency they failed. Singapore proved a dangerous challenge to banking competence, the chettiars, the uncertainty of the entrepot trade, and the risks of development in the Malay States proving fatal fascinations for successive managers. With the resignation of W.G. Greig in 1888, the departure of L.C. Balfour in 1892 and the take-over by G.W. Butt (East in 1878), and the sustained capability of T.S. Baker, the position there improved – but it would not peak until the managership of (Sir) John C. Peter (East in 1884) from 1911 to 1922.

By the early 1880s there were juniors in the East who would eventually assume leadership. François de Bovis opened the Tientsin agency in 1881 and in 1885 on the sudden death of J.M. Grigor (another early Hongkong Banker lost) took over

---

[b] Speaking at the Bank's 1909 Annual Dinner, Sir Thomas Sutherland, the founder of the Hongkong Bank, remarked that in any future history written of the Bank, David McLean would deserve a chapter to himself. This is a correct assessment of his importance but not, alas, of the space available.

Bombay. H.M. Bevis was a junior; he would succeed as Acting Chief Manager and as Manager in Shanghai until poor health drove him to seek a premature death in 1906. J.P. Wade Gard'ner would move up close to the top, ending his exceptionally long career in the 'East' (1873–1919) as Manager New York; R. Wilson would eventually reach Colombo, and David Jackson (TJ's younger brother) was moving up to the eventual managership of Yokohama; H.E.R. 'Harry' Hunter, a successful Shanghai Manager, 1907–1912, and Acting Chief Manager during J.R.M. Smith's leave in 1906, and the disappointed V.A. Caesar Hawkins were already in the East, as were J.R.M. Smith, Jackson's final successor, and C.S. Addis, E.G. Hillier, and less well-known, but important for the continuity of the Bank, such future managers as Charles W.May (East in 1888), T.McC. Browne (East in 1882), J.D. Smart (East in 1885), and H.D.C. 'Jumpy' Jones (East in 1884). A.G. Stephen, Chief Manager, 1920–1924, came East in 1885; his first appointment was as Accountant Batavia in 1896 and his career will be considered in Volumes II and III.

Despite this listing of future Bank managers, an examination of the Eastern staff of say 1880 when George Addis was passing judgement confirms that few survived the decade. The Bank needed a mix; and it is true that for a young man going East in 1883 there would be opportunity – not immediately, but it was there.

By 1891 when de Bovis as Chief Manager represented, tentatively, the take-over by a new generation, the Hongkong Bank had new managers. McLean and Kaye had gone from London to be replaced by the overly talented combination of Jackson and Cameron, both signing as 'Manager', but the former senior. John Walter was in the process of resigning from Shanghai in favour of Wade Gard'ner, Leith would soon have to leave Tientsin in favour of A.W. Maitland, H.M. Bevis had taken over Yokohama, G.W. Butt later of Singapore had his first agency in Hiogo, and the able J.R.M. Smith had completed setting up the new Bangkok agency; he was replaced by the very successful T.McC. Browne. Smith himself was assigned the task of opening Rangoon.

That same year Charles Addis went to Calcutta as Accountant to assist the Manager, Andrew Veitch; in Batavia M.C. Kirkpatrick began his long term as the Agent and Henry Hewat took over in Saigon.

The first departures had come in the last years of the 1880s. David McLean had begun the Jackson years virtually as the *éminence grise*; he had thrice been offered the chief managership which he did thrice refuse, but the shareholders had pressed the directors to send him on a tour of inspection and it was his report that reassured both them and the Bank's constituents. Then for many years he managed London, writing strongly worded letters of advice and criticism which could well mislead the casual reader into supposing he must have been the Chief Manager. McLean's main criticism was the handling of exchange with India, and, as the years passed his specialized knowledge, gained from life in the East and from the inspection tour, must have lost its immediacy and the letters are less sweeping in their scope. They remain to the end critical of error, but he has faded into the not unimportant role as London Manager; Jackson is by then clearly the chief. McLean in retiring acknowledged that Jackson was coming to replace him, even as Cameron was to replace Kaye.

McLean's actual retirement was marred by a misunderstanding. The Board in its report to shareholders, which was according to custom brief and formal, merely announced McLean's 'resignation', a word too often used to cover a discharge for poor performance. The Bank's Chairman made amends as planned in his address to the shareholders, but the original omission rankled. No doubt McLean was pacified by a gift of commemorative plate and the commissioning of Sir George Reid (1841–1913), President of the Royal Scottish Academy, to execute truly fine portraits of himself and his wife; these still hang in the dining room in Scotland in the house rebuilt on land he had rented for his shooting and which is now owned by the family (see Plate C5).

On May 3, 1889, Ewen Cameron, his departure delayed some eighteen months due to the problems of John Walter's brief chief managership, received a public address from the leading citizens of Shanghai. The *North-China Herald* described the scene:

The large and magnificent drawing room of the Bank [presumably the one the furnishing of which had aroused shareholders' ire in 1875] was thronged to overflowing by the friends of the popular manager of our great local institution, and his equally esteemed wife, and never perhaps in the history of Shanghai has there been such a general expression of regret at the disappearance of two of its residents from the everyday life of the Settlement.[22]

The Address itself was a tribute to Cameron's management:

When you arrived here in 1873, the 'Bank' of which you then assumed the management had a comparatively limited influence. You leave it to-day the great financial institution of Shanghai and the centre of a widely-extended system of Banking facilities in the North of China. This unexampled success is, we believe, largely due to your zealous care of its interests, and to the never failing courtesy extended to everyone who has had business relations with it. We may say, indeed, that by your exertions and under your guidance it has greatly contributed to the development of the trade of the port and to the prosperity of the community, a work of which you may be justly proud.

But there was a significant comment in the preliminary remarks: 'The duties of your office, Mr Cameron, no doubt prevented you from taking a very prominent or active part in the public affairs of this Settlement, but your counsel and advice have been always at the disposal of those who sought them . . .'[23]

The fact that such a comment should be made on such an occasion suggests, despite the flowery tributes which follow, a disappointment. Bankers simply did not stand for office but their advice, like that of the parson, was readily available in its proper sphere. Cameron was, however, an *ex officio* member of the Shanghai Recreation Fund, an early community project which, after financial difficulties, had been reorganized and was by then virtually a charitable foundation which provided funds to other non-profit organizations, clubs, libraries, and sporting facilities on varying terms. It was, in fact, a typical banker's honorary task.

Perhaps the Address was sincere in suggesting that if a banker made a success of his bank, he was doing all and more than the community expected. In his response Cameron praised the trustworthiness of the Shanghai businessman and the Chinese in particular, and when he and his wife sailed down the river on the *Tokio Maru* the Chinese 'also mustered in strong force and gave him the usual orthodox celestial send-off amidst a fusillade of fire crackers . . .'

This is not the place to evaluate Ewen Cameron; his was not a journey to retirement. His role in London belongs to another period and his story must, therefore, be concluded in Volume II. His role in the great loans of the period from 1895 was based, however, on his experience in Shanghai. He had the vision to open in Peking and to notice both Hillier and Addis. Perhaps it was this reaching into the staff and selecting the right man that differed from the perceived policy of his immediate successors; some would complain that only seniority mattered. And yet, he left as the Bank staff was growing. Whatever role the Bank was subsequently to play in and with China, the foundations were laid in Shanghai by Cameron, supported certainly by Jackson and the Board, but the work was his.

There is, in the folklore of the corporation, the assumption that the Shanghai Manager, not the Chief Manager, was the key figure in the Bank. This was never true, although when the focus was on China, naturally the Shanghai Manager was most prominent in the public news. Jackson, Cameron, and McLean were a team. When that broke up, the combination of Jackson and Cameron in London, while perfectly understandable as an historical development, was unsound. In the 1890s there was Jackson again in Hong Kong, Cameron in London assisted for a time by John Walter and G.E. Noble, and Wade Gard'ner in Shanghai.

When Jackson too departed for London in 1902, he was sufficiently senior to permit a sounder arrangement. He would be Chairman of the London Committee, leaving Sir Ewen Cameron, now aided by the Bank's first junior to go East, A.M. Townsend, as London Manager; and in Shanghai there was H.M. Bevis. G.E. Noble had died in 1901 and John Walter had joined the London Committee.

In 1902 at the end of the Jackson Era there were 162 on the Eastern staff; Sir Newton J. Stabb was still a 'junior' in Shanghai – eight years later he would be Chief Manager; A.G. Stephen was Agent in Sourabaya, A.H. Barlow a 'junior' in

Hong Kong, and A.C. Hynes in Bangkok. As a contrast, (Sir) John C. Peter, the Bank's successful Singapore Manager, 1911–1922, was already Chief Accountant; his successor in Singapore would be Hynes. In London Office awaiting 'orders' for the East were (Sir) Vandeleur M. Grayburn and his future Shanghai Manager A.S. Henchman. The succession was in place.

CAREERS WITH THE BANK – ADDIS, KOELLE, AND THEIR CONTEMPORARIES[24]

One way to bring institutions and regulations to life is through biography. Unfortunately in the Hongkong Bank (i) careers were distinctive and generalization difficult and (ii) only one man, Charles S. Addis, left an archive with letters and diaries, and his very successful career can hardly be presented as the story of a typical Hongkong Banker. F.T. Koelle left journals, and these can be inserted to flesh out a story, but he too is unique. Both Addis and Koelle were sons of preachers, the former's father a minister of the Free Kirk, the latter's a German missionary in Turkey for the Church of England; both wrote what must be untypically concerning missionaries and even for the age were unrepresentative in their interest in the theological basis of morality.

Addis came East in 1883, Koelle in 1894; both began their careers in Singapore. Addis went on to Hong Kong for experience under Jackson, and then to Peking, Tientsin, Calcutta, Rangoon, Shanghai, Hankow, Shanghai, and London. Koelle was shunted early to Batavia, never worked in China, and began his second tour in Colombo. In 1903 his knowledge of German was the probable cause in his temporary assignment to Hamburg where, in fact, he spent the rest of his career with the Hongkong Bank.

While outlining these careers some glimpse of the others can be taken – but naturally only on their terms and through their eyes. But for time before memory, this is the best that can be offered.

Recruitment and London Office

Charles Addis must have first learned about the East from the letters of his brother George, who as early as 1873 when George was already East with the Chartered Mercantile Bank and Charles had just entered Edinburgh Academy was stressing the 'need for good handwriting' and deploring the 'tendency nowadays to down play it'. Three years later Charles had left school and joined a merchant firm as shipping clerk; he led a low life until he turned about, became for the time teetotal, and finished as private secretary to the senior partner, Peter Dowie.

In 1880 at the age of nineteen he applied to the Hongkong Bank. George, home on leave in January had discussed the prospects with William Kaye, who stated a long-standing preference for taking men from banks as they were more familiar with calculations – prompting George's suggestions to Charles already quoted. 'If you are sent for and not employed,' added George with a banker's attention to detail, 'they will refund your railway fare.'

By the time G.H. Burnett wrote to Addis in October setting an appointment for an interview, Addis had toyed with the idea of going to Africa or of joining a New Zealand Bank at £100 a year. But there is an undated memo in the Addis papers reading simply, 'Please arrange to join the Office at ten . . .'

In London Addis roomed with J.C. Peter, the future Singapore Manager, and, as already recorded, studied Chinese. Rent was eighteen shillings a week for three rooms. His brother-in-law Peter Graham lent him, without interest, sufficient to enable an expenditure of £130 a year, repayable once he had reached the silver East. George sent him sound advice from Penang (November 26, 1880) on the good life he might expect and its dangers; George also wrote practical suggestions from which other juniors might well have profited.

Working as you are in some department of a big bank with special routine duties, you cannot grasp the why and wherefore of its operations, but master all the details you can both of your own department and of others and look forward to the day when you will be considered fitted to be sent abroad and pull the strings.

George added, 'The Hongkong Bank is the strongest in the East.'

After work Addis, in addition to studying Chinese, attended and was examined on the Gilbart lectures – passed and received one guinea from the Bank – and joined the Birkbeck Institution, with its reading room and library of 9,000 volumes. Unwisely Addis, who was not in any case in good health, frequented a vegetarian restaurant for lunch, partly for reasons of economy, and to which the doctor ascribed his various illnesses, concluding that he must, as a growing boy, have meat in the middle of the day.

At the same time Addis was sizing up his fellow juniors, one of the purposes, one might conclude, of the London experience. Thus on Harry Lamond, who would be appointed Accountant in 1886, study the Jurado case in Manila, assist the Bank in Madrid, work in New York, and resign in 1891 in favour of a more senior position with the Anglo-Argentine Bank, Addis wrote, 'A good hearted pleasant fellow, amusing in his frankness. Clever in a way, but as thoughtless and rash as a child . . . But love of adventures, his own selfish schemes, his lofty ideas – all are betrayed in the most amusing style.' Peter he described as speaking with a strong accent but with a warm Highland heart, not the verdict of all juniors who worked under him in the 1900s.

As the months went by senior London Office juniors left for the East. There were W. Adams Oram 'a particularly fine fellow' who eventually became the Bank's Inspector of Branches (1910–1917), Harry Hunter, V.A. Caesar Hawkins, then Gershom Stewart, and Lamond. One junior was found to have a 'secret disease'; McLean and Kaye would, Addis recorded, have let him go East with the disease on him, but the London Committee, in an interesting and hitherto unrecorded role, were against it; he left the Bank. Instead Gordon How was sent to Singapore. 'Hurrah for old Gordon.'

Meanwhile Addis was moving from department to department, commenting on the work, attending further Gilbart lectures; then he notes the prospective departure of his friends H.M. Thomsett and D.H. Mackintosh (later the long-time Manager of the Tientsin agency), but Mackintosh was temporarily rejected by the doctor.

Thus it was that on February 20, 1883, Addis himself visited Dr Thin and was passed. Henry Robert Sutton of the London Office ordered the trunks and, wrote Addis in his diary, 'will see to the packing'; Thomsett's mother went with him to the Army and Navy Stores. There was the final leave in Scotland and farewells with parting gifts – including a complete set of Scott's novels – and the Mother staying at home weeping.

On March 8 with snow on the ground and piercing cold, some 30 turned up to see Addis and Thomsett off from Charing Cross for an awful, bitterly cold and tempestuous crossing, then by train to Brindisi and the P&O's *Mongolia* to the East.

With the exception of a note about boxing, there is nothing in the Addis London diaries referring to sports, although the question of health pervades the account. Ten years later F.T. Koelle was a London junior, but his account is too brief for comparison, and his background differed in that (i) he had attended Marlborough (an English public school) and (ii) had obtained his experience as a bank clerk in Canada, returning on the news that he had been accepted for the Bank. The major role the sports grounds at New Beckenham played in the life of London juniors was something still for the future (see Volume II).

Nor is there anything in the records suggesting that the later requirement relative to 'experience' with another bank or business firm was a formalized prerequisite to entry into the Hongkong Bank as a junior. Nevertheless, this was already quite customary.

Koelle like Addis refers to the 'great and useful Sutton' – he had been with the Bank since 1868 and would retire in 1900 as senior messenger with a pension 'at the directors' pleasure' of 30 shillings a week; Cameron was at liberty to increase the amount at his discretion. Koelle then describes a pre-send-off dinner, providing a list of those who saw him off by boat train for Brindisi. He left together with A.J. McClure, a Shanghai junior in 1904, who like several others, left the Bank to join his brother as an exchange broker, and E.W. Townend, Agent Bangkok in 1920.

En route Addis showed his ability to retain a sense of judgement under emotional strain. At Suez he records, 'Saw nude Arab girls dance to tom-tom. Dancing poor.' Koelle's experience in Port Said was similar – 'Don't see the Kan Kan! it's a bally fraud and costs something.' Koelle's description of the voyage with its games, sports, and days in port more closely resembles the 'First Trip East' of the inter-war period as told in the oral histories. The pattern was developing.[c]

Life as a junior in the East

Singapore, first posting

When Charles Addis reached Penang in April 1883 a letter from his brother announced he would be taken off for duty at Singapore. The Hongkong Bank Manager had passed the news on to the competition, George Addis, manager of the Chartered Mercantile Bank. Thus Addis began life in the East at Chatsworth, the Mercantile manager's home.

Addis's contemporary Gordon How (East in 1882) was already in trouble. The current account ledger, which was his responsibility, had not been balanced since January. 'Lazy beggar' and no 'hurrah' was Addis's evaluation, but W.G. Greig, who was taking over from J.J. Winton, had How withdraw his resignation and transferred him to Shanghai. The last reference to this officer is in 1902; he had become Agent, Penang, and he retired for reasons of health with a satisfactory record.

Addis's first impression of Greig as a banker was favourable; he saw Winton in decline and virtually carried to the ship; he died two days off Penang. 'My first Manager was John Winton, a shrewd clever Scotchman, at one time a handsome man, but now bloated and swollen with drink.' Winton had been in Singapore as early as 1862 when he made his acting debut on the local amateur stage. He was first an assistant in the Chartered Mercantile Bank; he was appointed accountant and finally manager of the short-lived Asiatic Banking Corporation in Singapore; joined the Chartered Bank in a junior position, probably in India, from which position he resigned in 1873 and, on Ewen Cameron's instigation joined the Hongkong Bank, serving under Morriss in Calcutta and Cameron in Shanghai before returning as Manager Singapore in 1879.

As for work Addis began on the current account ledger, taking over *after* it had been balanced, and then, with the arrival from London of his friend D.H. Mackintosh, recently cleared by the doctor, Addis moved up to Inward and Outward Bills. The newly arrived junior traditionally took over the easier job – or the chores.

Addis had already bought a pony and been initiated into the formality of

[c] See the edited oral history account of the 'First Trip East – P&O via Suez' by Catherine E. King in Frank H.H. King, ed. *Eastern Banking* (London, 1983), pp. 204–29.

colonial society, when, in November, he was ordered up to Hong Kong. There he would meet Jackson.

The contrast in Koelle's journal is only partly a matter of personality; as a former public school boy he records meeting former Marlborough men, is very much involved in team sports, and joins the Volunteers. On the day of arrival Koelle is practising cricket at the nets and his description of his first rugger game in the tropics is vivid. His attitude to the local population is more detached; whereas he would pick up 'kitchen Malay' there is no suggestion that he wishes, as Addis did first in Singapore and then in China, to learn of their language and civilization on a formal basis.

He lived in a chummery, or 'mess' as it was coming to be called by Hongkong Bankers, but not one officially run by the Bank; rather it was a group of bachelors, probably from several firms, living together. Koelle recorded one special event:

The King [Chulalongkorn] of Siam [Rama V] came to look over the Bank here [Singapore] today, & the Mess had him in the drawing room & put up 'Fizz'. He went over the whole house & into my room, examining all the pictures carefully. He asked if my piece of the Golden Pagoda of Rangoon was from a Siamese temple. He wd probably have been annoyed if it had been.

I don't take much stock in 'aristocracy' myself, but the list of people the Mess has entertained here since the new buildings were opened is worth keeping: HM the King of Siam, HH the old Sultan of Johore, HH the Crown Prince (now Sultan) Abu Bakir, HH Prince Dramrong of Siam, HE the Governor Sir Chas Mitchell & Lady M, Lord and Lady Randolph Churchill, and sundry baronets, honourables, rajahs, tunkus, &c and the Crown Prince of Siam.

Koelle recorded that his new Bank work was much the same as in the Canadian bank where he had so recently served his apprenticeship; he had experience with decimals. But his main Bank interest is in the movements of his fellow juniors, going out on the P&O pilot's launch to surprise incoming friends, noting the death of R.A. Niven, a London junior friend who had been taken ill in Bangkok and died after an operation in Hong Kong, recording conversations with colleagues in the Mess, or recounting adventures to the islands or a cricket team trip to the Malay States.

One of his fellow juniors in Singapore was Newton Stabb who had joined the Bank in New York in 1888 and served a year as a London Office junior; he would be Chief Manager when Koelle's German nationality forced his resignation in 1919. At the time he was Manager Hamburg. Addis would be London Manager.

A glimpse of Hong Kong
Addis was in Hong Kong for a little more than two years and the description is of a Head Office whose small junior staff numbered only eight; the whole Hong Kong staff numbered thirteen. There is little wonder, therefore, that he can write: 'We had a grand Manager, Tom Jackson. He and his wife were father and mother to us young fellows. There were ten or eleven of us and we lived together (it was before

the new Bank was built) in an enormous house called Beaconsfield overlooking the Queen's Road.'

There is little of the detail of banking in Addis's writings of this time and his activities relative to the Chinese language and his friends have already been considered. When he resumed his diary in early 1886 on the eve of his own – as yet unknown – departure for Peking, he records wistfully the departure of other juniors for the North – Tientsin would provide a 'fine chance' for Chinese. His chance would soon come, but in the meantime there was a dance at the home of the Chief Manager at St. John's Place.[d] The 240 male guests outnumbered the ladies four to one, the hazard of a bachelor's life in the East. 'House beautifully decorated. A superb supper. Left about 2:30 a.m. full up.'

There are two further entries relating entertainment at Jackson's. In March Addis mentions merely 'dining', but he already knew that Cameron, whom he had met in Hong Kong, had sent for him to go to Peking – 'Horrible suspense. I cannot sleep.'

On April 9, 1886, there was a farewell dinner for Thomas Jackson. 'The best jamboree I have ever had. 32 sat down. Military band played outside. Finally entered house and marched us round – even on to the roof. Carried Jackson shoulder high home, preceded by band.'

The next day the news broke; Addis was to go north. He was examined by the Bank's doctor, Patrick Manson, brother-in-law of David McLean, and then there were the final events relative to the departure of his beloved Chief Manager. 'Enthusiastic meeting in Town Hall to present address to Jackson. Sir George Phillippo [Attorney-General] presented it in a fair speech. Jackson made a manly simple reply. A tremendous crowd went on board to say good-bye.'

And this all before Jackson had completed his life's work. He had, with his colleagues, saved the Bank, but he had not as yet placed it on what he himself was to consider an assured footing; this was to come, as noted in Chapter 13, at the end of 1898. When Jackson finally departed in 1902, the farewells were equally sincere, but perhaps more solemn, as befitted a man who by that time was known not only as a bank manager but as the premier British commercial representative in the East.

Two further matters arise from the materials available: Addis, in common with most other Hongkong Bankers, did not press for a particular assignment, and the Bank as family, or more prosaically 'career service', comes across clearly in the frequent references to staff passing through, their entertainment, and the undoubted mutual appraisal.

Koelle was never assigned to Hong Kong, but on his first leave from Batavia he returned to England via North America. Passing through Hong Kong in 1899, Koelle was asked by the Sub-Manager, Caesar Hawkins, if he had a preference

---

[d] Actually the house was off Lower Albert Road, next to where the American Consulate-General now stands (1986), the latter being on the site of the sub-manager's house).

for his next tour. He requested China; he was sent to Colombo. Whatever the formal policy, the staff was small and had to be allocated to the vacancies which existed. There were by now fifteen juniors in Hong Kong and Koelle himself was but at the end of his first tour. Harry Hunter was also on board and so –

... as we approached the anchorage launch after launch dashed out to us from the jetties along the harbour, until there were six launches abreast of one another at the gangway. They included the Customs, 'Ewo', and B&S [Butterfield and Swire] and the Hongkong and other hotels. At last the cleanest, fastest and prettiest of all steamed up, the 'Way-fung' or H&SBC's own launch which we had built a year ago. It took the seventh place in the line and discharged the distinguished party who had come to meet us: the great TJ, Chief Manager, Hawkins, sub-manager, Peter, Accountant and [A.] Coutts, sub-accountant, and Thompson Brown who is 'the gardener' and therefore took us through the garden across the road in front of the Bank, which is the Bank's property and worth one million dollars, and is now full of very pretty carnations, roses, heliotrope and other flowers. We all had a cup of tea together in the drawing room ...

By 1899 the junior mess was on the Peak – 'Cloudlands'.

[We] finally landed at 'Cloudlands' where there are about 15 bedrooms ... a hot toddy was just the thing and undressing before a roaring fire, I jumped into bed under four blankets, in my warm pyjamas and slept like a top. The room was one which [Harry] Hunter had given a Chinaman $15 and carte blanche to 'decorate' seven years ago and the effect, which has lasted perfectly, is a very good example of Chinese fresco art.
    ... The Peak is 1800 feet high. We were up at about 1500 and the thermometer at midnight outside [in March] was $58\frac{1}{2}°$, exactly the same as on the Papendayang crater at about 10 a.m.

All this was under the guidance of C. Stockwell, an enthusiastic 1896 junior, whose name disappears from the Staff List in 1901.

The path to an appointment

Addis's return to a normal career path
When Addis reached Shanghai in April 1886 he was again on a round of visits, even to the point of meeting Mrs A. Veitch, the wife of his manager-to-be in Calcutta. John Moffat, who would die en route home in Vancouver in 1892, R. Wilson, the future Colombo Agent, and H.E.R. Hunter lived together and entertained Addis; at the wharf he also met Jackson's 'near relative' T.McC. Browne (retired 1905), A. Coutts (retired 1902), and F.F. Raper (retired with a nervous breakdown, 1901), who served in San Francisco and New York. But he also had dinner and intimate business talks with Cameron.
    Once in Tientsin, which he characterized unflatteringly but accurately as 'a most hideous, depressing, sterile, dirty, dusty, dung-heap, in the centre of which we live in a trim and well kept little oasis of about a mile long and a few hundred yards wide. We have literally only one road two miles long on which to ride or drive.' Addis had contact again with J.R.M. Smith, and he stayed with

J.C. Nicholson (East in 1880) who would serve under him for a time in London. The Agent then was Alexander Leith, who was also responsible for the 'sub-agency' of Peking; Addis described his wife as 'a pleasant American woman'.

For a time Addis's career was dictated by his role as 'China specialist', and his appointment as Agent at this time was extraordinary; with one exception no member of the Eastern staff with seniority from 1879 had received an appointment; he had 'jumped' some 22 men. When on his return from leave and in the aftermath of sickness and a bad riding accident he had given up Chinese, leaving the Peking agency in the care of Hewat who would hold it for E.G. Hillier, Addis was appointed first a junior in Tientsin, then, after a brief return to Peking, sent to Shanghai in 1889 and finally, with a seniority of eight years, to Calcutta as Accountant in 1891 – his first 'ordinary career' appointment. Jackson had promised him five years, but that was probably an accurate 'seniority' forecast for the time; the growth of staff caused the delay of three years, for the Calcutta appointment was strictly in accordance with seniority – even G.T. How was an Accountant in Manila.

Addis had originally been ordered from Tientsin to be Agent in Saigon. If the story of H. Hewat is a sound parallel Addis could, despite any latent ability, have been left there many years. Instead John Walter, the Shanghai Manager, specifically pressed for his reassignment to his branch, and Addis's opportunities thus remained open. But G.E. Noble, not Jackson, was the Chief Manager, and François de Bovis was his Sub-Manager; the latter may well have made the initial assignment, and the pressure applied on de Bovis may have set the stage for an unfortunate difference of opinion when Veitch left Addis in charge in Calcutta in 1892.

What is striking again in the Addis biography is the progress from port to port, as, for example, when he took his leave in 1888, he met the key people in the Bank. Not only was there the impromptu Bank reunion in Yosemite and San Francisco, but in New York he visited A.M. Townsend, with whom he would work for over six years in London, and G.W. Butt. Once in London Addis called at the Bank and had a drink with George Mackie, then a London Office department head – he died in 1895. More to the point Addis had long meetings with John Walter, who was to urge his transfer to Shanghai the following year. Addis was only a one-tour junior, but his contacts covered the entire range of seniority; he even had tiffin with the recently retired David McLean, sitting between him and Howard Gwyther of the Chartered Bank. It was heady company for a young man, but in Peking Addis had met with Viceroys and Ministers; he was ready for it.

The contrast with F.T. Koelle

When Koelle left for Batavia in 1897 after three years in Singapore, he had no such opportunities. He did settle into the routine of a small agency and, as later juniors were to testify, there were advantages for the ambitious young man who wished to obtain a more comprehensive view of a bank's operations. In the great offices of Hong Kong and Shanghai there could be intense specialization.

A small agency also offered an opportunity to play a role in the community, especially in the minority English community of Dutch Batavia. Nowhere is this more apparent than in Koelle's contribution (and those of a banker before him and of one who followed) to the Church of England.

On Tuesday morning (July 12, 1898) as I was dressing I wondered when we should get a service here from some tourist or travelling parson. Two hours later I was told by the cashier that an old gentleman was waiting upstairs in the office. . . he had heard there was no clergyman here & he would be glad to hold a service in our church. . . the congregation numbered about 17, some of them being Dutch. . . The last service held here before today was in 1894. . . young [J.C.] Robertson in the Mercantile Bank here some years ago used not only to read the service every Sunday, but to preach an excellent sermon and, I believe, fill the church. He was moved before long. The same man had been told by his boss in Calcutta that that sort of thing would not do in the bank & he must give it up or leave. He said he would stick to it & take the risk, & he is now or has been Agent in Calcutta. It is very few laymen in the East who could, or would dare to, preach a sermon.

19 July . . . After all we know ourselves very little, as since writing the last two lines I have written my first sermon and am going to deliver it DV on Sunday.

His church work continued and the congregation grew, but it apparently did not long survive his departure in 1899, for it was said of a subsequent Hongkong Bank Manager, J.C. Nicholson, that his:

great claim to the gratitude of his own and succeeding generations of British people in Java is the conception and success of his work in reviving Church life in Batavia and gradually throughout Java. Within a year of his arrival in 1909, the Java Chaplaincy Fund re-established Java as a live part of the Diocese of Singapore.

After completing his first trip home to England, Koelle wrote nothing further in his journal; the records indicate, however, that he was assigned to Colombo, where, although not formally 'Accountant', he was the second senior officer and referred to locally by the title. There he played cricket, headed the Church of England's Boys' Brigade, and founded a mission to the aborigines.

An article in the *Ceylon Observer* of 1903 is a 'farewell' so typical of the local newspapers of the time:

We regret to find that the popular Accountant of the Hongkong and Shanghai Bank is leaving Colombo on promotion having got the appointment of Acting Accountant to the important branch of the Bank in Hamburg. Mr Koelle's knowledge of German has no doubt led to this result . . . Mr Koelle will be missed in several capacities outside the Bank: as an officer of the Boys' Brigade, a member of the Galle Face Church and especially as Hon Treasurer for a little Veddah Mission begun a few years ago and the responsibility of which in Colombo for funds, practically lay latterly with Mr Koelle. We can only thank him for his good work in the past and wish him health and prosperity in the future – at the same time congratulating the Directors of the Hongkong and Shanghai Bank on having so good, efficient and reliable an Officer on their staff.

Koelle had also been lay representative of the Tamil Cooly (now Church) Mission at the Diocesan Council of 1901.

Then in 1903 the Hongkong Bank's Hamburg Manager, J. Brüssel, was in poor health, A.J. Harold, who had been Accountant in Hamburg for thirteen years, had just died, and the Bank needed a backup; Koelle was chosen, jumping at least twenty senior to him. This and subsequent developments suggest that the appointment was expected to be temporary, until Brüssel either recovered or was replaced. Koelle was bi-lingual, the obvious reason for his selection. Even these factors would hardly have proved operative had not Koelle received excellent reports and been considered capable. In 1905 Koelle became Acting Manager Hamburg.

Charles Addis in Calcutta

Addis remained in Shanghai during 1890 but in March 1891 he left for Calcutta; he had received his first 'normal career' appointment – Accountant. But first there had been a temptation.

Uncle John Thorburn had struck at a dangerous moment. The ambitious Addis had made some calculations and estimated his time to an Accountantship would be five years – could he wait? His brother George had been correct in telling him that not all Hongkong Bankers were of high quality, but, as Addis observed, these men had now retired and their places filled by younger and more qualified persons, leaving his own chances worse than before. In early 1890 Thorburn wanted Addis for what the latter refers to as 'Russell and Co.'s Trust and Loan Company', but, as stated in Chapter 12, Addis after consultation and consideration turned down the offer. There would be many young men in the even slower days to come who would, however, leave the Bank having received offers in the East or in overseas banking in other regions.

Addis left Shanghai and his uncle was to have the task of winding up Russell and Co. at the request of the Hongkong and Chartered banks; John Thorburn would also keep the consequently rudderless National Bank of China afloat until a permanent chief manager was found in G.W.F. Playfair.[25]

En route, Shanghai to Calcutta

Before leaving Shanghai, where he had played a prominent role in the Settlement's intellectual life, contributing to the *North-China Herald* and becoming involved in various esoteric, that is, non-banking, controversies, Addis was present during a more mundane activity, an inspection of the branch by Harries – 'a smart clever man, a bit coarse but a good fellow'. Fortunately, all was in order. He was then off to Calcutta to be Accountant.

En route Addis spent time in Hong Kong with the new Chief Manager,

François de Bovis, with L.C. Balfour the Sub-Manager, and with Caesar Hawkins the Chief Accountant. All this should certainly have led to mutual understanding. But Addis did not hold a high opinion of either of the chief's assistants; perhaps it showed through. At one point Addis records a long chat with A.G. Stephen, who would be Chief Manager in the early 1920s at the time Addis took over the chairmanship of the London Committee.

While still in Shanghai Addis had heard of Alexander Leith's breakdown. Leith had been active in loan negotiations since 1874 and had been Agent Tientsin while Addis was in Peking. In Hong Kong Addis met him aboard the ship taking him home; the man was broken mentally and physically, his wife 'dreadfully crushed and broken'.[26] Leith recognized Addis but then broke into confused talk about the China loans and other business. Happily Addis's assumption that this was terminal proved wrong; the Bank directors' special grant of £10 a month for proper care was to be well spent, and within two years Leith had recovered. His son, A.C. Leith, was himself to have a career in the Bank, 1907–1940, reaching the position of Sub-Manager Shanghai under A.S. Henchman.

Addis then sailed for Singapore where he was met by his London Office colleague, W.B. Thomson (East in 1879), whose promising career – he was Agent Bombay, from 1897 – was cut short in 1905 through ill-health. There was dinner at the manager's home, 'Mount Echo', and a reunion with Thomsett.

R. Wilson, who had been Agent Tientsin at the time of Addis's accident, was then Agent in Penang, Addis's next stop en route to Calcutta.

The case of T.S. Baker

Also in Penang was T.S. Baker who came East in 1883 a few months after Addis and was an unusual case. He had joined the London Office as a clerk at the age of 25, already married with one child, and on the distinct understanding the Bank would not send him East. He then requested the Bank to send him East. He failed to pass Dr Thin's rigid examination but persisted by submitting the certificates of two other doctors.

McLean was strongly behind him on the grounds of excellence, pressing his case on Jackson, stressing his regular habits and his ability to write a good hand; finally in 1883 McLean informed Jackson that he was sending Baker out to Bombay 'unless you object'.[27] McLean covered himself by requiring Baker to agree to repay his passage should he have to return to England on health grounds within a two-year period.

Having thus broken every precedent, Baker proceeded to prove himself; still a junior when Addis passed through Penang, he soon went to Yokohama as Accountant when H.H. Vacher (son of W.H. Vacher and East in 1881) was taken ill. He was appointed Agent Nagasaki in 1896 and returned as Sub-Manager

Yokohama to play a leading role in negotiating Japanese Government loans; he then succeeded Nicholson as Manager Singapore in 1906 and moved from there in 1911 to take over from Harries in San Francisco, eventually retiring in 1921 after nearly 40 years 'in the East'.

Unfortunately not everyone proves the doctor wrong and even Dr Thin could be overly optimistic.

I enclose Dr Thin's report on one of our young men (John McChlery) who is anxious to proceed to the East. He is a first rate clerk & has pleased all the heads of departments. . . . Dr Thin told me the other day that he thought he would have quite [as good] if not better [health] in the East. If he breaks down, no more will be sent out unless the Doctor Certificate is a clean one.[28]

The young man in question came out to Shanghai in 1886 and was dead within two years.

To return to Addis: the trip across to Calcutta was not up to P&O standards, and the Captain gave Addis his cabin, himself sleeping in the chart room. Arriving on April 18, 1891, Addis took over the securities on the 19th (Sunday) and began studying Hindustani on the 22nd.

Death of a young banker
Addis commented on the fine new office, the marble floor, and noted that there were 36 Baboos and two excellent young fellows, A. Hassell (East in 1890) and William K. Dods (East in 1889).

As for Dods, he would spend most of his Bank career in Calcutta, as junior and Accountant, becoming Agent in 1905. Already he was a noted sportsman, and snipe shooting was particularly popular in Bengal. In fact W.K. Dods's record of 262 birds in a single day with one gun, made on February 11, 1900, at Doulatpur, Khulna District, Bengal, still holds today according to Bill Crowen's 'Big Game Records'. In 1922 Dods retired in Calcutta, and Sunil Singh Roy, first Indian to be made an officer of the Mercantile Bank of India, Limited, remembers:

Mr Dods was a friend of my grandfather, and both of them were regular visitors to the Zoological Gardens [of which Dods was the sometime Curator]. I, as a boy, used to accompany my grandfather to the Zoo and met Mr Dods. They were both keen snipe-shooters . . . he used to tell us that he could shoot a bird thrice before it dropped, which was quite good, particularly at his advanced age, but I never saw him do it because we were too small at that time to be taken to the snipe-shoot.[29]

Hassell had come East in 1890 and Addis developed a high regard for him; they used to walk together on the Maidan. It was with Hassell that Addis first learned to play golf. But office health had been generally poor; Hassell was ill and sent on a sea voyage to Colombo, at another time he was at the Hill Station of Darjeeling. All this was very trying for Addis, who as Accountant was responsible for the staff, and he had in any case a low fever himself.

On March 4, 1892, Hassell was down with a fever of 104, Dods was on holiday, and Addis was 'running the office alone'. It is here that Addis notes 'young Bishop has turned out a treasure, so considerate and thoughtful'. But on the 7th a nurse was called in and on the 16th Addis wrote: 'Poor chap, this is the fourth week. They can only keep down his temperature with iced sheets and so on. But altho 105° when I saw him, he looked fairly well though thin and white.' The story continued, 'Hassell making a brave fight for his life . . . looking pinched a bit but chirpy enough . . . Hassell very bad this morning. Just as ill as he can be. I fear his case is hopeless.' On the 27th Addis, who was himself taking 'arsenic three times a day on the top of quinine', received a cable from Hong Kong that the compradore had absconded; the following day, Hassell summoned up enough strength to ask, 'How is everything at the Bank?'; he died at 7:30.

'He was a sterling chap. Busy all morning arranging about funeral, etc. Scorching hot. We buried him in the Scotch cemetery at 5 p.m.'[30]

That there is more to a managerial position than banking had come through dramatically. Writing a few years later to his confidant, Dudley Mills, Addis confessed:

It is extraordinary how unreflective the average man is! During the past year we have had almost constant sickness in the Bank building. Two Europeans have died and of our men all have been laid up with the single exception of myself, although I from time to time have had spells of low fever which it is difficult to shake off & which kept me in a harassingly low state of vitality.

All this was apparent. It was clear too that the sickness was similar in character, viz., typhoid-malarial. And yet until a few days ago when one man was found to be suffering from sore throat, it never occurred to us that it might be well to examine our sanitary surroundings and see if they were not to blame. The sickness was always ascribed to the beastly climate or the abnormal drouth or damp or heat, never to the right cause.

At last, however, on a hint from the doctor I woke up and called upon a couple of doctors to make an independent examination of the premises and to embody their results in a report which would be laid before the health officer of the municipality. I need not go into details. The revelations are sufficiently shocking and when one thinks of young and promising lives sacrificed to the want of a little observation and reflexion, sufficiently sad.

My only excuse is that I have become so inured to stinks in China that I have grown olfactorily callous. It appears that the very soil of our compound is so soaked and saturated with sewage that there is nothing for it but to have it dug up to the depth of two or three feet and removed, fresh rubble being used to replace it.[31]

Andrew Veitch and Charles Addis

Andrew Veitch had joined the Chartered Mercantile Bank in 1864 and had been a good friend of George Addis, walking to the City together and nearly always spending Sunday evenings supping in each other's rooms. 'In those days,' George wrote to Addis on the occasion of Veitch's death, 'Andrew was a particularly warm-hearted, ingenuous little fellow.'[32] Surprisingly, he had switched to the Hongkong Bank in 1870 and come East in 1871 and spent the next fifteen years in Shanghai, first as a clerk or banker's assistant, under David McLean, then as Accountant and Sub-Manager. He moved to Hong Kong as Sub-Manager in 1887, spent some time in London Office relieving John Walter, and returned East in 1891 as Agent Calcutta. Charles Addis had met both Veitch and his wife; they invited him to live with them.

Addis's reactions were mixed; he admitted Veitch's experience and 'cunning of a cautious kind', and at first expressed the opinion that he deserved great credit for the sound view he had taken of exchange during the past four months. Commenting generally on Calcutta, Addis took a career viewpoint: 'The way business is done here, the magnitude of the operations and the scientific financing lend quite a new interest to the monotony of Banking life. I am sure a year in India is worth a good deal to a China hand in throwing a new light on exchange.'[33] But he added, 'I am not anxious at all to strike roots in Calcutta where my stay is not likely to be very long . . . I like the place, but I like China better.'[34]

After months of large parties in the hot climate, intimate talks, and watching his operations, Addis reevaluated Veitch, concluding he was shockingly illiterate and dull in the uptake. Indeed, life in Calcutta could be that of the exile. In the grand agent's house, Andrew Veitch used to sit in the evening pouring over magazines from home, especially *Field*, seeking for his ideal retirement home – after 21 years in the East, this would be his final tour.

It was not to be.

Shortly after the death of Hassell in 1892, Veitch himself was taken ill and had to return to England to recover from recurrent fever. Thus his calculations were already upset, even as the value of silver was falling – he did not have enough for retirement. He would agree to go East once again, and his assignment as Manager Yokohama was a measure of his seniority and the respect the Bank had for his abilities. There was to be one final frustration. Three days after arriving in Yokohama he was dead of meningitis, his dreams of retirement to the British countryside ended forever.[35]

Addis as Acting Agent – a run on the Bank

Veitch had on occasion taken time off on health grounds. It was two months after the death of Hassell that Veitch announced he was going home. He had cabled Head Office applying for four months' leave of absence and added, 'Addis quite competent Acting Agent'.

Being young, ambitious, and very excited, Addis recorded on June 2, 1892, 'Veitch. Saw him on board the P&O SS *Bengal* at 9 a.m. But oh! What a joy to see him go.' Addis was once again an Acting Agent, again in advance of his contemporaries, but this time on purely 'banking grounds'.

During Veitch's absences Addis had already gained considerable experience with Calcutta exchange operations. This was fortunate as Addis was not to be allowed an easy initiation. Within two weeks, while he was attempting, with one man short, to make up the half-yearly accounts and the Hongkong Bank was being carefully watched after the absconsion of the compradore in Hong Kong, a firm in which the Bank was largely interested failed in Calcutta and, worst blow of all, the New Oriental Bank Corporation, Ltd, closed its doors, causing a lack of confidence in general and, beginning June 10, a run on the Hongkong Bank.

'I feel,' Addis wrote, 'like the Captain of a ship in a storm. The main thing is to keep cool oneself and allay excitement in others.' This he did successfully, aided by local merchants who lent him funds and by Jackson's effecting an emergency telegraphic transfer of £100,000 from London, 'like the trump he is'. His instructions to the cashier had been to fill the till and keep it full, paying out as quickly as possible. The 'small crowd of natives . . . followed all day by Babus and half-caste women and even, I am ashamed to say, by some white men and women' continued. Addis was 'trying to carry on exchange business in the usual way, see constituents, replying to questions, and all the time the perpetual clink clink of the rupee across the counter. Is it ever going to stop? How much longer is it possible for us to hold out?'[36]

A friend in the New Oriental Bank wrote a memo which fell into Addis's hands: 'I hear that a severe withdrawal of deposits is going on at the Hongkong Bank. I feel for Addis very much and we here are deeply sensible that it is our collapse that has brought this trouble upon him.'[37]

The writer offered to help out gratis, but added, 'If he is not in trouble, please suppress this letter.'

Eventually the run subsided and the tide turned. As one lady told him, 'When I saw you took it so coolly, I thought everything must be all right.' But it had been a difficult time.[38]

A career in danger

Despite these initial successes and a letter of congratulations, de Bovis, then Chief Manager, did not intend that Addis should remain for long in charge. The plan was for Robert Wilson to come to Calcutta, Veitch would go, as noted, to Yokohama. At this point, perhaps unwisely, Jackson and Cameron intervened, strongly urging that Addis should be left as Agent.

I have no doubt that this telegram, which Jackson and Cameron followed up with letters, annoyed Bovis who felt that his plans were being unwarrantably interfered with. His letter to Jackson pointed out in the coldest manner that, in deference to his and Cameron's representations, Wilson's appointment had been cancelled and I was to remain. There was not one word to show that he himself approved of the change.[39]

From Hong Kong Addis's friend, Stewart Lockhart, warned him that comments were being made 'outside' – 'Clever fellow Addis and all that but not much of a banker you know . . .'[40]

The fact is that de Bovis, whatever motives may be ascribed him by Addis, acted in the normal way and his resentment against interference by subordinates in London, be they Jackson and Cameron or not, was natural. His subsequent moves may be more open to question.

A month after de Bovis had changed his arrangements to permit Addis to remain in Calcutta he attacked his policies in a semi-official letter copied to all branches. Addis was accused of 'over-trading, of taking undue risks, of giving excessive credit, of speculating in rupee paper'. Addis responded immediately, copying his reply to all branches receiving the accusations. His self-defence provides an insight into his operations.

1 That Addis had caused a strain on London resources. In September China and the Straits drew on Calcutta TT for Rs37 lacs. As Addis's deposit base had not been restored since the run and since he had no income and could not borrow, he was forced to debit these branches and agencies in London. In doing this he was following de Bovis's policy of requiring Calcutta to serve the Far Eastern branches. 'To this China/Straits drawing and not to Calcutta "plunging" must the strain of London resources be ascribed.'

2 Overtrading. November to April only £109,000 net altogether and the trade risk has not been increased; it has been decreased by purchasing bills very selectively.

3 Profits. June through August was the barren quarter of the year. This and the ruinous finance required following the failure of the New Oriental Bank Corporation caused the poor results, but the agency was regaining lost ground and July would turn the corner.

All this was apparently true, but not likely to further one's personal position at Head Office, indeed, as Addis noted, 'This [defence] was ignored and attacks took a new form. So virulent, so unscrupulous, so sustained. It was plain I must contemplate leaving the Bank.'[41]

Then Addis made a banking error, passing an item handed him by his Accountant without checking, and although Addis caught the error a few days later and reversed it, the damage had been done. De Bovis in a moderately complimentary letter 'promoted' Addis to Agent Rangoon. He was to replace J.R.M. Smith. Regardless of how Addis judged the move, the Rangoon agency was an appointment more in keeping with Addis's seniority, and in any case the meaning of such an assignment is difficult to assess. Being appointed agent in a small agency may be a terminal assignment, as Addis apparently chose to assume; it may on the other hand be a testing ground. Addis, despite a later encouraging letter from Smith assuring him that de Bovis did not harbour any animosity, and an admonishing letter from brother George that he might be making too much of it, considered he had been shelved.[42]

The events described suggest that all was not well. De Bovis sent L.C. Balfour to take over Calcutta, and he performed poorly, forcing his retirement from the

Bank. At one point Addis laments, 'Doesn't he know his men at all?'[43] And this may have been the problem. De Bovis, proven competent as a banker, able as a Sub-Manager at Head Office, indeed an obvious choice for Jackson's successor, may not have had all the necessary qualities of a chief executive. With Jackson still active and holding the confidence of the Board, de Bovis was in a difficult position. This might have been the moment for Head Office to move to London; instead, Jackson returned to Hong Kong.

Charles Addis remained in Rangoon until his leave in 1894, by which time Jackson was again Chief Manager. Addis was assigned as Sub-Manager Shanghai, served briefly in Hankow as Agent, and then returned to Calcutta as Agent in 1897. But he was a China hand and he was reassigned to Shanghai as Sub-Manager under H.M. Bevis and, subsequently, Wade Gard'ner, took an extended leave to study economics at the University of Edinburgh in 1899–1900, and returned for a final tour in the East as Sub-Manager Shanghai, 1901–1904, with Bevis again the Manager. Appointed to the key post of Manager Shanghai while on leave in 1905, he never took it up; Cameron's illness forced him to remain in London. First appointed junior Manager London, Addis became the senior in 1912 on the retirement of A.M. Townsend; his career had taken an extraordinary course – but this is a subject for Volumes II–IV.

EPILOGUE TO VOLUME I

At the end of 1901 the Hongkong and Shanghai Banking Corporation was the premier bank in the East. With total published shareholders' funds of $25.4 million (£2.33 million), including a paid-up capital of $10 million (£0.93 million), there was a third 'hidden' reserve approximately equal to $10 million. The Bank's operations spread out from the hub of Hong Kong to North and Central China, to the China coast, Japan, the Philippines, the Straits Settlements, French Indo-China, the Netherlands East Indies, Siam, Burma, and India, with agencies in France, Germany, and the United States. There was an important, but not overshadowing branch in the City of London.

The policy of the 'even keel', reinforced by an Eastern Head Office, accounts in silver, and a sound management, had served the Bank well. The Bank succeeded, as Heard predicted, because of its local support, but it could not have survived had it restricted its activities to the East. From the first it was involved in exchange; if the Bank were to grow to meet local requirements, it had to supplement its capital from equity funds originating in gold areas. On occasion the Bank had been caught, but it managed to weather the crises, and its conservative write-off policy placed it always in a strong position for a fast recovery.

Many of the old banks had fallen or been humbled. Although the Chartered Bank proved that it was possible to run a successful exchange bank from London, there were other aspects to the Hongkong Bank's success.

Based in the East it had nevertheless established a reputation as a British overseas bank in the City of London. Based in the East it had made contacts which no other bank could rival, and yet, with its sound London connection, its Eastern base had proved no handicap. Exactly how the Bank developed its position in the London market is a subject for Volume II. In the present volume the strength of the Bank has been established; what follows will consequently appear a logical and parallel development.

The Bank grew with British trade in the East, but it was never simply a bank for British traders. The international composition of its Board of Directors was a signal of its intent. Then through the compradores the managers established elusive though partially documented contacts with the local Chinese money markets and the bankers, with the local officials, and, finally, in Tientsin and Peking, with the great names of the Chinese Empire.

Despite the autonomy of its managers and the spread of its 26 offices, the Bank, after initial trial and error, established a three-level personnel system which was well-adjusted to the social factors behind China-coast and Eastern business in general. The establishment of a service, the learning on the job and years of routine, the socialization of the executive or Foreign staff were key to the problem of 'control' which all joint-stock banks faced in the early years of their development. The local Portuguese or Burghers or their equivalent were the clerical staff; the compradore's staff unlocked the doors to China – although they, virtually alone, kept the keys. Charles Addis, a young man in Peking, could glimpse into the world of Chinese business and politics; there were other breakthroughs, but despite Treaty privileges and the development of the foreign settlements, this was still Treaty-Port China, with the foreigner controlled and limited, consistent with traditional Chinese policy, to 'frontier trading posts'.

Like most foreign businessmen in the East, the Hongkong Bankers awaited the 'opening' of China; they sought evidence that China's expected modernization had begun. The proof, they thought, was to be sought in China's intentions relative to railways; the tentative experiments with factories, even the substantial China Merchants' Steam Navigation Company, which the Bank helped to finance, were not yet a commitment to modernization. The Bank stood ready to assist the Chinese; the Bank anticipated mutual benefits.

Instead, the Bank found itself supporting China's internal struggles and defence requirements. A high percentage of the funds made available went for non-productive purposes, but the hope remained.

In Volume I the Hongkong Bank developed the resources, the management skills, and the position. In Volume II these will be used, first to assist China in defeat, and then to finance a reluctant China in her first efforts at modernization as then understood.

Although Hong Kong and China have always dominated the history of the Bank, the Bank was active in different ways in Japan; its managers were sought for advice by governments; its agents moved into small settlements and brought them into contact with world trade. In some areas, particularly the Straits Settlements and the Malay States, the Bank shared with other British banks or, as in India, played a subordinate role. In French and Dutch territories the Bank was particularly dependent on the few British and the Chinese merchants. But its network and facilities often made it indispensable, despite national preferences.

All this has been only partly dealt with in Volume I. The Hongkong Bank had become bankers to the British Government in the Far East; but the main theme has been the Bank itself and the Bank in China. The theme must be fleshed out and completed to the Great War during new problems with silver and a redefinition of the 'even keel'. Then Volume II will turn back to consider the role of the Hongkong Bank as counsellor to governments, in currency reform, and as a 'focus of wealth' (*hui-feng*) for the early modernization of China.

The Hongkong Bank had fulfilled the expectations of its founders; it was the local bank; its funds were available for local development; its interests were regional. But despite an early 'good press' and sense of inevitability, the Bank had dangerous moments. These passed, it was ready to play its most public role in the Period of 'Imperialism' and War in the years from 1895 to 1914. And then the Bank's contribution, as Europe's, was checked. The events after 1918 are for Volumes III and IV.

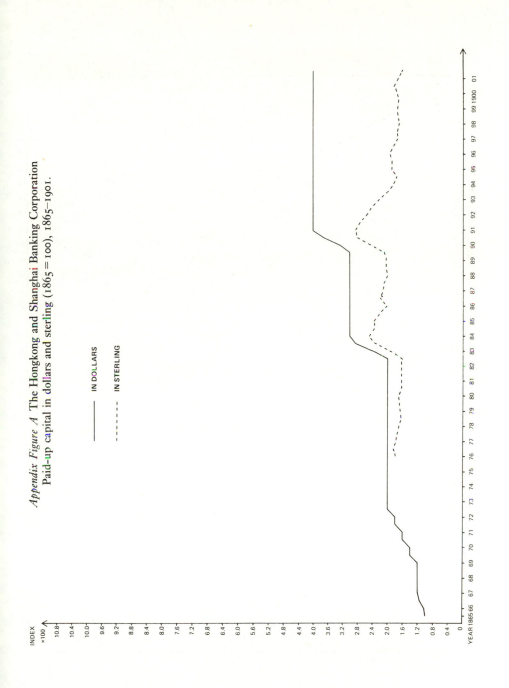

Appendix Figure A The Hongkong and Shanghai Banking Corporation
Paid-up capital in dollars and sterling (1865 = 100), 1865–1901.

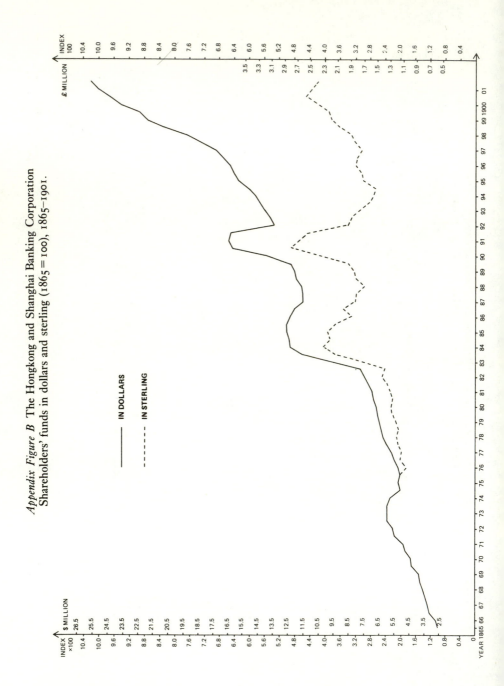

Appendix Figure B The Hongkong and Shanghai Banking Corporation
Shareholders' funds in dollars and sterling (1865 = 100), 1865–1901.

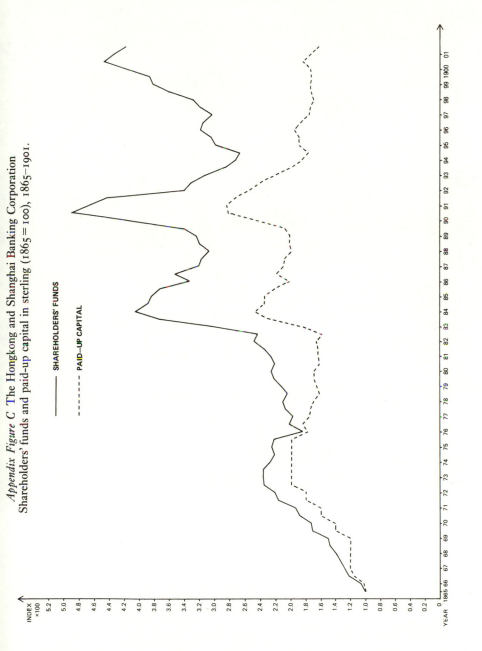

Appendix Figure C The Hongkong and Shanghai Banking Corporation
Shareholders' funds and paid-up capital in sterling (1865 = 100), 1865–1901.

SHAREHOLDERS' FUNDS

PAID–UP CAPITAL

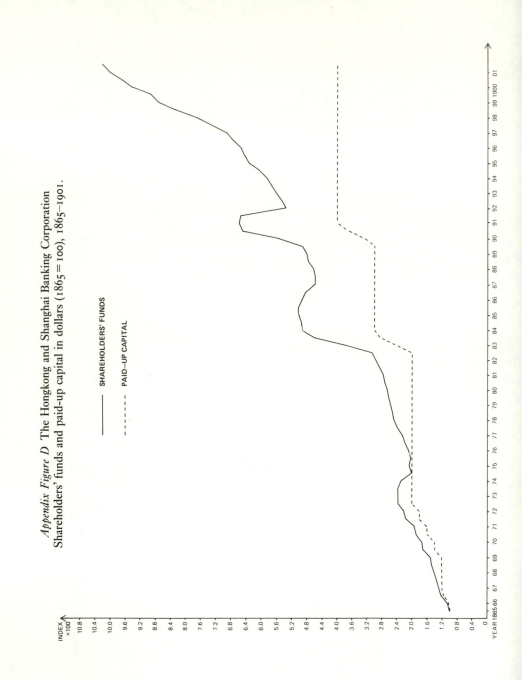

Appendix Figure D The Hongkong and Shanghai Banking Corporation
Shareholders' funds and paid-up capital in dollars (1865 = 100), 1865–1901.

SHAREHOLDERS' FUNDS

PAID–UP CAPITAL

INDEX
×100

10.8
10.4
10.0
9.6
9.2
8.8
8.4
8.0
7.6
7.2
6.8
6.4
6.0
5.6
5.2
4.8
4.4
4.0
3.6
3.2
2.8
2.4
2.0
1.6
1.2
0.8
0.4
0

YEAR 1865 66 67 68 69 70 71 72 73 74 75 76 77 78 79 80 81 82 83 84 85 86 87 88 89 90 91 92 93 94 95 96 97 98 99 1900 01

624

APPENDIX: THE HONGKONG BANK'S ORDINANCE OF INCORPORATION

No. 5 of 1866

An Ordinance enacted by the Governor of Hongkong, with the Advice of the Legislative Council thereof, for the Incorporation of the Hongkong and Shanghae Banking Company.

[14th August, 1866.]

WHEREAS the several Persons hereinafter named and others have agreed to form a Joint Stock Company under the name or style of "The Hongkong and Shanghae Banking Corporation," for the purpose of carrying on the business of Banking and of conducting all business usually transacted by Bankers: And Whereas for the purpose of establishing and carrying on the said undertaking they have agreed that a Capital of Five Millions of Dollars divided into Forty Thousand Shares of One Hundred and Twenty-five Dollars each shall be raised in the first instance with power to increase such Capital to the extent and in manner hereinafter mentioned: And Whereas the said several Persons have for some time been carrying on the business of Bankers as an un-registered and un-incorporated Company: And Whereas for the better accomplishing and carrying into effect the objects and purposes of the said Company they have applied to His Excellency the Governor of Hongkong to grant to them and all other the [*sic*] Subscribers of such Capital an Ordinance of Incorporation, which His said Excellency the Governor has consented and agreed to do, under and subject to the conditions, restrictions, and provisions hereinafter contained: Be it therefore enacted by His said Excellency the Governor of Hongkong, with the Advice of the Legislative Council thereof, as follows:

I. This Ordinance may be cited for all purposes as "The Hongkong and Shanghae Bank Ordinance."

II. In the Interpretation of this Ordinance, the Expression "The Governor" shall mean His Excellency the Governor of the Colony of Hongkong, or the Officer for the time being administering the Government of the said Colony; and the Expression "The Company" shall mean "The Hongkong and Shanghae Banking Corporation;" and the Expression "The Colony" shall mean the Colony of Hongkong and its Dependencies.

III. The Honorable John Dent, the Honorable Thomas Sutherland, Albert Farley Heard, Esquire, George Francis Maclean, Esquire, Douglas Lapraik, Esquire, Woldemar Nissen, Esquire, Arthur Sassoon, Esquire, George John Helland, Esquire, Palanjee Framjee, Esquire, Henry William Wood, Esquire and Caleb Tangier Smith, Esquire together with such and so many other Persons and bodies politic and corporate as now are, or shall hereafter become, proprietors of any Share or Shares of or in the Capital, for the time being, of the Company hereby established, shall be one body politic and corporate, in name and in deed, by the name of "The Hongkong and Shanghae Banking Corporation," and by that name shall and may sue and be sued, in all Courts, whether of law or of equity, and shall have perpetual succession with a Common Seal, which may be by them varied and changed at their pleasure.

IV. The Company is and shall be established for the purpose of carrying on under the management of a Court of Directors the business of Banking for the term of Twenty-one Years, commencing from the day of the date of this Ordinance, in the Colony: Provided always that nothing herein contained shall restrict the said Company, with the consent of the Commissioners for the time being for executing the Office of Lord High Treasurer in England, from establishing any Banks or Branch Banks at London or at any Port, Town, City or Place in India, Penang and Singapore, or in the Dominions of the Emperor of China, or of the Tycoon of Japan, in or at which any British Consulate or Vice-Consulate is or may be hereafter established, and also without such consent as aforesaid from establishing at London or any such Port, Town, City or Place as aforesaid, Agencies for Exchange, Deposit and Remittance.

V. The Capital of the Company shall consist of Five Millions of Dollars divided into Forty Thousand Shares of One Hundred and Twenty-five Dollars each, and such further Capital not exceeding Two Millions Five Hundred Thousand Dollars, as the Directors for the time being shall deem necessary for the purposes of the said undertaking: And for the creation of which they shall have previously obtained the consent of the Governor, such consent being signified in writing under the hand of the Governor; but such further Capital shall be divided into Shares of One Hundred and Twenty-five Dollars each and be paid up in full as hereinafter mentioned. And until such further Capital be raised as aforesaid, the aforesaid Sum of Five Millions of Dollars, shall be taken to be the fixed Capital of the Company – And whenever and so often as any further Capital shall have been raised then a Notification or Proclamation to that effect under the hand of the Governor shall be published in the *Hongkong Government Gazette*, and the said Sum of Five Millions of Dollars together with such further

Capital, shall thenceforth be taken to be the fixed Capital of the Company, but with power, nevertheless, to further increase such Capital as hereinafter mentioned.

VI. It shall not be lawful for the Company to commence or carry on the said business of Banking, until it shall be made to appear to the satisfaction of the Governor that the whole of the aforesaid Capital of Five Millions of Dollars has been subscribed for by Deed, under hand and seal; and that one-half (at the least) of such Sum of Five Millions of Dollars has been actually paid up, such satisfaction to be evidenced by a Notification or Proclamation under the hand of the Governor, to be published in the said *Hongkong Government Gazette*.

VII. Unless it shall be made to appear to the satisfaction of the Governor (to be evidenced as aforesaid), that the whole of the said Capital of Five Millions of Dollars has been subscribed, under hand and seal, before the expiration of a period of Two Years, to commence and be computed from the date of this Ordinance, and unless the whole of the said Capital of Five Millions of Dollars shall be actually paid up within the period of Three Years to be reckoned from the date of the Notification or Proclamation to be published as aforesaid of the payment of one half of the said Capital of Five Millions of Dollars (but so that such payment in full be not in any case delayed beyond the period of Four Years, to be reckoned from the date of this Ordinance), it shall be lawful for the Governor with the Advice of the Legislative Council of the Colony, at any time thereafter, by an Ordinance to be passed for that purpose to repeal this Ordinance and declare that the Incorporation hereby granted to the Company shall cease and determine and become absolutely void.

VIII. Until, as hereinbefore provided for, the Governor shall so publish in the *Hongkong Government Gazette* a Notification or Proclamation under his hand, that one half of such further Capital has been paid up, the Company shall not be entitled, by advertisement or otherwise, to hold out to the Public that the amount of its Capital has been increased.

IX. The remainder of the instalments on the Shares constituting such further Capital shall be wholly paid up within Two Years, to be reckoned from the date of such Notification or Proclamation (so to be published as aforesaid) of the payment of one half of such further Capital, and that the same shall be made to appear to the satisfaction of the Governor to be evidenced as aforesaid.

X. Within Twelve Calendar Months from the date of this Ordinance the persons who shall have subscribed for at least one half of the said Capital of Five Millions of Dollars, shall, to the satisfaction of the Governor, to be evidenced as aforesaid, enter into and execute a Deed of Settlement (and so as each such person so executing shall hold at least Five Shares in the said Capital), which Deed of Settlement shall be filed with the Registrar of Companies within Twelve Calendar Months from the date thereof, whereby provision shall be made for carrying on the business of the Company by a Court of Directors to be elected by the Shareholders of the company, as by the said Deed shall be provided, and, until such election, by a Court of Directors to be named in the said Deed, and whereby provision shall also be made for the payment, by the Shareholders, of all Monies to become due in respect of the instalments on the Shares taken by them, and also of such further or other Sums as are hereinafter provided, and in which said Deed of Settlement shall be contained (in addition to all such further provisions as shall be by the Governor considered necessary and usual in like cases for the management of the Affairs of the Company) provisions for effectuating the following objects, that is to say:

First. For holding General Meetings of the Company once at least in every Year at an appointed time and place.

Second. For holding extraordinary General Meetings of the Company upon the requisition of Nine or more Shareholders, holding in the whole at least Two Thousand Shares in the Company.

Third. For the management of the Affairs of the Company and the election and qualifications of the Directors.

Fourth. For the retirement of at least one-fourth of the Directors of the Company Yearly.

Fifth. For preventing the Company from purchasing any Shares, or making advances of Money, or securities for Money, to any person, on the security of a Share or Shares in the Company.

Sixth. For the publication, as shall be directed in the said Deed, of the Assets and Liabilities of the Company, and of the amounts of Promissory Notes in circulation, and of the Coin held in the Establishments of the said Company in the Colony or elsewhere.

Seventh. For the verification of such statements, and for the furnishing of such further information as the said Governor of Hongkong may require, respecting the state and proceedings of the Banking Establishments of the Company in the Colony or elsewhere.

Eighth. For the Yearly Audit of the Accounts of the Company by Two or more Auditors, not being Directors at the time.

Ninth. For the Yearly communication of the Auditors' Report, and of a Balance Sheet, and Profit and Loss Accounts to every Shareholder.

Tenth. For the appointment of Managers, or Agents, or other Officers, to perform the duties of Managers or Agents.

XI. The provisions of this Ordinance, and the provisions to be contained in the said Deed of Settlement, or in any Supplemental Deed to be made in pursuance thereof, or to be contained in any Bye-Laws to be made in pursuance of such Deeds, or any of them, shall be taken to be the existing Rules and Regulations of the Company, except so far as the same may be repugnant to the laws of the Colony, or of any Ports, Towns, Cities or Places where the Company may carry on business, or to the provisions of this Ordinance. Provided nevertheless that no Bye-Law or Supplemental Deed that may be made, shall have any force or effect until the same shall have been approved of by the Governor and a certificate of such approval shall have been given under the hand of the Governor.

XII. It shall be lawful for the Company to make, issue and circulate Notes or Bills payable to Bearer on demand in Coin lawfully current in the Colony and to re-issue the same: Provided that no such Notes shall be issued for any other Sums than the Sum of Five Dollars, or some multiple of such Sum, or other equivalent amount, unless the issuing of Notes of other amounts shall be sanctioned by the Governor: Provided also that nothing herein contained shall exempt the Company from the operation of any existing or future laws of the Colony or of any Port, City, Town, or Place beyond the limits of the Colony where they may with such consent as aforesaid establish Banks or Branch Banks, restricting or regulating the issue of such Notes, by Banks established therein. And provided also that the Shareholders of the Company shall be subject to unlimited liability in respect of all or any such issues or issue of Notes, and, if necessary, the Assets of the Company shall be marshalled for the benefit of the general Creditors of the Company, and the Shareholders shall be liable for the whole amount of such issue, in addition to the Sum for which they are liable under the other and general provisions of this Ordinance.

XIII. The total amount of the Bills and Notes of the Company payable to Bearer on demand actually in circulation shall not at any time exceed the amount of the Capital of the Company actually paid up, and there shall always be kept by the Principal Establishment in the Colony, an amount of Coin and Bullion equal to one-third at least of the Notes and Bills of the Company for the time being in circulation.

XIV. The total amount of the Debts and Liabilities of the Company of what nature or kind soever shall not at any time exceed the aggregate amount of the then existing *bonâ fide* Assets and property of the Company, and the Sum for which its Shareholders are liable under the provisions herein contained.

XV. If at any time there shall be a Suspension of Payment of any of the Notes or Bills of the Company, it shall not be lawful for the said Company from and after the commencement, and during the continuance, of such Suspension of Payment, to make any fresh issue of Notes or Bills.

XVI. The Company shall not Discount, or in any manner Advance Money upon Bills of Exchange, Promissory Notes, or other Negotiable paper, in or upon which the name of any Director, or Officer, of the Company, shall appear as Drawer, or Acceptor, either on his individual or separate account, or jointly with any partner or partners, or otherwise than as a Director or Officer of the

Company, to an amount exceeding one third of the amount of the Sum for the time being under discount, or advanced by the Company, nor shall any Director be allowed to obtain Credit on his own personal guarantee.

XVII. It shall be lawful for the Company notwithstanding the statutes of Mortmain or any other statutes or laws to the contrary, to purchase, hold, take, and enjoy to them and their successors, such Houses, Offices, Buildings, Lands and Hereditaments, as shall or may be thought necessary or proper for the purpose of managing, conducting, and carrying on the affairs, concerns, and business of the Company, but not for the purpose of speculation, or any other purpose than as aforesaid, and so as no such Houses, Offices, Buildings or Land shall be more than the Yearly value of Thirty Thousand Dollars at the time of acquiring the same, or of such further Yearly value as shall be sanctioned by the Governor, and to sell, convey, and dispose of the said property or any portion or part thereof, when not wanted for the purposes of the said business.

XVIII. All and every Person and Persons, and bodies, politic and corporate who are or shall be otherwise competent, shall be and are hereby authorized and empowered to grant, sell alien and convey in Mortmain unto, and to the use of, the Company and their successors, any such Houses, Offices, Lands, and other Hereditaments whatsoever as aforesaid accordingly.

XIX. It shall not be lawful for the Company to make any purchase of Messuages, Lands or Hereditaments in the Colony or elsewhere beyond the annual value of Thirty Thousand Dollars at the time of acquiring the same, or of such further annual value as shall be sanctioned by the Governor and when and as any such purchase shall be made by the Company, the Directors of the Company, shall, in all cases, within Three Calendar Months from the making and completing of any such purchase report the same in writing to the Governor, stating the amount of the purchase Money paid for the same and giving a description of the Lands and Hereditaments so purchased, and such other particulars relating thereto as may from time to time be required by the Governor; and in case any Hereditaments so purchased be re-sold by the Company, they shall within Fourteen Days after every such sale, give notice in writing to the Colonial Secretary of the Colony of such re-sale and of the price obtained for the same.

XX. Except for the purposes aforesaid it shall not be lawful for the Company to invest, lay out, employ, advance or embark any part of their Capital or Funds in the purchase of any Lands, Houses, or other real property, nor in any trading or mercantile speculation or business whatsoever (not usually considered as falling within the ordinary and legitimate purposes and operations of a Banking Establishment), but it shall nevertheless be lawful for the Company to take and accept any Lands, Houses, or other real or personal property in satisfaction, liquidation or payment of any debt absolutely and *bonâ fide* previously due and owing to the Company, and also to take any mortgage or other lien or charge on real or personal property as security for any Monies actually and *bonâ fide* previously due to the Company, or for which any Person or Persons may have rendered himself or themselves liable to the Company, and to hold such Lands, Houses, and other real and personal property respectively, for such reasonable time as shall be necessary for selling and disposing of and converting the same into Money.

XXI. It shall be lawful for the Company to sell, dispose of, and convert into Money, any Goods, Wares, or Merchandize, which shall or may be taken by them in satisfaction, liquidation or payment of any debt: And also to sell and convey any Lands, Houses, and other real property whatsoever, Goods, Wares, or Merchandize, which they shall or may have acquired in manner aforesaid.

XXII. It shall be lawful for the Company from time to time to extend or increase their Capital for the time being by the creation and sale of new Shares, in the manner to be specified and set forth in the Deed of Settlement, to be prepared and executed as hereinbefore directed, so as the same be made with the consent of a General Meeting of the Shareholders of the Company to be specially called for that purpose, and with the consent previously obtained of the Governor and under such Conditions and provisions as he shall think fit, such consent being evidenced as hereinbefore provided for with respect to other requirements of a like nature, and so as the total amount of the Capital of the Company shall not exceed the Sum of Ten Millions of Dollars and until it shall be certified by the Governor in like manner as aforesaid that one-half of such new Capital has been so paid up, the Company shall not be entitled by advertisement or otherwise, to state or hold out to the Public that the amount of the Capital has been increased.

XXIII. The remainder of the instalments on the Shares constituting such increased Capital shall be wholly paid up within Two Years from the date of the Certificate, to be granted as aforesaid, of one-half thereof having been paid up, and the same shall be made to appear to the satisfaction of the Governor, to be certified as aforesaid.

XXIV. The Directors of the Company shall, if, and whenever, they shall be required so to do, by the Governor, produce and submit to him, or to such persons or officers as he may appoint for that purpose, for his or their inspection and examination, the several accounts and statements which by the said Deed shall be directed to be made and furnished.

XXV. If the Company shall become insolvent, every Proprietor for the time being of Shares in the Capital thereof shall, in addition to his liability for the amount of the issue of Notes under the Provisions of the Twelfth Clause of this Ordinance, be liable to contribute to the payment of the debts, engagements, and liabilities of the Company not only such parts of the Shares held by him or her respectively, in the Capital of the Company, as shall not have been theretofore called for and paid up, but also such further Sums of Money not exceeding the amount of the Shares so held by him or her, as shall be requisite and necessary to satisfy and discharge the debts, engagements, and liabilities of the Company.

XXVI. In the said Deeds so to be executed as aforesaid, and in every Transfer of any Share or Shares in the Company, due provision shall accordingly be made for the payment by the Shareholders of such amounts as aforesaid.

XXVII. In the event of the insolvency of the Company, or of any Suspension in the Payments of the Company, for the space of Sixty Days in succession, or for any number of Days, at intervals which shall amount altogether to Sixty Days within any One Year, or if the Company shall not have well and truly maintained, abided by, performed and observed, all and every the rules, orders, provisions, and directions herein contained and set forth, or to be contained and set forth in the said Deed, so to be executed as aforesaid; Then, and in any of such cases, it shall and may be lawful for the Governor with the Advice of the Legislative Council of the Colony by an Ordinance to be passed for that purpose to repeal this Ordinance and declare that the Incorporation hereby granted to the Company shall cease and determine and become absolutely void.

XXVIII. Subject as hereinafter mentioned the Company may be wound up by the Supreme Court of Hongkong in its Equitable Jurisdiction and all the provisions of "The Companies Ordinance 1865" with respect to the Winding up of Companies registered thereunder shall apply to this Company as if expressly re-enacted in this Ordinance save and except in such respect as the same may be altered or modified as hereinafter mentioned or provided for:

1. The circumstances under which the Company may be wound up are as follows; that is to say:

A. In the event of the Company being dissolved, or ceasing to carry on business, or carrying on business only for the purpose of winding up its affairs.

B. Whenever the Company is unable to pay its debts.

C. Whenever the Court is of opinion that it is just and equitable that the company should be wound up.

2. The Company shall be deemed unable to pay its debts:

A. Whenever a Creditor to whom the Company is indebted at Law or in Equity, by assignment or otherwise, in a Sum exceeding Three Hundred Dollars then due, has served upon the Company, by leaving the same at the principal place of business of the Company, or by delivering to the Manager or some Director or principal officer of the Company, or by otherwise serving the same in such manner as the Court may approve or direct, a demand under his hand requiring the Company to pay the sum so due, and the Company has for the space of Three Weeks succeeding the service of such demand neglected to pay such Sum or to secure or compound for the same to the satisfaction of the Creditor.

B. Whenever execution or other process issued on a judgment, decree, or order obtained in any Court in favor of any Creditor, at Law or in Equity, in any proceeding instituted by such Creditor against the Company, is returned unsatisfied in whole or in part.

C. Whenever it is proved to the satisfaction of the Court that the Company is unable to pay its debts.

XXIX. On the determination of the Term of Twenty-one Years from the date of this Ordinance the powers and privileges hereinbefore conferred on the Company shall cease, unless the Governor with the Advice of the Legislative Council of the Colony declare to the contrary and by an Ordinance to that effect authorize the Company to continue incorporated under the aforesaid provisions for a further term of Ten Years, or for such period and under such provisions and conditions as may be contained in the Said Ordinance.

XXX. The Incorporation of the Company by this Ordinance shall not affect or prejudice the Liability of the Company to have enforced against it, or its Members, or its right to enforce, any debt or obligation incurred or any contract entered into, by, to, with, or on behalf of the Company previously to such Incorporation, but the Company may sue and be sued in respect of all or any such Debt or Debts, Obligation or Obligations, Contract or Contracts, by or under its Corporate name and in precisely the same manner as if the Debt, Obligation, or Contract had been incurred, made, or entered into after the Incorporation of the Company by this Ordinance.

NOTES

Material from the Hongkong Bank Group Archives is not fully cited; the archives were in the process of cataloguing during the writing of this history.

Abbreviations used in the notes

BPP	*British Parliamentary Papers*
BT	Board of Trade records in the PRO
cf.	compare
CO	Colonial Office records in the PRO
DG	Disconto-Gesellschaft
DNB	*Dictionary of National Biography*
f.	folio
ff.	folios
ibid	the same
I.G.	Inspector General (of the Imperial Maritime Customs)
IMC	Imperial Maritime Customs
FO	Foreign Office records in the PRO
IOR	India Office Records, London
MA	Massachusetts
NA	National Association
n.d.	no date
p.	page
pp.	pages
PP.MS.14	[Sir Charles] Addis Papers, the Library, School of Oriental and African Studies, University of London
P&O	Peninsular and Oriental Steam Navigation Company
PRO	Public Record Office, London
rpt	reprinted
SNA	Singapore National Archives
SOAS	School of Oriental and African Studies, University of London
SS	Straits Settlements
SSLCP	Straits Settlements Legislative Council Proceedings
T	Treasury records in the PRO
Ts	Taels
vol.	volume

There are no notes for Chapter 1.

2 THE PROVISIONAL COMMITTEE AND THE FOUNDING OF THE HONGKONG
BANK, 1864–1865

1 The initial statement on the purposes of the Hongkong Bank is dated 23 December
  1864 and is found in CO 129/101, f. 238.
2 Sir Thomas Sutherland, Speech at the Third Annual Dinner of the Hongkong and
  Shanghai Banking Corporation, London, 16 December 1909. Hongkong Bank Group
  Archives. The story in the next few pages is based on this account, but certain
  differences, especially on the timing of the ships, their names and captains, have been
  made in the light of information from contemporary references noted below.
3 A.F. Heard to his brother, John Heard III, 29 July 1864, HL-40, in the Augustine
  Heard Collection, Baker Library, Harvard Business School, Boston, MA.
4 'The Scottish Banking System', *Blackwood's Edinburgh Magazine* 41:671–86 (1844).
5 A.F. Heard to John Heard III, 29 July 1864, HL-40. See also George F. Heard to
  C.A. Fearon (in London), 29 July 1864.
6 *Hongkong Daily Press* (28 July 1864).
7 See Frank H.H. King, 'The Bank of China is Dead', in King, *Asian Policy, History and
  Development* (Hong Kong, 1979), p. 33 and 33n40.
8 A.F. Heard to C.A. Fearon, 27 July 1864, HL-40.
9 28 July 1864, HL-40.
10 A.F. Heard to John Heard III, 29 July 1864, HL-40.
11 A.F. Heard to G.B. Dixwell, 5 August 1864, HL-24.
12 A.F. Heard to John Heard III and Augustine Heard, Jr, 25 November 1864, FM-5.
13 A.F. Heard to Dixwell, 17 May 1865, HL-25, warning him to be careful with Dent's
   and expressing similar feelings about other firms. Dent's problems were sufficiently
   well-known outside the firm to be only too obvious within.
14 Austin Coates, *Whampoa, Ships on the Shore* (Hong Kong, 1980), pp. 55–57.
15 Ibid, pp. 48 and 55.
16 Stanley Jackson, *The Sassoons* (New York, 1965), pp. 42–43; see also Cecil Roth, *The
   Sassoon Dynasty* (London, 1941).
17 Edward LeFevour, *Western Enterprise in Late Ch'ing China, a Selective Survey of
   Jardine, Matheson & Company's Operations, 1842–1895* (Cambridge, MA, 1968),
   pp. 26–29.
18 A.F. Heard to Dixwell, 19 December 1864, HL-25. A.F. Heard makes frequent
   references to the allocation of shares, the time-consuming nature of the task, the
   system of priority, the number of applications and the state of the market, for which see
   his letters to C.E. Endicott of 7 December 1864, HL-25, and to his brothers John and
   Augustine of 30 November 1864, FM-5.
19 Minutes of a Special General Meeting of Shareholders, 27 March 1865, in Hongkong
   Bank Group Archives.
20 Information kindly provided by and quoted with the permission of Fr J. Verinaud,
   Archivist, Missions Étrangères de Paris, in a letter to Professor Patrick Tuck, 31
   January 1985, at the request of the author.
21 A.F. Heard to Dixwell, 6 August 1864.
22 See notice by B. and A. Hormusjee as agents of the Hongkong Bank in the *Times of
   India* (23 January 1865). The Indian Peninsular Bank, originally designated 'Imperial
   Bank of India and China', see ibid (19 May 1864), was suspended due to losses in
   February 1867, see ibid, Overseas Supplement (28 February 1867).
23 A.F. Heard to John III and Augustine Heard, Jr, 30 November 1864, FM-5.
24 See the account in my 'The Bank of China is Dead', pp. 31–32, based on letters to
   Whittall from Lidderdale, in Bombay, private, B/4/2, 13 July 1864, p. 181, and 12

September 1864, p. 187, Jardine Matheson Archive, Cambridge University Library.

25 Frank H.H. King and Prescott Clarke, *A Research Guide to China-Coast Newspapers, 1822–1911* (Cambridge, MA, 1965), p. 135.

26 W. Nissen to G.T. Siemssen, 25 October 1864, in Siemssen and Co. Archives, Hamburg; translation by D.J.S. King.

27 See, for example, the claim that the Bank was not living up to its role as a 'local bank' in the *Hongkong Daily Press* (23 October 1865).

28 Biographical material in Group Archives under J.R. Jones, 'Personalities and Narratives'. The Shanghai letter books of McLean (Early Letters) are part of the David McLean Papers (MS 380401), Library, School of Oriental and African Studies, University of London. For further information on McLean, see Chapter 7.

29 (10 December 1864), p. 996.

30 Information on the Scinde, Punjaub and Delhi Bank is found in the *London and China Express* (10 May, 10 December 1864, 10 December 1866); the *Bankers' Magazine* (January 1865) and in ibid 26: 432–35 (1866). On Porter's introduction to Whittall, see Remington and Co. to Jardine Matheson, in Bombay to Hong Kong non-private, B1/55, 28 September 1864, Jardine Matheson Archive.

31 Sassoon's investments in the Bank of Hindustan are listed in BT 31/654/2759.

32 *Times of India* (13 October 1866), and *Bankers' Magazine* 26: 1330–31 (1866); see also my 'The Bank of China is Dead', p. 38.

33 A.F. Heard to C.A. Fearon, 27 July 1864, HL-40. The Prospectus is reproduced as an Appendix to this chapter.

34 Plate 2, opposite p. 144 in Judith Sear, 'Variety in the Note Issues of The Hongkong and Shanghai Banking Corporation, 1865–1891', in King, ed., *Eastern Banking* (London, 1983).

35 Kresser to Colonial Secretary, 27 May 1865, CO 129/106, f. 81.

36 In CO 129/101, f. 241.

37 See Frank H.H. King, 'The Mercantile Bank's Royal Charter'. In *Asian Policy, History and Development* (Hong Kong, 1979), pp. 42–43.

38 Gerald C. Fischer, 'Wall to Wall Banks, the Marine Midland Story', draft history, p. 1.9 and Table 1.1. A copy was made available through the courtesy of Arthur Ziegler, Marine Midland Bank, NA.

39 John A. Gibbs, *The History of Antony and Dorothea Gibbs . . .* (London, 1922), p. v; M.C Reed, *A History of James Capel and Co.* (London, 1975), Chapter 1 and p. 120.

3 THE HISTORY OF THE HONGKONG AND SHANGHAE BANKING COMPANY, LTD

1 A.F. Heard to G.B. Dixwell, 5 August 1864, HL-24, Augustine Heard Collection, Baker Library, Harvard Business School, Boston, MA.

2 A.F. Heard to Torrey in Manila, 15 September 1864, HL-24.

3 James Gilbart, *A Practical Treatise on Banking* (London, 1856), II, 545–56, 566–72, and 572–78.

4 'The Scottish Banking System', in *Blackwood's Edinburgh Magazine* 41: 671–86 (1844).

5 The Prospectus is reprinted at the end of the text of Chapter 2 above.

6 Order in Council, 9 January 1863, effective from 16 February 1864; see *Hongkong Government Gazette* (13 December 1863).

7 See, for example, the *Hongkong Daily Press* (8 April 1865), hoping the Bank would provide clearing accounts but fearing it was becoming just another exchange bank.

8 See Carl T. Smith, 'Compradores of The Hongkong Bank', in King, ed. *Eastern*

Banking (London, 1983), pp. 93–111; H.L.D. Selvaratnam, 'The Guarantee Shroffs, the Chettiars, and The Hongkong Bank in Ceylon', in ibid, pp. 409–20, and comments on the system in Malaysia in Chee Peng Lim *et al.*, 'The History and Development of The Hongkong and Shanghai Banking Corporation in Peninsular Malaysia', in ibid, pp. 358–62. For a general discussion of the compradore's importance, see Yen-P'ing Hao, *The Comprador in Nineteenth-Century China* (Cambridge, MA, 1970).

9 The economic report for 1868 in *A Retrospect of Political and Commercial Affairs in China during the Five Years 1868 to 1872* (Shanghai: North-China Herald, 1873), pp. 99–100.

10 This list is taken from Manfred Pohl, *The Deutsche Bank's East Asian Business, 1870–1875*, Studies on Economic and Monetary Problems and on Banking History, No. 15 (Frankfurt, Deutsche Bank (1977), p. 38.

11 Stanley Jackson, *The Sassoons* (New York, 1965), pp. 42–43.

12 See Woldemar Nissen to Georg T. Siemssen, 26 August 1866, Archives of Siemssen and Co., Hamburg, for a discussion of the issue. Citations from this archive are based on translations undertaken by David J.S. King. See also, Hongkong Bank semi-annual report issued in August 1867, and *London and China Express*, e.g. 26 June, 10 July 1866.

13 See *The Bill on London* (Gillett Bros Discount Co., Ltd, London, 1952), pp. 23–24.

14 This controversial issue is discussed in W.T.C. King, *A History of the London Discount Market* (London, 1936), pp. 124–26, and in numerous articles in such newspapers as the *London and China Express* and the *Times of India*.

15 J.W. Maclellan, 'Banking in India and China', *Bankers' Magazine* 55: 735 (1891).

16 Ibid. The notice announcing the shorter usance period and signed on behalf of the Chartered, the Chartered Mercantile, the Bank of Hindustan, the Delhi and London, the Comptoir d'Escompte, and the Oriental banks was published as a private announcement in the *Hongkong Government Gazette* 21: 412 (6 October 1866). The Hongkong Bank was conspicuous in its absence.

17 Sir Richard Graves Macdonnell to Earl of Carnarvon, 14 November 1866, CO 129/116, No. 156.

18 Robert Hart to James Duncan Campbell, 2 and 16 November 1877, 3 January 1878, in J.K. Fairbank *et al.* eds. *The I.G. in Peking: Letters of Robert Hart, Chinese Maritime Customs, 1868–1907* (London, 1975), I, 253, 255, and 259.

19 See reference in note 17 above.

20 A.F. Heard to Dixwell, 4 January 1856, HL-25, p. 221, in which he notes the premium on Bank shares and summarizes his firm's position on agencies.

21 HL-25, p. 339.

22 27 July 1864, HL-40.

23 See A.F. Heard to Dixwell, 29 June 1865, H-26, and Augustine Heard, Jr, to A.F. Heard, 3 and 6 June 1865. On the Peking discussions, see A.F. Heard in Peking to George Heard in Hong Kong, 13 April 1865, and A.F. Heard in Tientsin to Robert Hart, 25 April 1865, HL-25, pp. 402–04, with memo dated 21 April.

24 In HQ-1, Miscellaneous, 1848–89.

25 To Augustine Heard, Jr from Boston, MA, 23 April 1866, OFL-13, pp. 32–35.

26 John Heard, III, to A.F. Heard, 9 October 1864, HM-8.

27 A.F. Heard to Russell of Russell, Sturgis and Co., 3 September 1864, HL-24, and to Dixwell, 22 May 1865, HL-26.

28 Woldemar Nissen to Georg T. Siemssen, 1 December 1865, from the archives of Siemssen and Company, Hamburg. Translation by D.J.S. King.

29 Nissen to Siemssen, 10 August and 25, 31 October 1864, in ibid.

30 BT 31/1081/2009ᶜ, and subsequent press reports.

31 A.F. Heard in Shanghai to G.F. Heard in Hong Kong, 8 June 1866, HL-28.

32 *Young Japan: Yokohama and Yeddo* (Yokohama, 1880), II, 13.

33 From the staff list, London Office, Hongkong Bank Court minutes, 26 July 1865; and biographical data, Hongkong Bank Group Archives.

34 Letter dated 8 October 1868 in the private collection of Dr Henry C. Wallich, Federal Reserve Board, Washington, D.C. (summary translation by D.J.S. King).

35 John G. Cattley and Charles Freeman for the Board of Directors to Thomas Dent and R.J. Ashton, 13 February 1865, London and Westminster Bank Board minutes (B2893), National Westminster Bank Archives.

36 Ibid.

37 Vacher to the London and Westminster, 1 June 1865, in London and Westminster Bank Daily Committee minutes, B2904, p. 355.

38 London and Westminster Bank, minutes of a Special Board Meeting, 8 July 1865, B2893, p. 275; see also previous minutes of 8 June and 6 July, pp. 360 and 372.

39 Hongkong Bank Board minutes, 5 August 1865, initiating the search; 24 August 1865, receiving the Westminster's negative decision of 8 July (see above); and 28 December 1865, noting success of Vacher's negotiations with the London and County Bank. In 1867 Vacher recommended and the Board agreed that he be styled 'manager' rather than 'agent'. Hongkong Bank Board minutes, 10 May 1867.

40 Vacher to W. McKewan, General Manager of the London and County Bank, letter dated 28 October 1865; the modifications arise in the latter's reply dated 3 November, approved 7 November 1865. National Westminster Bank Archives, B2358, pp. 357 and 361–71.

41 Although this provision was effective from the first, Hongkong Bank Board minutes indicate that the Hongkong Bank recorded formal change of status of the London operation at a Board meeting on 10 May 1867.

42 Hongkong Bank Board minutes, 5 August 1865.

4 THE HONGKONG BANK'S SPECIAL ORDINANCES – TO 1873

1 *China Mail* (28 July 1864). See also, Frank H.H. King, 'The Bank of China is Dead', in King, *Asian Policy, History and Development* (Hong Kong, 1979), pp. 19–41.

2 A.F. Heard to Charles A. Fearon, 27 July 1864, HL-40, in Augustine Heard Collection, Baker Library, Harvard Business School, Boston, MA; minutes of the Provisional Committee, Hongkong Bank Group Archives.

3 For the Bank of China's plan, see their prospectus in *Times of India* (23 June 1864) or *London and China Express* (26 July 1864).

4 F. Chomley to W.T. Mercer, 23 December 1864, CO 129/101, ff. 237–40.

5 'Report from the Select Committee on Chartered Banks (Colonial) Bill', *British Parliamentary Papers* (*BPP*), (1880), VII, 175–208. See also, E.W. Hamilton, 'Memorandum on Chartered Banks' (confidential), Treasury, 1877.

6 MacDonnell to Cardwell, 19 December 1864, CO 129/101, ff. 233–34.

7 F. Rogers in the Colonial Office to G.A. Hamilton in the Treasury, 1 March 1865, CO 129/101, f. 242.

8 See, e.g. BT 1/462 of 1846 or T.1/5153/7791. For a general discussion of the regulations and their background, see A.S.J. Baster, *Imperial Banks* (London, 1929), especially Appendix B, pp. 47–48, where the regulations of 1840 are reprinted.

9 For Arbuthnot's letter to Rogers, 19 May 1865, see CO 129/108, ff. 307–08. The Asiatic Banking Corporation's charter was forwarded to Hong Kong, 2 June 1865, see CO 403/12. The Asiatic's draft charter with manuscript amendments is in T 64/381ᶜ; the Bank of China's draft charter is in T.1/6545A/4242/65.

10 Colonial Office to Governor, Hong Kong, 2 June 1865, CO 129/108, and CO 403/12, #92. The need for changes is stated in Treasury to Colonial Office, 16 November 1865, CO 129/118, ff. 351–54.

11 For a biography of Baron Sir Julian Pauncefote (1828–1902), Attorney General, Hong Kong, 1865–72, see *DNB*, II, 2828. He was a member of the Legislative Council from 19 May 1865 and substantiated as Attorney General, 21 July 1866.

12 Legislative Council Proceedings, 25 July 1866, and *passim*, CO 131/6.

13 Minutes of 6 February 1865. Hongkong Bank Group Archives.

14 'Minutes of proceedings of a special general meeting of shareholders in the Hongkong Bank and Shanghae Banking Company (Limited)', 27 March 1865.

15 Ordinance No. 1 of 1865.

16 Private letter from W.T. Mercer (then the Officer Administering the Government), dated 1 November 1865, CO 129/108.

17 Colonial Office to Governor, Hong Kong, 11 December 1865, CO 403/15 and CO 129/108.

18 See reference in T.1/6737A/18254, a minute dated 31 October 1865 referring to item 18028 of 1864.

19 26 April 1865, CO 129/118, ff. 220–21.

20 'Minute of proceedings of a special general meeting of shareholders in the Hongkong and Shanghae Banking Company (Limited)', 27 March 1865.

22 For a full account of the extraterritorial argument, see Peter Wesley-Smith, 'The Hongkong Bank and the Extraterritorial Problem, 1865–1890', in King, ed. *Eastern Banking* (London, 1983), pp. 66–76.

22 Chomley to Mercer, 23 December 1864, CO 129/101, ff. 239–40; F. Peel in the Treasury to F. Rogers, 19 April 1865, CO 129/108, ff. 305–06.

23 For the Hongkong and Shanghai Bank Ordinance, No. 5 of 1866, see, for example, CO 129/124 with Governor's despatch of 2 August 1867.

24 See 20 April 1838, BT 6/274; Board of Trade to Colonial Office, 24 November 1837, T.1/3474. See also, 'Report on . . . Chartered Banks', cited.

25 5 June 1857, T.7/7, pp. 211–14.

26 'Appendix to Report from the Select Committee on Chartered Banks (Colonial) Bill', pp. 19–20, *British Parliamentary Papers*, 1880, Vol. VII, pp. 197–98.

27 T.1/5624/25, 562/1850.

28 MacDonnell to the Earl of Carnarvon, 24 August 1866, CO 129/114, ff. 333–35.

29 *China Mail* (8 March 1866), p. 39.

30 Noted in J.R. Jones's draft, TS, 'The Bank, 1865–1885' p. 15, in Hongkong Bank Group Archives.

31 See note 10 above.

32 T.64/381ᶜ, draft charter, pp. 6–7.

33 Minutes of 9 June 1865, Hongkong Bank Group Archives.

34 Rule 9, Memorandum in T.1/3475. For the Bank of Hindustan, see BT 1/654/2759.

35 Minutes of the General Meeting in the *North-China Herald* (28 August 1869), p. 148.

36 Kresser's memo and the Governor's despatch of 31 January 1867, CO 129/120, ff. 276–84, and Treasury response on ff. 275–76; see also T.1/6561A/1253.

37 MacDonnell to Duke of Buckingham, 2 August 1867, CO 129/124, paras. 6–12. ff. 4–6, and draft response, f. 7.

38 BT 1/516/1753, file dated 25 September 1854.

39 *Cf.* comparative tables analysing charters by subject, in Appendix to 'Report on . . . Chartered Banks', cited. The analysis does not include the charters of banks not in operation at the time of the report, so for the Asiatic's charter see T 64/381ᶜ.

40 All references are to the Ordinance No. 5 of 1866 and the revised Deed of Settlement in CO 129/124.

41 Kresser to MacDonnell, 4 December 1867, CO 129/126, f. 107.

42 No. 68 of 14 April 1868, CO 403/17 in response to Kresser's letter of 4 December 1867; see CO 129/126, ff. 101–11.

43 Officer Administering the Government, Hong Kong, to Earl of Kimberley, 16 October 1882, CO 129/203, ff. 69–70 and enclosures following. Circular dated 13 September 1882, J18.1, in Hongkong Bank Group Archives.

44 Treasury to Colonial Office, 16 April 1865, CO 129/118.

45 Wesley-Smith, p. 72.

46 No. 16 of 27 January 1868 in response to Hong Kong's No. 355 of 26 August 1867, CO 403/17, and Kresser's letter of 21 August 1867 to Colonial Secretary, Hong Kong, CO 129/124, ff. 188–91. The India Office instruction is dated 24 January 1868, CO 129/134, f. 629. The Bank's communications with India are noted in the minutes of the Court of Directors.

47 The draft Ordinance No. 1 of 1872 and a draft of the proposed ordinance in 1873 are in T.1/7304A. See also correspondence between Hong Kong and the Colonial Office dated from 28 March 1872, CO 129/157, ff. 389–402, and Treasury to the Colonial Office, 15 August 1872, CO 129/160, ff. 263–64. For the 1873 correspondence, see CO 129/166, especially ff. 173–74. The withdrawal of the draft ordinance of 1873 is reported from Hong Kong in CO 129/167, ff. 37–41, and considered in CO 129/168, ff. 175–78. A summary minute, dated 19 September 1887, is in T.1/8302B.

48 Minute of Rogers, Colonial Office, 13 June 1874, CO 129/168, f. 715. For correspondence relative to the draft ordinance of 1873, see T.1/7304A, especially the minute of 3 September 1873.

49 Treasury to Colonial Office, 26 November 1878, CO 129/183.

5 THE COURT AND ITS POLICIES, 1867–1875

1 Reprinted in the *North-China Herald* (19 December 1872).

2 See J.B. Jefferys, 'The Denomination and Character of Shares, 1855–1885', in E.M. Carus-Wilson, ed. *Essays in Economic History* (London, 1954), pp. 344–57, reprinted from the *Economic History Review* 16: 1 (1946).

3 A.F. Heard to G.F. Heard, 3 September 1864, HL-24, pp. 390–92, Augustine Heard and Co. Archives, Baker Library, Harvard Business School, Harvard University, Boston, MA.

4 *China Punch* (Hong Kong), 27 August 1874.

5 The *Hong Kong Times* (30 June and 1, 2, 3, 6, 7, 9, 13 July 1874), p. 2 or pp. 2–3. See also the editorial in ibid (14 July 1874), p. 2.

6 A.F. Heard to Low, 9 December 1874, HL-32, p. 506.

7 James W. Gilbart, *History and Principles of Banking* (London, 1865), in his Collected Works, IV, 239–40; *The Logic of Banking*, ibid, III, 223.

8 Woldemar Nissen to Georg T. Siemssen, 12 April and 1 December 1865, in Archives of Siemssen and Co., Hamburg; George F. Heard to his brothers in Massachusetts, 28 January 1868, FM-10.

9 Sheila Marriner and Francis E. Hyde, *The Senior, John Samuel Swire, 1825–98* (Liverpool, 1967), p. 106.

10 Jean Bouvier, *Le Crédit Lyonnais de 1865 à 1882: les années de formation d'une banque de dépôts* (1961), II, 529.

11 James W. Gilbart, *A Practical Treatise on Banking*, 6th edition (London, 1856).

12 Yen-P'ing Hao, *The Comprador in Nineteenth-Century China: Bridge between East and West* (Cambridge, MA, 1970), p. 53, and Carl T. Smith, 'Compradores of The Hongkong Bank', in King, ed. *Eastern Banking*, p. 101.

13 On the impracticality of operating the New York/London exchanges through a New York agency of the Hongkong Bank, see George F. Heard (who was then Chairman of the Hongkong Bank) in a letter to his brothers, 27 April 1871, FM-11, writing on the views of Kresser, the Chief Manager, and the Hongkong Bank Board of Directors.

14 Manfred Pohl, '*The Deutsche Bank's East Asian Business, 1870–1875*', in Studies on Economic and Monetary Problems and on Banking History (Frankfurt, 1977), No. 15, pp. 25–49; reference to the Deutsche National Bank can be seen in advertisement form in, e.g. the 6 January 1873 issue of Hong Kong's *Daily Advertiser*.

15 'Banking in India and China', *Bankers' Magazine* 55: 217 (1891).

16 David McLean to Thomas Jackson, 29 April 1881, Private Letters (London) II, 168, and 21 July 1882, IV, 93, in David McLean Papers (MS 380401), Library, School of Oriental and African Studies, University of London.

17 London and County Bank Board Minutes, Vol 14, p. 341, 2 Feb 1869, National Westminster Bank Archives. For decisions on previous Hongkong Bank requests for varying facilities, see pp. 112–13, 145, 158, 162, 221, 272 and 337. For the period 1875 to 1888, see also McLean, Private Letters, *passim*.

18 Ibid, 23 February 1869, p. 352.

19 Minutes of the Court of Directors, Hongkong Bank; Stock Exchange, minutes of the Committee for General Purposes, 26 November 1867, p. 398, deposited in the Guildhall Library, City of London.

20 See Takeshi Hamashita, 'A History of the Japanese Silver Yen and The Hongkong and Shanghai Banking Corporation, 1871–1913', in King, ed. *Eastern Banking*, p. 324.

21 *Hongkong Daily Press* report enclosed with despatch of 25 February 1868, CO 129/129, f. 281.

22 CO 129/129, ff. 378–82.

23 Kresser to MacDonnell, 16 March 1868, CO 129/129, ff. 445–47.

24 Treasury to Colonial Office, 26 May 1868, CO 129/135, f. 374.

25 Kresser to Colonial Secretary, Hong Kong, 11 April 1868, CO 129/130, f. 100.

26 MacDonnell to Earl of Kimberley, 19 June 1872, CO 129/158, ff. 145–47. See also C.C. Smith, Act. Col. Sec., to James Greig, 20 May 1872.

27 Minute by A. Lister, p. 6, dated 11 December 1889, CO 129/242, f. 615.

28 MacDonnell to the Duke of Buckingham, 10 June 1868, with accompanying documents, CO 129/131, ff. 102–06.

29 The correspondence, tenders and final Agreement are in T.1/6974B, 1870.

30 Agreement between the Lords Commissioners of Her Majesty's Treasury and the Directors of the Hongkong and Shanghai Banking Corporation . ... registered 12 April 1878, in T.1/7693A.

31 Ibid, clause 10.

32 For references and narrative relative to the China loans prior to 1896 see David J.S. King, 'China's Early Loans 1874–95, and the Role of the Hongkong and Shanghai Banking Corporation', TS in the Hongkong Bank Group Archives. See also his 'China's First Public Loan: The Hongkong Bank and the Chinese Imperial Government "Foochow" Loan of 1874', in King, ed. *Eastern Banking*, pp. 230–64.

33 Hart to Campbell, 30 December 1883 (letter No. 455), in J.K. Fairbank *et al.*, eds *The I.G. in Peking: Letters of Robert Hart, Chinese Maritime Customs, 1868–1907* (Cambridge, MA, 1975), I, 512.

34 18 September 1874, FO 228/546, f. 74; D.J.S. King, 'China's First Public Loan', p. 240.

35 A.F. Heard to Daly, 10 September 1874.

36 Court minutes, 29 June 1875, in Hongkong Bank Group Archives.

37 See the Prospectus in the *London and China Express* 6: 78b (26 January 1864).

38 BT 31/1089/1058ᶜ; capital was nominally £300,000 in 15,000 shares of £20 each. Nothing was paid up. For further details on the actual proposals, see Sir Macdonald Stephenson, *Railways in China: Report upon the Feasibility . . . Empire of China* (London, 1864), in Foreign Office Library.

6 SUCCESS, CRISIS, AND REORGANIZATION, 1867–1876

1 A.F. Heard to Fraser, 31 January 1875, in Augustine Heard Collection, HL-32, p. 605, Baker Library, Harvard Business School, Boston, MA.

2 A.F. Heard to Fearon, 4 February 1875, HL-32, p. 622.

3 Austin Coates, *Whampoa, Ships on the Shore* (Hong Kong, 1980), pp. 57, 80–82, 84.

4 See a translation in Group Archives from Chapter 16 of Etienne Dénis, *Bordeaux et le Cochinchine sous la restauration et le second empire* (Bordeaux, 1965).

5 David McLean to Foster, 23 February 1870, McLean to James Greig, 2 May 1870, McLean to T. Jackson, 16 May 1870, 19 July 1870, and *passim* in Early Letters (Shanghai), IV, 4, 10, 11, and 92, in the David McLean Papers (MS 380401), Library, School of Oriental and African Studies (SOAS), University of London.

6 References to the public companies are scattered throughout the newspapers of the period in overall summaries, court cases, annual meetings, etc. For the Indo-Chinese Sugar Company particular use has been made of articles in the *North-China Herald* (25 August 1871), p. 639; (18 May 1872), pp. 385–86; (11 March 1875), pp. 222–23; *The Hong Kong Times* (16 June 1874), pp. 2–3; (17 June 1874), p. 2. A visit to the Hong Kong Distillery is described in ibid (18 August 1874); the *China Mail* (15 January 1874), p. 3, deals with the legal problems of the Hongkong Bank and the Sugar Refinery of Wahee Smith and Co.

7 *North-China Herald* (18 May 1872), pp. 385–86.

8 *North-China Herald* (24 August 1872), report of meeting, p. 152 and ibid (20 February 1873), p. 161.

9 *North-China Herald* (23 August 1873), p. 160.

10 *China Punch* (30 August 1873), Hong Kong.

11 David McLean to Thomas Jackson, 16 May 1870, 20 June 1870; McLean to H.B. Lemann, Chairman, Hongkong Bank, 21 June 1870, in the Early Letters (Shanghai), IV, 53, and 65; IV, 66.

12 David McLean to Thomas Jackson, 11 May 1876, Private Letters (London) I, 76.

13 McLean to Jackson, 3 January 1872, in Early Letter Books (Shanghai), IV, 532, 578.

14 *North-China Herald* (6 July 1872 and 20 and 27 May 1876); McLean to J.S. Louden, 12 January 1872, Early Letters, IV, 563; Wang Qingyu 'Shih-chiu shih-chi wai-kuo chin-hua shih-yeh Chung ti Hua-shang fu-ku huo-tung' (The activities of Chinese merchants to buy capital shares in the aggressive foreign enterprises in China during the late 19th century), *Lishi Yenjiu* 4: 39–74 (1965), esp. pp. 51–55.

15 McLean to W.H. Vacher, 12 January 1872, Early Letters, IV, 564.

16 McLean to John Grigor, 21 July 1870, ibid, IV, 95.

17 McLean to James Greig, 16 February 1872, in ibid, p. 613; see also McLean to Greig, 9 March 1872, in ibid, p. 643.

18 See the dispute between Shanghai's *Celestial Empire* and the *Hong Kong Times* in the latter's issue of 23 September 1874, p. 2.

19 Discussion of the loan of 1874 is based on David J.S. King, 'China's First Public Loan . . .', in Frank H.H. King, ed. *Eastern Banking* (London, 1983), pp. 230–64. Comments on the loan's profitability are from this reference.

20 See Charles Rivington's share letter of 28 November 1878, from Shanghai in Hongkong Bank Group Archives, MB Hist. 470/63.

21 See, for example, the leading article in the *North-China Herald* (22 August 1874), p. 184.

22 The cartoon is found in *China Punch* (January 1875); as no extant copy of this issue has been located, the only source is the copy of the cartoon in the Group Archives.

23 Sources for the comments which follow in the text are found mainly in the *Celestial Empire*, but similar editorials and letters are found in all China-coast newspapers of the period: the relevant references to the former are, 12 September 1874, pp. 246–49; 10 December 1874, p. 259; 31 December 1874, p. 335; 7 January 1875, p. 4; 14 January 1875, pp. 29–30; 21 January 1875, pp. 52–54; 28 January 1875, p. 71; see also, *London and China Express* (26 February 1875), pp. 225–26; (18 June 1875), p. 660; (8 October 1875), p. 1067.

24 A.F. Heard to Augustine Heard, Jr., 17 December 1874, HL-51, pp. 239 ff.

25 See not only the letter books referred to in note 5 above, but also Kresser's letter to McLean which survives in the Group Archives.

26 Quoted in the *London and China Express* (26 February 1875), p. 225.

27 Reprinted in the *Celestial Empire* (31 December 1874), p. 335.

28 27 July 1875, Private Letters, I, 5.

29 *North-China Herald* (28 August 1875), pp. 198–99.

30 16 July 1875, Private Letters, I, 3.

31 Reported in the *Hong Kong Times* (24 February 1876), pp. 2–3; for editorial comment, see the issue of 25 February 1876, p. 2.

32 *Cf.* the summary in the Court minutes, 11 May 1875, and in the Chairman's report to the General Meeting, August 1875.

33 McLean to Jackson, 11 May 1876, Private Letters, I, 76.

34 26 May 1876, in ibid, p. 91.

35 31 May 1876, in ibid, p. 96.

36 McLean to Cameron, 8 September 1875, Private Letters, I, 9.

37 Ibid.

38 McLean to Jackson, 11 May 1876, Private Letters, I, 76.

39 McLean to Jackson, 31 May 1876, Private Letters, I, 93.

40 Comment by T.W. O'Brien, acting Manager Foreign Exchange and Treasury, Hongkong Bank, to Controller Group Archives, 10 August 1983. This was based on his reading of McLean's letters cited in notes 38 and 39 above.

7 THE EARLY HONGKONG BANKERS

1 A.M. Townsend, 'Early Days of the Hongkong and Shanghai Bank', privately reproduced, copy in Hongkong Bank Group Archives. These are his reminiscences, written at the age of 90, and referred to frequently in this chapter.

2 *Bankers' Magazine* 23: 574 (May 1863) and the complaint of Gordon Macpherson, chairman of the Agra and United Service Bank in ibid 23: 364 (April 1863). For the Deutsche Bank, see Manfred Pohl, *The Deutsche Bank's East Asian Business, 1870–1875*, Studies on Economic and Monetary Problems and on Banking History, No. 15 (1977), p. 47.

3 The main sources are the Shanghai Branch Charges Account Book, Hongkong Bank Group Archives; Jury Lists published in the *Hongkong Government Gazette*, various directories, and the Early Letters (Shanghai), David McLean Papers (MS 380401), Library, School of Oriental and African Studies (SOAS), University of London; typescript in Hongkong Bank Group Archives.

4 D. McLean to Jackson, 16 May 1884, Private Letters (London), V, 31.

5 Biographical information from J.R. Jones, 'Branches, San Francisco', in Hongkong

Bank Group Archives. For Bank of California, see advertisement in *China Mail* (3 November 1864) and *Hongkong Daily Press* (31 March 1866).

6 See previous chapter under 'Reassessment of Greig', and McLean to Jackson, 31 May 1876, Private Letters (London), I, 96.

7 McLean to Jackson, Private Letters, I, 134 and 151.

8 McLean to W.H. Vacher, 9 June 1870, Early Letters (Shanghai), IV, 62; McLean to James Greig, 21 July 1870, p. 75; McLean to Greig, 30 September 1870, p. 159; and McLean to Greig, p. 585. On a general criticism of Kresser's recruitment policy, see McLean to Greig, 23 November 1871, ibid, p. 506.

9 McLean to T. Jackson, 11 May, 10 August 1876, and *passim*, Private Letters, I, 76 and 120.

10 Sheng Hsuan-huai to Tsungli Yamen, 2 February 1897, in Mai Chung-hua, comp. *Huang-ch'ao ching-shih-wen hsin-pien*, 10B, 21b (Vol. I, p. 530 of Taiwan, 1965, reprint); a summary translation of the draft regulations is available in Albert Feuerwerker, *China's Early Industrialization: Sheng Hsuan-huai (1844–1916) and Mandarin Enterprise* (Cambridge, MA, 1958), pp. 228–29; A.W. Maitland is Mei-te-lun.

11 There is a reference to Mitchell in McLean to Jackson, 24 November 1876, Private Letters, I, 163.

12 Hermann Wallich, 'Aus meinem Leben', in *Zwei Generationen im deutschen Bankwesen* (Frankfurt/M, 1978), II, 52; Nissen to G.T. Siemssen, 25 October 1864, in Siemssen and Co.'s archives, Hamburg; translations by D.J.S. King.

13 Information on Kresser in Cochin-China is found in Chapter 16 of Etienne Dénis, *Bordeaux et le Cochinchine sous la restauration et le second empire* (Bordeaux, 1965).

14 Yasuo Gonjo, *Hurans teikokushugi to ajia – Indoshina ginko-shi kenkyu* (French imperialism and Asia – a history of the Banque de l'Indo-Chine; Tokyo, 1985), pp. 18–22.

15 McLean to Jackson, 10 August 1876, Private Letters, I, 120, and ibid, 2 March 1883, IV, 192.

16 Typescript copy – original not found – in section on Kresser in J.R. Jones compiled collection 'Personalities and Narratives', Hongkong Bank Group Archives.

17 T. Jackson, Speech at First Annual Bank Dinner, London, 18 February 1908, p. 4, in Hongkong Bank Group Archives.

18 From a sketch of McLean written at the time of his retirement in 1889, journal unidentified, but possibly *Bankers' Magazine*, p. 691. The balance of the biographical material is from material in the Group Archives provided by D.C.H. McLean, grandson of the London Manager.

19 McLean, 15 August 1864, Early Letters, I, 46.

20 Ibid, 29 August 1864, I, 47.

21 Charles B. Buckley, *An Anecdotal History of Old Times in Singapore, 1819–1867* (reprinted, Kuala Lumpur, 1965), p. 711.

22 McLean to Jackson, 13 April and 15 June 1877, Private Letters, I, 224 and 241.

23 This account of Greig's later life is based on an unpublished sketch of the history of Brown, Janson and Co. by T.S. Allen, now in the Archives of Lloyds Bank, A39d/3, and kindly brought to my attention by the Archivist J.M.L. Booker; information from H.A. Greig is derived from his oral history interview in Group Archives; for family relationships, see the chart in Volume III, under 'Joe' Cautherley.

24 One of the lost accounts was that of N.M. Rothschild, for which see Harry Tucker Easton, *The History of a Banking House (Smith, Payne and Smiths)* (London, 1903), p. 76; for the unfolding story, see articles in the *London and China Express* (e.g. 26 March and 16 June 1866). See also W.T.C. King, *A History of the London Discount*

Market (London, 1936), p. 244; *The Times* (26 May 1866), *Bankers' Magazine* (1866), pp. 790–802; and *Money Market Review* 12: 754–55 (9 June 1866).

25 Jackson's letter is now in the Hongkong Bank Group Archives.

26 Buckley, p. 374.

27 For the Bank of Hindustan, see *London and China Express* (17 November and 17 December 1866); for biographical information on Cameron, see compilation by J.R. Jones in Hongkong Bank Group Archives.

28 Chung-kuo jen-min yin-hang Shang-hai-shih fen-hang (The Chinese People's Bank, Shanghai), comp. *Shang-hai ch'ien-chuang shih-liao* (Historical materials on the native banks in Shanghai; Shanghai, 1960), pp. 28–29. The editors do not vouch for the story. Wah Sam's age is based on his note on the back of a picture, reproduced in this volume, sent to Mrs McLean in 1874 – he was then 37. The picture is from the private collection of D.C.H. McLean; a copy is in Group Archives.

29 Chung-kuo . . . (note 28), p. 29.

30 Arnold Wright, ed. *Twentieth Century Impressions of Hongkong, Shanghai, and Other Treaty Ports of China: Their History, People, Commerce, Industries, and Resources* (London, 1908), p. 754, as cited in Yen-P'ing Hao, *The Comprador in Nineteenth-Century China: Bridge between East and West* (Cambridge, MA, 1970), p. 276n146.

31 Quoted on pp. 475–76, Appendix II, in Edward Kann, *The Currencies of China* (Shanghai, 1927).

32 Sir Charles S. Addis diary entry for 13 March 1939, PP. MS. 14/57, Addis Papers, Library, SOAS.

33 McLean to Jackson, 1 March, 24 August 1877, and 13 September 1878, Private Letters, I, 211, 273, and II, 96; Court of Directors minutes.

34 This material and the specific quotations are identified as from Townsend, 'Early Days . . .', except where stated to the contrary.

35 McLean to Jackson, 10 August 1877, Private Letters, I, 268.

36 Typescript copy covering 1 January to 6 February 1871 is in the Hongkong Bank Group Archives; location of original unknown. Extracts are quoted in this section without further notes.

37 Material in the Bank's archives and especially in the Minutes of the Court of Directors has been supplemented by information kindly provided by Carl T. Smith taken from his extensive card file on Hong Kong residents: his sources include, marriage from *Friend of China* (15 October 1857); bankruptcy, *Daily Press* (17 February 1884); see also ibid (2 May 1884).

38 On duffers in general, see e.g. McLean to Greig, 15 April 1871, Early Letters, IV, 310; on Ellis, see McLean to Greig, 27 January 1872, ibid p. 585. See also references in note 8.

39 *North-China Herald* (6 July 1872 and 20 and 27 May 1876); Wang Qingyu 'Shih-chiu shih-chi wai-kuo chin-hua shih-yeh Chung ti Hua-shang fu-ku huo-tung' (The activities of Chinese merchants to buy capital shares in the aggressive foreign enterprises in China during the late 19th century), *Lishi Yenjiu* 4:39–74 (1965), esp. pp. 51–55.

40 *Celestial Empire* (7 January 1875), p. 4, and Townsend, p. 14.

PART II THE AGE OF JACKSON, 1876–1902, AND THE FALL OF SILVER

1 These matters were the subject of various Royal Commissions and Parliamentary inquiries. David McLean made a substantial contribution, on which the above material is based, for which see British Parliamentary Papers, *First Report of the Royal Commission appointed to inquire into recent changes in the relative values of the Precious Metals with Minutes of Evidence, and Appendices*, Vol. XXII, C. 5099 (1887). The

problem has been considered in the context of imperial currency problems in W. Evan Nelson's 'The Imperial Administration of Currency and British Banking in the Straits Settlements, 1867–1908', PhD Thesis (Duke University, 1984), and the analysis following page 200, with its additional references, is particularly interesting.

8 JACKSON'S FIRST TERM, I: RECOVERY AND GROWTH, 1876–1882

1 David McLean to Thomas Jackson, 17 December 1880, McLean Private Letter Books (London), III, 102, McLean Papers (MS 380401), Library, SOAS, University of London.

2 On missing church, McLean to Jackson, 22 February 1878, Private Letters, II, 21; on House of Commons, to E. Morriss, 30 July 1880, III, 54; McLean to Townsend, 23 December 1881, III, 296.

3 Calculated from the deposit figures in McLean to Jackson, 30 June 1882, Private Letters IV, 70.

4 J.W. Maclellan, 'Banking in India and China', *Bankers' Magazine* 55: 738–39 (1891).

5 Information on this subject has been assembled conveniently in two contemporary pamphlets, J.A. Angus, *Letter to the Proprietors of the Oriental Bank Corporation and of the Chartered Mercantile Bank of India, London and China* (Edinburgh: privately published, 1882), and H.J. Marsden, *The Decline of Indian Banking: the cause and the remedy* (London: Wm Clowes and Sons, Ltd, 1882). Both are available in the Hongkong Bank Group Archives.

6 McLean to Jackson, 7 January 1881, Private Letters, III, 121, and *passim*.

7 On the Hong Kong losses, McLean to John Walter, 8 June 1882; to Jackson, 9 June and esp. 23 June 1882, Private Letters, IV, 63, 65 and 68; on the cash balances, McLean to Jackson, 22 December 1882, ibid, p. 165.

8 2 May 1884, Private Letters, V, 23.

9 Robert R. Campbell, *James Duncan Campbell. A Memoir by his Son* (Cambridge, MA, 1970).

10 McLean to Jackson, 23 February 1883, Private Letters IV, 188.

11 Robert Hart to James D. Campbell, letters dated 14 May and 7 May 1884 respectively, in John K. Fairbank *et al.*, eds *The I.G. in Peking: Letters of Robert Hart, Chinese Maritime Customs, 1868–1907* (Cambridge, MA, 1975), I, 546 and 545.

12 Compton Mackenzie, *Realms of Silver, One Hundred Years of Banking in the East* (London, 1954), pp. 161–62.

13 McLean to Jackson, 9 May 1879, Private Letters, II, 190.

14 See references in note 5.

15 McLean to Jackson, 29 December 1881, Private Letters, IV, 1.

16 See for this and the trade figures cited, Liang-lin Hsiao, *China's Foreign Trade Statistics, 1864–1949* (Cambridge, MA, 1974), Tables 8.9A and 8.11.

17 Ibid, Table 8.3 for exports, Table 8.2 for imports, and Table 8.11 for adjusted figures providing a sounder basis for comparison.

18 On cash balances see, for example, McLean to Jackson, 24 September 1880, Private Letters, III, 79.

19 For Thomas Jackson's own description of the crisis, see his letter of 1 October 1882 to the Colonial Secretary, CO 129/203, ff. 548–51.

9 JACKSON'S FIRST TERM, II: NEW CAPITAL AND GROWTH, 1882–1888

1 The Officer Administering the Government, William Henry Marsh, reported the affair to the Secretary of State in a despatch dated 16 October 1882; he enclosed a letter from Jackson with a Statement from the Directors. See CO 129/203, ff. 71–72.

2 David McLean to J.J. Winton (Singapore), 22 August 1879, Private Letters

(London), II, 225, David McLean Papers (MS 380401), Library, School of Oriental and African Studies, University of London.

3 Board Minutes of the London and County Bank, 1 March 1879, XVII, 307–08, National Westminster Bank Archives.

4 Ibid, 31 July 1883, XVIII, 550.

5 McLean to T. Jackson, 7 December 1883, Private Letters, IV, 278.

6 See, for example, Committee minutes, London and County Bank, #2445, 6 June 1882, p. 156.

7 Sir John Clapham, *An Economic History of Modern Britain: Free Trade and Steel, 1850–1886* (Cambridge, 1952), p. 352, and references cited there.

8 McLean to Jackson, 30 December 1881, Private Letters, IV, 7.

9 McLean to John Walter, 12 March 1886, Private Letters, V, 253.

10 McLean to Jackson, 18 August 1882, Private Letters, IV, 121.

11 For a general description of the situation in Shanghai, see Kwang-ching Liu, 'Credit Facilities in China's Early Industrialization: the Background and Implications of Hsü Jun's Bankruptcy in 1883', in Chi-ming Hou and Tzong-shian Yu, eds. *Modern Chinese Economic History* (Taipei, Taiwan), pp. 499–509. The reference to the gift to Wah Sam is from the HSBC Board of Directors minutes.

12 C.S. Addis to his father, 27 February 1886, PP. MS. 14/64/19, (Sir Charles) Addis Papers, Library, School of Oriental and African Studies, University of London.

13 *North-China Herald* (10 September 1886), pp. 273–74 and 287–88.

14 Ibid, p. 288.

15 Ibid.

16 Ibid.

17 Ibid, p. 274.

18 Addis to his father, 28 February 1887, PP. MS. 14/64/141.

19 Reprinted in the *North-China Herald* (19 August 1887).

20 Frank H.H. King (ed.) and Prescott Clarke, *A Research Guide to China-Coast Newspapers, 1822–1911* (Cambridge, MA, 1965), pp. 98–99, 137.

21 This is reflected in Jardine correspondence with Michie, for which see, for example, press copy books Private Shanghai to Coast, C42/1–2 series, *passim*, Jardine Matheson Archives.

22 A. Gollan, HBM Consul, Manila, to Secretary of State for Foreign Affairs, 25 March 1889, FO 72/1851, enclosure 5, letter from British Merchants.

23 Reprinted in the *North-China Herald* (17 September 1887), pp. 317–18.

24 McLean to Jackson, 9 May 1884, Private Letters, V, 28; and even after the appointment was public and in operation, McLean felt called on to write again, 11 December 1884, V, 100.

25 John M. Willem, *The United States Trade Dollar* (Racine, WI, 1965), esp. Chapter X.

26 On Townsend's role, see *Banker's Magazine* (December 1911).

27 Addis to his father, 23 August 1887, PP. MS. 14/65/21.

28 McLean to Walter, 5 November 1886, Private Letters, V, 290.

29 McLean to Walter, 27 April 1887, Private Letters, VI, 30.

30 McLean to Walter, Private Letters, also dated 27 April 1887, ibid, VI, 30.

31 McLean to Walter, 10 December 1886, Private Letters, V, 299.

32 McLean to Jackson, 2 September 1887, Private Letters, VI, 49.

10 THE BOARD, POLICY, AND GOVERNMENT, 1876–1888

1 'Affairs of India', *Edinburgh Review* (April 1910), p. 154, quoted in William J. Barber, *British Economic Thought and India, 1600–1858* (Oxford, 1975), p. 138.

2 *British Parliamentary Papers* (1852–53), XXX, 301, quoted in Barber, p. 220.

3 R. Meade (Colonial Office) to Hamilton (Treasury), 15 December 1887, CO 192/233, ff. 5–8.

4 See Peter Wesley-Smith, 'The Hongkong Bank and the Extraterritorial Problem, 1865–1890', in King, ed. *Eastern Banking*, pp. 66–76.

5 A.F. Heard to Augustine Heard, Jr, 19 December 1874, HL-32, p. 506, in Augustine Heard Collection, Baker Library, Harvard Business School, Boston, MA.

6 David McLean to Thomas Jackson, 11 May 1877, Private Letters (London), I, 233, in the David McLean Papers (MS 380401), Library, School of Oriental and African Studies (SOAS), University of London.

7 Gershom Stewart to Addis, 1 April 1887, PP. MS. 14/107, (Sir Charles) Addis Papers, Library, SOAS.

8 There is nothing in the Arquivo Historico de Macau, e.g. in the *Boletim*, on the 'agency'; nor was there anything in *O Correio Macaense*, although there were full discussions and texts of the agreements and related correspondence of Sir Robert Hart and Campbell in London.

9 There were many routine transactions undertaken by the Hongkong Bank for the Macau Government, see *Arquivos de Macau*, Vol. I (Jan/Jun 1983), under 'Servicos de Finanças: *Inventario* do Codice de "Minutas de Oficios Expedidos em 1890"'; for the 1876 loan, see *Boletim da Provincia de Macau e Timor*, Vol. XXII, No. 18 (29 April); there is miscellaneous correspondence in only three other files.

10 Chartered Bank to Colonial Office, 5 March 1888, and draft reply of 27 November 1888, CO 273/157. See also Chartered Bank to Colonial Office, 14 November and 18 March 1895.

11 Alfred Dent to F. Graham with enclosures, 29 November 1888, included with Chartered Bank to Colonial Office, 5 November 1888, CO 273/157.

12 Acting Governor, Straits Settlements, to the Secretary of State, 28 May 1884, SS 207 in Singapore National Archives (SNA).

13 Straits Settlements Executive Council, minutes, 29 July 1884, CO 275/26; *Straits Settlements Government Gazette*, December 1844, *et seq.*

14 Acting Governor, Straits Settlements, to the Secretary of State, 18 June 1884, SS 265, SNA.

15 Acting Governor, Straits Settlements, to Secretary of State, 18 June 1884, SS 265, SNA.

16 A. Lister, then Treasurer and sometime Postmaster General, outlined his original plan for the Savings Bank as a government operation in Enclosure 2 of the Governor's despatch of 4 August 1884, CO 129/217, ff. 145–49.

17 Ibid, ff. 147–48. See also 'The Postmaster General's Report for 1884', dated 1 January 1885, and presented to the Legislative Council.

18 A. Lister's report, cited, f. 147.

19 Governor G.F. Bowen to the Secretary of State, 18 May 1884, CO 129/216, ff. 79–81.

20 Governor G.F. Bowen to the Earl of Derby, Secretary of State for the Colonies, 4 August 1884, CO 129/217, ff. 136–37, copied on ff. 138–42, in response to Derby's despatch of 16 June 1884.

21 Minutes on the affair in CO 129/217, f. 132.

22 The Earl of Derby to Governor Bowen, 8 November 1884, CO 129/217, ff. 150–51, and the Governor's response of 26 December 1884, CO 129/218, ff. 238–40.

23 Minutes on the ordinance, CO 129/218, ff. 220–21.

24 See draft of 9 February 1885, CO 129/218, ff. 228–29.

25 Letter from A.G. Crook, Deputy Postmaster General to the author, dated 14 January 1956, PO ref: 158/51/45.

26 Postmaster General's 1884 report, cited.
27 Ibid.
28 National Debt Office to the Secretary of the Treasury, 26 February 1885, copy furnished the author by the Colonial Office Research Committee; quoted with the Governor's response in his despatch of 28 May 1885, CO 129/221, f. 360.
29 Memorandum on the Savings Bank by the Hong Kong Treasurer, A. Lister, 4 August 1884, CO 129/218, ff. 223–24.
30 See, for example, the comment in his report on the banks in Hong Kong, dated 11 October 1883, CO 129/212, f. 53.
31 A. Lister, minute, 5 October 1887, Enclosure 1, in despatch of Governor William Des Voeux to the Secretary of State, CO 129/234, f. 439.
32 Governor W. Des Voeux to the Secretary of State, with enclosures, 14 October 1887, CO 129/234, ff. 436–41; see especially Enclosure 2 of the Treasurer, f. 440.
33 W.N. Marsh, Officer Administering the Government of Hong Kong, to Secretary of State, Earl Derby, 12 October 1883, CO 129/212, ff. 45–50.
34 Ibid., ff. 48–49.
35 Colonial Office minutes, 18 April 1887, CO 129/231, ff. 456–57.
36 See, for example, Governor Sir John Pope Hennessy to Secretary of State, 25 October 1877, CO 129/179, ff. 263–67; Colonial Office minutes and drafts. June-July 1879, Hong Kong No.11764, CO 129/185, ff. 67–75; and the response from W.H. Marsh which follows.

   On the question of the level of deposits and the subsidiary coinage, see Governor Des Voeux to the Secretary of State, 14 April 1888, with lengthy enclosures by Lister, CO 129/237, ff. 345–59. The saga is a continuing one, but see also the minute by the Auditor General, 11 December 1889, CO 129/242, ff. 613–16.
37 A favourite name bestowed on the building by R. Fraser-Smith, editor of the *Hongkong Telegraph.*
38 Christopher L. Yip, 'Four Major Buildings in the Architectural History of The Hongkong and Shanghai Banking Corporation', in King, ed. *Eastern Banking* (London, 1983), pp. 112–17. A technical description and professional references are included in this article; Yip had access to unpublished notes in the archives of Palmer & Turner, the successor firm.
39 *China Mail* (9 August 1886).
40 Ibid.
41 Ibid.
42 Ibid.

11 THE BANK AND ITS ORDINANCES – REVISION AND RENEWAL, 1882–1890

1 SS No. 275, 26 November 1879, in Singapore National Archives; also in T.1/7641.
2 Treasury to Colonial Office, 26 November 1878, CO 129/183.
3 Treasury to Colonial Office, 9 February 1888, CO 129/240 and T.1/8302B, the latter being the main file on this and related topics.
4 T.1/8504C, bundle 13168/90, file 13168, Chalmers' memo; see also Treasury to Colonial Office, 19 August and 10 October 1881, CO 129/196.
5 The principal correspondence relative to the one-dollar note debate is found in Hong Kong Government, 'Correspondence respecting the Issue of One Dollar Notes, presented to the Legislative Council by Command of H.E. the Governor', T.1/8130B (which is also a principal file for this and related matters) and in Hong Kong Legislative Council Sessional Papers.
6 Thomas Jackson, Chief Manager, the Hongkong Bank, to Colonial Secretary, Hong Kong, 2 November 1880, CO 273/109, f. 406.

7 R.H. Meade, Colonial Office, to Secretary to the Treasury, 27 May 1880, T.1/13006 – another principal file.

8 CO 273/109, f. 403.

9 Colonial Office minutes, Hong Kong/Straits No.14889, 20 August 1881, CO 129/196, ff. 77–120, esp. f. 81.

10 19 August 1881, CO 129/196, ff. 82–86.

11 Correspondence and minutes on this ordinance are found in CO 129/205, ff. 112–18.

12 W. Evan Nelson, 'The Hongkong and Shanghai Banking Corporation Factor in the Progress toward a Straits Settlements Government Note Issue, 1881–1889', in King, ed. *Eastern Banking*, p. 165. Reference has also been made to his valuable 'The Imperial Administration of Currency and British Banking in the Straits Settlements, 1867–1908', PhD thesis, Duke University, 1984.

13 Cited in ibid, p. 166, Treasury to Colonial Office, 27 September 1884, CO 273/131, and a minute by Lucas.

14 T.1/14873, petition dated 23 July 1883, see also T.1/803B.

15 Jackson to Acting Colonial Secretary, 21 May 1884, CO 129/216, ff. 425–26.

16 See the Sessional Papers, 1884, 'Correspondence respecting the Issue of One Dollar Notes', cited; the Finance Committee report is dated 22 May 1884. Also in T.1/8130B. The further opinion of Counsel is in file dated 18 November 1884, CO 129/128, ff. 385–86.

17 Hong Kong, No. 12276, minutes dated 12 June 1884, CO 129/216, ff. 419–20.

18 Lord Derby to Secretary of Treasury, 26 August 1884, CO 129/216, f. 436.

19 T.1/8130B is the main file and contains minutes on this subject.

20 Ibid.

21 'Case: The Hongkong and Shanghai Bank', 7 October 1884, in CO 129/218, ff. 378–82; and the Opinion, dated 4 November 1884, ff. 383–84. Also in T.1/8103B.

22 CO 129/218, 8 December 1884, f. 377.

23 See the summary history of the Hongkong Bank by R.F. Wilkins of the Treasury, dated 19 August 1898, T.1/9297A, esp. p. 9. This summary is accurate, but it was obviously not available to those considering the matters described in this chapter.

24 Treasury to Colonial Office, 31 March 1882, CO 129/205, ff. 93–94.

25 Colonial Office minute, Hong Kong no. 11266, 11 June 1887, CO 129/232, f. 270.

26 Secretary to the Treasury to Secretary of State, 9 August 1887, CO 129/235, ff. 151–52; for the relevant minutes see CO 129/232, ff. 270–74.

27 CO 129/235, f. 150.

28 Treasury to Colonial Office, 12 June 1874, CO 129/168, cited in Peter Wesley-Smith, 'The Hongkong Bank and the Extraterritorial Problem, 1865–1890', in King, ed. *Eastern Banking*, p. 70.

29 The information in this section is taken from a compilation in the Hongkong Bank Group Archives. The importance of the Jurado case caused J.R. Jones, the Bank's legal adviser charged with preparing material for the centenary history, to make a thorough search of the Board Minute Books and collect other documents to which this summary is indebted. No further notes will in consequence be provided; readers are referred to the appropriate file in Group Archives.

29 FO 72/1851, 25 March 1889.

30 Ibid.

31 Ibid.

32 In summary dated 12 April 1889, FO 72/1851/1855 (Manila).

33 FO 72/1846, 26 March 1889.

34 FO 72/1855, 10 April 1889; British Embassy, Madrid, to Foreign Office, 20 April 1889, FO 72/1847.

35 FO 72/1847, 24 June 1889.

36 Governor of Hong Kong to Colonial Office, cable dated 28 May 1891, copied in despatch dated 10 June 1891, CO 129/250, ff. 82–83.

37 10 June 1891, CO 129/250, ff. 82–84.

38 Compton Mackenzie, *Realms of Silver: One Hundred Years of Banking in the East* (London, 1954), p. 137.

39 CO 129/233, 17 May 1887, ff. 11–16.

40 CO 129/240, Treasury to Colonial Office, 9 February 1888, ff. 96–97, draft and related minutes in T.1/8302B.

41 CO 129/241, f. 479.

42 See note 40.

43 'Report from the Select Committee on Chartered Banks (Colonial) Bill', *British Parliamentary Papers*, Vol. VIII, from p. 175 (1880).

44 CO 129/240, cited, ff. 99–100. See also Treasury to Colonial Office, 19 April 1884, in Singapore National Archives.

45 15 December 1887, CO 129/233, ff. 5–8.

46 Ibid.

47 CO 129/241, ff. 467–69.

48 24 April 1889, CO 129/241, f. 465.

49 R. Welby (Treasury) to the Under Secretary of State for the Colonies, 22 February 1890, T.1/8504^c and CO 129/248, f. 275.

50 Colonial Office (two letters, from Wingfield and Meade respectively) to the Treasury, private, 14 and 17 February 1890, CO 129/242, ff. 556–61.

51 CO 129/243, ff. 529–30; also in T.1/8504^c.

52 McLean to R.H. Meade, Assistant Under-Secretary of State for the Colonies, 30 July 1889, CO 129/243, ff. 513–19; *cf.* G.E. Noble's letter to the Colonial Secretary, 8 June 1889, CO 129/241, ff. 621–24.

53 Treasury to Colonial Office, 14 September 1889, T.1/8504^c.

54 Governor William Des Voeux to Secretary of State, 12 June 1889, CO 129/241, ff. 616–20.

55 D. McLean, Manager, Hongkong Bank, London, to Colonial Office, 26 September 1889, CO 129/243, ff. 529–30; also in T.1/8504^c.

56 Treasury to Colonial Office, 17 June 1890, CO 129/248, ff. 288–89.

57 See T.1/8504^c.

58 Colonial Office draft, 10 July 1890, CO 129/248, ff. 290–91.

59 Ewen Cameron, London Manager, Hongkong Bank, to R.H. Meade, Colonial Office, 22 July 1890, CO 129/248, ff. 677–78.

60 See Governor of Hong Kong to Colonial Office, 25 July 1892, CO 129/255.

61 18 July 1890, CO 129/248, ff. 295–96.

62 Ewen Cameron to R.H. Meade, 25 July 1890, CO 129/248, ff. 681–82, and Hongkong Bank to Meade, 25 August 1890, CO 129/248, ff. 691–92.

63 Treasury to Colonial Office, 4 August 1890, CO 129/248, ff. 299–300, and related minutes to f. 308.

64 CO 129/248, ff. 316–17.

12 INTERREGNUM, 1889–1893

1 The memorials which sparked foreign enthusiasm are translated in the *North-China Herald* (6 July 1889), pp. 19–20; (7 September 1889), first page and p. 291; (4 October 1889), pp. 409–10, 419–20; (17 December 1889), p. 726; for the reactions from 'Home', ibid (1 November 1889), pp. 535–36; and discussions, ibid (22 November 1889), pp. 637–38.

2 John K. Fairbank, Edwin O. Reischauer, Albert M. Craig, *East Asia, the Modern Transformation* (Boston, 1965), pp. 380–81.

3 China Association, Minute Books, Vol. I, 1890, Archive of the China Association, Library, School of Oriental and African Studies (SOAS), University of London.

4 *Statist* (17 February 1893).

5 *North-China Herald* (17 January 1890).

6 Quoted in ibid.

7 C.S. Addis in Shanghai to his brother George, 15 February 1890, PP. MS. 14/65/143, (Sir Charles) Addis Papers, Library, SOAS.

8 The *Economist* wrote of a 'boom' in trust company promotion; see (6 April 1889), pp. 433–34, 443, and (13 April 1889), p. 479.

9 *North-China Herald* (17 January 1890).

10 Details are found in PRO Board of Trade company file BT 31/4611/30249.

11 For the change of name see, e.g. *North-China Herald* (13 March 1891), p. 309; the report on the company reprinted there is dated January 1891.

12 Meeting of 9 February 1893, reprinted in *North-China Herald*, 24 March 1893, pp. 425–26.

13 See company file, BT 31/6059/42877.

14 For an analysis of this bank's failure, see 'The New Oriental Bank Corporation, Ltd, a Lesson in Bad Banking', *Bankers' Magazine* 57: 69–81 (1894); see also ibid, pp. 226–27.

15 Company files BT 31/15145/33713; see also BT 31/4971/33210 and BT 31/4988/33367.

16 Pomeroy in London to Frank Blackwell Forbes in Paris, 20 June 1891, in the Forbes Papers, China Trade Collection, Massachusetts Historical Society, Boston, MA.

17 Ibid. The explanation of Pomeroy's letter was kindly supplied by T.W. O'Brien of the Hongkong Bank's Foreign Exchange Department.

18 F.B. Forbes to Ewen Cameron, 12 and 16 June 1891, in Forbes Papers, reel XXIV, No. 9.

19 See Board of Trade references in note 15 above.

20 For Jardine relationships, see the family tree in Maggie Keswick, ed. *The Thistle and the Jade: a Celebration of 150 Years of Jardine, Matheson and Co* (London, 1982), pp. 262–63.

21 For a contemporary comment, see e.g. *Hongkong Daily Press* (24 August 1891), quoted in the *North-China Herald* (4 September 1891), p. 318.

22 Biographical information in Group Archives has been supplemented by the research of Claude Fivel-Démoret; see his 'The Hongkong Bank in Lyon, 1881–1954: Busy, but too Discreet?', in King, ed. *Eastern Banking* (London, 1983), pp. 467–516, esp. p. 478.

23 (London, 1916), pp. 58–59.

24 C.S. Addis to Dudley Mills, 16 May 1895 and 10 February 1897, PP. MS. 14/156 and 158.

25 Jackson to McLean, 17 July 1891, in David McLean Papers, Hongkong Bank Group Archives.

26 London and County Bank, Board Minute Books, XX, 542 and 445 (5 September 1891 and 20 June 1891), item 2365 in National Westminster Bank Archives.

27 See David McLean, Private Letters (London), in David McLean Papers (MS 380401), Library, SOAS.

28 J.R. Jones, 'The Bank, 1876–1942', typescript in Group Archives. A copy of the Mercantile Bank's Agreement and the concluding letter from Baring Brothers and Co. to the Governor, Bank of England, 10 January 1895, is in Group Archives.

29 David McLean to G.E. Noble, 15 February 1889, Private Letters (London), VI, 141.
30 Addis diary entry, 8 March 1892, PP. MS. 14/10.
31 David McLean to Jackson, 14 April 1881, Private Letters, III, 154.
32 Hermann Wallich, 'Aus meinen Leben', *Zwei Generationen im deutschen Bankwesen* (Frankfurt am Main, 1978), and Wallich Papers, C/o Governor Henry Wallich, Federal Reserve Board, Washington, D.C.
33 For biographical details on Morel, see Fivel-Démoret, pp. 475–78.
34 Cited in Fivel-Démoret, p. 478n65.
35 *North-China Herald* (15 August 1890).
36 For biography, see Carl T. Smith, 'Compradores of The Hongkong Bank', in King, ed. *Eastern Banking*, pp. 101–03. The quote is from the *Hongkong Telegraph* (28 May 1892).
37 *Hongkong Telegraph* (28 May 1892), quoted in Smith, p. 103.
38 C.S. Addis to George Addis, 4 April 1892, PP. MS. 14/66/150.
39 Addis diary entry, 10 June 1892, PP. MS. 14/10, and C.S. Addis in Calcutta to Mills, 8 July 1892, PP. MS. 14/67/15.
40 C.T. Smith, pp. 103–08.
41 This controversy covers a period of several years, but the most relevant material is in the Public Record Office, CO 129/242, ff. 602–23, with a letter and enclosures from the Governor of Hong Kong to the Secretary of State, No. 381, 19 December 1889; CO 129/244, ff. 20–31, despatch No. 10 of 7 January 1890; CO 129/251, ff. 565–67; CO 129/254, ff. 720–25, 31 May 1892; CO 129/258, ff. 348–55, with despatch No. 36 of 3 February 1893.
42 Minute by the Acting Auditor General, A. Lister, 11 December 1889, CO 129/242, f. 615.
43 CO 129/258, f. 348.
44 CO 129/258, ff. 348–50.
45 See discussion in Chapter 11 on the 1889 Ordinance.
46 Thomas Jackson to R.H. Meade, Permanent Under-Secretary of State, 30 June 1891, CO 129/253, ff. 342–46.
47 R. Welby, Treasury, to Secretary of State, 11 August 1891, CO 129/253, f. 37. The Bank accordingly complied, see John Walter, signing 'pro Chief Manager', to Hong Kong Colonial Secretary, 19 April 1892, CO 129/254, f. 728.
48 12 August 1891, CO 129/253, f. 35.
49 Colonial Office minute, CO 129/253, ff. 35–37.
50 Minute in CO 129/257, f. 525.
51 Jackson to Treasury, 21 July 1892, copy in CO 129/257, ff. 519–21, and related minutes, ff. 492–518.
52 See S.J. Butlin, *Australia and New Zealand Bank* (London, 1961), p. 301.

13 THE BANK COMES OF AGE: JACKSON'S SECOND ADMINISTRATION, 1893–1902

The main sources for this chapter are the Minute Books of the Board of Directors, Group Archives, and reports of the semi-annual meetings. These latter are usually fully reported in the *Daily Press* or *North-China Herald*; the accounts usually two weeks earlier than the meeting itself. However, a full set of both accounts and reports, often photocopied from newspapers, is available in the Hongkong Bank Group Archives. References to these sources are obvious and therefore not specifically noted.

1 Albert Feuerwerker, *China's Early Industrialization, Sheng Hsuan-huai (1844–1916) and Mandarin Enterprise* (Cambridge, MA, 1958), pp. 226–42, esp. pp. 237–40;

Frank M. Tamagna, *Banking and Finance in China* (New York, 1942), pp. 35–36.

2 Sheila Marriner and Francis E. Hyde, *The Senior, John Samuel Swire, 1825–98* (Liverpool, 1967), p. 106. See also the discussion in my 'Establishing the Hongkong Bank: the Role of the Directors and their Managers', in King, ed. *Eastern Banking*, pp. 58–65, esp. note 81.

3 Information on the companies is taken generally from contemporary directories, etc., especially, Arnold Wright, ed. *Twentieth Century Impressions of Hongkong, Shanghai, and Other Treaty Ports of China* (London, 1908), J.M. Braga, comp. *Hong Kong Business Symposium* (Hong Kong, 1957), and W. Feldwick, ed. *Present Day Impressions of the Far East* (London, 1917).

4 For histories of Carlowitz and Co., see the following references from D.J.S. King's research report 'On the Relations of the Hongkong Bank with Germany, 1864–1948', in Group Archives: 'Carlowitz & Co.', in *Historisch-biographische Blätter der Staat Hamburg* (Berlin, 1905/6); *Carlowitz & Co. China, Hong Kong, Hamburg* (Hamburg-Zwickau: Föster & Barries, 1925); *Carlowitz & Co. Hamburg, Hong Kong, New York, China und Japan* (Hamburg, 1906); (Carlowitz and Co.), *Kurzer Auszug aus der Geschichte der Firma Carlowitz & Co.* (Shanghai, 1937).

5 For an assessment of Robert Shewan in another role, see Austin Coates, *Whampoa: Ships on the Shore* (Hong Kong, 1980), pp. 156–57.

6 7 November 1894, T.1/8875ᶜ.

7 For details, see D.J.S. King, 'China's Early Loans, 1874–95, and the Role of The Hongkong and Shanghai Banking Corporation', chapters 30 and 31, in Group Archives.

8 Treasury to Colonial Office, 18 July 1890, CO 129/248, ff. 295–96; Ewen Cameron to R.H. Meade, 25 July 1890, in ibid, ff. 681–82; Treasury to Colonial Office, 4 August 1890, in ibid, ff. 299–300; Governor of Hong Kong to Colonial Office, CO 129/250, ff. 28–30; ibid, 25 July 1892, CO 129/255, ff. 623–24; Ewen Cameron to Crown Agents, 28 May 1894, CO 129/264, ff. 271–72; and Crown Agents to Colonial Office, 30 May 1894, CO 129/264, ff. 670.

9 J.H. Stewart Lockhart, Colonial Secretary, Hong Kong, to J.A. Swettenham, Colonial Secretary, Straits Settlements, 5 February 1897, noting that the Proclamation had never been issued; it is probably this letter, in response to a query from Singapore, which led to the remedy being initiated; see *Hongkong Government Gazette*, 13 February 1897 for the actual Proclamation. For SS references see note 10.

10 For a full discussion of the controversy in Singapore, see W. Evan Nelson, 'The Hongkong and Shanghai Banking Corporation Factor in the Progress toward a Straits Settlements Government Note Issue, 1881–1889', in King, ed. *Eastern Banking* (London, 1983), esp. pp. 175–79, and the full documentation in his footnotes; see also his 'The Imperial Administration of Currency and British Banking in the Straits Settlements, 1867–1908', PhD thesis, Duke University 1984. The Swettenham letter is in SSLCP (Straits Settlements Legislative Council Proceedings) 1898, 'Correspondence with regard to the proposed Amendment of "The Hongkong and Shanghai Bank Ordinance 1881"', No. 51, 28 December 1898, p. C548. This is preceded by a letter of 5 February 1897 from J.H. Stewart Lockhart, Hong Kong Colonial Secretary, dealing with the omitted proclamation. Singapore National Archives.

11 R.M. Gray to the Under Secretary of State, Colonial Office, 8 July 1898, CO 129/288, ff. 117–18, and in Singapore National Archives, COD 118, transmitted to the Straits Settlements from the Colonial Office, 19 August 1898, cited in Nelson as SSLCP, p. C551.

12 Ibid. For minutes of the Chamber of Commerce in support of the Bank's position as proposed by T.H. Whitehead, Hong Kong manager of the Chartered Bank, see CO 129/284, ff. 84–87. A file on this subject is found in CO 129/284, ff. 78–87.

13 Telegram, Acting Governor [of Hong Kong, Major-General W.] Black to Mr Secretary [Joseph] Chamberlain, 12 July 1896, forwarded for information of Straits Settlements Government, 22 July 1898, SS 159, COD 118 in Singapore National Archives.

14 C.P. Lucas, Colonial Office, to Secretary to the Treasury, 13 July 1898, and response of 15 July 1898, under cover of letter to Straits Settlements of 22 July 1898, see note 10 above. See also T.1/9297H file for further material on this subject.

15 On the subject of poor drafting, see Hong Kong Legislative Council Proceedings, 1899 (25 January), p. 12. The various ordinances referred to are discussed as follows: No. 6 of 1898, CO 129/284, ff. 29–59, and CO 129/288, ff. 116–19, 392–98; for the revision of this ordinance, i.e. No. 1 of 1899, see CO 129/286, ff. 623–37 and CO 129/290, ff. 106–09, and also CO 129/315, ff. 58–59; for No. 17 of 1899, see CO 129/291, ff. 637–38, CO 129/292, ff. 579–81, CO 129/303, ff. 102–05, CO 129/315, ff. 60–61. See also T.1/9580BB, esp. H.M. Bevis to Colonial Secretary, 28 March 1900, and E.W. Hamilton to Under Secretary of State, 30 May 1900.

16 See J.A. Swettenham to the Secretary of State, 10 August 1898; disapproval is found in J. Chamberlain, Secretary of State, to Swettenham, 25 November 1898, SS No.282; the revised ordinance, repealing No. VI of 1898, was enclosed for approval; in SSLCP 1898, cited in note 10, pp. C550 and C552–53.

17 E.W. Hamilton to Under Secretary of State, 24 July 1899 and related correspondence in T.1/9402A.

18 For Hong Kong Legislative Council Proceedings, see the *Hong Kong Hansard*, 23 July 1900, p. 89. See also ibid, 25 July 1898, p. 43; 25 January 1899, p. 12; 1 February 1899, p. 15; 31 July 1899, p. 47; and 16 July 1900, p. 87.

19 Chief Manager, Mercantile Bank of India, to Secretary of State, 26 August 1898, T.1/9297.

20 See CO 129/336, ff. 519–36, and 652.

21 See CO 129/284, f. 311 and 129/286, ff. 605–06.

22 As Bevis predicted; see his letter of 12 April 1900 to the Under Secretary of State, T.1/9580BB or CO 129/303, ff. 299–301.

23 F.S. Taylor, 'Differences in Scottish and English Banking, I. The Note Issues', *The Banker*, 95:371. I am indebted to the comments of Dr C.W. Munn, author of *The Scottish Provincial Banking Companies, 1747–1864* (see esp. p. 95), in his letter of 21 March 1986 addressed to R.G. Baird, Bank's Economist, Royal Bank of Scotland, to whom I had addressed queries relative to Scottish practices.

24 The disaster of this P&O ship is referred to in Geoffrey R. Sayer, *Hong Kong, 1862–1919: years of discretion* (Hong Kong, 1975), p. 73. G.R. Sayer was the father of G.M. Sayer, Chairman of the Hongkong Bank, 1972–77.

25 R.T. Wright to Sir Thomas Jackson, May 1902, from the papers of Sir Michael Jackson in Group Archives. *Cf.* discussion of the charges by W.F. Skene in Chapter 1, Volume II.

14 THE HONGKONG BANK IN CHINA, 1874–1895

1 Robert Hart to James Duncan Campbell, letter No. 191 dated 3 January 1878, in Robert Hart, *The I.G. in Peking, Letters of Robert Hart, Chinese Maritime Customs, 1868–1907*, eds John K. Fairbank *et al.* (Cambridge, MA, 1975), I, 259.

2 Addis letter of 25 January 1886, PP. MS. 14/64/8, [Sir Charles] Addis Papers, Library, School of Oriental and African Studies (SOAS), University of London; presumably based on Addis research ordered by Thomas Jackson in connection with the Hong Kong exhibit at the Colonial Exposition, for which see Addis to his mother, 8 January 1886, PP.MS.14/64/2.

3 Quoted in the *North-China Herald* (11 May 1889), p. 581. See also references to Keswick in Banno's article, note 22 below.

4 See the accounts transmitted to David McLean during his inspection of the Bank, in Additional McLean Papers, Hongkong Bank Group Archives.

5 Robert P. Gardella, Jr, 'Fukien's Tea Industry and Trade in Ch'ing and Republican China: the developmental consequences of a traditional commodity export', PhD Thesis (University of Washington, 1976), pp. 143 and 147. The latter chart (reproduced as Figure 6) is adapted by Gardella from Nanshi chosa shiryo, *Fukkensho no chagyo* (The tea industry of Fukien; Taihoku [Taipei], 1938), p. 56, and 'Fukkensho chagyo no kekyu', in Nanshi chosa shjiryo, *Fukken kensetsu hokoku* (Taihoku, 1938), II, 222; see also Gardella's essay, 'The Boom Years of the Fukien Tea Trade, 1842–1888' in Ernest R. May and John K. Fairbank, eds, *America's China Trade in Historical Perspective: the Chinese and American Performance* (Cambridge, MA, 1986), pp. 34–75 and notes.

6 McLean, Additional Papers cited, see note 4.

7 *North-China Herald* (21 February 1883), p. 209.

8 Kwang-Ching Liu, a discussion of Han-sheng Chuan, 'The Economic Crisis of 1883 as seen in the Failure of Hsü Jun's Real Estate Business in Shanghai', in Chi-ming Hou and Tzong-shian Yu, eds, *Modern Chinese Economic History* (Taipei, 1979), pp. 499–509.

9 Ibid, p. 506.

10 See, for example, Yen-P'ing Hao, *The Comprador in Nineteenth-Century China: Bridge between East and West* (Cambridge, MA, 1970).

11 William Frederick Spalding, *Dictionary of the World's Currencies and Foreign Exchanges* (London, 1928), under 'Compradore'.

12 Information on Yap Ho Chiu comes from an interview with his great grandson, see later in this chapter under 'Amoy'; on Ch'en Lien-pai see Volume III, and on Sir Robert Ho Tung, see Carl T. Smith, 'Compradores of The Hongkong Bank', in King, ed. *Eastern Banking* (London, 1983), pp. 93–111.

13 For a specific case, Lau Wai Chün, see J.R.M. Smith to Addis, 12 May 1905, PP. MS. 14/352.

14 See note 3.

15 Michie to Addis, 12 May 1897, PP. MS. 14/143.

16 Hao, pp. 101 and 176. The Bank minutes for April 1905 (not 1907) record Chin Foo's death with the note that he had been compradore for 30 years and would be succeeded by his son 'Li Kung Sin'.

17 This information is based on the research of Carl T. Smith. See his article cited and oral history tape and transcript in Group Archives.

18 Chang Nan (Ch'ang Nan), 'Ying-kuo Hui-feng Yin-hang ti ching-chi lüeh-tou' (Economic plundering of the British Hongkong Bank), in *Wu-shih-erh chung wen-shih chih-liao pien-mou fen-lei suo-yin* (Shanghai 1982). Pp. 69–78.

19 Arnold Wright, ed. *Twentieth Century Impressions of Hongkong, Shanghai and other Treaty Ports of China* (London, 1908), p. 700. Addis to A.M. Townsend, May 1896, PP. MS. 14/69/22.

20 Chen Mong Hock, *The Early Chinese Newspapers of Singapore* (Singapore, 1967), p. 24, citing Song Ong Siang, *One Hundred Years of History of the Chinese in Singapore* (London, 1923), p. 104; see also Brooke Makepeace, *One Hundred Years of Singapore* (London, 1921).

21 The first reference is to McLean Private Letters (London), I, 237; the second to V, 85. See also, McLean to Jackson, 29 October 1875, Private Letters, I, 21; McLean to Wah Sam, 11 November 1875, p. 27; McLean to Jackson, 29 June 1876, p. 101, McLean Papers (MS 380401), SOAS.

22 See Masataka Banno, 'Ma Chien-chung's Mission to India in 1881: his Travel

Account, *Nan-hsing-chi*' (An account of a journey to the South), *Journal of Social Science* (International Christian University Publications), II-B, No. 17, pp. 108–24. In English with Japanese summary. The quotations below are from this article and clearly indicated. This report is supplemented by the *Nan-hsing jih-chi* of Ma's companion, Wu Kuang-p'ei.

23 Ibid.

24 Ibid, p. 118.

25 For a note on Chinese references consulted, see introductory notes to the bibliography.

26 H.E. Muriel's autobiography is in the Hongkong Bank Group Archives.

27 Alexander Leith to O'Conor, 20 June 1885, FO 228/816, f. 124.

28 J. Keswick to Irving, 18 November 1885, based on information from J.G. Dunn, letter in Jardine Matheson Archives.

29 C.S. Addis to Aunt Mansfield, 22 May 1886, PP.MS.14/64/47.

30 Quoted in Addis to his father, 4 April 1886, PP. MS. 14/64/33.

31 Addis to his father, 11 May 1886, quoted in Roberta A. Dayer, 'The Young Charles S. Addis: Poet or Banker?', in King, ed. *Eastern Banking*, p. 19.

32 Addis to Dudley Mills, 25 May 1886, PP.MS. 14/64/50; Edgar Allen Poe, 'The Haunted Palace', Stanza 2.

33 Addis diary, 2 May 1888, PP. MS. 14/6; and Addis to Mills, 16 May 1895, MS. 14/156.

34 Addis to Mills, 14 January 1890, MS. 14/64/134.

35 Addis diary, 12 May 1882, PP. MS. 14/2.

36 Ibid, 16 May 1882, PP. MS. 14/2.

37 Ibid, 19 and 23 May 1882, PP. MS. 14/2. *Tzu Erh Chi*, for an explanation, see the *Encyclopaedia Sinica*, ed. Samuel Couling (Shanghai, 1917, rpt. Hong Kong, 1983).

38 Ibid, 17 January 1883, PP. MS. 14/3.

39 Ibid, 1 April 1883, PP. MS. 14/3.

40 Addis to sister Etta, 1 March 1886, PP.MS. 14/64/22.

41 Addis to sister Annie, 23 January 1886, quoted in Dayer, p. 17.

42 Addis to sister Crop, 22 May 1886, PP. MS. 14/64/48.

43 Addis to sister Janie, 26 July 1886, PP. MS. 14/64/80.

44 Addis 'Diary' or journal, under 12 September 1887, PP. MS. 14/674.

45 Addis to Monro, 4 June 1886, PP. MS. 14/64/53.

46 Addis to J.S. Lockhart, 6 March 1887, PP. MS. 14/64/143.

47 Addis to Sister Etta, 20 September 1887, PP.MS. 14/65/28.

48 Addis to Mills, 3 January 1892, PP.MS. 14/66/19.

49 Addis's testimony before the Committee on Oriental Studies in London, 21 May 1908, minutes of evidence, p. 187, PP. MS. 14/643.

50 Addis, 'Leaves from a Diary', PP. MS. 14/67/152.

51 Addis to Mills, 24 November 1886, PP. MS. 14/64/111.

52 Addis in Peking to Captain Chiang Chiou Ying, Kalgan, 14 July 1887, PP. MS. 14/65/13.

53 Addis to Mills, 26 May 1889, PP. MS. 14/65/80.

54 See Dayer, pp. 20–21.

55 George Wilson, Shanghai manager, Chartered Mercantile Bank of India, London and China to C. Alabaster, Acting Consul-General in Shanghai, 23 September 1886, FO 228/836, ff. 253–58.

56 C. Alabaster to Sir John Walsham, British Minister, Peking, in ibid.

57 Addis to Robert Wilson, Agent Tientsin, draft (no date), PP. MS. 14/64/172; Wilson to Addis, 6 July 1889, PP. MS. 14/111.

58 Addis to brother Tom, 4 July 1886, PP. MS. 14/64/72.

59 Addis to sister Annie, 10 August 1886, PP. MS. 14/64/82.

60 Addis diary, August 1889, PP. MS. 14/7.

61 Gershom Stewart in Macau to Addis in Peking, 1 April 1887, PP. MS. 14/107.

62 Addis to Ewen Cameron, 18 November 1904, PP. MS. 14/352.

63 See for example a copy of the Addis memo on Chinese language instruction (note 62 above) sent by Cameron to Colin C. Scott of Swire's with the note that the plan was apparently working out, although it was too early to judge, PP. MS. 14/352. Also in Box 1183, Archive of John Swire & Sons Ltd, SOAS. See also the 'Report of the Committee on Oriental Studies in London', minutes of evidence for 21 May 1908 and Appendix III, PP. MS. 14/643.

64 Full references and argumentation will be found in this study which is part of the Hongkong Bank History Program. See also D.J.S. King, 'China's First Public Loan: The Hongkong Bank and the Chinese Imperial Government "Foochow" Loan of 1874', in King, ed. *Eastern Banking*, pp. 230–64.

65 See discussion in ibid, p. 235, and references cited.

66 Memo by Addis, n.d. but 1886/87 while he was in Peking, PP. MS. 14/343.

67 Ibid. The memo also includes the view of the German Minister, von Brandt.

68 See the discussion in Stanley F. Wright, *Hart and the Chinese Customs* (Belfast, 1950), pp. 363–67; a circular from Hart dated 16 March 1877 was reprinted in *The Times* (23 May 1877), p. 7a and is also in FO 233/73.

69 Long and intricate negotiations were held among foreign merchants and bankers on the terms to be allowed the Chinese, who may not have been contemplating a loan at all. On other occasions, there were debates on how China would proceed, quite without contact with the relevant Chinese authorities. See discussions in D.J.S. King's report on the Erlanger proposals in the 1870s and the Rothschild/DG discussions of 1885, pp. 25–30 and 304 respectively.

70 As late as 1875 the Oriental closed a private loan with Tso Tsung-t'ang for Ts2 million (=£625,000).

71 See discussion under 'The Hongkong Bank, Jardine Matheson, and Baring' and 'National consortiums and the Hongkong Bank', pp. 553–59. For information on Panmure Gordon and Co., see B.H.D. MacDermot, *Panmure Gordon and Co, 1876–1976, A Century of Stockbroking* (London, privately printed, 1976). In the first year the company was Gordon and Co.; between 1885–1902, Panmure Gordon, Hill and Co.

72 In 1883 the first repayment on the 1881 loan was delayed, and there was correspondence between de Bovis, Harry Parkes, and Thomas Jackson: see FO 228/776, ff. 81–82 and FO 228/775, ff. 20–21 and other material in D.J.S. King's report, 'China's Early Loans', Chapter 9, 'Difficulties in Repayment and Chinese Credit'.

73 Hart to Campbell, 13 January 1895, letter No. 960, in Hart, *The I.G. in Peking*.

74 See note 64.

75 FO 228/734, ff. 344.

76 FO 228/734, ff. 346–49.

77 Albert Feuerwerker, *China's Early Industrialization* (Cambridge, MA, 1958), pp. 134–35; for Hsü Jun's role, see Kwang-ching Liu, pp. 504–6.

78 Hart to Campbell, 3 February 1895, Letter No. 963, in Hart.

79 For a biography of Hu Kwang-yung and a note on the Shanghai Forwarding Office, see C. John Stanley, *Late Ch'ing Finance: Hu Kuang-yung as an Innovator* (Cambridge, MA, 1961).

80 Letter dated 28 December 1886, in J.R. Jones, ed. 'Personalities and Narratives', Thomas Jackson, p. 13, in Group Archives.

81 In Baring Bros Archives, Guildhall, City of London, letter dated 6 July 1874, HC17.312.

82 Letter of 11 June 1885, HC6.1.26 in Baring Bros Archives.

83 This and related matters are reported in David McLean private correspondence with Jackson, letters dated 17 April, 8 May, 15 May, 5, 12, 19 June; see also the discussion in Edward LeFevour, *Western Enterprise in Late Ch'ing China* (Cambridge, MA, 1968), p. 76.

84 20 June 1885.

85 Frank H.H. King, *Survey our Empire! A bio-bibliography of Robert Montgomery Martin (1801–1868)*, (Hong Kong, 1979), p. 190, and Geoffrey Jones, *Banking and Empire in Iran*, Vol. I of his *The History of The British Bank of the Middle East* (Cambridge, 1986).

86 See especially articles in the *Celestial Empire*, whose editor, J.G. Thirkell, admitted he had been in error.

87 23 November 1888.

88 Cameron to Addis, 16 August 1887, PP. MS. 14/107.

89 McLean to Jackson, 15 October 1884, Private Letters (London).

90 McLean to Jackson, 11 December 1885, Private Letters (London); *cf.* Maximilian Müller-Jabusch, *Fünfzig Jahre Deutsch-Asiatische Bank, 1890–1939* (Berlin, 1940), p. 15.

91 J. Keswick to E. Cameron, Private, 23 and 25 January 1886, Jardine Matheson Archives, Cambridge.

92 See Jardine Matheson Archives C41/8; correspondence between J. Keswick, W. Keswick, and E. Cameron of 16, 17, and 19 July 1886.

93 Chen Chung-sieu, 'British Loans to China from 1860 to 1913, with special reference to the period 1894–1913', PhD Thesis (University of London, 1940).

15 HONGKONG BANKERS IN THE AGE OF JACKSON

The main sources in this chapter are (i) the minute books and other records of the Hongkong Bank in Group Archives, (ii) J.R. Jones collections 'Personalities and Narratives' and appropriate ring-binder files, (iii) the (Sir Charles) Addis Papers, PP. MS. 14, in SOAS, which are fully catalogued, and (iv) the F.T. Koelle Papers, original with Dr W. Koelle in Hamburg, but a typescript of the sections important to the Hongkong Bank history is available in Group Archives, and this has been consulted in preparing the abstracts for this chapter. As the sources quoted are usually obvious and can be consulted on the basis of the information in the text, the notes have been kept to a minimum.

The Hongkong Bank's staff lists prior to 1890 were lost, presumably during World War II; they have been reconstructed by Catherine E. King from various sources including material in Group Archives, jury lists, China-coast directories, diaries, and correspondence. Actual dates may in the cases of posting to various outports be off by a year. She has also compiled other personnel data which makes it possible to provide at least a tentative description of the Bankers and their terms of service – especially the section on their career patterns.

1 Sir Newton Stabb to Lady Stabb, 25 December 1915, in Personalities files, Group Archives.

2 A.M. Townsend, 'Early Days of the Hongkong and Shanghai Bank', privately reproduced, copy in Hongkong Bank Group Archives. These are accurate reminiscences written at the age of 90.

3 C.S. Addis, letter to his father, 27 February 1886, PP. MS. 14/64/19, (Sir Charles) Addis Papers, Library, School of Oriental and African Studies (SOAS), University of London; see introductory note above.

4 Text available in Group Archives, also published in the *London and China Express*.

5 Addis to his father, 27 February 1886, PP. MS. 14/64/19.

6 This story is told in correspondence between Jackson's daughter, Mrs Raymond Marker, and J.R. Jones, in Jackson files, Group Archives.

7 David McLean to Jackson, 8 March 1878, Private Letters (London), II, 28, in David McLean Papers (MS 380401), SOAS.

8 *Hongkong Daily Press* (19 May 1902).

9 As told to Mrs Raymond Marker, Jackson's daughter, in J.R. Jones, 'Personalities and Narratives'.

10 Addis to Mills, 20 July 1893, PP. MS. 14/67/77.

11 McLean to Jackson, 13 April 1883, Private Letters, IV, 208.

12 Memoirs of W.S. Edwardson, the first 'skipper' of the Bank's London Office team, written in 1953 at the age of 92, in J.R. Jones file on 'staff'.

13 George Addis to C.S. Addis, 21 January 1880, after the former's interview with William Kaye in London Office, PP. MS. 14/70.

14 13 April 1883, Private Letters, IV, 208.

15 George Addis to C.S. Addis, 27 July 1886, PP. MS. 14/76.

16 J.H. Simpson, Bank of Liverpool, to C.S. Addis, 22 August 1901, PP. MS. 14/118.

17 George Addis to C.S. Addis, 7 November 1889, PP. MS. 14/79.

18 For Addis in Peking, see Roberta A. Dayer, 'The Young Charles S. Addis: Poet or Banker?', in King, ed. *Eastern Banking* (London 1983), pp. 66–76.

19 From the F.T. Koelle journals, see note above.

20 P.G. Wodehouse, 'Over Seventy, an autobiography with digressions', in *Wodehouse on Wodehouse* (London, 1981), pp. 476–77.

21 George Addis to C.S. Addis, 16 February 1881, PP. MS. 14/71.

22 *North-China Herald* (11 May 1889), pp. 581–82.

23 Ibid.

24 Based on the Addis and Koelle papers, see prefatory note above.

25 John Thorburn to C.S. Addis, 24 September 1881, PP. MS. 14/100.

26 Addis to Mills, 19 March 1891, PP. MS. 14/152, and Addis diary, 11 March 1891, PP. MS. 14/9.

27 28 September 1883, Private Letters, IV, 259.

28 11 September 1885, ibid, V, 195.

29 Interview by Frank H.H. King in Calcutta, April 1980; transcript and tapes in Group Archives.

30 Addis diary, March 1892, PP. MS. 14/10.

31 Addis to Mills, Calcutta, 8 July 1892, PP. MS. 14/67/15.

32 George Addis to C.S. Addis, 10 March 1893, PP. MS. 14/83.

33 Addis to E.G. Hillier, 12 March 1892, PP. MS. 14/66/137.

34 C.S. Addis to George Addis, 28 October 1891, PP. MS. 14/66/98.

35 C.S. Addis to Mills, 20 July 1893, PP. MS. 14/67/77.

36 Addis to Mills, 6 July 1892, PP. MS. 14/67/15.

37 Hamby to Chapman, 11 June 1892, PP. MS. 14/115.

38 C.S. Addis to Mills, 20 July 1893, PP. MS. 14/67/77.

39 Addis to Mills, 16 May 1895, PP. MS. 14/156.

40 Ibid.

41 Ibid.

42 George Addis to C.S. Addis, 10 November 1892, PP. MS. 14/82; and J.R.M. Smith to C.S. Addis, 31 December 1892, PP. MS. 14/115.

43 Addis to J.R.M. Smith, 31 July 1892, PP. MS. 14/67/16.

GLOSSARY OF TERMS

For current standard banking terms, see F.E. Perry, *A Dictionary of Banking*, 2nd ed. London, 1983; for terms special to the earlier period, see the works of W.F. Spalding cited in the Bibliography and earlier editions of standard exchange manuals, e.g. *Tate's Modern Cambist*. For Chinese terms and events, see, among others, Samuel Couling, ed. *The Encyclopaedia Sinica* (rpt. Hong Kong, 1983), the works of Edward Kann, and the biographical collection of Arthur W. Hummel, ed. *Eminent Chinese of the Ch'ing Period* (Washington, D.C., 1943).

ACCOUNTANT   The Hongkong Bank officer responsible, *inter alia*, for administration of the office; originally and in smaller agencies, the second-ranking officer; the actual accounting was done by the officer in charge of 'books'.

BANTO   office manager (Japan).

CASH   a Chinese copper coin, worth in theory 1,000th of a tael.

CHETTIAR   'chetty' – a South Indian caste of 'native' banker found also in Ceylon and the Straits Settlements.

CHOP   a mark or brand name.

CHUMMERY   a bachelors' mess, usually in India, but the term was erratically used by foreign firms in China.

CLEAN LOAN   one which is without specific security, *cf.* clean credits; see Perry.

COMPRADORE   a company's Chinese manager who also guaranteed transactions with Chinese customers, etc.; the word had other meanings in common usage, see Chapter 14.

COMPRADORIC SYSTEM   the adjectival form of 'compradore' is 'compradoric'; the 'compradoric system' is one in which the foreign business community acts through and depends on compradores.

CONCESSION   in an appropriate context the term refers to some area near a Chinese city which is under foreign administration, either separate or joint, as in Hankow and Tientsin. See also, French Concession, International Settlement.

CONSTITUENT   the term used by the Hongkong Bank for 'customer', suggesting the close relationship desired and the responsibility implied in becoming a customer's 'banker'.

EXTRATERRITORIALITY, EXTERRITORIALITY, EXTRALITY   used in this history in two particular senses: (i) the concept that the 'traveller' carries his own law with him or the fiction that he remains outside the territory of the state in which he resides and therefore is not amenable to its laws but remains subject to the laws of his own Sovereign, an arrangement formalized by treaty with, e.g. the Governments of China, Japan, and Siam; (ii) the policy relative to the authority of a British colonial legislature outside the territory of the particular colony.

FENG-SHUI (lit. wind-water) 'the art of adapting the residence of the living and the dead so as to cooperate and harmonize with local currents of the cosmic breath (Yin and Yang)' – *Encyclopaedia Sinica*.

FRENCH CONCESSION The part of Shanghai administered by French authorities; the French Concession and the International Settlement, *q.v.*, constituted foreign-administered Shanghai.

'GATEKEEPER' a bank regulator without authority to require a particular policy 'a', but who is able to force acceptance of 'a' when the bank requests permission for some policy 'b' over which the regulator does have authority.

GODOWN warehouse

GRIFFIN an untrained Mongolian pony; by extension, an inexperienced young foreigner on the China coast.

GUARANTEE SHROFF in Ceylon, the compradore, *q.v.*

HOLD OR KEEP THE RING, TO the policy designed to ensure that the rules of the contest (or commercial competition) are maintained but not to intervene otherwise.

HONG company.

INTERNATIONAL SETTLEMENT stated without qualification, the term refers to that portion of Shanghai delineated (for the British Settlement) by the Land Regulations of 1845, amended in 1854 to establish the Shanghai Municipal Council, and subject since 1863 to joint British/American jurisdiction (thus including the American Settlement) as subsequently modified. See also, French concession.

JOSS pidgin-English from 'dios': local gods; by extension, their protection and consequent good luck.

KUAN-TU SHANG-PAN 'official supervision, merchant management', referring to government sponsored enterprises, usually financed, at least in part, and managed by the private sector.

LAC (LAKH) one hundred thousand, written: 1,00,000.

LI Ts0.001, i.e. a one-thousandth part of a tael.

LIANG the Chinese for 'tael', *q.v.*

LIANG KWANG Kwangtung and Kwangsi provinces.

MASKEE pidgin-English: never mind, it's of no matter.

OPEN PORTS ports at which foreign trade and residence is permitted, see Treaty Ports.

SHROFF an employee responsible for handling the cash; sometimes 'the shroff', i.e. the second ranking Chinese after the compradore, *q.v. Cf.* the Hongkong Bank use of 'Accountant'. See also, guarantee shroff.

SHROFF, TO to sort out, examine, and classify coins and silver bullion.

SOVEREIGN RISK LOAN a loan where the risk is considered the willingness (and by extension the ability) of the State which has 'guaranteed' repayment.

SYCEE Chinese monetary silver, usually coined into the shape resembling a Chinese shoe, hence, 'shoe of sycee'.

TAEL a 'liang' or Chinese unit of weight; a Chinese silver unit of account. The tael weight and the silver content of the tael unit of account varied from place to place and market to market; the term had therefore to be qualified except where context made this unnecessary. *Cf.* ounce Troy and ounce avoirdupois; pound sterling and lira. See also various taels under Shanghai, Haikwan, Kuping.

TAEL, HAIKWAN an imaginary unit of account in which foreign Customs Revenues were denominated. (HkTs100 = ShTs111.4).

TAEL, KUPING Treasury tael (Kuping Ts100 = ShTs107.4).

TAEL, SHANGHAI an imaginary unit of account in which Shanghai-based commercial transactions were denominated (ShTs72 = $100).

TAIPAN chief executive.

TAOTAI (TAO-T'AI)   district officer/magistrate – intendant of a circuit.

TIFFIN   the noon meal; sometimes also a light snack.

TRANCHE   section or portion (of a loan); a 'drawing down' of an instalment or tranche of the sum agreed.

TREATY PORTS   before the first Sino-British War China had successfully limited Western sea-borne trade to the port of Canton; under the terms of subsequent treaties the Chinese agreed to open further ports – and in some cases opened them without foreign inducement (the so-called 'self-opened' ports). These were designated 'Treaty Ports' or 'open ports'. Until 1895 foreigners were free to settle only in designated areas of the open ports, in some cases under a local foreign administration, the foreign concessions.

UP-FRONT PROFIT   profit from a transaction which, despite the extended period of the transaction itself, is taken at the commencement.

CHINESE GLOSSARY

(This Glossary has been compiled with the assistance of Kitty Yu Wai Hing, Anita Lau Po Ling, and Cathy Wong Lin Yau. The characters for Chinese names and terms found in English-Language sources have not, in every case, been determined.)

AS IN TEXT WITH WADE-GILES	PINYIN	CHARACTERS
Amoy		
Hsiamen	Xiamen	廈門
Canton		
Kuang-chou	Guangzhou	廣州
ch'a-chan	chazhan	茶棧
ch'a-fan	chafan	茶販
ch'a-hang	chahang	茶行
ch'a-k'e	chake	茶客
ch'a-kuan	chaguan	茶館
Chang Chih-tung	Zhang Zhidong	張之洞
Chang Shu-sheng	Zhang Shusheng	張樹聲
chao-sang chu	zhaoshangju	招商局
ch'e-p'iao	chaipiao	拆票
Chefoo (i.e. *Yen-t'ai*)	Zhifu (Yantai)	芝罘(烟台)
Chekiang	Xijiang	浙江
Ch'en Chiung-ming	Chen Jiongming	陳炯明
Ch'en Lien-pai	Chen Lianbai	陳廉伯
Cheng Chou-fu	Zhengzhoufu	鄭州府
ch'ien-chuang	qianzhuang	錢莊
ch'ien-p'u	qianpu	錢舖
Chihli	Zhidi	直隸
Chin Foo, see *Hsi Cheng-fu*		
Ch'ing	Qing	清
Ch'ing, Prince	Qing Qinwang	慶親王
Chinkiang	Zhenjiang	鎮江
Chung-kuo jen-min yin-hang, Shang-hai-shih fen-hang	Zhongguo renmin yinhang, Shanghaishi fenhang	中國人民銀行 上海市分行
Chung-kuo t'ung-shang yin-hang	Zhongguo tongshang yinhang	中國通商銀行
Ewo (Jardine's)		
I-ho	Yihe	怡和
fantai		
fan-t'ai	fantai	藩臺

665

AS IN TEXT WITH WADE-GILES	PINYIN	CHARACTERS
feng	feng	豐
Foochow	Fuzhou	福州
Fukien	Fujian	福建
futai		
fu-t'ai	futai	撫臺
Haikwan		
hai-kuan	Haiguan	海關
Hangchow	Hangzhou	杭州
Hankow	Hankou	漢口
Heung Shan (now *Chung Shan*)		
Hsiang-shan (*Chung-shan*)	Xiangshan (Zhongshan)	香山(中山)
ho	he	曷
Ho Tung	He Dong	何東
Ho yin-hang	He yinhang	曷銀行
Ho-chia-la hui-li yin-hang	Hejiala huili yinhang	呵加剌匯理銀行
Honan	Henan	河南
'Hong Kong Uet Po'		
'Hsiang-kang Yueh-pao'	*Xianggang Yuebao*	香港粵報
Hongkew		
Hung-k'ou	Hongkou	虹口
hong		
hang	hang	行
Howqua		
Hao-kuan	Haoguan	浩官
See also *Wu Ch'ung-yueh*		
Hsi Cheng-fu (*Chin Foo*)	Xi Zhengfu	席正甫
Hsi Li-kung	Xi Ligong	席立功
Hsiang-kang Shang-hai hui-li yin-hang	Xianggang Shanghai huili yinhang	香港上海匯理銀行
Hsiang-kang Shang-hai yin-hang	Xianggang Shanghai yinhang	香港上海銀行
Hsiang-shang yin-hang	Xiangshang yinhang	香上銀行
Hsu Jun	Xu Run	徐潤
Hu Kwang-yung	Hu Guangyong	胡廣墉
Hu Yü-fen	Hu Yufen	胡橘棻
Hu-pu (*Hoppo*)	Hubu	戶部
Hua-li yin-hang	Huali yinhang	華利銀行
Hua-Ying shu-yuan	Huaying shuyuan	華英書院
hui	hui	匯
hui-feng	huifeng	匯豐
Hui-feng yang-hang	Huifeng yanghang	匯豐洋行
hui-li	huili	匯理
hui-lung	huilong	匯隆
hui-tui kuan	huidui guan	匯兌館
hui-yüan	huiyuan	匯源
Ichang	Yichang	宜昌
I-ho ch'üan	Yihequan	義和拳

AS IN TEXT WITH WADE-GILES	PINYIN	CHARACTERS
Kaiping		
K'ai-p'ing	Kaiping	開平
Kalgan		
Chang-chia K'ou	Zhangjiakou	張家口
Kansu	Gansu	甘肅
Kiangsi	Jiangxi	江西
Kiukiang	Jiujiang	九江
K'u-p'ing	Kuping	庫平
K'uai-fa-ts'ai	Kuaifacai	快發財
kuan-tu shang-pan	guandu shangban	官督商辦
Kuang-hsu	Guangxu	光緒
kuan-yu	guanyu	官語
kuei-p'ing	guiping	規平
Kuling	Jiuling	九嶺
Kuomintang	Guomindang	國民黨
kung-fa	gongfa	公法
kuo-yu	guoyu	國語
Kwangtung	Guangdong	廣東
Lee, Peter		
Li Shun-hua	Li Shunhua	李純華
'Lat Pau'		叻報
Lau Wai Chün		
Liu Wei-ch'uan	Liu Weichuan	劉渭川
li	li	厘
li	li	理
Li Ho-nien	Li Henian	李鶴年
Li-hua yin-hang	Lihua yinhang	麗華銀行
Li Hung-chang	Li Hongzhang	李鴻章
liang (taels)	liang	兩
Liang Kwang	Liang Guang	兩廣
Lo Hok Pang		
Lo Hou-peng	Lou Hepeng	羅鶴朋
Lo Pak Sheung		
Lo Po-ch'ang	Luo Bochang	羅伯常
Lo Sow Sung		
Lo Shou-sung	Luo Shuosong	羅壽嵩
ma-chen kuan	mazhen guan	媽振館
Ma Chien-chung	Ma Jianzhong	馬建忠
mai-pan	maiban	買辦
Manchuria		
Tung-san-shêng	Dongsansheng	東三省
mao-ch'a	maocha	毛茶
Mei-te-lun (Maitland)	Meidelun	美德倫
Mok Kon Sang		
Mo Kan-sheng	Mo Gansheng	莫幹生
Mok Cho Chuen		
Mo Tsao-ch'üan	Mo Zaoquan	莫藻泉

AS IN TEXT WITH WADE-GILES	PINYIN	CHARACTERS
Mu-tsung	Muzong	穆宗
'Nan-hsing-chi'	Nanxingji	《南行記》
'Nan-hsing jih-chi'	Nanxing riji	《南行日記》
Nanking	Nanjing	南京
Nei-wu-fu	Neiwufu	內務府
Newchwang	Niuzhuang	牛莊
Ng Choi	Wu Cai	伍才
Wu T'ing-fang	Wu Tingfang	伍廷芳
Ngai		
Ni Wen-wei	Ni Wenwei	倪文蔚
nien-fei	nianfei	燃匪
Ningpo	Ningbo	寧波
Peking	Beijing	北京
P'ing-hsiang	Pingxiang	萍鄉
Pingtu	Pingdu	平度
See Ewe Boon		
Hsueh You-wen		薛有文
See Ewe Lay		
Hsueh You-li		薛有禮
See Tiong Wah		
Hsueh Chung-hua		薛中華
See Hood Kee		
Hsueh Fo-chi		薛佛記
Shameen		
Sha-mien	Shamian	沙面
Shanghai	Shanghai	上海
Shantung	Shandong	山東
Shansi	Shanxi	山西
Shao-hsing	Shaoxing	紹興
Shasi	Shashi	沙市
shen-chi-ying	shenjiying	神機營
Shen Hsuan-huai	Sheng Xuanhuai	盛宣懷
shih-chiu shih-chi wai-kuo	shijiu shijiu waiguo qinhua	十九世紀外國侵華
ch'in-hua shih-yeh Chung ti	shiye zhong de Huashang fugu	事業中的華商附
Hua-shang fu-ku huo-tung	huodong	股活動
Shu Wen		
Hsiao Wen(?)	Xiaoyun	筱雲
Hsu Yung-i	Xu Yongyi	徐用儀
Soochow	Suzhou	蘇州
Soochow Creek		
Wu-sung-kiang	Wusong Jiang	吳淞江
Sung Chiang silver	Songjiang yin	松江銀
Swatow		
Shan-t'ou	Shantou	汕頭
sycee		
hsi-ssû	xisi	細絲
Taiping		
T'ai-p'ing	Taiping	太平

AS IN TEXT WITH WADE-GILES	PINYIN	CHARACTERS
Tang Kee Shang		
Têng Chi-ch'ang	Deng Jichang	鄧紀常
taotai		
tao-t'ai	daotai	道臺
Tientsin	Tianjin	天津
Tseng Chi-tse	Zeng Jize	曾紀澤
Tseng Kuo-fan	Zeng Guofan	曾國藩
Tsing Shan	Qingshan	青山
Tsingtau	Qingdao	青島
Tso Tsung-t'ang	Zuo Zongtang	左宗棠
Tsungli Yamen	Zongli Yamen	總理衙門
T'ung Chih	Tongzhi	同治
T'ung-chih Restoration		
T'ung-chih wei-hsin	Tongzhi weixin	同治維新
Tungchow Railway		
T'ung-chou T'ieh-lu	Tongzhou tielu	通州鐵路
Tung Wah Hospital		
Tung-hua I-yüan	Donghua Yiyuan	東華醫院
'Tzu Erh Chi'	*Zier ji*	《自邇集》
Wah Sam, see Wang Huai-shan		
Wang Huai-shan	Wang Huaishan	王槐山
Wayfoong		
Hui-feng	Huifeng	匯豐
Wei Sing	Weixing	闈姓(圍姓)
wei-yuan	weiyuan	委員
Wenchow	Wenzhou	溫州
Weng T'ung-ho	Weng Tonghe	翁同龢
Whampoa		
Huang-p'u	Huangpu	黃埔
wu		
hu	hu	滬
Wuchang		
Wu-ch'ang	Wuchang	武昌
Wuchow	Wuzhou	梧州
Wu Ch'ung-yueh (Howqua IV)	Wu Chongyao	伍崇曜
Wu Kuang-p'ei	Wu Guangpei	吳廣霈
Wu Jim Pah, see Wu Mao-ting		
Wu Mao-ting (Wu Jim Pah/'Jim Crow')	Wu Maoding	吳懋鼎
Wu Tiao-ch'ing	Wu Diaoqing	吳調卿
Yang Chin-tsin		
Yang Ch'ang-pao(?)	Yang Changbao	楊昌濬
yang-hang	yanghang	洋行
yang-p'ing liang	yangping liang	洋平両
yamen	yamen	衙門
Yangtze		
Ch'ang chiang	Changjiang	長江

AS IN TEXT WITH WADE-GILES	PINYIN	CHARACTERS
Yap Chai Ping		
Yeh Ts'ai-ping	Ye Caiping	葉采萍
Yap Ho Chiu		
Yeh Hou-ch'iu	Ye Heqiu	葉鶴秋
Yap Hong Siong		
Yeh Hung-hsiang	Ye Hongxiang	葉鴻翔
Yap Siong Lin		
Yeh Hsiang-lin	Ye Xianglin	葉祥麟
Yap 'Ta-jen'		
Yeh 'Ta-jên'	Ye 'daren'	葉'大人'
yin	yin	銀
Yingkow	Yingkou	營口
Ying-shang	Yingshang	英商
Ying-shang hui-feng yin-hang	Yingshang huifeng yinhang	英商匯豐銀行
You-li	Youli	有利
Yueh Hai-kwan Pu	Yue haiguan bu	粵海關部

ASSISTANTS
Au Yuk Han	區玉嫻
Cheng Mei Sze	鄭美施
Cheng Yim Mei	鄭艷媚
Chow Lo Sai	周蘿茜
Ip Yau Ching	葉幼清
Lau Wai Keung	劉偉強
Lee Chun Wah	李振華
Ng Wai Yee	吳慧儀
Wang Ke-wen	王克文
Yu Wai Hing	余蕙卿

CENTRE OF ASIAN STUDIES STAFF
Chan Yuen Yee	陳婉儀
Lam Tung Chun	林同春
Lau Po Ling	劉寶凌
Wong Lin Yau	黃蓮有

BIBLIOGRAPHY

The 'bibliography' is primarily a list of works consulted, prefaced by an explanation and a description of archival material obtained for the history. The list covers only those materials relevant to Volume I of the history of the Hongkong Bank. A separate bibliography will be provided for each volume.

The main explanation required relates to the lack of references to works in Chinese.

CHINESE SOURCE MATERIAL

The History Project employed two relatively senior assistants to search published collections of primary material, for example, Ch'ing dynasty memorials, books, and articles. The resources of the Fung Ping Shan Library in the University of Hong Kong were examined, and additional material was found in the Hoover Institution. Several ring binders of xeroxes and trays of note cards were produced. The results, with few exceptions, were disappointing.

This is a history of the Hongkong Bank. In the course of this study major events in Chinese history are referred to. For a study of such events reference to Chinese sources is essential, but not surprisingly their focus is not on the Hongkong Bank. The references are there, but they are too imprecise or too brief, being part of a correspondence and meaning little taken alone. Summaries of the Bank's activities and comments on the annual reports are better taken from more complete sources. As for the important China loans, there are frequent references, but they add little if anything to the Bank's own archival resources as far as material for a history of the Hongkong Bank is concerned.

In the Republican Period surveys of Chinese banking history were written, but their comments on any particular bank are brief and their political bias predictable. They are often inaccurate. Specific journal articles may, however, supplement information on a particular event and are, therefore, cited.

The most valuable contribution might have been references to Hongkong Bank financed modernization projects. These exist and the topic could have been further pursued. This remains, however, an area in which further research might well be undertaken using archives now becoming available to scholars in China itself. This history remained dependent on published sources.

The fifty or so collections and other studies actually surveyed have not been listed. No useful purpose would be served. Only Chinese references actually used in the text are included in the bibliography. The sources available, valuable as they may well be for many studies, were for the most part not appropriate to this particular history as defined.

Archival material, in China and unpublished, was not studied.

ARCHIVAL COLLECTIONS

The most important source for the history of the Hongkong Bank is the material in Hongkong Bank Group Archives. Briefly, they include for the period covered by Volume I: the Minute Books of the Provisional Committee and the Board of Directors from 1864, the semi-annual reports of the directors and abstracts of accounts, limited inter-branch correspondence, Shanghai and London share registers, miscellaneous charges books, ledgers from several branches, personnel reports, early photographs, and occasional letters. In addition there are the compilations of J.R. Jones and other bound reports (listed below under 'Works consulted') and boxes of personal memorials, manuscripts, etc. which are part social history, part banking.

There have been recent additions, including xerox copies of the journals of F.T. Koelle, which are relevant to Volume I. Specific studies are listed under 'Works consulted'.

The Bank's archives were enriched by the shipment of material from Shanghai, but that comprehended only that material actually taken from the Bund to the godown in 1955 and for the most part deals with post-1911 events. Other branch materials depend for their coverage on the chances of preservation, often confined to a 'sample' ledger or, as in Bangkok, to the first.

In this early period, therefore, the Bank's material must be supplemented by documents preserved elsewhere.

On the founding of the Bank, this includes the Augustine Heard Collection, Baker Library, Harvard Business School, Boston; the Siemssen and Co. Archives, Hamburg; and the Jardine, Matheson and Co. Archives in Cambridge University Library, England. The Forbes Papers, China Trade Collection, now deposited with the Massachusetts Historical Society, Boston, take up the story at a later period and have proved especially useful for the 1891/92 crisis.

The banking scene on the China coast may be seen through the papers of Hermann Wallich, manager of the Comptoir d'Escompte de Paris, Shanghai, in the private collection of Dr Henry C. Wallich of the Federal Reserve Board. There are references to the Bank's role in the China Merchants' Steam Navigation Co. in the papers of H.B. Morse, Houghton Library, Harvard University.

The London end of the Bank's operations can be noted in the archives of the London and Westminster Bank and the London and County Bank, both retained by the National Westminster Bank in London. Unfortunately, correspondence, not copied into the minute books, does not survive. Thus negative responses to Hongkong Bank requests are often not recorded – the request is withdrawn before it reaches Committee or Board level.

The early operations of the Hongkong Bank are best considered in the letter books of David McLean, now deposited in the School of Oriental and African Studies (SOAS), the McLean Papers (MS 380401), with a typescript copy by Catherine E. King. There are two sets, one covering Shanghai to 1872, the other London from 1875 to 1889.

Also in the Archival collections of SOAS Library are: the archive of John Swire & Sons Ltd (see Elizabeth Hook, *A Guide to the Papers of John Swire & Sons Ltd*, London, 1977), the [Sir Charles] Addis Papers, the China Association Archive, including minute books and correspondence, and the Papers of William Evans, Evans/Baker collection (PP.MS.11). The Addis Papers (PP.MS.14) are an important source for the Bank's history, broadly defined, from 1884 to 1944, a remarkable record of diaries, correspondence, and clippings, concerning which see Margaret Harcourt Williams, *Catalogue of the Papers of Sir Charles Addis* (London, 1986).

For the Hongkong Bank's relations with the Hong Kong and British Governments, the Public Record Office, London, is the main resource. Only one or two isolated documents have survived in Hong Kong and are in the Public Records Office here. The main files consulted were those of the Colonial Office (CO 129), the Foreign Office (FO 17, FO 288, and FO 233), and the Treasury (T.1 and T.7), but there is material as recorded in the endnotes in many other files, including the company records under the Board of Trade. There is relevant material in the India Office Library and Records. The Hongkong Bank did not, however, play a leading role; the Bank's agents co-signed letters from the Exchange Banks Association on matters of public policy and the Bank was on occasion very prominent in matters related to silver and India's trade with the East. There remains much in both the PRO and the India Office Library which is still neglected.

The German material is more important for Volume II, but material from the Auswärtiges Amt archives in Bonn has been used in the present volume. Limited information on the German companies represented on the Bank's pre-1914 Board of Directors was located in the Bremer Staatsarchiv and Hamburger Staatsarchiv. The archives of the Deutsche Bank have little on the Deutsch-Asiatische Bank and most of the material on the Disconto-Gesellschaft was destroyed during the war.

City materials are found in the Guildhall Library, and use was made of the archives of Baring Brothers and the London Stock Exchange. The N.M. Rothschild Archives were consulted for valuable background understanding, but actual references to Rothschild correspondence are to material in other archives. D.J.S. King also was granted access to documents in the archives of the Standard Chartered Bank.

List of Works Consulted for Volume 1

(The personal names of authors publishing in the People's Republic of China are listed alphabetically according to pinyin; the titles of such works are, however, in Wade-Giles. Other names of authors publishing in the Chinese language are listed either in the form found in the publication, if any, or in Wade-Giles.)

'Affairs of India'. *Edinburgh Review* (April 1910), p. 154, quoted in William J. Barber, *British Economic Thought and India, 1600–1858*. Oxford, 1975.

Allen, G.C. and Audrey G. Donnithorne. *Western Enterprise in Far Eastern Economic Development. China and Japan*. London, 1954.

Western Enterprise in Indonesia and Malaya. London, 1957.

Allen, T.S. 'A History of Brown, Janson and Co.'. MS. Archives of Lloyds Bank, London.

Andree, H.V. *Progress of Banking in Ceylon*. Colombo, 1864.

Angus, J.A. *Letter to the Proprietors of the Oriental Bank Corporation and of the Chartered Mercantile Bank of India, London and China*. Edinburgh, privately published, 1882.

Armstrong, F.E. *The Book of the Stock Exchange*. London, 1934.

Bangkok Times. 1888–1894.

[Bank of Chosen.] *Past and Present of the Hongkong and Shanghai Banking Corporation*. Bank of Chosen, 1915.

[Bankers Association of the Philippines.] *History of Banking in the Philippines*. Manila, 1957.

Bankers Magazine. London, 1863–1902.

Banno, Masataka, 'Ma Chien-chung's Mission to India in 1881: his Travel Account, *Nan-hsing-chi*'. *Journal of Social Science*. International Christian University Publications, II-B. No. 17, pp. 108–24.

Barber, William J. *British Economic Thought and India, 1600–1858*. Oxford, 1975.

Baster, A.S.J. *Imperial Banks*. London, 1929.

'The Origins of British Exchange Banks in China'. *Economic History* 3: 140–51 (1954).

[Behn Meyer and Co.] *Zur Geschichte der Firmen Behn Meyer & Co. und Arnold Otto Meyer*. 2 vols. Hamburg, 1957.

Beutler, Heinz. *Hundert Jahre Carlowitz & Co., Hamburg und China*. Diss. Hamburg, 1948.

Black, J.R. *Young Japan: Yokohama and Yeddo.* Yokohama, 1880. Vol. II.

Boletim da Provincia de Macau e Timor. Macau.

Born, Karl Erich. *International Banking in the 19th and 20th Centuries.* Leamington Spa, England, 1983. German ed. *Geld und Banken . . .* Stuttgart, 1977.

Bouvier, Jean. *Le Crédit Lyonnais de 1865 à 1882: les années de formation d'une banque de depôts,* II, 529 (1961).

Braga, J.M. comp. *Hong Kong Business Symposium.* Hong Kong, 1957.

Buckley, Charles B. *An Anecdotal History of Old Times in Singapore, 1819–1867.* Singapore, 1902. Rpt Kuala Lumpur, 1965.

Butlin, S.J. *Australia and New Zealand Bank.* London, 1961.

C. Melchers & Co. Bremen, Melchers & Co. China: Firmenschrift. Bremen, 1909.

Campbell, Robert Ronald. *James Duncan Campbell. A Memoir by his Son.* Cambridge, MA, 1970.

'Carlowitz & Co.'. *Historisch-biographische Blätter der Standt Hamburg.* Berlin, 1905/6.

Carlowitz & Co. China, Hong Kong, Hamburg. Hamburg-Zwickau, 1925.

Carlowitz & Co. Hamburg, Hong Kong, New York, China und Japan. Hamburg, 1906.

[Carlowitz & Co.] *Kurzer Auszug aus der Geschichte der Firma Carlowitz & Co.* Shanghai, 1937.

Carlson, Ellsworth C. *The Kaiping Mines (1877–1912).* Cambridge, MA, 1957.

Celestial Empire. Shanghai.

Ceylon Observer (article on Koelle), 10 January 1903.

Chandler, Alfred D., Jr. *The Visible Hand; the Managerial Revolution in American Business.* Cambridge, MA, 1977.

Chang, John K. *Industrial Development in Pre-Communist China.* Edinburgh, 1969.

Chang, Kia-ngau. *China's Struggle for Railroad Development.* New York, 1943.

Chang Nan (Ch'ang Nan) 常南. 'Ying-kuo Hui-feng Yin-hang ti ching-chi lüeh-tou' 英國滙豐銀行的經濟掠奪(Economic plundering of the British Hongkong Bank). In *Wu-shih-erh chung wen-shih chih-liao pien-mou fen-lei suo-yin*五十二種文史資料篇目分類索引. Shanghai 1982. Pp. 69–78.

Chang, Te-ch'ang. 'The Economic Role of the Imperial Household (Nei-wu-fu) in the Ch'ing Dynasty'. *Journal of Asian Studies* 31: 243–73 (1971).

Chapman, S.D. 'British-based Investment Groups before 1914'. *Economic History Review* 38: 230–51 (1985).

Chen, Chung-sieu. 'British Loans to China from 1860 to 1913, with special reference to the period 1894–1913'. Diss. University of London, 1940.

Chen, Mong Hock. *The Early Chinese Newspapers of Singapore.* Singapore, 1967.

Ch'en, Gideon. 'Tso Tsung-t'ang: The Farmer of Hsiang-shang'. *Yenching Journal of Social Studies* 1: 211–25 (1938).

'When was the First Foreign Loan to China?' *Yenching Journal of Social Studies* 1: 128–34 (1938).

'The Early History of China's External Debt'. *Yenching Journal of Social Studies* 2: 637–60 (1939).

Die China Export-Import-und Bank-Compagnie. Hamburg, 1959.

China. Imperial Maritime Customs. *Documents Illustrative of the Origin, Development, and Activities of the Chinese Customs Service.* 7 vols. Shanghai, 1940.

China Association. Minute Books. 1889–1902. Archive of the China Association, the Library, School of Oriental and African Studies, London.

China Mail (Hong Kong).

China Punch (Hong Kong). 1874–75.

Chung-kuo jen-min yin-hang·Shang-hai-shih fen-hang 中國人民銀行上海市分行 (The Chinese People's Bank, Shanghai). Comp. *Shang-hai ch'ien-chuang shih-liao*

上海錢莊史料 (Historical materials on the native banks in Shanghai). Shanghai, 1960.

Clapham, Sir John. *An Economic History of Modern Britain: Free Trade and Steel, 1850–1886.* Cambridge, 1952.

Coates, Austin. *Whampoa, Ships on the Shore.* Hong Kong, 1980.

Cole, W.A. 'The Relations between Banks and the Stock Exchange'. *Journal of the Institute of Bankers* (1899).

Collis, Maurice. *Wayfoong. The Hongkong and Shanghai Banking Corporation.* London, 1965. Rpt. with additional material by the Hongkong Bank, 1978.

Constantino, Renato. *A History of the Philippines: from the Spanish Colonization to the Second World War.* New York, 1975.

Cook, Christopher. 'The Hongkong and Shanghai Banking Corporation on Lombard Street'. In *Eastern Banking: Essays in the History of The Hongkong and Shanghai Banking Corporation.* Ed. Frank H.H. King. London, 1983. Pp. 193–203.

Coons, A.G. *The Foreign Public Debt of China.* Philadelphia, 1930.

Couling, Samuel. Ed. *The Encyclopaedia Sinica.* Shanghai, 1917. Reprinted, Hong Kong, 1983.

Currer-Briggs, Noel. *Contemporary Observation on Security from the Chubb Collectanea, 1818–1968.* London, n.d. Privately published.

Däbritz, W. *David Hansemann und Adolf von Hansemann.* Deutsche Bank, 1954.

Daily Advertiser. Hong Kong.

Daily Press. Hong Kong.

Dayer, Roberta A. 'The Young Charles S. Addis: Poet or Banker?' In *Eastern Banking: Essays in the History of The Hongkong and Shanghai Banking Corporation.* Ed. Frank H.H. King. London, 1983. Pp. 14–31.

Dénis, Etienne. *Bordeaux et le Cochinchine sous la restauration et le second empire.* Bordeaux, 1965.

Deutsche Bank. *Geschäftsberichte der Direction der Deutschen Bank.* 1872–1875, 1889–1894.

Dictionary of National Biography.

Diouritch, G. *L'Expansion des banques allemandes à l'étranger.* Paris, 1909.

Disconto-Gesellschaft. *Die Discontogesellschaft 1851 bis 1901: Denkschrift zum fünfzigjährigen Jubiläum.* Berlin, 1901.

Dujardin, Albert. 'The Hongkong and Shanghai Banking Corporation'. MA Thesis. University of St Louis, 1949.

Easton, Harry Tucker. *The History of a Banking House (Smith, Payne and Smiths).* London, 1903.

Economist. London.

Eitel, E.J. *Europe in China, the History of Hong Kong.* Hong Kong, 1895.

Endacott, George B. *A History of Hong Kong.* London, 1958.

Fairbank, John K., Edwin O. Reischauer, Albert M. Craig. *East Asia, the Modern Transformation.* Boston, 1965.
    See also: Hart, Sir Robert; Tseng, Ssu-yü

Feavearyear, Sir Albert. *The Pound Sterling: a History of English Money.* 2nd ed. Revised by E. Victor Morgan. Oxford, 1963.

Feldwick, W. Ed. *Present Day Impressions of the Far East.* London, 1917.

Feuerwerker, Albert. *China's Early Industrialization: Sheng Hsuan-huai (1844–1916) and Mandarin Enterprise.* Cambridge, MA, 1958.
    The Chinese Economy, ca. 1870–1911. Michigan Papers in Chinese Studies, No. 5. Ann Arbor, Michigan, 1969.

Fischer, Gerald C. 'Wall to Wall Banks, the Marine Midland Story'. (Unpublished typescript, copy with Marine Midland Banks, Inc.).

Fivel-Démoret, Claude. 'The Hongkong Bank in Lyon, 1881–1954: Busy, but too Discreet?' In *Eastern Banking: Essays in the History of The Hongkong and Shanghai Banking Corporation*. Ed. Frank H.H. King. London, 1983. Pp. 467–516.

Friend of China and Hongkong Gazette. Hong Kong, 1857.

'Fukkensho chagyo no kenkyu' 福建省茶葉の研究 (Research into the Fukien tea industry), in Nanshi chosa shiryo, 南支調査資料 *Fukken kensetsu hokoku* 福建建設報告 (Fukien reconstruction report). Vol. II. Taihoko (Taipei), 1938.

Gardella, Robert P., Jr. 'Fukien's Tea Industry and Trade in Ch'ing and Republican China: the developmental consequences of a traditional commodity export'. PhD Thesis, University of Washington, 1976.

'The Boom Years of the Fukien Tea Trade, 1842–1888'. In Ernest R. May and John K. Fairbank, eds. *America's China Trade in Historical Perspective; the Chinese and American Performance*. Cambridge, MA, 1986. Pp. 34–75 and notes.

Gibbs, John A. *The History of Antony and Dorothea Gibbs*. London, 1922.

Gilbart, James. *A Practical Treatise on Banking*. 6th ed. Vol. II. London, 1856.
The Logic of Banking. London, 1859. In *Collected Works*. Vol. III. London, 1865.
History and Principles of Banking. In *Collected Works*. Vol. IV. London, 1865.

[Gillett Bros Discount House.] *The Bill on London*. London, 1952.

Glade, Dieter. *Bremen und der Ferne Osten*. Bremen, 1966.

Gonjo Yasuo 権上康男. *Hurans teikokushugi to ajia—Indoshina ginko-shi kenkyu* フランス帝国主義とアジア―インドシナ銀行史研究―French imperialism and Asia — a history of the Banque de l'Indo-Chine). Tokyo, 1985.

Gunasekera, H.A. de S. *From Dependent Currency to Central Banking in Ceylon*. Colombo, 1960.

Gundry, R.S. *China Past and Present*. London, 1895.

Hamashita, Takeshi. 'A History of the Japanese Silver Yen and The Hongkong and Shanghai Banking Corporation, 1871–1913'. In *Eastern Banking: Essays in the History of The Hongkong and Shanghai Banking Corporation*. Ed. Frank H.H. King. London, 1983. Pp. 321–49.

Hänisch, Adolf van. *Jebsen & Co. Hong Kong: Chinas Handel im Wechsel der Zeiten 1895–1945*. Apenrade, 1970.

Hao, Yen-P'ing. *The Comprador in Nineteenth-Century China: Bridge between East and West*. Cambridge, MA, 1970.
The Commercial Revolution in Nineteenth-Century China, the Rise of Sino-Western Mercantile Capitalism. Berkeley, CA, 1986.

Hart, Sir Robert. *The I.G. in Peking: Letters of Robert Hart, Chinese Maritime Customs, 1868–1907*. Eds. John K. Fairbank *et al*. 2 vols. Cambridge, MA, and London, 1975.

Herrick, Tracy G. *Bank Analyst's Handbook*. New York, 1978.

Hoffman, R.J.S. *Great Britain and the German Trade Rivalry, 1875–1914*. Philadelphia, 1933.

Hong Kong, Government of. *Hongkong Government Gazette*.
Legislative Council Sessional Papers.
'The Postmaster General's Report for 1884'. 1885.
'Correspondence respecting the Issue of One Dollar Notes, presented to the Legislative Council by Command of H.E. the Governor'. 1884.
Finance Committee Report. 1884.
Legislative Council Proceedings. 1899.

Hongkong and Shanghai Banking Corporation. Semi-annual and annual reports. 1865–1985.

Hongkong Daily Press.

Hong Kong Hansard.

Hongkong Telegraph.

Hong Kong Times.

Hou, Chi-ming. *Foreign Investment and Economic Development in China, 1840–1937.* Cambridge, MA, 1965.

Hou, Chi-ming and Tzong-shian Yu. Eds. *Modern Chinese Economic History.* Taipei, Taiwan, 1979.

Hsiao, Liang-lin. *China's Foreign Trade Statistics, 1864–1949.* Cambridge, MA, 1974.

Hsü, Leonard Shih-lien, and others. *Silver and Prices in China: report of the committee for the study of silver values and commodity prices, Ministry of Industries.* Shanghai, 1935.

Huang, Feng-hua. *Public Debts in China.* Studies in History, Economics and Public Law, Vol. LXXXV, No. 2. New York, 1919.

Hummel, Arthur W. Ed. *Eminent Chinese of the Ch'ing Period (1644–1912).* 2 vols. Washington, D.C., 1943.

Hyde, Francis E. *Far Eastern Trade, 1860–1914.* London, 1973.

Jackson, Stanley. *The Sassoons.* New York, 1965.

Jefferys, J.B. 'The Denomination and Character of Shares, 1855–1885'. In *Essays in Economic History.* Ed. E.M. Carus-Wilson. London, 1954, pp. 344–57. Rpt. *Economic History Review* 16: 1 (1946).

Jenks, Leland H. *The Migration of British Capital to 1875.* London, 1963.

Jones, Geoffrey. *Banking and Empire in Iran.* Vol. I of his *The History of The British Bank of the Middle East.* Cambridge, 1986.

Jones, J.R. History Collections in the Hongkong Bank Group Archives:
'Personalities and Narratives'.
'The Bank, 1865–1885'.
'The Bank, 1876–1942'.
'Branches'.
'Chinese Loans'.

Kann, Edward. *The Currencies of China.* Shanghai, 1927.
'Early History of China's External Debt'. *Yenching Journal of Social Studies* 2: 637–60.
'The Foreign Loans of China'. *Finance and Commerce.* Vol. XIX, No. 85.

Keswick, Maggie. Ed. *The Thistle and the Jade: a Celebration of 150 Years of Jardine, Matheson and Co.* London, 1982.

Kiernan, E.V.G. *British Diplomacy in China 1880 to 1885.* Cambridge, 1939.

Kinder, T.W. Report in *Minutes of Evidence Taken before the Select Committee on Depreciation of Silver.* London, 1877.

King, Catherine E. 'The First Trip East – P&O via Suez'. In *Eastern Banking: Essays in the History of The Hongkong and Shanghai Banking Corporation.* Ed. Frank H.H. King. London, 1983. Pp. 204–29.

King, David J.S. 'China's First Public Loan: The Hongkong Bank and the Chinese Imperial Government "Foochow" Loan of 1874'. In *Eastern Banking: Essays in the History of The Hongkong and Shanghai Banking Corporation.* Ed. Frank H.H. King. London, 1983. Pp. 230–64.

'The Hamburg Branch: The German Period, 1889–1920'. In *Eastern Banking: Essays in the History of The Hongkong and Shanghai Banking Corporation.* Ed. Frank H.H. King. London, 1983. Pp. 517–44.

'China's Early Loans, 1874–95, and the Role of The Hongkong and Shanghai Banking Corporation'. Research report in Hongkong Bank Group Archives, Hong Kong.

'On the Relations of the Hongkong Bank with Germany'. 2 vols. Research report, 1981, in Hongkong Bank Group Archives, Hong Kong.

King, Frank H.H. *Money in British East Asia*. London, 1957.
Money and Monetary Policy in China, 1845–1895. Cambridge, MA, 1965.
Asian Policy, History and Development: Collected Essays. Centre of Asian Studies Occasional Papers and Monographs, No. 37. Hong Kong, 1979.
'The Bank of China is Dead'. *Journal of Oriental Studies* 7, 1: 39–62 (1969). Rpt. in *Asian Policy, History and Development: Collected Essays*. Hong Kong, 1979. Pp. 19–41.
'The Mercantile Bank's Royal Charter'. In *Asian Policy, History and Development: Collected Essays*. Hong Kong, 1979. Pp. 42–50.
Survey our Empire! A bio-bibliography of Robert Montgomery Martin (1801–1868). Centre of Asian Studies Bibliographies and Research Guides, No. 16. Hong Kong, 1979.
Ed. *Eastern Banking: Essays in the History of The Hongkong and Shanghai Banking Corporation*. Hongkong Bank Group History Series, No. 1. London, 1983.
'Appendix: an Outline of the Problems of The Hongkong and Shanghai Banking Corporation's Note Issue'. In *Eastern Banking: Essays in the History of The Hongkong and Shanghai Banking Corporation*. Ed. Frank H.H. King. London, 1983. Pp. 150–54.
'Establishing the Hongkong Bank: the Role of the Directors and their Managers'. In *Eastern Banking: Essays in the History of The Hongkong and Shanghai Banking Corporation*. Ed. Frank H.H. King. London, 1983. Pp. 32–65.
'Extra-Regional Banks and Investment in China, with Comments relative to other Far Eastern Territories, 1870–1914', in Rondo Cameron, Ed. Proceedings of a Conference on International Banking and Industrial Finance, Ballagio, 1985 (in the press).
and Prescott Clarke. *A Research Guide to China-Coast Newspapers, 1822–1911*. Cambridge, MA, 1965.
King, W.T.C. *A History of the London Discount Market*. London, 1936.
Koelle, F.T. 'Journals'. Copy in Hongkong Bank Group Archives.
Kuhlmann, Wilhelm. *China's Foreign Debt*. Hannover, 1983.
Kurgan-van Hentenryk, G. *Léopold II et les groupes financiers belges en Chine: la politique royale et ses prolongements (1895–1914)*. Bruxelles, 1972.
Laanen, J.T.M. van. 'A Preliminary Look at the Role of The Hongkong Bank in Netherlands India'. In *Eastern Banking: Essays in the History of The Hongkong and Shanghai Banking Corporation*. Ed. Frank H.H. King. London, 1983. Pp. 392–408.
Lambot, Ian and Gillian Chambers. *One Queen's Road Central: the Headquarters of HongkongBank since 1864*. Hong Kong, 1986.
Lavington, F. *The English Capital Market*. London, 1921.
Lee, T.A. 'The Financial Statements of The Hongkong and Shanghai Banking Corporation, 1865–1980'. In *Eastern Banking: Essays in the History of The Hongkong and Shanghai Banking Corporation*. Ed. Frank H.H. King. London, 1983. Pp. 77–92.
LeFevour, Edward. *Western Enterprise in Late Ch'ing China. A Selective Survey of Jardine, Matheson and Company's Operations, 1842–1895*. Cambridge, MA, 1968.
'Western Enterprise in China, 1842–1895'. Ph.D. Thesis, Cambridge University.
Lim, Chee Peng, *et al.* 'The History and Development of The Hongkong and Shanghai Banking Corporation in Peninsular Malaysia'. In *Eastern Banking: Essays in the History of The Hongkong and Shanghai Banking Corporation*. Ed. Frank H.H. King. London, 1983. Pp. 350–91.
Little, A.J. *Through the Yang-tze Gorges or Trade and Travel in Western China*. London, 1898.
Liu, Kwang-ching. 'Credit Facilities in China's Early Industrialization: the Background

and Implications of Hsü Jun's Bankruptcy in 1883'. In *Modern Chinese Economic History*. Eds. Chi-ming Hou and Tzong-shian Yu. Taipei, Taiwan, 1979. Pp. 499–509.

Liu, S.Y. 'China's Debts and Their Readjustment'. *Chinese Economic Journal* 5: 735–49 (1929).

London and China Express. 1864–1902.

MacDermot, B.H.D. *Panmure Gordon & Co., 1876–1976. A Century of Stockbroking*. London (privately published by the company), 1976.

McElderry, Andrea Lee. *Shanghai Old-Style Banks (Ch'ien-chuang), 1800–1935: a Traditional Institution in a Changing Society*. Ann Arbor, Michigan, 1976.

Mackenzie, Compton. *Realms of Silver: One Hundred Years of Banking in the East*. London, 1954.

Mackie, George (of the Hongkong and Shanghai Banking Corporation, London). Comp. *Dollar and Sterling Exchange Tables from 3s 4d to 6s 4d, ascending by one-eighth of a penny*. 3rd ed. London, 1881. (First ed. 1876).

McLean, David (Hongkong Bank). Letter Books. 'Early Letters', Shanghai, 1864–1872, and 'Private Letters', London, 1875–1889. McLean Collection, MS 380401, Library, School of Oriental and African Studies, University of London.

McLean, David A. (King's College), 'Commerce, Finance, and British Diplomatic Support in China, 1885–1886'. *Economic History Review* 26: 464–76 (1973).

'The Foreign Office and the First Chinese Indemnity Loan, 1895'. *The Historical Journal* 16: 303–21 (1973).

'British Banking and Government in China: the Foreign Office and the Hongkong and Shanghai Bank'. PhD Thesis, Cambridge University, 1976.

'Finance and "Informal Empire" before the First World War'. *Economic History Review* 29: 291–305 (1976).

'International Banking and its Political Implications: The Hongkong and Shanghai Banking Corporation and The Imperial Bank of Persia, 1889–1914'. In *Eastern Banking: Essays in the History of The Hongkong and Shanghai Banking Corporation*. Ed. Frank H.H. King. London, 1983. Pp. 1–13.

Maclellan, J.W. 'Banking in India and China'. *Bankers' Magazine* 55: 735–39 (1891).

Mai Chung-hua (Mai Zhonghua) 麥仲華. Comp. *Huang-ch'ao ching-shih-wen hsin-pien* 皇朝經世文新編. (New collection of essays on statecraft of the Ch'ing dynasty). Shanghai, 1898. Rpt. 2 vols. Taipei, Taiwan, 1965.

Makepeace, Brooke. *One Hundred Years of Singapore*. London, 1921.

Marriner, Sheila and Francis E. Hyde. *The Senior, John Samuel Swire, 1825–98*. Liverpool, 1967.

Marsden, H.J. *The Decline of Indian Banking: the cause and the remedy*. London, 1882.

Masuda, Takashi. *Japan, its Commercial Development and Prospects*. London, n.d.

Money Market Review. 9 June 1866.

Morgan, E. Victor. *The Stock Exchange: Its History and Functions*. London, 1962.

Möring, Maria. *Siemssen & Co. 1846–1971*. Hamburg, n.d.

Morse, H.B. *The International Relations of the Chinese Empire*. London, 1918.

Müller-Jabusch, Maximilian. *Fünfzig Jahre Deutsch-Asiatische Bank, 1890–1939*. Berlin, 1940.

Münch, Hermann. *Adolph von Hansemann*. München, 1932.

Myers, Ramon H. *The Chinese Economy, Past and Present*. Belmont, CA, 1980.

Nelson, W. Evan. 'The Hongkong and Shanghai Banking Corporation Factor in the Progress toward a Straits Settlements Government Note Issue, 1881–1889'. In *Eastern Banking: Essays in the History of The Hongkong and Shanghai Banking Corporation*. Ed. Frank H.H. King. London, 1983. Pp. 155–79.

'The Imperial Administration of Currency and British Banking in the Straits

Settlements, 1867–1908'. PhD Thesis, Duke University, 1984.
'The New Oriental Bank Corporation, Ltd, a Lesson in Bad Banking'. *Bankers' Magazine* 57: 69–81 (1894).
North-China Herald (Shanghai). 1869–1902.
[North-China Herald.] *A Retrospect of Political and Commercial Affairs in China during the Five Years 1868 to 1872*. Shanghai, 1873.
Ostasiatischer Verein Hamburg-Bremen zum 60-jährigen Bestehen. Hamburg, 1960.
Paish, F.W. 'The London New Issue Market'. *Economica* 18: 1–17 (1951).
Pelcovits, Nathan A. *Old China Hands and the Foreign Office*. New York, 1948.
Pohl, Manfred. *The Deutsche Bank's East Asian Business, 1870–1875: Proposals and preparations for establishing branches in Shanghai, Hong Kong and Yokohama*. Studies on Economic and Monetary Problems and on Banking History, 15. Frankfurt/M, 1977.
Pramuanratkarn, Thiravet. 'The Hongkong Bank in Thailand: A Case of a Pioneering Bank'. In *Eastern Banking: Essays in the History of The Hongkong and Shanghai Banking Corporation*. Ed. Frank H.H. King. London, 1983. Pp. 421–34.
[Pustau, Carl Wilhelm von.] 'Aus dem Lebenslauf von Carl Wilhelm von Pustau . . . Zusamengestellt aus Erinnerungen der Kinder, Urkunden und Zeitschriften in 1939'. (unpubl. located in Commerz-bibliothek, Hamburg.)
Quested, Rosemary. *The Russo-Chinese Bank*. Birmingham, 1977.
Radandt, Hans. 'Hundert Jahre Deutsche Bank: Eine typische Konzerngeschichte'. In *Jahrbuch für Wirtschaftsgeschichte*. Berlin (East), 1972. Pp. 37–62.
Reed, M.C. *A History of James Capel and Co.* London, 1975.
Reed, Richard. *National Westminster Bank, a short history*. London, 1983.
Reiß, Auguste. 'Das Bankwesen in China'. In *China, Wirtschaft und Wirt-schaftsgrundlagen*. Ed. Josef Hellauer. Berlin/Leipzig, 1921.
Roth, Cecil. *The Sassoon Dynasty*. London, 1941.
Ryder, F.R. and D.B. Jenkins. *Thomson's Dictionary of Banking*. 12th ed. London, 1974.
Sayer, Geoffrey R. *Hong Kong, 1862–1919: years of discretion*. Hong Kong, 1975.
'The Scottish Banking System'. *Blackwood's Edinburgh Magazine* 41: 671–86 (1844).
Sear, Judith. 'Variety in the Note Issues of The Hongkong and Shanghai Banking Corporation, 1865–1891'. In *Eastern Banking: Essays in the History of The Hongkong and Shanghai Banking Corporation*. Ed. Frank H.H. King. London, 1983. Pp. 139–49.
Seidenzahl, Fritz. *Hundert Jahre Deutsche Bank, 1870–1970*. Frankfurt, 1970.
Selvaratnam, H.L.D. 'The Guarantee Shroffs, the Chettiars, and The Hongkong Bank in Ceylon'. In *Eastern Banking: Essays in the History of The Hongkong and Shanghai Banking Corporation*. Ed. Frank H.H. King. London, 1983. Pp. 409–20.
'Servicos de Finanças: *Inventario do Codice de "Minutas do Oficios Expedidos em 1890"'*. In *Arquivos de Macau*. Vol. I, 1983.
Sheng Hsuan-huai 盛宣懷. *Hsin-hai ke-ming ch'ien-hou* 辛亥革命前後. Sheng Hsuan-huai tang-an tzu-liao hsüan-chi 盛宣懷檔案資料選輯. Eds. Chen Xulu (Ch'en Hsü-lu)陳旭麓, Gu Tinglong (Ku T'ing-lung)顧廷龍, Wang Xi (Wang Hsi)汪熙, Shanghai, 1980. Pp. 257, 298.
　　Chia-wu Chung-Jih chan-cheng 甲午中日戰爭 . 2 Vols. Eds. Chen Xulu *et al.* Shang-hai, 1980. I, 187, 197, 284, 322, 343; II, 173, 557.
Shenoy, B.R. *Ceylon Currency and Banking*. London, 1941.
Shinobu, Junpei. 信夫淳平, 韓半島 (The Korean Peninsula; 1901).
Slaughter, M. *Rules and Regulations for the Conduct of Business on the Stock Exchange*. London, 1873.
[Smith, Bell & Company.] *Under Four Flags, the Story of Smith, Bell & Company in the*

Philippines. Privately published in England, n.d., but early 1970s.

Smith, Carl T. 'Compradores of The Hongkong Bank'. In *Eastern Banking: Essays in the History of The Hongkong and Shanghai Banking Corporation*. Ed. Frank H.H. King. London, 1983. Pp. 93–111.

Song Ong Siang. *One Hundred Years of History of the Chinese in Singapore*. London, 1923.

Spalding, W.F. *Eastern Exchange, Currency and Finance*. 3rd ed. London, 1920.
  Dictionary of the World's Currencies and Foreign Exchanges. London, 1928.

Spector, Stanley. *Li Hung-chang and the Huai Army*. Seattle, 1964.

Stanley, Charles J. *Late Ch'ing Finance: Hu Kuang-yung as an Innovator*. Cambridge, MA, 1961.

Statist. London.

Stephenson, Sir Macdonald. *Railways in China: Report upon the Feasibility . . . Empire of China*. London, 1864.

Straits Settlements, Government of:
  Straits Settlements Government Gazette. 1884.
  'Correspondence with regard to the proposed amendment of the "Hongkong and Shanghai Bank Ordinance 1881"', Straits Settlements Legislative Council Proceedings, 1898, No. 51.

Syrett, W.W. *Finance of Overseas Trade*. 3rd ed. London, 1957.

Tamagna, Frank M. *Banking and Finance in China*. New York, 1942.

Taylor, F.S. 'Differences in Scottish and English Banking'. *The Banker* 95: 369–72; 96:99–103, 153–56 (1950–51).

Teng, Ssu-yü and John K. Fairbank. *China's Response to the West: a Documentary Survey, 1839–1923*. Cambridge, MA, 1954.

The Times.

Times of Ceylon.

Times of India.

Townsend, A.M. 'Early Days of the Hongkong and Shanghai Bank'. Privately reproduced. Copy in the Hongkong Bank Group Archives, Hong Kong.

'*Tzu Erh Chi*' 自邇集. *Encyclopaedia Sinica*. Ed. Samuel Couling. Shanghai, 1917.

United Kingdom. British Parliamentary Papers.
  House of Commons. *Report from the Committee on Loans to Foreign States; together with the proceedings of the committee, Minutes of Evidence, Appendix and Index*. 29 July 1875.
  1880, Vol. VII. 'Report from the Select Committee on Chartered Banks (Colonial) Bill'.
  Report of the Straits Settlements Currency Committee. Cd 1556. London, 1903.

Wagel, Srinivas R. *Finance in China*. Shanghai, 1914.

Wallich, Hermann. 'Aus meinem Leben'. In *Zwei Generationen im deutschen Bankwesen*. Schriftenreihe des Instituts für Bankhistorische Forschung e.v. Vol. II. Frankfurt/M, 1978.

Wang Qingyu (Wang Ching-yü) 汪敬虞. 'Shih-chiu shih-chi wai-kuo chin-Hua Shih-yeh Chung ti Hua-shang fu-ku huo-tung' 十九世紀外國侵華事業中的華商附股活動 (The activities of Chinese merchants to buy capital shares in the aggressive foreign enterprises in China during the late nineteenth century). *Yenjiu* (Li-shih yen-chiu) 歷史研究 4: 39–74 (1965).

Wesley-Smith, Peter. 'The Hongkong Bank and the Extraterritorial Problem, 1865–1890'. In *Eastern Banking: Essays in the History of The Hongkong and Shanghai Banking Corporation*. Ed. Frank H.H. King. London, 1983. Pp. 66–76.

Whale, P. Barrett. *Joint Stock Banking in Germany*. London, 1968.

Willem, John M. *The United States Trade Dollar*. Racine, WI, 1965.

Williams, Margaret Harcourt. *Catalogue of the Papers of Sir Charles Addis*. London, 1986.

Wing, Yung (Jung Hung). *My Life in China and America*. New York, 1909.

Wodehouse, P.G. 'Over Seventy, an autobiography with digressions'. In *Wodehouse on Wodehouse*. London, 1981. Pp. 467–645.

Psmith in the City. London, 1910. Penguin ed. 1970.

Wong, Kwai Lam. 'Anglo-Chinese Trade and Finance, 1854–1914'. PhD Thesis, University of Leicester, 1976.

Wright, Arnold. Ed. *Twentieth Century Impressions of Hongkong, Shanghai, and Other Treaty Ports of China: Their History, People, Commerce, Industries, and Resources.* London, 1908.

and H.A. Cartwright. *Twentieth Century Impressions of British Malaya*. London, 1908.

Wright, Stanley F. *Hart and the Chinese Customs*. Belfast, 1950.

Xu Yisheng (Hsü I-sheng). 徐義生. *Chung-kuo chin-tai wai-chai shih t'ung-chi tzu-liao* 中國近代外債史統計資料 (Statistical materials on the history of China's foreign loans, 1853–1927). Beijing, 1962.

Yang, Lien-sheng. *Money and Credit in China, A Short History*. Cambridge, MA, 1952.

Ybañez, Roy C. 'The Hongkong Bank in the Philippines, 1899–1941'. In *Eastern Banking: Essays in the History of The Hongkong and Shanghai Banking Corporation*. Ed. Frank H.H. King. London, 1983. Pp. 435–66.

Yip, Christopher L. 'Four Major Buildings in the Architectural History of The Hongkong and Shanghai Banking Corporation'. In *Eastern Banking: Essays in the History of The Hongkong and Shanghai Banking Corporation*. Ed. Frank H.H. King. London, 1983. Pp. 112–38.

Young, Walter. *A Merry Banker in the Far East*. London, 1916.

Zhongguo, see Chung-kuo

INDEX

Index

HONGKONG BANK GROUP HISTORY SERIES

General Editor: FRANK H.H. KING